The Jewish People in the First Century

Historical Geography, Political History, Social, Cultural
and Religious Life and Institutions

Volume Two

Edited by S. Safrai and M. Stern
in co-operation with D. Flusser and W. C. van Unnik

1976
Fortress Press - Philadelphia

Library of Congress Catalog Card Number 74-75908
ISBN 0 8006 0602 7

The publication of this book was made possible through a grant from the Prince Bernhard Fund of Amsterdam

First published in 1976 by Van Gorcum & Comp. B.V., Assen, the Netherlands
in association with Fortress Press, Philadelphia, U.S.A.
Printed in the Netherlands by Van Gorcum, Assen
Distributed in the U.S.A. and Canada by Fortress Press, Philadelphia
1-602

Compendia Rerum Iudaicarum ad Novum Testamentum

SECTION ONE
THE JEWISH PEOPLE IN THE FIRST CENTURY

Historical Geography, Political History, Social, Cultural and
Religious Life and Institutions

IN TWO VOLUMES

Editorial Board:
Y. Aschkenasy, R. Le Déaut, D. Flusser, J. van Goudoever,
B. S. Jackson, H. Kremers, M. Stone, W. C. van Unnik

General Editors:
M. de Jonge, S. Safrai

Executive Editors:
W. J. Burgers, H. E. Gaylord, Jr.

Published under the Patronage of the
Foundation Compendia Rerum Iudaicarum ad Novum Testamentum

The Jewish People
in the First Century

VOLUME TWO

Preface

This second volume completes the first section of the *Compendia* series. The first volume, published in 1974, mainly dealt with the political and legal aspects of Jewish society in the first century. This second volume describes its social and economic structure and its religious and cultural life and institutions. As in the first volume, much attention has again been paid to Jewish life in the Diaspora, because of its importance for Jewish history in the first century, especially in relationship with the history of Early Christianity. The influences from the Roman-Hellenistic milieu upon Jewish life have been indicated in the appropriate chapters, but special chapters are provided on paganism in Palestine and on the attitude of Greeks and Romans towards Judaism, as reflected in their literature.

The two volumes now published can be read as works in their own right, describing the *realia* of Jewish life in the first century. However, the volumes are definitely designed as part of the *Compendia* series, and should be seen particularly in the context of the third section entitled: *Social and Religious History of Judaism and Early Christianity*. The description of Jewish life in the first century as presented in the first section applies on the whole to the main stream of Judaism or reflects the common elements of the various groups and sects, whereas the third section will deal especially with historical changes and inner developments in Judaism in the same period, paying full attention to the variety of religious, social and political movements and groups. This is why, for instance, the history of the Pharisees, Sadducees and Essenes and the history of the Great Revolt have been omitted in the first section, to receive full attention in the third.

The publication of the first volume happily coincided with the appearance of the first volume of a revised English edition of Schürer's *History of the Jewish People*, edited by G. Vermes and F. Millar. We very much welcome this new edition of Schürer's work, which is an indispensable tool for all historians of Second Temple Judaism, in-

v

cluding the contributors to the *Compendia* project, which attempts a new synthesis, following new insights and new lines of approach. As many of the topics treated in the first section of the *Compendia* are also covered in Schürer's work, it is only natural that specialists will compare the two works, as some reviewers have already done for the first volume, though it should not be overlooked that the first section has been planned as part of a more complete history to be written in the sections to come.

Several contributors to the second volume have not lived to complete their work. Professor Kutscher, who had signed on for the chapter on 'Hebrew and Aramaic', died in 1971, and Professor Avi-Yonah, who contributed several chapters to the first volume, died in 1974, leaving the chapters on 'Economic life in Palestine' and 'Architecture and Art' unfinished. We also suffered the loss of Professor I. Abrams, who was translating the chapter on 'Home and Family', and of Mrs. Rivkah ben Yitzhak, who was translating the chapter on 'Aspects of Jewish Society'. Mrs. Rivkah ben Yitzhak was killed with her husband in a terrorist attack. May they all be remembered as a blessing.

M. DE JONGE
S. SAFRAI
General Editors

Editorial note and acknowledgments

The contributions by S. Safrai and M. Stern were translated from the Hebrew by Rabbi Klein, Mrs. Ch. Matza, Mrs. T. Rabin, D. R. Schwarz and J. Schwarz. The contribution by D. Flusser was translated from the German by K. Smyth, who also acted as language editor for the entire manuscript. The indices have been prepared by H. W. Hollander. Biblical quotations are according to the Revised Standard Version and Danby's translation of the Mishnah was used as a rule for the mishnaic quotations.

The Plan of the Second Temple on page 868 and the Map of Jerusalem on page 979 were specially designed for this volume by the late professor M. Avi-Yonah. The two illustrations of the Southern and

Western Wall on pages 981-2 have been reprinted from the periodical *Qadmonioth*, with kind permission of the publisher.

For the editorial preparation of this volume special grants have been received from the *Netherlands Organization for the Advancement of Pure Research* (*Z.W.O.*) and from the *Prins Bernhard Fonds*. Their help is gratefully appreciated.

Additional abbreviations

BMC, Palestine	G. H. Hill, *Catalogue of the Greek Coins of Palestine in the British Museum*, 1914
CIS	*Corpus Inscriptionum Semiticarum*
CRAI	*Comptes-rendus de l'Académie des Inscriptions*
DJD	*Discoveries in the Judaean Desert*, 1955 ff.
SCHÜRER	E. Schürer, *Geschichte des jüdischen Volkes im Zeitalter Jesu Christi*, 3 vls., 3rd-4th ed., 1901-11
SCHÜRER-VERMES-MILLAR	*The History of the Jewish People in the Age of Jesus Christ*, by E. Schürer. Revised edition, ed. by G. Vermes and F. Millar, volume 1, 1973
STRACK-BILLERBECK	*Kommentar zum Neuen Testament aus Talmud und Midrasch*, by H. L. Strack and P. Billerbeck, 6 vls., 1922-61
ZAW	*Zeitschrift für die alttestamentliche Wissenschaft*, 1883 ff.

Contents

CONTENTS

Chapter Eleven
Aspects of Jewish Society
The Priesthood and other Classes

The Hellenistic and the Hasmonaean periods

In the period of Hellenistic rule over Syria and Palestine, in the third and second centuries B.C.E., Jewish society continued to be organized along the lines established after the return from Babylon under the Persian empire. At the beginning of the Persian period, two families were predominant, the house of David led by Zerubbabel son of Shaltiel[1] and the high priestly house descended from Zadok, led by the high priest Joshua son of Yehozadak. With the disappearance of Zerubbabel, the high priestly dynasty remained in almost exclusive control of Judaea. This meant a further enhancement of the position of the priests, who formed the upper classes of society,[2] which then produced all the figures who were active and influential in public life, apart from Nehemiah. When the Hellenistic kings took over, an out-side observer, Hecataeus, could regard Jewish society as a theocracy, where the priests were in charge.[3] Among such priests were Simeon the Just and Onias III, both of whom were high priests, and several members of the priestly divisions of Hakkoz and Bilgah. A striking exception was the prominence of the 'sons of Tobias', an ancient, distinguished family of non-priestly origin, which already held an important position in the time of Ezra and Nehemiah.[4] The Tobiads co-operated closely with non-Jewish elements in Palestine. Their position was based on their extensive landed property and their

---

[1] On the fate of the Davidic dynasty after the exile see J. Liver, *The House of David from the Fall of the Kingdom of Judah* (1959; in Hebrew), pp. 68-104; R. Kittel, *Geschichte des Volkes Israel* III, 2 (1929), pp. 465-8.
[2] See E. J. Bickerman, in *The Jews. Their History, Culture and Religion*, ed. by L. Finkelstein, vol. I (1949), p. 74.
[3] See Hecataeus, in: Diodorus Siculus XL, 3, 4; for some remarks on Jewish society on the basis of Hecataeus cf. V. Tcherikover, *Hellenistic Civilization and the Jews* (1959), pp. 119-120.
[4] On the Tobiads see B. Mazar, in *IEJ* (1957), pp. 137-145; 229-38; O. Plöger, in ZDPV (1955), pp. 70-81; C. C. McCown, in *The Biblical Archeologist* XX (1957), pp. 63-76; Tcherikover, op. cit., pp. 126-142; M. Stern, in *Tarbiz* (1963), pp. 35-47 (in Hebrew); there is no warrant for the assumption of S. Schechter, *Studies in Judaism*, Second Series (1908), p. 65, that the Tobiads were priests.

influence in Ammon and Gilead.[1] Tobias' son Joseph was at the head
of a military colony in Transjordan and was a well-known figure at
the royal court of Alexandria under Ptolemy Philadelphus (283-
246 B.C.E.), maintaining important contacts with Ptolemy and his
finance minister. Following family tradition, he was active in Western
Palestine and Judaea as well as in Transjordan. It seems that he had
more influence in Jerusalem than his predecessors,[2] competing succes-
fully with the high priest Onias II. A public assembly in the Temple
authorized him to represent Judaea at the royal court of Ptolemy III
(Euergetes).[3] His connections with the latter gained him the post of
tax-collector for Syria and Phoenicia, which were ruled at the time by
the Ptolemies. It would appear that other Jews of the upper classes
were involved in his largescale financial activities. Like Joseph, these
too maintained close connections with the Gentiles of the upper
classes of Syria and Phoenicia. In contrast with the official leaders
since Ezra and Nehemiah whose viewpoint was strictly Jewish, people
like Joseph were Palestinian or Syrian in outlook like Tobiah the
Ammonite or Eliashiv the High Priest in the Persian period. Joseph
felt no less at home in Samaria than in Judaea or Gilead. Tendencies
that appeared to be on the wane before his time, were strengthened
once again under the Hellenistic ascendancy which such men as Joseph
represented in Judaea. Their activities brought a flow of capital into
Judaea and so furthered a significant change in the traditional mode
of life in Jerusalem.

The rise of the Tobiads, so closely associated with the priestly upper
class, aroused strong opposition among wide circles of the population.
This was particularly evident among the country folk who constituted
the majority of the population. These reacted strongly against the
alien atmosphere, that had come to predominate in Jerusalem. Class
tension between rich and poor grew as a result of economic and social
changes. The tensions in Jerusalem society at the time are clearly
reflected in the writing of Ben Sira. Ben Sira himself apparently
belonged to the priestly class,[4] and took its predominance for granted.
His book, written before the persecution of Antiochus, described the
Jerusalem of the time in this process of social transformation. As a

---

[1] See *CPJ* no. 1 on the cleruchy in Birtha of Ammanitis under Tobiah.
[2] Joseph's mother was the sister of the high priest Onias. See Jos. *Ant.* XII, 160.
[3] *Ant.* XII, 164-5.
[4] He probably belonged to the priestly division of Hakkoz; see below pp. 590-1;
cf. M. Z. Segal, *The Complete Ben Sira* (2nd ed., 1962), p. 1, n. 3.

priest, he esteems his social position highly and looks down with disdain on the ordinary farmer, labourer and artisan who constituted so large a portion of the Jerusalem population: 'How can he become wise who handles the plough, and who glories in the shaft of a goad, who drives oxen and is occupied with their work, and whose talk is about bulls? He sets his heart on plowing furrows, and he is careful about fodder for the heifers. So too is every craftsman and master workman who labors by night as well as by day; those who cut the signets of seals, each is diligent in making a great variety; he sets his heart on painting a lifelike image, and he is careful to finish his work. So too is the smith sitting by the anvil, intent upon his handiwork in iron; the breath of the fire melts his flesh, and he wastes away in the heat of the furnace; he inclines his ear to the sound of the hammer, and his eyes are on the pattern of the object. He sets his heart on finishing his handiwork, and he is careful to complete its decoration. So too is the potter sitting at his work and turning the wheel with his feet; he is always deeply concerned over his work, and all his output is by number. He moulds the clay with his arm and makes it pliable with his feet; he sets his heart to finish the glazing, and he is careful to clean the furnace. All these rely upon their hands, and each is skilful in his own work. Without them a city cannot be established, and men can neither sojourn nor live there. Yet they are not sought out for the council of the people, nor do they attain eminence in the public assembly. They do not sit in the judge's seat, nor do they understand the sentence of judgment.'[1]

Whatever the importance of craftsmen for the normal functioning of a city, they cannot be allowed to rule or act as judges in it. From his blanket condemnation, Ben Sira only excludes doctors: 'Honour the physician with the honour due him, according to your need of him, for the Lord created him; for healing comes from the Most High, and he will receive a gift from the king. The skill of the physician lifts up his head, and in the presence of great men he is admired.'[2] Ben Sira is fully aware of the problems set by social divisions and the hatred between rich and poor: 'Do not lift a weight beyond your strength, nor associate with a man mightier and richer than you. How can the clay pot associate with the iron kettle? The pot will strike against it, and will itself be broken... Every creature loves its like, and every person his neighbour; all living beings associate by species, and a man clings to

[1] Sir. 38:25-34.
[2] Sir. 38:1-3.

one like himself. What fellowship has a wolf with a lamb? No more has a sinner with a godly man. What peace is there between a hyena and a dog? And what peace between a rich man and a poor man? Wild asses in the wilderness are the prey of lions; likewise the poor are pastures for the rich. Humility is an abomination to a proud man; likewise a poor man is an abomination to a rich one.'[1]

There is little doubt that his sympathies are not with the rich. On the contrary, the rich are implicitly identified with the wicked. Though a priest and a writer, he does not see himself as belonging to the wealthy class whose profound hatred for the poor he describes in sombre colours.[2] He has much sympathy for the hired labourer, the poor and the oppressed.[3] One could argue here that he is clearly influenced by the Psalms.[4] In any case the passages quoted undoubtedly reflect the atmosphere of Jerusalem as created by the ascendancy of the Tobiads, the growing wealth of the upper classes and the penetration of Hellenism.

In the long run Hellenistic influence brought about far-reaching changes in Judaea. One must recall that Jewish settlements in Palestine, in Judaea and Samaria as well as in other regions, were surrounded by a hostile Gentile population. Ethnically, this population was heterogeneous but under Ptolemaic and Seleucid rule, its upper classes produced leaders who were thoroughly Hellenized. In the face of this Graeco-Syrian bloc, a fateful question confronted the Jews of Palestine. Would they retain their position as a distinct entity in Palestine or would they lose their national character with their religion and become just another of the many groups that were absorbed by the Hellenism of the Near East? The attractions of Hellenism were powerful enough to endanger the survival of Judaism or, at the very least, to efface the Jewish character of the leading classes as in Egypt and Babylonia. There, the leading classes became 'Hellenes', and left the lower strata of society without national leaders.[5] Indeed, even in Judaea, the beginnings of this process can be seen. Some of the upper

---

[1] Sir. 13:2-20.
[2] On Jerusalem society as depicted by Ben Sira see E. Bevan, *Jerusalem under the High Priests* (1904), pp. 49-68; Schechter, op. cit., pp. 55-101; Tcherikover, op. cit., pp. 142-151; M. Hengel, *Judentum und Hellenismus* (1973), pp. 241-52; E. T., vol. 1 (1974) pp. 131-153.
[3] Sir. 34:20-22.
[4] See R. Bultmann, *Theology of the New Testament* 1 (1952), p. 39.
[5] On the Hellenes of Ptolemaic Egypt see M. Rostovtzeff, *Social and Economic History of the Hellenistic and Roman World* II (1941), p. 912.

classes, priests and others, and members of the high priesthood itself, eminent priests of the house of Bilgah and, of course, the Tobiads, adopted a way of life and conduct very like that of their peers among the non-Jews of Syria and Phoenicia. In essence, this trend was opposed to any emphasis on Jewish particularity, and sought to merge with the upper classes of the non-Jewish population.

The movement was strongest in the time of Antiochus Epiphanes. The circles mentioned above, headed by Jason, the brother of the high priest Onias III, whose office he took over, sought to transform the life of Jerusalem. Far-reaching changes were introduced, to make Jerusalem a typical polis, with the name of Antiochia.[1] This they planned to do by introducing Hellenistic institutions into the traditional way of life of the capital of Judaea. The most important of these institutions was the gymnasion, the social centre for the citizens of a Hellenistic city.[2] The atmosphere of the gymnasion was essentially Greek and pagan, though one cannot of course assume that Jason actually introduced pagan worship into Jerusalem. However, many of the ceremonies of the Hellenistic world were performed in the gymnasion of Jerusalem. Soon enough, it replaced the Temple as the centre of social life. The second Book of Maccabees is bitter about priests forsaking the service in the Temple in order to view the competitions in the gymnasion.[3]

Jason followed the system of the Tobiad Joseph and his circles in attempting to assimilate the new polis to those of Seleucid Syria. Representatives of Antiochia (Jerusalem) were sent to the games in honour of the Sidonian Melkart (Heracles), a further step in the process of eliminating the unique character of Jerusalem. Jason was the last high priest from the line of Joshua son of Yehozadak, who was the legitimate successor to Zadok. He was deposed by Menelaus, a priest of the division of Bilgah. Menelaus was one of the greatest champions of Hellenism, and so co-operated with the Tobiads. He enjoyed the full confidence of Antiochus. A new chapter began in the history of the relations between Judaea and the Seleucid empire. The high priest who had once spoken for the Jewish people to the king, now became the spokesman of the king to the people. His role in the

---

[1] See Tcherikover, op. cit., pp. 404-9.
[2] On the Greek gymnasion see M. P. Nilsson, *Die hellenistische Schule* (1955); J. Delorme, *Gymnasion* (1960).
[3] II Macc. 4:12-15; cf. Ad. Wilhelm, *Neue Beiträge zur griechischen Inschriftenkunde* V (1932), pp. 45-6.

enforcement of the decrees against the Jewish religion is well known. Whoever planned these repressive measures,[1] it was Menelaus who led the radical Hellenizers in their whole-hearted co-operation with the king in their execution. This misled the king. He assumed that all the upper classes would support him against opponents of the decrees. It soon became clear however that Menelaus and his followers had no real support among the Jewish masses. Actually, the Hellenizers had lost all contact with the pillars of Jewish society and had cut itself off from the priestly class and the Jewish life. In opposition to the people as a whole, the extreme Hellenizers aligned themselves whole-heartedly with Seleucid policy. In the end, they were swept away by the reaction and left no trace on Jewish society. The country folk remained loyal to Jewish tradition. Even the moderate Hellenizers of the upper classes offered their energies, their talents and their experience in public affairs to serve the Hasmonaeans. They proved to be of considerable help in the war, and with contacts with the outside world.

The great achievement of the Hasmonaean revolt was the survival of the Jewish nation and religion. However, the new political situation brought about significant social and religious changes. Chief among these was the end of certain tendencies to assimilate which had been current in Hellenistic Jerusalem; contrary forces were strengthened and gave rise to new ideas. The tensions arising from Jason's innovations and Antiochus' repressive decrees resulted in an open split among the upper classes of Judaea. The failure of the royal policy brought about the fall of Menelaus.[2] He became the scapegoat whose death appeased the wrath of the Jewish community. Many of his supporters were killed, others lost their possessions and so their social standing. This process was reflected in the decline of the entire priestly division of Bilgah. It lost its prestige, and gained an evil reputation which remained an abiding memory.[3] One instance may be noted. How thoroughly all Hellenizing and idolatrous tendencies had been extirpated appears from the fact that a member of this priestly division who lived at the time of the revolt against Rome, threw himself into the flames of the burning Temple.[4] This self-immolation

[1] See E. Bickermann, *Der Gott der Makkabäer* (1937); I. Heinemann, in *MGWJ* (1938), pp. 145-172; J. C. Dancy, *A Commentary on I Maccabees* (1954), pp. 73-5.
[2] II Macc. 13:3-8.
[3] See below pp. 592-4.
[4] See Jos. *War* VI, 280.

expressed more eloquently than words his supreme loyalty to the Temple and all it represented. As for the descendants of the Tobiads, the faithful allies of the division of Bilgah and the only non-priestly family of influence in the Hellenistic period, they disappeared from the later history of Jewish Palestine. Only the branch headed by Hyrcanus son of Joseph, son of Tobias, may have survived. One may conjecture that its continued existence was due to the fact that it emigrated to Ptolemaic Egypt.[1]

The high priestly house of Zadok, descended from Joshua son of Yehozadak, likewise vanished in the wake of the Maccabean revolt. Having been the ruling dynasty of Judaea in the Hellenistic period, it proved inconsistent in its attitudes towards fundamental religious and social issues. Simeon the Just and Onias III, who was executed under Antiochus, were loyal to Judaism. But others of the same priestly clan maintained intimate contact with the Samaritan leader Sanballat and the Tobiads. These contacts were part of their effort to integrate with the ruling classes of non-Jewish Palestine. Thus Jason, the brother of Onias III, headed the opposition to his traditionalist brother and undermined his position. Jason himself died far away from Judaea. In Judaea itself, the sources are silent in regard to the subsequent history of this high priestly house. On the other hand, a brilliant future was reserved for the descendants of Onias in Egypt, where they served as statesmen and military commanders under the Ptolemies in the second century B.C.E. It was at their instigation that a Jewish temple was built in Egypt (the temple of Onias). At critical junctures in the beginning of the reign of Alexander Jannaeus they helped to strengthen Hasmonaean rule. The house of Onias, however, played no role in the life of Judaea. The Hasmonaean revolt brought new elements to the forefront as leaders of Jewish society, people who had supported the Hasmonaeans but who had hitherto played no significant part in the public life of Jerusalem. Towards the end of the Second Temple period, there were families, such as that of the historian Josephus, that could look back on the days of the Hasmonaean revolt as marking the beginning of their ascendancy.

These new social elements occupied a prominent place in the local élite, in the Temple and the sanhedrin, the latter having replaced the pre-

---

[1] This suggestion is based on the assumption that the *Tobiad Chronicle* from which Josephus derived his history of the Tobiads was composed in Ptolemaic Egypt during the second or the first century B.C.E. See M. Stern, in *Tarbiz* (1963), pp. 37-40.

Hasmonaean *gerousia*. Nevertheless, a sense of continuity with the past was quite palpable. The Hasmonaean family, itself of priestly origin, claimed descent from the distinguished priestly division of Yehoyarib. Members of other distinguished priestly families, such as that of the division of Hakkoz, threw in their lot with them. Two important personages of the latter clan played a prominent role in public affairs: Johanan who obtained a charter of privileges from Antiochus III, and his son Eupolemus who represented Judah Maccabee in negotiations with the Roman Republic. Thus the priestly division of Hakkoz remained loyal to Judaism and co-operated with the Hasmonaeans in winning freedom for Judaea. Another priestly clan joined forces with the Hasmonaeans, and produced a series of representatives who served the Hasmonaean kings. The first of such representatives was Jason son of Eleazar,[1] the companion of Eupolemus. It would appear that the three sons of this Jason (Antipater, Alexander and Diodorus) as well as his grandsons, filled important posts under subsequent Hasmonaean rulers.[2] In general, one may assume that the priestly class, having come to the fore in the Persian and Hellenistic periods, continued to be dominant in the Hasmonaean kingdom established by the Hasmonaean priests. At the same time, one can note an interesting development within Jewish society, the emergence of a class of sages from various social classes. The influence of the sages was now on the rise.

Two important priests of the time were the brothers Eleazar and Judah. The Palestinian Talmud says that Eleazar ben Pechora and his brother Judah used to seize the tithes by force, and that though he could have done so, John Hyrcanus did not protest against this illegal act.[3] Eleazar ben Pechora is probably to be identified with one of the prominent leaders of the Sadducees in the Hasmonaean period who urged John Hyrcanus to turn against the Pharisees.[4] The name

---

[1] 1 Macc. 8:17.

[2] On Antipater, the son of Jason, see 1 Macc. 12:16; on Alexander, the son of Jason, see Jos. *Ant.* XIV, 146; on Diodorus, the son of Jason, see Jos. *Ant.* XIII, 260. It seems also that Apollonius, the son of Alexander, mentioned ibid., and also XIV, 248, was a grandson of Jason. One should also note Aeneas, son of Antipater (also XIV, 248), who may be a son of Antipater, the son of Jason. Cf. already F. Ritschl, in *Rheinisches Museum* (1873), p. 597, n. 12.

[3] P. T. *Sotah* ix, 24a; P. T. *Maaser Sheni* v, 56d.

[4] It seems highly probable that this Eleazar is the same as the Saducee Eleazar ben Poira known from *B. T. Kiddushin* 66a, though the Babylonian Talmud dates the events related there to the time of Alexander Jannaeus. G. Alon, *Studies in Jewish History* I (1957; in Hebrew), p. 90 interprets somewhat differently the

Eleazar[1] and the incident of the tithes would point to the fact that the brothers were priests. Thus, we see a distinguished priestly house allied with the ruling house, a situation that was to be repeated towards the end of the Second Temple period. Eleazar and his brother seem also to have tried to take over tithes that actually belonged to the lower class of priests, without interference from John Hyrcanus.

From the time of Simeon the Hasmonaean, another development appears. The Hasmonaeans tried to establish ties with distinguished families that lived in the border areas of Palestine.[2] These efforts had marked effects on the political future of Judaea. The conversion to Judaism of an important Edomite family in the days of John Hyrcanus falls within this context. One of the members of this family, Antipas, was appointed *strategos* (governer) of Idumaea by the Hasmonaean rulers.[3] His son Antipater gained a leading position in the political life of Judaea at the end of Hasmonaean rule. We know too of his brother Phallion.[4] It was the grandson of the above-mentioned Antipas, Herod, who put an end to the Hasmonaean dynasty and established a new ruling house. From the same southern region came, so it would appear, the family of Malichus, who challenged Antipater's influence in Judaea under Hyrcanus II.[5] This conjecture is based on the Arabic sound of his name as well as on the important role that Malichus' brother played in the south of Palestine around Masada.[6] The Malichus family, like that of Antipas, were probably Edomite proselytes who had been converted to Judaism in the days of John Hyrcanus I. It is possible that this family, even before its conversion, had already competed for leadership with the family of Antipas.[7]

---

story in the Palestinian Talmud; he assumes that the Eleazar mentioned there is a Pharisee and that the Palestinian Talmud is close to the tradition which is found in Jos. *Ant.* XIII, 290-1.

[1] See M. Stern, in *Zion* (1961), p. 21 (in Hebrew).

[2] It is noteworthy that the son-in-law of Simeon was one Ptolemy, the son of Aboub (I Macc. 16:11), the *strategos* of Jericho. One should also mention the item in Syncellus I, p. 559 about Alexander Jannaeus sending the Galilean commander Digaios against the Nabataeans.

[3] Jos. *Ant.* XIV, 10.

[4] *Ant.* XIV, 33; *War* I, 130.

[5] *Ant.* XIV, 273-9; *War* I, 220.

[6] *Ant.* XIV, 296.

[7] Cf. B. Kanael, in *BJPES* XVIII (1954), p. 172 (in Hebrew), on Malichus' sphere of influence.

The Herodian and procuratorial period

In the Herodian period, certain transformations took place within Jewish society no less far-reaching than those after the Hasmonaean revolt. The families and social strata that had been the chief supporters of the Hasmonaean dynasty disappeared or suffered such severe losses as to nullify their influence. In any event, they lost their leading role in Jewish society. Herod confronted the problem of consolidating his rule over the nation by creating a new élite that would be loyal to him and have no especial ties with the Hasmonaean past. This élite was essentially drawn from two sources: the Diaspora of Egypt, and Babylonia, and the border areas of Palestine. Since Herod was not of priestly lineage, he could not assume the position of high priest.[1] The appointment of a high priest drawn from the remnants of the Hasmonaean dynasty would challenge the stability of his own rule. Hence Herod was compelled to look for candidates whose appointment would not threaten the Herodian dynasty. The first whom he designated was Hananel, a Babylonian. After him, we find high priests from the Hellenistic Diaspora in Egypt: Jesus son of Phiabi[2] and Simeon son of Boethus. These two were the founders of the high priestly oligarchy that held sway at the end of the Second Temple period. Thus, the foundation was laid for the characteristic phenomenon of Jewish society in that period, the oligarchy of the high priesthood.

It is clear that the house of Bathyra, headed by Zamaris, was of Babylonian origin. They migrated to Palestine, and settled in Transjordan, where they became the principal allies of the Herodian dynasty in Gaulanitis and Batanaea. The migration of the house of Hillel from Babylonia to Palestine is to be viewed as part of a general trend, which led Jewish families to migrate to Palestine and there assume a leading role in Judaean society. This process, initiated by the political and social demands of the time (Herod's struggle against the Hasmonaean dynasty), continued to some extent even after its original motives had largely disappeared.

We can trace the complex of relationships between the Diaspora and Palestinian Jewry throughout the period of the existence of the Second Temple. Pilgrimages to Jerusalem to celebrate the festivals, economic ties between Diaspora Jewry and Judaea, the attraction of

---

[1] Only in the *Geography* of Strabo (XVI, 2, 46) do we read that Herod tried to appear as a priest. Cf. W. Otto, *Herodes* (1913), p. 18; M. Stern, *Greek and Latin Authors on Jews and Judaism* I (1974), p. 310.

[2] Cf. chapter five, p. 274.

the famous 'houses of study' in Jerusalem, the ready absorption of immigrant Jews by Palestinian Jewry—all these factors prepared the ground for the integration of Diaspora Jews into Palestinian society. Some Jewish visitors from the Diaspora remained a relatively short time. Many, however, remained permanently and became an integral part of the Jewish scene. We have already seen that the founders of the house of Phiabi and that of Boethus had already settled in Jerusalem in Herod's time. Others like Hanan the Egyptian[1] or Nahum the Mede[2] settled somewhat later. The Jews of Hellenistic origin in Jerusalem built their own synagogues.[3] People such as Theodotus, son of Vettenus,[4] were completely integrated in local Jewish society. Indeed, it would be difficult to describe the development of Palestinian Jewish society without taking into account its penetration by Jews from the Diaspora.

But, as already indicated, Herod also relied on certain elements within Palestinian society itself. Some were of Edomite origin, like Herod himself. It was in Idumaea, it will be recalled, that his family had attained eminence. Here, the house of Antipater acted as one in their common interests. Herod depended on the Edomites more than on any other element within Jewish society. He had settled immigrants from Idumaea in Trachonitis even before Jewish-Babylonian settlement took place in the north-east areas of Transjordan. He continued to strengthen his family relationships with Idumaea through his sister Salome who had married Costobar, a scion of a distinguished family in Idumaea. It appears that the descendants of this couple played an active role in public affairs towards the close of the Second Temple period. By another husband, Alexa, Salome had a son by the name of Helcias, one of the most important personages in the days of Agrippa I. Not only Herod's direct descendants but those of the royal family in general appear as influential figures in Jerusalem in the days of the great revolt.[5]

---

[1] *M. Ketuboth* 13:1-2.

[2] *M. Nazir* 5:4; *M. Shabbath* 2:1.

[3] Acts 6:9.

[4] *CII* no. 1404 = E. Gabba, *Iscrizioni greche e latine per lo studio della Bibbia*, no. XXIII.

[5] Jos. *Ant.* xx, 214; *War* II, 418; 556. In Josephus we read about two brothers, Costobar and Saul, relatives of Agrippa II, who under the procurator Albinus, collected gangs of ruffians and led them to take part in the fighting in the streets of Jerusalem. Later, those two, as well as one Antipas, again stated to be relatives of Agrippa, incited both the king and Florus to come with military force and crush the revolt at its start. After the defeat of Cestius Gallus,

Herod also sought supporters among the Galileans, who on the whole regarded him with animosity. Nevertheless, we hear of influential people in Galilee (δυνατοί) who aided him in his struggle against Antigonus.[1] It was from Galilee that high priests emerged towards the end of Herod's reign, for example, Matthias, son of Theophilus and his relative Joseph, son of Ellem, who came from Sepphoris.[2]

A feature of Jewish society of the time is how some great families held on to certain views and a consistent political line, even outside the high-priestly oligarchy.[3] A striking example is afforded by the leaders of the central trend within the Pharisees, that of the house of Hillel.[4] The same phenomenon can be seen among Pharisaic groups outside the then existing establishment. An example of people with such traditions is the Galilean family that led the extreme wing of the freedom fighters at the end of the Second Temple period. The first member of this family known to us is the Ezechias who opposed Herod and was executed under Julius Caesar.[5] Ezechias, as described by Josephus, was leader of a band operating in the territory close to Syria. Forty years later, during the war against Varus, a Judas son of Ezechias was one of the leaders of the revolt, basing his military operations on Sepphoris.[6] Josephus also says that ten years later, when Judaea had become a Roman province, a certain Judas stirred up revolt against Rome under the governor of Syria Quirinius.[7] According to Josephus, this Judas was at the origin of the 'fourth philosophy', added to the three (Pharisaic, Sadducean and Essene) that had existed among the Jews before that time.

It is clear from Josephus, that active opponents of Rome in the later period, such as James and Simeon under the procurator Tiberius Alexander,[8] Menahem, the leader of the Sicarii and Eleazar son of Jair, the hero of Masada,[9] were relatives of the Judas who incited the people to

Costobar and Saul together with Philip, the son of Iacimus (Jachim), escaped from Jerusalem. Three men of the royal, i.e. the Herodian family were among the victims of the Zealots, one of them being the afore-mentioned Antipas (Jos. *War* IV, 140-1).

[1] *Ant.* XIV, 450.
[2] See chapter five, p. 272, n. 2.
[3] On the dynastic principle in the Jewish society of that time see also some of the articles bearing upon the history of early Christianity. Cf. E. Stauffer, in *Zeitschrift für Religions- und Geistesgeschichte* (1952), pp. 193-214.
[4] Cf. below, pp. 615-18.
[5] Jos. *Ant.* XIV, 159-60; *War* I, 204-5.
[6] *Ant.* XVII, 271-2; *War* II, 56.
[7] *Ant.* XVIII, 4-10.
[8] *Ant.* XX, 102.   [9] *War* II, 433.

revolts against the census of Quirinius. Our sources do not give us the name of the father of this Judas. However, it has long been assumed that Judas the Galilean, of the time of the census, is to be identified with Judas son of Ezechias who was active in the days of Varus.[1] It is likewise important to note that there is no mention in Josephus of Judas' death in the struggle against Varus. If he had been killed, it would be hard to explain why Josephus failed to mention this explicitly as he did mention the death of various leaders of the rebellion in other areas. Actually, from the famous speech of Gamaliel,[2] we know that Judas the Galilean was killed only as the result of his activities at the time of the census. The memory of Judas the Galilean (or the Gaulanite) overshadowed by far that of his father Ezechias. The members of the family who followed the ancestral tradition during the first century C.E. emphasized their relationship to Judas. When Josephus speaks of one of them as the son of Judas, it is not always possible to take him literally. It would thus appear that Menahem was the grandson of Judas and not his son, as Josephus would have it.[3] Another well-known member of the family is Eleazar son of Jair, the commander at Masada, a descendant of Judas the Galilean.[4]

We meet a similar instance of family tradition in the early history of Christianity, which again stresses the importance of this factor in Jewish society of Second Temple times. To some extent perhaps it is verified in the kinship between John the Baptist and Jesus.[5] Essentially, however, it appears in developments after the death of Jesus. The New Testament itself shows no trace of a 'dynastic' Christianity. On the contrary, one detects here and there an anti-dynastic note. In any event, it is emphasized that the closest members of Jesus' family, his brothers and mother, have no specific connection with his mission.[6] Nevertheless, we see a distinct reversal of this trend shortly after Jesus' death. It is seen in the rise of members of Jesus' family in

---

[1] Among the scholars who identify Judas, the son of Ezechias, with the Judas of the time of the census are E. Renan, *Histoire du peuple d'Israël* v (1891), p. 306, n. 1; K. Kohler, in *Festschrift Harkavy* (1908), p. 7; H. Dessau, *Geschichte der römischen Kaiserzeit* II (1930), p. 777; J. S. Kennard, in *JQR* (1945-6), p. 281; M. Hengel, *Die Zeloten* (1961), p. 337. Dissenting views have been expressed by Ed. Meyer, *Ursprung und Anfänge des Christentums* II (1921), p. 403, n. 1; H. Kreissig, *Die sozialen Zusammenhänge des judäischen Krieges* (1970), pp. 114-5.
[2] Acts 5:37.
[3] See Kennard, op. cit. p. 285, n. 5a.
[4] Jos. *War* VII, 253: Ἐλεάζαρος ἀπόγονος Ἰούδα.
[5] Luke 1:36.
[6] Mark 3:31-5.

Judaea, particularly the place held by James, the brother of Jesus.[1]
He figures prominently alongside of Peter and after a while over-
shadows the latter and becomes the recognized leader of the Christians
of Jerusalem until he is put to death by order of the Sadducean high
priest. Further, after the death of James, one of his cousins succeeded
him, according to tradition.[2] James is mentioned only once *en passant*
in Jesus' life time. and we have no reason to believe that Jesus assigned
him any particular position. The first source to emphasize James is the
First Epistle to the Corinthians.[3] In the Epistle to the Galatians,[4]
James appears as one of the three pillars of the Christian community
and his opinion is decisive in the supremely important matters that
confronted Christianity. Other brothers of Jesus also play an active
role in the community.[5] James did not play a leading part in the affairs
of the Christian community just because of his personal talents. It is to
be attributed to his association with Jesus' family as such. His
enlistment in the ranks of the new community entailed, in accordance
with the practice of the time, a certain hegemony of Jesus' family in
the Christian community.

The great revolt

The long internal peace within the Roman empire in the Julio-Claudian
period undoubtedly had its effects on Judaea. Peace encouraged
economic expansion in the Mediterranean world and strengthened the
ties between its various areas. But the prosperity was less shared by
Judaea. This was due to the tension between the Jews and the Roman
authorities, and between Jews and the non-Jewish inhabitants of
Palestine. It gave rise to periodic clashes over a long period of time.
To this must be added the growing tensions within Jewish society itself
towards the close of the Second Temple period in Jerusalem and elsewhere. Naturally, normal life was disrupted and economic growth
impeded. The Pax Romana had beneficial effects on the economy of
Judaea, by helping to create commercial ties with various countries.
But in the main, the communities that benefited by it were the cities
of the coast and certain cities in Transjordan, such as Gerasa.

[1] See in general H. Leclercq, in *DAC* VII, 2, cols. 2089-2109.
[2] Eusebius, *Historia Ecclesiastica* III, 11, 1.
[3] I Cor. 15:7.
[4] Gal. 2:9.
[5] I Cor. 9:5.

As at all earlier times, agriculture was the mainstay of the Jewish economy. In this connection, one may quote the well-known description of Josephus: 'Well, ours is not a maritime country; neither commerce nor the intercourse with the outside world has any attraction for us. Our cities are built inland, remote from the sea; and we devote ourselves to the cultivation of the productive country with which we are blessed.'[1] Allowing for the historian's exaggeration and one-sided picture, one must grant the essential truth of his statement. The vast majority of Jews were actually engaged in various branches of agriculture, which was held in high esteem, as appears from a passage in the *Testaments of the Twelve Patriarchs*: 'Bow down your back unto husbandry and toil in labour in all manner of husbandry.'[2]

The general picture that Josephus draws of Palestine at the close of the Second Temple period is that of a prosperous agricultural country supporting its inhabitants with ease.[3] He goes to great lengths in his description of the fertility of Galilee, Samaria and Judaea and devotes special attention to the Jericho valley and its famous groves of date palms and balsam trees, the products of the latter being highly treasured.[4] The three principal branches of agriculture were the cultivation of cereals, vines and olives. From Josephus' general description, one gathers the impression that he prefers wine and olive-growing to the cultivation of cereals such as wheat and barley. This predilection is likewise reflected in tannaitic sources. Olives ranked first among the produce of trees. A large part of the land of Palestine was in the hands of farmers who worked it together with members of their respective families. On the other hand, we hear of a concentration of land in the hands of the rulers of Judaea and large landowners. Thus, we hear of the collection of wheat in Beth Shearim from the surrounding villages, which belonged to Berenice. Beth Shearim was the centre of a private estate that had been inherited by Berenice from her forebears, the Hasmonaean kings and the kings of the Herodian house. Some agricultural lands, such as the famous balsam groves, passed directly into the hands of the Roman authorities. There were also some wealthy Jews who did not belong to the royal family but who nevertheless owned large tracts of land which they cultivated on a sharecropper basis. Alongside of agriculture, two other important

[1] Jos. *Against Apion* I, 60. See also chapter twelve, p. 632.
[2] *Testament of Issachar* 5:3; cf. 6:2.
[3] *War* III, 42-53. Cf. Kreissig, op. cit., p. 17-26.
[4] *War* IV, 459-75.

branches of the economy were cattle raising and fishing: 'And in the summer I caught fish, and in the winter I kept sheep.'[1] In addition to the various branches of agriculture, crafts occupied a prominent place in the economy. Ben Sira looked askance at the artisan, but towards the end of the Second Temple period, we hear of sages who had various handicrafts. Jerusalem generally was a city in which the crafts thrived. We hear of weavers, smiths and potters, in addition to such more artistic craftsmen as silversmiths and spicemakers. Many of the inhabitants were simple labourers working at the various building projects of the time. Some of them were occupied in the reconstruction of the Temple, begun in the days of Herod and finished a few years before the great revolt. The craftsmen directly connected with the Temple service would, at times, form a monopoly and demand a high price for their services. Such was the case of the house of Garmu and Avtinas who specialized in the making of the shewbread and the incense used in the Temple.[2]

It was in this period that Jewish participation in commerce increased. Owing to the special position of Jerusalem as the center of Jewish life, it became a commercial centre of importance. Many Jews in the coastal cities engaged in commerce. We thus hear of a significant number of wealthy Jews living in Palestine at the end of the Second Temple period. Among this wealthy class, members of the Herodian house as well as members of the oligarchy of the high priesthood figured prominently. Particularly noted for his wealth was the high priest Ananias ben Nedebaeus. A well-known tradition in the Babylonian Talmud speaks of three extremely wealthy men in Jerusalem: Nakdimon ben Gorion, Ben Kalba Sabbua and Ben Zizit Hakeset who could have provided Jerusalem with all its food for many years in order to withstand a siege.[3] In this connection, one should mention the father of Eliezer ben Hyrcanus.[4] We hear also of a number of Jewish settlements noted for their thriving economies. The Jews of Caesarea were especially noted for their wealth. Living close to the most important port of the country, they engaged in overseas trade as well as in tax farming. One of the leaders of the community was John, the tax collector. At times, the sources emphasize, in passing,

---

[1] *Testament of Zebulun* 6:8.
[2] *T. B. Yoma* 38a.
[3] *T. B. Gittin* 56a.
[4] On him and the other rich people of Jerusalem cf. *Avot de Rabbi Natan*, Version II, chapter 13; *Pirke de Rabbi Eliezer* 2.

the prosperity of certain villages, especially those in the north of the country. Thus, for example, the houses in the Galilean village of Chabulon aroused the amazement of Josephus, who compares them to the houses in the large Phoenician cities of Tyre, Sidon and Berytus.[1] On the other hand, we hear a great deal about the impoverishment of the masses and the debts that oppressed them towards the end of the Second Temple period. After the completion of the reconstruction work on the Temple, shortly before its destruction, many remained unemployed. Some of these, thanks to the initiative of Agrippa II, found employment in public works such as paving the streets of the capital. The roads between Jerusalem and various parts of the country were hazardous for travellers. This was true not only of the road that ran from Galilee through Samaria to Jerusalem but also of the road that connected Jericho to Jerusalem, where bands of high-waymen lay in ambush. The roots of this insecurity, evident in Judaean villages as well as in the streets of Jerusalem, could be traced to the bitterness of the masses and economic pressure. In turn, the fragile nature of security had its impact on the general situation. A heavy burden of taxation crushed the peasantry, and the exactions of such procurators as Florus added to the economic distress. Tenants were compelled to hand over a significant portion of the produce of the land they worked to its owners. Many of the farm-workers were only hired labourers engaged for seasonal work. The priests of the lower classes whose livelihood depended in large measure on the tithes they received were often driven to despair by the oligarchy of the high priesthood, who frequently took these tithes for themselves. Landless men, displaced persons and casual labourers who had lost their sources of livelihood, proved an unfailing source for the quarrels and public disturbances that broke out repeatedly.

The great revolt bore all the signs of an inner social upheaval. The social and revolutionary character of the great revolt was particularly manifest among the radical groups which produced messianic figures such as Menahem the Galilean and Simeon bar Giora. In Simeon's view, the revolt was not just a war against the Romans but a protest against the social order of Judaea. From the outset, the radical elements pursued a revolutionary objective. Thus, they set fire to the city archives which contained proof of their debts and engaged in open warfare against the leaders of the existing order.[2] The latter showed

---

[1] *War* II, 504.
[2] *War* II, 427; we know that cancellation of debts was one of the main slogans in

little enthusiasm for the revolt and in its early stages sought to stem the movement of the masses. However, a large proportion and perhaps a majority of the upper classes were embittered by Florus' policies. Florus had cut himself off from all contact with the Jewish élite, the representatives of the Herodian dynasty and the oligarchy of the high priesthood. The dangers facing the Jewish population throughout Palestine and its neighbouring areas and the action of the Roman authorities and the non-Jewish population stimulated even the moderates among the Jewish leaders and pushed them towards activism. The victory of the rebels over the legions of Cestius Gallus, the governor of Syria, made even the moderates enthusiastic for the rebellion. In the temporary government set up in Jerusalem following this victory, Ananus ben Ananus, the former high priest and leader of the Sadducees, played a leading role. He was charged with the task of organizing the country against the impending Roman onslaught. Other members of the high priesthood joined him in this task. Among them was Joshua ben Gamala, who was married to Martha, daughter of Boethus. They were joined by Rabban Simeon ben Gamaliel, the head of the house of Hillel and the leader of the Pharisees. Only after the loss of Galilee to the Romans and the Jewish defeat near Ascalon, did the Jewish leadership slip from the hands of the moderates and pass to the extremists. The latter came either from the circles of the Zealots in Jerusalem or drew support from other areas of the country.

It is important to dwell on the nature of the various groups of freedom-fighters who made up the activist elements at the beginning of the revolt and eventually succeeded to the leadership. To some extent, it is possible to recognize the social tendencies of some of the main groups who took an active part at the outbreak of the revolt and defended Jerusalem during its siege. Josephus, in his general summary, in *The Jewish War*, book seven, describing the fall of Masada, counts no less than five distinct groups.[1] The last group are the Zealots whose activities we can follow from the very beginning of the revolt. Their principal leaders were Eleazar ben Simeon and Zechariah ben Avkules, both of whom were priests.[2] Their principal base of

the social struggle in the Greek world. A well-known example of such a proceeding is revealed by a letter of a Roman proconsul to one of the cities of Achaia, Dyme (115 B.C.E.?). See R. K. Sherk, *Roman Documents from the Greek East* (1969), no. 43; cf. A. Fuks, in *Scripta Hierosolymitana* XXIII (1972), pp. 21-7.

[1] *War* VII, 259-74.
[2] *War* IV, 225.

operations was the Temple mount. It would appear that the Zealots were largely responsible for the suspension of the sacrifice brought for the well-being of the emperor.[1] It appears likely too that the name Zealots derives from their relationship to the priestly class and its choice harks back to the priest described as a zealot in the Torah, namely, Phineas son of Eleazar the priest. It is also possible to trace a relationship between the Zealots and the house of Shammai. Characteristically they sought to democratize the high priesthood. This they achieved by insisting on lots being cast for the office, which resulted in the office falling to Phineas ben Samuel, one of the priests of the lower classes.[2]

More radical in its social tendencies was the wing of the extremists led by the descendants of Judah the Gaulanite. Generally, members of this radical group are designated by Josephus as *sicarii*. It was led by Menahem. It was this group that raised the banner of social revolt, burned the memoranda of debts and, in general, fought relentlessly against the ruling class. From this point of view, Simeon bar Giora and his men had much in common with them. Simeon was a descendant of a family of proselytes of Transjordan. He called for the emancipation of slaves, fought bitterly against the rich and thus became the leader of the lower classes throughout Palestine. One notes in Simeon as well as in Menahem a relationship between social radicalism and the cult of personality, a combination which was already apparent in the war against Varus (4 B.C.E.).

A figure of an altogether different cast was Johanan ben Levi of Gischala. At first, he was a local leader in Upper Galilee who had prospered by his export of oil. He was a man of moderate views and not at all enthusiastic at the prospect of war with the Romans. He had important contacts throughout Upper Galilee and maintained close ties with the leader of the house of Hillel, Simeon ben Gamaliel.[3] Only the force of circumstances made him join the rebels, yet he was the last among the soldiers of Galilee to hold out against the Romans. Escaping to Jerusalem, he joined the Zealots and helped to depose the moderate

---

[1] This follows from the consideration that Zechariah, the son of Avkules plays a significant part in this act, as we know from *T. B. Gittin* 56a. It seems also that Eleazar ben Hananiah who was mainly instrumental in the cessation of sacrifices on behalf of the Roman emperor, according to Josephus (*War* II, 409) was also connected with the Jerusalem group of Zealots.

[2] *War* IV, 139-157.

[3] Jos. *Life* 192.

leaders. The life and struggles of Johanan ben Levi make a good example of how the idea of freedom could take a grip on all classes in the nation.[1]

The priesthood and the priestly divisions

The priesthood constituted the upper stratum of Jewish society in the Second Temple period.[2] It was a kind of Jewish nobility. 'For us,' says Josephus, 'the priesthood is a sign of nobility of origin.'[3] The priests conducted the affairs of the Temple and supervised its service. They were regarded as the natural and self-evident authorities in interpreting Scripture.[4] The superiority of the priestly class in Jewish society was the result of a long development whose origins go back to the return from Babylon. Under Persian rule, the position of the priesthood was further consolidated. After the disappearance of the house of David, the high priest held the central public office in Judaea. It appears that other positions connected with the administration and financial affairs of the Temple and of Judaea were handed over to the priests (the sons of Hakkoz). This process continued in the Hellenistic period, in whose early stages a Greek thinker and writer (Hecataeus) could describe Judaea as a country ruled by priests. Other Greek writers of the time view the Jews as a sect of priests.[5] Ben Sira could turn to his fellow Jews with such explicit counsel as: 'With all your soul fear the Lord, and honor his priests. With all your might love your Maker, and do not forsake his ministers. Fear the Lord and honor the priest, and give him his portion, as is commanded you.'[6] The families whose influence was predominant in the Hellenistic period belonged to the priesthood: the high priests, the sons of Hakkoz and the sons of Bilgah. It is likely that many sages and scribes came from a priestly background. Ben Sira himself may have been a priest, and so too probably the Jewish historian Eupolemus. Among the sages who became famous in later generations as members of the *zugot* (pairs), we find Jose ben Joezer who is characterized as the 'pious one

---

[1] Cf. Stern, pp. 147-9.
[2] See the surveys of E. Meyer, *Die Entstehung des Judentums* (1896), pp. 168-76; Büchler; Schürer II, pp. 277-357; Jeremias, pp. 147-207.
[3] *Life* 1: ἡμῖν ἡ τῆς ἱερωσύνης μετουσία τεκμήριον ἐστιν γένους λαμπρότητος.
[4] See e.g. Jos. *War* III, 352.
[5] See Clearchus, in Josephus, *Against Apion* I, 179.
[6] Sir. 7:29-31.

of the priesthood.'[1] The only family that played a decisive role in Hellenistic Judaea that was not of priestly origin was the house of Tobias. But it, too, was linked to the priesthood by marriage. The status of the priests was given official recognition by the secular authorities. All the priests of Jerusalem were exempted from taxation by order of Antiochus III. This exemption was included in the charter of privileges obtained through the efforts of the priest Johanan ben Hakkoz.[2] At times, the priests are referred to as a distinct category in the official letters included in the I Maccabees; for example, in the letter of Jonathan to Sparta: 'Jonathan the high priest, the senate of the Jews, the priests and the rest of the Jewish people, to our brothers of Sparta, greetings.'[3] The same is true of the Spartan response to Simeon.[4] Even in the famous decision of the assembly of the people that confirmed the rule of Simeon, the priests appear as the first group among those who made up the assembly.[5]

As one might expect, the hegemony of the priesthood continued after the rise to power of the Hasmonaeans. Moreover, for the first time in Jewish history, royal authority passed into the hands of the priesthood. Actually, this was the outcome of a process already at work earlier, by which the high priest became ruler of Judaea. This involved, however, to a large extent the displacement of the messianic hopes connected with the house of David. The assumption of royal authority by the Hasmonaeans enhanced the status of the tribe of Levi as contrasted with the tribe of Judah. The fact is reflected in a most interesting way in the pseudepigraphic literature of the period, especially in *The Testaments of the Twelve Patriarchs*.[6]

---

[1] Already from *M. Hagigah* 2:7 (יוסי בן יועזר היה חסיד שבכהונה) we may justly infer that Jose ben Joezer was a priest, and there is hardly any justification for the view that the reference here is to a later sage also called by the same name, who lived in the last decades of the Second Temple period, as maintained by H. Graetz, in *MGWJ* (1869), p. 30; Büchler, p. 9; I. Loeb, in *REJ* XIX (1889), p. 188, n. 1. There is much to be said for the view that Jose ben Joezer was an uncle of the high priest Alcimus. See the haggadic material in *Gen. Rabba* 65 (pp. 742-4), and *Midrash Psalms* 11, 7 (pp. 103-4). Cf. A. Geiger, *Urschrift und Übersetzungen der Bibel* (1857), p. 64; H. Graetz, *Geschichte der Juden* III, 2, p. 367; J. Derenbourg, *Essai sur l'histoire et la géographie de la Palestine* (1867), p. 65; W. Bacher, *Tradition und Tradenten* (1914), p. 50; H. Volkmann, in *Klio* XIX, p. 396, n. 2.

[2] II Macc. 4:11.

[3] I Macc. 12:6.

[4] I Macc. 14:20.

[5] I Macc. 14:28.

[6] Cf. *The Testament of Reuben* 6:7; *The Testament of Judah* 21:1-3; *The Testament of Issachar* 5:7; *The Testament of Naphtali* 5:3; *The Testament of Joseph* 19:11.

Alongside of this development, one must note a parallel one, that of the rise of the sages, many of whom could not point to priestly origins. This development comes into prominence towards the end of the Hasmonaean age and is particularly noteworthy during the Herodian period and that of the procurators. To this, one must add the rise of a royal dynasty of nonpriestly origin, that of the Herodians, though many of its members were descended from priests on their mother's side.[1] The leaders of the central body of Pharisees, the house of Hillel, were of non-priestly origin. The frequent changes in the office of the high priest reflected adversely on the prestige of the priestly class as a whole. Nonetheless, towards the close of the Second Temple period, the priesthood constituted the prestigious and élite class in Jewish society.

As a class whose prestige depended upon family origins, the priests sought to enforce exacting regulations which would bar doubtful elements from their company.[2] The priesthood among Jews was an hereditary affair and there was no other avenue through which one could become a member of this class. As a result, a rigorous system of genealogical purity had to be enforced, one that made it possible to investigate the lineage of priests, and ensure that all marriages had been with suitable classes. Josephus, for example, lists his family tree and bases it upon documents available in the public archives.[3] The marriage of priests is already limited in the Torah: 'They shall not marry a harlot or a woman who has been defiled; neither shall they marry a woman divorced from her husband.'[4] But in course of time, these limitations were extended.[5] The category of 'profane' and 'whore', came to include other types, such as the proselyte and the manumitted slave.[6] On the other hand, priests could freely marry any virgin or the widows of priests, Levites or Israelites whose family tree was unblemished. The offspring of a priest and an Israelite woman was regarded as a priest in good standing. This prevented any self-isolation of the priesthood, so that it did not become a caste. There was, however, a tendency among the priesthood toward endogamous marriage, especially among the upper classes. This was particularly

[1] Philo, *Legatio ad Gaium* 278 (in a letter of Agrippa I to Gaius).
[2] See Schürer II, pp. 279-83.
[3] *Life* 6.
[4] Lev. 21:7.
[5] Philo, *De specialibus legibus* I, 101; Jos. *Ant.* III, 276; M. *Yebamoth* 6:4 (concerning the marriage of the high priest).
[6] M. *Yebamoth* 6:5.

true of the high priests. Thus, for example, the high priest Joseph Caiaphas was the son-in-law of the high priest Ananus; and the high priest Joshua son of Gamala was the husband of Martha of the house of Boethus. According to Philo, a high priest could only marry a virgin who was a daughter of a priest,[1] But the traditional Halakah offers no support for such view. Nevertheless, such an impression as that of Philo could be gathered by an observer of the Second Temple period. And in fact, endogamous marriages were frequent in priestly circles. Thus, Rabbi Tarphon's uncle on his mother's side was a priest.[2] Both parents of John the Baptist were of priestly families; his father being Zechariah of the priestly division of Abijah.[3] The persistence of the tradition of endogamous marriage among those of priestly descent finds an echo in the later statement that 'the marriage of a daughter of a priest to an Israelite is bound to result in a bad marriage.'[4] It is clear, however, that this type of endogamous marriage was not the only type to be found among those of priestly origin. We hear of marriages between eligible Israelites and priests. A whole series of examples of such marriages, beginning with that of the house of Tobias into the high priesthood is to be found in the sources. The house of Herod married into the priestly family of the Hasmonaeans. Two examples from the history of the house of Hillel may be cited. The priest Simeon ben Nethanel and the last high priest, Phineas ben Samuel, chosen for the office by the Zealots, were both married into the house of Hillel.[5] In connection with the latter family, one can also perhaps point to Rabbi Eliezer ben Hyrcanus who was the brother-in-law of Rabban Gamaliel of Jabneh.[6]

To preserve the purity of the line, the priests themselves took stringent precautions. This extreme attitude of the priesthood aroused the ire, at times, of the sages. The latter declare: 'The priests would hearken to you in what concerns putting away, but not in what concerns

---

[1] *De specialibus legibus* i, 110; cf. I. Heinemann, *Philons griechische und jüdische Bildung* (1932), p. 32.
[2] *P. T. Yoma* i, 38d. *P. T. Horayoth* iii, 47d.
[3] Luke 1:5.
[4] *T. B. Pesahim* 49a; cf. S. Klein, *Jüdisch-palästinisches Corpus Inscriptionum* (1920), pp. 12-13; A. Büchler, in *Festschrift A. Schwarz* (1917), pp. 135-6.
[5] Cf. below, p. 618.
[6] The priesthood of R. Eliezer ben Hyrcanus is based on interpretation of *P. T. Sotah* iii, 19a. Cf. *T. B. Shabbath* 116a for his family connections with Rabban Gamaliel ii. For doubts on the priestly origins of R. Eliezer cf. A. Hyman, *History of the Tannaim and the Amoraim* i (1964; in Hebrew), p. 162.

bringing near.'[1] The lengths to which priests went to safeguard the purity of their families may be seen from the fact that priests living in Egypt, Babylonia and other lands outside of Palestine would, when a marriage was impending, make enquiries at Jerusalem in order to ascertain the lineage of the bride.[2]

A large percentage of the priests had their permanent residence in Jerusalem. Others were scattered throughout the various cities and villages of Judaea, Galilee and Transjordan.[3] From here, they would make their periodic pilgrimages to Jerusalem, serve in turn in which-ever of the twenty-four priestly divisions to which they belonged. From Origen's commentary on Matthew, we learn that there were villages entirely inhabited by priests. Such was the case of the village of Bethphage near Jerusalem.[4] Many priests lived in the cities of Judaea, among them Gophna: 'Eighty pairs of brothers (priests) married eighty pairs of sisters of priestly origin in one night in Gophna.'[5] There was a large concentrations of priests in Jericho. In exaggerated fashion, a baraita declares that 'twenty-four divisions of priests were in the Land of Israel and twelve of them were in Jericho.'[6] Important priestly houses in the Judaean villages Zevaim[7] and Mekoshesh[8] are mentioned in the Tosefta and the Palestinian Talmud.[9] The latter village was the birthplace of the high priest Caiaphas. Issachar, one of the chief priests, came from Kefar Barkai, situated in the northernmost point of Judaea in the direction of Samaria.[10] The Gospel according to Luke indicates that priests lived in the hills of Judaea.[11] We know of priests living in Galilee and Sepphoris who would go up to Jerusalem to participate in Temple services.[12] It was Sepphoris that provided a number of high priests towards the end of Herod's reign.

The priests enjoyed many material benefits from the dues fixed by the

---

[1] *M. Eduyoth* 8:3.
[2] Jos. *Against Apion* I, 32-3.
[3] The main discussion of the priests' residences is in Büchler, pp. 159-207.
[4] Origines, *Commentaria in Matth.* 16, 17 (ed. Klostermann 1935, p. 532).
[5] *P. T. Taanith* IV, 69a; *T. B. Berakoth* 44a.
[6] *T. B. Taanith* 27a. See Büchler, pp. 161-81.
[7] On Zevaim see F. M. Abel, *Géographie de la Palestine* II, p. 452. It is mentioned in Nehemiah 11:34 between Hadid and Naballat; it seems to have been situated to the north of Lydda. Büchler, p. 186, n. 3 connects the place with הר צבועים (*M. Hallah* 4:10).
[8] Mekoshesh is still unidentified.
[9] *T. Yebamoth* 1:10; *P. T. Yebamoth* I, 3a.
[10] *T. B. Pesahim* 57a; *Kerithoth* 28b.
[11] Luke 1:39.
[12] *P. T. Yoma* VI, 43c; *T. Sotah* 13:8.

Torah.[1] Throughout the Second Temple period [a practice was in vogue which began with the Hellenistic period, and continued even after the destruction of the Temple. It was the practice of the priests to control the tithes even though the Torah assigned the latter to the Levites who, in turn, had to give a tithe of what they received to the priests.[2] From the Book of Nehemiah we still get the impression that the tithes naturally belong to the levites.[3] But in the Book of Judith the tithes, like the wave offering, belong to the priests: 'They have decided to consume the first-fruits of the grain and the tithes of the wine and oil, which they had consecrated and set aside for the priests who minister in the presence of our God at Jerusalem.'[4] So too the *Book of Jubilees*.[5] And Hecataeus, at the beginning of the Hellenistic period, declares en passant that the Jews give their tithes to the priests.[6] We have concrete evidence of this practice from the last decades of the Second Temple period.[7] It is the practice known to Philo,[8] to the author of the Epistle to the Hebrews[9] and to Josephus. The latter says, incidentally, in his autobiography, that he renounced the tithes which lawfully belonged to him as a priest.[10] And he says that the high priests towards the close of the Second Temple period used to send their servants out into the fields in order to take possession of the tithes due to the priests: τὰς τοῖς ἱερεῦσιν ὀφειλόμενας δεκάτας.[11] A literal reading of the Mishnah leads to the same conclusion: 'A priest and a Levite who took possession of a granary—the tithes belong to them,[12] that is, the tithes are to be shared in equal measure between priests and Levites. In general, the tannaitic Halakah assumes, through several of its spokesmen, that the tithes belong not only to the Levites but also to the priests. We likewise

---

[1] Useful surveys of benefits accruing to priests are given in Schürer II, pp. 297-317; Strack-Billerbeck IV, 2, pp. 640-97.
[2] Num. 18:21. [3] Neh. 10:38-40. [4] Jud. 11:13.
[5] 13:25-26; cf. Ch. Albeck, *Das Buch der Jubiläen und die Halacha* (1930), p. 30; L. Finkelstein, in *HTR* (1943), p. 22.
[6] Hecataeus, in Jos. *Against Apion* I, 188. However, Hecataeus hardly distinguished between priests and Levites; cf. J. G. Gager, in *ZNTW* (1969), pp. 137-8.
[7] On the problem of the allotment of the tithes to the priests in the period of the Second Temple see in general Y. M. Grintz, *The Book of Judith* (1957; in Hebrew), pp. 191-2. Strack-Billerbeck IV, 2, pp. 655-7.
[8] *De virtutibus* 95.
[9] Hebr. 7:5.   [10] *Life* 80.
[11]*Ant.* xx, 181; xx, 206. On the other hand it follows from *Ant.* IV, 68. 205 that the tithes belong both to the priests and Levites.
[12]M. *Peah* 1:6.

meet with the opinion that the tithes belong primarily to the priests.[1] Some justification for the assignment of at least part of the tithes to the priests can be found in the fact that they far outnumbered the Levites, after the return from the Babylonian exile.[2]

It was the practice, from the times of Malachi and Nehemiah on, to collect the tithes and distribute them in Jerusalem.[3] This is corroborated by later writings like the Book of Tobit,[4] the First Book of Maccabees[5] and the edict of Julius Caesar.[6] But for various reasons, this practice was abolished and by the close of the Second Temple period it no longer existed.[7]

From various halakic sources we may well conclude that the giving of tithes was by no means universally observed by the mass of farmers in Jewish Palestine. The fact gave rise to some acute halakic problems.[8] Perhaps the practice of concentrating the tithes in Jerusalem originally implied that tithing was done only by those who went up to Jerusalem.[9] Yet even when this practice was in vogue, it was possible for the farmer to set aside his tithes for the priest and Levite wherever he happened to live. In any event, this problem no longer existed by the end of the Second Temple period. Still, the heavy burden involved from an economic viewpoint in tithing was felt throughout the Second Temple period and undoubtedly was responsible more than anything else for limiting the practice.[10]

Clearly, the priests were not able to maintain themselves merely from the tithes and the other dues connected with the Temple service. Hence we hear of priests who engaged in various types of gainful

---

[1] See the formulations of the views of Eleazar ben Azariah and Simeon ben Eleazar in *T. B. Ketuboth* 26a; *Hullin* 131b; *Yebamoth* 86ab.

[2] It is worth noting the explanation given for the change, namely that Ezra punished the Levites because they did not return from the Babylonian exile; cf. Graetz, in *MGWJ* (1886), pp. 97-108.

[3] Malachi 3:10; Neh. 10:38 seems to imply that only the *terumah* is to be brought to the Temple, while the tithes may be delivered at any place in the country. However, it follows from Neh. 13:5 that the tithes also were delivered to the Temple.

[4] Tob. 1:6-7; Jud. 11:13.

[5] I Macc. 3:49-51.

[6] Jos. *Ant.* XIV, 203 (the tithes should be delivered to Hyrcanus the high priest).

[7] On the problem of the concentration of tithes at Jerusalem cf. also G. Alon, *Studies in Jewish History* I (1957; in Hebrew), pp. 83-92; A. Oppenheimer, in *de Vries Memorial Volume* (1968), pp. 70-83 (in Hebrew).

[8] Cf. A. Büchler, *Der galiläische Am ha-Arets des zweiten Jahrhunderts* (1906), pp. 5-41.

[9] Cf. Oppenheimer, op. cit., p. 82.

[10] Cf. Oppenheimer, ibid.

employment. So, for example, the high priest Phineas ben Samuel, a man of humble origin, was a stone-cutter;[1] Eliezer ben Zadok engaged in the sale of oil;[2] and many priests certainly gained their livelihood by means of agriculture. At the beginning of the Hellenistic period, Hecataeus emphasizes the large land-holdings of priests in Judaea.[3] In light of the preponderant position of priests in Jewish society at the time, it may be assumed that not a few of them attained to the status of wealthy landowners. Such, for example, was the case of Hyrcanus, the father of the tanna Rabbi Eliezer.[4] The priest-historian Josephus owned an estate near Jerusalem.[5] The high priest Ananias ben Nedebaeus was particularly noteworthy by reason of his extreme wealth.[6]

The requirements of the Temple ritual necessitated the division of the priests into twenty-four divisions, each division conducting the ritual in turn. This method of division continued throughout the period of the Second Temple and it may be assumed that it had its origins during the period of the First Temple. A parallel to it may be found in the Egyptian temples during both the Pharaonic and Hellenistic periods.[7] These divisions of priests were known in Second Temple times as *mishmarot* (courses). From at least the end of the Persian period, the time of the composition of the Books of Chronicles, the Jewish priesthood was divided into twenty-four courses. This division was stable, and for its existence at the end of the Second Temple period we have the testimony of Josephus.[8] It continued to exist even after the destruction of the Temple and the Bar Cochba revolt, and can be traced from inscriptions to the very end of antiquity.[9] The names of

---

[1] *T. Yoma* 1:6; *Sifra, Emor* 2.

[2] *T. Betzah* 3:8.

[3] See Hecataeus, in Diodorus Siculus XL, 3, 7. Although according to the Torah the priest did not own land (Deut. 10:9; 12:12; 18:1; Num. 18:24; cf. Philo, *De specialibus legibus* I, 131; Sir. 45:22) we have evidence from the Bible that in the early period land was already owned by priests. See 1 Kings 2:26; Amos 7:17; cf. A. Alt, *Kleine Schriften* III (1959), pp. 359-60.

[4] On the legendary wealth of the priest Eleazar ben Harsum see *P. T. Taanith* IV, 69a; *T. B. Yoma* 35b.

[5] See Jos. *Life*, 422.

[6] On the wealth of Ananias ben Nedebaeus see Jos. *Ant.* xx, 205.

[7] See H. Kees, *Orientalia* (1948), pp. 71-90; 314-25.

[8] See Jos. *Life* 2; *Ant.* VII, 366. On the *mishmarot* of the Second Temple period see Schürer II, pp. 286-91; Strack-Billerbeck II, pp. 55-68; S. Klein, *Palestinian Studies* I, 2 (1924; in Hebrew), pp. 1-29; J. Liver, *Chapters in the History of the Priests and Levites* (1968; in Hebrew), pp. 33-52.

[9] Cf. S. Klein, *The Land of Galilee* (1946; in Hebrew), pp. 64-70; 191-202; S.

these divisions are mentioned in I Chronicles, chapter 24, and talmudic sources also add the names of various people associated with them in Palestine. The relationship of individual priests and their respective priestly families to these divisions is emphasized in the sources even where the priests in question are not mentioned in connection with the Temple service. According to Josephus' testimony in his autobiography, the prestige of a priest depended on the particular division to which he belonged.[1] The history of the various divisions reflects the social development quite clearly. However, the paucity of our sources permit us to follow the latter only to a limited extent. Only here and there do we get a glimpse of the views and activities of the members of the various divisions in the history of the period.

From the Bible itself, it is evident that before the division of the priesthood into twenty-four courses, ascribed in I Chronicles to king David,[2] the priesthood was divided between four priestly families. This emerges from the list of those who returned from the Babylonian exile, as given in the Books of Ezra and Nehemiah.[3] In this list, four divisions of priests appear: the sons of Jedaiah, of the house of Jeshua, the sons of Immer, the sons of Pashhur and the sons of Harim. The house of the high priest Joshua son of Yehozadak,[4] belonged to the sons of Jedaiah. Of these four divisions, three (Jedaiah, Harim and Immer) are mentioned among the twenty-four divisions, and only that of Pashhur is missing from the list in I Chronicles. It would appear that the organization of the priesthood into twenty-four courses was the result of an official decision according to which certain families were joined together, possibly on the basis of their previous connections. The latter assertion however must be seen as purely conjectural. In any event, henceforth, these divisions maintained their fixed character and as far as we know did not undergo any essential change in their composition in course of time. The conversion of the four priestly divisions into twenty-four is explicitly stressed in talmudic literature. 'Four courses went up from the Exile, Jedaiah, Harim, Pashhur and Immer. The prophets of that generation then subdivided them into twenty-four.'[5] We have perhaps an echo of this ancient

Abramson, in *Tarbiz* xv, pp. 50-5; M. Avi-Yonah, in *Eretz Israel* (1964; in Hebrew), pp. 24-8 (an inscription from Caesarea).
[1] *Life* 2.
[2] See Liver, op. cit. pp. 38-9.
[3] Ezra 2:36-9; Neh. 7:39-42. [4] Ezra 2:36.
[5] *P. T. Taanith* iv, 68a; *T. Taanith* 2:1; *T. B. Taanith* 27ab. See Liver, op. cit., pp. 43-4.

division into four groups in the following statement by Josephus: 'For although there are four priestly tribes, each comprising upwards of five thousand members, these officiate by rotation for a fixed period of days; when the term of one party ends, others come to offer the sacrifices in their places.'[1] It is quite evident that Josephus speaks here of the service in the Temple conducted by the four priestly divisions. There is no reason to assume that some error has occurred in the manuscripts and that the original spoke of twenty-four courses. Since Josephus declares that each of the divisions numbered five thousand priests, he hardly intended to speak of twenty-four divisions.[2] According to I Chronicles, chapter 24, the division of Yehoyarib appears at the head of the list, before that of Jedaiah to which the high priest-hood of that period belonged.[3] Some scholars attribute this to the rise of the Hasmonaeans, who belonged to the division of Yehoyarib.[4] The explanation is certainly plausible. However, an alternative explanation is possible. One recalls that the house of Yehoyarib was from its very beginnings a very distinguished one. There is therefore no need to regard the Hasmonaeans at the beginning of the rebellion as *homines novi* and the representatives of the lower classes of Jewish society. They were a branch of the Yehoyarib family which had risen to im-portance in Jerusalem many years before the signal for rebellion was given at Modiin.[5] It is quite likely that the prestige of this division and its entrenched position within Jewish society aided the Has-monaeans in heading the revolt. Nevertheless, if one assumes that the Chronicler gives the list of the divisions in the order of their relative importance, the precedence of the course of Yehoyarib over that of Jedaiah requires a special explanation. It is agreed among scholars that I Chronicles was given its final editing about the year 300.[6] Whatever the exact date, it was most certainly long before the Hasmonaean rebellion.[7] On the other hand, we know that the high

---

[1] *Against Apion* II, 108.
[2] Cf. L. Herzfeld, *Geschichte des Volkes Jisrael* III (1857), p. 193.
[3] Both these courses appear alongside each other also in the Mishnah. See e.g. *M. Baba Kamma* 9:12.
[4] I Macc. 2:1; 14:29.
[5] It is true that we do not know of any particular persons from the division of Jehojarib who were conspicuous in the life of Judaea before the revolt, as we know indoubtedly about the division of Hakkoz.
[6] See O. Eissfeldt, *The Old Testament: An Introduction* (1965) p. 529ff; E. L. Curtis and A. A. Madsen, *A Critical and Exegetical Commentary on the Books of Chronicles* (1910), p. 6.
[7] Some scholars still maintain that changes and additions could have occurred

priesthood belonged uninterruptedly to the division of Jedaiah, until the removal of Jason, the brother of Onias III, by Antiochus Epiphanes. We must therefore look for a time somewhere between the age of Ezra and Nehemiah and the year 300 B.C.E. in which the legitimate high priesthood, the house of Joshua ben Yehozadak, lost some of its prestige without thereby losing the office of high priest. It is reasonable to conjecture that just such period is to be found at the time of the internal quarrels of the high priesthood at the end of the fifth and the beginning of the fourth centuries B.C.E. These quarrels resulted in the murder of Jeshua the brother of the high priest and a certain loss of status for the high priesthood in the eyes of the Persian authorities.[1] This is offered, of course, merely as a conjecture.

As indicated, the high priesthood belonged to the division of Jedaiah and continued to do so in the Jerusalem Temple until deposed by Menelaus under Antiochus Epiphanes. The descendants of this high priestly family were to become subsequently the founders and the priests of the temple of Onias in Egypt. The course of Hakkoz, the seventh in the list of priestly courses enumerated in I Chronicles, played a leading role in the public life of Judaea during the Persian and Hellenistic periods. The priests of the sons of Hakkoz who returned from Babylonia had originally had some genealogical blemish which had cast doubt on their legitimacy.[2] Yet, with the lapse of time, they managed to attain a dominant position among the leaders of Jewish society. It appears that one of the sons of Hakkoz, Meremoth son of Uriah, as early as Ezra, had served as the treasurer of Judah. It was he who was appointed by Ezra to weigh the silver brought from Babylonia by the returning exiles. He is also mentioned among those who built the wall together with Nehemiah.[3] In this connection, mention should be made of the seals dating from the Persian period discovered in Jericho, on which the name of Uriah appears. It may confidently be assumed that he was the treasurer of Judah. It may further be presumed that this Uriah was the father of Meremoth, who filled a similar office in the days of Ezra. Another possibility is that

---

after the redaction of the bulk of the book. See Ed. Meyer, *Die Entstehung des Judentums* (1896), p. 174; Schürer II, p. 290, n. 45; W. Rudolph, *Chronikbücher* (1955), p. 161; id. in *Vetus Testamentum* IV (1954), p. 402; Eissfeldt, ibid.

[1] Jos. *Ant.* XI, 297-301; Cf. A. Schalit, in *Commentationes Iudaico-Hellenisticae in Memoriam Iohannis Lewy* (1949), pp. 252-72.

[2] Ezra 2:61-63.

[3] Ezra 8:33; Neh. 3:4.

this Uriah was a descendant of Meremoth son of Uriah.[1] The obvious conclusion is that the office of treasurer of the Temple frequently passed from father to son in the division of Hakkoz. Another important member of this division was Johanan. He represented Judaea in negotiations with the Seleucid monarch and obtained from him a charter of rights.[2] It was his son, Eupolemus, who, together with Jason son of Eleazar, was sent by Judah Maccabee to Rome in 161 B.C.E. to negotiate a treaty between Rome and Judaea.[3] One may conjecture that Ben Sira was also a member of the division of Hakkoz since the name *Sirah* is the Aramaic for the Hebrew *Koz*.[4] The division of Hakkoz is also mentioned in the *Copper Scroll* from the Judaean Desert.[5] The eighth division, that of Abijah, appears in the Gospel of Luke, mentioning Zechariah, the father of John the Baptist, of the division of Abijah.[6]

The eleventh course, that of Eliashib is mentioned in a document from a place called Hardona, five kilometers from Jericho, a marriage contract, probably from 117 C.E.[7] The groom was a priest of the house of Eliashib, whose father's name was Manasseh.

The sources relating to the division of Jeshebab are more numerous. It appears that one of the high priestly houses at the end of the Second Temple period, the house of Kimhit, belonged to this division.[8] The priests of the house of Kalon whose sarcophagi were discovered in Jerusalem,[9] undoubtedly belonged to this division. One of the inscriptions on the sarcophagi reads: 'Miriam, Joezer and Simeon, children of Jehzaq, son of Kalon, of the sons of Jeshebab.'[10] What stands out in these inscriptions is the fact that we have a family of priests called Kalon. This priestly family belonged to the house of Jeshebab, that is to say, to the division so named. In the talmudic sources, the division of Jeshebab is ranked higher than that of Bilgah.

---

[1] The first possibility is suggested by N. Avigad, in *IEJ* (1957), pp. 146-53; the second has been proposed by W. F. Albright, in *BASOR* CXLVIII (1957), pp. 28-30.
[2] II Macc. 4:11.
[3] I Macc. 8:17.
[4] See S. Klein, in *Leshonenu* I, p. 341 (in Hebrew).
[5] See *DJD* III (1962), pp. 258, 291, col. VII, line 9.
[6] Luke 1:5.
[7] See *DJD* (1961), p. 110, col. I, line 2; col. II, line 17.
[8] This supposition is based on *T. B. Yoma* 47a where Jeshebab appears as a name of one of the sons of Kimhit.
[9] *CII* nos. 1350-5.   [10] *CII* no. 1352.

The historical recollections in the tradition relating to the course of Bilgah bear a special character. This division supplied the priests who were the champions of Hellenism in Jerusalem. Thus, there was Menelaus, appointed high priest by Antiochus Epiphanes, and his brother Simeon, the chief of the Temple. The latter was responsible for intervention of the Seleucid authorities in the affairs of Jerusalem and the attempt on the part of Heliodorus to despoil the Temple treasury. The third brother died in the bloody encounter in the streets of Jerusalem with the outraged Jewish masses.[1] The affiliation of these three brothers to the division of Bilgah is based above all on the ancient Latin translation of II Maccabees.[2] This identification is further confirmed by the Talmudic tradition which speaks deprecatingly of the course of Bilgah and the punishment visited upon it because of its non-Jewish behaviour.[3]

The origins of Menelaus have long intrigued scholars. To begin with, he is the first of the high priests who did not belong to the established high-priestly family; that is, those who did not succeed by reason of their legitimate descent from Joshua son of Yehozadak. Furthermore, from the consensus of the Greek manuscripts of the Second Book of Maccabees, it is clear that Simeon, the father of Menelaus, belonged to the tribe of Benjamin (Σίμων δέ τις ἐκ τῆς Βενιαμιν φυλῆς). Accordingly, many scholars have concluded that the Menelaus, one of the three brothers mentioned above was of the tribe of Benjamin.[4] Some scholars have advanced the theory that Menelaus belonged to the house of Tobias,[5] a theory for which the sources offer no support.

However, it is quite difficult to accept the assumption that Menelaus and his brothers were not of the house of Aaron. True, one can readily believe Antiochus was capable of going so far as to appoint to the high priesthood someone who was not of priestly descent and that Menelaus

---

[1] II Macc. 4:29.
[2] See D. de Bruyne, *Les anciennes traductions latines de Machabées* (1932), p. 118: 'Simon autem quidam de tribu balgea (L, bargea x), praepositus templi constitutus.'
[3] *M. Sukkah* 5:8; *T. Sukkah* 4:28; *P. T. Sukkah* v, 55d; *T. B. Sukkah* 56b.
[4] II Macc. 4:23. See Schürer-Vermes-Millar I, p. 149.
[5] See e.g. Ed. Meyer, *Ursprung und Anfänge des Christentums II* (1921), p. 133; A. Schlatter, *Geschichte Israels von Alexander dem Grossen* (1925), p. 103. Also A. Büchler, *Die Tobiaden und die Oniaden* (1899), pp. 88-90, holds the view that Menelaus belonged to the Tobiads, and also emphasizes the connection between the Tobiads and the tribe of Benjamin. V. Aptowitzer, in *HUCA* v (1928), p. 296, maintains that Menelaus belonged to the tribe of Benjamin on his mother's side.

would readily accept such appointment. But if this were indeed the case then the sources hostile to Menelaus, and above all II Maccabees, would certainly have mentioned it among the great sins ascribed to him. Furthermore, the brother of Menelaus, Simeon, had already been appointed to the high office of chief of the Temple (προστάτης τοῦ ἱεροῦ),[1] a central position in the administration of the Temple, one that would certainly be reserved for a priest. One must bear in mind that this appointment was already made in the reign of Seleucus IV when as yet no policy hostile to Jewish religion had been launched. In the light of these facts, scholars have advanced the theory that an error has occurred in the Greek text and that instead of Benjamin one should read either Miniamin or Miamin, the name of a well-known priestly division.[2] More convincing is the suggestion based on the manuscripts of the ancient Latin translation of II Maccabees. From these manuscripts it appears quite plausible that the reference is to a 'tribe' (φυλή), that is, to the division of Bilgah.[3]

The latter suggestion is to be preferred on the following grounds. 1. Even though the manuscripts of the ancient Latin translation of II Maccabees are relatively late, they reflect an ancient tradition independent of the Greek manuscripts that have reached us.[4] 2. If the original reading was φυλή (tribus) of Bilgah, one can understand the change to Benjamin since the later scribes no longer understood the meaning of the term 'tribe' in connection with Bilgah. The reading Bilgah here is obviously the lectio difficilior. On the other hand, one cannot understand how the Latin translators came to change the unambiguous and perfectly clear and well known term 'the tribe of Benjamin' to the relatively unknown term 'the tribe of Bilgah.' 3. Here, we have to understand the term 'tribe' (φυλή) in the sense of division of priests. The term was current in Hellenistic Egypt[5] and it is in this sense that it is employed by Josephus.[6] Subsequently, this usage of the term was forgotten and it is perhaps this lapse into oblivion that explains the error that occurred in our Greek manuscripts.

[1] II Macc. 3:4; cf. E. Bickerman, in *Annuaire de l'institut de philologie et d'histoire orientales et slaves* VII, pp. 5-40.
[2] See Herzfeld, op. cit., II, p. 218; H. Graetz, in *MGWJ* (1872), p. 62; J. N. Epstein, in *MGWJ* (1934), p. 98, n. 3.
[3] See D. de Bruyne, in *RB* (1922), pp. 46-7; F. M. Abel, in *Miscellanea Mercati* I (1946), pp. 52-58; it has been received into the Göttingen text of Hanhart (1959). Cf. also Jeremias, p. 185.
[4] This is also attested elsewhere in II Macc., as e.g. in II Macc. 4:4.
[5] Cf. e.g. *OGIS* no. 56, lines 24, 26, 28-31.
[6] *War* IV, 155; *Against Apion* II, 108 (tribus).

4. The assumption that Menelaus belonged to the sons of Bilgah is indirectly supported by the talmudic sources which, as already observed, speak disparagingly of the course of Bilgah. The following is the account of the Babylonian Talmud: 'The course of Bilgah always divided it in the south. Our Rabbis taught: it happened that Miriam, the daughter of Bilgah, apostasized and married a soldier of the Greek kings. When the Greeks entered the Sanctuary, she stamped with her sandal upon the altar, crying out, 'Lukos, Lukos. How long wilt thou consume Israel's money'. And yet thou dost not stand by them in the time of oppression'.''[1]

As a result of the enthusiastic participation of the division of Bilgah in radical Hellenization under the aegis of Antiochus Epiphanes, its prestige suffered a sharp fall and it became the target of opprobrium in later times. Despite it, however, later members of the division took part in the life of the nation and revealed genuine loyalty to its sacred values. As we have already mentioned above, within the context of a description of the burning of the Temple by Titus, we hear that among the priests who threw themselves into the flames was a certain Meir son of Bilgah, one of the members of this priestly course.[2]

The presence of the seventeenth division, that of Hezir, is reflected in one of the famous inscriptions from the Kidron Valley, about fifty metres from the centre of the Tomb of Absalom. The family tomb of the sons of Hezir is apparently from the Hellenistic period. Architectural considerations lead to the conclusion that the tomb of the sons of Hezir was among the first Jewish tombs in Jerusalem to reflect Greek motifs.[3] Hence, it is to be regarded as the most ancient of the architectural monuments of the Jerusalem necropolis in the Second Temple period.[4] The three-line Hebrew inscription carved on the facade of the tomb reads as follows: 'This is the grave and memorial of Eleazar Honia Joezer Judah Simeon Johanan sons of Joseph son of Obed Joseph and Eleazar sons of Honia priests of the sons of Hezir.' It should be noted at once that the inscription was not all carved at once, when the tomb was dug. The date of the carving on the façade of the tomb does not lead us to assume that the inscription dates from the

[1] *T. B. Sukkah* 56b. There is no adequate reason for dating the story to the Roman period, as is done by Büchler, p. 76, n. 3.
[2] Jos. *War* VI, 280.
[3] See N. Avigad, *Ancient Monuments in the Kidron Valley* (1954; in Hebrew), pp. 37-78.
[4] See N. Avigad, op. cit., p. 57; cf. L. H. Vincent, in *Memorial J. Chaine* (1950), pp. 385-397.

same time. The script does not allow of any certain conclusions as to its date. Nonetheless, there is no sufficient reason to assent to the opinion of the scholars who connect this inscription of the sons of Hezir with the house of Boethus.[1]

The twenty-first division, that of Jachim, produced the last high priest of the Second Temple period, Phineas son of Samuel.[2] The same division also appears in the inscription 'Menahem of the sons of Jachim, priest.'[3]

The twenty-third division, that of Delaiah, is represented by Joseph son of Delaiah who threw himself into the flames of the burning Temple together with Meir son of Bilgah.

In a fragment of the Dead Sea Scrolls dealing with the calendar, the names of several divisions are preserved: Maaziah (Maoziah), Yehoyarib, Jedaiah, Seorim and Jeshua.[4]

It is difficult to estimate the actual number of priests during the Second Temple period and what fraction they formed of the total population of Jewish Palestine. Among those who returned from Babylon under Cyrus,[5] the priests made up close to ten per cent of the total, 4,289 priests out of a total of 42,360 men. To this number of priests there must be added those who remained in Judah and were not exiled to Babylonia. Presumably, the priests who had remained were a much smaller proportion of the local population than those who returned from exile. In the time of Nehemiah, the priests of Jerusalem alone numbered 1,192.[6] The First Book of Chronicles gives the figure as 1,760.[7] Hecataeus speaks of 1,500 priests and it appears that he has in mind only the priests of Jerusalem.[8] In the *Letter of Aristeas*,[9] we read of 700 priests who minister in the Temple. The reference is apparently only to the priests of a single division. Josephus speaks of 20,000 priests as the total number in Judaea.[10] It is clear that during the Second Temple period the percentage of priests to the total Jewish population decreased markedly, in contrast to their number just after the return from Babylon. The absorption and proselytization

---

[1] So e.g. S. Klein, *Jüdisch-palästinisches Corpus Inscriptionum* (1920), pp. 14-15; W. F. Albright, in *JBL* (1937), p. 159.
[2] Jos. *War* IV, 155 ('Ενιάχιν).
[3] See J. T. Milik, in *Studi Biblici Franciscani* (1953/4), p. 269.
[4] See S. Talmon, in *Scripta Hierosolymitana* IV (1958), p. 170.
[5] Ezra 2:36-9; 2:64.
[6] Neh. 11:10-14.   [7] I Chron. 9:13.
[8] Hecataeus, in Jos. *Against Apion* I, 188. Büchler, p. 49.
[9] *Letter of Aristeas* 95.
[10] *Against Apion* II, 108; Jeremias, pp. 204-5.

of large numbers of the non-Jewish population, especially in the time of John Hyrcanus, Aristobolus I and Alexander Jannaeus did not of course increase the number of priests. The latter could increase only through their birth-rate. Thus, the proportion of priests to the total population gradually decreased.

The Levites

The Levites continued to exist as a separate entity throughout the Second Temple period but their place in Jewish society is secondary to that of the priests.[1] Wherever the sources emphasize the importance of the Levites, it is essentially because of their affiliation with the house of Aaron. Non-Jewish sources, with one exception,[2] do not reckon with the Levites as such. The reason may be that these sources do not distinguish between priests and Levites since both are regarded as belonging to the same priestly class. One of the characteristic features of the development of the class of Levites in this period is the appropriation of their right to the tithes by the priests. There is a recurring struggle for prestige between priest and Levite in the Second Temple period. Our sources indicate generally the connection of the Levites with the Temple and the functions they performed in it. The sources dwell particularly on Levites who served as singers and door-keepers in the Temple.

Just after the exile, the paucity of the number of Levites who returned with priests is noteworthy. Here, the Levites numbered only 341 sons of Asaph, of whom 128 were singers, 74 doorkeepers, and 74 Levites without a specific function. This contrasts with the 4,289 priests who returned.[3] This disproportion may be the result of two factors. The priests looked forward more eagerly than did the Levites to the restoration of the Temple since they would be playing a central role there. Further, constituting as they did the upper stratum of Jewish society, a much larger proportion of priests was exiled. As a result, Ezra had subsequently to contend with the problem of the paucity of Levites: 'I gathered them to the river that runs to Ahava, and there we encamped three days. As I reviewed the people and the priests, I found there none of the sons of Levi.'[4] It was only when Ezra had

---

[1] On the Levites see Schürer II, pp. 293-7; Jeremias, pp. 207-13; R. Meyer, in *Theologisches Wörterbuch zum Neuen Testament* IV, pp. 245-7.
[2] Plutarch, *Quaestiones convivales* IV, 6,2.
[3] Ezra 2:40-2. [4] Ezra 8:15.

sent messengers to Iddo, the leader of the Jews at Cesiphia, did he succeed in adding 38 Levites to his entourage along with a number of Nethinim.[1] Nevertheless, in the Books of Ezra and Nehemiah, the Levites are invariably mentioned alongside of the priests[2] and it is they who exhort the people and supervise the Temple.[3] It is interesting to compare the number of Levites in Jerusalem after the *synoecismos* of Nehemiah: 456 Levites (284 singers and 172 doorkeepers) as contrasted with 1,192 priests.[4]

Under Nehemiah, it was taken for granted that the tithes belonged to the Levites even though we hear that the people neglected the tithing. 'I also found out that the portions of the Levites had not been given to them; so that the Levites and the singers, who did the work, had fled each to his field.'[5]

The importance of the Levites emerges from the description of them given in I Chronicles, which reflects the situation obtaining in the pre-Hellenistic period. By contrast, they are conspicuous by their absence in the basic sources of the Hellenistic and Hasmonaean periods. Such is the case, for example, in Ben Sira, who dwells on praises of the priestly class. And I Maccabees does not find it necessary even to mention the functions of the Levites. What is most striking is that they are not mentioned even in contexts where one would expect them to appear, such as the description of the dedication of the Temple by Judah Maccabee or in that of the celebration of the capture of the Acra.[6] This silence reflects the relative decline of the Levites as a social class in the Hellenistic period in contrast to the priests. This decline took on concrete form when the priests seized control, to some extent, of the tithes that had originally been the prerogative of the Levites. And then, all the outstanding personalities of the period came exclusively from the ranks of the priests. There is not a single Levite who occupies a significant position in the life of the period. The absence of the Levites from the basic literary sources of the period is only partially explained by the fact that the authors of these works were priests—Ben Sira and perhaps the author of I Maccabees, the latter the champion of the priestly house of the Hasmonaeans. Even

[1] On whom see R. Kittel, *Geschichte des Volkes Irsael* III, 2 (1929), pp. 417-9.
[2] Ezra 1:5; 2:70; 3:8; 6:18; 7:7; 7:13; 7:24; 8:15-18; 8:29-30; 9:1; 10:5; 10:23-24; Neh. 7:43-5.
[3] Neh. 8:11; 9:4-5.
[4] Neh. 11:18-19.
[5] Neh. 13:10.
[6] Cf. A. Büchler, in *ZAW* (1899), p. 123.

in the official documents included in I Maccabees, the Levites, in contrast to the priests, go unmentioned. Nor do they appear as one of the specific elements of the people in the great assembly that took place in Jerusalem in the days of Simeon the Hasmonaean. However, from a document not included in I Maccabees, an official Seleucid document from the time of the capture of Jerusalem by Antiochus III, preserved in the *Antiquities* of Josephus, we learn that even in the Hellenistic period the Levites occupied an important position in Jewish society.[1] This follows from the inclusion of some of the Levites (alongside of the members of the gerousia and the priests) among those who were exempted by Antiochus from paying the royal taxes. 'The Temple singers shall be relieved from the poll-tax and the crown-tax and the salt-tax which they pay.'[2]

The specific functions of the Levites were connected with the Temple. Most prestigious among the Levites was the class that served as singers. In this context, Philo's description of the functions of the Levites in the Temple is also most interesting.[3] They relate to the policing and sanitation of the Temple. 'Some of these are stationed at the doors as gate-keepers at the very entrances, some within in front of the sanctuary to prevent any unlawful person from setting foot thereon, either intentionally or unintentionally, some patrol around it by turn in relays by appointment night and day, keeping watch and guard at both seasons. Others sweep the porticoes and the open court, convey away the refuse and ensure cleanliness.' One notes that Philo does not mention the important role of the Levites as the Temple singers. As such, they participated in the services each morning and evening, and rendered special music during festivals, such as the festival of the Drawing of Water. The singers among the Levites are already noted in the Ezra, Nehemiah and Chronicles. It was they who viewed themselves as closest to the status of priests. An echo of the struggle of the Levitical singers to raise their status to that of the priests, at least as far as their vestments were concerned, is to be found in Josephus who describes the situation at the close of the Second Temple period.[4] He informs us that the singers persuaded Agrippa II to convene the sanhedrin in order that it might hear their suit. The sanhedrin decided

---

[1] *Ant.* XII, 138-44.
[2] *Ant.* XII, 142. Cf. E. Bickermann, in *REJ*, C (1935), pp. 4-35; A. Alt, in *ZAW* (1939), pp. 283-5; M. Stern, *The Documents on the History of the Hasmonean Revolt* (2nd ed. 1972: in Hebrew), pp. 32-41.
[3] *De specialibus legibus* I, 156.
[4] *Ant.* XX, 216-7.

that they might wear garments of linen similar to those worn by the priests. Josephus adds that at the same time the Sanhedrin ruled that other Levites who served in the Temple could be taught the art of song.[1] What is unquestionably alluded to here is the effort on the part of lower-class Levites to attain the prestigious status enjoyed by the singers. Josephus has nothing but disparagement for the changes that took place in the Temple service in the time of Agrippa II.

Together with the singers, the doorkeepers appear as the other specific group of Levites, in Ezra, Nehemiah and Chronicles. Their function was to open and close the gates of the Temple. Their status was lower than that of the singers as is particularly attested by the story related of Joshua ben Hananiah and Johanan ben Gudgeda in a baraita in the Babylonian Talmud.[2] 'It happened that Rabbi Joshua ben Hananiah went to assist Rabbi Johanan ben Gudgeda in the fastening of the Temple doors, whereupon he said to him: 'My son, turn back, for you are of the singers, not of the doorkeepers'.'' Thus, Johanan ben Gudgeda, while himself a member of the doorkeepers, seeks to preserve the traditional distinction between the latter and the singers, to which class Joshua ben Hananiah belonged, a higher class on the social ladder of the Levites.

While it is possible to point to many leading figures of the period who belonged to the priestly class, such is not the case in regard to Levites. Here, the sources mention only a few: Joshua ben Hananiah, referred to above, one of the singers at the close of the Second Temple period, and Joseph bar Naba of Cyprus, one of the first Christian missionaires.[3] Generally, those who bore the name Levi or son of Levi in this period may be assigned to the Levites. Among these, the outstanding personality was no doubt Johanan ben Levi of Gischala, one of the most important leaders of Galilean Jewry and one of its commanders in the great revolt.[4] Another Galilean was Jannai ben Levi who, according to Josephus, was a relative of Agrippa II.[5] One of Josephus' assistants and bodyguards in Galilee was a Levite.[6] Another Levite fell victim to the Zealots during the civil war in Jerusalem, at the time of the great revolt. Josephus informs us that the victim was close to

---

[1] *Ant.* xx, 218; cf. H. Vogelstein, *Der Kampf zwischen Priestern und Leviten seit den Tagen Ezechiels* (1899), pp. 139-40.
[2] *T. B. Arakhin* 11b.
[3] Acts 4:36.
[4] Jos. *War* ii, 575; iv, 85; *Life* 43; 122; 189.
[5] *Life* 131.
[6] *War* ii, 642; *Life* 171; 319.

the royal house.[1] The royal house meant here is that of the Herodians. It is possible that the affinity derived from his mother's family.[2]

The high priests

The period of Herod and the Roman procurators marks the consolidation of the priestly oligarchy, an oligarchy that included certain priestly families who held exclusive control of the high priesthood. At the time, it was taken for granted that the high priesthood could be taken from one of these families and given to another, as long as the position remained within the control of the same group of families. All of the latter made up the upper class of the priesthood. In previous generations, until and including the Hasmonaean age, the high priesthood was dominated by a single priestly family. In the days of Herod, this monopoly ceased and we witness a struggle for the high priesthood among a number of priestly houses, each regarded as of equal rank.

This new situation is clearly reflected in the sources related to the close of the Second Temple period. Thus, one of the current designations of the time was 'high priests' or 'sons of high priests' (ἀρχιερεῖς). In connection with these terms, it is manifest that not all those who are described as high priests in either the Talmudic sources or in the New Testament actually served in that capacity.

The period was marked by rapid, successive changes in the office of high priest. This situation naturally accounts for the presence of a certain number of former high priests who continued to bear the title even if they no longer held the office. Alongside of high priests who held the position for long periods of time, for example, Joseph Caiaphas (18-36 C.E.)[3] or Ananias ben Nedebaeus (47-59 C.E.), we hear of high priests whose term of office did not exceed a year or even a few months. This situation is the occasion of the patristic view that the term of the high priest was limited to one year.[4] However, it is quite clear from the sources that not all the persons described by them as high priests could possibly have served in that office even for a short period of time.

---

[1] *War* IV, 141.
[2] One should also mention the Levi of the Gospels (Mark 2:14; Luke 5:27).
[3] Cf. chapter six, p. 349.
[4] Cf. already the expression ἀρχιερεὺς ὢν τοῦ ἐνιαυτοῦ ἐκείνου in John 11:49; cf. 11:51; 18:13; Eusebius, *Historia ecclesiastica* I, 13; G. Alon, *Studies in Jewish History* I (1957; in Hebrew), pp. 57-60.

Some examples from the sources will indicate their very broad use of the term high priest.

In many instances, we read in the Gospels of the activities of the 'high priests' (note the plural).[1] Numerous similar examples may be cited from the Acts of the Apostles.[2] The term high priests in the plural likewise appears in the works of Josephus.[3]

Clearly in the passages in which specific persons are mentioned by their personal names, the people described as high priests were not such in the accepted meaning of the term. Moreover, one gets the impression that some of them not only did not serve in that office but that even the sources do not consider them as functioning high priests. So it would appear in the case of Scaeva of Ephesus (Acts 19:14) whose seven sons exorcised demons in the name of Jesus. There was certainly no high priest in the Temple in Jerusalem by that name. The same may be said of Simeon, one of the high priests who was among those sent to Galilee to depose Josephus from his post (*Life* 197). Josephus says of him that he was the youngest among the delegation. Another high priest who never actually held that office was Jesus ben Sapphias who was appointed commander of Idumaea by the revolutionary government in Jerusalem (*War* II,566). In *War* VI,114, Josephus speaks of high priests and of the sons of two high priests, both called Matthias. One of them can be identified with Matthias ben Theophilus. The second, however, cannot be identified with any priest by that name who served as high priest towards the close of the Second Temple period. Another high priest belonging to this category is a certain Levi who is mentioned in an Oxyrhynchus papyrus.[4] To this list there may be added several personages mentioned in Talmudic literature; Pniel,[5] Issachar of the village of Barkai,[6] and Eleazar ben Harsum.[7] Here too mention must be made of the high priest Akabiah whose name appears on one of the ostraca of Masada.[8]

[1] Matth. 2:4; 16:21; 26:14; 27:63; Mark 8:31; 14:53; 15:11; Luke 20:19; 23:10; John 7:32; 12:10; 19:6.
[2] Acts 4:6 (γένος ἀρχιερατικόν); 9:21; 19:14.
[3] *Ant.* xx, 180ff; xx, 207; *War* II, 316; II, 336; II, 410; IV, 151; *Life* 9; 194; 197.
[4] *The Oxyrhynchus Papyri* v, no. 840; cf. E. Preuschen, *ZNW* (1908), pp. 1-11; A. Sulzbach, op. cit., p. 175-6; L. Blau, op. cit., pp. 204-15; A. Marmorstein, in *ZNW* (1914). pp. 336-8.
[5] *T. B. Gittin* 58a.
[6] *T. B. Kerithoth* 28b.
[7] On Eleazar ben Harsum see *T. Yoma* 1:22; *P. T. Taanith* IV, 69a; *T. B. Yoma* 35b. Cf. J. Perles, in *MGWJ* (1872), pp. 268-71; A. Kohut, in *JQR* III (1891), pp. 549-51.
[8] See Y. Yadin, in *IEJ* (1965), p. 84.

All these examples force one to conclude that in addition to those who actually served in the office of high priest or had done so at one time, there was another category included among the ἀρχιερεῖς. Who were they? To this question, scholars have offered a variety of answers for more than a hundred years. One suggestion is that they were the heads of the twenty-four priestly divisions.[1] This interpretation is not supported by even the slightest hint to that effect in the relevant sources, even though the facts known to us do not explicitly contradict it. On the other hand, the facts do not necessitate limiting the number of these high priests to heads of the priestly divisions alone.

Another interpretation views these high priests as the priestly members of the Sanhedrin mentioned in the New Testament.[2] One of the most commonly accepted opinions in this matter is based on two assumptions: 1. that former high priests continued to bear the title; 2. that the title was extended to members of their families. Thus, the term high priest at the close of the Second Temple period would indicate someone who belonged to a distinguished family, a member of which at one time had held that office. This interpretation was accepted by Kuenen and Schürer among others.[3] In the twentieth century, this view has been contested. Jeremias has proposed an interpretation which has found acceptance by other scholars.[4] He sees in these high priests, the distinguished members of the priesthood of the Jerusalem Temple, people whom he describes as belonging to the *Oberpriesterschaft* or as *Erzpriester*; people who stood out from among the lower classes of common priests. These were the priests who fulfilled important functions in the Temple, such as treasurers, administrators and the like. These priests were members of a court that rendered legal decisions affecting the priesthood and constituted a distinct bloc within the Sanhedrin.

Some of the objections that Jeremias raised against Schürer's view are undoubtedly valid. He is unquestionably right when he asserts that the term 'sons of the high priests'[5] is not to be understood literally, but

[1] For a survey of older views see E. Schürer, *Theologische Studien und Kritiken* (1872), pp. 593ff.
[2] See K. Wieseler, *Beiträge zur richtigen Würdigung der Evangelien und der evangelischen Geschichte* (1869), pp. 205-30.
[3] See A. Kuenen, *Gesammelte Abhandlungen* (1894), pp. 57-8; Schürer II, pp. 274-7.
[4] Jeremias, pp. 175-81. See Schrenk, in *Theologisches Wörterbuch zum N.T.* III, pp. 271-2.
[5] *M. Ketuboth* 13:1-2; *T. Ohiloth* 17:8.

is to be taken rather as a generic term. That is to say, 'sons of the high priests' were themselves high priests much as the 'sons of the prophets' were themselves prophets.[1] But can this interpretation be accepted without reservation? Do we have to assume, for example, that a man like Scaeva whose sons exorcised demons in Ephesus was at one time one of the higher officials of the Temple? Or that the high priests whom Johanan ben Zakkai met in Galilee also belonged to the latter body?[2]

It seems to us, that in the search for a satisfactory explanation, one has to provide a framework broad enough to embrace all the phenomena and based on something more than a merely formal definition. We should assert, then, that at the close of the Second Temple period, any distinguished priest, distinguished by reason of his social standing, and in a majority of instances, one who belonged to the group of oligarchical priestly families of the high priesthood could be called a high priest. The members of such families presumably occupied the important positions in the Temple. Hence, in effect, the principal officers of the Temple could also be called high priests. What was decisive was not the specific function in the administration of the Temple but one's general social standing. Even someone who did not fulfil a definite function in the Temple could be called a high priest by reason of his social status. Thus, the term high priests serves as an expression *par excellence* of the social hierarchy that prevailed at the end of the Second Temple period. Similarly, it reflects the collective superiority of the oligarchical class of the priesthood.

These priestly families of high social rank managed to maintain their position and, in no small measure, shaped the character of Jewish society in those years, in spite of the rise of the Herodian house and the non-priestly families that prospered as the direct result of the latter's influence and in spite of the rise of the class of sages and the prestige of the Pharisees under the house of Hillel. From among these families, certain individuals stood out, people who constituted a kind of élite for the priestly class in general.

The Tosefta and the Babylonian Talmud give us a concise picture of the composition of this oligarchy. 'Abba Saul ben Bothnith said in the name of Abba Joseph ben Hanan: 'Woe is me because of the house of Boethus, woe is me because of their staves. Woe is me because of the house of Hanan, woe is me because of their whisperings. Woe is me

---

[1] Jeremias, p. 177; Alon, op. cit., p. 61, n. 41.
[2] *Avot de Rabbi Natan*, Version II, 12 (p. 56); cf. J. Neusner, *A Life of Johanan ben Zakkai* (1970), pp. 47-53, on the sojourn of Johanan ben Zakkai in Galilee.

because of the house of Kathros, woe is me because of their pens. Woe is me because of the house of Ishmael ben Phiabi, woe is me because of their fists. For they are high priests and their sons are treasurers and their sons-in-law are trustees and their servants beat the people with staves."[1] The priestly houses listed here in the Talmud are enumerated in the following order: the house of Boethus, the house of Hanan, the house of Kadros and the house of Ishmael ben Phiabi. These four houses are also known to us from Josephus. To this élite of the high priesthood, we must assign also the house of Kimhit.

The house of Boethus is mentioned first in the Talmud among the families of the high priesthood and rightly so. For it was this house above all others that put its stamp on the inner development of the Second Temple period. It came to the fore under Herod, produced from its ranks a high priest in the days of Agrippa I and played a leading role in Jewish society up to the destruction of the Temple. The house of Boethus became a kind of symbol of the age of Herod and the procurators. In miniature, it reflected the social development of Jewish Palestine at that time. The term Boethusians became famous in Jewish tradition, as a synonym for Sadduceans. The house of Boethus belonged to the new social élite that came to the fore with the Herodian house with whom its interests were joined. It was eminent enough to determine the way the high priesthood functioned from the time of Herod the Great. It had strong ties with the royal house and with other priestly families.

The house of Boethus was not the first non-Hasmonean priestly family that attained the high priesthood in Herod's time. It was preceded by Hananel the Babylonian and by the house of Phiabi whose representative, Jesus son of Phiabi, served as high priest under Herod. The ancestor of the house of Boethus had migrated from Alexandria some time before 23 B.C.E., as early as the thirties of the first century B.C.E. In the year 23 B.C.E., when Simeon ben Boethus was appointed high priest, he was already considered a Jerusalemite ('Ιεροσολυμίτης). From the beginning, the family was regarded as a particularly eminent one. Josephus explains its swift ascent by its marrying into the royal family.[2] Herod wanted to marry Simeon ben Boethus' daughter and

---

[1] *T. Menahoth* 13:21; *T. B. Pesahim* 57a. Cf. also on the high-priestly houses and politics E. M. Smallwood in *JTS* (1962), pp. 14-34. On Abba Shaul see W. Bacher, *Tradition und Tradenten in den Schulen Palästinas und Babyloniens* (1914), p. 674: Index of the names of the Tannaim.
[2] *Ant.* xv, 322.

in order to elevate the status of his father-in-law, appointed him high priest, after deposing his predecessor in the office, Jesus son of Phiabi. Simeon ben Boethus, however, did not continue to hold the position until Herod's death but was deposed as the result of a family quarrel in the royal household. It seems that Herod's wife, Mariamme, daughter of Simeon ben Boethus, was implicated in a plot hatched by Antipater.[1] Shortly afterwards, Herod removed Matthias son of Theophilus from the office of high priest and appointed in his stead Joazar of the house of Boethus, his brother-in-law. Subsequently, Archelaus deposed Joezer and replaced him by the latter's brother, Eleazar.[2] Agrippa I, at the beginning of his reign (41 C.E.), removed Theophilus son of Ananus from the office of high priest and replaced him by Simeon Cantheras of the house of Boethus, apparently the younger son of the Simeon ben Boethus who had served in that position in the days of Herod.[3] It would thus appear that the three sons of Simeon ben Boethus of Herod's time, Joazar, Eleazar and Simeon, served at one time or another as high priests.

During this entire period, even when members of the house of Boethus did not actually hold the position of high priest, the house of Boethus as such was regarded as a family of high priests. One of the prominent figures among the members of this family during the days of the great revolt was a man by the name of Matthias whom Josephus describes as Matthias ben Boethus.[4] He paved the way for the rise of Simeon bar Giora as leader of the revolt in Jerusalem, in order to weaken the

[1] In not a few passages Josephus says expressly that Simeon, the son of Boethus, was the king's father-in-law (*Ant.* xv, 320; 322; xvii, 78; xviii, 109; 136), and also that it was he who acted as high priest. But some scholars deny this and are of the opinion that it was Simeon's father Boethus who was Herod's father-in-law. See Schürer in his article in *Studien und Kritiken* (1872), p. 599; in his *Geschichte* ii, p. 270 he hesitates, and so does Bammel, p. 147, n. 5. However, this is hardly tenable. Cf. M. Stern, in *Tarbiz* xxxv (1966), p. 247, n. 83 (in Hebrew).

[2] Jos. *Ant.* xvii, 339.

[3] Jos. *Ant.* xix, 297. That a son should bear the name of his father, even if not born posthumously, is well in accord with the habit of the period. According to Luke 1:59 it was intended at first to call John the Baptist after his father, who was then living, and the historian Josephus, the son of Matthias (Josephus) had a brother also called Matthias (*Life* 8), though his father was certainly living when his brother was born, as he attained to an old age and was still alive at the time of the siege of Jerusalem (*War* v, 533). Cf. M. Stern, in *Zion* (1960), p. 8 (Hebrew); J. Mann, in *HUCA* i, p. 328, n. 14; Strack-Billerbeck ii, pp. 107-8.

[4] *War* v, 527; the son of Boethus should not mean literally the son of a man called Boethus, but rather signifies that he belonged to the family of Boethus.

influence of Johanan of Gischala. Josephus describes Matthias as a man popular with the people and indicates that he was one of the high priests. However, one is not to conclude from this that he is to be identified with Matthias ben Theophilus, the high priest at the outbreak of the revolt.[1] Subsequently, he and his three sons were put to death by order of Simeon bar Giora. A fourth son managed to escape to the Roman camp.

As was the practice of high priestly families at that time, the house of Boethus also married into distinguished priestly families. We know of at least one instance of such marriage. According to Talmudic sources, Martha, the daughter of Boethus, married the high priest Joshua ben Gamala.[2]

The house of Hanan appears on the scene somewhat later. It began its rise under the first Roman governors or, at the very earliest, in the time of Archelaus. It appears that the first member of this family to hold the position of high priest was Joshua ben Σεέ (?).[3] The latter served as high priest between Eleazar ben Boethus and the second term of office of Joazar. He had been appointed by Archelaus, son of Herod. His appointment to the office, like that of his predecessor, Matthias ben Theophilus I, marked a break in the exclusive hegemony of the house of Boethus that had prevailed under Herod. There is no reason to believe that Joshua was the first of the famous priestly house of Hanan and it is quite possible that he was the brother of the high priest Ananus ben Σεθί (?).[4] The names Σεέ and Σεθί[5] are variations of the same name whose origin is far from clear.

This Ananus not only served in the office of high priest for a considerable period of time but was also the father of five sons who were high priests. In addition, he was the father-in-law of a high priest. We

---

[1] *War* VI, 114 speaks of sons of two high priests called Matthias. It seems that one of them is Matthias, the son of Boethus, and the second is Matthias, the son of Theophilus.

[2] *M. Yebamoth* 6:4; *T. B. Yebamoth* 61a.

[3] Jos. *Ant.* XVII, 341.

[4] Jos. *Ant.* XVIII, 26.

[5] Σεθί and Σεέ are probably variations on the same name. Σεθί is read in the mss. AE, while Σεέ is the reading of MW. The Latin translation omits the name. J. Derenbourg, *Essai sur l'histoire et la géographie de la Palestine* (1867), p. 195, n. 3, suggests that the name should be identified with that of Ben-Zion (בן ציון) known from *M. Eduyoth* 8:7. Derenbourg on p. 196 also expresses the opinion that the family of Hanan, like that of Boethus, came from the Diaspora, and he identifies Ananus, the son of Sethi (or See) with Hananel the Egyptian (*M. Parah* 3:5), but it is hard to substantiate all these conjectures. Cf. also H. Graetz, in *MGWJ* (1851-2), p. 595.

know the names of his sons in the order of their succession to the office; Eleazar, Jonathan, Theophilus, Matthias and Ananus.[1] But, as we have already observed, the eminence of the house of Hanan was based not only on the high priests in its ranks but also on its marriages with other high priestly families. From the Gospel of John, we learn that the first Ananus was the father-in-law of Caiaphas.[2] Since it has been conjectured that the high priest Elionaeus was actually the son of Caiaphas, then this Elionaeus was a grandson of Ananus and the five high priests, the sons of Ananus, were his uncles. But even this does not exhaust the family ties of the house of Hanan. One may reasonably conjecture that the high priest at the time of the great revolt, Matthias ben Theophilus, was also somehow related to the house of Hanan. It is surely no mere coincidence that two of the sons of the first Ananus bore the names of Theophilus and Matthias.[3]

The eminence of the house of Phiabi is shown by the fact that no fewer than three of its members attained the office of high priest. The first, Jesus son of Phiabi, had been appointed by Herod. The second was Ishmael, son of the first Phiabi, who held the office in the days of the early Roman governors. The third was Ishmael son of the second Phiabi, who was appointed by Agrippa II.[4] The first of this house to attain the position, as has already been observed, was Jesus son of Phiabi.[5] He was removed from his position by Herod in order to make room for Simeon ben Boethus, Herod's father-in-law.

The house of Phiabi, then, was the first of the oligarchical families of the high priesthood and, in this regard, preceded the houses of Boethus and Hanan. We do not know why Herod considered Jesus son of Phiabi worthy of the position of high priest. It is probable, as the name Phiabi indicates, that he had come from Egypt.[6]

About the two other members of the house of Phiabi mentioned by Josephus, little information has been preserved. Of Ishmael ben Phiabi I, we know that he was appointed to his position by Valerius

---

[1] Jos. *Ant.* XVIII, 34; XVIII, 95; 123; XIX, 313-316; *War* II, 240; *Ant.* XX, 162-164; XIX, 342; XX, 197.
[2] John 18:13.
[3] Jos. *Ant.* XVIII, 123; XIX, 316; 342.
[4] Again, as in the case of Boethus, we should not take the name Phiabi as the name of the father of Ishmael, but rather assume that both the Ishmaels belonged to the house of Phiabi. Of course we have to suppose that there were two Ishmaels, and not to think of two mentions of the same Ishmael.
[5] Jos. *Ant.* XV, 322.
[6] See already chapter five, p. 274.

Gratus[1] and that after a short time was deposed, and replaced by Eleazar ben Ananus. We know a little more about Ishmael ben Phiabi II. He was appointed by Agrippa II[2] and yet headed a delegation of Jerusalem Jews when it seemed to them that the king had violated the sanctity of the Temple. The delegation achieved its purpose but Nero, to spare Agrippa's dignity, prevented Ishmael from returning to Jerusalem.[3] It is very likely that Ishmael ben Phiabi II was the grandson of the high priest who bore the same name. This identification would fit in with the chronology.

Of the four oligarchical families of the high priesthood noted by the Talmud, we know least about the house of Kithros. It is only by means of conjecture that we can assign several high priests to this family. One of them was Elionaeus, the last high priest appointed by Agrippa I, who took the place of Matthias ben Ananus.[4] We read in the Mishnah that this Elionaeus was one of the high priests (the others being Hananel the Egyptian and Ishmael ben Phiabi) who prepared a red heifer.[5] This Elionaeus is called Hakkof in the Mishnah. This suggests a connection between him and the high priest Joseph Caiaphas of whom it can be conjectured that he too belonged to the house of Kithros.[6]

One of the priestly families at the close of the Second Temple period was the house of Kimhit. This particular family is not included among those held up to opprobrium in talmudic literature. It provided at least two, and possibly three high priests towards the end of the Second Temple period: Simeon ben Kimhit,[7] Joseph ben Kimhit and perhaps Joseph Kabi.[8] No hasty conclusion can be drawn to the effect that the family was named after its maternal ancestor.[9] It must be stressed, however, that it does not appear among the high priestly

---

[1] Jos. *Ant.* XVIII, 34.

[2] Cf. chapter six, p. 367.

[3] On the end of Ishmael II, the son of Phiabi cf. also S. Applebaum, *Greeks and Jews in ancient Cyrene* (1969; in Hebrew), pp. 191-2.

[4] *Ant.* XIX, 342; the Greek manuscripts read here κιθαίρου or κιθαίου while the Latin translation reads here *Cantherae natum*. Niese follows here the Greek manuscripts, Hudson prefers the Latin translation.

[5] *M. Parah* 3:5.

[6] Cf. also Jeremias, p. 94, n. 21; J. Perles, in *MGWJ* (1872), p. 257, takes here הקייף in the meaning of monkey (קוף) which is hardly likely.

[7] *Ant.* XVIII, 34.

[8] In *Joseppi libellus memorialis* (*PG* CVI, col. 20) he is called Ἰώσηππος Κάμη. Both Schürer and Graetz equate Κάμης (= Κάμιθος) with קמחית See Schürer II', p. 273, n. 19; H. Graetz, *Geschichte der Juden* III, 2 (5th ed. 1905), p. 738.

[9] Thus e.g. Derenbourg, op. cit., p. 197, n. 2 following the talmudic sources.

families who are disparaged in talmudic tradition. On the contrary, here and there it appears in a positive light.[1]

An important question must be raised at this point; the relationship between the high priestly families of the oligarchy and the various sects of the Second Temple period. Were all such high priests Sadducees or affiliated in some way to them? Even if they were associated in general with the Sadducees, there is an important reservation to be made. One cannot affirm that all individuals followed the family tradition or that all of the families in the oligarchy always took the Sadducean view, though they naturally inclined to do so. With this reservation in mind, one can answer the question in the affirmative: the high priestly families at the close of the Second Temple period did identify themselves for the most part with the Sadducean attitude. This conclusion is based on several convergent arguments. To begin with, the very name Sadducee points to the priestly family of Zadok.[2] Against the argument that the name originated in an earlier age and that by our period it had lost its social connotation, it must be noted that the Sadducees were also called Boethusians, which certainly can not be earlier than the reign of Herod.[3] The talmudic sources that refer to the Boethusians regard them as a group at least akin to the Sadducees and even use the two names interchangeably.[4] This new name of Boethusians points unequivocally to the affiliation of at least a part of the élite of the high priesthood with the Sadducees. There is,

[1] See the talmudic sources on the house of Kimhit: *Avot de Rabbi Natan*, Version I, 35 (p. 105); *T. Yoma* 4:20; *P. T. Yoma* I, 38d; *P. T. Horayoth* III, 47d; *P. T. Megillah* I, 72a; *Midrash Num. Rabba*, 2 (the end); *T. B. Yoma* 47a; *Pesikta de Rav Kahana* 26, 10 (p. 398).

[2] Of the older literature see A. Geiger, *Urschrift und Übersetzungen der Bibel* (1857), e.g., p. 126; J. Wellhausen, *Die Pharisäer und die Sadducäer* (1874), pp. 45-47; G. Hölscher, *Der Sadduzäismus* (1906), pp. 102-3; Schürer II, p. 477. For a broad survey of the views about the origins of the Sadducees and their social connections see Le Moyne who summarizes his own views as follows (p. 348): 'Les Sadducéens n'étaient pas un groupe proprement sacerdotal. On peut cependant supposer que le groupe avait pour centre les grands prêtres et les prêtres en chef.' From twentieth century literature see also R. Leszynsky, *Die Sadduzäer* (1912); J. Z. Lauterbach, in *Studies in Jewish Literature, issued in Honor of K. Kohler* (1913), pp. 176-198; id. in *HUCA* (1927), pp. 173-205. Apart from Le Moyne's survey cf. also Marcus, who discusses the Pharisees in the light of modern scholarship, but implicitly the discussion bears on the Sadducees as well.

[3] *Avot de Rabbi Natan*, Version I, 5; Version II, 10 (p. 26), which traces the Boethusians to the times of Antigonus of Socho, has a legendary character.

[4] See e.g., Geiger, op. cit., p. 102: 'Eine Abart von ihnen oder vielmehr eine sich ihnen anrankende Schlingpflanze sind die Boöthusen.' Cf. Le Moyne, p. 337.

moreover, a general consideration to be drawn from sources which stress the fact that the Sadducees constituted only a minority of the nation, even though they had attracted to themselves the wealthy and the upper classes.[1] When one speaks of wealth and high social standing among the Jewish people in that period, one can be sure that the high priestly families enjoyed these prerogatives.

Besides, we have the testimony of a variety of sources, such as the New Testament, Josephus and talmudic literature, all of which in general terms describe the high priestly circles or individual high priests as belonging to the Sadducees. The basic sources in the New Testament in which Sadducees are mentioned are not explicit about the social distinctions we have drawn. From this viewpoint, some importance is to be ascribed to two particular passages. In the first passage, we hear of the activities of the priests, of the 'captain' of the Temple and of the Sadducees.[2] All act together, and seem to form one group. More important for our purpose is another passage which declares that the party of the high priest at that time was made up of Sadducees.[3]

With few exceptions, Josephus does not describe people according to their affiliation with either the Pharisees or the Sadducees. One of these exceptions is his description of Simeon ben Gamaliel as a Pharisee, like those who were sent to depose him from his post in Galilee.[4] He especially emphasizes the affiliation of certain people with the Essenes.[5] In only one instance does he explicitly characterize one of the high priests as a Sadducee. There is ground for the surmise that by reason of his origin, Josephus was related to the distinguished circles of the priesthood even though he proclaims himself a Pharisee in his viewpoint. It would seem that Josephus was determined to some extent to conceal the general affinity between the priestly aristocracy and Sadduceism.[6]

In one passage, as indicated, Josephus breaks his silence in this matter.

---

[1] Jos. *Ant.* XIII, 298; XVIII, 17; cf. *Avot de Rabbi Natan*, Version I, 5, (p. 26): 'And they used silver vessels and gold vessels all their lives.'

[2] Acts 4:1.

[3] Acts 5:17: Ἀναστὰς δὲ ὁ ἀρχιερεὺς καὶ οἱ πάντες οἱ σὺν αὐτῷ, ἡ οὖσα αἵρεσις τῶν Σαδδουκαίων. See Jeremias, pp. 179-80.

[4] *Life* 191; 197.

[5] *Ant.* XIII, 311; *War* II, 113; II, 567; III, 11.

[6] On Josephus and the religious parties of his time see H. Rasp, in *ZNW* (1924), pp. 27-47; Le Moyne, pp. 28; 326 supposes family connections of Josephus with the Sadducees, and even thinks that Josephus was still a Sadducee when appointed to his command in Galilee.

He says that Ananus ben Ananus belonged to the Sadducean sect.[1] This item of information tallies with what may be gleaned from the New Testament, which makes his father, the elder Hanan, a Sadducee.[2] Taken together, these two statements confirm the Sadducean character of the house of Hanan in general. Thus, we may say that the two most eminent high priestly families, those of Hanan and Boethus, were completely identified with the Sadducean sect. The character of the house of Hanan is deduced from two specific references cited; that of the house of Boethus from its name.

The information to be gathered from talmudic literature confirms the conclusions to be drawn from the New Testament and Josephus. But nowhere does the Talmud identify all high priests as Sadducees, nor can this be inferred from the disparaging remarks about the high priestly oligarchy.[3] However, from a series of passages one can conclude without hesitation that Sadduceism was predominant in the high priestly circles. From this viewpoint, special significance attaches to the tradition that it was the practice to have the high priest take an oath that on the Day of Atonement he would not burn the incense outside the Holy of Holies as was the wont of the Sadducean and Boethusian high priests.[4] The reason for the oath was that a certain high priest followed the Sadducean practice and met a tragic end as a result.[5] Another high priest is mentioned in connection with the burning of the red heifer. The Sadducees, in contrast to the Pharisees, insisted that the ritual must be performed only after sunset.[6] The Tosefta mentions an instance in which a Sadducean high priest, having waited for sunset after the ritual purification, came to burn the red heifer and met with opposition on the part of Rabbi Johanan ben Zakkai.[7] There is ground for the assumption that the high priest in question belonged to the house of Phiabi.[8] If the conjecture is correct, we would have another example of the affiliation of a high priestly family—that of the house of Phiabi—with the Sadducees.

---

[1] *Ant.* xx, 199.
[2] Acts 5:17. In view of Acts 4:6 where Ἅννας is called ἀρχιερεύς it seems that also in 5:17 it is he and not Caiaphas who is implied by this term.
[3] *T. Menahoth* 13:21; *T. B. Pesahim* 57a; *T. B. Yoma* 9a; *T. B. Kerithoth* 28.
[4] *P. T. Yoma* I, 39a; *T. B. Yoma* 19b.
[5] Cf. H. Graetz, *Geschichte der Juden* III, 2, pp. 749-52.
[6] *M. Parah* 3:7.
[7] *T. Parah* 3:8.
[8] See Jeremias, p. 229, n. 30. On Rabbi Johanan ben Zakkai as a militant Pharisee in the struggle against the Sadducees see also E. Rivkin, in *HUCA* (1969-1970), pp. 221-2.

One must take into account that all the Sadduceans mentioned by name were priests. So were all who took the Sadducee line according to our sources. It is virtually certain that in this period the high priestly oligarchy were the leaders of the Sadduceans, as is also clear from the synonym, Boethusians. Likewise, one should bear in mind that where the Talmud speaks favourably of something a high priest did, it does not necessarily follow that the high priest in question was not a Sadducee. Finally, it must be observed that the Sadducees, generally speaking, were never able to put their views into practice even when they were in power. On several occasions, the leaders of the Pharisees co-operated with the leaders of the Sadducees, as when Ananus ben Ananus, a declared Sadducee, co-operated with Rabban Simeon ben Gamaliel.[1] The talmudic sources have nothing but praise for the public activities of the high priest Joshua ben Gamala.[2] That is no reason however to designate him as a Pharisee. Not only did he have family ties with the house of Boethus but in his public activities he was an outright supporter of Ananus ben Ananus.[3]

The non-priestly élite

Along with the arrival of several high priestly houses from the Hellenistic Diaspora, we note in the same period that several non-priestly families rose to prominence in Judaea, associated in one way or another with the Herodian regime. In this process, Diaspora Jewry came to the fore. Among those close to the Herodian house who played a central role in the life of Jewish Palestine at the end of the Second Temple period were the descendants of Salome, Herod's sister, by her second marriage, to a man by the name of Alexa of whose origins we know nothing.

This Alexa was among those close to Herod and in one place he is described as one of the friends of the king.[4] In order to draw their respective families closer, Herod married one of Salome's daughters by a previous marriage, to a son of Alexa by a former wife. It is apparent that Alexa belonged to the new Herodian aristocracy that emerged together with the new dynasty. Alexa held his special position until the very end of Herod's reign. The king relied on him

---

[1] Jos. *Life* 193.
[2] *T. B. Baba Bathra* 21a. Cf. Derenbourg, op. cit., p. 248, n. 2.
[3] Jos. *War* iv, 160.
[4] Jos. *War* i, 566.

to enforce his final testamentary dispositions.[1] It was Alexa and his wife who assembled the people in the amphitheatre after Herod's death. The son of Alexa and Salome, Helcias, married Cypros, the daughter of Salome's son Antipater, the offspring of Antipater's marriage to the daughter of Herod and Mariamme. In other words, Alexa's son married Herod's granddaughter.[2] This Helcias became one of the most influential figures in Jewish public life and was known as Helcias the Great. When Gaius Caligula issued his repressive decrees, Helcias, together with Aristobulus, Agrippa's brother, was a vigorous supporter of the efforts to have the decrees revoked.[3] Helcias was also active in the time of Agrippa I and was undoubtedly one of the leading figures during the latter's reign.[4] In keeping with the family tradition, Helcias further strengthened his ties with the house of Herod by additional links of marriage. Agrippa I, betrothed one of his three daughters, Mariamme, to Julius Archelaus, a son of Helcias.[5] The marriage took place, however, only in the days of Agrippa II.[6] A daughter, named Berenice, was born to the couple. Shortly afterwards, Mariamme abandoned her husband Julius and married Demetrius, an important figure in the Jewish community of Alexandria.[7] The name Julius Archelaus shows that its bearer was a Roman citizen. We do not know to what extent Julius managed to assume an important position in the life of Jerusalem in the Second Temple period. We hear of him even after the destruction of the Temple. He is mentioned by Josephus as one of the Jews who were versed in Greek culture and to whom he sold copies of his work, *The Jewish War*.[8] To the same family there belonged a certain Alexa of whom the Tosefta relates: 'When Alexa died in Lod, the people of the nearby villages came to eulogize him.'[9]

Herod's policy of encouraging the migration of families from the Diaspora to Judaea and of appointing them to key positions in his administration, made special provision for families that hailed from Babylonia. One such family, that of Zamaris, played a significant role in the defence and administration of northern Transjordan. The leaders of this family implemented the policies of Herod, Agrippa I and Agrippa II.

[1] *Ant.* XVII, 175; *War* I, 660.
[2] *Ant.* XVIII, 138.   [3] *Ant.* XVIII, 273.   [4] *Ant.* XIX, 353.
[5] *Ant.* XIX, 355.   [6] *Ant.* XX, 140.   [7] *Ant.* XX, 147.
[8] *Against Apion* I, 51.
[9] *T. Hagigah* 2:13. Cf. H. Graetz, in *MGWJ* (1885), pp. 205-9.

The man who laid the foundations for the subsequent ascendancy of his family was Zamaris.[1] He had a son called Iacimus, whose son Philip is known from the various tasks he performed for Agrippa II at the time of the great revolt. Zamaris' migration to Judaea is not to be viewed as that of a single family. A whole clan arrived, headed by Zamaris. He crossed the Euphrates at the head of five hundred mounted archers, along with a host of relatives. His standing became hereditary. His sons maintained his pre-eminent position among these Babylonian Jews, who continued to exist as a separate community for a long time. They were known as the Babylonians in the days of the great revolt.[2]

Herod's invitation to the Babylonian Jews was motivated by his concern to ensure the defence and peace of Trachonitis and Batanaea. It is therefore understandable that their principal base was located in the area of Batanaea.[3] We hear of the Babylonian (Zamaris) building fortresses, and a village named Bathyra.[4] Though mainly based on Batanaea, the family spread in the course of time to adjacent areas. Nearby Gamala in Gaulanitis served as their main area of settlement. Chares and Jeshua, two close friends of Philip, son of Iacimus, lived in Gamala.[5] At the time of its conquest by the Romans, only two of the population survived—the two daughters of the sister of this Philip.[6] The family had widespread connections which reached to western Palestine. Chares' brother, a relative of Philip, married a member of an important Tiberian family. Justus of Tiberias was his brother-in-law.[7]

The suggestion was made some time ago that Zamaris the Babylonian, founder of the settlement in Batanaea, was somehow linked to the elders or sons of Bathyra mentioned in talmudic literature, which ascribes to them an important role in the religious life of Jerusalem at

---

[1] Jos. *Ant.* XVII, 29-31.
[2] E.g., Jos. *Life* 54, 177.
[3] *Ant.* XVII, 25.
[4] On the location of Bathyra see F. M. Abel, *Géographie de la Palestine* II, 261; for previous attempts cf. K. Furrer, in *ZDPV* (1899), p. 151; S. Klein, *The Jewish Trans-Jordan* (1925; in Hebrew), p. 17.
[5] Cf. H. Drexler, in *Klio* (1925), p. 310; A. Schalit, in *Klio* (1933), p. 83.
[6] Jos. *War* IV, 81.
[7] Jos. *Life* 177. One of the important persons in the entourage of Agrippa II, Silas, possibly came from among the Jewish military colonists of Transjordan. In any case in the time of the revolt he deserted the king for the rebels. See Jos. *War* II, 520.

the time of Hillel's rise to eminence in the city.[1] Various sages, shortly before and after the destruction of the Temple are described as sons of Bathyra.[2] They are active in Jerusalem in Hillel's time and in Jabneh at the time of Rabban Johanan ben Zakkai.[3]

Among the families that came into prominence in the Herodian age, one should include the house of Hillel. Its rise to a position of commanding influence constitutes a unique phenomenon in the period of the Second Temple. Gradually, a family with no connections with the priestly class, became hereditary leaders of the nation until eventually, in the time of Rabbi Judah the patriarch, it gained official recognition by the Roman Empire. But even before the destruction of the Temple, when other leaders, religious and secular, were available, either members of the Herodian dynasty or high priests from very distinguished families, the house of Hillel comes to the fore. It produced three or four pre-eminent personalities in succession and came to be regarded as the hereditary leader of the Pharisees, who constituted one of the main forces in Judaea. This impressive rise was based, in the first instance, on the personality of Hillel himself, a man endowed with many talents, displayed in his halakic and social activity. Secondly, his descendants appear to have been similarly gifted and were thus able to continue his tradition and be similarly influential in the same spheres. There is hardly any parallel in the whole history of the Halakah to this close succession of distinguished figures from the same family. These factors alone are hardly sufficient to explain this phenomenon. A fuller explanation must take into account the development of Jewish society from the days of Herod onward.

The high priests continued to enjoy outstanding prestige and official recognition. But the constant change in the office of high priest, and the quarrels and plots within the oligarchy served to undermine respect which the people normally had for their priestly leaders. In addition, the people began to look on the leaders of the Pharisees as the spiritual authorities. And here it was the house of Hillel which guided the Pharisaic movement. For a century, the sages of this family were

---

[1] *P. T. Pesahim* VI, 33a; *T. B. Pesahim* 66a. See already H. Graetz, in *MGWJ* (1852), pp. 115-20.

[2] From the talmudic sources also, we should infer that 'Bnei Bathyra' do not mean the sons of a man called Bathyra, but is a *gentilicium* (against Fürst, in *MGWJ* (1852), p. 560.).

[3] *T. B. Rosh-Hashanah* 29b. We know of various scholars belonging to this house, e.g. Jonathan or Johanan ben Bathyra, or Judah ben Bathyra, Simeon ben Bathyra, Jehoshua ben Bathyra.

widely regarded as the leaders of the nation. But what of Hillel's family background? Was his phenomenal rise aided by his supposedly Davidic origins?[1] Actually, we know nothing of his origins. Even his father's name has not been preserved. We know only that he had a brother by the name of Shebna.[2] There is no doubt that Hillel was not a native Palestinian and that he had migrated from Babylonia, a fact on which the Talmud and Midrash unanimously agree.[3] The central question relating to the family background is his relationship to the house of David. Various talmudic sources assert that Hillel was descended from David,[4] but there is no confirmation of this elsewhere. Hillel is not mentioned in non-Jewish sources, though Rabban Gamaliel the Elder is praised in the Acts of Apostles, according to which Paul was one of his disciples.[5] Gamaliel is here described as an honoured teacher of Torah but no allusion is made to his origin. No far-reaching conclusions are to be drawn from the author's silence in this matter. As a Christian, the author of Acts could have no possible interest in stressing the Davidic origin of a Jew who, though respected by Christian tradition, did not belong to Jesus' family. Josephus fails to mention Gamaliel altogether though he refers in his autobiography to his son Simeon.[6] Josephus describes the family of Simeon ben Gamaliel as most distinguished.[7] But again there is no reason to conclude that the historian alludes here to the Davidic origin of the family. Josephus is referring to the family's eminence in the past and present. From Josephus' writings, we learn that Simeon ben Gamaliel maintained broad social ties which included such people as Johanan of Gischala[8] and the leaders of the high priesthood.[9] On the other hand, one must bear in mind that Josephus was extremely

---

[1] As maintained by G. Goitein, in *Magazin für die Wissenschaft des Judentums* (1884), p. 6.

[2] *T. B. Sotah* 21a.

[3] *T. Negaim* 1:16; *Sifre on Deut.* 357 (p. 429); *P. T. Pesahim* VI, 33a; *T. B. Pesahim* 66a; *T. B. Sukkah* 20a. A. Kaminka, in *Zion* IV, p. 259 (in Hebrew), sees Hillel as coming from Alexandria, and not from Babylonia. However, this assumption seems wholly unwarranted and hardly supported by *T. Ketuboth* 4:9 (a parallel tradition is to be found in *T. B. Baba Metzia* 104a), on Hillel's decision concerning the betrothal of women in Alexandria.

[4] *P. T. Taanith* IV, 68a; *Gen. Rabba*, 98 (p. 1259); 33 (pp. 305-6); *T. B. Sanhedrin* 5a; *T. B. Ketuboth* 62b; *T. B. Shabbath* 56a.

[5] Acts 5:34; 22:3.

[6] *Life* 190-196; 216; 309; *War* IV, 159.

[7] *Life* 191; ὁ δὲ Σίμων οὗτος ἦν πόλεως μὲν Ἱεροσολύμων, γένους δὲ σφόδρα λαμπροῦ.

[8] *Life* 189-96.

[9] *War* IV, 159.

reticent about messianic hopes and avoids any reference to the house of David in Second Temple times.

Obviously, there is little to be learned about Hillel's ancestry outside the Talmud and Midrash. Our conclusion must depend on a critical examination of these sources. When we examine them, we find that no source maintaining Hillel's Davidic origin dates from before the time of Rabbi Judah the patriarch. Moreover, these sources do not attribute Davidic origin to any member of the house before Judah's time. The only exception apparently is Rabbi Levi, an Amora of the school of Rabbi Johanan, who declares that there was a genealogical record in Jerusalem saying that Hillel was a descendant of David.[1] There are some talmudic sources that mention this relationship in general terms and others that are quite specific, indicating that Hillel's Davidic descent was on his mother's side.[2] Furthermore, it is clear from a comparison of the sources that the house of the patriarch, in the time of Rabbi Judah, was interested in emphasizing its relationship to the house of David. It is no less clear that there were reasons that compelled it not to deny its descent from the tribe of Benjamin on the father's side. To do so would have been to deny a widespread tradition of the time.[3]

But even the traditions of the Davidic origin of the house of Hillel on the maternal side are late, and not earlier than the days of Rabbi Judah the patriarch. As for the tradition handed down by the Amora Rabbi Levi to the effect that Hillel was descended from David, it is to be regarded as a late haggadah without a kernel of historic fact.[4] It is certainly not worthy of being considered an authentic tradition that derives in part from the official archives of Jerusalem or from a family archive discovered by Rabbi Levi in the ruins of Jerusalem.[5] To this one must add the telling silence of the sources precisely in those passages in which there was reason to link Hillel with David, as in the appointment of Hillel as *nasi* of the Sanhedrin.[6] We may therefore conclude that the relationship to David, even on his mother's side,

---

[1] *P. T. Taanith* IV, 68a; *Gen. Rabba*, 98.

[2] See *P. T. Kilaim* IX, 32b; *P. T. Ketuboth* XII, 35a; *Gen. Rabba* 33 (p. 306).

[3] The Gaon R. Sherira already saw that the Talmuds are inconsistent about the origins of Hillel. He himself decided in favour of direct Davidic ancestry against the Benjamin one. See the *Letter of R. Sherira*, ed. Lewin, Appendix XV, pp. XI-XII.

[4] See the defence of the tradition by S. Klein, in *Zion* IV, pp. 30-50 (in Hebrew).

[5] See I. Lévi, in *REJ* XXXI (1895), pp. 202-11; J. Goldin, in *Journal of Religion* (1946), p. 263.

[6] *T. B. Pesahim* 66a.

was no factor in the ascendancy of Hillel and his descendants in Jewish society. Moreover, such relationship, if it did indeed exist, could only have served as an obstacle during the Herodian regime. It would be a grave error to imagine that Herod would have elevated anyone of the Davidic house to counterbalance the Hasmoneans. Such promotion would have been a two-edged sword that might readily be turned against Herod himself; with messianic hopes so lively, to advance a family related to the Davidic house would have been to create a future threat to the Herodian line.

Having risen to prominence in Jerusalem, the Hillel family sought to intermarry, it seems, with distinguished families, and so included itself in the tribe of Benjamin in whose territory Jerusalem was located.[1] This affiliation was well known and could not be ignored. If members of the Hillel family did seek to establish a link between themselves and David on the maternal side, such efforts never received official recognition before the time of Rabbi Judah the patriarch.

Our information on the sons and grandsons of Hillel has many gaps. In one passage in the Babylonian Talmud, we read: 'It was taught: Hillel and Simeon, Gamaliel and Simeon wielded their patriarchate during one hundred years of the Temple's existence.'[2] This would make Simeon, Hillel's son, his successor in the patriarchate. This Simeon is not mentioned elsewhere nor is any halakah quoted in his name. Thus, his very existence has come to be doubted.[3] Presumably the name Simeon slipped in erroneously into the Baraita.

In any event, the outstanding personality, after Hillel, in the family, in the period of the Second Temple, was Rabban Gamaliel the Elder.[4] It was his opinion that was decisive in many circles of Jerusalem society. By his time, the house of Hillel was linked through marriage with a number of priestly families. This emerges from a passage in the Tosefta.[5] Rabban Gamaliel the Elder married his daughter to Simeon the son of Nethanel, the priest. This intermarriage between the house of Hillel and priestly families is reflected also in the fact that the last high priest of Second Temple times, Phineas ben Samuel of Kefar Habta, is regarded in the sources as the son-in-law of a Hillelite, apparently the son-in-law of Rabban Simeon ben Gamaliel.[6]

[1] So Paul considered that he belonged to the tribe of Benjamin.
[2] *T. B. Shabbath* 15a.
[3] Cf. J. Kämpf, in *MGWJ* (1854), pp. 98-9; Schürer II, p. 429, n. 47; cf. also A. Geiger, *Nachgelassene Schriften* IV (1876), p. 297.
[4] See *M. Gittin* 4:2-3; *M. Rosh-Hashanah* 2:5; *T. Sanhedrin* 2:6; *M. Sotah* 9:15.
[5] *T. Yoma* 1:6.   [6] *Sifra, Emor* 2.

The sages

One of the features of the religious and social development of the Second Temple era is undoubtedly the rise of the sages, the interpreters of the Torah. 'And the rough he-goat is the king of Greece...' (Dan. 7:21), that is, Alexander of Macedon who rules twelve years—until now the prophets prophesied in the holy spirit, from now on turn your ear and hear the words of the sages.'[1] It is certain that we can already discern the influence and activities of the sages in the second century B.C.E. as the direct heirs of the scribes of the previous period. Ben Sira displays his sympathy to them when he describes the scribes in the following passage: 'On the other hand he who devotes himself to the study of the law of the Most High will seek out the wisdom of all the ancients, and will be concerned with prophecies; he will preserve the discourse of notable men and penetrate the subtleties of parables; he will seek out the hidden meanings of proverbs and be at home with the obscurities of parables. He will serve among great men and appear before rulers; he will travel through the lands of foreign nations, for he tests the good and the evil among men. He will set his heart to rise early to seek the Lord who made him, and will make supplication before the Most High; he will open his mouth in prayer and make supplication for his sins. If the great Lord is willing, he will be filled with the spirit of understanding; he will pour forth words of wisdom and give thanks to the Lord in prayer. He will direct his counsel and knowledge aright, and meditate on his secrets. He will reveal instruction in his teaching, and will glory in the law of the Lord's covenant. Many will praise his understanding, and it will never be blotted out; his memory will not disappear, and his name will live through all generations.'[2] The scribe Ben Sira is still immersed in the Eastern tradition of wisdom.[3] He thus stresses the need for being able to 'penetrate the subtleties of parables' and 'seek out the hidden meaning of proverbs.' At the same time, he says that 'he will serve among great men' and 'travel through the lands of foreign nations.' With all this, 'he devotes himself to the study of the law of the Most High.'

The sage is the scribe who has been tempered in the crucible of the repressive decrees of the time of Antiochus. He is the scribe whose moral stature has grown and who sees his central task as the promotion

[1] *Seder Olam Rabba* 30 (pp. 139-140).
[2] *Sir.* 39.
[3] On the 'Wisdom' in Ben Sira see M. Hengel, *Judentum und Hellenismus* (1973), pp. 284-92.

of the Torah and its dominance in all aspects of life. His chief occupation is its interpretation. The rise of the sage meant the almost total obliteration of the class distinctions created by the aristocracy. At the same time, the former disdain for the labourer and craftsman vanished to a large extent. The teaching of the Torah and the direction of the spiritual life of the people ceased to be the prerogative of the priest and became the province of men who did not belong exclusively to the priestly class. The 'crown of the Torah' could be won by anyone who desired it and who, of course, possessed the necessary intellectual and moral qualifications. However, the number of priests among the sages in the coming generations continued to be significant. Alongside of them, there were notable figures from a variety of elements in Jewish society in both Judaea and the Diaspora. Moreover, according to talmudic tradition, some of the outstanding sages were descended from proselytes. The title 'disciple of Aaron' carried more prestige than 'a son of Aaron.' The following is the most striking illustration of the revolution in Jewish society whereby the sages became its élite, deriving their influence from learning and personality rather than heredity: 'Our Rabbis taught: It happened with a high priest that as he came forth from the Sanctuary, all the people followed him; but when they saw Shemaiah and Abtalion, they forsook him and went after Shemaiah and Abtalion. Eventually, Shemaiah and Abtalion visited him to take their leave of the high priest. He said to them: 'May the descendants of the heathen come in peace.' They answered him: 'May the descendants of the heathen, who do the work of Aaron arrive in peace but the descendant of Aaron who does not the work of Aaron, he shall not come in peace.''[1]

The sages put their stamp on every aspect of religious life, its legal system and its social institutions. Their 'houses of study' in which they taught Torah attracted numerous students. Aside from their importance in the formation of the Halakah, in the eyes of the masses there was an aura of sanctity and moral grandeur about them. Their way of life and their moral attitudes were no less influential than their halakic decisions. Some of them were labourers and managed to sustain themselves by hard work.[2] Their halakic enactments, whether or not they had the approval of the Sanhedrin, were generally accepted as normative and became widely practised by the people, because of

[1] *T. B. Yoma* 71b.
[2] On the other hand M. Beer, in Annual of *Bar-Ilan University* II (1964), p. 143, n. 57 (in Hebrew) gives examples of well-to-do sages.

the prestige and authority of the 'great sages.'[1] They were the back-bone of the pharisaic sect,[2] which was by far the largest, and the one with the deepest roots among the nation from the time of the Has-monaeans until the end of the Second Temple era. The pharisaic sages formed a bloc in the Sanhedrin,[3] and so were an influential factor in its decisions.

We have a long list of great sages who were active in the two centuries B.C.E. and in the first century C.E.. They came from various localities in both Palestine and the Diaspora. Their social origins were equally varied. A brief chronological list of some of the more prominent figures among them shows the different parts from which they came. Anti-gonus of Socho was from Judah,[4] Jose ben Johanan from Jerusalem, Jose ben Joezer was a priest from Zeredah, in the south of Samaria;[5] Nittai the Arbelite came from Arbel in eastern Galilee. Simeon ben Shetah was probably the most eminent figure before Hillel and played a leading role in the struggle between the Pharisees and Sadducees under Alexander Jannaeus and Salome Alexandra. According to one tradition he was this queen's brother.[6] Other traditions, however, imply that he was of lower-class origin.[7] Shemaiah and Abtalion are said to be descended from proselytes.[8] If the tradition is well-founded, it may be conjectured that they were descended from non-Jewish inhabitants of Palestine who were converted in the time of the Has-monaean conquests. Hillel came from Babylonia. He was the only sage to found a 'house' that became an institution in the social life of the nation. In the course of time, they were recognized by the Roman authorities as the official leaders of the people.[9]

---

[1] See Ch. Albeck, in *Zion* VIII (1942-3), pp. 168-170 (in Hebrew).

[2] Examples of sages who are expressly defined as Pharisees: Pollio—Abtalion (*Ant.* xv, 3); Gamaliel the Elder (Acts 5:34); his son Simeon ben Gamaliel (*Life* 191); Rabban Johanan ben Zakkai (*M. Yadaim* 4:6).

[3] On the scribes among the members of the Sanhedrin cf. Jeremias, pp. 236-7.

[4] On Socho see F. M. Abel, *Géographie de la Palestine* II (1938), p. 467.

[5] On Zeredah see S. Klein, *The Land of Juda* (;1939 in Hebrew), p. 45.

[6] The notion that Simeon ben Shetah was a brother of the queen Salome Alexandra is mainly based on *T. B. Berakhot* 48a and *Kohelet Rabba* 7, 11. Cf. the comments of Ch. Albeck to *Gen. Rabba* 91 (p. 1116).

[7] We learn from *T. P. Baba Metzia* II, 8c that he rather lived in humble conditions. On the problem of the sources for Simeon ben Shetah see Y. Afron, in *Essays in Jewish History and Philology in Memory of Alon* (1970; in Hebrew) pp. 69-132.

[8] See below p. 623.

[9] On the sages cf. E. Urbach, *The Sages*; id. in *Proceedings of the Israel Academy of Sciences and Humanities* II (1968), pp. 38ff.

Proselytes

An interesting and instructive aspect of Jewish society in the period under discussion is that while one royal family, the Hasmonaean, was of priestly origin, the other, the Herodian, was descended from proselytes. Attempts were subsequently made to conceal the origins of the Herods and to give them Jewish ancestry.[1] These two dynasties represent the two poles of the development of Jewish society at that time; on the one hand, the rise in prestige and influence of the priestly class, and on the other, the absorption of non-Jewish elements. This absorption came about through proselytization, which took place in both Palestine and the Diaspora. In the Diaspora, conversion was a voluntary act by masses of Gentiles who wished to join the Jewish people and faith. In Palestine, it was only partially so. An instance of this process was the conversion of Achior the Ammonite, described for us in the Book of Judith: 'And when Achior saw all that the God of Israel had done, he believed firmly in God, and was circumcised, and joined the house of Israel, remaining so to this day.'[2] Strabo says that the conversion of the Idumaeans was voluntary,[3] and such conversions continued throughout the Second Temple period and even after the destruction.[4] There was, however, another aspect to conversion, proselytization by force, something typical only of Palestine, where Semitic elements such as Idumeans in the South and Itureans in the North were forcibly assimilated.[5] The Judaized South, Idumaea, produced Antipater, Herod and their relatives but also Antipater's rival, Malichus. Among the proselytes from Transjordan, there is Simeon bar Giora of Gerasa whose name shows that he was descended from proselytes.[6] This Simeon, it will be recalled, became the leader of the lower classes at the time of the great revolt and was the outstanding commander of Jerusalem when it was besieged by the Romans. Descendants of proselytes were even to be found among the

[1] An attempt of this kind was made by Herod's court historian, Nicholas of Damascus, in Jos. *Ant.* XIV, 9; cf. W. Otto, Herodes (1913), pp. 1-2.
[2] Judith 14:10.
[3] *Geographica* XVI, 2, 34, p. 760; cf. M. Stern, *Greek and Latin authors on Jews and Judaism* I (1974), p. 304.
[4] See B. J. Bamberger, *Proselytism in the talmudic period* (1939).
[5] On the circumcision of the Ituraeans see Jos. *Ant.* XIII, 319 which derives from Strabo, and ultimately from Timagenes. Cf. Stern, op. cit., I, p. 225.
[6] M. Avi-Yonah, *Historical Geography of Palestine* (1962; in Hebrew), p. 122 suggests that Simeon bar Giora came from a town in Samaria (Jureish), also transcribed Gerasa in Greek, but his descent from proselytes would rather suggest the Hellenistic city of Gerasa.

great sages. The most famous were Shemaiah and Abtalion. Haggadic tradition, as well as a baraita, describe them as descendants of Sennacherib: 'Naaman was a resident alien, Nebusaradan was a righteous proselyte; descendants of Haman studied Torah in Benei Beraq...; descendants of Sennacherib gave public lectures on the Torah. Who were they? Shemaiah and Abtalion.'[1]

More problematical are the proselyte origins of Abba Saul ben Bothnith and of Johanan, son of the Hauranite.[2] The fact that they are called by their mother's names rather than their father's is not sufficient ground for assuming that they were of proselyte origin.[3] Talmudic literature mentions other proselytes towards the end of the Second Temple period.[4] To this must be added the information to be gleaned on the subject from the New Testament.[5] One can hardly speak of proselytes in this period without mentioning the most famous of all, the royal dynasty of Adiabene.[6] Members of this family played a significant role in the public life of Jerusalem (Queen Helena, in particular). Some of them participated actively in the great revolt.

In principle, the proselytes became an integral part of the Jewish nation with all that this implied.[7] But certain limitations applied, which curtailed the possibility of marrying into priestly families. The latter had strict rules about marriage, in order to preserve the purity of their pedigrees and so the marriage of a priest to a proselyte was forbidden.[8] The prohibition is explicit in talmudic sources, though there was a tendency to permit the marriage of a priest and a proselyte if the latter was less than three years of age at the time of conversion.[9] And some held that the daughter of proselytes could marry a priest.[10] In these matters, the priests were more rigorous than the sages. These limitations did not apply to the daughter of a priest, who could be married to a proselyte.[11] One gathers the impression that while

---

[1] T. B. Gittin 57b; T. B. Sanhedrin 96b. Cf. also T. B. Yoma 71b; M. Eduyoth 5:6.
[2] Jeremias, p. 324, thinks that they are sons of proselyte mothers.
[3] See Bamberger, op. cit., pp. 230-1.
[4] See for proselytes in tannaitic literature, Bamberger, op. cit., pp. 222-50.
[5] Acts 6:5.
[6] Cf. Chapter three, pp. 172-8.
[7] T. B. Yebamoth 47b.
[8] P. T. Yebamoth XIII, 9b; cf. T. Kiddushin 5:3. This is also implied by Jos. Against Apion I, 31 (a member of the priestly order must, for the sake of his offspring, marry a woman of his own race).
[9] Cf. T. P. Kiddushin IV, 66a.
[10] Cf. Bamberger, op. cit. p. 84.
[11] T. B. Kiddushin 72b (the view of R. Judah).

theoretically there were certain limitations that restricted a proselyte from filling public offices, in practice, these were not enforced and proselytes could and did attain to the crown and were, as we have seen, to be found in the ranks of the outstanding sages.

Slaves

Slavery was characteristic of Jewish society in our period just as it was an accepted institution in antiquity in general.[1] But slavery in Judaea was never so important and widespread as it was, for example, in Athens in the fifth and fourth centuries B.C.E. or in Rome at the end of the Republic. The situation in Judaea, however, was certainly not much different from that which prevailed in the neighbouring countries. One may assume that slaves played a significant part in the economy, particularly in domestic service.[2]

The relatively large numbers of slaves in Jewish society is already emphasized in the census of the first exiles who returned after the Cyrus' proclamation. 'The whole assembly together was forty-two thousand three hundred and sixty, besides their men-servants and maidservants, of whom there were seven thousand three hundred and thirty-seven.'[3] That is to say, the slaves were one sixth of the whole population. There are no comparable figures for the Jewish population that had remained in the Land. But since these were mostly the poor, it is safe to assume that there were relatively fewer slaves among them. In the time of Nehemiah, we witness a situation in which many Jews had become impoverished, either through droughts or the heavy burden of taxation or a combination of both. As a result, not only were they compelled to sell their fields and vineyards but to stand helplessly by and see their sons and daughters impressed as slaves by the upper classes of their own people. Nehemiah reacted strongly to this situation and spoke out boldly: 'We, as far as we are able, have bought back our Jewish brethren who have been sold to the nations;

---

[1] Out of the huge literature dealing with ancient slavery in general Cf. W. W. Buckland, *The Roman Law of Slavery* (1908); W. L. Westermann, *The Slave Systems of Greek and Roman Antiquity* (1955); R. Schlaifer, 'Greek Theories of Slavery from Homer to Aristotle,' in *Harvard Studies in Classical Philology* (1936), pp. 165-204; M. I. Finlay, 'Was Greek Civilization based on Slave Labour', in *Historia* (1959), pp. 145-164; J. Vogt, *Sklaverei und Humanität* (2nd ed. 1972).
[2] Cf. also A. H. M. Jones, in *The Economic History Review* (1956), p. 185, who correctly says that the proportion of slaves engaged in domestic service must at all periods have been considerable.
[3] Ezra 2:64-5.

but you even sell your brethren that they may be sold to us. They were silent, and could not find a word to say.'[1] Later sources do not speak of a recurrence of the phenomenon, the enslaving of Jews by fellow-Jews.

The Hellenistic period brought about a large increase in the slave population as a result of the constant warfare between the Hellenistic powers. Many prisoners were sold as slaves. Another reason for the increase was the enslaving of members of the lower classes by the Greek settlers.[2] It is clear, however, that the non-Greek population also continued to keep slaves and even to engage in the slave trade. Thus Tobias informs Apollonius the finance minister of Ptolemy Philadelphus, in a letter dated 257 B.C.E., that he has sent him a eunuch and boy slaves, two of whom are uncircumcised.[3] The son of Tobias, the famous Joseph, required the services of Arion to manage his affairs in Alexandria. Arion was apparently either a slave belonging to Joseph or had been freed by him.[4]

Slavery in Judaea on the eve of Antiochus' decrees is clearly reflected in the work of Ben Sira which gives the impression that slavery was a very widespread institution in Jerusalem in his time. Hence Ben Sira advises his readers how to deal with their slaves. The advice is humane: 'Let your soul love an intelligent servant; do not withhold from him his freedom.'[5] But in a later chapter, Ben Sira takes a utilitarian view.[6] Yet, even here, he adds a few reservations to his harsh attitude.[7]

Other books, from the later Persian or Hellenistic-Hasmonean periods, take slavery for granted. To Judith, her husband Manasseh bequeathes 'gold and silver, male and female slaves, flocks and fields.'[8] Similarly, the story of Susanna refers to her five hundred male and female slaves.[9]

---

[1] Neh. 5:1-12. Cf. W. Rudolph, *Esra und Nehemia* (1949), p. 129 for the interpretation of the passage.
[2] See above all the Rainer Papyrus, first published (1936) in *Aegyptus* XVI by H. Liebesny and now in Th. Lenger, *Corpus des Ordonnances des Ptolémées* (1964), Nos. 21-22.
[3] *PCZ* no. 59076 = *CPJ* no. 4.
[4] This may be surmised from Jos. *Ant.* XII, 203 where it is related that Joseph put Arion into chains.
[5] Sir. 7:21.
[6] Sir. 33:27-9.
[7] Sir. 33:31-3.
[8] Judith 8:7; cf. also 12:19 - the expression ἡ δούλη αὐτῆς; at the end of her life Judith sets her maid free (16:23).
[9] Susanna 30.

Objections to slavery as an institution are voiced only rarely in Jewish literature of the Second Temple period. One of these is in the *Book of Jubilees*. When captives are sold into slavery, a crime like murder is committed, according to the author. 'And the sons of Noah began to war on each other, to take captive and to slay each other, and to shed the blood of men on the earth, and to eat blood, and to build strong cities, and walls and towers, and individually (began) to exalt themselves above the nation, and to found the beginnings of kingdoms, and to go to war people against people, and nation against nation, and city against city, and all (began) to do evil, and to acquire arms, and to teach their sons war, and they began to capture cities, and to sell male and female slaves.'[1] But the passage does not condemn slavery as such, merely the slavery resulting from capture in war. Slaves are mentioned in the *Damascus Covenant* as an accepted feature of the life of the sect.[2] In accord with Greek philosophical ideals Philo says that the Essenes opposed slavery in principle. 'Not a single slave is to be found among them, but all are free, exchanging services with each other, and they denounce the owners of slaves, not only for their injustice in outraging the law of equality, but also for their impiety anulling the statute of Nature, who mother-like has borne and reared all men alike, and created them genuine brothers, not in mere name, but in very reality though this kinship has been put to confusion by the triumph of malignant covetousness, which has wrought estrangement instead of affinity and enmity instead of friendship.'[3] This is the most radical critique of slavery in the whole Jewish literature of the age, one based as much on principle as on the social consequences of slavery. Philo asserts that the Therapeuts likewise rejected slavery.[4] Interestingly enough, in other passages in his writings, Philo accepts slavery as a self-evident institution and does not react unfavourably.[5]

---

[1] *Jubilees* 11:2.
[2] *The Zadokite Documents*, ed. Ch. Rabin, XI, p. 56: 'Let no man urge on his slave or maidservant or hired labourer on the Sabbath;' XII, p. 60: 'And his slave and his maidservant he must not sell to them (scil. to Gentiles).'
[3] *Quod omnis probus liber sit* 79. Also Jos. *Ant.* XVIII, 21 emphasizes the Essene objection to slavery on principle.
[4] *De vita contemplativa* 70. The objection on principle to slavery occurs also in Greece and Rome. Thus already the thetor Alcidamas declared in 370 B.C.E. that nature made nobody a slave, and the same idea occurs in the writer of comedies Philemon. Cf. J. M. Edmonds, *The Fragments of Attic Comedy* IIIA (1961), fr. 22, p. 14.
[5] But in his *De specialibus legibus* II, 67 Philo emphasizes the importance of a day of rest for slaves. Cf. also II, 90-91 and III, 137: Servants rank lower in

We do not hear of slaves combining for common purposes, let alone of any revolt. But slave revolts were not frequent in antiquity. They occurred only under certain circumstances, such as those obtaining towards the end of the Roman Republic. Only in the days of the great revolt do we hear of a general emancipation of slaves, and this was done by Simeon bar Giora.[1] However, it is not at all clear whether it was a matter of principle or derived merely from the desire to increase the number of his supporters.[2] The Hasmonean conquests brought a large number of slaves into Jewish hands. And possibly many slaves were bought in territories not conquered by the Hasmoneans in an era in which piracy and the sale of freemen to distant countries were prevalent. Presumably, Herod's wars against the Nabataeans further increased the supply of slaves. From then on, the number of slaves could increase according to their birth-rate. The sources speak of slaves and manumitted slaves in the retinues of Herod and his descendants and the high priests. Josephus relates, for example, that the high priests used to send their slaves to the granaries to seize the tithes that were the due of the lower order of priests.[3] A wellknown baraita recounts how the slaves of the high priests maltreated the people. 'They are the high priests, their sons are the treasurers, and their sons-in-law are the Temple trustees, and their slaves come and beat us with sticks.'[4] Whatever the historical accuracy of the information, we do know of the large number of slaves belonging to Pashur ben Immer.[5] We hear of other landowners who possessed many slaves.[6] Moreover, talmudic traditions assume, as a matter of course, that the ordinary man has at least one slave. 'When he entered the Bet Midrash, he would send his lulab by the hand of his son, his slave or

---

fortune, but in nature can claim equality with their masters, and in the law of God the standard of justice is adjusted to nature and not to fortune. And therefore the masters should not make excessive use of their authority over slaves by showing arrogance and comtempt and savage cruelty. It seems to me that E. R. Goodenough, *An Introduction to Philo Judaeus* (2nd ed. 1962), pp. 124-6 emphasizes perhaps too much that Philo has throughout the typical attitude of a slave owner.

[1] Jos. *War* IV, 508.
[2] For cases of liberation of slaves in the Greek world when the necessity arose in time of war cf. L. Robert, *Etudes épigraphiques et philologiques* (1938), pp. 118-26.
[3] *Ant.* XX, 181; 206.
[4] *T. B. Pesahim* 57a; *T. Menahoth* 13:21.
[5] *T. B. Kiddushin* 70b.
[6] Cf. the traditions on Eleazar ben Harsum mentioned above.

his messenger.'[1] 'It was related of Hillel the Elder that he bought for a certain poor man who was of a good family a horse to ride upon and a slave to run before him.'[2]

One may presume that the majority of slaves in Jewish Palestine in the Second Temple period were of foreign origin, or, in terms of the Halakah, 'Canaanite' and not 'Hebrew' slaves. This, too, was no unusual phenomenon in the world of antiquity. For we know that according to certain Greek laws, it was forbidden to enslave citizens in their own cities.[3] At the same time, one must stress the fact that these slaves of foreign origin became a part of the Jewish nation and that it was customary to circumcise them.

What were the status and rights of the 'Canaanite' slave? It is quite certain that he was regarded as the absolute possession of his master and was put by law in the category of his chattels or real estate.[4] Here the Halakah was similar to Roman law which recognized the absolute ownership of the slave by his master. On the other hand, in the course of time, Roman law came to recognize the right of a slave to acquire property of his own (*peculium*). We note a similar tendency in talmudic literature.[5] This need not to be viewed as the influence of Roman law but simply the result of a development within Jewish society parallel to one which we also meet in the Greek world and in Egypt.[6]

The 'Canaanite' slave was circumcised and underwent ritual immersion and thus, in effect, became a Jew from a religious and national viewpoint.[7] In his competence as a witness, a slave had the same

---

[1] *T. B. Sukkah* 41b; *T. Sukkah* 2:10; cf. *M. Pesahim* 8:2.

[2] *T. Peah* 4:10; *T. B. Ketuboth* 67b. And in fourth-century Athens even the poorest of those who paid the war-tax usually owned a maid-servant. See Demosthenes XXIV, 197.

[3] Dittenberger, *Sylloge* no. 45, lines 32-41—a law from Halicarnassus provides for selling into slavery outside the city anyone planning to disrupt recent arrangements for peace and whose property is below ten staters. Cf. also the law of Alexandria in *Dikaiomata*, ed. *Graeca Halensis* (1913), pp. 122-4.

[4] *Sifra on Lev.* 25:45; *T. B. Kiddushin* 22b; *M. Baba Bathra* 3:1; *T. B. Megillah* 23b; *T. B. Pesahim* 88b.

[5] See A. Gulak, in *Tarbiz* I, 4, pp. 20-26 (in Hebrew).

[6] On *peculium* in Roman law see W. W. Buckland, *The Roman Law of Slavery* (1908), pp. 187-216. On Egypt see R. Taubenschlag, *The Law of Graeco-Roman Egypt in the Light of the Papyri* (1955), pp. 87-8.

[7] *T. B. Shabbath* 137b; *T. B. Yebamoth* 48b; *Mekhilta on Ex.* 20:10 (p. 230). On the 'Canaanite' slave in general cf. also A. Büchler, in *Occident and Orient, Gaster Anniversary Volume* (1936), pp. 549-70 (in Hebrew); Jeremias, pp. 345-51; E. E. Urbach, in *Zion* (1960), pp. 156-166 (in Hebrew).

status as that of a woman.[1] His obligation to perform the commandments was the same as that of a woman.[2] The Torah had already
ordained the penalty of death for a master who beat his male or female
slave to death.[3] In this regard, the Jewish practice stands out in a
most favourable light.[4] At times, we hear of most cordial relations
between slaves and their masters. Some slaves were emancipated by
their masters as a token of regard. Freed slaves are fairly numerous,
especially in the retinues of the Herodian rulers for whom they
performed important services. This accorded with Roman practice.
One must bear in mind that the Julio-Claudian era was a golden age
for freedmen at the imperial court and in the administration of the
state.

Our discussion would be incomplete if we failed to consider the
presence of Jewish slaves in Jewish Palestine. One thing is certain.
In principle, the institution of Jewish slavery was never abolished.
This appears from the extensive discussions of this problem in the
Halakah.[5] On the other hand, it is quite evident that Jewish slaves
were not common. Actually, in the last century of the Second Temple
period, we have no concrete example of a Jewish slave. One can
possibly speak of a gradual withering away of the institution of Jewish
slavery and its almost total disappearance.[6] One of the causes, and
perhaps the chief cause, is to be seen in the inconvenience involved in
maintaining a Jewish slave. The Torah had already endowed him
with a number of important rights. It is no wonder that a Canaanite

[1] *T. B. Hagigah* 4a.
[2] *M. Sukkah* 2:8; *M. Hagigah* 1:1.
[3] Exod. 21:20.
[4] For humane tendencies in Roman law under the Empire in the second and
third centuries C. E. cf. Westermann, op. cit., p. 115.
[5] Strack-Billerbeck IV, 2, pp. 698-716.
[6] In fact the most definite example of the existence of the Hebrew slaves was
under the policy of Herod (Jos. *Ant.* XVI, 1-5) who provided that housebreakers
should be sold into slavery abroad. Cf. A. Schalit, *König Herodes* (1969), pp.
230-7. Josephus remarks on this that the laws order a thief to pay a fourfold
fine, and that if he were unable to do so, he was to be sold, but even in that
case he was to be set free after six years. Another case in point is the parable
in Matth. 18:23-25. Strack-Billerbeck IV 2, p. 698 asserts categorically that the
'Hebrew slave' was a real institution at that time. Cf. Jeremias, pp. 312-6.
See also Ramon Sugranyes de Franch, *Etudes sur le droit palestinien à l'époque
évangélique* (1946). On the other hand G. Alon, *History of the Jews in Palestine
in the Period of the Mishnah and the Talmud* II (1955), pp. 228-9 wholly denies
the existence of 'Hebrew slaves' in the time of the Second Temple. Urbach, p.
166 thinks that the unlimited possibilities to buy Canaanite slaves made the
acquisition of Hebrew slaves unprofitable from the economic point of view.

slave was preferred. In any event, when one speaks of slavery in this period, the reference is essentially to Canaanite slaves. But again, one must stress that in effect these foreign slaves became a part of the Jewish people.

BIBLIOGRAPHY

One of the best surveys of the Jewish society at the end of the Second Temple period is the book by J. JEREMIAS, *Jerusalem in the time of Jesus*, 1969 (English translation of: *Jerusalem zur Zeit Jesu*, 3rd ed. 1962). Of much value is still SCHÜRER II which has chapters on the high priests and priesthood and A. BÜCHLER, *Die Priester und der Cultus im letzten Jahrzehnt des jerusalemischen Tempels*, 1895.

Two more recent articles elucidate the problem of the high priesthood in the Herodian and Roman periods: E. BAMMEL, 'Die Bruderfolge im Hochpriestertum der herodianisch-römischen Zeit,' in *ZDPV* (1954), pp. 147-153 and E. M. SMALLWOOD, ' High Priests and Politics in Roman Palestine,' in *JTS* (1962), pp. 14-34.

For the world of the sages and the part played by them in Jewish society see E. E. URBACH, *The Sages*, 2 vls, 1975 (translation from the Hebrew).

Also some of the works bearing upon the sects and their social background should be consulted: L. FINKELSTEIN, *The Pharisees*, 3rd ed., 1962; R. MARCUS, 'The Pharisees in the Light of Modern Scholarship,' in *Journal of Religion* (1952). pp. 153-164; J. LE MOYNE, *Les Sadducéens*, 1972; M. HENGEL, *Die Zeloten*, 1961; M. STERN, 'Zealots', in *Encyclopaedia Judaica*, Year-Book 1973, pp. 135-152. There are also relevant chapters in: S. W. BARON, *A Social and Religious History of the Jews* I, 1952, pp. 250-285.

See also the recent work of J. NEUSNER, *The Rabbinic Traditions about the Pharisees before 70*, 3 vls, 1971; and the chapter 'Jesus and Galilee', in G. VERMES, *Jesus the Jew*, 1973, pp. 42-57.

Chapter Twelve
Economic Life in Palestine

In writing of the Jewish economy of the first century c.e. in Palestine, and of the non-Jewish economic sector in the same country, we are under an obligation to declare the limitations and qualifications of our theme. The Land of Israel of the period that concerns us had become an integral part of the Hellenistic economy of the eastern Mediterranean, and of the Roman Empire that succeeded it. But the country had its own limitations and its own contributions to make; its Jewish society further retained some characteristics which made it deviant and even exceptional within the Empire. It imposed upon itself certain religious restrictions which limited its own free consumption and production and encouraged economic autarky. Its craftsmen were organized in a more advanced and active way than most of their Gentile confrères; its leading intelligentsia earned their livings to a growing extent by manual labour; in the period we are discussing the Jews of Palestine were less urbanized than the population of other equally developed Roman provinces, and their outlook on slavery was strongly tinged with moral reservations.

The literary sources from which any picture can be drawn of the Jewish economy of Palestine in the first century c.e., present certain difficulties, and their use requires discrimination.[1] The evidence of archaeology has been but sparely applied to build a reasoned picture of the ancient Jewish economy of Judaea in the period which concerns us, and much of the work of analysis and synthesis remains to be carried out. An endeavour will nevertheless be made here to use some of the available material.

Several enquiries have utilized the literary sources to construct a comprehensive account of the Jewish economy before and during the talmudic period (Herzfeld, Krauss, Klausner, Heichelheim, Baron, Avi-Yonah, Kreissig, Ben-David), but where the talmudic material is concerned, not all these scholars have distinguished between earlier and later material. The consequence has been that accounts have not

[1] See chapter one, pp. 8-15.

always described Jewish economy as a process of historical development. We shall endeavour to build our discussion, where the talmudic material is concerned, exclusively on information dated to the first century C.E. unless specific grounds can be discovered for relating given undated or later statements to the same earlier period.

The agrarian development of Palestine from Alexander the Great to the coming of the Romans

In the ancient world only a few exceptional urban centres depended for their foodstuffs upon imports from overseas, and the subsistence of all other inhabited units and areas was derived from their own local agriculture. We shall therefore mainly deal with the part played by agricultural production in the life of first-century Palestine. Inevitably we must open with Flavius Josephus' well known statement that 'we the Jews neither inhabit a coastal territory nor welcome the commerce or the association with others which it brings, for our towns are built far from the sea, and we cultivate the excellent rural region which we occupy...moreover there was nothing in ancient times to induce us to associate with the Greeks as did the Egyptians, induced by their exports and imports, or the Phoenicians of the coast, induced by their love of mercantile and commercial gain.'[1] It has often been pointed out that Josephus' statements were here influenced by his endeavour to buttress his claim for the priority and independence of the Jews as pioneers of culture, by explaining why they had not come into earlier contact with the Greeks. Although in fact the implication that the Jews of his own period were not engaged in commerce cannot stand up to criticism, Josephus' claim rested on a measure of contemporary fact: the coastal towns of Palestine, ever since Pompey's activity in the country, had been overwhelmingly repopulated by Greek-speaking Phoenicians and Syrians;[2] the Jews were preponderantly a people of the hinterland, preoccupied with agriculture and hardly maintaining a single significant urban centre beside Jerusalem; the other two Jewish towns of some importance, Tiberias and Sepphoris, were, significantly, in Galilee, and on the coast only one harbour town may have contained a preponderantly Jewish population, namely Joppa.

This represented, nevertheless, a situation created by Pompey in 63

[1] *Against Apion* I, 60.
[2] *Ant.* XIV, 74-6; *War* I, 155-6.

B.C.E. and was very far from reflecting the situation existing after the conquests of Alexander the Great and the Maccabean expansion. To understand the economic situation in Judaea in the period between the accession of Herod and the destruction of the Temple, it is necessary briefly to survey the country's agrarian development between Alexander and the coming of the Romans. Josephus' above-cited statement might indeed have applied to the economic position of the Jews of Judaea under Persia, which deliberately placed the coastal towns in the hands of the Phoenician seafarers.[1] But the country's inclusion in the Hellenistic world involved Judaea in an increasingly cosmopolitan society of free movement and accelerated trade; the Mediterranean Jewish Diaspora began to develop, and with it a small but influential Jewish group in Jerusalem with international contacts and financial interests.[2] But the Hellenizing movement initiated by these men was opposed and ultimately defeated by a combination led by the rural priesthood, the sages, the urban lower class and above all by the peasantry, who vindicated their national faith and independence, and perpetuated the leadership of the Hasmoneans in the form of a new high-priestly dynasty.

Not enough is known of the relationships between the Jewish peasantry and their Hasmonean rulers. The statement of Kreissig that the Maccabean rising prevented the Hellenization of land-tenure in Judaea and the conversion of rural areas into royal lands ($\beta\alpha\sigma\iota\lambda\iota\varkappa\grave{\eta}$ $\gamma\tilde{\eta}$) is at least debatable;[3] there is evidence of the all-embracing taxation of livestock as early as 261 or 260 B.C.E.,[4] and in 258 B.C.E. there was royal land in Upper Galilee or in Bashan.[5] The Hephtziba inscription indicates that extensive estates in the eastern Plain of Esdraelon and in the Plain of Beth Shean had been in royal hands under the Ptolemies, who had transferred them, part in hereditary lease, part as gift-land, to the high official Ptolemy son of Thraseas.[6] Antiochus III gave him further tracts here and elsewhere.[7] There is no doubt that the peasants tilling the above estates were *laoi*, ie. villagers virtually bound to the soil and possessing little or no internal autonomy. It would be a bold

---

[1] *CIS* 1, 3; Scylax, ed. Müller, *Geographi Graeci Minores*, p. 79, par. 104.

[2] Cf. V. Tcherikover, *Hellenistic Civilization and the Jews* (1959), pp. 127-42.

[3] Kreissig, p. 26.

[4] *Aegyptus* XVI (1936), pp. 257ff.

[5] Rostovtzeff I, p. 342; III, nos 139 and 149; Tcherikover, op. cit. pp. 43ff.

[6] Y. Landau in *IEJ* (1966), pp. 58-61.

[7] Ibid. pp. 54ff.

assumption that they included no Jews.[1] While on the other hand Antiochus IV's order to Lysias to convert Judaea into royal *katoikiai*[2] indicates that not all its cultivable areas belonged to the category of royal land in the year 166-5, in the letters of the later Seleucid kings Demetrius I and II announcing various concessions of taxes and territory to the Maccabean rulers,[3] the dues remitted bear a close resemblance to those paid by the peasants (*laoi basilikoi*) of the royal lands of Egypt, and there are strong reasons for supposing that the toparchies conceded by the same Seleucids to the Maccabees (Ekron,[4] Aphaerema, Lydda[5] and Ramatayyim) constituted royal property.[6] This being the case, it would be less accurate to decide with Kreissig that the Maccabean rising prevented the conversion of the Judaean rural areas to royal domain, than to conclude that it was generated by the actual extent existence of such lands, and the oppressive régime by which they were characterized. The reform of Nehemiah had secured the tenure of the independent peasant smallholder,[7] who constituted the backbone of the Jewish nation in its homeland, and of the successful resistance to the Seleucids. An awareness of this situation will contribute to an understanding of subsequent events, whether under the Hasmoneans, the Herods, or the Roman procurators.

As stated, we are ill-informed of what occurred in this sphere under the successors of Simeon, the last of the Maccabean brothers. The operative known facts are that the later Jewish high priests, Hyrcanus, Aristobulus and Alexander Jannaeus, annexed extensive territories, needed considerable manpower to conduct their campaigns, and no little revenue to finance them. Jannaeus, moreover, if Josephus can

---

[1] I can see no evidence to confirm Avi-Yonah's belief (p. 373), that these estates were transferred to the city lands of Scythopolis (government lands could exist within the bounds of such), or that the status of the peasants was so ameliorated. This theory rests entirely on the analogy of Seleucid policy in Asia Minor, as visualized by Rostovtzeff (I, p. 507). An inscription found at Beth Shean (*SEG* xx, no. 455, 305/311 c.e.) suggests that considerable state domain (δεσποτικαὶ χῶραι) still existed in the vicinity of the city in the later Roman period. For the meaning of δεσποτικαὶ χῶραι cf. Perdrizet, in *Mélanges de l'école française de Rome* (1900), p. 229.

[2] I Macc. 3:36.

[3] I Macc. 10:30; 11:34.

[4] *Ant.* XIII, 102. ceded to Jonathan by Alexander Balas.

[5] Cf. *Ant.* XIV, 200.

[6] A. Alt, *Kleine Schriften* II (1953), pp. 384ff., believed that most of Galilee, Golan and Bashan were composed of royal domain land from the era of Ptolemaic rule, due to the backwardness of urban development in those regions.

[7] Neh. 5:1-12; cf. Diodorus XL, 3, 7-8.

be trusted, was in dire conflict with an important section of his own people.[1] The nominal recorded field of conflict was religious, and no doubt this aspect was important, but economic factors may be suspected; Schalit, indeed, accepting the predominance of royal land in Judaea under the Seleucids, believes that the Maccabees freed the Jewish peasants from the oppressive taxation associated with that régime, and distributed newly acquired lands among them in return for the obligation to military service, though part of the lands acquired became royal property leased to cultivators in tenancy.[2] The cause of conflict under Jannaeus, in Schalit's view, may have been that the King attempted to reassert the Seleucid claim to proprietorship of the soil,[3] thus reintroducing the conditions of the Hellenistic 'royal land,' presumably (we would add) under the pressure of financial needs created by continuous warfare.

Schalit's views on the agrarian position under Jannaeus are entirely hypothetical, but if they are not provable, they are at least in conformity with objective conditions and with the practices of the Hellenistic régimes that had ruled Judaea and continued to influence her. Moreover, we do have evidence of villages held by Hyrcanus and his successors in the Plain of Esdraelon,[4] and of special rights exercized by the Hasmoneans in the district of Lydda;[5] it is also reasonable to infer that Jonathan had received Ekron as a personal appanage. Tradition moreover attributes to Jannaeus numerous villages in the 'King's Mountain Country' (הר המלך),[6] a tract ultimately extending over much of the western foothills of Judaea and Samaria between Wadi Ara and Beth Govrin, with an eastern spur extending to the Judaean watershed north of Jerusalem and to the west shore of the Dead Sea.[7] Luria has noted that the later of the two mishnaic lists of localities from which produce for the Temple service was derived,[8] contains names not earlier than the time of Jannaeus, including *Har ha-Melek* and Beth Yannai; he concludes that the area referred to constituted the territories annexed in Jannaeus' campaigns of conquest.[9] The precise status of these lands after their incorporation

[1] *Ant.* XIII, 372-83.
[2] *Herod, the Man and his Work* (1960; in Hebrew), pp. 95-6.
[3] Ibid. p. 400, n. 92.
[4] *Ant.* XIV, 207.   [5] *Ant.* XIV, 200.
[6] *T. B. Gittin* 57a.
[7] *M. Menahoth* 9:13; *M. Shebiith* 9:2; *P. T. Maaser Sheni* I, 52d; *P. T. Taanith* IV, 69b; *T. Demai* 1:11; *Sifre Deut.* 6; *T. B. Gittin* 57a.
[8] *T. Menahoth* 9:13.
[9] B.-Z. Luria, *King Yannai* (1961; in Hebrew), pp. 39ff., esp. p. 43.

into Judaea must remain a subject of guided conjecture, but it is clear from the name that part at least remained Hasmonean royal property, and part must have been estates transferred in gift to Jewish notables including, for instance, the priestly family whose scion Eleazar ben Harsum appears in possession of broad tracts of *Har ha-Melek* worked by tenants after the destruction of the Second Temple. Their estates apparently reached the coast somewhere near Caesarea.[1] Other lands of this area were doubtless given to Jewish peasant proprietors in full possession, but most of the Jewish holdings in the plainland would have been lost in 63 B.C.E. when Pompey reconstituted the Greek coastal cities.

Luria has suggested that John Hyrcanus' abolition of the 'avowal' connected with the payment of tithe to the priests[2] may have been motivated, *inter alia*, by the existence on Hasmonean royal land in Idumaea of Jewish tenants who, because they did not own the soil, were not obliged to discharge this obligation.[3] On the other hand Schalit has voiced the conjecture, that it was Hyrcanus or Jannaeus who raised to one half the one-third shekel contributed to the Temple from Nehemiah's time,[4] and that this was one of the issues behind the clash between Jannaeus and the popular opposition which reached the point of civil war in the year 88 B.C.E.[5]

The evidence of Jannaeus' coinage, which indicates the restoration of representative institutions late in his reign, and possibly also of Pharisaic influence,[6] would suggest that a compromise had been reached between the parties before his death, but we do not know what form this took with regard to agrarian problems. The fact remains, that the subsequent reign of Alexandra is described as one of consistent agricultural prosperity, presumably to be explained by the absence of costly warfare.[7]

---

[1] *P. T. Demai* VI, 28b.

[2] *M. Maaser Sheni* 5:15; *M. Sotah* 9:10.

[3] *Molad* XXIII (1965), pp. 697ff. (in Hebrew).

[4] Neh. 10:33.

[5] Op. cit. p. 140. A new perspective of this struggle may be gained if it is viewed against the socially disturbed situation prevailing in the entire eastern Mediterranean in the same year (Italy, Cyrene, Egypt, Asia Minor.) Cf. Tarn and Griffith, *Hellenistic Civilization* (2nd ed. 1952), p. 42.

[6] Y. Naveh, in *IEJ* XVIII (1968), pp. 20-5.

[7] It is notable that the one recorded campaign of Alexandra's reign, that against the Iturean Ptolemy Mennaeus near Damascus (*Ant.* XIII, 418), could be explained as aimed to protect, in cooperation with that city, the profitable trade-route from Elath via the Decapolis, controlled by the Hasmoneans, and doubtless a valuable source of state-revenue (cf. below, p. 667).

The loss of the coastal plain following Pompey's drastic reorganization of the affairs of Judaea and Syria, must have meant the creation of a very considerable class of landless Jewish peasants, as Schalit has seen.[1] This phenomenon may serve as a key to an understanding of the entire development of the agrarian problem in Judaea down to the great rebellion of 70 C.E. Indeed, combined with the seismic effect of the sudden and massive loss of commerce caused by the cutting off of the coastal towns and the Decapolis from the Judaean state, which must have thrown a considerable group of Jews back upon agriculture, this situation (widely ignored by historians) would have done much to foment the stormy revolutionary atmosphere of the subsequent period.

The period which followed Pompey's coming was one of nearly continuous disturbance and conflict which lasted down to the effective seizure of rule by Herod in 37 B.C.E. The conflict between Hyrcanus II and his brother Aristobulus resulted in armed Roman intervention and the storming of Jerusalem; following Pompey's drastic reduction of the area of Judaea, the governor Aulus Gabinius cut the country into *synhedria* dominated by oligarchies; the economic effect of such a cantonization can only be conjectured. This short-lived régime was prudently abolished by Julius Caesar, who reconstituted Hyrcanus as ethnarch, but not before the country had been further disturbed by the unsuccessful rebellions of Aristobulus and his son Alexander, and heavily mulcted by Crassus, a process repeated during the civil war after Caesar's death by Cassius. In 40 B.C.E. came the successful Parthian invasion and the temporary restoration of Antigonus Mattathias, whose rule ended with a long drawn out battle against Rome's tool Herod, and with another and bloodier capture of Jerusalem by the Roman forces. It may be stated with a measure of assurance that every Hasmonaean rebel against Roman rule found powerful support among the Jewish peasantry, more especially among the discontented landless elements, which doubtless furnished all these leaders with good military material.[2] Several years before Herod's accession to the throne of Judaea, moreover, a sign appeared of things to come. This was the activity of Ezechias, father of Judah of Galilee, on the borders of Phoenicia, where he led a struggle against the villages of the area of Tyre, till he was caught and executed by Herod

[1] Op. cit. pp. 168-9.
[2] Cf. explicitly Josephus, *War* I, 153; also, perhaps, *Ant.* XIV, 334.

in his capacity of governor of Galilee (47 B.C.E.).[1] It is clear from Mark Antony's subsequent decision that the lands at issue had been seized from the Jews in the confused days of the civil war, and were restored to Hyrcanus' jurisdiction by the Triumvir.[2] Ezechias' struggle was part of a long drawn out conflict produced by an acute shortage of cultivable land at a time when the tracts at the disposal of the Jewish population had been drastically curtailed: it was natural that this conflict should find its earliest and acutest expression in the marginal areas, where the Jewish and non-Jewish rural populations met. It was to be perpetuated as a Jewish movement, and the conflict itself was to be continuous until the rebellion of 66, of which it was an important component.[3]

Climate and physical characteristics

Palestine shares the climatic and physical characteristics of all the Mediterranean countries: it consists of a limestone mountain massif and a limited maritime plain; the soil cover of the massif consists chiefly of the residues of the limestones and chalks in dissolution, and the plainlands soils, of the transported material washed down from the uplands.[4] Rainfall is confined to the winter months as the rain-bearing Atlantic winds move southward, but the southern half of the country, the Negev, screened from the Atlantic by Africa and Sinai, is desert, cultivable only in certain areas by irrigation and by conservation of run-off.

In the rest of the country, the possibilities of successful cultivation depend on rainfall, water supply, seasonal temperatures, and soil. The winter months are the season of sowing. While early growth is favoured by sunny days between the rains, the arid east winds of the seasonal transition from winter to summer endanger crop-development in its critical period. The karstic character of the Judaean uplands and the permeability of its rock create a deep watertable and few permanently flowing rivers; but springs break out at various points, more particularly in the marginal areas of the coastal plain. Possibilities of irrigation are therefore localized, except in the northern

---

[1] *Ant.* XIV, 159; *War* I, 204.

[2] *Ant.* XIV, 313-6.

[3] S. Applebaum, 'The struggle for the soil and the revolt of 66-73 C.E.', in *Eretz Israel* XI (1975), pp. 125ff.

[4] For the following brief account of the country's soils, I am much indebted to Y. Qarmon, *Eretz Israel, a Regional Geography* (1973; in Hebrew), pp. 41-4.

Jordan rift, which is watered by the snows of Mount Hermon. But the winter rains are sufficient to create a permanent vegetational cover, productive of cultivable soil; only the steep eastern slope, lying in the rain-shadow of the massif, is arid. The most extensive soil of the uplands of Judaea, Samaria and Galilee is constituted by the terra rossa, the residue of the limestones in dissolution, which composes about forty per cent of the soils of the country west of Jordan. Terra rossa is one of the most fertile soils of the country, but tends to be shallow and difficult to work due to the steep slopes of the mountain-country, a feature which must be counteracted by terracing. Part of the terra rossa, nevertheless, occupies considerable areas of level plateau close to the watershed north and south of Jerusalem. The rendzina soils, which occupy some ten per cent of the country's cover, are the by-product of limestones and chalks; they are distributed in the Shepharam (south-west Galilee) and south Carmel regions, also in central Samaria, and in the south-western Shephelah between Latrun and Beth Govrin. The rendzinas are less fertile than the terra rossa, but easier to work with simple tools and well supplied with water where they are shallow and overlie porous rock. The volcanic basalts of eastern Galilee are parent to a heavy grain-growing soil, which, however, is full of rock fragments and hence laborious to clear. The korkar, a very recent precipitate of limestone and sand, forms two parallel belts along the central coastal plain; it responds to careful cultivation and has been occupied since ancient times. Marl soils, on the other hand, are confined almost entirely to the Jordan rift, the Dead Sea area and the Araba. They are highly salinated and uncultivable except in the region of Beth Shean and the Sea of Galilee, where they are leached by rain.

The lowlands are covered, in the main, by the fertile tertiary soils brought down by spate from the hills. The soils derived from the terra rossa are to be found chiefly in the Lower Galilee valleys, in Samaria and on the western mountain margins. Those derived from the rendzinas occupy the broad streambeds of those areas and the foot of the hillslopes to west of them. The alluvial soils brought down by the streambeds and deposited in the valleys, are distributed preponderantly in the maritime plain and in the Valley of Esdraelon; their fertility depends on adequate drainage, neglect of which during long periods has resulted in the formation of swamps due to the blockage of streambeds. Smaller alluvial deltas are to be found on the west shore of the Dead Sea. In the central maritime plain swamp-formation was further encouraged by the korkar ridges which, running parallel with the coast, act as natural barriers to seaward drainage. The wind-transported soils include the coastal sand-dunes, which have invaded a considerable belt of the coastal plain between Caesarea and Sinai. These sands are completely barren, but were certainly less extensive in the ancient period. The redsand soils, also wind-borne in origin, and extending west of the Shephelah from Binyamina to Gadera, were wooded and uncultivable till the present century due to hard-pan and poor water-retention. The loess soils of the northern Negev and the valleys of the central Negev mountains are also wind-borne in origin, but part has been transported by wadi-spate. Despite the area's low and variable rainfall, diminishing from 300 mm. per year north of Beersheba to less than two mm. at Elath, this soil is fertile when cultivated and irrigated with the correct techniques; thus the stream-beds of the central Negev were successfully exploited in ancient times,[1] but historically the Negev must be regarded as a marginal area apt to be colonized only when peculiar circumstances necessitate its exploitation.

It follows from the foregoing brief survey that the mountain massif, which was the heartland of Jewish settlement before the time of the monarchy and again prior to the Hasmonaean expansion, demanded the greatest hardihood and skill on the part of those who wished to wrest a living from it. It required careful and laborious terracing to conserve the soil, and the skilled regulation of the torrent beds in order to check soil-erosion and water-wastage due to uncontrolled spate in the rainy season. Cisterns had to be quarried and maintained to supply drinking water for man and beast, and run-off conserved to supplement springs for irrigation. Natural woodland had to be safeguarded, and cultivated fruit-trees fostered, in order to anchor the soil and to retain moisture. Woodland had been greatly reduced since the era of the Israelite takeover, and in large areas of the hills no doubt had been replaced by plantations and arable land, but the Carmel, the Sharon and considerable areas in the Hebron area and north of Jerusalem were still wooded in the Second Temple period, the natural climax woodland consisting chiefly of the Mediterranean oak, the terebinth, the Aleppo pine and the carob.[2]

[1] M. Evenari, L. Shaanan and N. Tadmor, *The Negev; the Challenge of a Desert* (1971); P. Mayerson, 'The ancient agricultural régime of Nessana in the central Negev,' *Nessana* III (1960); S. Applebaum, 'Investigations into the ancient agriculture of the central Negev,' in *BIES* XXX (1966), pp. 224ff.

[2] See especially L. Rost, 'Jüdische Wälde,' in *Palästinajahrbuch* XXVII (1931),

In mountain and plain alike, careful dry farming methods involving constant summer ploughing to conserve soil-moisture, were necessary to fertility. But where the hill country was concerned, it is to be noted that both grain and fruit could be produced successfully in quantities adequate for subsistence thanks to the qualities of the terra rossa, the rendzina and the alluvial soils.

The Transjordanian massif is more exposed to desert influences and its rainfall more fitful, but it possesses extensive areas of terra rossa and several permanently flowing rivers. The incentive of an international trade route connecting Elath with Damascus further encouraged the population to make their agriculture productive. Extensive ancient irrigation works are reported;[1] of their date less is known, but much is doubtless to be attributed to the Roman period.

The settlement pattern in the first century

When we turn to examine the agricultural economy of Judaea in the first century, our first question must be, what was the settlement distribution over the countryside, or, to use the agrarian historian's expression, the settlement pattern? As a starting point we may consider the terms applied by rabbinic literature to the rural settlements. They are כפר (kefar), עיר (ir), עירה (ajarah) and קריה (kirjah).[2] Ir, in contrast to the modern usage of the word, meant primarily a rural settlement, and, in the first instance, an isolated farm.[3] This meaning is demonstrated by two mishnaic halakot: 1) 'If an ir having a single ownei became an ir having many owners' etc.;[4] 2) 'If a man sold an ir, he has sold also the cisterns, trenches, vaults, bath-houses, dovecots, oil-presses and irrigated fields...but if it is said, 'It and all that is in it,' even if cattle and slaves were in it, all these were sold also.'[5]

pp. 111ff. For information on the natural woodland cover of the Judaean hills, I am also indebted to G. Douer.

[1] See generally N. Glück, 'Explorations in Eastern Palestine 4,' in *AASOR* XXV-XXVIII, parts 1 and 2 (1951).

[2] See S. Krauss, in *He-Atid* III (1923), pp. 10ff.; S. Applebaum, in *Papers of the Sixth Congress of the World Union of Jewish Studies* (1973).

[3] An exact parallel in English is the word 'town', which originally meant a single farm enclosed by a fence. Cf. J. Morris, *The Age of Arthur* (1973), pp. 470-1, on this placename element (-tun): 'Its basic meaning 'fence' is perpetuated by the modern German word *Zaun*. In old English it usually means a fenced area, sometimes agricultural. But its ordinary meaning in the seventh century and later...was 'village', a collection of houses, compact or scattered... It is regularly translated in Latin by the word *villa*.'

[4] *M. Erubin* 5:6.   [5] *M. Baba Bathra* 4:7.

There can be little doubt, that this type of farm, consisting of residence, baths, agricultural outbuildings and installations, corresponded roughly to the Roman *villa*. It is not clear how far this form existed in the country in the pre-Hellenistic period; in the Hellenistic period this type was not uncommon in the coastal plain as is suggested by the archaeological surveys of the Soreq valley conducted by Kaplan and Dothan;[1] here a chain of Hellenistic sites is seen along the alluvium of the lower Soreq valley between the sea and Beth Oved; from there it turns southward along the korkar ridge to Qatra, and it is tempting to see in these settlements a planned colonization by military settlers carried out either to protect the territory of Jamnia and Azotus (Ashdod)[2] from Jewish attack, or to protect Jewish territory from the Greek coastal population of the same area.

In the foothills between Lydda and Antipatris (Rosh ha-Ayyin) several Hellenistic sites are to be found, of which Tirat Jehudah was one.[3] They occupy medium soil enclaves, and it is reasonable to assume that they were individual farms. Among the ancient sites recorded in this belt, they are a minority as compared with the later Roman and Byzantine settlements. On the maritime plain to west, a nucleated village at Nebbi Kifil may have existed in the Hellenistic period, on the evidence of pottery; in the early Roman period isolated farms certainly were to be found on the plain, one being the first-century *villa* part of which was excavated by Kaplan near Nahlat Jehudah.[4] The Shephelah foothills also contained nucleated villages in the earlier Roman period, such as that at Hirbet el-Hamman south of Kefr Qasm, where the buildings were concentrated and covered a considerable area.[5] Much of the surface pottery from this site is early Roman.

In the Judaean and Samaritan mountain country, on the other hand, both isolated farms and nucleated villages were present in the earlier Roman period. Thus on the hill known as Hirbet Furadeis north of the present village of Qirwat bene-Hassan, there is a considerable ancient nucleated village consisting of solid masonry buildings built

[1] Y. Kaplan, in *IEJ* II (1952), pp. 104ff.; M. Dothan, in *BIES* XVII (1953), pp. 138ff.; XXI (1957), pp. 199ff.

[2] Cf. the towers of Ashdod (I Macc. 16:10). For towers as parts of ancient farmsteads, see Preisigke, in *Hermes* LIV (1919), p. 423; cf. Rostovtzeff, in *Anatolian Studies in Honour of W. Ramsay*, p. 334.

[3] Migdal Jabba, Nakhshonim (two sites), Hirbet Lebbed.

[4] Y. Kaplan, *Two Groups of Pottery of the First Century C.E. from Jaffa and its Vicinity* (1964).

[5] I am indebted to M. Kokhbi for drawing my attention to this site.

on the terraces cut into the entire south side of the hill. The surface pottery begins in the early Iron Age, but some is early Roman. A road communicates directly between this settlement and Qirwat bene-Hassan, in the centre of which are a Herodian fortified building and elsewhere a large ancient cistern of impressive construction, which may well mark the residence of the proprietor to whose estate the village at Hirbet Furadeis belonged. His magnificent tomb with rock-cut ornamental façade faced northward from the escarpment to the south of Qirwat bene-Hassan; typical of the later Second Temple period, it reflects a family of wealth and distinction. To the east of the area lay Haris, the ancient Arous, which late in the first century B.C.E. was part of the estate of Ptolemy, minister of Herod.[1] Here then we have an area of nucleated villages attached to the estates of large landed proprietors. The fortified *villa* at Hirbet al-Moraq, west of Hebron,[2] on the other hand, appears to be an isolated unit, although it may well have dominated an estate; it consisted of a walled enclosure containing rooms surrounding an internal court; attached to it on the east were a second court and a tower. The columns of the structure bore masons' marks cut in Hebrew and Greek, and the occupation was dated in the first and second centuries.[3]

The association of nucleated villages with large estates, as found at Qirwat bene-Hassan and Haris, may well illustrate the meaning of the mishnaic '*ir*' owned by a number of people which became the property of one man.[4] Both mishnaic and archaeological evidence, at any rate, indicates that two parallel processes were at work in the country in the first century B.C.E.; on the one hand the growth of large estates which assimilated complete villages in tenancy,[5] and on the other hand, the conversion of single farmsteads into agglomerations of a number of homes by the addition of settlers or by natural increase of the population.

---

[1] *Ant.* XVII, 289. The above sites have been visited in the course of archaeological reconnaissance work carried out with S. Dar.
[2] *Archaeological News* XXXIII (Jan. 1970), pp. 5ff. (in Hebrew).
[3] Other examples of large fortified farms, Hellenistic or early Roman, are known in western Galilee, but have not been published. I have to thank R. Fraenkel for this information.
[4] *M. Erubin* 5:6.
[5] In this context may be recalled the Zamarid, Philip son of Iacimus, who owned villages in the vicinity of Gamala. (Jos. *Life* 47; 58). The inhabitants of such villages, it is to be assumed, were not the Babylonian military settlers settled as *katoikoi* by Herod (*Ant.* XVII, 23-31), as the latter were independent tenants of the king.

How far the other terms for settlements possessed a precise juridical or classificatory character is difficult to say, but they do seem to apply to settlements which stood in a certain relationship to given centres, whether as villages of an urban territory in relation to the city with which they were associated for purposes of justice and taxation, or as tenurial units in relation to the centre of an estate. Thus we hear of the *ajarot* of the territory of Sepphoris;[1] of the *kerajot* around Lydda inhabited by cultivators who possess a special attachment to Rabban Judah the patriarch;[2] and of the thousand *ajarot* owned by Rabbi Eleazar ben Harsum in *Har ha-Melek*.[3] All the above-cited instances belong to the second century C.E., but Rabbi Eleazar's holdings in *Har ha-Melek* certainly went back to the period before 70 C.E. It follows that the *ajarah* and the *kirjah* had in common, that whether or not they possessed an internal organization of their own, they were administratively dependant on a larger centre, whether the residence of a landlord, the headquarters of a state domain or a city possessing a municipal territory.[4]

Of the field systems of the settlement pattern whose first faint lines we have endeavoured to trace above, little is known as yet. Most of the cultivated areas of the mountain country occupied hillside terraces pursuing the natural contours; only where the valleys and plateaux offered relatively level tracts could normal field systems obtain. The Mishnah tells us that 'where it is the custom to fence, it is obligatory; but in the plainland, where it is not customary, it is not obligatory.'[5] The inference is that on the maritime plain and in similar valleys where the land was level, walled or fenced plots were exceptional. This means that strict control had to be exercized over

---

[1] *P. T. Gittin* II, 43c.
[2] *P. T. Sanhedrin* I, 18c.
[3] *T. B. Yoma* 35b; *P. T. Taanith* IV, 69a.
[4] A further nexus between the term *ajarah* and tenancy on crown domain or on large estates is indicated by the Syrian Gentile encountered by Rabban Gamaliel in western Galilee, who defined himself as 'from the *ajarot* of *burganin*', ie. from villages whose inhabitants were grouped round *burgi*, fortified points established for defensive purposes in disturbed districts (*T. Pesahim* 1:2). On *burgi* in the Roman Empire, see Winckelmann, *Germania II*, 54; Labrousse, *Mélanges de l'école française de Rome* LVI, p. 151; M. Schwabe, in *Tarbiz* XX (1950), pp. 273ff. (in Hebrew); S. Applebaum, in *BIES* XVIII (1954), pp. 202ff.; S. Safrai, in *Roman Frontier Studies* 1967 (1971), p. 230. Ben David, p. 49, cites various talmudic sources which suggest that the population of *ajarot* might vary from 600 to 7,500 souls, but all these sources are post-70, and most do not precede the second century.
[5] *M. Baba Bathra* 1:2.

livestock after sowing and in the season of growing crops; further that communal grazing on the stubble after harvest was almost certainly practised. What cannot be established is whether holdings were concentrated or held in parcels scattered over the entire village area. The latter pattern appears to have existed in Syria in the fourth century, side by side with strictly individual plots or areas.[1] It existed among the Palestinian Arabs in the British Mandatory period.[2] Communalism of the seasonal cropping plan, at any rate, has left no trace in the sources; what we do possess is a short but vivid record of total communalism of harvesting, storage and distribution in the sabbatical year in the pre-70 period.[3] This scheme is operated by the emissaries of the local court among the *ajarot*, and the produce collected is stored in the *ir* for systematic distribution. We would be glad to know whether the word *ir* in this passage means an estate-centre or an actual town. There is no means of gauging how far this striking instance of socialist cooperation was applied or when it originated.

In the hill-country, where stone was abundant, fencing of the plots was, according to the passage cited, the rule, and was doubtless further encouraged by the greater incidence of the goat.[4] The main factor, however, would have been that the terrain dictated a greater dispersal of arable plots where these did not take the form of terraces. In the period of the Second Temple nucleated villages must nevertheless have predominated in the mountain areas, for reasons of security and because of the need to concentrate near water.[5] It is also evident that for physical reasons some villages possessed fields which lay at a distance from them. An instance of this sort, cited in

---

[1] Libanius, *Orationes*, ed. Förster XLVII, 11; for commentary, L. Harmand, *Libanius, discours sur les patronages* (1955), pp. 124ff.

[2] At Nessana a cultivated tract including both vineyard and arable was in the Byzantine period divided among three brothers; each of the two respective divisions takes the form of contiguous strips. See Mayerson, in J. Kraemer, *Nessana* III (1958), no. 31, fig. 3, p. 97.

[3] *T. Shebiith* 8:1. The relevant passage begins with the word *Ba-Rishonah*.

[4] In north-western Samaria, the terraced slopes are dotted with isolated tower-like structures normally regarded as mausolea. Many however are associated with oil and wine-presses. Whatever the case, their existence may well be interpretable as pointing to holdings held in severalty.

[5] In the Byzantine period isolated farms are to be found in the Judaean mountain country; an example is the valley between the Hebrew University and Beth Haccerem, south-west of Jerusalem, where at least two villas of that period existed. Another such farm is known to me west of Ein Kerem.

the Palestinian Talmud,[1] is that of Baalat, whose houses lay in Judaea, and its land in Dan. The phenomenon is illustrated in the same vicinity at Hirbet al-Hammam, the ancient village south of Kefr Qasm (above); this lies on a rocky hill, and the nearest level arable is 1,5 kilometres to the west, and here a large area of field-divisions is still visible, abutting upon the Roman road connecting Migdal Jabba (Apheq) with Qirwat bene-Hassan. These fields, small and squarish in shape, are divided from one another by rows of large stones, sometimes by roadways marked in a similar manner; such roadways are interpretable as indicating plots held in severalty rather than collectively. Much of the surface pottery is early Iron Age, but the Roman period is also represented, and the field pattern may be the result of a Roman resurvey, perhaps for the allotment of land to the inhabitants of several villages situated in the surrounding hill-country. Two kilometres to eastward, among the hills, is the Arab Dir Balut, which can hardly be other than Baalat.[2]

Agriculture

The actual area of Judaea and Idumaea covered 730,000 hectares; with Galilee and Peraea, the area was nearer 1,055,000 hectares. Reifenberg calculated that 65-70 percent of the area was cultivated in ancient times.[3]

Tosefta Menahoth (8:3). which lists localities whence prime agricultural produce was furnished for the Temple worship, may be utilized as a first pointer to the potentialities of the country's various regions. The finest flour was supplied from Mihmash north of Jerusalem, from Zenoah, probably south of Beth Shemesh, and from Hapharaim in Lower Galilee; the earliest barley and the shewbread from Bikat Beth Makalah (near Jerusalem), from Sarafand between Lydda and Joppa, and from Bikat Ein-Soker east of Shechem; wine from Kuratajjim (Qirwat bene-Hassan?) and Beth Rimah (both in Samaria), from Hattulim, perhaps north of Gilgal, from Beth Lavan in Samaria and Kephar Sagneh, perhaps near Joppa. Oil came from Tekoa of Upper Galilee, from Regev (Rijab west of Gerasa), and from Gush Halav in Upper Galilee. Rams are sent from Moab, calves from the Sharon, lambs from the desert of Hebron, young chicks from *Har ha-Melek*.

---

[1] *P. T. Sanhedrin* 1, 18c.
[2] I am indebted to M. Kokhbi for drawing my attention to this complex.
[3] A. Reifenberg, *Soils of Palestine* (1938), pp. 113ff.

This list, attributable to the first century B.C.E., shows that much of the grain came from the Judaean uplands and Lower Galilee; much of the wine from Samaria and the Judaean hills; the oil from Transjordan and Upper Galilee, the cattle from Moab and the Sharon. But cereals and wine were also produced by the maritime plain.[1] Talmudic and non-Jewish sources add information on the agricultural produce of Galilee—wine, figs, flax, vegetables and other fruit; Josephus describes the entire region as cultivated;[2] Samaria, according to him, was fertile and endowed with rich pasture.[3] A reference to fertility is absent in Josephus' account of Judaea itself,[4] but elsewhere he dwells on the palms and balsam of Jericho.[5] Idumaea was better known for barley than for wheat,[6] and produced vinegar rather than wine.[7]

As to Transjordan, as early as the time of David the Rabbath-Ammon region could supply the king with an appreciable quantity of wheat, barley, lentils, honey, butter, mutton and beef at short notice;[8] Peraea, by contrast, Josephus calls rugged and in part desert, but containing fertile regions that produced olives, vines, and palms.[9] The livestock branch certainly bulked large in these parts, sending many head to Judaea in the Second Temple period. The basalt areas of Golan, Bashan and Hauran, bordering with Gilead on the north, also began to produce ample cattle, wheat and wine when they were pacified and their semi-nomadic populations compelled to settle at the end of the first century B.C.E.[10] The livestock branch across the Jordan, nevertheless, was always bound up with a great measure of seasonal transhumance and a semi-nomadic tribal way of life.

Of the agriculture of the specifically Greek areas of the country east and west of Jordan from the Hellenistic period onward we know little.

---

[1] The wines of Gaza and Ascalon were held in high esteem in the fourth century of the present era (*Expositio totius mundi et gentium*, ed. Rougé, par. 29), and the corn-growing potentialities of the Sharon are known to us from a document of the Persian period (*CIS* I, 3). Cf. the large granary of the Roman period found at Tell Ibrektas near Hadera by the writer.

[2] *War* III, 42-3.   [3] *War* III, 48.   [4] *War* III, 51-8.

[5] *War* I, 138-40.   [6] *M. Ketuboth* 5:8.

[7] *M. Pesahim* 3:1.   [8] II Sam. 17:27-9.   [9] *War* III, 44-5.

[10] We hear from Strabo (XVI, 4, 21), of the products of Nabataea, ie. the Negev and Transjordan, during the first century B.C.E. The area according to his information was fertile but produced no olive oil, oil of sesame being used instead. Its livestock included large oxen, the white-haired sheep, but no horses; aromatic plants were also grown. Was the white-haired sheep known to Strabo the originator of the fine fleece which ultimately gave Europe its first refined wool? (Cf. M. L. Ryder, in *Agricultural Hist. Review* XII (1964), pp. 1ff, esp. p. 5; also below, p. 656.

We cannot tell from the records embodied in the correspondence of Zeno in the mid-third century B.C.E. to what extent the exports of grain and oil there recorded came from Jewish or from non-Jewish sources.[1] The village of Beth Anat in Galilee or Bashan, granted to the minister Apollonius by Ptolemy II, at any rate, was intensively cultivated, producing wine, some of which was exported, also wheat and figs—partly by irrigation.[2] It may be assumed that during the three centuries following the conquests of Alexander, the Greek areas of the country were laying the foundations of the prosperous production reflected in later sources. Ascalon is known to have produced grain, henna, onions, and, one suspects, other market-garden produce and herbs;[3] Ptolemais, grain,[4] Caesarea, wine and cattle,[5] and Lydda wine, figs and linen;[6] the neighbourhood of Antipatris grain, pumpkins and pulse;[7] Emmaus wine and grain;[8] Samaria wine and fruit;[9] Scythopolis, the only Decapolis city west of the Jordan, grain, linen and olives.[10] The Decapolis cities east of the Jordan cultivated olives of repute;[11] among its individual members, Gerasa furnished wine and linen.[12] Near Gadara swine were herded and the territory is recorded to have yielded high yields of wheat;[13] Abila[14] and Capitolias produced wine,[15] and the wine of Ammon is referred to in the Talmud.[16] Unfortunately little has been done to study such agricultural sites of the period, nor is it always possible to distinguish between Jewish and non-Jewish settlements.

Various literary evidence indicates that the Hellenistic period was a time of agricultural development and that a number of new utility

---

[1] For the records showing the purchases of barley and wheat from various places in Judaea, Transjordan, Bashan and Galilee, *CPJ* I, nos. 2a-b.
[2] *PSI* VII, nos. 43; 594.
[3] *T. Ohiloth* 18:18; Pliny, *Natural History* XII, 51; XIX, 23.
[4] Herondas, *Pornoboskos* (Naira), lines 16-17.
[5] *P. T. Megillah* I, 72d.
[6] *T. B. Ketuboth* 111b; *T. B. Nazir* 52a.
[7] *T. Terumoth* 1:15 (Pegae); *T. Kilaim* 2:11-12 (Kefar Pegae).
[8] *BMC, Palestine* pl. XVII, 10.
[9] *M. Demai* 8:4; *P. T. Abodah Zarah* v, 44d; *M. Arakhin* 3:2.
[10] *SEG* VIII, 43; *M. Abodah Zarah* 4:12; *P. T. Kiddushin* II, 62c; *M. Peah* 7:1.
[11] Pliny, *Natural History* XV, 15.
[12] *IGR* III, 1341; *SEG* VII, 827.
[13] Mark 5:2; Varro I, 44, reading Gadada for Garara.
[14] Eus. *Onom.* 32, 17.
[15] F. de Saulcy, *Numismatique de la terre sainte* (1874), p. 310.
[16] *T. B. Sanhedrin* 108b.

plants were introduced into Judaea under Hellenistic influence. The expansion of royal land, the planting of Greek military and civilian settlers in the country, and the general tendency of the Hellenistic rulers to control agriculture and to bring it to a maximum production, are bound to have influenced both Jewish and non-Jewish agriculture in the country in this period. Among the plants that may be considered to have been introduced from Greek countries on the strength of their Greek-derived names, were the lupin (תורמוס, θέρμος),[1] some variety of cabbage,[2] the *crustomelos* (a variety of pear)[3] and the so-called Greek marrow.[4] A number of cultivated plants specifically named in the Mishnah as Egyptian are further likely to have been introduced from there at a time when both lands were under Ptolemaic rule; these were the Egyptian mustard,[5] lentil,[6] bean[7] and marrow.[8] The Libyan bean[9] is likely enough to have been derived from the same quarter. *Tiltan*, known in Judaea in the first century B.C.E., may not have been fenugreek (*trigonella faenum Graecum*—Arab *hilbeh*), as sometimes assumed,[10] since this plant occurred in early Iron Age strata at Lachish;[11] it may have been lucern (*medicago sativa*, ἡ Μηδικὴ πόα), said to have been introduced into Greece from Persia in the fifth century B.C.E., and known in Italy in the first century B.C.E.;[12] as rulings on its use are made by the sages,[13] it was probably brought to Judaea in the Hellenistic period.

In the same period Judaea may have contributed something to Hellenistic agriculture. In December 256 B.C.E. the Egyptian minister Apollonius is found transmitting royal instructions to his estate manager at Philadelphia of Fayum, to sow a second crop of irrigated three-month wheat (τὸν τρίμηνον πυρόν).[14] This appears to correspond to the 'early' and 'second' Syrian wheat alluded to in Egyptian records

---

[1] *M. Kilaim*, 1:3 etc.
[2] Cf. *M. Nedarim* 6:10; Nicander, *Ther.* 813.
[3] *M. Kilaim* 1:4.   [4] *M. Kilaim* 1:5; 2:11.
[5] *M. Kilaim* 1:2.   [6] *M. Maaseroth* 5:8.
[7] *M. Kilaim* 2:11 etc.   [8] *M. Kilaim* 1:.5
[9] *P. T. Kilaim* VIII, 1, 31b.
[10]E.g. Danby, *The Mishnah*, ad *M. Maaseroth* 1:3.
[11]Tufnell *et alii*, *Lachish* IV (1958), pp. 309ff (Helbaek).
[12]Pliny, *Natural History* XVIII, 43; cf. Aristotle, *Historia animalium* III, 21. See I. Löw, *Aramäische Pflanzennahmen* (1881), p. 234.
[13]*M. Orla* 3:6.
[14]*PCZ* 27; cf. Schnebel, *Die Landwirtschaft im hellenistischen Ägypten* (1925), pp. 145-60; C. C. Edgar, in *Ann.d.Serv.* XVIII-XXIV (1918-24), Zenon Papyri II, 59155, pp. 156ff; Thompson, in *Arch.f. Pap.* IX (1928-30), pp. 207ff. Cf. Theophrastos, *Historia plantarum* VIII, 4.

of 15 C.E.,[1] and the term 'first' (early) wheat occurs also in the Zenon papyri. Tosefta Menahoth, 9: 2-3 describes a rapidly maturing wheat produced at Rehajjim and Kefar Ahus north of Jerusalem: '(the land) was ploughed the first year and sowed the second seventy days before Passover to be near the heat, and produced abundant fine flour.' This then was a Jewish spring wheat that matured in a little over two months on fallow land. It was probably the 'three-month' Syrian wheat sown on Apollonius' estate in the middle of the third century B.C.E., and it possessed the importance of furnishing a rapid early crop on fallow land in an economy in which the farmer faced the permanent problem of a non-productive summer arable. Such a crop, indeed, probably formed part of the Hellenistic process of intensification and was a step towards a three-field course.

In addition to direct Hellenistic introductions from Egypt certain other cultivated plants are thought to have been transmitted to Italy from the east in the Hellenistic period and to have returned to the Levant under Roman rule. Such were the apricot, first heard of in Italy in the first century,[2] and referred to in rabbinic literature in the earlier second century;[3] and probably the peach.[4] The etrog (citron), was certainly known in Palestine in the second century B.C.E.,[5] but the orange, though present in Italy in the first century C.E., does not seem to have been grown as an edible fruit till the fourth century C.E.[6] Rice, both homegrown and imported, is mentioned frequently in the Mishnah;[7] judging by one such reference,[8] it was introduced after the lifetime of Hillel, who was a contemporary of Herod, and its Hebrew name is derived from the Greek; Strabo, writing under Augustus, reports that it then grew in Syria.[9] Among industrial crops, cotton is evidenced in Judaea in the early decades of the second century C.E.,[10] though known earlier in Persia and Egypt,[11] and may

[1] P. Lond. II, 256(a); ibid. (d); cf. Thompson, loc.cit.
[2] PW II, s.v. Aprikose, cols. 270-1 (Olck).
[3] M. Maaseroth 1:2.
[4] Dioscorides 1, 165; M. Kilaim 1:4 (פרסק).
[5] Ant. XII, 372.
[6] PW III, 2, s.v. Citrone, cols. 2612ff (Olck); V. Hehn, Kulturpflanzen und Haustiere in ihrem Übergang aus Asien nach Griechenland und Italien sowie in das übrige Europa (1911), pp. 445ff.
[7] M. Demai 2:1; M. Shebiith 2:7, 10; M. Hallah 1:1; 3:7; 4:3.
[8] M. Tebul Yom 1:1.
[9] Strabo XV, 1, 18. It may not be chance that it was later grown in the Huleh Valley, granted to Herod by Augustus in 20 B.C.E. (Ant. XV, 360).
[10] M. Kilaim 7:2.
[11] Rostovtzeff II, p. 1166.

therefore have been an introduction of the Roman period. Hemp is not mentioned as present in Italy before about 100 B.C.E., though grown much earlier in Central Europe[1] and Thrace.[2] As the Mishnah refers to a ruling concerning this plant by the sages,[3] it is likely to have entered Judaea before the Roman conquest; the same applies to woad, which is referred to by the Mishnah under its Greek name.[4]

Although it belongs to the third century, R. Johanan's advice, 'Let your holdings be divided into three parts, a third grain, a third olives, and a third vines,'[5] would certainly have been accepted also in the first. Of these, the cereals branch was the most essential to subsistence; the chief winter-sown crops were wheat, emmer, barley and *shippon* (perhaps einkorn).[6]

The mishnaic plough[7] was a beam-ard,[8] that is, the stilt and sharebeam were made of one timber, which was inserted through a hole in the ploughbeam. The sharebeam ended in the plough point, normally but not invariably consisting of an iron share socketed onto the beam. The ploughbeam was lengthened by the attachment of an additional pole known as the יצול, which was attached to the yoke when the plough was drawn by two oxen. The rear part of the sharebeam was often equipped with laterally projecting blades or wings, to ridge up the soil each side 'of the furrow. Their Hebrew name (עריין) is perhaps the Latin *aures*, whose function corresponded exactly to that of the *arajin* of the mishnaic plough; this suggests that they were introduced under the influence of Roman techniques.[9]

Ploughing was careful and thorough;[10] the first breaking of the stubble after the harvest took the form of furrows opened with broad bands between them to facilitate the absorption of the rains. In the ploughing after the first rain, closer furrows divided by ridges were opened for

[1] Willerding, in Jahnkuhn, *Deutsche Agrargeschichte: Vor- und Frühgeschichte* (1969), pp. 226ff.
[2] Hehn, op.cit., p. 190.
[3] *M. Kilaim* 5:8.
[4] *M. Kilaim* 2:5; *M. Shebiith* 7:1; *M. Shabbath* 9:5; *M. Megillah* 4:7.
[5] *T. B. Baba Metzia* 107a.
[6] Not *triticum spelta* (Felicks p. 177), which was not known in the Mediterranean area till the later third century c.e. Y. Helbaeck and Jessen, *Cereals in Great Britain and Ireland in Prehistoric and Early Historic Times* (1941), p. 41.
[7] *M. Kelim* 8:2; Felicks, pp. 72ff.
[8] For an explanation of the main structural types of ancient ploughs and the terminology applied to them, see K. D. White, *Agricultural Implements of the Roman World* (1967), pp. 127-9.
[9] Cf. Virgil, *Georgica* I, 172; Palladius I, 43, 1.
[10] Felicks, pp. 30-51.

drainage; only at the third ploughing, before sowing, were the furrows close-set without intervening bands. The final working was to cover the seed. The mishnaic plough could cut to a depth of some 27 centimetres,[1] which in antiquity ranked as deep working, and shows that the implement was larger and heavier than the modern Arab plough, which it in general resembled.[2]

We have little information on rotations. The normal course appears to have been the biennial crop-fallow succession.[3] We have one reference to the planting of barley after onions (onions need plenty of dung).[4] We know that the sages instructed conditions of lease that safeguarded against the exhausting effects of flax on the land;[5] but rather strangely regarded clover as harder on the soil than barley; their order of preference was barley, clover, cucumbers, woad,[6] which therefore might be regarded as following each other in reverse order if an ordered rotation was ever used. The seventh-year fallow[7] safeguarded the soil from exhaustion, but created difficulties for small farmers without reserves in hard years.[8] We have noted social action to meet such situations. The seventh-year fallow was observed in the Hasmonaean period, as is evidenced both in Judah the Maccabee's time[9] and under Hyrcanus II.[10] Whether Julius Caesar's remission of tribute in the seventh year was perpetuated under Herod we do not know; I have suggested that the withdrawal of such remission when Judaea became a Roman province may have been among the causes of Judah of Galilee's revolutionary movement.[11] Nevertheless, the fact that Judah the patriarch failed to abolish the practice,[12] and that it was still observed in the fourth century,[13] indicates that its voluntary observance continued down to 70 C.E. (as Tacitus testifies);[14] it was further enforced by Bar Cochba's régime.[15]

[1] M. Baba Bathra 2:12.
[2] Felicks, p. 28.
[3] M. Shebiith 3:4; M. Menahoth 8:2.
[4] T. Shebiith 4:13.
[5] T. Baba Metzia 9:31.
[6] T. Baba Metzia 9:32.
[7] Exod. 23:10; Lev. 25:2-7; 20-2; Deut. 15:1-3.
[8] It might cause the farmer to suppress his fallow to avoid non-productivity for two years running.
[9] 1 Macc. 6:49.
[10] Ant. XIV, 202.
[11] JRS LXI (1971), p. 162.
[12] See Alon, History of the Jews II, pp. 154-5, where the relevant extracts are discussed.
[13] Lev. Rabba, beginning.   [14] Hist. V, 4.   [15] DJD II, no. 24B, pp. 13ff.

One of the problems of the Mediterranean cultivator is to maintain field-production in the rainless months, especially when possibilities of irrigation are restricted. The principal Jewish spring-sown crops were millet, pannic and sesame;[1] we have seen that a seventy-day spring wheat was also grown. In addition irrigated rice was cultivated where sufficient water was available.

Intensive working and soil shortage made manuring a vital factor in the country's agriculture, and animal manure was the most important source of organic fertilizer; it was applied both by carting from the farmyard[2] and by direct grazing, when livestock was penned on the fallow, the pens being moved systematically over the area.[3] In addition to the animal manure derived from cattle, goats and draft animals, the dovecots present on most Jewish farms further augmented the supply.[4] The information that in some districts the corn was cut whereas in others it was uprooted,[5] may also be taken to mean that in the former case the stubble was left for the livestock to graze on—a practice more appropriate to the open fields of the lowlands than to the hill-country—and the land was thus manured for the coming year. In addition to animal manure, the fertilizers used were wine-lees, oil-residues, leaves and marl; straw and stubble were also ploughed in to increase fertility.[6]

In addition to his cultivation of winter and summer grains, the Jewish farmer supplemented his income by growing rice, industrial crops, vegetables, herbs and legumes. Rice was of course confined to level areas where irrigation was available (see above); intensive vegetable growing (cabbages, beetroot, leeks, turnips, onions, cucumbers)[7] was probably carried on chiefly within the range of urban markets or for personal use. Much the same would apply to the growing of table herbs such as mustard, cummin, coriander, chicory and garlic.[8] The legumes contributed to human and animal diet, and were the main source of proteins for the poorer part of the population;

---

[1] M. Shebiith 2:7.
[2] M. Shebiith 3:1.
[3] M. Shebiith 3:4; T. Shebiith 2:15-19.
[4] I do not find specific references to pigeon manure in the relevant literature, but there are numerous references to dovecots (e.g. M. Baba Bathra 2:5).
[5] M. Baba Metzia 9:1.
[6] M. Baba Metzia 9:1.
[7] M. Kilaim 1:2-3. Many more garden vegetables are mentioned; for an exhaustive list, see Felicks, in Encyclopedia Hebraica XVII, col. 970.
[8] M. Kilaim 1:2-3; M. Demai 2:1.

they were the lupin, peas and beans of several varieties,[1] lentils, vetch and lucern.[2] It is not clear whether the value of legumes as field-crops to be rotated with cereals and to be used as fodder and restoratives of the soil was understood. Amongst the industrial crops must be numbered woad and madder for dyeing hemp, flax and cotton.[3] Flax was much grown, more especially in Galilee,[4] but with a full awareness of its high demands upon soil fertility, and formed the basis of a textile industry widely known outside the country by the second century c.e.[5] Hemp and cotton appear to have been less developed. On the other hand marrows, radishes, pumpkins and sesame[6] formed a significant source of vegetable oil, like the olive, which constituted so important a branch side-by-side with viticulture. It is needless to recapitulate the numerous uses of olive oil in daily life, in diet, as a soap, as fuel for lighting and as a component of medicines and cosmetics.[7] Ritual dictates, moreover, presumably gave Judaea's oil a considerable market in the neighbouring Diaspora countries.[8] The best olives came from Galilee and Judaea, but, as we have seen, olive plantations also flourished in Transjordan, and there are few parts of the country where olive-presses have not been found.[9] The shortage of good land is nevertheless emphasized by the fact that intercultivation of olive groves, i.e. the growing of cereals between the trees, is referred to in our sources.[10] Judaean wine was reputed, its main areas of production being the Carmel, Samaria, Judaea, the Sharon and the area round the Sea of Galilee.[11] Vineyards produced not only red wines but also liquors (including absinth) reinforced with aromatics and honey[12], likewise raisins.[13] Orchard fruits were not wanting, serving also as a source of fruit-drinks and cordials.[14] The fig was a major article of diet,

[1] M. Kilaim 1:3.
[2] M. Kilaim 1:5.
[3] M. Kilaim 2:2; 5:8; 7:2; M. Shebiith 5:4.
[4] M. Baba Kamma 10:9.
[5] Pausanias v, 5, 2.
[6] M. Kilaim 1:2; M. Shebiith 2:7.
[7] See Avi-Yonah, pp. 137ff.
[8] Cf. Sifre Deut. 355 (p. 420).
[9] Tchalenko, Villages antiques de la Syrie du nord II (1953), pl. cxvii-cxxiii; III, index, s.v. pressoires, p. 183; huile, p. 181; Z. Yeivin, 'Two Ancient Oil-Presses,' in Atiqot III (1966), pp. 52ff, with bibliography.
[10] E.g. M. Kilaim 4:9; M. Peah 3:1.
[11] See pp. 646 and 675. For the Sea of Galilee see Ant. III, 517-9; T. B. Ketuboth 111b.
[12] T. B. Abodah Zarah 30a.
[13] Maaseroth 1:6.
[14] Cf. Pliny, Natural History xiv, 14.

regarded as an obligatory component of the sustenance to which a married woman was entitled.[1] Date-growing, on the other hand, like the production of herbal medicaments and perfumes such as opobalsam, was mainly confined to the Jordan Valley—more especially to the Jericho and Dead Sea areas, and to state domain; government plantations of opobalsam existed also in Transjordan. But there were date-plantations in private ownership down to the earlier second century near Zoar at the south end of the Dead Sea.[2] Judaean dates, indeed, were world-famed, and reached the imperial table of Augustus.[3] Animal husbandry played an important part in Jewish agriculture. The ox and the cow were valued first and foremost as plough animals, and the Jewish sages would have concurred with Hesiod that the ox is the farmer's best friend. But the need of sacrifices must have been a permanent incentive to run cattle and sheep for sale in Jerusalem. Cattle were stalled both in the farmyard and apart, and in the winter, at least, those not needed for work were in the open. Maximum grazing range of cattle is defined by the sages as sixteen 'miles' (a Roman unit of measure).[4] Since this halakah precedes an addition by R. Meir, it probably applied also to the first century c.e. In Bashan and Hauran the relatively restricted accommodation provided by the byres, which can be accurately measured, indicates predominantly open-range grazing for meat and hides.[5] Cow's milk, in effect, was little reputed as a drink, and with that of the ewe and the goat, used mainly for cheese.[6] The prominence of the Judaean wool industry indeed, shows that sheep were no less important;[7] the Babylonian Talmud's regulations limiting the rearing of 'small livestock' to the Accho Plain and the Judaean Desert,[8] belong to the post-70 period,[9] and probably applied mainly to the black goat, whose depredations are so dangerous to woodland and to all vegetational cover. But goats and sheep were customarily grazed together, and if the rabbinical prohibitions applied to both animals, I believe that they were directed more especially against the speculative transhumance of large flocks, mainly non-

[1] M. Ketuboth 5:8.
[2] Yadin, in Ex Oriente Lux XVII (1964), pp. 230-1.
[3] Athenaeus, Deipnosophistal XIV, 66f. (p. 652).
[4] M. Bekhoroth 9:2. Cf. The Testament of Zebulun 6:8. The mention of a cattle-bell (M. Nazir 6:2) is further evidence of open-range grazing.
[5] Cf. Jos. Life 58.
[6] E.g. M. Nedarim 6:5.
[7] M. Baba Kamma 10:9.
[8] T. B. Baba Kamma 79b.
[9] For the earlier period, see below, p. 670.

Jewish in origin, which accompanied the taking over of wide tracts of Jewish land after the year 70, and was the more destructive since it was unintegrated with fixed agriculture.[1] Some large Jewish owners certainly grazed big flocks before 70,[2] but the average farmer's flock was doubtless more modest[3] and spent part of the year (the autumn) penned on the home fields. The evidence of parchments from the Nahal Hever cave showed the presence of a medium-woolled sheep which Ryder thinks may have been the fine-woolled Mediterranean animal of ancient authorities.[4] It is possible that this animal is referred to by Strabo when he writes of the white-woolled sheep of Nabataea.[5]

Winter feeding of livestock was a serious perennial problem that faced the stockowner in all Mediterranean lands. To solve it resort was had to a variety of fodder such as straw, branches, young shoots,[6] hay, rice-stalks, unripe corn-stalks, carobs and gourds,[7] and the pods of peas and lentils.[8] The Jewish farmer's livestock included, besides pigeons, poultry[9] and geese. He also kept bees, to produce honey and wax.[10]

The situation of the Jewish cultivator

There is very little doubt that Jewish Judaea suffered from an acute land shortage from the time of Pompey onward. The cutting off of the coastal plain and much of Transjordan from the Jewish area must have created a considerable rural proletariat; it is difficult to estimate the average size of a small holding at this period, or the proportion of free peasant holders to tenants and large landed proprietors. Ben David's estimate of the viable Jewish smallholding as averaging seven

---

[1] Recent field-work in Samaria and north-west Judaea by S. Dar has shown that many inter-village rural roads, some later 'adopted' by the Roman administration, were fenced each side by standing stones and boulders, presumably to enable the controlled transfer of livestock without damage to trees and crops.
[2] *P. T. Betzah* II, 61c.
[3] *Luke* 15:3-6.
[4] E.g. Dionysius Periegetes. Yadin, 'The Cave of the Letters,' in *Judaean Desert Studies* (1963), pp. 165-90; M. L. Ryder, in *Agricultural Hist. Review* XII (1964), pp. 1ff.
[5] Strabo XVI, 4, 21.
[6] *M. Shabbath* 18:2.
[7] *M. Shabbath* 24:2.
[8] *M. Shabbath* 21:3.
[9] *M. Betzah* 1:1; *M. Hullin* 12:1.
[10] *M. Baba Bathra* 5:3.

hectares[1] may be too optimistic. The tract held by the two kinsmen of Jesus of Nazareth, 39 plethra or 4.78 hectares,[2] supported two families, and Second Temple holdings in Western Samaria, indeed, seem to have averaged about 2.5 hectares.[3] The Mishnah and the Bar Cochba contracts show that some units measured as little as 0.3 - 0.1 hectares.[4]

The ranks of the day-labourers consisted of landless elements, but labour was also contributed by slaves and tenants. On the evidence, few smallholders could have afforded slaves, who like the tenants belonged chiefly to the large estates; the crown domains were also worked by the latter category. A labourer might be hired by the day (*poel*)[5] or he might be a poor peasant contracted for a longer period to a wealthier farmer.[6] Piece-work[7] was also common when seasonal jobs such as harvesting had to be done. Work was from dawn to sunset;[8] food was normally provided by the employer.[9] Payment was sometimes made in produce,[10] and there may have been bargaining over rates.[11] The Gospels indicate that unemployment existed,[12] at least in the first decades of the first century.

The situation and number of tenants was dependant on the existence of large estates, whether private or in the possession of the rulers. The later Hasmonaeans accumulated considerable tracts of royal domain; Herod confiscated the estates of his political opponents,[13] and acquired the date groves and opobalsam plantations of Jericho first in lease, later as a direct appanage.[14] It seems probable that he treated the major part of the Peraea, Hulata, Bashan, Golan and the Trachonitis as crown domains, and his family held land in Idumaea,[15]

---

[1] *Ben David* pp. 135ff.
[2] Hegesippus ap. Eusebius, *Historia ecclesiastica* III, 20, 1-2.
[3] According to work carried out in the region by a team of the Israel Archaeological Survey.
[4] *M. Baba Bathra* 1:6; *DJD* II, p. 145; *Biblica* XXXVIII (1957), p. 260; Felicks, in *Encyclopedia Hebraica* XVII, col. 967.
[5] *M. Baba Metzia* 9:11.
[6] *M. Baba Metzia* 9:1; cf. Krauss II, p. 101.
[7] *T. B. Baba Metzia* 76b.
[8] *M. Baba Metzia* 9:11.
[9] *M. Baba Metzia* 7:1.
[10] *M. Baba Metzia* 9:12.
[11] Cf. Matt. 20:2 (συμφωνήσας μετὰ τῶν ἐργατῶν).
[12] Matt. 20:3-7.
[13] *Ant.* XVII, 305, 307.
[14] *Ant.* XV, 96; *War* I, 362.
[15] *Ant.* XVI, 291.

in the western Plain of Esdraelon[1] and round Jabneh.[2] Other such tracts may be indicated by the allocation of territories to Herod's new cities of Antipatris and Caesarea; his son Antipas owned estates in Narbata east of Caesarea.[3] It is further probable that the Herods regarded the entire countryside, not excluding the city territories, as legally their own to do as they liked with in given circumstances; only this assumption can explain to us the allocation of rich lands to the veterans settled by Herod at Samaria-Sebaste, where, since they were merged with the existing citizens and local peasantry,[4] a total redistribution of holdings would have become necessary; or Antipas' establishment of Tiberias by the drafting in of landless and even unfree elements and the forcible transfer of peasants from Galilee.[5] Of similar significance was Herod's arbitrary transfer of 3,000 Idumaeans to Hauran.[6]

We know little or nothing of social or economic conditions on the very considerable royal domains, but the fact that three of the foci of revolt after the death of Herod in 4 B.C.E. were located in the royal domains of Peraea and in Jericho[7] can hardly be without significance. Whether the Herodian domains were sold up when Judaea became a province in 6 C.E. is controversial; Josephus' expression ἀποδωσόμενος τοῦ Ἀρχελάου χρήματα[8] can also be interpreted to mean that they were leased out, which is more in conformity with the practice of the period,[9] and would have meant a perpetuation of tenancies.

Large private estates certainly existed. Apart from the wide possessions of Eleazar ben Harsum in *Har ha-Melek* and the lands of Flavius Josephus,[10] we know of the estate of Ptolemy, minister of Herod, centred in the village of Arous (Haris) in Samaria,[11] and of a second impinging on it on the west, centred on Qirwat bene-Hassan; Compsos, a well-to-do citizen of Tiberias, owned estates over the Jordan,[12] as did Philip son of Iacimus near Gamala.[13] The Idumaean Costobar

---

[1] Jos. *Life* 119 (Besara = Beth Shearim).
[2] *Ant.* XVIII, 32.
[3] Georgius Cedrenus, *Hist. Comp.*, PG CXXI, p. 369, 330C.
[4] *Ant.* XV, 296; *War* I, 204-5; 403.
[5] *Ant.* XVIII, 37.
[6] *Ant.* XVI, 285.
[7] *Ant.* XVII, 274; 277; *War* II, 57.
[8] *Ant.* XIV, 2.
[9] For Josephus' ἀποδωσόμενος, cf. Strabo IV, 13, C 188.
[10] Jos. *Life*, 422; 429.
[11] *Ant.* XVIII, 289; *War* II, 69.
[12] Jos. *Life*, 33.   [13] *Life* 47.

possessed farms in his own country.[1] A number of Jesus' parables allude to large landowners who both leased lands and employed wage-labourers.[2] Nor is it likely that the three Jewish wholesalers of Jerusalem, Nakdimon ben Gorion, Kalba Sabbua and Ben Zizit Hakeset said to be capable of provisioning the city for ten years,[3] were simply merchants; they would have derived at least part of their produce from their own lands.[4]

There were several categories of tenants: the אריס[5] paid his rent as a fixed percentage of the harvest (generally a half or a third); sometimes he received seed from the landlord and this he repaid; the שוכר or the חוכר,[6] on the other hand, paid a fixed amount, the former in money, the latter in produce. The *shatla*[7] took over the development of a plantation until it reached profitability and then received part of it; he paid half the produce in rent, but his lease could only be terminated earlier if he was compensated for the labour he had invested. While the *aris* and *hoker* are referred to in the Mishnah, the *soker* appears only in Tosefta.[8] Leases were normally for five or six years: we hear of rents of ten kors of grain (about 40 hectolitres) per annum; also of 100 zuz (100 drachmae)[9] and of various other rents from the lease contracts of Bar Cochba's administration found in the caves of Wadi Murabbaat and Nahal Hever, but in no case is the area of the plot recorded.[10] It is probable that the five-year leases signed by tenants of state land in the

---

[1] *Ant.* xv, 264.
[2] Luke 16:1-8; Mark 12:1-11; Luke 17:7; 19:19; Matt. 20:1-15.
[3] *Midrash Lament. Rabba* I (p. 65. cf. p. 663, n. 4).
[4] How Kreissig (p. 29) manages to deduce that Simon of Cyrene, Barnabas and Ananias were large landowners, because they held land outside Jerusalem, I do not understand. The ownership of plots of various sizes (often small) by city-dwellers was a common phenomenon in the ancient world; cf. Finley, p. 95.
[5] *M. Peah,* 5:5.
[6] *M. Baba Metzia* 9:2; *T. Demai* 6:2.
[7] The *shatla* is first mentioned specifically in the Babylonian Talmud (e.g. *Baba Metzia* 109a-b), but cf. *T. Baba Metzia* 9:17-18, suggesting that this type of tenant existed earlier.
[8] *T. Demai* 6:2.
[9] *M. Baba Metzia* 9:7-10.
[10] Yadin (*IEJ* xii (1962), pp. 249ff.), publishes rents of 8 shekels 16 drachmae, 39 denarii (drachmae), and 65 zuzim (= 65 drachmae), recorded in documents from the Nahal Hever cave, but the size of the plots, if recorded, is not referred to by him. Milik, in *DJD* ii, records rents of 4 kors 8 sa'ah (no. 24B); 6 kors 3 saah (no. 24D); and 3.5 kors (no. 24E); these are from the Murabbaat cave; the documents do not specify the size of the plots. I have a suspicion that the quantities of grain paid as annual rent are equivalent to the amounts of seed-corn sowed in each plot, in which case the approximate areas leased could be calculated.

time of Bar Cochba's administration[1] were modelled on the practices of Roman state domain, where plots were leased for a similar term (the *lustrum*).[2] In addition to rent, these tenants paid tithe, and in one case, apparently, in addition, a tenth part to the treasury. Otherwise, however, we have no direct information on conditions of lease on Roman state land in Judaea in this period.[3] In general, the increase of state domain from the later Hasmonaean epoch onward and the expropriation of Jewish settlers from the coastal region and Transjordan by Pompey, must have greatly increased the tenant-class, and have created tensions such as are illustrated not only by the events of 4 B.C.E. in Peraea, but also a few decades later by the evidence of the Gospels. It suffices to cite the famous parable of Matt.21:30-40, which indicates a state of enmity between landlord and tenants, the logical outcome of which is the readiness on the part of the latter to kill the proprietor's heir and to take over his property. From this situation to the events of 66-70 a direct line can be drawn.

There were also groups of cultivators who, while not owning large tracts, nevertheless enjoyed a privileged position and constituted a minor aristocracy. These were the military settlers, whether serving *katoikoi* or time-expired veterans; they included Herod's Sebastenes settled in Sebaste-Samaria and other veterans at Gaba, Heshbon, and perhaps Ashdod;[4] further the Jewish *katoikoi* from Babylonia and Idumaea settled by the same king in Bashan and Golan. These enjoyed special tax-concessions and their property could not be distrained upon for arrears of payment;[5] they were joined by numerous landless Jews, but it is unknown whether these shared the same privileges.[6] After 70, 800 Roman veterans were settled at Amasa

---

[1] *DJD* II, p. 124, no. 24B.

[2] Hyginus (ed. Lachmann), 116; Cicero, II *Verres* 3:13; 5:53.

[3] Why tithe should have to be paid on rented land raises an interesting halakic problem. As regards conditions on Roman state land, Jabneh, the centre of imperial property from the early first century C.E., possessed a granary where the *annona* was paid to a centurion (*T. Demai* 6:3; cf. 1:13). The information is post-70, but we hear that grain could also be purchased there. This suggests an analogy with a situation described by Tacitus (*Agric.*19) in Britain under the Flavians, in which tax-payers unable to pay grain were made to buy it at the government granary. See Marquardt, *Staatsverwaltung* (1881), II, p. 102, n.1; Furneaux and Anderson, *Agricola* (1922), p. 97 ad 19, 4.

[4] Azotus Hippinus: Hierocles 5; Georgius Cyprius 23.

[5] *Ant.* XVII, 25.

[6] On the Zamarid settlement, see the present writer, *Studies in the History of the Jewish People and the Land of Israel* I (1970; in Hebrew), pp. 79ff. (Eng. résumé, *ibid.* p. 8).

(Motza)[1] west of Jerusalem, and this element formed a sort of aristocracy present alike in cities such as Ascalon,[2] Caesarea, Gerasa[3] and Ptolemais-Accho,[4] and in the countryside, especially, but not only, in Bashan and Hauran, where their inscriptions appear from the second century onwards.[5]

These were privileged minorities which grew considerably after the great rebellion; of the conditions of the other non-Jewish population of Judaea in the pre-70 period we know very little. But Jones noted the tendency of the Greek cities to be parasitic on their rural territories,[6] and Rapaport has argued that the forcible Judaization of Idumaea and Galilee by the Hasmonaeans may have been accepted without demur by the rural populations of those areas because they saw the Hasmonaeans as liberators from Hellenistic city exploitation.[7]

Another elementary fact is germane to an understanding of the situation of the Jewish cultivator. The Jewish peasantry, which had been virtually free of fiscal exactions since the liberation of Judaea by Simeon, and certainly never, even under Jannaeus, had borne taxation equivalent to that of the Seleucids, found themselves crushed with merciless exactions under Pompey and his successors and no less under Herod. In the latter's reign, indeed, they had to bear the double yoke of Roman tribute and the taxation required to finance Herod's ambitious programme of internal public works and aid to Greek cities outside his kingdom. That Judaea was exempt from tribute under Augustus (as may be understood from Josephus), when it had been imposed by Julius Caesar, is hardly credible.[8] We do not

[1] Jos. *War.* VII, 217. [2] *SEG* I, 552.
[3] C. Kraeling, *Gerasa*, p. 399, no. 52.
[4] Pliny, *Natural History* XIX, 75; *Dig.* XV, 1, 3; Ekhel, *Doctr. Numm.* 1794, III, 423-5.
[5] *JRS* XXI (1931), pp. 269 ff.; A. H. M. Jones, *The Cities of the Eastern Roman Provinces* (2nd. ed. 1971), p. 464, n. 79; Rostovtzeff, p. 666, n. 35. For Samaria, we may note T. Mucius Clemens, veteran officer of Agrippa II, buried near Moshav Habonim, evidently on his own estate (*IEJ* XVI, (1966), pp. 258-64), and for Judaea, Flavius Ouales, an ex-decurion of horse, buried with his wife at Beth Nattif ἐν τοῖς ἰδίοις (on his own property: *IGR* III, 1207; 1208).
[6] *The Greek City from Alexander to Justinian* (1940), pp. 268; 274.
[7] U. Rapaport, *Jewish Religious Propaganda and Proselytism in the Period of the Second Commonwealth* (1965; in Hebrew with Eng. résumé), pp. 65ff.
[8] For what is known of Roman taxation, see chapter five, pp. 239; chapter six, pp. 324-34; 372-3. On the question of whether tribute was paid for Judaea: Appian *BC* IV, 5, 75 says Herod paid on Samaria and Idumaea; here Idumaea might be a corruption of Judaea (see A. Schalit, *King Herod*, p. 90); against payment: Mommsen, *Römische Geschichte* V (9th ed.), p. 501, n. 1; Schürer-Vermes-Millar I, p. 317 and n. 108; Otto, *Herodes* (1913), p. 55; for payment:

know enough of the full incidence of Roman taxation in Judaea in either the pre-provincial or in the procuratorial period, but it may be assumed that down to 4 B.C.E. the combination of Roman tribute and Herodian taxation, with religious dues, would have been extremely oppressive. In addition, at some point in Herod's reign the pressure to obtain loans on the part of the common people, among whom the peasants certainly constituted the majority, had become so great that Hillel formulated the *prozbul*, which enabled the official circumvention of the seventh-year cancellation of debts.[1] The widespread effects of this step is made apparent by the burning of the debt-records in Jerusalem during the revolutionary movement of 66.[2] How far this situation was aggravated by the social and economic structure of Judaea in this period must now be discussed. Kreissig certainly errs in minimizing the part played by Roman taxation or by the taxation of Herod, but more plausibly lays responsibility at the doors of the landowners and the agents of progressive commercialization. His premises, nevertheless, are controversial.[3] His two chief claims are, that the peasant suffered 1) from the competition of the big landowner and lessor on the market, due to the superior quantity and quality of their produce; and 2) from the progressive commercialization of Jewish society, whose abuses Jewish religious influence failed to curb by its social legislation. That the big owners could undersell the small peasant is true enough, but if he was more interested in inflating prices by 'cornering' the market or witholding stocks in times of shortage (as certainly did occur),[4] the small man might also profit from this situation. But the entire theory rests on the assumption of a countrywide price-structure, or at least of a large urban market. In effect anything like a large market was restricted to Jerusalem and some of the larger coastal cities such as Caesarea, Gaza and Ascalon; transport-restrictions and the ubiquitous and oppressive inter-urban customs network made the long-distance transfer of bulk-produce difficult and unprofitable.[5] Where agricultural produce was concerned,

Schalit, *Herod*, p. 90 and 396, n. 64; Momigliano, *Ricerche sull'organizazzione della Giudea sotto il dominio romano*, 63 a.C.—70 p.C. (1934), pp. 49-51; Stern, above, chapter five, p. 239.

[1] *M. Shebiith* 10:3.

[2] *War* II, 427.

[3] Kreissig, pp. 36-51.

[4] Cf. *T. B. Baba Bathra* 90b.

[5] Finley, pp. 126-7; 206, notes 6-10 for bibliography on the question of transport; also Westermann, in *Amer.Hist.Rev.* XX (1915), pp. 724ff.; Meyer, *Kleine Schriften*, pp. 79ff.

practically all the towns depended on their immediate rural hinterlands, and in this respect we have something like a detailed picture of
the district of Ephraim extending from western Samaria to Lydda.
The local markets mentioned here are Antipatris, Patros (Badrus)
near Lydda, and Yishuv;[1] Caesarea also absorbed some of the agricultural produce and much was sold along the highway connecting Lydda
with the north. In proportion as markets were local the big man's
influence might have been felt, but it would have been restricted, not
countrywide.

More important, perhaps, was the antagonism between town and
country. It has left its traces in an interesting tradition which purports
to explain why Beitar was destroyed: the townlet rejoiced at the
destruction of Jerusalem, because the wealthy men there had de-
frauded the cultivators of Beitar of their land by forged contracts.[2]
The preponderantly rural basis of the great rebellion is generally
acknowledged, but the alleged antagonism can be exaggerated. A
high proportion of city-dwellers cultivated holdings in the immediate
vicinity of the town, and the urban upper class's economic basis was
almost invariably landed property. Antagonisms cut across the urban
and rural population alike, and the non-agricultural urban craftsmen
and petty traders were also a politically radical factor. What is true
is that city-life tended to be identified with its ruling group,[3] inevitably (and especially under Roman rule) largely identical with the
landed aristocracy which was predominantly non-commercial;[4] in them
the peasantry saw the main authors of oppression. It was the city
authorities who fixed the grain and other prices of both the urban
centre and the city's rural territory,[5] hence, theoretically, both

[1] T. Demai I:II.

[2] P. T. Taanith IV, 69a. In the form this account has come down to us it contains
late elements, but I believe preserves a genuinely ancient tradition.

[3] In talmudic literature the word bouleutes (city-councillor) is often synonymous
with 'man of wealth'; the term occurs as early as Megillath Taanith 9 and Sifre
Deut. 309. See Krauss, Griechische und Lateinische Lehnwörter (1898), p. 628.

[4] See Finley, pp. 35ff. for the non-commercial rôle of the ruling landowning
groups of the Roman Empire. But the Phoenician and oriental cities in general,
I think, may have offered exceptions; among them Jerusalem would not have
been a prominent example, yet cf. the cases of the three Jerusalem tycoons
referred to above (p. 659); the prerogatives enjoyed by the high priests in
providing certain requisites for sacrifice; that Herod's minister Ptolemy held
an estate near Kuratajjim where some of the best wine in the country was
produced (above, p. 646) and that in the early second century Eleazar ben
Harsum, of high priestly family, combined extensive landholding with maritime
commerce in his own ships.

[5] M. Baba Metzia 5:7; P. T. Baba Metzia V, 10c.

proprietors and smallholders obtained a uniform rate. This might well be to the advantage of the men with the larger stocks to sell, yet it is far from certain that it was invariably their interest to obtain lower prices. The stronger factor in this tension was the tenant-landlord relationship, and pressure exercized by the extension of loans in money or grain.[1] Kreissig emphasizes the small peasant's desire for self-sufficiency, frustrated by his lack of reserves against a lean year. The moral is highlighted by the great famine of 25 B.C.E.,[2] when Herod had to distribute seed and clothing to a starving rural population; Heichelheim may be correct when he suggests that the grain was no gift, but a repayable loan of a type well documented in the ancient world.[3]

The Pharisees, who were the progressive party devoted to the interests of the common people, could perhaps have succeeded in stemming the abuses of commercialization if Herod had not placed legislation on a secular Hellenistic basis, purging the sanhedrin of all non-subservient elements, and making the high priests his personal nominees. It was, after all, a Pharisee, Saddok, who with Judah of Galilee founded the first militant social and anti-Roman movement in 6 C.E. On the other hand, Hillel devised or sanctioned the *prozbul*, but he was opposed in much that he did by the school of Shammai.[4] Herod could forcibly separate the established institutions from the traditional forces of social religious legislation, but he could not suppress the desire to legislate, which continued to operate underground as a future force.[5] And if it failed to mitigate the social evils of the economy under the Herods and the procurators, it burst forth as a powerful revolutionary movement in 66, and whatever the attitude of individual Pharisees to it, the great rebellion was very largely the reaction of rural Judaism to social injustice.

The economic achievement of Herod

It is in this connection that a brief endeavour must be made to appraise the economic achievement of Herod as a whole, and to arrive at some estimate as to whether he left the country more prosperous than he

[1] E.g. *M. Baba Metzia* 5:8.
[2] *Ant.* xv, 299-316.
[3] p. 227.
[4] *P. T. Shabbath* 1, 3c.
[5] For halakic activity under Herod, see Alon, in *Scripta Hierosolymitana* vii (1961), p. 69.

found it. Ideally, the method to be adopted would be to draw up an account of his income and expenditure, in order to gauge his solvency; unfortunately we do not possess sufficient figures and not all those we have are credible. What is clear is that his expenditure was extremely heavy; the list of his public works at home and abroad, including city-building and aid or donations to cities abroad, is long and impressive. His gifts to such prominent men as Augustus, and to his relatives and friends, were handsome and numerous; his court was conducted with all pomp, his army, fleet and civil service were costly. We hear that Herod's annual revenue was 900 talents,[1] a figure approximately confirmed by the statements of Agrippa II and, indirectly, Strabo.[2] If Palestine had a population of three million, this meant an average yearly payment per head of 3.3 drachmae, not counting religious dues. As the Egyptian fellah, who was miserably poor, paid the equivalent of 2 drachmae per head, amounting to about 34 percent of his income,[3] it is probable that Herod's taxation was actually higher, and he certainly needed sums much in excess of the stated revenue.

Beside direct taxation several other sources were at his disposal; he derived a very considerable income from the crown domains, which we have seen were not small; the date-plantations and balsam groves of Jericho are said to have furnished enormous returns;[4] he also leased from Augustus the copper-mines of Cyprus, and retained half their output.[5] The customs and excise of his ports and inland duties must have yielded no mean revenue, and he advanced loans, for instance, to the Nabataeans.[6] While the detailed economic implications are not clear when Herod made gifts of entire cities to his relatives—e.g. Salome received Jabneh, Azotus, and Phasaelis—revenue was definitely involved and the cities concerned paid 60 talents per year to the beneficiary.[7]

Herod certainly increased the agricultural production of his kingdom by his irrigation works round Jericho and by his colonization work in several regions, especially in Bashan, Hauran and Trachonitis, which must have contributed appreciably to the settlement of landless Jewish peasants. Yet in 25 B.C.E. his treasury was empty,[8] and if he

---

[1] *Ant.* XVII, 317-18. [2] *War* II, 386; Strabo, XVII, 1, 13.
[3] A. C. Johnson, in *Economic Survey of Ancient Rome*, ed. by T. Frank, II (1936), p. 304.
[4] Diodorus Siculus II, 48; Strabo, XVI, 2, 41.
[5] *Ant.* XVI, 128. [6] *Ant.* XVI, 279.
[7] *Ant.* XVII, 321. [8] *Ant.* XV, 303.

remitted taxation by one third,[1] this does not prove that he had balanced his income and expenditure. Nor do the ample sums which he shared out among his heirs and kindred prove solvency, merely that his privy purse was full. Josephus states succinctly at one point that he spent more than he could afford, and was so compelled to exploit popular hostility to justify further forced exactions and confiscations.[2] After his death a Jewish delegation to Augustus claimed that he had ruined Judaea; and Tacitus, no sympathizer with Jews, confesses that the country had been exhausted by taxation by 17 c.e., when Tiberius found it advisable to lighten payments.[3] This is the more striking in view of the assumption that under procuratorial rule the parallel payment of Roman tribute and royal taxation would have been replaced by the payment of tribute only, and that we would therefore expect there to have been some alleviation.

We do not know whether Herod used the very large resources deposited in the Temple of Jerusalem to finance some of his enterprises, and more particularly the rebuilding of the Temple itself. Klausner thinks that he did.[4] Yet Josephus has no reference to such an act, although he records that Agrippa II, invested with the formal supervision of the cult,[5] used some of its funds to pave the streets of Jerusalem.[6]

The acid test of Herod's ultimate economic achievement must be, whether the productive results exceeded the investment in unproductive monuments, and further, whether in the course of the latter he took from the producers—who were predominantly the tillers of the soil—more than they needed for a tolerable existence. Two pieces of evidence, if not decisive, may contribute to a negative verdict. One is the testimony of his coinage: many of Herod's bronze pieces are stated to be of short weight,[7] and Reifenberg found that they possessed a high percentage (ten per cent) of tin,[8] all the more remarkable if one considers that he had his own resources of copper. The second piece of evidence concerns Herod's programme of urbanization.

---

[1] *Ant.* xv, 365.

[2] *Ant.* XVI, 154-6.

[3] Tacitus, *Annales* II, 42.

[4] Klausner IV, pp. 101 ff. It may be noted that Josephus, *Ant.* xv, 380, writes of Herod, that he undertook τὸν νεὼν τοῦ Θεοῦ κατασκευάσθαι. Marcus translates δι' αὐτοῦ 'at his own expense'.

[5] *Ant.* XX, 15: τὴν ἐξουσίαν τοῦ νεώ; cf. 222.

[6] *Ant.* XX, 219-21.

[7] Y. Meshorer, *Jewish Coins of the Second Temple Period* (1967) pp. 64ff.

[8] *ZDPV* (1927), pp. 175ff.; id., *Coins of the Jews*, (1947; in Hebrew), pp. 17-18.

Two of the more important towns which he built or rebuilt, were Antipatris and Sebaste-Samaria. Recent excavations show that Antipatris was destroyed during the great rebellion of 66-73, and not—as far as the present evidence goes—rehabilitated till the time of Severus.[1] It is uncertain whether Sebaste was damaged in the same revolt,[2] but whatever occurred, the city was found by two successive archaeological expeditions to have been in a state of neglect and even ruin prior to the Severan revival.[3] Neither city, therefore, was thought worthwhile maintaining during the century after the Jewish war, and evidently part at least of Herod's city-building programme was regarded as not having justified itself. Caesarea and its port were certainly his most successful achievements.

With few exceptions, ancient cities were based on agriculture, with whose proceeds they covered most of their tax-obligations, imports and amenities.[4] If the cultivators of their territories were forced to contribute more than was needed to maintain a minimal standard of living, they ceased to use the services which the city had to offer, and decline set in, to be further accelerated by excessive taxation. Thus ultimately only those cities continued to flourish which were entrepôts of commerce.

Palestine's commerce: import and export

The Hasmonaeans broke through to the sea when Simeon finally made Joppa Jewish in the year 141 B.C.E.[5] John Hyrcanus, by penetrating Moab to capture Medaba and Samaga, and by taking Scythopolis (111-110 B.C.E.),[6] drove a wedge into the important trade route along which the wares of Arabia and India, coming via Elath or Petra, reached Damascus, Syria and Asia Minor. In the following decade Alexander Jannaeus gained control of the entire coast from Dora to Rhinocolura,[7] and consolidated the Jewish hold on the Elath-Damascus

---

[1] I owe this information to M. Kokhbi, the excavator.
[2] As stated by Josephus, *War* II, 460.
[3] Reisner, Fisher and Lyon, *The Harvard Excavations at Samaria* (1924), III, p. 211: the columns of the forum and its attached basilica had fallen before the Severan rehabilitation. Crowfoot, Kenyon and Sukenik, *The Buildings at Samaria* (1942), p. 41: the Herodian stadium had been ruined by flood from the city above.
[4] Cf. Finley, op.cit., pp. 123ff.
[5] I Macc. 13:11.
[6] *Ant.* XIII, 255-7.
[7] *Ant.* XIII, 395-6.

highway and the Dead Sea, by taking Libbah, Agalain, Oronaim and Zoar,[1] probably also Rabbat Moab and Kir Moab. The domination of this route and of the coast, including especially Gaza, whence merchandise from Arabia and the East reached Alexandria and the Mediterranean in general (only Ascalon remained independent, but normally friendly to the Hasmonaean dynasty),[2] gave Judaea complete control of the oriental and African trade which entered the country by the Red Sea or by land via Petra. These wares consisted chiefly of highly profitable luxury articles such as incense, perfumes, spices, silk, precious stones, gold, expensive textiles, animal skins, and rare woods. Previously the Nabataeans had held a monopoly on these as far as the Mediterranean seacoast; now Ascalon and Ptolemais, in so far as they did not obtain them from the northern Euphrates route, controlled by Parthia, were, like the Syrian ports, dependent on Jewish favour. The Greek towns of Asia Minor and the eastern Mediterranean basin as a whole were forced to accept Red Sea and Arabian wares from Judaean harbours and perhaps through Jewish middlemen operating in Delos and in such Asiatic ports as Miletus, Ephesus, Smyrna and Tarsus. It is possible that this situation was one of the main causes for the political anti-Semitism manifested by the Greek cities of Asia in the second half of the first century B.C.E. after the local cities of Judaea had been separated from Jewish rule.

Pompey's revision of Jewish territory in 63 B.C.E. restored the handling of the Arabian and oriental trade to the Greek coastal and Decapolis cities, but Julius Caesar returned Joppa to Hyrcanus II, while Herod acquired Gaza, the trade's key-entrepôt, from Antony, lost it temporarily to Cleopatra, and finally recovered it by the favour of Octavian,[3] who subsequently, in 30 B.C.E., gave him also Straton's Tower, Joppa and Anthedon.[4] Hence Jewish commerce continued to enjoy a slice of the oriental luxury trade. Its value should not, of course, be overestimated; its profits were shared among a number of intermediaries over a vast distance, but it brought in a considerable income in customs dues[5] and certainly obtained for Judaea a regular

---

[1] *Ant.* XIII, 397.

[2] For the political situation which preserved Ascalon's independence vis-à-vis the Hasmonaeans, see M. Stern, in *Tarbiz* XXXIII (1963), pp. 183ff. (in Hebrew).

[3] *War*, I, 396; *Ant.* XV, 217.

[4] Chapter five, pp. 236 and 306.

[5] We read in Pliny, (*Natural History* XII, 63) that Arabian frankincense, after having paid dues to various Arab rulers and their officials on its way across the Arabian desert, also for water and fodder, totalling 688 denarii per camel-load,

supply of gold and silver currency. It may have been one of the factors which influenced Herod to cultivate good relationships with the Greek cities of Asia Minor;[1] his live interest in this trade may also be indicated by the peculiar fact that he is not recorded by Josephus to have conferred any mark of favour upon the Decapolis cities which were concerned in transferring eastern goods from the Red Sea to Syria, and the two of them which he controlled, Gadara and Hippos, displayed hostility and resentment towards his rule.[2] The earlier interest of his family in the Decapolis route, nevertheless, may be evidenced by the burial at Scythopolis of his cousin, Antiochus son of Phallion.[3]

An examination of Judaea's commerce in the two centuries before the destruction of Jerusalem must attempt to compare imports with exports, and to determine in what measure the country was self-supporting. Such a survey must, of course take cognizance of the transit trade which, owing to Judaea's geographical position, was considerable.

While there is some evidence for the import of Egyptian grain into the country in the second century B.C.E.,[4] it is uncertain if such imports were normal except in times of shortage or famine, or in sabbatical years when the current year's supplies proved inadequate.[5] Herod's importation of 80,000 kors (28,155.6 tons) of grain from Egypt during the famine of 25 B.C.E.[6] was clearly exceptional, as were the supplies of Alexandrian grain and Cypriot figs obtained by the proselyte Queen Helena of Adiabene in the similar conditions of 46-47 C.E.[7] As to the seventh-year imports from Syria, those of vegetables, fruit, olives, figs and raisins were said to have been prohibited by Halakah down to 70 C.E., but rice was perhaps already imported.[8] Apart from the above—largely emergency—imports, the country appears to have

finally discharged customs to the Roman publicans of Gaza. Probably additional rates were paid to the city itself. As a cumulative result the best incense cost the consumer six denarii the pound.

[1] Rhodes, Chios, the cities of Cilicia, Pamphylia and Lycia, Pergamum, Cos.
[2] *Ant.* xv, 351; 356-9.
[3] *RB* (1923), p. 484; A. Rowe, *Topography and History of Beth Shean* (1930), p. 48.
[4] *T. Makshirim* 3:4.
[5] The grain imports of Joppa and Sepphoris referred to by *T. Demai* 1:11 may possibly go back to the first century, since they are followed by a statement of R. Eleazar concerning the markets of Yishuv, Antipatris and Patro sin the same century.
[6] *Ant.* xv, 299-316.
[7] *Ant.* xx, 51, 52.
[8] *P. T. Demai* 11, 22d, not datable.

been reasonably self-sufficient, and most of the other contemporary foods known to have been brought in during this period were in the nature of luxuries. An exception was salt, some of which was brought from Ostrakene on the north shore of Sinai,[1] and much, one assumes, from Mount Sodom.[2] The remoter commodities were largely sea-food, such as tunny-fish from Spain, possibly but not certainly referable to the period,[3] also roes and fish-entrails in brine from Pelusium[4] and Spain, and fish from Egypt.[5] A number of vegetables and legumes attributed to Egypt and other countries by the Mishnah (eg. Egyptian beans, Greek gourds) were introduced from those lands, but not necessarily imported from them. On the other hand limited imports of the seed of these plants would have been necessary in order to prevent local crops from degenerating.

The extremely heavy demands on domestic livestock occasioned by the Temple sacrifices doubtless explain the import of cattle and sheep into Judaea from the neighbouring areas. The importation by the Idumaean notable Baba ben Buti of 3,000 head of sheep and other cattle from beduin areas[6] to Jerusalem for sacrifice, though recounted in haggadic form, doubtless represented a regular trade. The rabbinical prohibition to bring small stock (sheep and goats) from Syria, on the other hand, though attributed to the sages,[7] and therefore possibly going back to Gamaliel, would seem to apply in the main to conditions after 70.

Judaea also furnished most of its own clothing, and it may be taken for granted that imported garments and footwear, on the whole, were to supply specialized and fashionable tastes. This remains true in spite of the considerable number of talmudic words applying to human dress which are of Greek or Latin derivation, such as *itztala* (στολή), *sudar* (*sudarium*) and *sagin* (*sagum*). This merely means that they were originally Greek or Roman introductions, whose manufacture had long been taken over by local producers. It should not be deduced, however, that some extraneous articles were not available for those

---

[1] *T. Menahoth* 9:15.
[2] Krauss I, pp. 499-501.
[3] *M. Shabbath* 22:2; *M. Makshirim* 6:3, possibly but not certainly a second-century reference.
[4] *B. T. Abodah Zarah* 39a, not closely dated.
[5] *M. Makshirim* 6:3, first or second century.
[6] *P. T. Hagigah* II, 78a.
[7] *M. Baba Kamma* 7:7.

with money to spend; among such were sandals from Tyre and Laodicea,[1] goathair cloths from Cilicia[2] and the fine linens of Pelusium and India worn by the high priests.[3] The import of precious stones, pearls etc. from Arabia referred to in the third century B.C.E. in the *Letter of Aristeas* may be taken to have continued down to the end of the first century C.E.

Among the articles of everyday use to which words of Greek or Roman derivation were applied furniture figures prominently; such were *saphsal* (*subsella*), *kuphsah* (κυψέλη), *kathedra* (κάθεδρα), and *tavlah* (*tabula*). But the earliest available list of such objects[4] contains articles, namely chests (or cupboards), ovens, (doubtless portable clay ovens of the sort found, for instance, in the Athenian agora),[5] benches and clay vessels, which are mentioned in such a way as to indicate that they were imported from abroad.

The last commodity raises the question, to what extent pottery, the commonest class of use-object in the ancient world, was purchased from outside the country. Avi-Yonah demonstrated how extensively changes of political régime in the Hellenistic period affected the direction of trade and trade-objects.[6] Thus from Alexander's conquest down to the middle of the third century B.C.E., Attic imported pottery was abundant at Samaria, and Rhodian stamped jarhandles constituted 60 per cent of those found in the excavation. But from about 250 B.C.E. local imitations of Greek imported types appeared in increasing quantities. With the Seleucid annexation the source of imported wares shifted to Asia Minor and Syria, and 'Megarian' bowls became prominent. Although the city fell to the Maccabees in 108/107 B.C.E., eastern *terra sigillata* (red glaze) was still represented in the Hasmonaean levels and dominated the Herodian occupation strata, but was increasingly superseded by Roman imported pottery and Arretine red glaze from Italy. Subsequent excavations at Shechem, Ptolemais and Ashdod[7] have shown that eastern red glaze appears

---

[1] *M. Kelim* 26:1. [2] *M. Kelim* 29:1. [3] *M. Yoma* 3:7.

[4] *T. Hullin*, 1:22; cf. *T. Ohiloth* 18:5.

[5] Cf. B. A. Sparkes, in *Journal of Hellenic Studies* (1962), pp. 127-8, fig. 2, pp. 133-4, which, however, date from the sixth and fifth centuries B.C.E.

[6] *IEJ* XI (1961), pp. 158-9, reviewing Crowfoot, Kenyon and Sukenik, *Samaria-Sebaste* III: *The Objects from Samaria* (1957).

[7] For the relevant information derived from Tell Mor and Tell Balata I am indebted to H. V. Kee; these results concur with the results of my own excavations at Akko New Post Office in 1959. (Cf. *IEJ*. IX (1959), p. 274). E. Oren, who extended the investigation of the same area in 1972, reached similar

first in the second century B.C.E. at Ptolemais as a direct evolution from the 'Megarian' styles. With the Roman conquest some of the finer wares, more particularly red glaze, begin to be imported from Italy and even from Gaul. But in the manufacture of pottery, Judaea rapidly recovered its relative independence, possessing as it did a long-established local industry for the manufacture of coarse household pottery, many of whose types can be traced back to the early Hellenistic and even to the Persian period. On one type of imported Italian coarse pottery, however, light has recently been cast by a new discovery. The Mishnah prohibits the wine of idolators, also 'Hadrianic' pottery;[1] Rabbi Judah (d. 299 C.E.) explained the term as relating to pottery of the Emperor Hadrian.[2] The clue has now been furnished by a stamped jar found by Kaplan in a stratum at Joppa not later than the second century C.E., bearing the words FAN(um) FOR(tunae) COL(onia) HADR(iana).[3] Although Hadria in Italy possessed a pottery industry praised by Pliny,[4] the stamp in question appears to be that of a potter of Colonia Hadrumetum in North Africa;[5] evidently by the later second century the real meaning of the stamp had been forgotten in Judaea, and the import of this ware, therefore, must have begun some time before the reign of Hadrian.[6] It may indeed be assumed that *amphorae* and store-jars continued to be imported containing the wine and other commodities which the Roman occupation army was not prepared to forego.[7]

The clay lamps of Palestine tell a clearer story. In the Hellenistic period Greek types of the closed oil lamp were prevalent in Judaea, mainly as imports. One type of lamp in this period, open but with

conclusions. That Gerasa was one of the local centres of the manufacture of Megarian ware is perhaps suggested by a unique Megarian spherical bowl with handles and pedestal from that town, shown to the writer by M. Dayyan. A local pottery industry is evidenced there by inscriptions (Kraeling, *Gerasa*, no. 79, third century C.E.).

[1] *M. Abodah Zarah* 2:3.
[2] *T. B. Abodah Zarah* 32a.
[3] I am grateful for Y. Kaplan's permission to refer to this find, adding my own interpretation of it.
[4] Pliny, *Natural History* XXXV, 16.
[5] *CIL* VIII, nos. 62; 104772.2; XV, no. 3375.
[6] I am indebted to V. Grace and to E. L. Will for their expert assistance and advice on the origin of the above stamp.
[7] Longstanding inhabitants who remember mandatory Palestine will recall the famous stores of Spinney's, purveyors of British foods to the administration and the army.

pinched spout, is thought to be a specifically Jewish form.[1] With the Roman period came the cheaper mould-made lamp, frequently produced in Greece or Asia Minor; it was imitated in Palestine, and the so-called Herodian type was used down to the first decades of the second century. It was seldom decorated; only after the fall of Jerusalem did the *menorah* begin to figure as a decorative motif, and a class of lamp was evolved bearing motifs derived from plant-life, agriculture and the symbology of the Temple cult, its area of manufacture being centred in south-western Judaea.[2] But in the pagan areas the normal Roman lamps of the period, adorned with various mythological and genre scenes, in which human and divine figures abounded, were widely used. It is possible that some Jewish lamps were exported in this period: a clay lamp of Herodian type, at any rate, has been found in France.[3]

Foreign glassware was being imported before the first century C.E., for its use was prohibited by the pre-tannaitic sages Jose ben Joezer and Johanan of Jerusalem,[4] but the mishnaic references to glass are difficult to date and do not tell us to what extent it was from abroad, although it was widely used and it is natural to suppose, that while some of it came from Phoenicia, its fragility and its commonness in tombs of this period indicate local manufacture.

Other articles of use whose origin abroad is reported (but not all certainly before 70 C.E.) were Egyptian baskets,[5] rope,[6] papyrus containers,[7] wickerwork[8] and small shields from Arabia.[9] The only metal which the country possessed was copper in the Araba and Transjordan—not certainly worked in this period—hence it is not surprising to find that at a later date pig-iron was being obtained from India,[10] and the import of all necessary metals must be assumed in the Second Temple period. Other raw materials certainly or probably coming into Judaea at the time were flax from Syria (chiefly in the

---

[1] V. Sussman, *Ornamented Jewish Oil Lamps* (1972; in Hebrew), p. 20.
[2] See generally Sussman, *op. cit.*, chapters 2 and 3.
[3] *Archives Juives: Cahiers de la commission française des archives juives* III (1968), pp. 29-30, fig. 3, from Orgon, B. du Rhône, between Avignon and Marseilles.
[4] *T. B. Shabbath* 14b.
[5] *M. Sotah* 2:1.
[6] *M. Sotah* 1:6.
[7] *M. Kelim* 2:5; but they may have come from Lake Hulah.
[8] *M. Kelim* 16:5.
[9] *M. Kelim* 24:1.
[10] *T. B. Abodah Zarah* 16a.

sabbatical year),[1] earth from the Cycladean isle of Kimolos, for bleaching purposes;[2] naphta[3] and marble.[4] A variety of building materials and metals from abroad are likely to have been needed for the construction of the Temple.

The regular Temple service also required considerable commodities only obtainable from a distance, to wit, incense, which was consumed in great quantities, and whose constituents included nard, frankincense from Hadramaut, aloe wood (*tarum*), cassia, cinnamon (the last two from Ethiopia), costum from India, and galbanum. Of these, aloe-wood and galbanum were also produced in Judaea.[5]

Judaea's main exports in this period were olive oil, dates and opobalsam. The monopoly sale of a large quantity of oil from Galilee at an inflated price to the Jews of Caesarea Paneas[6] (or Syria)[7] by the astute John of Gischala in the sixties, at least shows that a machinery for such largescale purchases and their transport existed. The olives of the Decapolis towns also went overseas.[8] In respect of the export both of oil and wine, however, restrictions were imposed in the seventh year or in times of dearth.[9] The same presumably applied to grain, but here the needs of the conquering power and of Phoenicia imposed permanent obligations on the economy; the export of 20,675 modii of grain per year (except in the sabbatical years)[10] from Joppa to Sidon, was stipulated by the treaty between Rome and Hyrcanus II under Julius Caesar,[11] and appears to be referred to again in the time of Agrippa I,[12] while the government took regular grain contributions both from the imperial domains[13] and from other cultivators.[14] Both these deliveries were taxes,[15] and therefore in the nature of unrequited

[1] T. Shebiith 4:19.   [2] M. Shabbath 9:5.
[3] M. Shabbath 2:2.   [4] M. Kelim 22:1.
[5] For all these, see J. I. Miller, *The Spice Trade of the Roman Empire*, (1969), especially pp. 3ff. and 102ff. Most of them are listed together in T. B. Kerithoth 6a.
[6] War II, 591.
[7] Life 74ff.
[8] Pliny, *Natural History* xv, 15.
[9] T. Abodah Zarah 4:2; T. B. Baba Bathra 90b. The latter may be first century, but these restrictions are not referred to in the Mishnah.
[10] Eight modii are one bushel. 20,675 modii = 2,584 bushels = 1,292 hectolitres.
[11] Ant. xiv, 206.
[12] Acts 12:20.
[13] Jos. Life 71.
[14] The stipulated regular supply to Sidon demonstrates the virtual dependance of the Phoenician cities on the surrounding countries for grain, due to their restricted agricultural hinterlands, and Rome's concern for the welfare of these centres, doubtless due to their industrial importance.
[15] φόρους τε τελεῖν (Ant. xiv, 206).

exports. Dates were also exported, expecially from Jericho, and some varieties, particularly the 'caryotos'[1] and the 'Nikolaos' (named after Nicholas of Damascus),[2] were highly regarded in Rome; here again, the Jericho plantations passed to the Roman treasury after the deposition of Archelaus in 6 C.E. Other known plantations were to be found at Zoar,[3] Beth Nimrin[4] and Abila.[5]

The renowned wines of Gaza and Ascalon do not appear in the records as exports till the fourth century, but Horace had a high opinion of the products of Syria in Augustus' time,[6] and Pliny refers to Syrian wine reinforced with myrrh;[7] taken with earlier references, and the Sharon pottery industry (below), these mentions suggest that Judaea's wines were already known abroad in the first century C.E.

While most of the oriental and African incenses, spices and medicaments were part of Judaea's transit-trade, handed on through her harbours for re-export, some were products of the country itself; these included rose oil,[8] henna, a speciality of Ascalon[9] and Engeddi,[10] myrobalanus, grown near Jericho,[11] aloe-wood,[12] sweet flag (Galilee),[13] lentisk (Gilead),[14] terebinth resin (Gilead),[15] galbanum,[16] styrax,[17] and balm of Gilead (a Commiphora).[18] Of the above products, henna, lentisk, terebinth resin, galbanum—and also mustard—are referred to by Pliny, and may therefore have been exported from the country. Nabataea yielded mastic, resin of the terebinth, and ladanum.[19]

A special note is required concerning opobalsam. This was the sap of a low bush (Hebr. *afarsamon*) grown in the Dead Sea area, also in Gilead and Ramata of Transjordan;[20] it was extracted from the stem

---

[1] Strabo XVI, 763, 41; Pliny, *Natural History* XIII, 44-9.
[2] Pliny, *Natural history* XIII, 44.
[3] *M. Yebamoth* 16:7.
[4] *T. Yoma* 5:3.
[5] *Ant.* IV, 176.
[6] *Od.* I, 31.
[7] Pliny, *Natural History* XIV, 103; *T. B. Abodah Zarah* 30a.
[8] *M. Demai* 1:3.
[9] Pliny, *Natural History* XII, 51.
[10] Cant. 1:13; 4:13.
[11] Pliny, *Natural History* XII, 100.
[12] Num. 24:6.
[13] Strabo XVI, 754.
[14] Pliny, *Natural History* XXI, 96.
[15] Pliny, *Natural History* XII, 121.
[16] *T. B. Kerithoth* 6a.
[17] *War* IV, 469.   [18] Gen. 23:35. etc.   [19] Miller, op.cit., p. 22.
[20] Pliny, *Natural History* XII, 111; Engeddi: *T. B. Shabbath* 26a; Ramata: ibid.; Zoare: Eusebius, *Onomasticon* 42, 4.

with a piece of glass or stone. The twigs and bark were also sold at high prices, costing as much as 800 sesterces per pound in 75 C.E. A sextarius of the sap itself, marketed by the Roman treasury at 300 denarii, was resold in Rome for thousands of denarii.[1] It was thought to be a sovereign remedy for headaches, dimness of vision and incipient cataract.[2]

Since the small onions of Ascalon were well known to Strabo[3] and to Pliny,[4] it may be accepted that they too were exported abroad. Pliny's knowledge of Syrian fruit-cordials[5] suggests the same conclusion concerning them.

As to manufactured goods, although woollens and linen garments were widely produced in Judaea,[6] the earliest extraneous mention of locally woven linens belongs to the later second century.[7] Reference to the production by Jews of purple-dyed fabrics does not appear in the Mishnah before the second century,[8] but according to Pliny[9] a considerable expansion of murex fishing took place in the later first century B.C.E., leading to a fall in the prices of the dye, hence it is more than possible that Jews had joined the industry then if not earlier. It may be noted that archaeological evidence of the activity has been observed as far south as Ashdod.[10] Allon, indeed, understood Rabbi Joseph's interpretation of Jeremiah 52:16, as referring to the murex-fishers between the Ladder of Tyre and Haifa,[11] to mean that the Jewish industry in that tract of coast was taken over by the Roman treasury after 70.

Some plants and minerals were traded abroad as raw materials in the first century C.E.; those recorded are Galilean rushes used for ropemaking;[12] Dead Sea asphalt, sent to Egypt for the embalming of the dead and for the caulking of shipshulls,[13] and amethyst from Petra.[14] It is extremely probable, though not strictly proven, that the silica

---

[1] Pliny, *Natural History* XII, III.
[2] Strabo XVI, 763.
[3] XVI, 759.
[4] *Natural History* XIX, 105.
[5] *Natural History* XIV, 103.
[6] *M. Baba Kamma* 10:9.
[7] Pausanias V, 2.
[8] *M. Kilaim* 9:9 (R. Jose); *M. Baba Metzia* 2:1 (R. Meir).
[9] *Natural History* IX, 138-9.
[10]*BIES* XXIV, 1959/60, p. 129; cf. I Macc. 4:23: πορφύραν θαλασσίαν.
[11]Alon I, pp. 97-8 on *T. B. Shabbath* 26a and *Sifre Deut.* 354.
[12]Strabo XVI, 754; Pliny, *Natural History* XXXV, 178.
[13]Strabo XVI, 764.
[14]Pliny, *Natural History* XXVII, 121.

sand of the Haifa-Ptolemais shore was exported for glass-making.[1] It should however be noted that the last four products were administratively outside Judaea and that Petra was outside the empire till Trajan's day. It seems probable that the sulphur and alum mined near Machaerus were also sent abroad.[2]

Joppa had the reputation of being a pirates' nest; Strabo adds that the pirates controlled the Sharon (ὁ δρυμός) and the Carmel.[3] How far this state of affairs was perpetuated into the first century C.E., is impossible to say. Piracy and the slave trade were inseparable, and in the Hellenistic period instances are found of slaves named after Joppa port.[4] Clearly, for the Gentile towns, a considerable import of slaves may be assumed, and Gentile slaves were certainly not absent from Jewish society.[5]

The country's transit trade was important, but entirely confined to profitable long-distance luxury articles, such as have been referred to; they were derived from East Africa, Arabia, India and the Far East. The list of these wares is long and impressive, and some of the spices have been alluded to.[6] The trade benefited a relatively small group of specialist merchants, also the treasuries of the empire, the kings and the ports; as a near-monopoly of the Nabataeans, many of its profits accrued to traders outside Judaea prior to 106 C.E., when Rome laid her hand on the westernmost sectors of the trade-routes concerned by the establishment of the province of Arabia. But it may be noted that the discovery of the monsoons and the direct sailing route to India in the first century B.C.E. considerably lowered the prices of Indian spices; spikenard is quoted at 300 denarii the pound by Mark (14: 3) but at 100 denarii by Pliny.[7]

The Temple tax, that is the half-shekel, paid by every male Jew

[1] Cf. Strabo XVI, 758.
[2] *War* VII, 189.
[3] Strabo XVI, 759.
[4] E.g. *Fouilles de Delphes* III, 4, no. 91; *SEG* XXIII, no. 381 (Zacynthus); *Corpus Inscriptionum Atticarum* III, 2, 2498. See also above, chapter eleven, pp. 624-30.
[5] See e.g. Danby, *The Mishnah* (1933), Index, p. 839, s.v. Slaves. The extent of the survival of Jewish slavery in Judaea in this period is highly controversial. To judge from Jos. *War* IV, 508, 510, their number may have been considerable on the eve of the Destruction. On the subject, Baron, *A Social and Religious History of the Jews* II (2nd ed. 1952) pp. 267-71; E. Urbach, 'Rulings on Slavery', in *Zion* XXV (1954), pp. 141-89 (in Hebrew).
[6] The chief sources are Pliny, Strabo, Dioscorides and Apicius; for details and references see Miller, op.cit., and the bibliography there assembled.
[7] Pliny, *Natural History* XII, 42-3.

from the age of 20 or 13,[1] invites further comment. Its payment by Diaspora Jews inside and outside the Roman empire constituted a steady flow of hard currency into Judaea and a certain loss of bullion to the Gentile communities where Jews dwelt. How far it served to create a favourable balance for the country's economy depends on the unresolved problem, to what extent its proceeds re-entered general circulation. Part of these funds certainly did so, because they were used to cover public sacrifices, the preparation of requisites (e.g. incense), the maintenance of buildings, the salaries of judges, support of the priesthood and the needy;[2] and the municipal services of the city of Jerusalem. Surplus supplies, moreover, were traded off outside the Temple.[3] The balance frequently roused the envy and covetousness of the Roman rulers; the wiser of them, nevertheless, may have perceived the advantage of the Temple contributions to the imperial economy, in that they guaranteed a steady flow of hard cash from Parthia and the other countries beyond the frontier where Jews were numerous;[4] in so far as the money re-entered circulation, it would have helped to balance the empire's outflow of currency in payment of its costly luxury imports from the Orient and East Africa.[5] In 70, when this flow ceased, it may have been Vespasian's awareness of the situation that caused him to impose his Jewish tax upon both sexes from the age of three to sixty, and also on Jewish-owned slaves,[6] multiplying several times over the previous proceeds from the Jewry of the Roman Diaspora and of Judaea.

Ben David concludes that on the whole the country's balance of imports and exports was favourable, but this relates to the entire talmudic period.[7] Examination of the strictly available evidence for the first century is not so decisive; a considerable part of Jewish Judaea's chief exports (dates, opobalsam, wheat) were the products of crown domain or paid as taxation, and hence unrequited. Except for oil, wine and native spices, we know of next to no home produce

---

[1] Exod. 30:14-15; M. Shekalim 1:3; Ant. III, 196.
[2] Cf. M. Shekalim 4:1-2; T. B. Ketuboth 105a; also chapter four, p. 190.
[3] M. Shekalim 4:3.
[4] Of the three areas rendering dues, the Land of Israel, the neighbouring countries, and Parthia, Media etc., the last yielded the richest income, including gold staters and darics. (T. Shekalim 2:3; chapter four, p. 189).
[5] Pliny, Natural History VI, 101 stated the annual Roman loss in this trade to have been 55 million sesterces; Tacitus (Ann. III, 53) also commented on this expenditure.
[6] Ginsburg, in JQR XXI (1930/1), p. 289, n. 43; Tcherikover, in CPJ I, p. 81.
[7] Ben David, p. 264.

or manufactures that were with certainty exported during this period. On the other hand the country was apt to be dependent on external agricultural produce in the sabbatical years or in times of drought, and always for metals, several raw materials and crafts products, and for a number of luxuries (fine clothing, furniture etc.). In the available record, items of imports exceed exports.

Against all this we have to set the fact that the Hasmonaeans evidently developed Jewish seafaring (compare Simeon's repair of Joppa port,[1] and the appearance of the anchor on the coins of the dynasty), while Herod both built a fleet[2] (perhaps predominantly manned by Gentiles), and gave the country its most successful harbour at Caesarea, being also careful to cultivate good relationships with the Greek seaboard towns of Phoenicia and Asia. Of the existence of Jewish mercantile seafaring there is no doubt (see p. 689); we are nevertheless forced to conclude, unless the written evidence is hopelessly distorted by its own lacunae, that the bulk of the objects of trade carried to and from the Greek coastal towns were produced or consumed by the Greeks themselves.

The Jewish population's chief advantage was its agricultural self-sufficiency, yet even this was sensitive to the fluctuations of nature and to overpopulation. Its surplus was absorbed under Herod by public works, much of them unproductive, later by direct Roman taxation. The contributions derived from Diaspora Jewry, whether in the form of the half-shekel payment, or of various other contributions, including money brought in by the yearly pilgrimages, must therefore have played a vital rôle in keeping the Jewish economy on an even keel, but here again, it was chiefly Jerusalem that benefited. The diversion of the tax to Rome after 70, coupled with the further expansion of Roman state land in Judaea, must have rendered more acute an already unenviable poverty, which could only be countered by the increase of the community's production for export.

The conclusion is that if Jewish Judaea suffered a degree of commercialization in the first century C.E., it was not very effective where export was concerned. Economic activity was predominantly internal. The position of the Greek population remains obscure; our information

---

[1] 1 Macc. 14:5.
[2] *Ant.* XVI, 16-21. Coins figuring a ship's prow, an anchor or an aphlaston, were struck by Alexander Jannaeus, Herod, Archelaus and Agrippa II; see Reifenberg, *Coins of the Jews*, pp. 14-15, pl. iii, 33; iv, 57; Meshorer, *Jewish Coins*, pp. 119; 129; 130; Ben David, p. 277.

is still too scanty to pass judgement, but such as it is, it suggests that they achieved a degree of prosperity by successful agriculture (chiefly at the expense of the cultivators of their territories) and above all as long-range commercial entrepôts. Their agriculture was free of the religious restrictions enforced by Judaism; they probably exercised initial monopolies in the manufacture of purple-dyed stuffs, glass, red-glaze and amphorae; we know of Ascalon's production of vegetables, henna, iron and leather equipment. The coastal towns doubtless engaged in fishing, and their ships would have obtained the lion's share of maritime commerce including the slave-trade. They would have been the chief purveyors of clothes and wine to the Roman army of occupation, and the sole producers of pagan *objets d'art* and figured lamps. They further furnished the Roman forces with all or nearly all the locally enlisted men serving in the auxiliary units (the Jewish population of Bashan and Hauran were exceptions to this rule), and from this point of view the Jews were for Rome a negative liability; there were few or no Jewish veterans to return to spread sentiments of loyalty or Roman skills and experience among their fellow countrymen.

Production and circulation of goods in Palestine

We now turn to the internal production and circulation of goods in Palestine. It may be said at once that the Jewish population, like the peoples surrounding it, possessed all the craftsmen, specialized workers and performers of simple manual tasks possessed by any other normal economy of the ancient world.[1] By the period that concerns us, the branches of production had achieved a certain differentiation, i.e. a functional division among groups of workers producing the same type of product. This feature appears both in the larger units of contemporary Jewish agriculture,[2] and among the handicrafts of the period.[3] Further, differentiation had also developed between craftsmen and those who supplied them with raw materials or sold their products, although craftsmen selling their own wares and 'home' industries conducted within the family or village were still common, and there were also travelling craftsmen who worked up the materials supplied to them by their customers in the latters' homes (tanners, potters).

[1] For full lists of occupations, see Krauss II, chapter 7, pp. 253-311; Ben David, pp. 149-150.
[2] Cf. Heichelheim III, p. 1109, n. 49.
[3] Ben David, pp. 143ff. and especially pp. 150-1.

The most pronounced differentiation within given handicrafts, however, is to be found after the first century C.E., and more particularly after the second revolt of 132-5.

Certain branches were preponderantly associated with rural areas; such were the pottery industry and the manufacture of silk, and in this feature the Jewish economy anticipated a trend which was to become pronounced in the third century of the Roman Empire.[1] Pottery had of necessity to seek localities close to clay, water and fuel (i.e. woodland); it was also closely linked with the production of wine, oil, perfumes, and the fish-salting industry. We have already observed that Judaea supplied most of her own coarse wares; contemporary literature records industries in the Sharon,[2] at Lydda,[3] Bethlehem,[4] Modiin,[5] Kefar Hananya and Sihin (the latter two in Galilee).[6] The Qumran community also appears to have turned out much of its own domestic earthen-ware during the first century B.C.E.[7]

While glass-making was certainly carried out in the country before 70 C.E., the few known production sites excavated hitherto, all within range of Haifa Bay, belonged to the third century or later. The time of origin of the industry evidenced at Tiberias by talmudic references has not been established.[8]

Most of the clothing worn by the Jewish population was woven at home,[9] but surpluses were often sold, and we have already a picture of a well-organized home industry turning out wollen garments, belts and carpets for the market in Proverbs (21:10-29), which probably belongs to the Persian period; weaving mills of some size are known from excavation, one at Nir David of the early Iron Age.[10] Consequently, similar mills may be taken to have existed also in our period, and this is confirmed, for the years immediately after 70, by regulations governing wool-weavers and dyers in the average townlet recorded in

[1] See Rostovtzeff I, pp. 174-5; Finley, pp. 138; 160.
[2] *M. Baba Bathra* 6:2.
[3] *M. Kelim* 2:2.
[4] Ibid.
[5] *M. Pesahim* 9:2.
[6] *T. Baba Metzia* 6:3; *T. B. Shabbath* 120b.
[7] *RB* LXIII (1956), p. 543 (period 1b, from the end of the second century till 31 B.C.E.).
[8] *P. T. Niddah* 11, 50b; *T. B. Niddah* 21a.
[9] *M. Ketuboth* 5:9.
[10] G. Edelstein, *Weavers' Settlements of the Period of the Hebrew Monarchy* (1972; in Hebrew).

the Tosefta,[1] and earlier by the name Migdal Tzebia on the Sea of
Galilee,[2] indicating a centre of the dyeing industry. Silk appears to
have been woven at Migdal Tzebia and at Sihin in Galilee, according
to a tradition transmitted by Rabbi Johanan (third century) referring
to the period before 70.[3] Two sorts of silk are mentioned in the Mishnah;[4] the fabric turned out in Galilee must have been derived from
the cocoons of the moth *Pachypasa otus Dr.*,[5] which could be fed with
the leaves of the Galilee oak (*Quercus coccifera*).

The leather industry also possessed centres in the countryside; we
know of a shoe-making industry at Amki in western Galilee.[6] The
trade of tanning is amply evidenced by the halakic regulations
restricting those engaged in it to a given distance from inhabited
areas.[7] Further rural occupations were rope-making and basket-
making, from such materials as osier, straw, palm-fibre and flax; one
centre of this activity was Arbela, west of the Sea of Galilee.[8]

The manufacture of basalt millstones and mortars, often found on
ancient sites of the period, must also have been localized somewhere
in eastern Galilee or Bashan. Such a centre appears to have existed
at Khabab (ancient Abiba) in the western Lejja.[9] Of interest in this
connection is a type of chalk measuring-cup found mainly in the
Jerusalem district and within an area enclosed by Hebron, Masada
and Jericho.[10] Some 15 examples have been recorded, and are analysed
by Ben David.[11] They were made from material present east of
Jerusalem in the Herodian period, and come preponderantly from one
workshop, which marketed its products over an area of no less than
1,400 square kilometres, with a maximum radius of about 30 kilometres. Among the specialized manufactures in stone must be added
ossuaries for the bones of the dead, more particularly centred on

[1] *T. Baba Metzia* 11:24.
[2] *P. T. Taanith* iv, 69a.
[3] *P. T. Taanith* iv, 69a. For a discussion of the problem of the related passages,
see Herzfeld, pp. 108; 310.
[4] *M. Kilaim* 9:2.
[5] S. Bodenheimer, 'Silk and Silk-Weaving in Palestine', in *Eretz Israel* i (1951),
pp. 171ff. (in Hebrew).
[6] *M. Kelim* 26:1.
[7] *M. Baba Bathra* 2:9.
[8] *M. Parah* 12:8 (reading כוש שלרובן); *T. Parah* 12:16.
[9] Dussaud and Macler, *Rapport sur une mission scientifique dans les régions
désertiques de la Syrie moyenne* (1901), p. 417.
[10] *Archaeological News* xxx (April 1969), p. 24 (Jebel Mukbar near Beth Hananiah).
[11] Ben David, pp. 334-43; Mazar, in *BIES* xxx (1966), pl. xxxvi, 9 and pp.
183ff; Ben David, in *IEJ* xix (1969), pp. 158ff.

Jerusalem, and sarcophagi.[1] In general, quarrying and masons' work must have employed a considerable number of hands in this period.[2] Fish-salting at Migdal Nunaiyya on the Sea of Galilee also seems to have attained an industrial scale,[3] combined with fishing, for which the Gospels,[4] rabbinic literature and archaeological finds (net-sinkers, anchors) provide adequate evidence. The Greek name of the townlet, Tarichaeae (saltings),[5] seals the testimony.

The largest concentration of economic activity, both productive and commercial, was naturally in Jerusalem. A considerable part of the handicrafts was conducted in connection with the Temple, which constituted an economic unit in its own right. Besides purchasing considerable quantities of livestock for the public sacrifices, and supporting annually 7,000 priests and Levites, it kept busy a notable staff of physicians, scribes, maintenance workers, butchers, weavers, metal-workers, incense-makers and bakers of the shewbread. In the decades prior to 66, the remodelling of the shrine employed, in addition to trained priests, 10,000 other labourers.[6] The bakers, incense-specialists and metal-workers were organized in their own guilds, constituting closed family monopolies which guarded their trade secrets jealously and transmitted them from one generation to the next.[7] About the Temple gathered numerous money-changers connected with the changing of the money of pilgrims for the purchase of sacrifical animals,[8] also purveyors and traders concerned with the sale of such, and with the purchase of Temple surpluses. But the high priests also furnished requisites at a price, and retained the profits.[9] The Temple further acted as a deposit bank.[10]

The productive crafts were well represented in Jerusalem to serve the city and its innumerable visitors. Workshops included those of weavers,[11] cheesemakers,[12] woolcombers,[13] bakers,[14] copper-smiths[15] and

---

[1] 177 Jewish ossuaries from the Jerusalem area were published by Frey (*CII* II, nos. 1210-1387); since then a number of others have been discovered.
[2] *M. Shebiith* 3:5 etc.
[3] Strabo XVI, 764.
[4] Mark 1:16 etc.
[5] Strabo XVI, 764.
[6] *Ant.* XV, 390.
[7] *M. Shekalim* 5:1; *M. Yoma* 3:11.
[8] Matt. 21:12; Mark 11:15.
[9] E.g. *Midrash Lam. Rabba* 2 (pigeons); cf. *M. Kerithoth* 1:7.
[10] II Macc. 3:11.   [11] *M. Eduyot* 1:3.
[12] *War* I, 140.   [13] *M. Erubin* 10:9.
[14] *Ant.* XV, 309.   [15] *War* V, 331.

cobblers;[1] potteries existed in the vicinity of the city.[2] The establish-
ments of these craftsmen, often producing by piecework, varied from
large workshops employing a number of hands, to individual families
who both produced and sold their wares. Characteristically, each craft
tended to occupy its own street, vaulted bazaar or quarter; thus we
hear, additionally, of the clothes market,[3] the poultry market,[4] the
wool market,[5] the flour market,[6] the timber market,[7] and the fruit
market.[8] Similar crafts quarters are recorded in other cities of the
country, now or later.[9] In the Jerusalem of Herod and his successors
much sumptuous building went on, and besides the quarrymen and
the masons, the artists, decorators and skilled metalworkers would
have found plenty to employ them.

The sages valued work as a basis of the honest life, and by 'work'
they meant first and foremost manual labour;[10] they made education
to a craft a moral commandment.[11] The manual employment of the
larger part of the Jewish intelligentsia which exercised the decisive
social and moral influence on the Jewish community after 70, was
probably a unique phenomenon in the world of its time, and certainly
in the Roman empire. Most sons followed their fathers' callings;
alternatively they could be apprenticed.[12] Several of the common
crafts were organized in guilds, and these must be distinguished from
the hereditary monopoly-groups working for the Temple. The earliest
allusions to the genuine crafts guilds occur in the Tosefta, none in the
Mishnah, but a synagogue of *Tarsiim*, i.e. linen-workers, is referred to
in Jerusalem,[13] indicating that they originated before 70.[14] Other

---

[1] *Midrash Lam. Rabba* 1:3.
[2] Matt. 27:7.
[3] *War* v, 331.
[4] *M. Erubin* 10:9.
[5] *War* v, 331.
[6] *M. Menahoth* 10:5.
[7] *War* ii, 530.
[8] *M. Maaser Sheni* 5:2.
[9] Ascalon had a special wheat exchange (*T. Ohiloth* 18:18); a grainmarket also
existed at Beth Shean (*SEG* viii, 43 - ἀμφόδου σειτικῆς); Sepphoris appears to
have possessed several markets *T. B. Baba Bathra* 75b; *T. B. Erubin* 54b), likewise Tiberias (*T. B. Erubin* 29a; *T. B. Sotah* 45a etc.), where one was devoted to
the carpenters.
[10] E.g. *M. Aboth* 1:10.
[11] Cf. *M. Kiddushin* 4:14. See chapter nineteen, p. 958.
[12] See Krauss ii, p. 255; Ben David, p. 170.
[13] *T. B. Megillah* 26a.
[14] They are recorded among the Jewish crafts guilds of Alexandria before 115
(*T. Sukkoth* 4:6).

guilds of *Tarsiim* are heard of at Lydda[1] and Tiberias[2] in the later second century, and the account in Tosefta of the functions of the organizations of woolmakers, dyers, donkey-drivers and ship-owners,[3] shows that they were an integral part of the structure of the Jewish town and that their practices were approved in Halakah; it may therefore be supposed that they were of long standing. According to the same source weavers could collectively acquire the raw materials of their trade entering the locality, and share it out amongst themselves; bakers could allot different days of work amongst their members. The guilds of ship-owners, donkey-drivers and camel-drivers also insured their members, compensating them for loss of vessels or animals so long as this was not the result of negligence. Fishermen and well-diggers too were organized,[4] although the fishermen sometimes retained a kinship organization.[5] These activities show that the Jewish craftsmen's organization differed fundamentally from their Roman and Greek counterparts, in that they were active in promoting and protecting the interests of their members, and practised a measure of cooperation among themselves.

When we come to discuss the internal circulation of goods, we must first consider communications and transport. The country possessed a developed road-system, many centuries old, but although it was subject to maintenance,[6] it was the Roman government which initiated systematic paving. The network has been described by Avi-Yonah;[7] paving began late, from military necessity in Nero's reign, with the coastal route from Gaza to Caesarea and Ptolemais.[8] How a Roman road developed can be seen from a study of the one connecting Antipatris with Caesarea.[9] The earliest section was a prehistoric track, but the line began to develop in the late Hellenistic period with the colonization of the Sharon woodlands and with the foundation of Herodian Caesarea. It was formally adopted, paved and equipped with milestones only at the end of the second century.

Over these highways transport of goods was mainly by donkey,[10] mule

---

[1] *T. Ohiloth* 4:2; cf. *T. B. Nazir* 52a.
[2] *P. T. Shekalim* II, 47a.
[3] *T. Baba Metzia* 11:24.
[4] *P. T. Pesahim* IV, 30d etc.; *T. Hullin* 3:2.
[5] E.g. the fishermen's group at Joppa, which was a βόλος συγγενική (*CII* II, 945).
[6] *M. Shekalim* I:I.
[7] Chapter two, pp. 80-113 and map, pp. 100-1.
[8] *ZDPV* (1917), p. 18, no. 9a.
[9] *IEJ* (1973), pp. 91ff.
[10] *M. Baba Metzia* 1:6; 5:5.

or wagon, or, when deserts had to be traversed, by camel.[1] Grain and other agricultural produce went mainly by donkey. Transport cost one denarius a parasang (variously estimated at 4.5 to 6.5 kilometres). It took about four days to travel from Galilee to Jerusalem.[2] There was doubtless coastwise traffic, and transport by small boats on the Sea of Galilee, the Jordan[3] and the Dead Sea[4] is attested.

Circulation of goods in Judaea encountered two obstacles. One was the ubiquitous customs-tariff, which had to be paid not merely at the ports but also at the boundaries of individual cities and tetrarchies.[5] The other, applicable after the division of Herod's kingdom in 4 B.C.E. and for the next 45 years, arose from the nature of the currency. Meshorer notes that Archelaus' coins are found in the Jerusalem, Jericho, Caesarea and Masada areas;[6] those of Antipas (who began to mint in 19/20 C.E.) in the north, but not in Judaea; those of Philip, who minted from the first century C.E., entirely outside Judaea. As the tetrarchs struck only bronze coins, that is, those of the lesser denominations, while the gold and silver currency was entirely imperial Roman, it would follow that there would have been considerable difficulties in small trading between the three tetrarchies, and only large quantities of goods which could be paid for in silver or gold, could be transferred without exchange difficulties. Alternatively, barter was resorted to (an unlikely procedure with bulk consignments) or the city bronze coinage, of whose distribution I am ignorant, was used. The arrangement, on the whole, favoured the bigger men, possibly the city-treasuries. It made the community much dependent on the obtaining of imperial currency. The situation described may have been the expression of a situation not characterized by extensive largescale countrywide commerce; it certainly would not have en-

---

[1] M. Baba Bathra 2:14.

[2] The normal distances traversed may be deduced from the mishnaic injunction (M. Ketuboth 5:6) that a donkey-driver should have marital intercourse once a week, implying a six-day stretch (say 180 kilometres), a camel-driver every thirty days. According to Pliny (Natural History XII, 109) the camel covered twenty-five Roman miles (c. 28 kilometres) per day; a twenty-six-day caravan would therefore have travelled some 730 kilometres. Destinations 90 and 365 kilometres distant are therefore implied. The marital injunction to camel-drivers seems to have made a virtue of necessity.

[3] Strabo XVI, 754.

[4] War IV, 438-9; cf. T. Sukkah 3:9.

[5] See chapter six, pp. 332-3.

[6] Y. Meshorer, The Coins of the Jews in the Second Temple Period (1966) pp. 41, 46.

couraged it.[1] Jerusalem alone attracted large supplies; the three wholesalers who could supply the city with food for ten years have been alluded to. Grain, oil, to a lesser extent wine and smaller bulk luxuries were the principal wares requiring transport over distances; much of the oil and livestock came from Jerusalem's immediate vicinity.[2]

Market-places existed in a number of towns; notable outside Jerusalem were those at Shechem, Sepphoris, Lydda and Antipatris; no Greek town would have been without its *agora*. Municipal market control had been a feature since Hellenistic times; Jerusalem had an *agoranomos* even before the Hellenizing 'reform' of Jason;[3] some smaller places, not known to have possessed Greek city status, also appointed these officers.[4] The Halakah empowers the community to fix prices, weights and measures;[5] the *agoranomos* certainly controlled the last two and inspected wares; he may have influenced prices, which we hear[6] could not be fixed in the rural area till they had found their level in the urban centre.[7] The old Jewish market-day was Friday, but by mishnaic times it had moved to Mondays and Thursdays.[8] In addition to these urban institutions, there were periodical fairs at fixed dates, nearly always pagan, and nominally associated with pagan cults, hence visited by Jews with reluctance and under precautions enjoined by Halakah.[9] Much of the information stems from the post-70 period, but some of it—for example in relation to the markets of Patros,

[1] The cessation of city minting at several cities during the second revolt (132-5 c.e.) and the overstriking of Greek city issues by Bar Cochba, suggest, indeed, that in the second century, at least, circulation of city-coinage encountered no geographical restrictions. On the other hand the regional scope of the local bronze issues is confirmed by the fact that Agrippa I's issues, for instance, carried no human figures, i.e. they were meant primarily for the Jewish areas. On the whole matter, F. Heichelheim, *An Ancient Economic History* (1970) III, p. 213, who confirms that the Roman policy of promoting the circulation of the denarius and the aureus hampered trade and exchange, making traffic in many wares impracticable.

[2] *M. Shekalim* 7:4: cattle for sacrifice from a radius of 40 kilometres round Jerusalem.

[3] II Macc. 3:4.

[4] E.g. Gezer: Macalister, *Excavations at Gezer* II (1912), p. 286.

[5] Chapter seven, p. 417.

[6] See Ben David, p. 214.

[7] *P. T. Baba Metzia* v, 10c. The reference is to Tiberias and its fish; under Antipas its *agoranomos* was a royal nominee (*Ant.* XVIII, 149). The information of *T. P. Baba Metzia* hardly confirms Jones' belief (*CERP*, p. 277) that Tiberias did not control a territory.

[8] *M. Megillah* I:1, cf. III:6; *Ketuboth* I:1.

[9] Cf. *M. Abodah Zarah* I:1.

Antipatris and Yishuv, is pre-70; they were certainly visited by Jews.[1] The fairs dealt chiefly in cattle, slaves, immobilia and caravan luxury imports.[2] Caravanserais also attracted improvised markets furnishing provisions for travellers.[3]

Much agricultural produce was sold by the peasants themselves when they came to market, just as many craftsmen sold their own products. But middlemen (תגרים)[4] existed, who bought and sold the peasants' produce, also purchasing crafts products and supplying craftsmen with raw materials. Some of these men dealt on a large scale, and worked with agents. The shopkeeper, on the other hand, dealing in a few wares (e.g. bread, supplied to him by the baker) ranked closer to the smaller dealer. Much petty trade was conducted in the village areas by itinerant peddlers,[5] or by small dealers resident in rural centres to which they daily returned.[6] Itinerant potter swere numerous.[7] It is significant that the Hebrew word for the big merchant (סיטון)[8] was derived from the Greek term for a wholesaler in the grain trade, and to this class doubtless belonged the wealthy purveyors of Jerusalem to whom allusion has been made. The wealthy ship-owners engaged in long-distance import and export and handling a variety of goods simultaneously, were also known by a Greek term (πραγματευτής),[9] and most of them were Gentiles.[10] But there is no doubt that Jewish

---

[1] *T. Demai* 1:11-14.
[2] See especially Krauss II, pp. 356-7.
[3] E.g. Emmaus: *M. Kerithoth* 3:7, a report dated to Hadrian's reign.
[4] *M. Baba Metzia* 4:3.
[5] *M. Maaseroth* 2:3.
[6] *P. T. Maaseroth* II, 49d; Krauss II, p. 349.
[7] *M. Baba Kamma* 5:2; *M. Hagigah* 3:5.
[8] *M. Demai* 5:6; *M. Baba Bathra* 5:10.
[9] The oldest occurrence of this word appears to be in *Sifre Deut.* 315,: see Krauss, *Griechische und Lateinische Lehnwörter* II, p. 478, ad vocem; by far the majority of the works in which it is used are late.
[10]The not very abundant evidence, mainly epigraphical, for the trade connections of the Greek cities of Judaea with Greece and Italy, is scattered throughout the Greek and Roman periods; Ascalonites honoured at Naples and Delos (Laidlaw, *History of Delos* (1933), pp. 210ff); at Athens (*IG* II, 1028; another at Rheneia (*SEG.* IX, 930); at Puteoli (*CIL* X, 1746); for the banker Philostratos of Ascalon (first century B.C.E.): Launey and Roussel, *Inscriptions de Délos* (1937), nos. 1717-24, 2283; Gaza honours Gordian at Portus Ostia (*IGR* I, 837); citizen of Gerasa at Pergamum (*IGR* IV, 374, end first century C.E.); Athenians at Accho (Demosth. LII, 20, late fourth century B.C.E.); a woman of Joppa at Athens (*SEG* XXV, no. 275); a Neapolitan at Tomi (*SEG* XXIV, 768); a woman of Caesarea at Puteoli (*CIL* X, 1985); an Azotan in Greece (*SEG* XVI, 57, 178/7 B.C.E.). For slaves from Joppa in Greece, see above p. 677, n. 4.

ship-owners existed (cf. p. 686), and a word must be said concerning them.

The participation of Jews in Mediterranean trade as far as Alexandria and Italy is sufficiently attested by the fact that the Tobiad family of Jerusalem held credits in Alexandria in the third century B.C.E.,[1] and the Jewish alabarchs of Alexandria at Puteoli under Tiberius.[2] We have seen that Jewish ship-owners combined for mutual insurance. The merchant ships of Eleazar ben Harsum belong to the Hadrianic epoch, but his family and his large estates go back to the pre-70 period.[3] The Mishnah has rulings relating to the sale of ships,[4] and the Jewish craft wrecked at Joppa in 67 were certainly not all pirate vessels.[5] Halakic rulings on bottomry loans and agreements between shore-merchants and skippers, on the other hand, are preponderantly recorded in post-70 sources.[6] If our previous conclusions are justified, cargoes would have been mainly oriental luxury goods, passengers (Jewish pilgrims), grain for Sidon, and the foodstuffs periodically needed for seventh-year consumption or by the Roman forces. Much cargo may have been carried for Greek dealers, Jewish oil and wine for the Jewish Diaspora. Coastwise traffic would have been brisk.[7]

As regards business relationships, sleeping partnerships were not infrequent, and cases occur in which a dealer is found working in order to support the studies of a sage.[8] While interest was nominally prohibited, credits were extended not only to finance mercantile ventures on the sea,[9] but also to cultivators on the strength of the purchase of future crops,[10] when the prohibition was sometimes

---

[1] *Ant.* XII, 199.
[2] *Ant.* XVIII, 159-60.
[3] For his wealth, *T. B. Kiddushin* 49b etc.
[4] *M. Baba Bathra* 5:1.
[5] It may be pointed out that the Romans would have called any hostile mariners acting on their own account 'pirates'—cf. Hengel, *Die Zeloten* (1961), pp. 25ff. In any case, the dividing line between the astute maritime trader and the privateer was always a fine one in the ancient Mediterranean.
[6] See in greater detail, Ben David, pp. 245ff.
[7] Even over paved roads inland transport was slow and expensive, and water transport the most efficient form known to the ancient world. Excluding the Greek port towns, there were anchorages for light craft at the mouths of the rivers Sorek, Yakqon, Poleg, Alexander and Hadera, and small ports at Mikmoret (Abbu Zabbora), Sykaminum, and at Shavei Tziyyon near Nahariyyah.
[8] Cf. *Gen. Rabba* 99 (p. 1263).
[9] *T. Baba Metzia* 5:13.
[10] *T. Baba Metzia* 6:12.

circumvented.[1] The halakic regulations designed to safeguard the customer and to prevent sharp practice are very numerous, and if the number of discussions and rulings are any guide as indicators, the grain-trade took first place in importance, next came the wine trade, and oil came third,[2] although this distribution may reflect a later age. Space precludes a discussion of the attitude of the sages to the ethics of commerce and employment as it comes to expression in talmudic legislation, but one point may be of more than usual interest. They had grasped the principle of the added value of the product arising from the labour invested in it, and ruled, accordingly, that in disputed cases the product belonged to the worker until the improvement resulting from his work was fully paid for.[3] Numerous other rulings are directed to public health and hygiene, restricting the number of craftsmen permitted to reside in one street,[4] prohibiting the propinquity of dyeing and baking to granaries,[5] and removing tanneries from inhabited areas.[6] There is also legislation regulating the relations of employer and employee: overtime was regulated,[7] prompt and regular payment enforced,[8] and the right to food[9] and perquisites[10] emphasized. This does not mean that the position of the wage-labourer was ideal. But it is doubtful if the legislative effort to improve it was to be found contemporarily elsewhere. The perennial discussion on how far these rulings, and many others, were purely academic or actually enforced, seems pointless, and the stand taken on the question generally depends on prejudice. Probably the reality varied from period to period according to conditions. If under the first Herods and the procurators the halakic decisions counted for little, the situation had changed by the end of the second century, when an effective Jewish autonomy had developed under the aegis of the patriarchate.

[1] *T. Baba Metzia* 5:1.
[2] Ben David, pp. 186-9.
[3] *M. Baba Kamma* 9:4. Additional comments by R. Meir and R. Judah make it probable that the ruling goes back to the first century c.e.
[4] *T. B. Baba Bathra* 21a.
[5] *M. Baba Bathra* 2:3.
[6] *M. Baba Bathra* 2:9.
[7] *M. Baba Metzia* 7:1.
[8] *M. Baba Metzia* 9:11-12.
[9] *M. Baba Metzia* 7:1.
[10] E.g. *M. Maaseroth* 2:1-8.

The social revolution and the rising against Rome

We may endeavour to sum up the results of our enquiry. The greater part of Judaea's income, at least as far as the Jewish sector was concerned, was derived from agriculture and its ancillary industries rather than from commerce, which fulfilled a more important rôle in the economy of the maritime and Transjordanian cities, Herodian and Roman taxation drained off the greater part of Judaea's most profitable home-production (dates, opobalsam, wheat), and much of Herod's revenue was expended on non-productive enterprises. If a balance was maintained between the country's income and expenditure, this was mainly due to the extensive Jewish contributions from the Diaspora and the exports of the Greek cities, also to the great skill and grit of the hard-working Jewish cultivator in wresting production from a minimal plot of ground. But overpopulation reduced the Jewish peasant unit of cultivation and endangered the cultivator's margin of livelihood. This was further curtailed by climatic instability and taxation, leading to chronic indebtedness, and the growth of a landless tenantry and labouring class, whose ranks were also enlarged by political developments—Rome's reduction of Jewish territory and Herod's policy of confiscation—and whose existence is indirectly evidenced by the vast increase of 'bandits', more particularly in the years between 40 and 66 C.E.[1]

The Temple represented a large capital accumulation; despite considerable expenditure, only part of its income was ploughed back into production; the scale, direction and purpose of such mortgages as it granted are unknown. The Temple rendered some social aid,[2] but a considerable share of the assistance furnished to the poverty-stricken came from the peasantry and the small-town communities themselves, by medium of *peah*, *leket*, second tithe and the other obligatory dues. The upper échelons of the priestly families enriched themselves from the Temple perquisites and exploited the poorer priests,[3] in conformity with the opportunistic and egotistical character of those high-priestly families which were prepared to respond to the requirements of the Herodian rulers and the Roman government.[4]

In so characterizing the salient trends of the Jewish economy of Judaea in the first century, we have gone a long way towards indicating

[1] See chapter six, pp. 366-72.
[2] *M. Shekalim* 5:6.
[3] *Ant.* xx, 180-181; cf. *T. Menahoth* 13:21.
[4] Cf. chapter five, pp. 271-2, for the origins of this element.

the chief causes of the social revolution that coincided with the rising against Rome in 66-73. Two currents of the revolutionary movement, that of the Sicarii and of John of Gischala, though a century divides their beginnings, had their origin in the same circumstances: Ezechias father of Judah of Galilee[1] died fighting the Tyrians for Jewish cultivable land,[2] and John's band was recruited among refugees from the villages of the Tyrian rural area.[3] His townlet, Gischala, inhabited preponderantly by Jewish cultivators,[4] was deeply involved in a chronic feud with the Tyrian townlet of Cadasa.[5] The struggle for cultivable land further reasserted itself on the east in the year 44 C.E., in the clash between the Jews of Peraea and the Greeks of Zia in the territory of Philadelphia.[6] Subsequently the activists in Jerusalem burned the debt contracts in the public archives,[7] and Simeon bar Giora attacked the houses of the large estate-owners.[8]

Rabbi Johanan ben Torta, a contemporary of Rabbi Akiba, pene-tratingly summed up the situation which had led, in his view, to the catastrophe of the Destruction, when he said: 'But as to the recent Temple, we acknowledge that they were diligent in the Law and attentive in the payment of tithes; why then were they exiled? Because they lusted after money and hated one another.'[9]

The economic situation after 70 C.E.

The economic situation of the Jewish community of Judaea after the Destruction must be briefly surveyed. Josephus put the Jewish losses at 1,100,000.[10] His figures are seldom accurate, and this is certainly an exaggeration. The figure of 97,000 prisoners in Jerusalem[11] is possible; if Tacitus' figure of 600,000 besieged in the city is real,[12] then some half a million perished in Jerusalem alone. The decisive fact is, that the Judaean mountain massif and Galilee remained extensively Jewish,[13]

---

[1] Despite doubts, *Midrash Lam. Rabba* 1:16 confirms the descent of Menahem, the Sicarian leader of 66, from Hezekiah, thus showing the latter to have been the father of Judah, co-founder of the Sicarii.
[2] *War* I, 204; *Ant.* XIV, 159; cf. *Ant.* XIV, 313-6.
[3] *War* II, 587.   [4] *War* IV, 84.   [5] *War* IV, 84.
[6] *Ant.* XX, 2.   [7] *War* II, 427.   [8] *War* II, 652.
[9] *T. Menahoth* 13:22.   [10] *War* VI, 460.
[11]*Ibid.*   [12] *Histories* V, 13.
[13] However Dio Cassius' figure (XIX, 14) of 985 villages taken by the Roman army in Judaea in the war of 132-5 is to be evaluated, it demonstrates that the highlands had remained predominantly Jewish.

and even the surrounding territory of Jerusalem, which became the preserve of the tenth legion (Fretensis), would not have lost many of its Jewish inhabitants.

Damage was severe, but localized. Besides Jerusalem, two cities, Antipatris and Samaria, suffered heavily, and Antipatris was not revived till the Severan age; Samaria may have been in like case (see above, p. 666). Joppa became, now or under one of the Flavians, a titular Roman colony;[1] her territory had been devastated, yet by the early second century she certainly again possessed a sizeable Jewish community.[2] Caesarea Maritima likewise received colonial rank, though not exempted from the land tax.[3] Vespasian founded a new municipality at Neapolis,[4] near the site of Shechem, and settled 800 Roman veterans at Amasa west of Jerusalem.[5] The main areas which had suffered real damage in the rebellion besides Jerusalem, Joppa and Antipatris, were Narbata, Upper Galilee, Lydda and some parts of the Peraea. The large Jewish population of Caesarea was for the time being annihilated or dispersed, and Jews had been driven out of most of the Greek cities of the Decapolis. The village areas of a number of Greek towns attacked by the Jews at the opening of the rebellion had presumably suffered to some extent, while a number of country estates in Judaea, both Jewish and Gentile, had been plundered and burnt by the Jewish revolutionaries, particularly those led by Simeon bar Giora. The Idumaeans appear to have been wiped out,[6] possibly as an object lesson to would-be proselytes; at any rate they disappear from history as a recognizable unit, and it has been suggested that Idumaea was organized at this time as a military district to prevent the Nabataeans filling the empty region.[7]

With the stationing of the tenth legion at Jerusalem[8] the surrounding area became its commissariat area (*prata legionis*), implying that supplies were levied consistently upon the remaining population, who

---

[1] Head, *Hist. Nummorum* (2nd. ed. 1911), p. 803.
[2] Y. Kaplan (*JQR* LIV (1963), p. 111) found at Jaffa a burnt-out building whose destruction was closely dated to Trajan's time; the finds included three weights stamped with the name of the *agoranomos* Judah in the year 106/7 C.E.
[3] Ulpian, *Dig.* 50, 15, 8, 7.
[4] Pliny, *Natural History* v, 69; *War* IV, 449.
[5] *War* VII, 212.
[6] Cf. *War* IV, 446-8. It is significant that Vespasian celebrated a separate triumph over the Idumaeans (Statius, *Silvae* III, 3, 140-1).
[7] Applebaum, in *Zion* XXVII (1962), pp. 7-8.
[8] *War* VII, 5.

became the tenants of the army, administered by its officers.[1] The results were no doubt hard, but not entirely negative; the legionary command would have been interested in reviving and maintaining the district's productivity. The legionary tilery has been found at Givat Ram on the southwest fringe of Jerusalem,[2] but the administrative centre of the legion, which became the nucleus of a new townlet at Ramat Rahel, probably the ancient Beth Haccerem, did not begin to develop before the third century.[3]

Josephus says that Vespasian, founding no city in Judaea itself, reserved the rural area (χώρα) for himself, and ordered it to be leased out.[4] This policy would have excluded the area assigned to the tenth legion and various tracts allotted to Roman veterans and individual aristocratic Roman beneficiaries who received personal grants of property from the emperor in reward for their support during the civil war of 69. The evidence for these grants is to be found in the rabbinic literature, which contains an interesting contemporary picture of the new agrarian régime as the Jews saw it. The changes are reflected by two phenomena, firstly by the appearance of a new social figure, the *matzik* and secondly, by the new halakic rulings called forth to counter the dangers threatening the Jewish population and its hold on the land. The *matzik* is a new type of landlord, or his agent,[5] who expels the Jewish peasant or converts him forcibly into a tenant, afflicting him with constant and exhorbitant exactions.[6] He has the support of the Roman government,[7] but as in many cases he ultimately abandons his new holding,[8] it must be assumed that he could legally dispose of it, and therefore had received it in full legal proprietorship, that is, in [Roman legal language, *optimo iure*. The *matzikim* are to be found over the entire country, according to the sources;[9] they are chiefly Romans, but certainly included some Jews. The Midrash

---

[1] For the *prata legionum*, see S. Móczy, *Studien zu den Militärgrenzen Roms* (1967), pp. 211ff.

[2] See *Encyclopedia of Excavations* I (1970; in Hebrew), p. 227.

[3] Y. Aharoni et alii, *Excavations at Ramat Rahel*, I-II (1962-4).

[4] *War* VII, 216-7.

[5] For a different interpretation of the term's derivation and significance, M. Gil, in *Revue international des droits de l'antiquité* XVII (1970), pp. 40ff. For other discussions, Klein, *Palästinensische Studien, Beiträge zur Geschichte und Geographie Galiläas* (1923), pp. 28ff.; Applebaum, in *Eretz Israel* VIII (1957), pp. 283-7.

[6] *Sifre Deut.* 317; *Midrash Tannaim* (pp. 193; 223ff.).

[7] *M. Baba Kamma* 10:5; *Midrash Tannaim* (pp. 223-4).

[8] *Midrash Tannaim* (p. 198).

[9] *Sifre Deut.* 357.

tells us who the former were: they were consuls and senators, women of the aristocracy (*matroniot*), high-ranking officers and other military settlers.[1] The more aristocratic of these proprietors were doubtless represented by their procurators and *villici*, but we hear quite independently of a Roman matron who personally held a big estate near Lydda, and inclining to Judaism, dutifully paid Rabbi Eliezer ben Hyrcanus tithes on her land.[2] This sage, however, was a wealthy man, and enjoyed privileged treatment. The *matzikim* appear to have carried out, in the course of their tenures, military intelligence work,[3] and to have behaved with extreme oppressiveness.

The halakot of this period were framed to deal with the new agrarian situation by restricting the conditions on which Jews might acquire the land of Jewish holders surviving or deceased, from whom it had been confiscated under the Roman *Lex Cornelia de sicariis et veneficis*. Such at any rate is the most reasonable interpretation of the so-called *sikarikon* regulations discussed in rabbinic literature relating to conditions between 70 and the later second century. The law concerned was that under which rebels against Roman rule became liable to the death-penalty and to confiscation of property.[4]

Mishnah Gittin (5:6) says succinctly that 'there was no *sikarikon* in Judaea in respect of those killed in the war, [but] from the [second] war onward the *sikarikon* applied to those killed in the war.' Palestinian Talmud Gittin (v, 6) adds: 'In Galilee the *sikarikon* has always applied.' This would seem to mean that a considerable area of confiscated land was being sold up only in Galilee, and that in Judaea, as most land was held by the authorities or by new Gentile settlers, options were left open for any tract that came on the market. To judge by the wording of another passage, however, this situation changed in the second war of 132-5, due to the number of casualties, and an application of the *sikarikon* regulations became imperative.

Thus, while numerous Jewish peasants were forced off the land or compelled to become tenants on their own holdings, other tracts continued to be held as imperial domain (*praedium Caesaris*).[5] Confiscations doubtless applied mainly to sectors which had been directly involved in the rebellion, and other Jewish elements who had favoured

[1] *Midrash Tannaim* (p. 193).
[2] *P. T. Sotah* III, 19a.
[3] *T. Betzah* 2:6.
[4] See Safrai, in *Tarbiz*, XVII (1952), pp. 56ff. (Hebrew). For the Lex Cornelia: *Pauli Sententiae* V, 31, 1.
[5] *T. Demai* 6:2; *M. Demai* 6:2.

Rome or come over to her side at the critical juncture (e.g. Flavius Josephus,[1] Rabbi Johanan ben Zakkai) retained their lands or received new estates. The latter were chiefly the well-to-do, but there were also simpler peasants who were resettled, like those who received new holdings from the Roman commander Placidus in Peraea.[2]

One of the imperial domains was that of Jamnia, originally the property of Livia, wife of Augustus;[3] its cultivators became, as on the crown domains in other Roman provinces, tenants (*coloni*) of Caesar, and the affairs of the estate were handled by his agent, the procurator.[4] Here, and at Lydda, Vespasian resettled a group of loyalist elements,[5] mainly well-to-do, to be under the direct surveillance of authority. On the estate of Jamnia was also located a government granary into which grain levied in taxation was paid.[6] As already stated, (above, p. 676) the Jewish purple-fishers of the Galilean coast seem now to have become tenants of the imperial treasury, and the same occurred with the workers of the opobalsam plantations at Ein Geddi and Beth ha-Ramtah (Livias) in Peraea.[7]

More difficult is the problem of the status of *Har ha-Melek*. As it embraced much of the western Judaean uplands, it is possible that as a Hasmonean term it was synonymous with the Hellenistic term βασιλικὴ χώρα (ie. the royal land outside the city-territories) and also with the χώρα which Vespasian retained in imperial ownership. Part, at any rate, appears to have been restored to Jewish collaborators, in particular to Eleazar ben Harsum, who held extensive estates there.

[1] Jos. *Life* 422.
[2] *War* IV, 438.
[3] *War* II, 167.
[4] *Ant.* XVIII, 158. The normal form of tenure on imperial domain, intensified and reorganized under Vespasian (Rostovtzeff, *Geschichte des römischen Kolonates* (1910), p. 327; A. Schulten, *Die römische Grundherrschaft* (1896), pp. 62ff.), was to lease to *conductores*, or contractors, who collected rent from the *coloni* as their subtenants, each farming a larger estate in the area for which he was responsible. But we have no evidence that such a system operated in Judaea; Alon, indeed, thought the *matzikim* were *conductores* (Alon I, p. 37), an opinion followed by the writer in his article in *Eretz Israel* VIII (1957), pp. 283-7, but generally applied the assumption is unacceptable, because the *matzikim* had free disposal of their land; it is not, however, beyond possibility that some of them were *conductores* of imperial land; imperial legislation records the oppressive behaviour of such men during the second century and later in Africa and Asia Minor; cf. *CIL* VIII, 10570 (Shuq el-Hamis, Africa) etc.
[5] *War* IV, 444.
[6] For a parallel case of a granary as the centre of an imperial estate, *CIL* VIII, 8426 (Ain Zada, Mauretania): 'caput Saltus horreorum.'
[7] *T. B. Shabbath* 26a.

Other tracts here, however, may have been retained by Agrippa II as Herodian royal domain derived from the Hasmonaeans; it is significant that he seems to have held property in central Galilee, outside his kingdom,[1] just as Antipas had held some in Narbatta, within the *Har ha-Melek* itself.[2]

Büchler has studied the Jewish social group at Jabneh and Lydda in this period in some detail.[3] It included many of the sages who became prominent in the course of the later first century, such as Rabbi Johanan ben Zakkai, Rabbi Tarphon, Rabbi Eliezer ben Hyrcanus, Rabbi Eleazar ben Azariah, Rabbi Akiba and Raban Gamaliel II. On the evidence which he reviewed, Büchler concluded that there were no restrictions on the full proprietorship and transfer of lands by Jews in the decades after 70 C.E. It must however be remembered that the majority of the cases cited concern a privileged group of people, most of whom enjoyed abundant means, and nearly all of whom were resident in the immediate vicinity of Lydda and Jabneh. The contemporary rabbinic literature itself reveals a different picture among the broad sections of the rural population of other districts.

The Lydda-Jabneh group's chief economic interest lay in the livelihoods of its members. Rabbi Tarfon owned land and slaves,[4] and received priestly dues from other Jewish landowners in the vicinity of Lydda.[5] Other Jewish landowners here were Rabbi Simeon Shazuri,[6] Rabbi Eleazar ben Azariah, who is reputed to have owned a vast herd of cattle,[7] and to have dealt in wine and oil;[8] Rabbi Ishmael, who held land in Kefar Aziz;[9] Rabbi Eleazar, owner of a vineyard, who also grew flax, olives and dates;[10] Rabban Gamaliel II, who owned land and let it to tenants.[11] Boethus ben Zenon of Lydda imported figs from abroad and lent money.[12]

The last case, indeed, is probably symptomatic, and indicates the

---

[1] Jos. *Life* 126; *T. B. Shabbath* 121a; *T. B. Sukkah* 27a.
[2] Georgius Cedrenus, *Hist. Comp.*, *PG* CXXI, p. 369, 330C.
[3] *The Economic Conditions of Judaea after the Destruction of the Second Temple* (1912), pp. 46-7.
[4] *T. B. Nedarim* 62a.
[5] *T. Ketuboth* 5:1 etc.
[6] *T. Demai* 5:22.
[7] *T. B. Shabbath* 51b.
[8] *T. Abodah Zarah* 4:1.
[9] *M. Kilaim* 6:4.
[10] *T. B. Sanhedrin* 68a.
[11] *M. Baba Metzia* 5:8.
[12] *M. Abodah Zarah* 5:2; *M. Baba Metzia* 5:3 etc.

same trend as that reflected in the activity of Rabbi Eleazar ben Harsum, with his large estates and his fleet of merchant ships.[1] The trend among the leading men of the community was to associate agriculture with overseas trade, possibly in the awareness that Jewish economic dependence and poverty could only be reduced by strengthening the country's commercial ties with the provinces. In the future, the commercial and industrial element among the Jews of the country was to grow, along with their increasing concentration in the maritime towns.

Undoubtedly the destruction of Jerusalem dealt a shattering blow to the Jewish economy, eliminating the principal hub of Jewish commerce and crafts and the community's largest source of internal and external income. The livelihoods derived from supplying the products required for sacrifices and the numerous Temple requisites were lost; also the income received from the vast public which had flowed yearly to the capital. The economic basis of a large hierarchy had vanished, and with it the regular contributions and dues furnished by the Diaspora; these were now diverted to Rome and the burden, vastly increased, fell on Judaea and Diaspora Jewry equally.

The remaining population was afflicted by loss of land and the ravaging of its villages and townlets, while a series of drought years and increased taxation exacerbated the existent poverty. On the taxes little need be added to the information furnished elsewhere.[2] The *tributum capitis* appears to have been increased,[3] and to this was added the augmented Jewish tax of Vespasian. When Rabbi Johanan ben Zakkai cited the payment of fifteen shekels i.e. 60 denarii,[4] as a punishment for neglect of Temple dues before 70, he may have been summing up the approximate average total sum paid yearly by the contemporary Jew of Palestine.[5] Nor should it be forgotten that the

---

[1] *T. B. Yoma* 35b.

[2] Chapter six, p. 335.

[3] So, at least, it seems Appian, *Syriaca* 50 (viii) is to be interpreted: having referred to the capture of Jerusalem by Ptolemy Lagos, Vespasian, and Hadrian, Appian continues by saying that the Jews paid a heavier φόρος τῶν σωμάτων than the surrounding region διὰ ταῦτα. This suggests that a progressive increase of the tax took place after each of the above three events.

[4] *Mekhilta, Behodesh* 1 (pp. 203-4).

[5] Sixty drachmae was the average sum paid in taxes out of an income of 210-80 drachmae by the Egyptian peasant in the late first century c.e. according to A. C. Johnson, in *Economic Survey of Ancient Rome* II (1936), Egypt, p. 304. This was the equivalent of 15 denarii outside Egypt. (Cf. *ibid.*, p. 532). This would mean that if Rabbi Johanan's figure approximated to the truth, the Jews in contemporary Judaea paid four times as much.

voluntary payment of priestly dues was continued, at least by those whose faith was unimpaired by their unenviable situation.[1]

The shocking poverty resulting from these circumstances is well documented. It is sufficient to repeat the story of a contemporary sage who was riding on a donkey with provisions, when he was accosted by a Jew who begged him for food. He dismounted to unload his beast, but the man had died before he could do so.[2] Well known too are the contemporary disputes among sages as to whether the obligation existed to rear orphans or even young girls.[3]

Some notions of food-prices in this period can be derived from the scales of income[4] which, in the view of Rabbi Eleazar ben Azariah, permitted a man to add meat to his meals; according to him, only a yearly income of 10,000 denarii justified eating meat every day, and this situation was hardly mitigated by the effect on prices of the flood of gold released by the plundering of the Temple. One can understand the recurrent emergence of groups of outlaws and bandits which was one of the factors leading ultimately to Bar Cochba's rising in the reign of Hadrian.

If the economic situation in Judaea after the war of 70 is grasped, therefore, it will be seen as one of the elements that contributed to the outbreak of the last desperate revolt of 132.

BIBLIOGRAPHY

The most important comprehensive works written on the Jewish economy of the Second Temple and talmudic periods as a whole are: L. HERZFELD, *Handelsgeschichte der Juden des Altertums*, 2nd ed. 1894; S. KRAUSS, *Talmudische Archäologie* I-III (1910-1912), esp. II, pp. 248ff; F. HEICHELHEIM, in *An Economic Survey of the Roman Empire* ed. by T. Frank, IV (1938), pp. 123ff.: Roman Syria (for corrigenda see D. SPERBER, *Roman Palestine 200-400, Money and Prices* (1974), pp. 18-9; id. in *Journal of Economic and Social History of the Orient* VIII (1965), pp. 248-9); A. BEN DAVID, *Talmudische Ökonomie* I (1974). To the latter the writer owes a special debt; his disagreements with some of Ben David's conclusions in no way detract from his appreciation of this very useful work. None of the above mentioned studies differen-

---

[1] *M. Shekalim* 8:8.
[2] *T. B. Taanith* 21a.
[3] *M. Ketuboth* 4:6.
[4] *T. Arakhin* 4: 27.

tiates sufficiently between the various periods reflected in talmudic literature. J. KLAUSNER has a very useful survey in *The Second Temple in the Days of its Greatness* (1930; in Hebrew), pp. 42ff. (English translation in *The World History of the Jewish People* VII: *The Herodian Period*, 1975, chapter V, pp. 180ff.), which however is written on the assumption that most of the mishnaic evidence is applicable equally to the pre-70 epoch. Important information will also be found in M. AVI-YONAH, *Essays and Studies in the Lore of the Holy Land* (1964), esp. section 3, pp. 97-196, containing chapters on aspects of the Jewish economy in the Greek and Roman periods. Interesting observations are embodied in F. HEICHELHEIM, *Wirtschaftsgeschichte des Altertums*, 3 vols., 1938 (The English translation of this work should be avoided). H. KREISSIG, *Die sozialen Zusammenhänge des jüdäischen Krieges*, 1970, an economic study written from a communist point of view, though an incredibly ill-natured book that from time to time abuses the evidence, is nevertheless a very useful accumulation of sources and examines the subject in greater detail than any previous work. A valuable short account of the economic position in Judaea after 70 is to be found in G. ALON, *History of the Jews of Eretz Israel in the Period of the Mishnah and the Talmud* (1950; in Hebrew) I, chapters 1-2. J. FELICKS, *The Agriculture of Eretz Israel in the Period of the Mishnah and the Talmud* (1963) is a profound study of the cereals branch of that economy. General works on the ancient economy which formed the setting of the present theme are: M. FINLEY, *The Ancient Economy* (1972); M. ROSTOVTZEFF, *Social and Economic History of the Hellenistic World*, 3 vols. (1941).

Chapter Thirteen
The Social and Economic Status of the Jews in the Diaspora

Manifold as are the difficulties encountered in attempting to survey the economic life of the Jews in Palestine in the first century C.E., an account of the economic activities of Diaspora Jewry in the same period faces even acuter problems. The ample ancient rabbinic material that assists an understanding of the subject with regard to Judaea also contains information on Babylonia, but the data furnished by the Babylonian Talmud are almost entirely confined to the third and following centuries; The Mishnah and Tosefta contain only occasional evidence bearing directly or indirectly on the Diaspora. Other ancient sources, whether Jewish or Gentile, rarely cast light on the Jewish Diaspora before the third century and information becomes fuller for the fourth century. No complete picture can be drawn of the earlier period, and to project backwards from the fourth century in the Roman empire or from the third century in Babylonia and its neighbouring lands is methodologically dangerous. The destruction of Jerusalem in 70 C.E. certainly affected the other, chiefly Mediterranean, provinces of the empire, in so far as it discharged and dispersed into several of them and into Italy thousands of Jewish refugees and prisoners of war, whose presence, besides giving rise to some new Jewish settlements, created a new Jewish social stratum or reinforced one that already existed, and also imposed a certain financial burden upon existing Diaspora communities that felt duty-bound to redeem Jewish slaves. Manumission of these also had the effect of limiting the freedom of the first generation of freedmen and of confining most of them to the lower occupational grades.

Within the Roman empire a drastic change in the Jewish economic position took place under Trajan in Egypt, Cyrenaica and Cyprus, and repercussions of this upheaval may also have been felt in Syria. Trajan's invasion of Mesopotamia and Babylonia, moreover, caused the Jewish communities there considerable losses and can hardly have left their economies unscathed. How far, therefore, the occupational pattern that emerges in the Babylonian Talmud reflects the first century distribution, is a question to which no comprehensive answer can be given. Nor can we follow the method of Herzfeld, who, having established the branches of trade in a given land of the Diaspora in ancient times, and the contemporary presence of Jewish communities there, assumes, with the occasional assistance of the somewhat meagre Jewish evidence, that these were the branches in which Jews engaged. All that can be said is, that in those countries which did not suffer the direct shocks of 70 or 115,—and whose Jewish populations were large and established for centuries (this applies particularly to Asia Minor and Syria), the main lines of the Jewish economy no doubt remained relatively stable throughout the first two centuries C.E. The third century, and more particularly its second half, witnessed important economic and social changes in the Roman empire, into which it is unwise to trespass when evidence is sought relating to the first century. The Jewish economy of the Hellenistic and Roman periods is best known in *Egypt*, thanks to the papyri, which are supplemented by some written sources and by inscriptions and ostraka. The available evidence shows that while the general occupational distribution of Egyptian Jewry did not alter with the Roman conquest (31 B.C.E.)., Roman rule nevertheless wrought certain changes in the Jewish economy, and this constitutes a warning to those who are content to read from earlier to later periods in this context. Under Ptolemaic rule Jews served in some numbers in the armed forces, being found as cleruchs or *katoikoi* in rural districts;[1] from the mid-second century B.C.E. in several cases they constituted their own military units, concentrated in areas of blok-settlement (e.g. Leontopolis, Pelusium, and perhaps elsewhere).[2] They also composed, at some period, a unit of the garrison of Alexandria.[3] They further served in the police. Jews took their share in government service, among them being, besides high-ranking commanders and other officers such as district governors, tax-collectors, tax-farmers, managers of governmental storehouses and banks.[4] These, however, were a minority; Jews were numerous in agriculture, whether as landowners, tenants or labourers. Many were tenants on royal land. Among the military settlers, they included various ranks and the areas of their holdings varied accordingly. The

---

[1] *CPJ* I, pp. 12-13; Lesquier, *Les institutions militaires de l'Egypte sous les Lagides* (1911); M. Launey, *Recherches sur les armées hellénistiques* (1949-50).
[2] Tcherikover, p. 39.
[3] *CPJ* I, pp. 14-15.
[4] Ibid., pp. 17ff.

military settlers as a class were mostly prosperous and privileged landowners. There were also Jewish shepherds and herdsmen.[1]

On the other hand there is little evidence for Jewish commerce in the pre-Roman period, and it may be assumed that much of what there was, was concentrated in Alexandria; some Jews may have been shipmasters carrying grain down the Nile according to a document of the first century B.C.E.[2] We have instances of petty trade and the advancing of small personal loans among Jewish soldiers and civilians.[3] Nor are many allusions to Jewish craftsmen to be found in Ptolemaic sources. Nevertheless, the guilds of Jewish craftsmen listed by Tosefta Sukkah and its parallels,[4] as holding places in the Great Synagogue of Alexandria, and including linen-weavers, gold and silversmiths, blacksmiths and wooldressers, certainly existed under Ptolemaic rule.[5] Papyri mention individual weavers, tanners, a dyer and a fluteplayer,[6] and Philo speaks of Jewish workshops (ἐργαστήρια) in Alexandria.[7] Talmudic literature refers to bronzeworkers, bakers and incense makers who were sent to Jerusalem to replace the traditional employees of these branches in the Temple.[8] One or two Jewish slaves are recorded in the third century B.C.E., when they would have been numerous.[9] Other recorded occupations in the pre-Roman epoch are those of horsedealer,[10] a building worker or contractor,[11] and (probably) a prostitute.[12] The intelligentsia are curiously absent from the papyri, but several authors are known, whose works have survived.[13] A general conclusion emerging from the surviving records is that the

[1] Ibid., pp. 15, 16, 26, 43, 54; and especially Pap. no. 28, p. 171.
[2] Tcherikover, p. 65.
[3] E.g. *CPJ* II, Section vii.
[4] *T. Sukkah* 4:6; *T. B. Sukkah* 51b; *P. T. Sukkah* v, 55a.
[5] It may be recalled that the Roman government did not favour craft-organizations of this type, hence the formation of these Jewish guilds of Alexandria may be assumed to have taken place in pre-Roman times. It may be that these bodies were deliberately incorporated into the synagogue framework in order to avoid suppression by the authorities; as religious societies they could claim the privileges accorded to the Jewish organizations by Julius Caesar (Suetonius, *Aug.* 32; Jos. *Ant.* XIV, 215). For a synagogue of linenweavers at Jerusalem, see *T. B. Megillah* 26a.
[6] *CPJ* I, p. 17.
[7] *In Flaccum* 56.
[8] *T. Yoma* 1:5-6; *T. B. Yoma* 38a; *T. B. Arakhin* 10b.
[9] *Letter of Aristeas* 12-14.
[10] Tcherikover, p. 70.
[11] *CPJ* I, no. 10, p. 136.
[12] CPJ III, no. 1429, p. 139.
[13] See generally *Schürer* III, pp. 420ff.; Y. Guttman, *Jewish Hellenistic Literature* 2 vols. (1958-1963; in Hebrew).

economic and occupational structure of Egyptian Jewry under the Ptolemies was normal to the extent that they were represented in all callings, well represented on the land, in the armed forces and in the government services. There is no evidence of the 'inverted occupational pyramid' that has characterized Diaspora Jewry for so long a period in various countries, more particularly in mediaeval and modern times.

This same normality of structure, so far as the evidence goes, continued in the Roman period, but some changes may nevertheless be noted. The later second and first centuries B.C.E. in Egypt were an era of internal political and social conflict, and of social change. Having lost much influence abroad, and being therefore forced to increase taxation at home, and facing a resurgent Egyptian nationalism, the monarchy came under new pressures; the Egyptian clergy and the Greek middle class demanded greater freedom of economic activity, the Egyptian peasantry rights and concessions. Greek Alexandria became hostile to the royal house.[1] With this worsening situation, and with the growth of a freer economy within the previous étatistic framework, came a tendency to eliminate the most prominent section of the population that could be regarded as an alien element, the Jews.[2] This attitude was not modified by the fact that the Lagids, in their growing isolation, tended in the later second century B.C.E. to lean upon the Jews militarily and politically,[3] and by the contemporary assertion in Judaea of Jewish national and religious independence, which involved a long struggle against the Greek cities of the country and the ultimate destruction or subjection of most of them.

Thus under Roman rule, which began in Egypt after the battle of Actium in 31 B.C.E., some modifications can be observed in Jewish occupational structure.[4] The Roman government restored free economic enterprise, but maintained the existing oppressive range of taxation, and much of the Ptolemaic bureaucratic administration, with the difference that many functions previously discharged by a paid officialdom became obligatory upon private citizens, to be performed as unremunerated duties at their own expense.[5] With a few exceptions, Jews virtually disappeared from the civil service

[1] M. Rostovtzeff, *Social and Economic History of the Hellenistic World* (1941), pp. 711-918.
[2] S. Applebaum, in *Tarbiz* (1959), pp. 420-1.
[3] V. Tcherikover, *Hellenistic Civilization and the Jews* (1959), pp. 280-2.
[4] *CPJ* I, pp. 52-3.
[5] Milne, 'The Ruin of Egypt by Roman Mismanagement,' in *JRS* (1927), pp. 1ff.

(which might be taken as an indication that the affluent element amongst them was not numerous); Tiberius Julius Alexander, who served as *strategos* of a nome and ultimately rose to be prefect of Egypt, was, if not actually a renegade, at least a studious neglecter of Judaism.[1] The nature of the distinguished post of Alabarch, filled by at least two members of Philo's family, is obscure. All that can be said is that it was a rich man's function in the municipal administration of Alexandria. It is generally thought to have been the control of customs, perhaps on the Nile.[2] The Jewish garrison-settlers and military cultivators became civilians, losing their privileged military status, and their holdings were now regarded as private property. The military district of Leontopolis was presumably liquidated with its temple in the year 73 C.E. A solitary Jewish centurion, Aninios, is known to have been serving in the Roman army in the year 116 C.E.[3] It is not clear how far Egyptian Jews continued their service in the police; Josephus attributed to them the guard on the Nile.[4]

Two important changes took place, therefore, in relation to the Jews of Egypt. They were eliminated as a military factor and ceased to be an appreciable element in the government service. Whether their position deteriorated in other branches is difficult to say. Most of them were subject to heavier taxation than the Greeks, who remained a privileged section.[5] By and large Jews are still found in most branches of the economy; they continued numerous in agriculture, whether as labourers, tenants, landowners or shepherds, also in transport, being found as boatowners on the Nile.[6] The Alexandrian craftsmen's guilds are referred to by the Tosefta (above) in the Roman period, and Philo too alludes to the city's Jewish artisans.[7] More problematic is the degree of Jewish participation in commerce. The

---

[1] τοῖς γὰρ πατρίοις οὐκ ἐνέμεινεν οὗτος ἔθεσιν (*Ant.* XX, 100).

[2] Cf. Strabo XVII, 800; for literature on the subject till 1909, *Schürer* III, pp. 132ff.; till 1957, *CPJ* I, p. 49, n. 4.

[3] *CPJ* II, no. 229.

[4] *Against Apion* II, 64. The canals leading to Lake Mareotis, Alexandria's inland port, from the south and east, were guarded by various customs posts (*phylakai*) under the Ptolemies. See P. M. Fraser, *Ptolemaic Alexandria* (1972) I, p. 144. Possibly Josephus was referring to the manning of these points. Near one of them, Schedia, a Jewish settlement had existed at an earlier period (*OGIS* 726).

[5] *CPJ* I, pp. 60-2.

[6] Ibid., pp. 48-55.

[7] The discovery, probably otherwise unrecorded, of an Alexandrian Jewish workshop turning out figurines and lamps, is reported in the Haifa Municipal Museum's *Handbook of the Collection of Ancient Art* (1959), p. 35; cf. *Tarbiz* (1959), p. 419.

very wealthy Jewish group in Alexandria is represented by the family of the alabarchs, to which belonged Demetrius, Alexander, Marcus and Tiberius Julius Alexander.[1] The source of their great wealth can only be conjectured, but it cannot have lain in the levying of customs, which under the Ptolemies was closely controlled by the government and allowed the taxfarmers little profit. But the fact that Alexander could lend Agrippa I a considerable sum and make half of it payable on presentation of a letter of credit at Puteoli,[2] can only be interpreted to mean that one of the family's sources of income was commerce. Alexandria's close trade connections with Puteoli dated from the end of the Second Punic War (201 B.C.E.), and continued under Roman rule; through this port passed the bulk of Alexandria's exports to Italy.[3] The Jewish merchant group of Alexandria is referred to by Philo when he mentions Jewish businessmen and shipowners;[4] his ἔμποροι were probably merchants who travelled in other men's vessels. Some of these businessmen were in partnership with Gentiles.[5]

In the second half of the second century B.C.E. the loose organization of the Levantine merchants trading with Rome was replaced by a more closely-knit structure, in which the 'factories' (οἶκοι, stationes) of merchants from the various eastern ports (Alexandria, Tyre, Berytus, etc.) were an important feature. Such institutions are found at Delos, Puteoli, Perinthos, Tomi and elsewhere. After the battle of Pydna (167 B.C.E.), importance shifted from Rhodes, with which Alexandria had close commercial ties, to Delos, and simultaneously, within the new political framework, Alexandria's primary rôle in Mediterranean commerce was consolidated.[6] It is now that Jews, and what was probably their synagogue, are found at Delos[7] and it is to be concluded that Alexandrian Jews were now party to the maritime trade based on the Alexandria-Delos-Puteoli triangle.

How far the Jewish merchant group was involved in the Egyptian grain trade cannot be determined; despite Josephus, who ascribes to

[1] *Ant.* XVIII, 159; 259; XIX, 276; XX, 100; 147.
[2] *Ant.* XVIII, 160.
[3] Cf. Strabo XVII, 793, par. 7; Fraser, op.cit. I, p. 156.
[4] *In Flaccum* 57; cf. *M. Kelim* 15:1 for the measurements of a flatbottomed Egyptian vessel (a lighter), which must have been used for cargo either on the Nile or in harbour.
[5] 3 Macc. 3: 10.
[6] Fraser, *op.cit.* I, p. 186.
[7] E. Goodenough, *Jewish Symbols in the Greek and Roman Period* I (1954), pp. 71ff. The Jewish identity of the building and its inscriptions is disputed; the pro and con are equally balanced.

Jews a share in the *administratio tritici*,[1] and the views of some modern scholars,[2] there is no confirmation from papyri that the Jews possessed any special influence in this branch. On the other hand it is reasonable to assume that the wealthy group also engaged in banking activities. Here too, exaggerations must be avoided: in a list of Egyptian bankers of the Roman period, no identifiable Jews appear.[3] Needless to say, papyrology records various small loans advanced by individual Jews to other Jews in the course of everyday life throughout the country, but these have little bearing on the general economic structure of the community. Small loans were in demand among the poorer Jewish stratum in Alexandria, among which wet-nurses, a freed slave and a servant girl are recorded;[4] the same stratum doubtless included also petty traders, labourers, porters, beggars and all the other components of the bazaar proletariat.

The intelligentsia had their own stratification. Philo Judaeus, philosopher, apologist and statesman, belonged to the uppermost aristocracy; Dorotheus, son of Cleopatrides of Alexandria, who pleaded the cause of the Jews of Asia,[5] probably came from a well-to-do milieu. The Boethids and Ishmael ben Phiabi who held the high priesthood in Jerusalem under the Herods and the procurators, were of Egyptian origin and doubtless derived from affluent families.[6] The Jewish community councils and organizations, especially in Alexandria, would have concentrated public workers and lesser paid functionaries from several classes, and their scholars and judges doubtless were drawn from no one social stratum. At the other end of the scale, probably, stood the Egyptian prophet whose messianic zealot activities in Judaea are reported by Josephus and the Book of Acts.[7]

The economic position of Egyptian Jewry as a whole would have been affected by the new conditions of Roman rule. They now paid the *laographia* or poll-tax from which the Greeks were exempted or which, in the *metropoleis* of the nomes, they paid on a reduced scale.[8] Rome

---

[1] *Against Apion* II, 64.
[2] E.g. Milne, *loc.cit.*, p. 6.
[3] Calderini, in *Aegyptus* (1938), pp. 244-78.
[4] *CPJ* II, nos. 146-9.
[5] *Ant.* XIV, 236.
[6] See chapter five, p. 274.
[7] *War* II, 261-3; Acts 21:38; cf. Eusebius, *Ecclesiastical History* II, 21.
[8] It has now been argued, however, that some Jews resident in the *metropoleis* also paid on this reduced scale, according to the evidence of tax-receipts (A. Kasher, in an unpublished doctoral thesis, *The Civic Status of the Jews in Egypt and their Rights in the Hellenistic and the Roman Period*, Tel Aviv University,

restored order and rebuilt the irrigation system, but the province was looked upon by the emperors as their personal estate and treated accordingly. Its main product, grain, was an unpaid export directed preponderantly to feed Rome.[1] Its other exports suffered from the deliberate undervaluing of the Egyptian drachma, which was worth a quarter of the corresponding issues circulating outside the province.[2] The upper and middle classes struggled under the increasing governmental and municipal duties thrust upon them without remuneration by the authorities. Before the end of the first century C.E., according to Milne, the Egyptian middle class had been completely impoverished.[3] As to the peasantry, under continued gruelling taxation the average fellah's annual income was a quarter of the lowest income classified in the Mishnah as above the charity line;[4] the abandonment of Egyptian villages by their peasantry, so common in the critical times of later Ptolemaic rule, had begun again before the end of the first century C.E. The Jews, clearly, suffered from this oppressive situation like the non-Jews; from 73 they discharged in addition the notorious Jewish tax. Greek anti-Semitism, incipient under the later Ptolemies,[5] was exacerbated under Rome by the humiliation of servitude;[6] it was intensified by the events of 66-70 C.E., but owed little to them, as the pogroms of 38 C.E. in Alexandria showed. That it was not confined to that city is made clear by the bloody conflict of 115-117.

No vast body of papyrological evidence exists to illumine the economic position of *Cyrenaican Jewry* in the first century C.E., but careful enquiry yields some information. This considerable community had originated with the settlement of Jews as supporters of Ptolemaic rule in and round the five cities of the country by Ptolemy Lagos;[7] it is safe to assume that these were groups of cleruchs, and the language of the sources makes it plain that they lived both in the towns and

---

1972, Chap. iii, pp. 84ff.). If this is correct, it would imply *a fortiori* that the well-to-do section of Alexandrian Jews also received this reduction—for what it was worth.

[1] Milne, *loc.cit.*, p. 6.
[2] A. C. Johnson, in *Economic Survey of Ancient Rome*, ed. by T. Frank, II (1936), p. 433.
[3] Milne, *loc.cit.*, p. 7.
[4] *M. Peah* 8:8.
[5] Cf. the literature typified by Manetho; the year 88 B.C.E. may have witnessed anti-Semitic repercussions in Alexandria. The evidence is disputed, I think erroneously, by I. Lévy, in *HUCA* (1950-1), pp. 127ff.; cf. *CPJ* I, p. 25, n. 63.
[6] No psychological situation breeds a stronger anti-Semitic potential than loss of status.
[7] *Against Apion* II, 44.

throughout the countryside.[1] The presence of Jews in the rural areas is independently attested both by literature[2] and by archaeology.[3] On the other hand the provisions of the timocratic constitution of Cyrene dictated by Ptolemy Lagos at the end of the fourth century,[4] are strongly in favour of the upper income groups, revealing a pronouncedly conservative prejudice against craftsmen, traders, and other nonlandholding elements.[5] Clearly the Jewish settlers would not easily have obtained Cyrenean citizenship, or the right to acquire land in the city's territory. This being so, their holdings would have been predominantly on those lands which came under the control of Ptolemy, and were converted to *ager publicus* when taken over by Rome in the year 96 B.C.E.[6] We learn from Tacitus that many of the holdings in these areas had become vacant and had fallen into the illegal possession of Cyrenean citizens by Nero's time,[7] a process probably initiated by the indiscriminate grazing of the *ager publicus* by the Roman *publicani*.[8]

Something is indirectly known of the standard of living of the Teucheira Jewish community thanks to its epitaphs,[9] which belong chiefly to the first centuries B.C.E. and C.E. These indicate that their Greek literacy, if existent, was elementary, though their superficial Hellenization, to judge from their names, was considerable. This did not however apply to a small group of families whose sons are found as members of the city's *ephebeia*. The Jewish families, in so far as they can be reconstructed, were limited to three children, and only in two cases can we trace more. Their mortality up to the age of twenty was forty per cent. Under Rome some of them were Roman citizens, probably

---

[1] Chapter eight, p. 425 and n. 6; Applebaum, *Jews and Greeks*, p. 170.
[2] Severus of Ashmunein, *The Coptic Lives of the Patriarchs of Alexandria*, cited by Goodchild, *Kyrene und Apollonia* (1971), p. 33, n. 33.
[3] Jewish inscriptions at al-Bagga, (Applebaum, *Jews and Greeks*, p. 171), Jewish agricultural settlements at Ain Targhuna (ibid., p. 197), Kapparodis (see chapter eight, p. 426), Iscina Locus Augusti Iudaeorum (see below), and probably at Topos Magdalis (Ptol. IV, 5); the general character of the Jews of Teucheira as evidenced by the Jewish tombs there (see below), and the absence of evidence that Teucheira performed any commercial function, pointing to its predominantly agricultural character (Applebaum, 'The Jewish Community', p. 47).
[4] *SEG* IX, 1.
[5] Applebaum, *Jews and Greeks*, pp. 44-55.
[6] Livy, *Epit.* LXXXI; Tacitus, *Annales* XIV, 18.
[7] *Annales loc.cit.*
[8] Pliny, *Natural History* XIX, 3, 15.
[9] Applebaum, 'The Jewish Community'. Some of the deductions made here have now been modified by subsequent readings of epitaphs, but the general conclusions hold good.

freedmen; one or two slaves can be identified. A few Libyan proselytes are also traceable. A section of the community certainly hailed from Egypt, and probably most of its members were descended from the second wave of Jewish emigration from Egypt after the reunion of Cyrene and Egypt in the mid-second century. The economic character of Teucheira, which seems to have been overwhelmingly agricultural, would make most of the community labourers or tenants, and an element of military settlers seems probable.

The admission of small groups of Jews to the ephebates of Cyrene, Teucheira and Ptolemais in the last decade of the first century B.C.E.[1] suggests that there were now well-to-do Jews who owned land in these cities, and such proprietorship would have been the outstanding qualification for the citizenship to which the gymnasium education furnished access. Josephus gives the number of 3,000 for the wealthy Cyrenean Jews executed in 73 C.E. by the proconsul Catullus, after their property had been confiscated to the treasury.[2] It is not clear whether this figure refers to Cyrene alone or to all five cities of the territory, and in any case it should be treated with caution. At the other end of the social ladder were the 2,000 indigent Jews of Cyrene recorded by Josephus to have followed the Sicarian Jonathan the Weaver into the desert in 73;[3] they were perhaps the second generation of the agricultural proletariat created by the expropriation of the Jewish settlers of the *ager publicus*.

Whatever the case, the source of the wealth of the upper Jewish group in Cyrenaica is quite obscure, and not enough is known of the country's economy in this period.[4] The Pentapolis is not thought to have participated directly in the Sahara caravan traffic, and if silphium was still exported under the Empire,[5] it was almost certainly state property.[6] There is one possible hint: Jonathan the Weaver's possible clash with the wealthy Cyrenean Jew Alexander[7] perhaps originated in a labour dispute, in which case the latter would have been the owner of a

---

[1] See chapter eight, pp. 446-7; *SEG* IX, 424, 439, 441; *CII* I, 556.

[2] *Ant.* VII, 445. Josephus writes that Catullus thought he could execute these Jews with impunity because he had confiscated their property for the treasury. Vespasian had in fact been *quaestor* (treasury representative) in Cyrene (Suetonius, *Vespasian* 2, 3) in his early career. Possible implications are sinister (cf. Suetonius, *loc.cit.* 16).

[3] *Life* 424.

[4] For discussion of the problem, Applebaum, *Jews and Greeks*, pp. 38-41.

[5] See W. Capelle, in *Rheinisches Museum* (1954), pp. 185ff.

[6] Cf. Pliny, *Natural History* XIX, 3, 15 (140).

[7] *War* VII, 445.

weaving mill. Cyrenean wool was reputed, and almost certainly exported.[1] Cyrene also produced a considerable quantity of olive oil in the ancient period,[2] and Jewish participation in this branch is conceivable, but entirely conjectural. Equally possible and unproven is Jewish participation in the production of the country's renowned perfumes,[3] as their manufacture had long been a traditional Jewish occupation elsewhere.[4] Among the lower income-groups of the Jewish community, besides the farmers, we have evidence of a slave-woman of the imperial household, of another who was in the service of *publicani*,[5] a stonecutter,[6] makers of clay lamps[7] and a painter of human and animal figures.[8] Indirect evidence evokes the possibility also of the presence of Jewish seamen[9] and mint-workers.[10]

Cyprus already had a sizable Jewish population in 140 B.C.E.,[11] and it must have been considerable under Trajan, to judge by the explosion of 115 C.E. Our information on its economic basis is negligible. The marriage of Timios, a Jew of the island, to Alexandra, daughter of Phasael, Herod's brother,[12] shows that the community included families of wealth with wide contacts. On the sources of this wealth history is silent, and all that can be said is that Cyprus was admirably situated for commerce between Asia Minor, Syria, Judaea and Greece.

[1] Cf. the Arkesilas kylix: Lane, in *Annual of the British School of Athens* XXIV (1933-1934), pp. 161-2; Homer, *Odysse* IV, 85-9; Herodotus IV, 155; Pindar, *Pyth.* 9, 6; Arrian, *Ind.* 43, 13; *Anab.* III, 28, 7; Pliny, *Natural History* XIX, 5 (43); O. Bates, *The Eastern Libyans* (1914), pp. 91-100.

[2] Theophrastus, *Causa plantarum* IV, 3; Diodorus III, 49; Scylax 110; numerous oil-presses in the central and eastern Jebel; the large cistern enclosure attached to the east wall of Cyrene is thought by some archaeologists to have been for the storage of olive oil. Cf. *SEG* IX, 4, lines 43-6. Olives and olive oil are regularly listed in the Demiurgi steles; see *Documenti antichi dell'Africa Italiana* I, *Cirene*. ii, 1933 (V-II centuries B.C.E.) which list the produce and revenues of the temple estates of Cyrene.

[3] Theophrastus, *Causae plantarum* VI, 1; 6; 18; Pliny, *Natural History* XXI, 6; Athenaeus XV, 29; Dioscorides I, 5 etc.

[4] Cf. e.g. *CII* II, 790-2; 1098.

[5] Pacho, *Relation du voyage en Marmarique* (1827-9), pl. lxxv; L. Robert, in *REG* (1969), p. 536, n. 618.

[6] *CIG* III, 5176 (89-99 C.E.): *IEJ* (1944), p. 10, (1955), p. 216.

[7] Wright, in *PEQ* 1963, pp. 28ff. (Teucheira); cf. *IEJ* (1957), pp. 154ff.; S. Stucchi, *Cirene 1957-1966* (1967), p. 163; *L'agora di Cirene* (1965), I, p. 277, pl. xlv, 5b.

[8] *REG* (1949), pp. 290ff. (Benghazi).

[9] Cf. Synesius, *Ep.* 4.

[10] E. S. Robinson, *British Museum Catalogue Greek Coins: Cyrenaica* (1927) p. clxi.

[11] I Macc. 15:23.

[12] *Ant.* XVIII, 131.

The illegal running in of 'pilgrims' to the Jerusalem Temple via Ptolemais and Antioch at the end of Trajan's reign or at the beginning of Hadrian's, as recorded in talmudic tradition,[1] seems to point to Cyprus as the place of origin of many of these 'illegals'—there is no evidence of contemporary ferment in Asia Minor; the episode would therefore testify to the existence of a Jewish sea-faring element on the island.

Jews seem to have lived over most of Cyprus, and not only in the larger towns; so much is indicated by evidence of a synagogue at Golgoi (Athenaiou)[2] and by possible epigraphic evidence at Lapethos and Carpasia of destruction in the rebellion of 115-117.[3] The building of a Roman fort at Knodara, between Salamis and Leucosia, during those disorders,[4] points in the same direction.[5] We may also note dedications to *Theos Hypsistos*, the fruit of Jewish influence, at several places in the island.[6] Whether there was a Jewish community at Soli, where Herod leased the copper mines from the Roman treasury, is questionable; a statue of Zeus was, however, restored here in 116-117,[7] and Herod may have worked with Jewish slaves,[8] but the overseers are more likely to have been Greeks.

Jewish settlement in *Syria* was very ancient, and would have been augmented by further immigration with the Seleucid conquest of Judaea shortly after 200 B.C.E. There can be little doubt that a very high proportion of this Jewish population was engaged in agriculture, as is indicated not only by numerous halakic rulings relating to Jewish cultivation in Syria,[9] but also by the very large number of place names recorded or still surviving which evidence the one-time existence of Jewish villages.[10] Prominent among these is a group

[1] *Gen. Rabba* 64 (p. 710).
[2] *REJ* (1911), pp. 285ff.; the renewal of the community is here recorded (fourth cent.), implying prior existence before 115.
[3] *IGR* III, 934; *AJA* (1961), p. 123, no. 25 (discussion, in *JJS* (1962), pp. 41-2).
[4] *CIL* III, (1), 215.
[5] Cf. further an inscription with the name Σαμβαι at Tremithos, west of Salamis: *SEG* XX, 128, dated 81 or 88 C.E.
[6] *SEG* XXV (1971), 1089 (Limassol); Mitford, *Inscriptions of Kourion* (1971) nos. 71, 160, 161.
[7] *Opuscula Archaeologica* VI (1950), p. 32. no. 16.
[8] These would not, however, have been the Jews of Herod's kingdom condemned for crime and sold by him abroad (*Ant.* XVI, 1-5), as Jewish slaves used to work at Soli would have been retained by him.
[9] E.g. *M. Hallah* 4:7; 11 (Jewish cultivation near Apamea); *T. Peah*; *M. Shabbath* 6:1-2.
[10] Luria, p. 10ff.

testifying by their names to the former presence of Babylonians.[1] The colonization in Syria of Jews as military settlers at such places as Zarephat (between Tyre and Sidon) is recorded by the Prophet Obadiah (vs. 20), possibly shortly after the annexation of Judaea by Antiochus III. The mortgaging of land to Jews by Gentiles in Syria is recorded in the Tosefta,[2] and Jewish tenants are also mentioned.[3] Reference to various types of tenures on Jewish land suggests that some Jews held large estates.[4] Although some of the rabbinical evidence of Mishnah and Talmud concerning Jewish cultivation in Syria is probably post-70 and even second century, there can be little doubt that the Jewish rural population had been well-established and considerable before 70 C.E.

The Seleucid military settler element would not have survived the Roman conquest as a distinguishable military factor, and without doubt became demilitarized, but this did not apply to the regions of Bashan and Hauran, which remained, except for short periods, under Herodian rule till late in the first century C.E. The Babylonian and Idumaean troops planted here by Herod[5] engaged in agriculture, the Babylonian villages and their cattle being referred to by Josephus,[6] and cattle-rearing was certainly one of their main sources of livelihood.[7] Their precise relation to the *Benei Bathyra*, an important halakic school, settled in Jerusalem,[8] is disputed, but R. Judah ben Bathyra, the first of the name, was settled at Nisibis and had close contacts with the Temple;[9] moreover, we are explicitly told that the Zamarid military settlers of Bashan, among their other duties, patrolled the western sectors of the pilgrim route from Babylon to Judaea.[10] The Zamarid mounted archers and the Idumaeans constituted the main nucleus of what had become by the end of the first century C.E. a considerable force under the command of Agrippa II.[11]

---

[1] Ibid., p. 58; cf. *M. Eduyoth* 6:2.
[2] *T. Terumoth* 2:9-11.
[3] *M. Hallah* 4:7.
[4] *T. Terumoth* 2:13.
[5] Chapter eight, pp. 432-4.
[6] *War* IV, 2.
[7] For a possible reference to the import of their livestock into Judaea, *T. B. Baba Kamma* 97b, cf. Jos. *Life* 58.
[8] *M. Peah* 3:6; *T. B. Rosh ha-Shanah* 19b.
[9] *T. B. Pesahim* 3b; *T. B. Zebahim* 63a, etc.
[10] *Ant.* XVII, 26.
[11] Applebaum, 'The Troopers of Zamaris', pp. 85-6.

They had by then undergone a process of Romanization,[1] and part of the Zamarids appear to have been transferred to Cappadocia and merged in the regular Roman army in the early second century, probably by Trajan.[2] The unit is still found in that province in the fourth century,[3] when it may be imagined that it had lost any Jewish complexion that it had formerly possessed.

There was also some direct recruitment of Syrian Jews to the Roman armed services. Matthaius, son of Polaus, joined the Roman fleet in 43 C.E., and was released from legion I Adiutrix in 68.[4] Since he is recorded as a Syrian, without any further notice of his birthplace, he evidently came from the countryside. Marcus son of Damas of Gerasa, less certainly a Jew, enlisted in the fleet in 46 C.E., to be released in 71 from the Misenum squadron; one of the witnesses to his discharge certificate[5] was Lucius Cornelius Simon of Caesarea Straton (i.e. Caesarea Maritima in Judaea), who appears with other soldiers from Antioch and Laodicea, and is therefore likely to have enlisted at Laodicea. It has already been observed (above, p. 676) that an interpretation of *Midrash Lamentations* suggests that there was a Jewish purple-fishing industry on the coast between Haifa and Tyre, which was converted to an undertaking of the Roman treasury after 70. Although the Jewish urban communities of Syria were large in such centres as Damascus, Antioch and Laodicea, there is virtually no evidence as to the sources of their livelihood. In the third and fourth centuries inscriptions record Syrian Jews as goldsmiths,[6] perfume-makers[7] and manufacturers of, or traders in silk.[8] Only in relation to the silk trade is there evidence suggesting that Jews may have engaged in this branch in the first century. The Galilean silk industry existed before the Destruction, and it has been conjectured (see chapter twelve, p. 682) that the material used was of local manufacture. Whatever the case, its existence makes it possible that Jews were then already active in the industry known to have flourished round Tyre

---

[1] Cf. *OGIS* I, 4251; *Syria* XLII (1965), pp. 31-9; cf. Applebaum, 'The Troopers of Zamaris', p. 86.
[2] Arrian, *Ektaxis* I, 9.
[3] *Notitia Dignitatum Orientis* XXXVIII, 21.
[4] *CIL* III, 2, Dip. 5 = *CIL* XVI, Dip. 8.
[5] *CIL* XVI, Dip. 15. For this and the previous instance of military service, see the *B.-Z. Katz, Memorial Volume* (1970), pp. 3-6 (in Hebrew).
[6] *CII* II, 865.
[7] *IEJ* (1955), p. 216 (Berytus).
[8] *CII* II, 873 (Berytus); *IEJ* (1957), p. 77.

and Berytus.[1] The question further arises, whether the silk woven there was local, or whether raw material (*serikon*) was imported from China. Nearly all the talmudic references to Chinese silk appear to belong to the third or fourth century; it is however mentioned in connection with one Menahem[2] who was a contemporary of Shammai, and as the material was already known to Horace under Augustus,[3] the word *serikon* here may not have been used anachronistically. But Parthia did her best to impede direct trade contact with the west, and much of the Chinese silk exported to the Mediterranean area went by sea direct from India to Egypt. As the earliest references to Jewish silk-trading at Tyre or elsewhere are of the second half of the second century, it is difficult to establish the scope of Jewish activity in this branch in Syria before that date.[4]

The relative antiquity of Jewish settlement in *Asia Minor*[5] makes it probable that in course of time Jews penetrated all the peninsula's normal occupations. Joel reports their sale as slaves to the Ionian Greeks, which would have been the work of pirate forays; at any rate it can hardly be considered coincidence that the third place in the frequency of known finds evidencing Jewish settlement in Asia Minor is held by Caria and Cilicia, both notorious as the haunts of piracy—Caria in the fifth century B.C.E. and earlier.[6] What this might mean in terms of subsequent occupational distribution can only be guessed; possibly participation in both piracy and slave-trading, but any other trade is as likely, and pirates were not above tilling the land between their forays.[7]

There is excellent evidence that Jews were engaged in agriculture in the later third century B.C.E.; this is furnished by Antiochus III's well-known settlement of 2,000 Jewish families as military settlers (*katoikoi*) in Lydia and Phrygia in the last decades of the century, and the assignment to them of arable land and vineyards is specifically provided for.[8] Lydia and Phrygia together head the list of known Jewish settlement points with nine and eleven localities respectively,

---

[1] E. S. Bouchier, *Syria as a Roman Province* (1916), pp. 112-20; 136-9.
[2] *T. B. Hagigah* 16b.
[3] *Epod.* 8, 15.
[4] The mention of the word *serikon* in *T. Negaim* 5:5 followed by an addition by R. Judah (mid-second century C.E.) might push the reference back to the earlier second century.
[5] Joel 4:6; Isaiah 66:19.
[6] Thuc. I, 8; Strabo XIV, 5, 2.
[7] Cf. the pirates of Lipara. Diodorus V, 9, 4.
[8] *Ant.* XII, 147-53; see chapter eight, pp. 468-9.

and this can hardly be coincidence. Naturally, there may have been other, earlier groups of Jewish military settlers: no less than three Jewish communities of Phrygia were located in places known to have possessed groups of Macedonians.

Later, in the first century C.E., epigraphical evidence of Jewish participation in the gymnasium at Iasos (Caria)[1] probably means that some well-to-do Jewish families in the town owned land, and the same interpretation would apply to the family of the distinguished and ambiguous Julia Severa of Acmonia, who both built a synagogue and was priestess in her city in the reign of Nero.[2] Additional evidence has been adduced in chapter nine (p. 486) pointing to a considerable Jewish rural population in Pamphylia in Roman times. Jewish inscriptions, mostly epitaphs, of various dates, more especially of the third and fourth centuries C.E., can also be cited from various remote places in Asia Minor where no city is known to have existed.[3] Cilician wine imported into Judaea,[4] at least originally, must have come from Jewish vineyards, and other agricultural products imported from Asia (Cilician groats[5] and beans[6]) are likely enough to mean Jewish farmers.

Paul of Tarsus' profession was tent-making, but tents of that period, despite misstatements, were made of leather, not textiles.[7] His friend Aquila of Pontus, whom he encountered at Corinth, practised the same trade,[8] so that evidently it was not uncommon among the Jews of Asia Minor. The two Jewish makers of hobnail boots (*caligae*) buried at Corycus[9] belong to a later period, but continued the same tradition, and might, like Paul, have been working for the Roman army.

Probably the commonest occupation of Jews in Asia Minor was the manufacture of textiles. The evidence for organized guilds of Jewish

---

[1] *REJ* (1937), pp. 73ff.
[2] See chapter eight, p. 443.
[3] As examples may be quoted Beyköy (O. H. E. Haspels, *The Highlands of Phrygia* I (1971), p. 176 and no. 67); Merdivenli Kaya (ibid., p. 183); Çeşmeli Zebir, Galatia (*MAMA* VII, 1956, no. 563); Alkaran, Lycaonia (*MAMA* VIII, 1962, no. 127); Chousaden-Karaly, Galatia (*CIG* 4087).
[4] *T. Shebiith* 5:2.
[5] *M. Negaim* 6:1.
[6] *M. Maaseroth* 5:8.
[7] Livy V, 2, 7; XXXVII, 39, 2; Cf. J. Curle, *A Roman Frontier Fort and its People* (1911), p. 66.
[8] Acts 18:1-3.
[9] *IEJ* (1953), p. 236.

dyers and carpet-makers at Hierapolis of Phrygia belongs to the third century C.E.,[1] but other considerations point to the industry as long established. The word *Tarseus* early became synonymous with a linen-weaver, and at Tarsus λινουργός in the first century meant any industrial worker;[2] there was a synagogue of *Tarsiim* in Jerusalem,[3] and such are referred to in connection with the Great Synagogue of Alexandria before 115 C.E.:[4] Isaac the linen merchant from Cappadocia was buried at Joppa not before the second century.[5] Hence it was probably no coincidence that at Philippi Paul met a godfearing woman from Thyateira (Lydia) who sold purple stuffs.[6] We may perhaps connect with the Jewish textile trade the import, at a date not determinable, but not before the late second century, of Cilician goathair cloths.[7] The woollen wares of Miletus, where a flourishing Jewish community existed,[8] are referred to several times in talmudic literature, but not, apparently, before the second century, nor is it clear whether Jews were actually engaged in their manufacture. The talmudic tractate *Sotah* tells us that 'he went to the land of the Hittites, which is Luz, where they dye (cloth) blue for all Israel.'[9] In this case, surely Luz is Lydia rather than Lydda. But probably the best evidence for Jewish participation in the textile industry is indirect and statistical: thirteen Greek towns of Asia Minor known to have engaged in this branch possessed Jewish communities in the Greek and Roman periods.

Other Jewish occupations known in Asia were the preparation of perfumes and the working of metals. Both are recorded among Jews at a late date at Corycus in Cilicia;[10] the Jews of Sardis held a notable place as goldsmiths in the late Empire.[11] Corycus was the *locus classicus*

---

[1] *CII* II, 777.

[2] Dio Chrysostom 34, 21.

[3] *T. B. Megillah* 26a.

[4] *T. Sukkoth* 4:6.

[5] Klein, *Jud. Pal. Corpus Inscriptionum* (1920), no. 132. The Joppa epitaphs must begin not much after 115-117, to judge from the presence of Jews from the Cyrenaican Pentapolis (*Sepher Ha-Yishuv*, s.v. Jaffa, no. 54); Klein identifies R. Judah ha-Cohen, commemorated on epitaph (ibid., no. 110) with R. Judah ha-Cohen of *M. Eduyoth* 8:2, who as a contemporary of R. Judah ben Baba belonged to the first half of the second century C.E. (ibid., p. 37).

[6] Acts 16:14.

[7] *M. Kelim* 29:1.

[8] *Ant.* XIV, 244-6; *CII* II, 748; *ZNW* XX (1921), pp. 177ff.

[9] *Sepher Ha-Yishuv* I, no. 54, p. 103 (Lydda).

[10] *CII* II, 790, 791, 792, 793.

[11] L. Robert, *Nouvelles inscriptions de Sardes* (1964), p. 54, no. 13; p. 55, no. 14.

for saffron, being recorded as such by Strabo[1] and Pliny,[2] hence Jewish participation in the industry may have begun earlier; on the other hand a Jewish bronze worker is heard of at Ephesus in the first century[3], showing that Jewish metalworking had begun in Asia before the late Empire. It has been suggested in the previous chapter (p. 668), that during the Hasmonean and Herodian periods and perhaps later, the Jews of the Asiatic ports were involved in the trade in the oriental luxury wares which reached the Judaean harbours from Arabia.

Something like a conspectus of Jewish occupational structure in Asia Minor is to be obtained by the statistical method; it applies not to the first century only,[4] but to the first four centuries. Jewish settlement during that period is found at four commercial centres and at ten towns situated at important crossroads. It is known at thirteen towns which manufactured textiles, and at six towns where metalworking was important, and at three of these Jews are recorded specifically as metalworkers. Jews are found in five centres of the perfumes branch. They lived in eight towns whose predominant basis was agricultural.

How far can this picture be applied to the first century? The period likely to have affected the economy of Asia adversely, with resulting occupational changes, was that between the revolt of Aristonicus (130/128 B.C.E.) and the accession of Octavian to full power over the Roman Empire (31 B.C.E.). During this period of revolt, annexation and republican rule, the cities of western Asia Minor were subject to crushing exactions and reparations, to heavy debts under exorbitant interest, and to mulcting by the Roman *publicani*. The pressure was increased during the civil wars that marked the twenty years before the emergence of Octavian as sole ruler. The not unfavourable economic situation of Asian Jews (or some of them) during the first part of the period is nevertheless indicated by Mithridates of Pontus' seizure of 800 talents of half-shekel dues deposited by the communities at Cos during his war of 88 B.C.E.[5] In 62-61 B.C.E., a year of stringency and currency shortage in Italy, the predatory Roman governor L. Va-

---

[1] XIV, 5 (5).
[2] *Natural History* XXI, 31.
[3] 2 Tim. 4:14.
[4] The information on the industries and economics of the Roman towns of Asia Minor here considered is derived from Broughton's chapter on Asia in *Economic Survey of Ancient Rome*, ed. by T. Frank, IV, pp. 715ff.
[5] *Ant.* XIV, 112-3.

lerius Flaccus confiscated similar dues collected by them.[1] The presence of a number of Jews who enjoyed Roman citizenship in the middle of the first century B.C.E. in Asia may be interpreted to indicate a comfortable group, and may further imply that a section of them had served in the Roman army.[2] Better conditions returned with the reforms of Augustus following Actium, so that in general it can be stated that information on the Jewish economy of Asia derived from the first century onwards reflects a situation which did not suffer any grave shock till the middle of the third century, and even in the third and fourth centuries, to judge from inscriptions, which now become more numerous, the Jewish communities of Asia contained families of wealth and even of distinction.

We have next to no information on the occupational structure of *Greek Jewry*. This applies equally to the mainland, including Thrace, the Aegean islands and the north coast of the Black Sea. Stern points out that economically Greece had declined since the later Hellenistic period, hence its absorptive capacity would not have been great.[3] But if a Samaritan woman is recorded in Attica between 330 and 322 B.C.E.,[4] Jews also had probably reached the Greek mainland by then. Several Jewish slaves were freed at Delphi in the second century B.C.E.[5] In the first century C.E. a Jewish woman Hannah, wife of Demetrius, an inhabitant of Histria in Moesia, appeared in a list of benefactors of the town who had contributed to its rehabilitation after a great disaster,[6] showing that there were well-to-do Jews in the Balkan Peninsula. Histria, indeed, would have been a notable entrepôt for trade up the Danube valley. Of the origin of the means of such families we have no secure information; but when Athens sent a diplomatic mission to announce to Hyrcanus I the city's decree acknowledging his previous affability to all Athenians, and honouring him with a crown and statues,[7] it may be assumed that this was not due to the High Priest's expertise in Greek philosophy or his enthusiasm for Greek art;[8] it is much more likely that Athens still retained an interest in the oriental goods available in the Judaean ports, then

[1] Cicero, *Pro Flacco* 28.
[2] See chapter eight, pp. 458-9.
[3] Chapter three, p. 157.
[4] *SEG* xxv, 180.
[5] *CPJ* I, 709; 710; 711.
[6] *SEG* xxiv, 1105.
[7] *Ant.* xiv, 147-55.
[8] His uncle Aristobulus had taken the title of *Philhellene* (*Ant.* xiii, 318).

under Hasmonaean control. Of Jewish livelihoods in the various smaller places of mainland Greece where they lived, we have no information. There is not a trace of agriculture.[1]

Among the islands, we have already spoken of Delos. Rhodes, though there were Jews there by 142 B.C.E.,[2] has not yielded earlier evidence, and by that time much of Rhodian trade had moved to Delos, (see above), so that the Jewish commercial element need not have been significant. Though there were Jewish communities on other Greek islands,[3] we possess possible evidence of their occupations only in two. Bleaching chalk or soapstone was imported into Judaea probably before the Destruction, from the Cycladean island of Kimolos,[4] about six kilometres to south-east of which lies the island of Sikinos.[5] It is perhaps to this place that the Jewish epitaph in the Catacomb of the Via Nomentana in Rome refers when it commemorates a γραμματεὺς Σεκήνων;[6] the suggestion is supported by the existence on the island of a cult of Dionysos Sabazios.[7] If it is accepted, then the export of soapstone from Kimolos to Judaea may have been the chief occupation of the Jews of Sikinos.

At whatever time the first Jews reached *Italy*, they were certainly numerous in Rome in 63 B.C.E., and Pompey's conquest of Judaea must have enlarged the number of Jewish slaves in the capital city. Some of the Roman synagogues whose names have come down to us may have taken their names from the Roman masters from whom their first congregants received their freedom, but the epitaphs help us little here; relatively few names of Roman citizens occur in the known Jewish catacombs of the city.

The view of Frey is that the earliest known Jewish burial places, the

---

[1] Kahrstedt, commenting on Mantinea (*Die Wirtschaftliche Gesicht Griechenlands in der Kaiserzeit* (1954), p. 134; *IG* v, 2, 295), with its woodlands, its horserearing, and its synagogue, and transferring nineteenth-century Silesia to Roman Greece, suggested dryly that 'the timber and horse-trading Jew was here in place.' And on Hermione (Argolis), where purple-dyeing was carried on and Jews are evidenced (ibid., p. 189 *Hesperia* XXII, p. 156, no. 9), that they had perhaps invested in that industry. Both cases belong to the third century C.E.; neither suggestion is more than a conjecture.

[2] 1 Macc. 15:23.

[3] See chapter three, pp. 151-5.

[4] *M. Shabbath* 9:5; followed by an addition by R. Judah ben Ilai.

[5] *IG* I, 2, 223; *SEG* V, 30, etc.

[6] *CII* I, no. 7. None of the identifications so far suggested is convincing. See Leon, pp. 149-61.

[7] See *PW* IIA, s.v. The inhabitants, however, are referred to in the inscriptions as Σεκινεται.

Monteverde and Via Appia Pignatelli, originated in the first century C.E., and continued in use in the 2nd; the Via Appia catacomb belonged to the second and third, that of the Via Nomentana to the second century C.E.[1] Hence it is not easy to ascribe the very meagre information furnished by the epitaphs specifically to the first century C.E. The only definitely first-century occupational evidence is that of an ex-soldier, and his Jewish origin has been doubted. From other sources we know that Paul's friend Aquila made tents at Rome for a period; in addition the synagogue of the Calcaresians may have belonged to a group of limeburners.[2] There is no reason to believe that Jews refrained from unpleasant manual work in those days;[3] it was precisely the low grade of many Jewish occupations and Jewish poverty that evoked the contempt of Roman authors.[4] Clearly the catacomb record is not a cross-section; hardly more so the testimony of the Roman satirists; Statius[5] and Martial[6] noticed the city's Jewish peddlers who traded broken glass for sulphur; Juvenal the beggars and fortune-tellers.[7] All these writers gibed at Jewish poverty. A more productive Jewish occupation of the time may be represented by the Jewish lamps found in Rome; one belongs to an early type, probably between 70 and 115 C.E.[8] Other Jewish lamps of undefined, probably later date, recovered on the Palatine,[9] may well indicate the presence of Jewish imperial slaves, some of whom are mentioned specifically in the first century by Josephus.[10] The strength of the Jewish slave-class in Rome in the first century is perhaps to be gauged by the deportation under Tiberius of 4,000 freedmen who inclined to Judaism.[11]

There was also a Jewish intelligentsia, which included the actor

---

[1] Leon, p. 65; *CII* i.
[2] Leon, p. 142.
[3] We may consider in this connection the Jewish community at the Nitriai (*SEG* VIII, 366) in Ptolemaic Egypt. Even Tacitus (*Hist.* V, 6) pays tribute to Jewish physique (*corpora salubria et ferentia laborum*).
[4] A. G. D. Askowith, *The Toleration of the Jews under Julius Caesar and Augustus* (1915), pp. 94-8.
[5] *Silvae*, I, 6.
[6] I, 41.
[7] *Sat.* VI, 542-7.
[8] Reifenberg, in *JPOS* (1936), pl. xi; cf. p. 177; Goodenough, *Jewish Symbols* III (1953), no. 934.
[9] *Boll. d'arch. cristiana* V (1867), pp. 9-16.
[10] *Ant.* XVII, 134, 141; XVIII, 103.
[11] Tac. *Ann.*, II, 85. For epitaphs of Jewish freedmen at Rome and in its vicinity, *CII* i, nos. 68, 70, 73, 74.

Menophilos, known to Martialis,[1] and a poet disliked by him for stealing both his verses and his boy-friend.[2] Another poet, Aristius, who had become a Jew, belonged to Horace's circle.[3] The actor Aliturus, whom Josephus met at Puteoli,[4] was more probably resident in Rome, since he was in favour with Nero.

The synagogue found in recent years at Ostia is of the Lower Empire,[5] but it was preceded by a first-century building sufficiently substantial to argue a well-to-do element of the community, which it is natural to interpret as engaged in the import and export business of the harbour town. There were probably also Jews among the portworkers. Among the other towns of Italy one of the earliest to see Jews was certainly Puteoli (Dicaearchia), the chief port for the orient.[6] Its strong commercial links with Alexandria and the coastal cities of Judaea make it probable that Jewish merchants and their agents were resident there. An inscription from Puteoli is a tombstone set up by a Jewish freedman, Acibas, to his pagan master P. Caulius Coeranus, a *negotiator ferriarum et vinariariae* in the first or second century.[7] The only commodity required both by iron mines and vineyards is timber for pit props and vine stakes, respectively. Some occupational evidence is also forthcoming from Pompei, destroyed in 79 C.E. Here the words for 'kosher fish sauce' and 'kosher fish pickle' inscribed on amphorae indicate that Jews there were engaged in producing these relishes for Jewish consumption.[8] A Hebrew graffito from the same town recording a sale mentions two Jewish names (Joshua and Felix Iudaeus),[9] and Jewish feminine names occur in graffiti of weaving operatives.[10] Lastly, we have an epitaph that shows that Jews were also to be found as cultivators in Italy in the earlier Empire:[11] Iaso who buried his daughter Mariamme near Rome, was a *colonus* of a farm belonging originally to Marius. Marius had owned very extensive estates at Baiae, Salonium (Salerno) and elsewhere;[12] a procurator of

[1] VII, 82. [2] XI, 94.
[3] *Sat.* I, 9, 60ff.
[4] *Life* 3.
[5] D. M. F. Squarcapino, *La sinagoga di Ostia* (1964).
[6] Cf. *Ant.* XVII, 328; XVIII, 160; *CIL* X, 1893; 1971; G. Giordano and J. Kahn. *Gli ebrei in Pompeii e Ercolano* (1960).
[7] *CIL* X, 1931; *CII* I, 75.
[8] *Comptes-rendus de l'Académie des Inscriptions* (1885), p. 146.
[9] *CII* I, no. 562.
[10] *CIL* IV, 1493, 1507: *Technology and Culture* X (1969), p. 564.
[11] *ILS* 7453 = *CIL* VI, 9276.
[12] Plut. *Marius* 34, 35, 45.

Augustus in charge of one of the *massae Marianae* is found at Ostia.[1] Our only information connected with Jewish occupations in *Spain* in the first century C.E. is the tradition that a weaver of the Temple tapestries migrated to Spain after the Destruction.[2] Little more satisfactory are the sources on the Jews of *North Africa* west of Cyrene. Finds on the coast of the Syrtis (Tripolitania) indicate that Jews had reached the region by the third century B.C.E.[3] As the Ptolemaic frontier stood at the Tower of Euphras (Gasr Ziphrin) on the Syrtis in the early years of that century, it seems probable that the Jews were settled in this part by Ptolemy Lagos as military settlers.[4] In the same area a Jewish settlement was established in the late first century C.E.; its name, Iscina Locus Augusti Iudaeorum, shows that it was situated on imperial domain land.[5] Goodchild noted the traces of ancient fields near this site (Medinat es-Sultan),[6] and its inhabitants were therefore cultivators. It is reasonable to connect this settlement with the tradition preserved in a mediaeval chronicle that 30,000 Jews were deported from Jerusalem to Carthage after 70 C.E.;[7] this tradition survived till recently also among the Jews of Tripolitania. In the Syrtis area, an agricultural basis would have been inevitable for such a colonization.

Further west, in the Roman province of Africa Vetus, there appears to be no reliable evidence to show how the Jewish population earned its living, and in any case there is no dependable evidence for its existence until the second century C.E.[8]

The occupational structure and economy of *Babylonian Jewry* offer no less difficult a problem. The bulk of the information concerning the economic activities of this Jewish Diaspora is derived from the Babylonian Talmud, whose contents relate to the third century onwards. At the beginning of the same century, in 227-229, a new

---

[1] *ILS* 1592.
[2] See chapter eight, p. 432, n. 6.
[3] See Applebaum, *Jews and Greeks*, p. 110.
[4] Ibid., p. 49.
[5] Ibid., pp. 172, 201-2. Cf. chapter nine, pp. 489-90.
[6] *Geog. Journ.* CXVIII (1952), p. 146.
[7] R. A. Zakkut, *Midrash Sepher Yuhsin; Midrash Lam. R.* 1:31; A. Neubauer, *Mediaeval Jewish Chronicles* I (1887), p. 190; Applebaum, *Jews and Greeks*, pp. 201-2.
[8] For a full discussion of traditions bearing on an earlier Jewish settlement in north Africa, see Hirschberg, *History of the Jews of North Africa* (1965; in Hebrew), pp. 7-8.

régime, that of the Sassanids, replaced the old Arsacid dynasty which till then had ruled the Parthian Empire of which the Jews of Babylonia were a part. The new rulers introduced various economic and social changes into the life of the country; the loose feudal structure of the Arsacids, which allowed for a large measure of local autonomy, was replaced by a hierarchical ruling caste, a bureaucratic administration, rigorous taxation and a considerable degree of étatistic supervision of economic affairs. The dynasty further founded a number of new cities on new unexhausted land, leading to a considerable transmigration of urban populations, in which the Jews participated.[1] It follows that the economic picture of Babylonian Jewry drawn by the Talmud cannot be referred in any detail to the preceding Arsacid period or to the first century C.E., and even the transfer of its general lines should be treated with caution, the more so since Trajan's Parthian War of 115-117 caused numerous losses among Mesopotamian and Babylonian Jewry and is bound to have disrupted their economy. This being the case, we must confine the present account to the meagre information that relates directly to the earlier period.

That period too must be divided into two phases; the second begins after the extensive anti-Jewish movement of the years between 20 and 37 C.E., centring initially on Nehardaea and Seleucia-on-Tigris, commencing with the establishment of the miniature Jewish state of Anilaeus and Asinaeus, and ending with the massacre of the Jews of Seleuceia in the time of the Emperor Gaius. (See chapter three, pp. 178-9; 433-44). This disturbance probably had repercussions beyond its initial centres, and must have caused a degree of disruption of the Jewish population. Hence even in the 1st century, the Jewish economic structure of the first half of the century may not have been the same as that of the second. The reports relating to the first half-century indicate a large urban population, a not inconsiderable element with a strong military tradition, a merchant class, and an agricultural population of uncertain size, part of which was derived, in all probability, from groups of military settlers planted by the Seleucids and perhaps by the Arsacids.

As early as the third century B.C.E. we hear of Babylonian Jews fighting with distinction in the Seleucid forces;[2] the planting by

---

[1] Neusner II, pp. 11ff.
[2] II Macc. 8:20. See now B. Bar-Kokhba, in *Proc. Cambridge Philol. Soc.*, 119, ns. 19, (1973), pp. 1-8, for the proposed connection of the engagement concerned with the war between Seleucus II and Antiochus Hierax, probably in Babylonia.

Antiochus III of 2,000 Babylonian Jewish families in Lydia and Phrygia in the later third century B.C.E. has been referred to. The settlement of Jewish *katoikoi* in Osroene in Seleucid times is probably to be traced in the name of Sina Iudaeorum,[1] possibly too in that of Tovia contra Birtha in the same district.[2] Whether the mounted archers of the Jewish Zamaris originated under the Seleucids or under Parthia (the latter seems more likely), they must represent a Jewish community occupying a horse-rearing area: their place of origin is perhaps to be traced in the name Saviri, appearing as Samri in one of the manuscripts of the *Ravenna Cosmography*,[3] and situated somewhere in Mesopotamia. Anilaeus and Asinaeus, on the other hand, were weavers of Nehardaea,[4] in this representing the Jewish craftsmen element. As the same town, largely Jewish and autonomous in this period, was a collecting centre for the half-shekel tax,[5] the departure point for the organized caravan which conveyed the treasure to Jerusalem,[6] and a seat of Jewish money-changers,[7] it was clearly a centre both of commerce and manufacture in the Arsacid period. The Jewish commercial element is further represented by the merchant Ananias who is found proselytizing at Spasinou Charax,[8] the chief port for the Indian trade on the Persian Gulf in the middle of the century. It may therefore be legitimate to see the Jewish traders as already active in the import and transfer westward of oriental wares (silk, spices, condiments, precious woods, etc.), which flourished throughout the ancient period, and whose chief stations in Babylonia, Mesopotamia and Adiabene were Seleucia on the Tigris, Nisibis, Singara and Edessa. At all these places Jewish communities were to be found.

Jewish settlement in southern *Arabia* began in biblical times. New inscriptions from Anatolia show that among the military colonists planted by Nabonidus of Babylonia in northern and central Hedjaz in the 6th century B.C.E., Jews played a considerable part.[9] These communities, which included the towns of Tema, Dadanu, (Hagra), Padakku, Hibra, Iadihu and Yitrab, continued to be Jewish centres

---

[1] *Not. Dig. Orientis* XXXV, 19.

[2] Ibid. XXXV, 28.

[3] J. Schnitz, *Ravennatis Anonymi Cosmographia* I (1939), pp. 4ff.; II, p. 13, line 10.

[4] *Ant.* XVIII, 314.

[5] Ibid. 212.

[6] Ibid. 313.

[7] *P. T. Yebamoth* XII, 12c.

[8] *Ant.* XX, 34-7.

[9] C. J. Gadd, 'The Harran Inscriptions,' in *Anatolian Studies* (1958), pp. 35-93.

down to the end of the Byzantine period. The Jews of northern Hedjaz were chiefly agriculturalists and semi-nomadic, those of the south mainly town-dwellers.[1] Both were probably associated with the trade in oriental luxury goods which continued throughout the Hellenistic, Roman and Byzantine periods, and part of which traversed Arabia by the caravan-routes leading to Petra, Gaza and Damascus.

BIBLIOGRAPHY

No general work on the economy of the Jewish Diaspora in ancient times has been produced. L. HERZFELD, *Handelsgeschichte der Juden des Altertums* (2nd ed. 1894), contains a chapter on Jewish commerce with special reference to the first century C.E, (pp. 185-98); its method is criticized at the opening of the present survey. J. JUSTER, *Les Juifs dans l'Empire Romain* II (1914; repr. n.d.), chapter 22, has some useful information. For the inscriptions, see *CII*, *MAMA*, *SEG* and L. ROBERT, *Hellenica* (for older and newly-discovered inscriptions). The Beth Shearim epitaphs (B. Mazar, *Beth Shearim* I (1958); M. SCHWABE and B. LIFSHITZ, *Beth Shearim* II (1967); N. AVIGAD, *Beth Shearim* III (1971); also *IEJ* and *BJES*, *passim*), contain much information on later Diaspora occupations.

For *Egypt* see A. TCHERIKOVER, *The Jews in Egypt in the Hellenistic and Roman Age in the Light of the Papyri* (2nd ed. 1963; in Hebrew), containing comprehensive information on the occupations of the Jewish population; see also *CPJ*.

For *Cyrenaica* see S. APPLEBAUM, *Jews and Greeks in Ancient Cyrene* (1969; in Hebrew), with some material on Tripolitania; id. 'The Jewish Community of Hellenistic and Roman Teucheira in Cyrenaica,' in *Scripta Hieroslymitana* VII (1961), pp. 27ff.

For *Cyprus* see S. APPLEBAUM, op.cit. p. 254. No other attempt has been made to consider the ancient Jewish economy of the island.

For *Syria* the only extensive work on the Jews in our period available is B.-Z. LURIA, *The Jews of Syria in the Period of the Return and the Talmud* (1957; in Hebrew); it contains, however, little economic information besides that on agriculture. For the Zamarids of Bashan see S. APPLEBAUM, 'The Troopers of Zamaris', in *Studies in the History of the Jewish People* I (1970), pp. 79ff. (in Hebrew).

The evidence on *Asia Minor* and *Greece* is derived from historical

---

[1] Ben Zevi, in *Eretz Israel* VI (1960), p. 133.

texts and inscriptions; the chief material is to be found in *CII* II, (1952); L. ROBERT, *Hellenica* I (1940), pp. 25-29; III (1946), pp. 90-108; and *MAMA* (1928-62).

No investigation of the economic aspects of the Jewish settlement in *North Africa* for the first century appears to have been attempted relating to the territory west of Cyrenaica.

For *Italy*, the evidence of the Roman catacombs is discussed by H. J. LEON, *The Jews of Ancient Rome* (1960).

For *Babylonia* see J. NEUSNER, *A History of the Jews in Babylonia* I-II (1965-6).

For *Arabia:* Y. BEN-ZEVI, 'The origin of the settlement of Jewish tribes in Arabia,' in *Eretz Israel* VI (1960). pp. 130ff. (in Hebrew, with Eng. résumé).

Chapter Fourteen
Home and Family

The courtyard

The vast majority of the Jewish people in Palestine during the first century lived in middle-sized or small towns which in the talmudic literature were usually called *arim* (ערים) and only occasionally 'villages' (כפרים).[1] But there were two laige Jewish cities, Jerusalem and Tiberias; Jews also resided in the coastal Hellenistic cities, such as Gaza, Ascalon and Caesarea, and in the Hellenistic Decapolis in Galilee and Transjordan; but the greater part of the population lived in the smaller towns of Judaea, Galilee and Transjordan.[2] In general streets were extremely narrow. This can be demonstrated from the halakic literary sources and archaeological discoveries in various Galilean towns, such as Chorazin and Usha. The widths varied from two to four metres for small streets, although there were even narrower paths, and eight metres for major roads.[3] From a street an alley (מבוי) led into the courtyard; often this alley was merely a cul-de-sac, ending in the courtyard. This entrance might be closed off by a gate or mat; but this was unusual because the alley was public domain and its improvement required the consent and participation of all the residents of the alley and the courtyard.[4] In some cases alley residents would contract to prohibit the opening of a tailor shop, tannery, or other type of workshop within that alley. On the sabbath the Halakah prohibited the removal of articles from private to public domain; nothing could be moved from a house to the alley. However, one resident could 'form a partnership' (*erub*) and declare one of his cooking utensils in the alley to be common property of all the residents; in this way the alley ceased to be public domain and became joint property during that time, and articles could be moved between the houses and the alley. Nevertheless, this required the unanimous agreement of

---

[1] For the meaning of *ir* and *kefar* in talmudic literature, see above chapter twelve, p. 641.
[2] Cf. Jos. *War* III, 43 and *Life* 235.
[3] *M. Baba Bathra* 6:7; see Yeivin, pp. 136-9.
[4] *T. Baba Metzia* 11:15; *T. B. Erubin* 8a.

728

the residents; if one of them was a Sadducee, disapproving of this Pharisaic arrangement, it could not be done. Rabban Gamaliel tells of such a situation in his father's courtyard in Jerusalem.[1]

Unlike this limited partnership within an alley, that between residents of a courtyard (חצר) was much more comprehensive. The courtyard, an area in which one or more rows of houses adjoined each other, was the basic residential unit. The entrance could open onto the yard; or, if there was a single row of houses, it sometimes led into the back of the houses which faced an inside yard. Some yards were owned by individuals, but most were owned jointly by several people, sometimes relatives. A fence, usually containing both doors and gate-houses, separated the yard from the street; these were kept in good condition. Gate-keepers guarded the entrances of the yards of more wealthy people. These more lavish yards were often constructed in imitation of the Tyrian style and, hence, called 'Tyrian courtyards'.[2] Large yards sometimes had surrounding pillars: the row of pillars, popular in Hellenistic and Roman construction, was widespread throughout Palestine, in public buildings and in yards attached to residences.[3]

Various buildings and structures in addition to the houses were round the courtyard. These could be either the common property of all residents or the private property of a single household. They included straw-sheds, cattle-sheds, woodsheds and storehouses of various commodities.[4] Many also contained dovecots and chicken coops.[5] Other items, such as toilet facilities, sewage gutters and refuse stores were placed in the courtyards. In most cases sewage was poured into specially constructed pits, from which it flowed into the gutter.[6] When the town did not possess a public water supply, cisterns were hewn under the courtyards. If the town had a public water supply, channels connected the courtyards to it. Tannaitic halakic sources discuss the legal problems arising in the case of a water channel which passed through a courtyard.[7] In larger courtyards the residents grew vegetables and trees. Sometimes there were rows of trees for fruit and

---

[1] *T. Baba Metzia* 11:16; *M. Erubin* 6:2.
[2] *M. Baba Bathra* 1:6; *M. Maaseroth* 3:5. See Yeivin, pp. 155-7.
[3] *M. Sukkah* 1:10; *T. Sukkah* 1:8.
[4] *M. Erubin* 8:4; *Sifre Deut.* 194.
[5] *T. B. Pesahim* 6a-b; cf. Krauss I, p. 46.
[6] *T. Erubin* 9:18; *T. Baba Metzia* 11:20.
[7] *M. Baba Bathra* 2:1; *T. Baba Bathra* 2:16; *M. Erubin* 8:7.

shade; it was possible to find fig and pomegranate trees, grape and watermelon vines and other fruits and vegetables.[1]

House structure and climatic conditions encouraged the residents to spend much time outdoors in the courtyards. In places where it was customary for women to launder, they were permitted to do this in the courtyard, 'out of respect for the daughters of Israel', even if it disturbed the other neighbours; and they were not required to go to the well outside for this task.[2] During the long summer season and the greater part of the winter, when it did not rain, ovens, stoves, and millstones were set up in the courtyard for cooking and grinding.[3] Eating in a public place was considered ill-mannered, but it was common to eat in a walled courtyard, especially one in the Tyrian style.[4] Even whole groups would sit down to eat together here in the open air; and during Passover in Jerusalem parties would eat their meals together in courtyards.[5] Larger courtyards could have a shop, often with entrances from the courtyard and the street.[6] Another important use of the courtyard was for unloading burdens which were brought from the fields.[7] The number of houses to a courtyard varied. Halakic sources mention some containing only two, which were rare. A greatly exaggerated statement, recorded in several places in talmudic literature, states that before the destruction of Jerusalem each of its courtyards contained twenty-four houses.[8] Archaeological excavations indicate that the number was much smaller. The houses adjoined one another, as a rule, to save building materials and space; the roofs were either continuous or slightly set off from each other.[9]

The house

From the literary sources and archaeological excavations one finds that most houses had at least two storeys, and sometimes even three. Generally a single owner built a house and its upper chambers; but because of inheritance and sales divided ownership developed. This

---

[1] T. Maaseroth 2:20; M. Maaseroth 3:8; T. B. Erubin 24a.
[2] P. T. Baba Bathra I, 13a.
[3] M. Baba Bathra 3:5; T. Baba Bathra 2:13.
[4] M. Maaseroth 3:5; P. T. Maaseroth II, 50d.
[5] T. Pesahim 6:11.
[6] M. Baba Bathra 2:3; T. Baba Bathra 1:4.
[7] P. T. Baba Bathra I, 13a.
[8] Lam. Rabba I (pp. 43-4).
[9] Cf. Yeivin, pp. 155-68.

caused friction between neighbours and led to endless litigation.[1] The steps leading to the upper rooms were generally jointly owned; so, too, the entrance to a house or the entrance to the rooms of the upper storey. These steps led to a balcony along the whole upper floor; entrance to the upper rooms and apartments was from this common veranda. This balcony was on the outside of the house and was supported by pillars resting on the ground or beams braced against the wall. The upper floors were not always full storeys; sometimes they consisted of single rooms on a roof or an attic with its entrance from a ladder inside the house. These attics could be used for a member of the household or as a guest room.[2] Upper chambers also served as meeting-places for small groups; numerous traditions from the Temple period and later tell of assemblies of sages or heads of schools which took place in such chambers. 'These are among the halakoth which were taught in the upper rooms of the house of Hananiah ben Hezekiah ben Gorion.'[3] 'And this was already established when the elders of the school of Shammai and the school of Hillel went up into the chambers of Johanan ben Bathyra and declared...'[4] Whether or not original plans called for upper storeys, it was common to add rooms or small structures to the roofs of houses and to the courtyards, as it became necessary.[5] The most frequent reason was the expansion of a family; a newly married son customarily brought his wife to live in the family house. The father would set aside a room within the house for the couple or build a marital house (בית חתנות) on the roof. On such an occasion relatives, friends, and neighbours came to assist the father and celebrate the new arrangement. A widowed daughter also returned to her father's house, especially if she were childless. She did not live with the rest of the family but in a special room set aside for her or in an upper chamber, a widow's house (בית אלמנות), built especially for her.[6]

Roofs of houses and upper chambers were usually flat and utilized for various purposes. The roof provided space for future expansion, and was a comfortable place to sit, particularly in the evening. Rooms within the houses, as we shall see, were very small, and the tiny

---

[1] M. Baba Metzia 10:1-3; T. Baba Metzia 11:1-3.
[2] Judith 8:5; Mark 14:15 (= Luke 22:11); Pirke ben Azzai 3:3 (p. 190); T. B. Kiddushin 81a; cf. Acts 9:37.
[3] M. Shabbath 1:4.
[4] T. B. Menahoth 41b; cf. Acts 1:3; 20:8.
[5] M. Baba Bathra 1:4; T. B. Baba Bathra 5b.
[6] T. B. Taanith 14b; M. Baba Bathra 6:4; T. Ketuboth 11:5-7.

windows did not provide adequate ventilation. The courtyards were used, but rooftops gave more privacy and the temperature was cooler than below. Although the ascent to them was more difficult, they were above surrounding walls and evening breezes made them quite comfortable, especially during the long hot summer months. People ate their meals there and gathered there for communal festivities and the study of the Torah. We are told of assemblies of people who ate their Passover meals on the rooftops of Jerusalem. Fruits and vegetables were spread out on roofs for drying and safekeeping; some roofs had pots of aromatic plants.[1]

It is very difficult to form a true conception of a house and the measurements of its various rooms. From the archaeological surveys and literary sources we can reconstruct complete houses. The variety of house construction depended mainly upon economic disparities and regional conditions. The northern settlements near Phoenician cities and other close to the Greek cities on the West reflected the styles of the surrounding areas; the interior hill country and southern regions also developed individual styles in construction. Houses were of stone in areas where this was easily accessible; elsewhere, as in the Sharon Valley, the poorer people built their houses with non-durable mud and clay bricks. In Galilee one could find beautiful houses in the style of residences in Tyre, Sidon, and Berytus.[2]

Although there were many families whose dwellings comprised only one room which served as living quarters for the entire household— kitchen, dining and living room and bedroom—most families had more than one. Among other factors conducive to the provision of additional rooms, was the halakic ruling that a woman must remain apart from her husband during the period of her menstrual impurity. Entrance to a house was through a vestibule (פרוזדור) which led to the *triclinium* (טריקלין) or dining-room. In a large house the *triclinium* was in the centre; all other rooms adjoined it. The extended family often lived together in one house, including the father and the families of his married sons. Even if the sons lived in upper storeys or side chambers not directly adjoining the *triclinium* it still served as the

---

[1] *T. Maaseroth* 2:10; *M. Erubin* 10:3; *T. Pesahim* 6:11; *P. T. Pesahim* VII, 35b; *T. Maaseroth* 2:19; *T. Shebiith* 1:12; cf. Luke 5:18-19.
[2] *M. Sotah* 8:3; *P. T. Sotah* VIII, 23a; *T. B. Sotah* 44a. The unstable houses of the Sharon Valley were also mentioned in the prayer of the high priest on the Day of Atonement: *P. T. Yoma* V, 42c. On the fine architecture of the houses in Galilee, which impressed Cestius Gallus, see Jos. *War* II, 503-4.

hub of the home's activity.[1] It was, of course, the largest room in the house: normal rooms were three by four metres, but *triclinia* were usually five by five metres. In many houses each couple had its own bedroom, but in some cases all the members of a household slept in the same room. More spacious houses had separate rooms for males and females and also a guest room, either in the house or the upper chambers.[2]

A kitchen was not a necessity in the house. When weather permitted, all baking and cooking was done in the courtyard in the open air or under a structure.[3] During the rainy winter season permanent ovens and stoves were also kept indoors; these were usually in the *triclinium*. They were placed beside a wall below a window or with an outlet (עשן in mishnaic parlance) for the smoke to escape.[4] In a later period we hear of a special room as the kitchen, the *mageireon*, set aside for cooking and baking, which also served for small meals for individuals.[5] Houses were plastered, and care was taken that the plaster would remain clean. Sooty walls were evidence of either poverty or a special occupation of the owner which dirtied the walls with smoke. Toilets were not found in houses; it was considered to be a luxury to have one even near one's house. They were normally only in courtyards and other public places.[6] Public buildings and the palaces of the wealthy and government officials contained elaborately decorated floors. Some floors were made of multicoloured marble, but stone floors were more common. More simple types of flooring were of plaster, earth and so on. Plastered floors were difficult to keep in good condition because they were easily damaged and required periodic replastering. Among the common people an earthen floor was normal in both towns and villages. It was sprinkled with water and stamped down with an instrument or by foot. At times it was covered with a woollen carpet or straw mat. When a piece of furniture was moved, it left furrows on the floor; one constant household task was the sweeping and watering of a floor to keep it presentable. Because of the scarcity

---

[1] *M. Aboth* 4:16; *M. Niddah* 7:4 (see the commentary in Albeck's edition, p. 589); *T. Erubin* 7:8.
[2] *M. Baba Bathra* 10:4; *T. B. Kiddushin* 81a.
[3] *M. Nedarim* 5:1; *M. Kelim* 5:1.
[4] *T. Kelim Baba Kamma* 7:9.
[5] *P. T. Betzah* v, 63b. The evidence for the *mageireon* is late, and it is doubtful if it existed in the first century C.E.
[6] *T. B. Shabbath* 25b.

of wood in and around Palestine, the exorbitant cost prevented the use of wooden tiles for flooring.[1]

No dwelling, except temporary structures and guard-houses in the fields, was considered fit for residence if it did not contain a proper door, including a bolt and lock. Careful attention was paid to the form of the entrance or doorway, the lintel, the doorposts, and the door itself. The single doorway was usually in the centre of the house front, but in a large *triclinium* or in public buildings additional entrances could be added on the sides. Whether from fear of theft or simply from good manners, the doors remained locked; the appearance of a guest was announced by his knock or the ringing of a bell at the door. At night the courtyard gates were bolted and the doors of houses were also bolted from within. During the day, however, they were only locked with a key. Large keys of crude design and more complex ones existed and we hear of a keychain which was used to keep several together. Not all rooms were separated by doors; some families contented themselves with dividing the rooms by means of straw mats and curtains. Doors were often left open during the day in summer and a curtain was spread across the entrance. Since windows were small, the doors were left open to provide the necessary light and air; the curtain gave privacy to a family from the courtyard or alley.[2]

The construction of windows in antiquity was difficult; the basic problem was the material to be used to fill the space. Under the climatic conditions of Palestine, this material had to be durable for the winter months and removable during the summer. Two types of material were used: glass and translucent stone. Tannaitic sources mention the use of flat glass panes fixed into the window to let in light; these were generally small and disshaped. However, the dating of these descriptions and archaeological evidence concerning the use of glass in Palestine suggest that its use began considerably after 70 C.E. Another solution was the use of brightly polished alabaster.[3] The expense of both these items rendered them accessible only to wealthy households. Most windows in houses were quite small, and there was a tendency to leave many walls entirely blank. There were large

---

[1] The pavement in the Temple and in palaces is mentioned many times in the sources, and remnants have been uncovered in many archaeological sites. On other types of flooring see *T. Ohiloth* 17:8 and 18:10; *T. Yom Tob* 2:13; *T. Kelim Baba Metzia* 11:10.

[2] Luke 13:25; *T. Kelim Baba Metzia* 1:13; *M. Parah* 12:9; Jos. *Ant.* III, 129.

[3] *T. Kelim Baba Bathra* 7:7.

windows, as well, which were blocked off during the winter months. But during the summertime one could sit and cool oneself in an open window. The thick walls provided large window-seats. When cool breezes began to blow late in hot summer afternoons, men and women in the greater houses could be seen in their windows with servants fanning them.[1] The Book of Acts tells that during one of Paul's journeys to Troas, he spoke so long with his disciples after supper that a young man sitting in the window dozed off and fell out.[2] This picture also fits conditions in Palestine. Various types of lattice-work, usually of wood, were also fitted into the window as a protection against burglars; and curtains were also hung over the windows for decoration and protection against the sun.[3]

Household articles

Palestine enjoyed the benefits of a long cultural tradition in the manufacture and use of diverse household articles. Moreover, the styles and traditions from neighbouring kingdoms such as Tyre and Sidon in the north and Egypt in the south, and influences from the conquering powers of Persia, Greece and Rome, also contributed greatly to the techniques and design for such furnishings. Because of its geographical position as a crossroad between the Mediterranean and the East and with a constant influx of pilgrims and settlers from Egypt, Parthia, Asia Minor, Greece and the western Mediterranean many beautiful goods and the technical skills to make them were available in the Land of Israel. In the first century there was no widespread poverty or famine in Palestine, except for years of drought and the ups and downs of the years preceding 70 C.E. The standard of living in villages and small towns was not luxurious; but because food, clothing and furnishings were simple they were in adequate supply. They did not usually come up to the standard of elegance to be found among the upper classes in Hellenistic and Roman society; furnishings in particular in Jewish households were as a rule devoid of the decorations and reliefs commonly found in Hellenistic cities.

The bed was considered one of the essential items for a minimum

---

[1] *P. T. Yoma* i, 38c.
[2] Acts 20:9.
[3] *T. Erubin* 11:17; *T. Kelim Baba Metzia* 11:10. See R. J. Forbes, *Studies in Ancient Technology* v (1957), pp. 183ff; S. Safrai, in *Yediot* xxxi (1967), pp. 231-5.

standard of living as is proved by several halakic rulings. Trustees of charity, responsible for the marriage of poor orphans, ensured that they were each provided with a bed. Even when a debtor's property was taken in pledge, his bed had to remain in his house. In nearly every house there were several beds; sleeping on the ground was a sign of the most extreme poverty.[1] Beds were usually high, and were entered by a footstool. In wealthy houses the beds were adorned with gold, ivory and other decorations. The space under a bed could be used for storage, but this was considered to be bad taste. 'How can one recognize the bed of a scholar? Any bed which has nothing beneath it except sandals in the summer and shoes in the winter. But the bed of an ignoramus is like a packed storeroom.'[2] Beds were wide enough to accomodate not only husband and wife but several young children as well.[3] It was customary for a mother to keep her small infant in her bed; the child's cradle, often mentioned in the sources, was intended for daytime use only.[4] There were also other types of smaller beds which were usually dismantled during the day.[5] Not every bed had a canopy, but canopies were not unusual.[6] They gave privacy as well as the necessary protection from flies and mosquitoes. Various figures were drawn or woven into the fabric of the canopy, and occasionally small bells were hung from it. In addition to the larger beds, smaller and simpler ones, designated by several names, could be found in a house; these were used by the sick or anyone who wished to lie down.[7]

Couches were used for reclining at meals. They were lower and smaller than beds. Following the custom prevailing among the Greeks, diners reclined on individual couches; this meant that an average household contained a fairly large number of them, stored in the *triclinium*. These couches were used for festive banquets, as well as for regular meals and also for the reception of honoured guests. In wealthy households, these, like the beds, were decorated with gold or other embellishments.[8] Although couches were used at formal and festive occasions, the more usual seat was a chair. The seats were constructed

---

[1] *T. Ketuboth* 6:8; *T. B. Baba Metzia* 113b.
[2] *T. B. Baba Bathra* 57b-58a.
[3] *T. Nedarim* 2:7.
[4] *P. T. Makkoth* II, 31c.
[5] *Aboth de Rabbi Nathan*, Version A, 6 (p. 27).
[6] *T. B. Sukkah* 10b-11a; *T. B. Sukkah* 26a; *T. B. Niddah* 17a.
[7] *T. B. Sanhedrin* 20a; Acts 5:15.
[8] *T. Berakoth* 5:5; *T. B. Yebamoth* 16a.

of wood, leather or straw which rested on four legs. Folding chairs were also very common. These had three legs and a leather seat and were collapsible for storage against a wall when not in use.[1] Benches were used to accomodate many people in a room. These consisted of a long board which rested on two broad legs; unlike some types of chairs, they had no arm-rests or back. They did, however, have 'heads', supports at each end: These are similar in construction to those found in various parts of the Roman world. Benches were the most common seating in public places such as schools, synagogues, bath-houses and inns; but they were also very common in private houses since they were the least expensive form of seating.[2] 'If a man has a close friend, the first time he gives him a couch to sit on; the second time the friend visits, he gives him a chair; the third time, a bench; and the fourth time he says: what a bother and a nuisance this fellow is!'[3] Sitting on the floor was very uncommon, being reserved for mourners and those under a ban. Only at public assemblies or large gatherings of students around their rabbis would people sit on mats spread on the ground because of the lack of other seats or out of respect for the speaker.[4]

In wealthy households one or more wooden armchairs with backs (*cathedrae*) could be found. Those in synagogues and other public places for sages and community leaders were permanent fixtures and made of stone.[5] Neither private or public *cathedrae* were permanently upholstered, but they were covered each time they were used. To sit in a *cathedra* was a sign of wealth and power. A halakah which enumerates a wife's household responsibilities says, 'If she brought in one bondswoman, she need not grind or bake or launder; if two, she need not cook or nurse her child; if three, she need not make the bed or work in wool; if four, she may sit [all day] in a *cathedra*.'[6] From a description of diners in rich homes, we learn that at a feast the guests first sat on *cathedrae* and benches before moving to the couches to lie down and eat.[7]

[1] *M. Eduyoth* 1:11; *M. Kelim* 22:4-7; *T. Baba Kamma* 10:8; *T. B. Shabbath* 138a.
[2] *M. Kelim* 22:3; *T. Baba Kamma* 2:9; *T. Kelim Baba Bathra* 1:11.
[3] *Midrash Psalms* 4 (p. 42).
[4] *Aboth de Rabbi Nathan*, Version A, 6 (p. 27); *T. B. Moed Katan* 16b; *P. T. Moed Katan* III, 83a.
[5] *Lam. Rabba* 1:3 (p. 63). On a *cathedra* in the synagogue, see Matt. 23:2. For the evidence from talmudic literature and archaeological discoveries, see E. L. Sukenik and J. N. Epstein in *Tarbiz* I (1929), pp. 145-52.
[6] *M. Ketuboth* 5:5.
[7] *T. Berakoth* 4:8.

Tables did not remain in fixed positions in the house for diners to sit around them, but were brought to the sides of the couches. When a meal was finished, they were removed and stored. They were composed of a tripod with removable top.[1] The ancients were not always capable of building level floors for their houses and the construction of four perfectly straight legs was also difficult; but the tripod could be used on any sort of floor. It is true that four-legged tables were used in the Temple in Jerusalem, but inferences cannot be made from the shape of sacred furniture to the type used in secular life. The shapes and measurements of the sacred articles were based on unalterable regulations from ancient times. Furthermore these were permanently fixed, and in general the design and workmanship of these tables were of higher standard than in ordinary houses. The detachable table-top could be used as a tray to bring food into the *triclinium* and placed on the tripod. After a meal it could be cleaned simply by shaking. Both sides could be used as table-tops.[2] Although most tables were made of wood, marble or wood with marble inlay were also quite common. Tables of metal, including such precious metals as silver and gold, were rare and are mentioned as a sign of great wealth. Marble tables had the added advantage for a Jewish householder of not being susceptible to impurity.[3] It was quite common to eat directly on the table-top which had been scraped with a knife earlier;[4] but those who were meticulous in the proper presentation of meals used tablecloths. A second cloth, was used as a napkin for hands and mouth during the meal, and ancient controversies from the Temple period are recorded concerning their ritual purity.[5] One source informs us that it was not customary to cover the entire table, but only two-thirds of it, for plates and bread, the outer edges being reserved for pots.[6]

Stoves and ovens were vital to nearly all cooking. They were generally made of clay and stone which were readily available, and less often of metal.[7] Some localities specialized in the manufacture of pottery, such as Shihin (Asochis) and Kefar Hananiya in Galilee, Lydda and Bethlehem in Judaea. Craftsmen here and elsewhere were famed for

---

[1] *M. Kelim* 22:2.
[2] *M. Shabbath* 21:3.
[3] *T. Kelim Baba Bathra* 1:10; *T. B. Taanith* 25a. See chapter fifteen, p. 830.
[4] *T. Kelim Baba Bathra* 1:9.
[5] *M. Berakoth* 8:3.
[6] *T. B. Baba Bathra* 57b.
[7] *M. Kelim* 5:11.

the designs of their vessels and ovens.[1] The fact that many made
their own ovens is confirmed by a story about Onias the Circle-Maker,
who lived at the end of the Hasmonaean period. When once he stood
up to pray for rain in Jerusalem, he instructed all the people to take
inside the new ovens drying in the sun, which they had prepared for
Passover.[2] Another report tells of an old woman who made her own
stove and took it up to the roof to dry.[3] Stoves were in the form of
elongated rectangles or ellipses, a few handbreadths high, and they
could accomodate two pots. An opening on the side facing the room
was used to stoke the fire, and one facing the wall, slightly higher
served as the exit for smoke via a chimney or a window in the wall.[4]
The stove was kept in the living room or kitchen; often an additional
stove was kept in the courtyard. The oven, for the baking of bread
and various sorts of cooking and roasting, usually stood next to the
stove. In the large cities professional bakers made most of the bread;
it was sold either on the premises or in shops in the marketplace.[5]
However, even in the large cities bread was also baked at home.
Already in the first century c.e. the Jews were familiar with the
Roman *furnus* (פורני), a large, well-built oven, similar to the ovens
of today. It contained a lower opening for fuel and an upper one for
the bread which was placed on a shelf two to three metres deep. These
ovens were principally to be found in the larger cities, especially in
the Hellenistic cities, and were owned by the professional bakers. The
oven usually found in Jewish cities and houses was made of clay and
cylindrical in shape. Its diameter at the base was 65 cm. and at the
top approximately 40 cm. Wood or other fuel was inserted at the
bottom and dough was placed in a separate upper compartment on a
shelf or against the walls. This was done from an opening above.
Ovens were normally fixed permanently to the ground, but some
smaller varieties could be carried to and fro between house and
courtyard or neighbouring houses.[6] Most ovens were made from clay;
but some houses were equipped with ovens of stone, brick or metal.
The ovens of the Temple were made from metal.[7] Such metal ovens
were imported and not manufactured in Palestine. Ovens were even

---

[1] *T. Baba Metzia* 6:3; *M. Kelim* 2:2.
[2] *M. Taanith* 3:8.
[3] *Agadath Bereshit* 44.
[4] *M. Kelim* 7:3; *T. B. Shabbath* 38b.
[5] *T. B. Abodah Zarah* 35b.
[6] *T. Ketuboth* 7:4.
[7] *T. B. Zebahim* 95b.

hewn from single blocks of stone, the requisite openings being hollowed out.[1]

The baking of bread was a weekly task for the whole family. The wife was responsible for kneading and baking the dough, while the husband tended the fire; sometimes the husband would do it all himself. The biblical picture of 'the children gathering wood, the fathers kindling the fire, and the women kneading the dough' (Jer. 7:18) remained the custom in the first century as well.[2] The weekly bread was baked before the Sabbath and then eaten during the whole week. Only for special festivities, such as weddings, or in the wealthy households was bread baked more often.[3] During the rest of the week the oven was used for other cooking. The paschal sacrifice of a small kid, born that year, was lowered whole in the oven. Kettles and pots of various foods could also be lowered into the oven for cooking or baking.[4] Tannaitic sources mention numerous other utensils in connection with the oven, including the mill for grinding the flour, kept next to the oven, the kneading trough and the basket in which bread was kept for use during the week.[5]

The shape and size of vessels used in the first century differed widely. Each one was particularly designed for its specific use. Although manners were simple, food and drinks were stored, prepared and served and consumed in different containers; these included special serving dishes, vessels for mixing wine and water, separate vessels for the storage of wine. Wine and oil were not kept in the same type of container; water was stored in a third type and served in yet another. The Jewish way of life, including family meals and social banquets, particularly the meals on sabbaths and feast-days, funeral meals and wedding banquets, encouraged the development of a dining etiquette which included many types of utensils. The observances connected with ritual purity and pollution were practised by wide strata of the population and exercised considerable influence on the number of vessels used and on the manufacture and material of those vessels.

The materials used in the manufacture of utensils in Palestine did not

[1] A hollowed out rock oven, apparently of the type mentioned in *M. Kelim* 5:11, was discovered by G. Dalman near Jerusalem, see *Arbeit und Sitte in Palästina* IV (1935), p. 93.
[2] *Mekhilta, Pisha* 10 (p. 35).
[3] *P. T. Orlah* II, 62b; *P. T. Megillah* IV, 75a.
[4] *M. Pesahim* 7:1-2; *T. Kelim Baba Kamma* 6:10.
[5] *M. Nedarim* 5:1; *Sifre Deut* 3 (p. 11); *T. Kelim Baba Kamma* 6:6. See Brand, pp. 544-6.

differ from those in use throughout the Roman empire at that time. It is reported that the Sadducees and the Boethusians 'used silver and gold vessels all their days';[1] despite the exaggeration of this statement the use of gold and silver vessels was not uncommon among the wealthy as is attested by many other sources. The use of less expensive metals was very common. Glass vessels were also very common, even the poor possessed them. A baraita relates that 'Formerly, the rich brought [food] to the house of mourning in silver or gold baskets; but the poor used wicker baskets made from peeled willow branches, and the poor felt shamed. It was therefore enacted that all should bring [their gifts] in wicker baskets, made from peeled willow branches, out of deference to the poor... Formerly, when drinks were served in a house of mourning white glasses (which had been purified from all pigmented materials) were used for the rich and coloured glasses for the poor, and the poor felt shamed. It was therefore enacted that all should be served with coloured glasses, out of deference to the poor.'[2] Glass vessels in use were chiefly cups and jars, blown by craftsmen.[3]

Of course, many cooking implements were made from wood, such as spoons, table-tops and mixing bowls; wooden dishes are known only from a later period. In general the use of wooden utensils was not very common. In some Jewish houses stone utensils could be found. Millstones for grinding flour were always of stone, as were other large permanently fixed utensils. Stone had the great advantage of not being susceptible to ritual pollution.[4] Even those who did not follow the meticulous observances of laws of purity, as practised by the associations (חבורה) of the Pharisees, certainly kept the laws of purity which are specifically mentioned in the Torah. Thus the use of stone had its distinct advantage. Similarly in the Temple stone utensils were frequently used where special precautions against impurity had to be taken.[5] Stone utensils from the first century are particularly numerous among the finds at the yet unpublished archaeological excavations of the southwest wall of the Temple Mount in recent years.

The most common vessels were made from clay. Potsherds of diverse

---

[1] *Aboth de Rabbi Nathan* version A, 5 (p. 26).

[2] *T. B. Moed Katan* 27a.

[3] On the spread of glass utensils before 70 C.E. especially in Jerusalem, cf. *P. T. Ketuboth* VIII, 32c and *P. T. Sukkah* V, 54d.

[4] *M. Kelim* 10:1.

[5] *M. Parah* 3:1.

types are found in great abundance at every excavated site. Liquids, such as water, wine and oil, as well as dry and moist foods were almost always stored in large and small clay containers. The ancients believed that wine could be properly preserved only in pottery. The popularity of pottery was undoubtedly due primarily to its low cost compared to other materials and the ease with which pottery vessels could be manufactured. Food and drink were usually served in pottery.

Most vessels were simple in form, but some were artistically fashioned and glazed on the surface. The latter were particularly common in richer households near the Hellenistic cities.[1]

Wine, oil and water were stored in large quantities for use at home. Water was brought either from outside sources, such as springs, brooks, or wells, or from the cistern in the courtyard or nearby. It was stored in large jars which were permanently embedded in the ground. Girls usually had the responsibility of keeping these jars filled,[2] but if a man happened to be near the well, he was expected to draw the water. 'The custom of the world is that men draw the water and women serve it.'[3] Wine and oil were bought in great quantities, usually once a year, and stored in large casks; for these two commodities were important parts of the daily menu and essential for cooking. All the containers for water, wine, and milk were provided with wooden or pottery lids to ensure that they were not left uncovered; it was strictly forbidden to drink anything which had been left uncovered.[4]

Drinks and their containers played an important role in dining. Hot drinks were not very popular; but much wine was drunk, usually diluted by a large quantity of water. It was customarily served in cups. A cup (כוס) in Tannaitic literature without any further qualification denotes a glass, made in a glassmaker's shop. Although there is reason to doubt that glass was very common at this time, it is certain that glass cups were in general use. Pottery cups also existed, and in wealthy households cups of copper, silver and gold were also in use. The usual cup of this period bore little resemblance to that of today: it had a wide mouth but the base was so narrow that it could not be set on the table when filled. It was served directly into the diner's

---

[1] *P. T. Baba Bathra* v, 15c; *P. T. Peah* VIII, 21a.
[2] *T. Niddah* 6:9.
[3] *Aboth de Rabbi Nathan*, Version A, 20 (p. 72).
[4] *M. Terumoth* 8:5; Jos. *Against Apion* I, 161 (for its interpretation cf. S. Liebermann, *Ha-Yerushalmi ki-Pshuto* (1934), p. 49.

hand, and when he was finished with it, he placed it in a special metal stand, called the 'cup container'[1] or laid it on the table.

Because of the multiplicity of uses for oil, it was kept in several different types of containers. Oil was used for cleaning and anointing the body; anointment with oil also served several medicinal functions, such as a cure for headache and as a precaution against several diseases.[2] Oil was stored in containers appropriate to its use. Separate vessels held oil for the table, for the bath-house and anointment at home. The cruse (פך) of oil is frequently mentioned. A Tannaitic halakic tradition which defines the essential articles to be supplied to a woman when her husband has gone abroad, leaving money with a trustee for her maintenance, includes as basic items: a cup, a jar, a pot, a cruse, a lamp and a wick.[3] Dining ware was used strictly at the table because proper manners forbade the use of the same dishes for cooking and eating.

Occasionally reference is made to a chip of wood or similar object which was used for eating and there might be a small knife on the table; but usually spoons and knives were used in the preparation, cooking and arrangement of food rather than at the meal.[4] Dishes were often pottery, but metal and glass dishes also existed. A tannaitic halakah ruled that when a man had to apply for public assistance he must first lower his standard of living. 'If he formerly used golden vessels, he must sell them and use silver vessels; silver vessels he must sell, and use copper vessels; copper vessels he must sell and use glass vessels.'[5] Even the poorest, apparently, were not required to go below the standard of glass vessels. Wooden plates are mentioned only in later sources and apparantly did not exist in the first century. A dish held the portions for several diners; as a rule two or three diners reclined on their couches around a single table and ate from a common dish.[6]

Chests were used for the storage of clothing, sundry household articles and jars of food. Bulk food storage, such as for oil, wine, flour and grain, was in large clay casks. Smaller items, such as pickled foods,

---

[1] *T. B. Pesahim* 55b; *M. Kelim* 16:2.
[2] *T. Shabbath* 12:11-2. Pliny also reports that the Jews anoint their heads with oil as a remedy for headaches: *Natural History* XXIII, 28. Cf. also *Aboth de Rabbi Nathan*, Version A, 12 (p. 56).
[3] *T. Ketuboth* 5:8.
[4] *M. Shabbath* 17:2; *T. Shabbath* 14:1.
[5] *T. Peah* 4:11.
[6] *T. Berakoth* 5:7-8.

spices and other specialties from the market were kept in jars of clay, metal or glass in wooden cupboards. The sources mention several types of chests. Several bore Greek or Latin names, such as the *theke* (תיק) and the *kamptra* (קמטרא); other principal types frequently mentioned include the strong-box (שדה), the chest (תיבה) and the closet (מגדל). Although we cannot give detailed descriptions of these pieces of furniture because none have been recovered, we know that they were all large. The largest was the closet, which was high and apparently resembled a tower.

A rim was added to its top for decoration or support for storage above it. Both the strong-box and the closet had hinges and could be locked with a key. The chest was the smallest of the three. Some were opened from the top, others from the side. Most strong-boxes and closets, and some chests contained removable drawers.[1]

Baskets and mats were woven from willow or palm leaves. Fruits, vegetables and the weekly bread supply were all kept in baskets. Produce was transported to the markets in baskets, and they served many purposes on farms.[2] The Mishnah describes a procession with the first fruits to the Temple, 'The rich brought their first fruits in baskets overlaid with silver and gold, while the poor brought theirs in wicker baskets made of peeled willow branches.'[3] The baskets of Bar Cochba's time found in the caves of the Judaean desert are mostly made from palm leaves, which were readily available in that vicinity.[4] A large number of mats were found in the same caves, also made from palms. Mats were spread on floors of houses, which were of earth or even stone. Poor people used mats to sleep on.[5] They were also used at the entrances of shops facing public streets and at the entrances to houses and to partitioned-off rooms.[6] The mats found in the Judaean desert range up to two metres in length and a metre wide; these are oval rather than rectangular in shape, but this may not have been universal.[7]

Lamps were among the most common household items. Whole or fragmented lamps are found in great abundance in the remains of every settled area. Furthermore, they are often mentioned in the

---

[1] *M. Baba Kamma* 9:3; *M. Kelim* 19:7; *M. Erubin* 3:3.
[2] *M. Shabbath* 16:3; *M. Shebiith* 1:2; *T. Baba Kamma* 11:8.
[3] *M. Bikkurim* 3:8.
[4] Yadin, pp. 136ff.
[5] *M. Ketuboth* 5:8; *Lev. Rabba* 27 (p. 618).
[6] *T. Erubin* 11:12.
[7] Yadin, pp. 150ff.

744

literary sources in contexts ranging from accounts of daily activities to parables which provide many details on the preparation, kindling, care and extinguishing of the lamp and on the lamps themselves. The burning lamp served the Jew in his daily activities and religious observance. The lighting of lamps functioned as an important part of the beginning and end of the sabbath.[1] Lamps accompanied the Jew throughout his life; custom required the kindling of lights at every significant occasion from birth, betrothal and marriage, to death. Many lamps have been found at graves, put there either for the use of visitors or—in accordance with various beliefs—to be used by the soul of the deceased.[2] Not only within the Jewish community itself, but also among Gentiles who had some attachment to Judaism this custom became widespread.[3] The presence of many lamps in Jewish homes is probably related to the practice of studying Torah at night, which was current among many strata of the Jewish population. The lamp is numbered among the most essential articles, part of 'the exile's baggage' (Ez. 12:3), which a man should take with him when embarking upon a long journey; to be left 'in want of all things' (Deut. 28:48) is according to one tradition nothing other than to be without a lamp.[4]

The shape of a lamp was elliptical; the oil was poured into a hole in the middle of the top, and the wick was inserted through a smaller opening on the side. Numerous lamps of this type, plain and decorated, have been found in Palestine. Pagan symbols predominate on the lamps from Gentile areas and Jewish symbols on those from centres of Jewish population. Lamps of various metals have been found, but they were not as common as in Pompei; most of the lamps are of pottery, and some are simply glass or pottery cups. In these the wick was leaned against the side.[5] Several common oils were used as fuel, even fats which were prohibited for consumption were permitted for use in lamps. Olive oil was the choicest, and some Jews took care to use this exclusively in the sabbath lamps and on festive occasions: 'All oils may be used in the lamp, but olive oil is preferred.'[6] If left on

---

[1] *M.* and *T. Shabbath* ch. 2; *T. B. Shabbath* 23b and 119b; *P. T. Berakoth* VIII, 12b. On the history of sabbath lights, see M. Levin in *Studies in Memory of L. R. Miller* (1938), pp. 55-68.
[2] *T. B. Sanhedrin* 32b; *P. T. Shabbath* 11, 5b; *M. Berakoth* 8:6.
[3] Jos. *Against Apion* II, 282; Tertullian, *Ad Nationes* I, 13.
[4] *T. Ketuboth* 5:8; *T. B. Nedarim* 40b-41a.
[5] *T. B. Pesahim* 14b; *M. Kelim* 2:5. Cf. Brand, pp. 337-8.
[6] *M. Shabbath* 2:2; *T. Shabbath* 2:3; *T. B. Shabbath* 23a.

the floor, a small lamp could not illuminate an entire room; thus, lamps were often placed in a recess in the wall, on a projecting shelf or upon a slightly elevated pedestal, as indicated in Jesus' parable: 'Nor do men light a lamp and put it under a bushel, but on a stand, and it gives light to all in the house.'[1] Often these lampstands were large enough to bear several lamps. In some cases a few branches extended from the lampstand, each branch having a receptacle for oil and wick, in the style of the Temple candelabrum.[2] Candelabra with several lamps apiece were of course common in public places, such as synagogues and 'houses of study', but they were also not unusual in private homes. In public places there were even gold and silver candelabra, and the literature mentions gold or silver candelabra more frequently than it does any other article made from those metals.[3] Excavations of various synagogues of later periods have uncovered bronze, stone, and marble candelabra; the usual candelabrum in the Jewish home, however, was made of wood in the Roman style.[4]

Torches and lanterns were used by pedestrians at night and for illuminating the courtyards. The lantern was basically just a lamp placed within a closed container which protected it from the wind, a small hole at the top allowing air to enter. The sides of some lanterns were made of translucent materials, while other lanterns had holes pierced in their otherwise opaque sides; by the first century glass-sided lanterns were also known. At times lanterns were used indoors as well, in particular to move from one room to another and to illuminate the house in the summertime, when open windows allowed the breezes to enter.[5]

Food

Food production changed radically from the First Temple to the Second Temple period. The cultivation of vegetables is not mentioned in the earlier period, but in the latter this was a major item of farming.[6] Likewise, in the earlier period honey was only a chance find in forests; but later it became an organized element in agricultural production.

---

[1] Matt. 5:15 and par.
[2] *M. Oholoth* 13:4; *Sifre Num.* 93 (p. 94).
[3] *M. Sukkah* 5:2.
[4] *M. Kelim* 2:2-3. For the assumption that candelabra were wooden unless otherwise noted, cf. esp. *Sifra, Shemini* 6 (p. 52d).
[5] *M. Kelim* 2:4; *T. Kelim Baba Bathra* 7:11; *Sifre Num.* 83 (p. 80).
[6] II Sam. 16:1; I Kings 5:2-3; *M. Uktzin* 1:2.

Fishing both along the coast of the Mediterranean Sea and in the interior lakes, especially in the Sea of Galilee and the lakes of the Huleh Valley was highly developed.[1] Fish products, such as fish brine, salted fish and fish gravies, are often mentioned in tannaitic sources.[2] The importance of these industries for Galilee is indicated by the name of the most distinguished town of eastern Galilee, Tarichaeae ('salt-ings')

With the change of available food products came adjustments in the daily diet. Vegetables and fish became more fundamental and meat was a luxury which families of average means could seldom afford. A minimum weekly diet is described in Mishnah, tractate Ketuboth, which specifies the required provisions for a woman when her husband is absent; it includes two cobs of wheat,[3] half a cob of pulse, half a log[4] of oil, one cob of dried figs or other fruits.[5] The lists of provisions for the poor[6] and the daily labourer[7] include bread, pulse, oil and dried or fresh fruit. On the sabbath fish and vegetables were added to these.[8] Meat was generally limited to feast-days[9] and family festivities;[10] Only the most wealthy households were accustomed to meat also on the sabbath.[11] But a strong custom prevailed that fish should be eaten on the sabbath, and many stories and legends tell of the difficulties which poor men overcame to have fish on their tables for sabbaths and feast-days.[12] Wine is not mentioned as a necessity in these lists, but it held a prominent place on the table on sabbaths and feast-days. Not only was it necessary for *kiddush* and *habdalah* and at weddings, circumcisions and funeral meals, but it was increasingly a part of feast-days and even cooking. The omission of it in the basics for a woman may be due to delicacy or because women simply did not drink wine. However, women from wealthy families did have a wine allotment; a provision of wine is specifically mentioned for Martha of

---

[1] *Sifre Deut.* 39 (p. 79); *P. T. Shekalim* VI, 40a.
[2] *M. Kelim* 10:5; *M. Terumoth* 11:1; *M. Nedarim* 6:4.
[3] 1 cob = 2.2 litres.
[4] 1 log = 0.5 litre.
[5] *M. Ketuboth* 5:8; *T. Ketuboth* 5:8; *P. T. Ketuboth* V, 30a; *T. B. Ketuboth* 64b.
[6] *T. Peah* 4:8; *M. Peah* 8:7.
[7] *M. Baba Metzia* 7:1.
[8] *T. Peah* 4:8; *T. Sukkah* 4:11.
[9] See esp. *M. Hullin* 5:3-4.
[10] *M. Hullin* 5:3-4; *M. Kerithoth* 3:7.
[11] *T. B. Betzah* 16a (a pre-70 tradition).
[12] *T. B. Shabbath* 119a.

the House of Boethus, the wife of Nakdimon ben Gorion.[1] On feast-days no fewer than four cups of wine were drunk.[2] Wine was not drunk neat but was mixed with water.[3] The use of vinegar was restricted to sauces in which bread was dipped.[4]

The family

There were scattered cases of men and women who remained unmarried or who married only at an advanced age. Various reasons lay behind these very rare cases, such as economic difficulties or the wholehearted dedication to some goal or project, e.g. Torah study.[5] The accepted ideal, however, was that of marrying and building up a family at a young age.[6] Tannaitic literature is full of comments and statements on the value of family life. The sages saw in the family not only the fulfilment of a divine commandment but also the basis for social life, and they tried to invest family life with an aura of holiness. Family life is held in high value in most of the literature of the Second Commonwealth. None of the ascetic trends within Pharisaic Judaism advocated celibacy, neither did most other movements.[7]

Family life was generally built around a monogamous marriage. Tannaitic literature contains no discussion of contemporary concubinage; when concubinage is discussed only the legal institution mentioned in the Bible is meant. Neither did tannaitic law take cognizance of a man's sexual relations with his female servant. By this time there were no longer Jewish maidservants, and a Gentile maidservant was forbidden to both her master and his sons until she had been freed and then converted, thus gaining the legal status of any other

---

[1] *T. Ketuboth* 4:8; *P. T. Ketuboth* v, 30a; *T. B. Ketuboth* 64b.
[2] *T. Berakoth* 4:8, cf. *M. Pesahim* 10:1.
[3] *M. Niddah* 2:2; *T. B. Shabbath* 77a.
[4] Ruth 2:14; *Ruth Rabba* ad loc.
[5] *Testament of Issachar* 3:5; Sirach 42:9 (cf. esp. the quotation of this in *T. B. Sanhedrin* 100b); *M. Ketuboth* 13:5 (a pre-70 controversy); *T. B. Ketuboth* 82b (also pre-70). It is known that Simeon ben Azzai, in the generation immediately after 70, did not marry because 'my soul lusts for the Torah' (*T. B. Yebamoth* 63b).
[6] Tobit 4:13; Sir. 7:25; *Testament of Naphtali* 8:9; Jos. *Against Apion* II, 199-203; *T. B. Sotah* 17a; *T. B. Sanhedrin* 76b; *Gen. Rabba* 22, 1-2 (pp. 204-6). See also the many sayings in *Gen. Rabba* 68:3-5 (pp. 771-4) and *T. B. Yebamoth* 61b-64. On Philo's attitude, see I. Heinemann, *Philons Griechische und Jüdische Bildung* (1932), pp. 261-5.
[7] See E. Urbach, 'Ascesis and Suffering in Talmudic and Midrashic Sources,' in *Baer Jubilee Volume* (1960), pp. 48-68 (in Hebrew) and Heinemann, op.cit., p. 265, n.3.

Jewish woman. From the fact that our sources record many sharp sermons against the practice of having sexual relations with maid-servants, we may deduce that it was not unknown. This, however, was simply a sin into which men fell, and it should not be seen as a regular form of family life similar to the legal situation described in the Bible, according to which a wife could be of either lesser or equal status with a maidservant.[1]

According to biblical law a man was allowed to take more than one wife, and talmudic law did not limit this right. In his account of the marriages of Herod and his relatives, Josephus adds: 'For it is our ancestral custom that a man have several wives at the same time.'[2] This practice is noted as a charge against the Jews by Justin Martyr.[3] Tannaitic literature mentions some actual cases of bigamy in upper class circles,[4] and only within certain Jewish schools of thought was bigamy explicitly forbidden.[5] Various halakic and haggadic statements, however, are based upon the assumption of monogamy, and also plainly recommend the practice;[6] one halakah explicitly states that if a married man takes a second wife, the first wife is entitled to demand payment of the *ketubah* (money which the husband had agreed to pay her in the event of divorce), and the husband must comply.[7] Among

---

[1] At the beginning of the first century C.E. a saying of Hillel refers to this: 'The more maidservants, the more lewdness' (*M. Aboth* 2:7). Cf. *M. Yebamoth* 2:8; and *Lev. Rabba* 25, 8 (p. 585).

[2] Jos. *Ant.* XVII, 14; cf. also *War* I, 477.

[3] *Dialogus cum Tryphone* 141.

[4] *T. Yebamoth* 1:10; *T. B. Sukkah* 27a; *T. B. Yebamoth* 15a. All these cases are from the Temple period or shortly after 70.

[5] As is well known, early Christianity did not forbid re-marriage to everyone (cf. 1 Tim. 3:2; 1 Cor. ch. 7). The members of the Qumran sect explicitly required monogamy; cf. *Damascus Document* 4:20. On the history of monogamy, see E. Roth in *Jewish Studies in Memory of Michael Guttmann* (1946), pp. 114-36, Hebrew section. Cf. also S. Lowy, 'The Extent of Jewish Polygamy in Tannaitic Times', *JJS* 9 (1958), pp. 115-38. On anti-polygamy tendencies in early Christianity, see D. Daube, *The New Testament and Rabbinic Judaism* (1956), p. 75. On the anti-polygamy attitude of Jewish Christians, see H. J. Schoeps, 'Ehebewertung und Sexualmoral der späteren Juden-Christen' in *Studia Theologica* II (1959), pp. 99-101.

[6] The Halakah ruled that if a man served as a judge or witness in a divorce proceeding he was forbidden to marry the woman; this was held even if he had been married at that time and his wife died later. The sages did not think it possible for a married man to be interested in taking another wife. Cf. *M. Yebamoth* 2:9-10 and the relevant discussions in *T. B. Yebamoth* 25a-26a and *P. T. Yebamoth* II, 4a-b; also *T. B. Ketuboth* 62a-b. For haggadic statements cf. *Aboth de Rabbi Nathan*, Version B, 2 (p. 9); *Targum Ruth* 4:6, etc.

[7] This was the Palestinian halakic ruling, which contrasted to the Babylonian practice: cf. *T. B. Yebamoth* 65a.

all the stories about the married life of the Tannaim and Amoraim, finally, there is not a single case of bigamy. It may therefore be assumed that monogamy was the widespread norm, although here and there, particularly in non-Pharisaic aristocratic classes, there were cases of families built around two wives or of men who maintained two wives in separate households.[1]

The ideal of marriage was the perpetuation of the family line, and so the number and survival of children was seen as the family's chief blessing.[2] An early, pre-70 mishnah bases the obligation of procreation upon Isaiah 45:18: 'He did not create it (i.e. the earth) a chaos, he formed it to be inhabited.'[3] This concept is repeated elsewhere in the literature of the Temple period and especially in the later tannaitic and amoraic works. If after ten years his marriage had no issue, a man was required to divorce his wife and take another.[4] Jewish tradition prohibited abortion and considered it to be possibly equivalent to murder,[5] and any idea of abandoning children after their birth was apparently quite alien.[6] Male children were seen as particularly important in the building of families, as a baraita rules: 'Without both male and female children the world could not exist, but blessed is he whose children are male and woe to him whose children are female.'[7] A very early mishnah which codifies the duties of a father towards his children and vice versa, mentions only sons,[8] and the tradition similarly reports that although it is true that the parents rejoice when a girl is born, the greatest rejoicing is upon the birth of a son.[9] Many reports testify to the existence of large families including children of both sexes; in most cases naturally, we hear of families with several sons because of their positions in communal life.

Male and female slaves may generally be counted among members of the family. Slaves were held in large numbers by very rich families

---

[1] King Agrippa's guardian had two wives, one in Tiberias and one in Sepphoris: *T. B. Sukkah* 27a. In *T. B. Yebamoth* 15a we are told that Abba, the brother of Rabban Gamaliel had two wives, but he was not one of the sages.

[2] Sirach 26:19-21; Jos. *Against Apion* II, 199-203.

[3] *M. Eduyoth* 1:13.

[4] *M. Yebamoth* 6:6.

[5] The prohibition of abortion is found in the Jewish part of the *Oracula Sibyllina* III, 765, Pseudo-Phocylides, Philo (cf. Heinemann, op.cit., pp. 392-4), Josephus and the rabbinic sources: *T. B. Sanhedrin* 57b; *Gen. Rabba* 34, 14 (p. 325); cf. also *Didache* 2:2.

[6] See *M. Makshirim* 2:7 and *T. Makshirim* 1:8.

[7] *T. B. Baba Bathra* 16b.

[8] *M. Kiddushin* 1:7.

[9] *Lev. Rabba* 27:7 (p. 639); cf. *M. Berakoth* 9:3 and many other passages.

and by those owning large estates; but their numbers were limited on the other hand, among middle-class families. The literature gives the impression that the average household included a manservant or a maidservant. A male or female servant belonging to a Jewish family was not employed in agricultural labour or in manufacturing; they were personal servants for the man or woman of the house.[1] These servants or maids were Gentiles who were either bought at the various markets in the environs of Palestine or born to parents who were slaves in a Jewish house. It may be assumed that at this time no Jewish slaves were held by Jewish masters, and the male and female servants mentioned in Jewish and other literary sources were Gentiles. These Gentiles, upon entering into service in the Jewish household, accepted the obligation of certain laws of the Torah. Manservants were circumcised and maidservants underwent ritual immersion, and those who refused to accept these rules had to be resold, according to the Halakah. Slaves who were circumcised or immersed and practiced some of the commandments were to a large extent considered as Jews and privileged to perform many religious functions. Frequent reports inform us of various religious activities and missions, such as the bringing of sacrifices, which were performed by slaves for their masters. If the master was a *haber*, that is, if he was particularly rigorous in his observance of the laws of ritual purity, then his servant or maid was also considered trustworthy in those matters.[2] Although Gentile slaves, both male and female, generally remained in that status throughout their lives, they were freed on various occasions, e.g. when their master was on his deathbed. According to the Halakah, male or female slaves upon manumission became Jews, converts like other converts. It often happened that the freed slaves remained with or near the families which had formerly owned them, and continued in their labours as before, with the difference that now their legal status had changed: being free, they received payment for their services and could leave their employment whenever they chose.[3] Frequently the former slave would become a permanent member of the household and even marry into the family. An old tradition,

[1] *M. Sukkah* 2:9; *M. Baba Bathra* 10:7; *T. B. Ketuboth* 96a; Luke 17:7-10.
[2] For information regarding the religious status of Gentile slaves see A. Büchler in *M. Gaster Anniversary Volume* (1936), pp. 549-70.
[3] A tannaitic tradition records that a matron named Veloria converted her slaves and freed them, but they continued to serve her throughout her life. In *M. Rosh ha-Shanah* 1:7 Tobiah the physician, his son, and his freed slave came to Jerusalem together, to testify regarding the new moon.

ascribed to 'the men of Jerusalem', counsels: 'If your daughter has come of age, free your slave and give him to her'.[1] It also often happened that even without valid halakic manumission slaves became assimilated within the family, which is attested at least for certain families. Despite the fact that slaves were for many purposes considered as Jews, in marital matters they were considered to be gentiles until they had been granted their freedom. Therefore, members of those families within which servants or maids had become assimilated but not been freed, were considered to be of impure lineage and thus disqualified from marriage, particularly within priestly families. This problem is often mentioned in the rabbinic sources, and many public discussions ensued.[2]

Betrothal and marriage

Betrothal and marriage were accompanied by a long series of customs and colourful practices. Numerous sources deal directly with betrothal and marriage and many popular stories, sayings and parables are woven around these subjects.

The young Jewish woman in Palestine was not imprisoned in her house or courtyard: she went to the well to draw water or to the market to shop and older girls might even find employment in shops or other concerns.[3] Tannaitic literature includes a lifelike description of a folk festival on the Fifteenth Day of Ab, when young women went to dance in the vineyards. 'And he who was yet unmarried would direct himself thither.'[4] Youths could certainly meet women on their own. A late midrashic source indicates that marriage brokers existed in the second century C.E.,[5] but it is not known whether the use of an intermediary was general in the first century.

There was an early halakic argument as to whether the parents were allowed to negotiate and agree on the financial side of the marriage on the sabbath.[6] Both families had the responsibility of helping the

---

[1] *T. B. Pesahim* 113a.

[2] *T. Kiddushin* 5:2 and *T. B. Ketuboth* 14b. This claim was also used to slander Herod's family, see *T. B. Baba Bathra* 3b. Cf. also A. Büchler, 'Familienreinheit und Familienmakel in Jerusalem vor dem Jahre 70', in *Festschrift Schwarz* (1917), pp. 133-62 (English translation in Büchler, *Studies in Jewish History* (1956), pp. 64-98.

[3] *M. Ketuboth* 1:10; 9:4; *Gen. Rabba* 49, 6 (p. 504); *P. T. Yebamoth* XIII, 13c.

[4] *M. Taanith* 4:8; *T. B. Taanith* 30b-31a; *P. T. Taanith* IV, 69c.

[5] *Ex. Rabba* 6, 3; 43, 1.

[6] *T. Shabbath* 16:22; *T. B. Shabbath* 12a; 150a.

young couple to establish its household; it seems, however, that it was particularly the groom who was interested in his in-laws' accepting this obligation, as it was in the household of the groom's parents that the couple would begin its married life and the major expenses therefore fell upon the groom and his father.[1] Characteristically Jewish in courtship and matchmaking was concern for purity of lineage, that is, the certainty that in neither family was there any suspicion of irregular ancestry which could make the present descendants forbidden or undesirable marriage partners; this was especially important in priestly families.[2] There are legendary accounts of Jerusalem customs on this matter.[3] A special ceremony was that of 'cutting off' (קצצה) a couple from the family. If a man married a woman of a family whose lineage was questionable his relatives would fill containers with nuts and roast corn and then break the containers before small children, who would gather up the prizes and say: 'So and so has been cut off from his family.' But if he divorced her, the relatives would repeat the procedure and the children would say: 'So and so has returned to his family.'[4] This ceremony was intended to ensure that there would long be witnesses to testify to the fact of the improper union and thus preclude its offspring from marrying into the family.

Josephus reports that the priests living in Babylonia, Egypt, and other places used to send certificates to Jerusalem attesting to the lawfulness of their marriages, and that whenever the Temple was damaged in the course of a war or outbreak of violence, these genealogical records were restored by the priests.[5] The tannaitic sources include excerpts from a genealogical scroll from Jerusalem.[6] It is doubtful, however, if there were ever complete and orderly genealogical lists regarding all the priests, much less all Jews. From the sum of tannaitic evidence, one gets the impression that in conjunction with genealogical lists, all investigations of descent also made use of oral testimony, such as: 'A, a priest, participated in the sacrificial service in the Temple and saw there B's son', or 'A, of a family of priests which participated in the sacrificial service in the Temple, saw B's son', or 'Members of A's family took spouses from priestly families'

[1] *T. B. Moed Katan* 18b; *T. B. Kiddushin* 9b.
[2] *M. Kiddushin* ch. 4; *T. Kiddushin* ch. 5; Jos. *Ant.* IV, 244-6.
[3] E.g. *Lam. Rabba* 4:2 (p. 141).
[4] *P. T. Ketuboth* 11, 26d and par.; cf. also *T. Ketuboth* 3:3.
[5] Jos. *Against Apion* I, 30-36.
[6] *M. Yebamoth* 4:13; fictional citations are found in *P. T. Taanith* IV, 68a.

(which indicates that A's family was of pure descent), etc.[1] These cases are from a period after 70, but by their nature it seems probable that the situation was similar during the Temple period.

The importance of taking a wife from one's own family is very much emphasized in the early literature of the Second Temple Period. The Book of Judith, for example, informs us that the heroine's husband, Manasseh, was also of her family and clan.[2] This endogamy is particularly emphasized in the Book of Tobit;[3] the author of the *Book of Jubilees* likewise stresses the importance of it, although he does not specifically require it, and in his usual manner he tells us that the patriarchs adhered to this norm.[4] The later literature apparently did not emphasize the importance of endogamy but marriage with one's sister's daughter was considered to be a very pious act;[5] several actual cases of such are known.[6] A young man was therefore at times subjected to great pressure to marry his sister's daughter, a demand from which he himself may have been trying to escape.[7] The Damascus sect, Samaritans, Christians, Falashas, Karaites, and Moslems forbade the marriage of a man and his sister's daughter.[8] Apart from marriage with one's sister's daughter, marriage within the family or tribe is emphasized in the Talmud only for the priestly tribe, and there are many reported instances of priests taking wives from priestly families.[9] It should, however, be pointed out that marriage with a sister's daughter or the marriage of a priest within his tribe were not actually required. Some priests took their wives from among the Levites or Israelites, and women of priestly families married Levites or Israelites.

Law and custom distinguished between betrothal, where the husband 'sanctified' his bride and she became as if formally married, and the wedding ceremony, called the *chuppah* (חופה) because it was held under a canopy. Not until the second ceremony did the bride move into her

---

[1] *M. Kiddushin* 4:5; *M. Eduyoth* 8:3. See Büchler op. cit., pp. 133-62.
[2] Judith 8:2.
[3] Tobit 1:9; 3:15-17; 4:12.
[4] *Jubilees* 4:15, 16, 20, 27, 28, 33; 8:6; 11:7, 14.
[5] *T. Kiddushin* 1:4; *T. B. Yebamoth* 62b and par. in *T. B. Sanhedrin* 76b, etc.
[6] Rabbi Eliezar ben Hyrcanus married his sister's daughter: see *Aboth de Rabbi Nathan*, version A, 16 (p. 63); there are many more examples.
[7] *M. Nedarim* 8:7; 9:10.
[8] S. Krauss, 'Die Ehe zwischen Onkel und Nichte', in *Studies in Jewish Literature in Honour of K. Kohler* (1913), pp. 165-75; Ch. Rabin, *Qumran Studies* (1957), pp. 91-2.
[9] Cf. esp. *P. T. Ketuboth* 1, 22c; cf. Luke 1:5.

husband's home. During the interval between betrothal and wedding the young woman remained in her father's house.

The various talmudic statements regarding the proper age for marriage deal with the groom's age when his wife moves into his house, but do not mention his age at the time of betrothal. An early talmudic saying states, 'At five one is ready to study the Bible... at eighteen for the wedding.'[1] Another tradition, originating in the school of a sage who lived at the time of the destruction of the Temple, informs us that God waits patiently for a man to marry before he is twenty, but if he remains single after that age God becomes angry.[2] There were, however, known cases of men remaining single past this age, often the higher age of marriage reflecting a poor economic situation.[3] Commenting on Deut. 20:5-6, a baraita concludes that 'The Torah here teaches us that a man should build a house and plant a vineyard, and only afterwards should he marry;'[4] certainly building a house and planting a vineyard, and becoming established economically, would imply an age higher than eighteen or twenty. It seems that girls married at a younger age; many laws deal with the right of the father to marry off his daughter while she is yet a minor, which means less than twelve years of age. In case of a betrothal during her minority, however, she had the right to refuse the final stage of marriage until she reached her majority.[5]

The betrothal took place in the home of the bride's father, where she was to remain following the ceremony.[6] Betrothal was actually a formal act of property transfer, wherein the groom gave his bride money or something else of monetary value and told her that through it she became betrothed to him 'according to the law of Moses and Israel.'[7] The money in question was at times merely symbolic: an early argument shows the house of Shammai claiming that the mini-

---

[1] *M. Aboth* 5:21. The received text attributes this saying to Judah ben Tema, whose time is unknown; but another version attributes it to Samuel the Small from the first generation after 70. Cf. A. I. Katsh, *Ginze Mishnah* (1970), pp. 122-3; C. Taylor, *An Appendix to Sayings of the Jewish Fathers* (1900), p. 171.
[2] *T. B. Kiddushin* 29b. The tradition is ascribed to the school of Rabbi Ishmael.
[3] Rabbi Eliezer ben Hyrcanus, who lived in the last years of the Second Temple period, came from a rich family, but was still unmarried at the age of twenty-two or twenty-eight. Cf. *Aboth de Rabbi Nathan*, Version B, 13 and Version A, 6 (p. 30).
[4] *T. B. Sotah* 44a.
[5] *P. T. Ketuboth* v, 29d.
[6] *M. Pesahim* 3:7; *M. Ketuboth* 5:2.
[7] *T. Ketuboth* 4:9.

mum value permitted was one *dinar*, whereas the house of Hillel held that even a *perutah* would suffice.[1] A late source mentions that inhabitants of Palestine were accustomed to betroth their wives with rings, in contrast to the practice of the Babylonian Jews. It is not impossible that this was the early Palestinian practice, as indeed was accepted in the Roman world, but tannaitic sources only mention money or its equivalent, never rings, in view of betrothals.[2]

The betrothal took place towards evening, and was a festive occasion: candles were lit, the beds were specially covered, many people gathered for the celebration,[3] and, as was customary at least in southern Palestine, special betrothal blessings were said in the presence of a quorum of ten men.[4] It was customary for the husband to present on this occasion a written marriage contract to his wife in which he enumerated in detail his responsibilities toward her and stipulated a sum of not less than two hundred dinars which he agreed that she receive in the event of divorce or his death.

This practice is cited by Philo, and in rabbinic literature as early as Hillel the Elder.[5] The Mishnah and Tosefta quote some excerpts from contracts of the Temple period; those from Galilee and Jerusalem are in Aramaic, but the excerpts from a Judaean contract are in Hebrew.[6] Several years might separate the betrothal from the marriage. During this interval it was customary for the groom to bring gifts of food to his in-laws when he went to their house for festive meals; he would also add presents for the bride which she would take with her upon moving to her husband's home.[7]

The Talmudic sources reflect differences between the practices in Galilee and in Judaea in the relationship of husbands and wives. According to the southern custom the groom, prior to marriage, was allowed to stay alone with his bride 'in order that he might become

---

[1] *M. Kiddushin* 1:1.
[2] M. Margoliot, *The Disagreements Between the Residents of the East and those of the Land of Israel* (1938; in Hebrew), p. 139. See B. M. Lewin, *Otzar ha-Geonim* IX (1939), p. 9 and B. Cohen, *Jewish and Roman Law* I (1966), p. 312, n. 181.
[3] *T. B. Gittin* 89a.
[4] *T. B. Ketuboth* 7b; *M. Megillah* 4:3.
[5] *T. Ketuboth* 4:9 and parallels—*P. T. Ketuboth* IV, 28d-29a and *T. B. Baba Metzia* 104a; Philo, *Spec. Leg.* III, 311. Cf. A. Büchler 'Das jüdische Verloben' in *Festschrift zu Israel Lewy* (1911), pp. 122-9. The first mention of a *ketubah* is in Tobit 7:14; cf. also *DJD* II, nos. 20, 21, 116.
[6] *M. Ketuboth* 4:7-12; *T. Ketuboth* 4:2.
[7] *M. Kiddushin* 2:6; *M. Baba Bathra* 9:5; *T. Baba Bathra* 10:10; *T. B. Baba Bathra* 146a.

attracted to her' and if he did, he could not complain to the court after marriage that his wife had lost her virginity.[1] Further, according to one Tanna, if the groom died, even before marriage, a Judaean bride was required to wait at least three months before marrying again to be certain that she was not already pregnant.[2]

When the bride and groom felt ready for marriage, they would suggest that the wedding be held. 'A virgin is granted twelve months to provide for herself; and like as such time is granted to the woman, so is it granted to the man to provide for himself.'[3] The bride prepared her clothes and adornments; the groom and his parents had greater responsibilities, including the preparation of the couple's home and of the feasts connected with the wedding. The groom could avail himself of the financial help of an institution called *shushbinut*, an organization each of whose members agreed to contribute a sum of money whenever one of the members or his sons married. *Shushbinut* money was not simply a free gift; it was an obligation enforceable at law and detailed laws were composed to deal with the various problems arising in connection with the institution.[4] Although membership in such an organization naturally resulted in ties of friendship between the men, they were certainly not simply the 'groom's men' who appeared at the wedding; contrary to the accepted view, *shushbinut* was a characteristic form of financial structure.[5] Tannaitic sources report that the ancient custom was for virgins to be wedded on Wednesdays, and widows on Thursdays; this custom, however, disappeared at the time of the religious persecutions under Hadrian.[6] The principal stages of the wedding celebration were: 1) preparation of the bride, 2) transfer of the bride from her father's home to that of the groom, 3) the bride's introduction into the home of the groom, and 4) blessings and festivities within the husband's home.

[1] *M. Ketuboth* 1:5; *T. Ketuboth* 1:4.

[2] *M. Yebamoth* 4:10.

[3] *M. Ketuboth* 5:2; cf. *T. Ketuboth* 5:1.

[4] *M. Baba Bathra* 9:4; *T. Baba Bathra* 10:7-9; *T. B. Baba Bathra* 145a.

[5] For later discussions on this institution, see the commentary of Rabbenu Gershom ad *T. B. Baba Bathra* 144b and Maimonides, *Laws of Ownership and Gifts*, chapter 7, which deals with the friendship among *shushbinim*.

[6] *M. Ketuboth* 1:1; *T. Ketuboth* 1:1. The Mishnah and Tosefta state that the reason for holding marriages of virgins on Wednesdays was that, if the bride were discovered not to be a virgin, the husband could immediately go to the court to complain on the following day. Both Talmuds, however, give additional reasons to explain the law. See the notes of Ch. Albeck in his edition of the Mishnah ad loc. *Nashim*, p. 345 and S. Lieberman's commentary on the Tosefta ad loc., p. 185ff.

The bride's preparation consisted mainly of bathing, perfuming and anointing, and the arrangement of a complicated array of clothes and adornments.[1] This completed, she was seated in a decorated carriage and, crowned with a wreath,[2] driven through the main streets of the town to the accompaniment of song, dance, musical instruments and applause.[3] When the bride was a virgin, it was customary for her to wear her hair loose, and special hymns were sung.[4]

The most highly-respected people saw it as their duty to accompany the bride on her way, and the sages even interrupted their study so that they and their students could meet a bridal procession and dance before the bride.[5] The houses of Hillel and Shammai had a long-standing dispute concerning the permissibility of exaggeration of the bride's beauty by those who sang before her.[6] Roast ears of corn were cast on the way before a virgin's procession, and wine and oil weie poured before all brides and grooms.[7] Wedding processions and festivities were held towards evening, and it was customary to accompany the bride with torches to add to the festivity.[8]

The groom would go out to receive the bride and bring her into his house;[9] in fact the wedding ceremony was essentially the groom's introduction of the bride into his house. Often, particularly in early sources, only the introduction into the house is mentioned, and this is supported by the formulae of early wedding contracts from the Temple period.[10] In the early tannaitic literature, however, there is already frequent mention not of the bride's introduction into the house, but into the *chuppah*. This was a festively decorated structure within the

[1] *Aboth de Rabbi Nathan* Version A, 41 (p. 133); *Cant. Rabba* 4.
[2] *M. Sotah* 9:14 reports that during the war against Vespasian the use of wreaths by grooms was suspended; during the war with Quietus (this is the better reading), i.e. the rebellion against Trajan, 115-8 C.E. bridal wreaths were also abandoned.
[3] *M. Sotah* 9:14; *M. Ketuboth* 2:1; *Pesikta Rabbati* 20 (p. 95a).
[4] *M. Ketuboth* 2:1; *P. T. Ketuboth* 11, 26b.
[5] *Aboth de Rabbi Nathan*, Version A, 4 (p. 18); *T. B. Ketuboth* 17a.
[6] *T. B. Ketuboth* 16b-17a and parallels in *Pirke ben Azzai* ch. 4, (p. 208).
[7] *P. T. Ketuboth* 11, 26b; *T. Shabbath* 7:16; *T. B. Berakoth* 50b; *Semahoth* 8:3-4 (pp. 150-1); cf. *Pesikta Rabbati* 37 (p. 163a).
[8] This is apparently the proper explanation of Matt. 25:1; cf. *Pesikta Rabbati* 43 (p. 182b and Friedmann's comments there, n. 28).
[9] *Mekhilta, Massechta de Bahodesh* 3 (p. 214); *T. B. Berakoth* 59b. This is also the scene described in 1 Macc. 9:39; cf. Matt. 25:1.
[10] *M. Yebamoth* 5:4; *T. Ketuboth* 4:9. See A. Büchler, 'The Induction of the Bride and the Bridegroom into the *Chuppa* in the First and Second Centuries in Palestine,' in *Livre d'hommage à la memoire du Samuel Poznanski* (1927), pp. 83-97.

house, the symbolic home into which the groom brought his wife; she remained there during the seven days of the wedding feast.[1]

Blessings, requiring a quorum of ten men, were recited during the wedding ceremony and during the whole festival.[2] The participants in the feast included the *shushbinin* and other invited guests, known as *bene chuppah*; this latter term is discussed in the halakic literature.[3] The feast was an important part of the wedding ceremony. It included the recital of verse.[4] The fact that Rabbi Akiba spoke against the singing of Canticles at wedding celebrations implies that this was the custom in some circles at least at the beginning of the second century.[5] All who were present at the celebration did their best to be merry and to add to the rejoicing of the wedded couple as well; the traditional sources repeatedly emphasize the obligation of 'gladdening' the bride and the groom.[6]

The groom's place was at the head of the table;[7] it is improbable that the bride sat among the male celebrants, as there was always separation of the sexes at such feasts, which were conducted in a semi-reclining position. The bride was not hidden, however; she remained visible to the guests throughout the days of celebration.[8] The feast concluded with a special blessing for the bridegroom, in some cases the drinking ended only at a very late hour.[9]

Talmudic sources report early differences between Judaea and Galilee as regards the first wedding night, for the southerners were very suspicious and exacting in all that regarded the confirmation of the bride's virginity. The Judaeans would examine the groom and the bride, prior to the wedding, in order to preclude all fraud as regards virginal blood; in some places it was customary for the two families to each send one *shushbin* who slept in the same house as the bride

---

[1] *T. B. Yebamoth* 89b; *P. T. Sotah* IX, 24c; *Pesikta de R. Kahana* (Appendix 6, p. 470).
[2] *M. Megillah* 4:3; *T. B. Ketuboth* 7b-8a; *P. T. Ketuboth* I, 25a.
[3] *P. T. Sukkah* v, 53a; *T. Berakoth* 5:10; cf. Matt. 9:15, Luke 5:34. On the practice in Jerusalem concerning invitations, see *Lam. Rabba* 4 (pp. 141-2).
[4] *M. Sotah* 9:11; cf. *Lev. Rabba* 28 (p. 653); *Sifre Deut.* 38 (p. 75).
[5] *T. Sanhedrin* 12:10.
[6] *T. B. Berakoth* 6b.
[7] *T. B. Moed Katan* 28b.
[8] *T. B. Ketuboth* 17a; see Büchler, op.cit., pp. 124-6.
[9] *T. B. Ketuboth* 7b-8a. *M. Berakoth* 1:1 relates that once Rabban Gamaliel's sons returned from a wedding celebration and had forgotten to recite the Shema; their father told them that they were obliged to recite it if the morning star had not yet risen.

and groom in order to serve as witnesses in case it was claimed that virginal blood had not been found. Of these varying customs the tradition adds that 'but in the Galilee such was not customary,' for the Galilean customs regarding many matters relating to sex and marriage were more delicate than those of the south.[1]

Providing hospitality for the many guests apparently posed no problem as a rule. The guests all crowded into the groom's house for the celebration, but before retiring they all returned to their homes. There is a report of a man who used to lend out wooden planks for use as serving trays at wedding celebrations,[2] and of the loan of an entire inn, apparently to house the guests.[3]

Wedding festivities lasted seven days. During this period neither the bride or groom went to work, and many of their friends and relatives, including both *shushbinin* and *bene chuppah*, also stayed with them.[4] The Halakah rules that if any 'new faces' came during the seven days of the festivities, guests who had not joined in the celebrations previously, the blessings of the groom were repeated, which included a prayer for the gathered crowd.[5] Only for a widow's remarriage was the celebration limited to three days or even one.[6] The festivities did not conclude even after the seventh day. On the second sabbath the bride's parents customarily came to visit the couple in their new home.[7] It is not surprising that our sources recall the careful preparations of the father of the groom prior to the wedding: we find more than one reference to fathers purchasing a whole cow for the wedding feast.[8] Although the bride lived in her husband's house, it was customary for her to return to her parents for the first Passover festival following her marriage.[9]

---

[1] Accounts of these practices appear in *T. Ketuboth* 1:4 and parallels in *P. T. Ketuboth* 1, 25a and *T. B. Ketuboth* 12a. For their explanation, see the commentary of S. Lieberman, *Tosefta Kipeshuta* ad loc., pp. 193-4.

[2] *T. Kelim Baba Metzia* 5:3. The reading 'sprigs' (נזרים) must be a mistake for 'planks' (נסרים). See Lieberman's discussion in *Hasde David, Seder Tohoroth* 1 (1970), p. 4, n. 6.

[3] *T. Baba Metzia* 8:28.

[4] *T. Berakoth* 2:10.

[5] *T. B. Ketuboth* 7b-8a.

[6] *P. T. Ketuboth* 1, 25a.

[7] *T. Baba Metzia* 8:28.

[8] *M. Keritoth* 3:7; *Sifre Deut.* 107 (p. 168).

[9] *M. Pesahim* 8:1. This is also implied in *M. Ketuboth* 7:4 and the variant versions of this mishnah in *P. T. Ketuboth* VII, 31b and *T. B. Ketuboth* 71b.

The married woman

The Mishnah lists the various duties of a married woman: she had to grind flour, bake, launder, cook, nurse her children, make the beds and spin wool.[1] It also lists the husband's obligations towards his wife when he is absent, including the provision of food, clothing and shoes for winter and summer, and a sixth of a dinar weekly for her personal expenses.[2] The Mishnah further rules that if the wife brought with her a maidservant her own duties were diminished accordingly.[3] If she brought with her a great sum of money, she was entitled to an increased allowance for perfumes. Tannaitic tradition indeed records the large perfume allowance which was granted to the widowed daughter of Nakdimon ben Gorion.[4] The Mishnah adds, however, that all the obligations it enumerates are minimal and a man is expected to exceed them according to his means.[5]

No legal obligation for wives to assist their husbands at work in the fields is mentioned, but this seems to have been the custom, particularly during the seasons of fruit collecting and harvest, and some even obtained employment together with their husbands, as fruitpickers.[6] We also hear of cases of married women who performed minor services at the markets, although this was considered to be a disgrace.[7] A wife could work at crafts or horticulture at home and then sell the fruits of her labours. This was sometimes done in order to supplement the husband's income, but some wives kept their income as pocket money for their own personal use.[8]

Although a housewife was kept very busy with her work in the house, she was still expected to dress and adorn herself properly; this point is stressed in many traditions.[9] The early law held that during menstruation a woman was forbidden to paint her eyes or put on rouge until she had ritually immersed herself after her period. Rabbi Akiba, however, subsequently ruled that a woman could use make-up even during that time, so as not to lose her charm in her husband's

---

[1] *M. Ketuboth* 5:5. In mishnah 9 the amount of wool a wife must spin is given. The different customs of Judaea and Galilee are cited.
[2] *M. Ketuboth* 5:8-9; *T. Ketuboth* 5:8.
[3] *M. Ketuboth* 5:5.
[4] *T. Ketuboth* 5:9.
[5] *M. Ketuboth* 5:9.
[6] *M. Yebamoth* 15:2 and par. in *M. Eduyoth* 1:11; *M. Baba Metzia* 7:6.
[7] *T. Baba Kamma* 11:7.
[8] *M. Baba Kamma* 10:9; *T. Baba Kamma* 11:5-6; *T. B. Pesahim* 50b.
[9] Cf. *P. T. Taanith* 1, 64b-c and its par. *T. B. Taanith* 23b.

eyes.[1] One halakic tradition ascribed to Ezra an ordinance 'that peddlers may go about in towns, so that they may sell woman's jewelry and thus wives will not lose their charm in their husband's eyes.'[2]

A married woman was expected to conduct herself with modesty, and a husband was compelled to divorce his wife if she appeared in public in torn clothing or bathed together with men, as was the Roman custom.[3] A husband could not forbid his wife to visit her parents even if they lived in another city, nor could he prevent her from attending celebrations or making condolence calls. Tradition condemns a certain famous man for locking the door on his wife when he left his house for market.[4] The married woman did not usually go shopping at the market, as such was considered the responsibility of the husband.[5] A man who prevented his wife from going to the bathhouse at a reasonable time was required to divorce her and pay the full sum stipulated in the marriage contract.[6]

Apart from her strictly household work the wife was also responsible for hospitality and the care of guests. Inns were not numerous, and those who travelled from place to place were dependent upon private homes for lodgings. The Jewish way of life contributed to making such hospitality necessary, because teachers of Torah used to go from place to place to speak, and those who gathered in the towns to hear the sages' words needed places to stay. Providing lodging for travellers became one of the characteristic ideals of the Jewish people. Tradition includes much discussion about the relations between guests and the woman of the house, on whose shoulders fell the responsibility for hospitality. It was said that wives looked with more grudging eyes upon guests than did their husbands, but it was also assumed that it was the woman of the house who could more accurately judge the character of guests.[7] The woman's duties as a mother included preparing the children for school. Truancy seems not to have been unknown, for mothers are advised to take their children to school to ensure their arrival.[8] Various sources indicate that women were

[1] *Sifra, Mezora* 9 (p. 79b) and par. *T. B. Shabbath* 64b, *P. T. Gittin* IX, 50d (end).
[2] *T. B. Baba Kamma* 82b.
[3] *T. Ketuboth* 7:6; *M. Ketuboth* 7:6. Cf. *T. B. Gittin* 90a-b; *P. T. Gittin* IX, 50d.
[4] *M. Ketuboth* 7:4-5; *P. T. Kiddushin* IV, 65d.
[5] *T. B. Abodah Zarah* 38a-b.
[6] *P. T. Ketuboth* VII, 31b.
[7] *T. B. Baba Metzia* 87a; *T. B. Berakoth* 10a.
[8] *T. B. Berakoth* 17a; *P. T. Yebamoth* 1, 3a *Pesikta Rabbati* 43 (pp. 182a-b).; *P. T. Hallah* 1, 57b.

active in charitable work. They gave alms to the poor who came to their homes and participated in charitable projects outside the home.[1] A few sources report the charitable labour of the 'worthy women' of Jerusalem.[2]

From a legal point of view, one could certainly point out some aspects in which the wife's status was inferior to that of her husband. There is no doubt, however, that socially the woman's position in the house was highly esteemed, a fact reflected not only in various laws and sayings but also in many facts reported in talmudic tradition and in other contemporary sources. A husband's marital obligations were not only monetary: he was also required to maintain sexual relations with his wife; if he took an oath of abstinence, for two weeks, according to the house of Shammai, or even for one week, according to the house of Hillel, he was required to divorce his wife.[3] The Mishnah states further that he must eat with her at least every sabbath eve.[4] The Halakah also rules that a husband may not move from one part of the country to another without his wife's permission, neither may he leave home except for certain periods demanded by his work; even for Torah study a married man was not allowed to leave home for more than thirty days.[5] A law frequently inculcated required the man whose wife came from a home richer than his own, to maintain the standard of living to which she was accustomed. If his wife's family was poorer than his own, however, he was required to maintain her according to his own status, the rule being: 'His wife ascends with him but does not descend with him.'[6] Early and late sources repeatedly emphasize that sexual relations required the wife's consent, the husband having no right to force himself upon her even on her first night of purity after menstruation.[7] Similarly, respect for one's wife was seen as a basic family duty: 'He who loves his wife as himself and honours her more than himself and teaches his sons and daughters honest ways and arrange their marriages just before they attain puberty, of him the

---

[1] *T. B. Taanith* 23b; *P. T. Horayoth* III, 48a.
[2] *T. B. Ketuboth* 106a; *T. B. Sanhedrin* 43a.
[3] *M. Ketuboth* 5:6.
[4] *M. Ketuboth* 5:9. In the discussions in both Talmuds ad loc. some took 'eat' literally and others as a euphemism for sexual relations. From other tannaitic sources it appears that the literal meaning is probably the original one. Cf. *P. T. Ketuboth* v, 30b and *T. B. Ketuboth* 65b.
[5] *M. Ketuboth* 13:10; 5:6.
[6] *P. T. Ketuboth* v, 30a; *T. B. Ketuboth* 48a, 61a.
[7] See the collected sayings from the beginning of the third century C.E. and later in *T. B. Erubin* 100b.

Bible says (Job 5-24): 'You shall know that your tent is safe.'[1] The woman is once called 'the mistress of the house'[2] and this picture suits many stories recorded in the rabbinic literature and the New Testament which reflect on the role of the woman in the home.

Pregnancy and childbirth

Pregnancy was regarded as a blessing and women as a rule made no effort to avoid it. Some methods of birth control were known, however, and in certain cases the Halakah allowed their use, at times even by the husband. According to a baraita which appears a number of times in the Tosefta and the Babylonian Talmud, a married woman who was yet a minor and fearful of pregnancy was allowed to use a cloth or wool tampon in order to prevent pregnancy, as was a nursing mother. The husband was allowed to spill his semen outside for twenty-four months after a childbirth, to prevent a new pregnancy and subsequent cessation of lactation.[3] Concern for the health of pregnant women was duly stressed in the early sources; they were regularly exempted from participation in all public fasts except the most solemn, such as the Ninth of Av and the Day of Atonement.[4] A mishnah rules that a 'pregnant woman who began to crave food after smelling it was allowed to eat until she recovered herself', even on the Day of Atonement,[5] and in another source we read that 'pregnant women were allowed to eat a small amount for fear of fatality.'[6] The fact that 'no woman ever miscarried due to the smell of the sacrificial flesh' was counted among the miracles which occurred in the Temple, for it was believed that a pregnant woman whose appetite is whetted by the smell of food is liable to miscarry if she does not eat it.[7] Miscarriages were very common and frequently mentioned in our sources;[8] as was common among other peoples also, Jewish women used to

---

[1] *T. B. Yebamoth* 62b.
[2] *P. T. Hagigah* ii, 77d.
[3] *T. Niddah* 2:6 and the parallel in *T. B. Yebamoth* 12b.
[4] *T. Taanith* 3:2.
[5] *M. Yoma* 8:5.
[6] *T. Mikwaoth* 7:6, cf. *T. Yoma* 4:4 (ed. Lieberman and his commentary ad loc. p. 819) and *T. B. Keritoth* 13a, with the classical commentaries. The commentators are divided in interpreting this: either a pregnant woman may eat on the Day of Atonement or she may eat unclean food on that day.
[7] *M. Aboth* 5:5; *Aboth de Rabbi Nathan*, Version A, 35 (p. 103) and Version B, 39 (p. 105).
[8] E.g. *Gen. Rabba* 20 (pp. 188ff.).

wear a small stone amulet, called 'stone of preservation' to ward off miscarriages.[1] Among the various prayers recited daily by the deputations of Israelites to the Temple, the Thursday prayers included one 'for the pregnant women, that they might not miscarry.'[2]

According to Josephus one group of Essenes married; but since they did so only to beget children, they abstained from marital intercourse throughout their wives' pregnancies.[3] Tannaitic tradition emphasizes the dangers of marital intercourse during the first three months of pregnancy, when it would endanger both the mother and the foetus; during the second three months, however, intercourse was considered to be difficult for the mother but good for the child, and during the final three months it was considered to be good for both.[4] The hour of birth was awaited anxiously, because it often resulted in suffering and grief, particularly with the very high maternal mortality rate. The Mishnah claimed that death in childbirth resulted from negligence in religious obligations specific to women: the kindling of the sabbath lights, the separation of the dough-offering (cf. Num. 15:17ff.), and the laws of menstrual purity.[5]

Midwives assisted at childbirth, and the Halakah allowed the preparation of the mother's every need even on the sabbath, including bringing a midwife from a distant place.[6] The woman was first settled into a reclining 'travail chair';[7] at times her state was already such that she could not manage the move on her own and had to be lifted into the chair by other women, who grasped her under the arms.[8] Preparations included the heating of water, and in wintertime a large fire was also kindled. In addition, oil was brought, apparently to be spread on the mother's natal orifice, and at night lamps were lit; these sundry details won halakic mention primarily because they were all listed as being permissible on the sabbath.[9] Many stratagems were

---

[1] These are mentioned in *T. Shabbath* 4:2; see the important note in Krauss, *Talmudische Archäologie* II, p. 425, n. 16.
[2] *P. T. Taanith* IV, 68b and par. *T. B. Taanith* 27b.
[3] Jos. *War* II, 161.
[4] *T. B. Niddah* 31a.
[5] *M. Shabbath* 2:15; *P. T. Shabbath* II, 5b; *T. B. Shabbath* 32a; *Aboth de Rabbi Nathan*, Versim B, 9 (p. 25). On the frequency of death during childbirth, see especially *Lev. Rabba* 27:7 (pp. 638-9).
[6] *M. Shabbath* 18:3; *M. Rosh ha-Shanah* 2:5.
[7] *M. Kelim* 23:4; *M. Arahin* 1:4.
[8] *M. Oholoth* 7:4.
[9] *M. Shabbath* 18:3; *T. B. Shabbath* 128b-129b; *P. T. Shabbath* XVIII, 16c (end); *T. B. Berakoth* 53a.

used to assist women who had difficulties in childbirth, and after the birth other measures were taken to protect the newborn infant from possible injury. Tosefta, tractate Shabbath, lists a numer of such measures; some were forbidden as pagan customs, while others were permitted, chiefly on the basis of hints found in biblical verses. Practices forbidden at childbirth included blocking the window to prevent the entrance of demons who were supposed to suck children's blood, tying a piece of iron to the mother's bedposts, and setting out a meal on a table—probably for the enjoyment of demons or magical spirits. It was permitted, however, to place a cup of water before a woman in confinement, and to tie a hen to her.[1] Another stratagem was to whisper into the mother's ears; although this practice is mentioned a few times in our sources, we are never told what was whispered. [2] In addition to caring for the mother throughout the whole procedure, the midwife was also responsible for quieting her, encouraging her, and, eventually, for informing her that the child had safely emerged.[3] The father was not always present at the moment of birth, and had to be notified of it.[4]

Following the severance of the umbilical cord the infant was washed and his limbs were shaped, that is, straightened out and swaddled, a common opinion of the ancient world holding that such was necessary to ensure that the limbs grew properly.[5] One final detail of childbirth may be mentioned: the afterbirth was not discarded, but buried, the belief being that this would help to warm the newborn baby.[6] 'On a sabbath, the rich preserve the afterbirth in oil, and the poor in straw, but on week-days all bury the afterbirth in the ground, in order to give the earth a pledge.'[7] Infants were swaddled and left in their cradles during the day.[8] One passage in the Babylonian Talmud indicates that in southern Judaea it was customary to plant a cedar tree at the birth of a son and an acacia tree for a daughter; when the children

---

[1] The list appears in *T. Shabbath* 6:4; see Lieberman's commentary ad loc. pp. 84-5, in which he provides comparative material from non-Jewish sources.
[2] *Eccles. Rabba* 7 and parallel in *T. B. Sotah* 11b. Incantations are mentioned in *T. B. Shabbath* 66b, a later discussion; cf. *T. B. Yoma* 82b.
[3] *Gen Rabba* 82 (p. 986).
[4] *T. B. Baba Bathra* 141b.
[5] *M. Shabbath* 22:6; *T. B. Shabbath* 123a, 129b, 147b (with the classical commentaries).
[6] *T. Shabbath* 15:3 and par. in *T. B. Shabbath* 129b.
[7] *P. T. Shabbath* XVIII, 16c (end), and previous note.
[8] Cradles are mentioned in *M. Oholoth* 12:4 and *M. Niddah* 4:1.

were eventually married branches from these trees were used in constructing the wedding canopy.[1]

As some laws were concerned with a child's exact age, it may be assumed that Jewish families usually remembered the date of birth, but birthdays were not celebrated. Josephus even informs us that the Torah forbids the practice of turning the occasion of one's birth into an opportunity for celebration and drink.[2] The Gospels note the birthday celebrations of Herod Antipas,[3] but tannaitic literature mentions the celebration of birthdays only as a Gentile practice.[4]

Following the birth of a boy guests gathered nightly until the circumcision. Tannaitic reports tell of attempts to preserve this custom, known as the 'son's week,' even during the persecutions following Bar Cochba's revolt, and lament the fact that the Roman authorities did not allow assembling for its celebration.[5] One source mentions a 'daughter's week' as well, but it is doubtful that this single report, in a medieval quotation, justifies the assumption that such a celebration was also usual at the birth of a girl.[6] The circumcision on the eighth day was a festive occasion, and various traditions from the second Temple period already report that it was accompanied by the gathering of many people for celebration and feasting.[7] Although only the later sources mention the requirement of a quorum of ten men for circumcision and the accompanying blessings, it seems that in actual practice this was the ancient rule as well.[8] Circumcision was performed by a professional physician. Tannaitic sources discuss such questions as whether a Samaritan doctor is preferable to a Gentile.[9] The naming of sons at circumcisions is not mentioned in rabbinic sources, apart from a late midrash; the practice is mentioned by Luke, however,[10] and it is certain that this custom, which has continued until our own time, was part of Jewish practice in the first century.

[1] *T. B. Gittin* 57a.
[2] Jos. *Against Apion* II, 204.
[3] Mark 6:21; Matt. 14:6.
[4] *M. Abodah Zarah* 1:3; *T. B. Abodah Zarah* 10a; *P. T. Abodah Zarah* I, 39c.
[5] *Semahoth* 12:5; *T. Sotah* 15:10 (according to the best reading); *T. B. Baba Bathra* 60b; *P. T. Ketuboth* I, 25c; *T. B. Sanhedrin* 32b.
[6] The quotation is from Nachmanides in *Torat ha-Adam*, taken from *Semahoth*. See W. Brüll, *Jahrbücher für Jüdische Geschichte* I (1874), p. 12; A. Büchler, *JQR* XVI (1904), p. 158. For a fuller discussion see Higger pp. 20 and 231.
[7] Elisha ben Abuya told of the feast at his circumcision in Jerusalem before 70 C.E.: *P. T. Hagigah* II, 77b. See also *T. B. Shabbath* 130a.
[8] *Halakoth Gedoloth* (Berlin ed., pp. 106-7, Jerusalem ed. 1972, p. 216).
[9] *T. B. Abodah Zarah* 26b and par. in *T. B. Menahoth* 42a.
[10] Luke 1:59-60; 2:21.

The Mishnah lists, among the obligations of a wife, her duty to nurse her children;[1] it seems that no other method of feeding infants was known and in case of the mother's sickness or death there was no choice but to find a wet-nurse. Richer families would sometimes turn over the nursing of their children to capable maidservants, or hire nursemaids.[2] The nursing mother was granted special treatment: her household work was diminished and her food supplemented, the addition of wine to her diet being especially noted. Foods, such as onions and garlic, on the other hand, were considered to be injurious to the infant.[3] Nursing continued for a lengthy period. Most tannaitic sources mention twenty-four months; but a variant tradition states that the period is eighteen months, as is testified by a halakic decision, which says that, if a man dies while his wife is nursing, she may not remarry for eighteen months in case a new pregnancy should cause the cessation of lactation.[4] In a Jewish contract of 18 B.C.E. from Egypt, the length of a nursemaid's employment was set at eighteen months.[5] We also hear, however, of longer periods of nursing, even three years or more. In the story of the martyrdom of Hannah and her seven sons, Hannah tells one of the boys that she nursed him for three years, and this period is also mentioned in tannaitic traditions.[6] In the case of a firstborn son the commandment to 'redeem' him was to be fulfilled on the thirtieth day as required by the Torah (Num. 18:16). This obliged the father to pay a redemption fee of five *selas*. There are many laws regarding this practice, and tannaitic literature also contains much evidence of its actual observance.[7]

According to tannaitic law, redemption money for the firstborn son was included among the priestly dues which could be given 'in the country', that is to say to any local priest, and need not be taken to Jerusalem.[8] The earlier practice, however, called for bringing priestly dues to Jerusalem as is mentioned in the literature from the beginning of the Second Temple period until the Hasmonaeans, and it remained common, to a certain extent, until the latter days of the Temple.[9] Of

---

[1] *M. Ketuboth* 5:5; *T. B. Ketuboth* 59b.
[2] *Deut. Rabba* 7 (p. 113). In *Testament of Benjamin* 1:13 Benjamin was nursed by Bilhah after his mother, Rachel, died.
[3] *M. Ketuboth* 5:9; *P. T. Ketuboth* v, 30b (end).
[4] *T. Niddah* 2:1-6; *P. T. Niddah* 1, 49b; cf. *T. B. Ketuboth* 60 a-b.
[5] *CPJ* II, no. 146.
[6] II Mac. 7:27; for the Tannaitic tradition, cf. *Deut. R.* loc. cit.
[7] E.g. *M. Bekhoroth* 8:1, 8; *T. Bekhoroth* 6:1, 14; *T. Kiddushin* 1:11.
[8] *T. Hallah* 2:7-9.
[9] See infra, p. 822 n. 6.

the redemption of the firstborn son the Torah explicitly states (Exod. 34:20): 'All the first-born of your sons you shall redeem. And none shall appear before me empty.'[1] The Gospel of Luke indicates that Jesus was taken to Jerusalem for redemption in the Temple.[2] Although presumably some or perhaps most Jews did not do so in the first century, it is very probable that some did go to Jerusalem in order to perform the ceremony of redeeming their firstborn sons 'before the Lord in the Temple in Jerusalem.'

In accordance with the laws of Leviticus, a mother became impure for seven days following the birth of a boy and two weeks in the case of a girl; after the 'days of purity,' thirty-three for boys and sixty-six for girls, she was required to complete her purification with a sacrifice of either a lamb or young doves.[3] The wife was permitted to engage in sexual relations with her husband, however, before she brought the sacrifice; she was only prevented from entering the Temple and partaking of sacrificial meals. A clear and detailed tradition of the Temple period informs us that women did not usually go to Jerusalem following the birth of each of their children, but would rather go after a few births, bringing all the sacrifices together. The Mishnah reports that at one time the price of doves was so high Rabban Simeon ben Gamaliel ruled that a woman could fulfill with a single sacrifice her obligations for five births or miscarriages, whereupon the price of doves immediately dropped.[4]

Childhood and adolescence

Halakic sources frequently discuss a father's duty to feed and support his children; the extent of the father's legal responsibilities towards his sons and daughters were in dispute. An old marriage contract recorded the father's obligation to provide for his daughters' food

---

[1] An amoraic halakic midrash understands this verse to say that if a man is obliged to redeem his son and at the same time to go on a festival pilgrimage, the former obligation takes precedence (see *T. Bekhoroth* 6:10 and *T. B. Kiddushin* 29b). This is not, however, what the words mean; the plain meaning of the verse is that one must go to redeem his son in the Temple before the Lord, as is recorded in the covenant in Neh. 10:37.

[2] Luke 2:22, see S. Safrai, *Pilgrimage in the Second Temple* (1965, in Hebrew), pp. 128-9.

[3] Lev. 12:1-8. The Mishnah seems to indicate the place (*M. Sotah* 1:5) and the time in the daily worship (*M. Tamid* 5:6) when this ceremony took place. Cf. also Luke 2:22-24.

[4] *M. Kerithoth* 1:7.

until they married,[1] but some of the Tannaim from the Jabneh period said that this legal obligation affected only the father's estate, should he die, but not the father while he was alive.[2] In fact, however, fathers supported their daughters as well as their sons, and only rarely do we hear of exceptions; even if it was held that strictly according to the Halakah a father could not be required to provide for his children, the realities of moral and social demands forced him to do so.[3] From both legal and practical points of view, minor daughters were more dependent upon their fathers than were sons, and also more sheltered. The Mishnah rules that a father could accept the tokens of betrothal for a daughter who was a minor, appropriate the fruits of her labours, and annul her oaths.[4] According to an early mishnah, which was, however, rejected by certain sages of the Temple period, the provision of food for daughters takes precedence even over inheritances for the sons, in case the estate of the deceased father did not suffice for both purposes.[5] After the death of the father the elder brothers and their mother inherited his right to marry off the minor girls.[6] Generally the younger sisters had to respect their elder brothers just as they had to respect their parents.[7] A father was required to provide for the instruction of his sons and daughters and to teaching them good behaviour. We have already referred to the anonymous baraita which appears a few times in our sources: 'He who loves his wife as himself and honours her more than himself and teaches his sons and daughters honest ways and marries them off just before they attain puberty, of him the Bible says (Job 5:24): 'You shall know that your tent is safe.'[8] Whipping was accepted, along with other disciplinary measures; the father's right to inflict stripes on his son was given legal recognition, and the famous admonition of Proverbs 13:24, 'He who spares the rod hates his son, but he who loves him is diligent to discipline him', is frequently

[1] *M. Ketuboth* 4:11.
[2] *M. Ketuboth* 4:6.
[3] *T. Ketuboth* 4:8; *P. T. Ketuboth* IV, 28d; *T. B. Ketuboth* 49a-b; *T. B. Baba Bathra* 141a.
[4] *M. Ketuboth* 4:4.
[5] *M. Ketuboth* 13:3 and the parallel in *M. Baba Bathra* 9:1.
[6] The legal validity of such betrothals was not, however, identical with that of betrothals arranged by the father; the daughter was allowed to reject her brother's choice. Our texts record various controversies and traditions of the Second Temple period regarding this right of rejection, e.g. *M. Yebamoth* 13:1-6; *T. Yebamoth* 13:1-6. The basic statement is found in *T. Yebamoth* 13:1.
[7] *T. B. Ketuboth* 103a and elsewhere.
[8] *T. B. Yebamoth* 62b and par. in *T. B. Sanhedrin* 76b.

recalled in our sources, various parables from everyday life being woven around it.[1] Mothers too administered discipline and they were even capable of using a raised shoe.[2] Our literature also reports a large number of incidents indicating the father's love and care for his children, however, such as feeding them and treating them with compassion and tenderness.[3] The grandfather as well contributed to the child's education, talmudic sources emphasizing the grandfather's role in teaching the Torah or in taking the child to school.[4]

Throughout tannaitic and other Jewish literature, stress is placed on the honour and respect due to parents, and various stories are told about particularly praiseworthy conduct in this regard by both Jews and gentiles. It should be noted, however, that this preaching was usually directed not towards young children, but rather towards adult men and women, including those who were married, who were obliged to care for and honour their aging parents. Some of these traditions, originating precisely in our period, emphasize respect for the mother even more than for the father.[5]

Religion and society made no sharp distinction between childhood and adolescence. The Jewish practice of celebrating the Bar Mitzva when a boy reaches the age of thirteen, marking the fact that at this age he received the obligations to observe all the commandments, originated in a later period. In the first century both boys and girls began to participate in social life and observe the law as soon as they were mature enough to be able to perform and understand these activities. A baraita which often appears in the sources expresses this idea as follows: 'A minor who is no longer dependent on his mother is obliged by the commandment to sit in a booth (during Tabernacles); if he can wave it he is obliged to take a palm branch; if he can wrap it around himself he is obliged to wear a prayer shawl; if he can care for them, his father should buy phylacteries for him; if he can talk, his father should teach him the *shema* and Torah and the sacred language;... if he knows how to slaughter animals, his slaughtering is kosher; if he can keep his body clean, he may eat pure foods; if he can keep his hands

---

[1] *M. Makkoth* 2:2; cf. also *Midrash Tanhuma, Parashat Shemot* (traditional edition) beginning, and the anonymous parable in *T. B. Kiddushin* 30b.

[2] *T. B. Kiddushin* 31a; *Esther Rabba* 1.

[3] *T. Yoma* 5:2; *Gen. Rabba* 63 (p. 678); *T. B. Yoma* 30b.

[4] This duty is mentioned in tannaitic literature, but recorded instances are from later periods. Cf. *P. T. Kiddushin* I, 61a; *T. B. Kiddushin* 30a.

[5] *Mekhilta de R. Ishmael, Bahodesh* 8 (pp. 231ff), *P. T. Kiddushin* I, 61a-b, *T. B. Kiddushin* 31a; *P. T. Peah* I, 15c; Jos *Ant.* IV, 260ff.

clean, one may eat pure food from them; if he can eat…a piece of meat the size of an olive, one may slaughter a paschal lamb for him…'[1] Girls and boys participated in every religious and social ceremony, in the synagogue and at celebrations at home, in pilgrimages and at every public gathering, as much as possible, if only 'so as to bring a reward to those who brought them.'[2] The passage from childhood to adolescence was perhaps not felt in the home, as the process was slow and gradual, but we should not underrate the religious and legal significance of the formal definitions of attaining majority. According to a law which was already well known and defined during the Second Temple period, the criterion for children's majority was the beginning of physical adolescence.[3] The ancient assumption was that such signs of maturity appeared at twelve among girls and thirteen among boys, and so the ages of twelve years and a day and thirteen years and a day were the respective legal ages of majority, following the confirmation of the physical indications. The tannaitic traditions reported differences in the appearance of signs of maturity among city girls 'whose lower signs appear first because they are in the habit of taking baths, [as opposed to] the country girls among whom the upper sign appears first, because they grind with mill stones and carry jars on their sides.'[4] The respective bounds of twelve and thirteen years served to define the beginning of a youth's independent legal status, his acceptability as a witness, his eligibility for marriage and marital relations; only after the age of thirteen was a boy permitted to serve as a leader in prayer and perform many other functions forbidden to minors.[5] It was only in a few specific matters, such as some punishments and the sale of inherited real estate, that twelve or thirteen years were considered to be insufficient, the minimum age for these matters being eighteen or twenty.[6] Similarly, it was strictly required that judges should be at least twenty years of age. Youths among

---

[1] *T. Hagigah* 1:2 with par. in *Sifre Zuta* on Num. 16:38 (p. 288); *P. T. Sukkah* III 54a; *T. B.* ibid. 42a.

[2] *M. Hagigah* 1:1; *P. T. Hagigah* 1, 75d; *Tractate Soferim* 18:8.

[3] *M. Niddah* 5:7-9; *T. Niddah* 6:4.

[4] *T. Niddah* 6:9; *T. B. Niddah* 48b.

[5] *M. Terumoth*. 1:1, 3; *Megillah* 2:4; 4:6; *Ketuboth* 2:3; *Sanhedrin* 8:1; *Shebuoth* 6:4; *Keritoth* 2:6.

[6] *T. B. Baba Bathra* 155a-156a; *T. B. Gittin* 65a; *T. B. Shabbath* 56b. In talmudic literature these advanced ages do not appear except in sources later than the first century, but the age of twenty as the lower limit of majority does appear in the apocryphal literature, cf. Ch. Albeck, *Das Buch der Jubiläen und die Halacha* (1920), p. 14.

whom physical signs of maturity had not appeared were legally considered as adults, from the age of twenty according to the Hillelites, or the age of eighteen, according to the house of Shammai.[1]

Death, burial and mourning

Jewish literature in general and talmudic literature in particular include numerous details of the practices regarding the care of corpses, funerals, interments and mourning. Very frequently we may speak with certainty about practices common during the Second Temple period, as our sources include reports of incidents which occurred in that period, as well as traditions relating to burial practices attributed to contemporary sages. Although the Tractate *Semahot*, which is entirely devoted to the laws of burial and mourning, is not part of the Mishnah, it includes many early traditions, some of which are known from other tannaitic sources as well, others from this tractate alone.[2] Tannaitic sources repeatedly emphasize that it is forbidden to treat a person as dead until it is clearly ascertained that he has expired.[3] One of the first acts done for the dead person was the closing of his eyes: the Halakah again warns that this must not be done until after the departure of the soul.[4] Later sources note that this was performed by the son or the closest relation present, linking this practice to the divine promise to Jacob (Gen. 46:4): 'Joseph's hand shall close your eyes;'[5] we may assume that this was also the early custom, as it was also known in Roman and Hellenistic practice.[6] Care was taken to ensure that the body did not become distorted: this was done by binding the cheeks, in order to keep the mouth closed, and by closing the orifices of the body to prevent swelling. Placing the corpse on cold sand was another measure taken to inhibit swelling.[7]

A death in the family immediately caused grief and lamentation, expressed in numerous forms some of which were required by the

---

[1] *M. Niddah* 5:9; these traditions are ascribed to second century sages in *T. Niddah* 6:3.
[2] The earlier opinion, which held that the tractate was of late origin, appears to be unfounded. See the introduction of Zlotnick pp. 1-30 esp. pp. 1-9.
[3] *Semahoth* 1.
[4] *M. Shabbath* 23:5; *Semahoth* 1:4.
[5] *Midrash ha-Hafetz* (cited in Kasher, *Torah Shelemah* VIII (1940), p. 1675; *Aruk ha-Shalem* s.v. אמץ.
[6] On the Greek practices, see Plato, *Phaedo* 118a.
[7] *M. Shabbath* 23:5; *Semahoth* 1.

Halakah, including the obligations of the husband to his deceased wife. Others were merely customs or even just tolerated practices. Among the first signs of grief and mourning was the obligatory rending of garments by the members of the family, male and female alike;[1] this obligation was particularly grave in the case of mourning for a parent. Those who were present at a death rent their garments even if they were not members of the family, while members of the family rent theirs either at the time of death or when they received notification of it.[2] Our literature stresses the fact that it was customary to assign someone to attend the corpse continuously;[3] and candles were lit at the head or feet of the corpse out of respect for the dead.[4] After these first arrangements, the family immediately began preparations for funeral and burial. The traditions about the customs of Jerusalem report that 'one should not keep the corpse through the night,' but rather bury it on the very day of death,[5] and outside of Jerusalem efforts were also made to bury the dead as speedily as possible. Leaving a corpse unburied through the night, for any reason, was considered to be sinfully disrespectful, and was permitted only if more time was needed for the preparation of shrouds or a coffin.[6] This haste may also be seen in the New Testament's account of the death of Ananias, the husband of Saphira, who was buried three hours after his death.[7]

In addition to preparation of shrouds and a coffin, burial arrangements included the acquisition of keeners and pipers. A halakhah informs us that, as a minimum, a husband was expected to provide one keening woman and two pipers for his wife's funeral, and this

---

[1] The detailed laws of this practice, as well as various early traditions about the rending of clothing are set forth in *Semahoth* 9. See also *M. Moed Katan* 3:7; *T. Moed Katan* 2:17 and both Talmuds.

[2] *T. B. Moed Katan* 25a. Cf. also *Semahoth* 12:2; *M. Yebamoth* 15:1.

[3] *T. Shabbath* 17:19; *T. B. Berakoth* 18a.

[4] *M. Berakoth* 8:6; *T. B. Berakoth* 53a; *T. Shabbath* 6:2.

[5] The customs of Jerusalem are preserved in four versions: 1) *Aboth de Rabbi Nathan* Version A, 35 (p. 104); 2) *Aboth de Rabbi Nathan*, Version B, 39 (p. 107); 3) *T. Negaim* 6:2; 4) *T. B. Baba Kamma* 82a. The antiquity of these customs has been disputed, but undoubtedly they preserve ancient traditions. See the recent discussion of A. Gutman in *HUCA* XL/XLI (1969/70), pp. 251-75 and the literature cited there.

[6] See *M. Sanhedrin* 6:5; *Semahoth* 11:1.

[7] Acts 5:6-10. In the story about the death of Tabitha in Joppa, the disciples await Peter's arrival from Lydda; the account emphasizes that Lydda was only a few hours' walk from Joppa (Acts 9:36-41).

was required of even the poorest Jew.[1] In some places pipes, shrouds, coffins and other requisite items were not readily available, and various regulations dealt with problems which arose in connection with the acquisition of such items on the sabbath, to be arranged with the assistance of gentiles, so that everything would be ready for a funeral upon the conclusion of the sabbath; other laws deal with the problems which arose if the pipers had not arrived by the scheduled start of the funeral.[2]

Josephus and Matthew mention male keeners,[3] but in the tannaitic literature only female keeners are mentioned.[4] A slightly later source lists the different uses of various languages, and Aramaic was appropriate for lamentations.[5] This need only imply that keening was performed by women. The keening women began their lamentations in the house of the deceased, even sitting upon the bed on which the corpse lay,[6] and continued their wailing all along the route of the funeral procession. The practice of having keening women also explains the fact that women customarily walked at the head of the procession. This was at least the most common practice, although tannaitic sources also mention the existence of a different custom, according to which men walked at the head of funeral processions.[7] Keening women probably received wages for their work. In most towns if not in all there existed charitable societies whose purpose was to care for the dead and aid the mourners, thus doing works of righteousness (גמילות חסד) for both; a sage of the Jabneh period referred to such groups in Jerusalem.[8] These charitable groups also took care of the preparation of the corpse for burial: there was a fixed tradition regulating the preparation of the corpses, and certainly not everyone knew how to care for the corpse and perform such required functions as bathing it and wrapping it in shrouds. In an inscription

[1] M. Ketuboth 4:4. Semahoth 14:7 mentions 'two pipers and keening women', but the reading 'a keening woman' (singular) appears in all readings of the Mishnah.

[2] M. Shabbath 23:4; T. Shabbath 17:14; M. Baba Metzia 6:1.

[3] Jos. War III, 437; Matt. 9:23.

[4] In addition to the preceding notes, cf. also M. Moed Katan 3:9; T. Yebamoth 14:7; T. Nedarim 2:7 and many other passages.

[5] P. T. Megillah I, 71b; P. T. Sotah VII, 21c.

[6] T. Kelim Baba Bathra 2:8.

[7] See P. T. Sanhedrin II, 20b; T. B. Sanhedrin 20a. In Aboth de Rabbi Nathan Version B, 9 (p. 25) the preacher assumes that women lead funeral processions.

[8] The charitable societies of Jerusalem are mentioned in T. Megillah 4 (3): 15 and Semahoth 12:5; cf. also T. B. Moed Katan 27b, see J. Mann, 'Rabbinic Studies in the Synoptic Gospels', HUCA (1924), p. 325.

at Beth Shearim, apparently from the synagogue, two people are mentioned; one of these is described as συστελλον(τος), probably the one who covered the eyes or wrapped the body in the shrouds, the other as κοιμ(ωντος), either the one who prepared the body for burial or the eulogist.[1]

Preparation of the corpse for burial consisted mainly in washing it and wrapping it in shrouds. The Mishnah states that the corpse is anointed and rinsed.[2] The body was first anointed with oil to clean it and this was followed by a bath with water.[3] The Book of Acts, reporting the death of Tabitha in Joppa also mentions the washing of her corpse as part of the burial preparations.[4]

The Gospel of John notes that as part of the preparation for Jesus' burial, his body was 'bound in linen cloths with spices, as was the burial custom of the Jews';[5]

Luke and Mark also mention the spices.[6] Josephus records the use of spices at Herod's funeral; these spices were carried before the body in the procession and buried during the funeral.[7] The funeral use of spices is not conspicuous in talmudic traditions, but various forms of the practice are referred to,[8] and there is no reason to doubt the existence of this custom either in the form of wrapping the corpse in spices, burning spices before the funeral procession, or sprinkling them on the bier along with myrtle branches.[9] The preparation of the corpse

---

[1] B. Lifschitz, in *RB* (1960), p. 62; M. Schwabe and B. Lifschitz *Beth Shearim* II (1967), no. 202; G. Allon, *Studies in Jewish History* II (1958; in Hebrew), pp. 106-10. Cf. also Acts 5 : 5-6.
[2] *M. Shabbath* 23 : 5.
[3] Inaccuracy in translation has caused some to reverse the order in the Mishnah so that the corpse was first washed and then anointed with scented oil. The proper order was one anointing prior to the washing, which rinsed off the oil; the second anointing following the washing was to perfume the body. See A. Büchler in *S. Krauss Jubilee Volume* (1937), pp. 36-54 (in Hebrew).
[4] Acts 9:36-7. In the accounts of the burial of Jesus no mention is made of washing the body before it was wrapped in a shroud (Matt. 27:59 and parallels). It is possible that it was omitted because of the imminent approach of the Sabbath. Nonetheless this custom of washing the corpse was already well established in the first century. Cf. *Lev. Rabba* 34, 10 (p. 794); *Ruth Rabba* 2.
[5] John 19:39-40; cf 12:5-7.
[6] Mark 16:1; Luke 24:1.
[7] Jos. *Ant.* XVII, 199 and *War* I, 673; the earlier rumour of Herod's death mentions this also, cf. *Ant.* XV. 61.
[8] *M. Berakoth* 8:6; *T. B. Berakoth* 53a; *P. T. Berakoth* VIII, 12b-c; cf. Maimonides, *Mishneh Torah, Laws of Mourning* 4:1.
[9] For spices alone, cf. *P. T. Shekalim* II, 47a; on the use of myrtle cf. *T. B. Betza* 6a; spices placed under the bed of a corpse are mentioned in *T. B. Moed Katan*

for burial further included trimming the hair,[1] the only exception being unmarried girls, who were buried with their hair loose, just as brides were brought to their wedding.[2] The body was wrapped in shrouds, which are frequently mentioned in Jewish sources.[3] These were garments specially prepared, or freshly laundered, for the purpose of wrapping the dead.[4] The Hebrew word for these burial garments, (תכריכין) connotes wrapping and binding more than dress, as is indicated also by tractate Semahot: 'Men may wrap and bind men but not women, but women may wrap and bind both men and women.'[5] This same activity is explicitly indicated by John: 'They took the body of Jesus and bound it in linen cloths.'[6]

During the late Second Temple period it apparently became common to spend great sums on expensive shrouds, just as other expenses for funerals such as for funeral meals grew, and various traditions recall that the nation's sages attempted, by personal example, to brake this process and reduce expenses. The *Testament of Judah* reports that Judah demanded that he should not be buried in expensive clothes,[7] and the Talmud reports that 'formerly, the funeral expenses were even harder for the family to bear than was the death itself, until Rabban Gamaliel treated himself lightly: he was buried in flaxen shrouds, and following him the whole people regularly buried its dead in flax.'[8] It cannot be determined whether the reference is to Rabban Gamaliel the Elder, who lived before 70 C.E., or to his successor Rabban Gamaliel II, of the Jabneh period. A similar tradition reports that Rabbi Judah the patriarch who died in the early third century C.E., commanded that numerous shrouds should not be used for his burial.[9] The *Book of Adam and Eve* informs us that God instructed the angels to bring three sheets of expensive fine linen for enshrouding the dead

27b; *T. Niddah* 9: 16. Cf. also *Testament of Abraham* A, 20; *Life of Adam and Eve* (Latin version) 40:2.
[1] *T. B. Moed Katan* 8b.
[2] *Semahoth* 8:7.
[3] Cf. *M. Kilaim* 9:4; *M. Maaser Sheni* 5:12; *T. Nedarim* 2:7. See also the following notes.
[4] *T. B. Moed Katan* 8b; *T. B. Menahoth* 41a.
[5] *Semahoth* 12:10.
[6] John 19:40; cf. Matt. 27:59 and parallels; also in the case of Lazarus, cf. John 11:44.
[7] *Testament of Judah* 26:3. Its omission in the Armenian version does not prove that this passage is secondary.
[8] *T. B. Ketuboth* 8b and par. in *T. B. Moed Katan* 27b; cf. the abridged form in *T. Niddah* 9:17.
[9] *P.T. Kilaim* IX, 32a (end) and par. in *Gen. Rabba* 100 (p. 1285). Cf. *Semahoth* 9:23.

Adam's body;[1] it is difficult to determine, however, if the latter source reflects contemporary funeral practice or is only an extravagant description of Adam's divinely directed burial.

Coffins, usually wooden, were used for burial, but the body was brought to the graveside, in a כליבא, a sort of knitted covering. A tannaitic tradition relates that 'Formerly, a *dargash* (type of couch) was used for the burial of the rich and a *kliva* for the poor, and the poor felt shamed: it was ruled that out of respect for the poor, all burials should be in *klivas*.'[2]

After the corpse was removed from the house, it was customary to lower all the beds in the house onto the ground, a procedure known in tannaitic literature as 'overturning the bed.' This was the most conspicuous sign that the house was in mourning, and is frequently mentioned in talmudic literature. According to some usages, the beds were overturned as soon as the dead body was removed from the house, but according to others it was done only following the burial.[3]

The coffin was borne on the shoulders of pall-bearers (כתפים). Although the mourners themselves were permitted to wear shoes during the funeral, removing them only after the interment, the coffin-bearers walked barefoot as a sign of mourning;[4] the pall-bearers were exchanged a few times along the way.[5] As the burial of the dead was not only the concern of the relatives and friends of the deceased, but an important commandment as well, all who heard of a funeral procession or saw one in progress, men and women alike, joined those accompanying the coffin.[6] We are told that in Babylonia it was customary to blow horns in order to publicize funeral processions, but it is not known whether this was common in Palestine as well.[7]

In addition to the keening women, there was sometimes also a male eulogist who accompanied the coffin. In contrast to the women, who constantly repeated general expressions of grief which were only slightly adjusted to fit each individual deceased, the eulogist's laments were in each case composed just for the person he was accompanying to burial. Eulogists took various passages from the Torah and oral tradition and applied them to the deceased, or to the particular

---

[1] *Life of Adam and Eve*, Latin version; cf. parallel versions.
[2] *T. B. Moed Katan* 27b; *T. Niddah* 9:16.
[3] *M. Moed Katan* 3:7; *P. T. Moed Katan* III, 83a-b.
[4] *P. T. Berakoth* III, 6b; *P. T. Nazir* VII, 56c; *Gen. Rabba* 96 (p. 1238).
[5] *M. Berakoth* 3:1; *P. T. Berakoth* III, 6b.
[6] *T. B. Ketuboth* 17a.
[7] *T. B. Moed Katan* 27b.

circumstances of the death. The eulogists were on occasion sages or students of the Torah, and talmudic traditions have preserved passages from such eulogies from various times.[1] Usually, however, eulogists were professionals who received fees for their work.[2] Eulogies were not generally delivered all at once, but split among various stations along the route of the funeral procession; the funeral procession of Rabbi Judah the Patriarch made eighteen such stops.[3] Our sources also mention a 'eulogy house', a sort of permanent courtyard, near the family burial plot, where it was customary to eulogize deceased members of that family.[4] If the deceased person was notable in the community, and the mourning for him public, his coffin was also taken into the synagogue for the eulogy. As may be well understood, there was a tendency to exaggerate the qualities and achievements of the dead, and we find some statements denouncing any falsehood. One report informs us that the inhabitants of Galilee and Jerusalem differed from the Judaeans in this matter, the former limiting themselves to statements which truly pertained to the deceased, while the latter allowed even unwarranted praise. The tradition further states that in Galilee and Jerusalem eulogists preceded the bier, while in Judaea they followed it.[5] In some places only men were eulogized, but elsewhere there were funeral orations for women as well. In places where eulogies were customary for women, the husband was obliged to give the speech in memory of his wife, in addition to his other responsibilities regarding her burial.[6] An inscription from a later period, found in Venosa, Italy, records that the death of a fourteen year old girl was the cause of general mourning, and she was eulogized by two sages and two *apostoli* who apparently happened to be there at the time.[7]

Cemeteries or burial sites were usually private and belonged to individual families; this fact becomes obvious from the plans of the many graveyards around Jerusalem and elsewhere, as well as from inscriptions, historical references, and halakic discussions. The Halakah

---

[1] See E. Feldman, 'The Rabbinic Lament', *JQR* (1972), pp. 51-75.
[2] *M. Moed Katan* 1:5 as understood in *T. B. Moed Katan* 8a.
[3] *T. Megillah* 3 (4): 14 and the parallels cited by Lieberman's commentary ad loc.; *M. Baba Bathra* 6:7; *M. Ketuboth* 2:10; *M. Megillah* 4:3; *T. B. Baba Bathra* 100b. On the funeral of Rabbi Judah the Patriarch at the beginning of the third century, cf. *P. T. Kilaim* ix, 32b.
[4] *T. B. Moed Katan* 21b and previous note.
[5] *Semahoth* 3:6; *T. B. Shabbath* 153a.
[6] *T. Ketuboth* 4:2; *P. T. Ketuboth* iv, 28d; *Semahoth* 14:7.
[7] *CII* no. 611.

779

stresses the importance of family burial plots, and the Tannaim simply assumed that all those who dug or hewed graves did so for families. Often the family gravesites were concentrated in an area or areas outside of the city, and, according to the accepted Halakah, graves had to be at some distance from the city, preferably on the eastern side but in any case not on the west, from which side came the prevailing winds,[1] Jerusalem's necropolis was bowshaped, surrounding the city on all sides except the west; only the Herodian family graves lay to the west of the city.[2]

The dead were buried in coffins, many sources mentioning shrouds and coffins together as the principal requirements of the dead; usually the reference is to wooden coffins.[3] Burials in the first century differed from those of later Jewish practice. Graves were usually niches hewn in rows in a cave or one of its chambers; the construction of a family tomb thus involved digging out a chamber or exploiting an existing cave and carving one or two rows of niches into the mountainside or within the cave. Some burial caves were more complex: a hall was first hewn out, and the niches were then carved into the different rooms branching off the hall. This design is discussed in a mishnah, which specifies the plan and dimensions of burial caves, and the number of niches they must include, in cases when a man contracted to construct such a cave.[4] There is also evidence of burial in fields. Great efforts were made to ensure that these graves would not disappear. It was forbidden to plow such fields as this might destroy the graves, and the graves themselves were marked in order to prevent passers-by from being ritually defiled by them.[5]

Whether the burial was in field or cave, Jews took pains to ensure that the body was interred with the limbs unbent, and it therefore was

---

[1] On family burial, cf. the baraita in *T. B. Baba Bathra* 100b and parallels; on the graves outside cities, see *M. Baba Bathra* 2:9, cf. also Luke 7:12 and Matt. 8:28.

[2] Summaries about the necropolis of Jerusalem are given by K. Galling, 'Die Nekropole von Jerusalem', *PJB* 32 (1936), pp. 73-101; N. Avigad, 'The Necropolis', in *Sefer Jerushalaim*, pp. 320-48.

[3] *M. Moed Katan* 1:6; *M. Kilaim* 9:4; *M. Maaser Sheni* 5:4; *T. Nedarim* 2:7; cf. also *Gen. Rabba* 19, 8 end (p. 178). Stone coffins are mentioned in *T. Ohiloth* 2:3.

[4] *M. Baba Bathra* 6:8. On the type of burial cave we have described see M. Cohen, *The Grave of the Kings* (1947); in Hebrew; J. Rotschild, in *PEQ* 84 (1952), pp. 23-38; 86 (1954), pp. 16-22.

[5] *M. Oholoth* chaps. 17-18; *T. Ohiloth* chaps. 16-18. On grave markings, see *M. Shekalim* 1:1; *M. Moed Katan* 1:2; *T. B. Moed Katan* 6a; Matt. 23:27.

assumed that any corpse found in this state was Jewish.[1] The grave
was not filled with dirt: it was blocked with a large rock, although
some also built a stone door for the grave as well. As we shall see,
however, the usual burial cave was simply blocked with a heavy
boulder, which could be rolled aside by the combined efforts of a few
people in order to open the grave; sometimes both doors and movable
boulders were used.[2] The Tosefta gives a lifelike description of a
burial which took place in the Beth Dagon of Judaea. Because the
burial took place on the eve of Passover and the men had to avoid
incurring impurity, the women took care of the burial and tied ropes
around the entrance boulder, so that the men could pull while remaining outside.[3] Such entrance boulders or the depressions which
received them have been found in the many graveyards discovered in
Israel.

Various articles were sometimes placed or thrown into the grave
along with the body, particularly the personal accessories of the
deceased, although the tannaitic tradition tended to restrain this
practice as much as possible. Some sages completely forbade throwing
such articles into graves, while others only limited the practice to
things of merely symbolic value, such as the inkstand, reed pen, and
writing tablets of the deceased.[4] In extraordinary cases it was even
customary to burn valuable articles, as the tannaitic Halakah rules:
'One burns for kings... just as one burns for kings, one burns for
patriarchs, but not for common people. And what was burnt for him?
His couches and his objects of service... When Rabban Gamaliel the
Elder died, Onkelos the proselyte burnt articles valued at more than
seventy *manas*.'[5]

Following the burial a ceremony took place in which condolences were
offered: the public ranged itself in a row, or rows, and the mourners
passed among the rows while the public expressed their condolences.

---

[1] *M. Nazir* 9:3 as understood in the Talmuds, cf. *P. T. Nazir*, IX, 57d and *T. B. Nazir*, 65a.
[2] *M. Oholoth* 2:4; *M. Nazir* 7:3; Matt. 28:2; *P. T. Moed Katan* III, 83a.
[3] *T. Ohiloth* 3:9.
[4] *Semahoth* 8:2-7 and the notes in the translation of Zlotnick, p. 137; *T. B. Sanhedrin* 48b; *T. Ohiloth* 9:5.
[5] Allon, *Studies* II, pp. 99-105; Zlotnick pp. 15-17. *T. Shabbath* 7:18 and parallels mentioned in Lieberman's commentary ad loc. The story about Rabban Gamaliel is contained in *T. Shabbath, Semahoth* 8:6 and *T. B. Abodah Zarah* 11a. Most readings mention Rabban Gamaliel the Elder, but this conflicts with the date of Onkelos. The story refers to the death of his grandson, Rabban Gamaliel II in the early part of the second century; cf. Lieberman, op. cit., p. 100.

A passage recalls that 'formerly the mourners used to stand still while the people passed by. But there were two families in Jerusalem who contended with one another, each maintaining: We shall pass first. So the sages established the rule that the public should remain standing and the mourners pass by.'[1] In fact, the traditions from the Second Temple period usually speak of the consolers filing by the mourners;[2] while the later traditions speak of the former being ranged in rows and the latter passing among them, as is still the Jewish practice.[3]

The funeral did not conclude with the consolation ceremony. People continued to express condolences, either standing or sitting down. They walked a short distance, stopped, sat down, said some words of comfort to the mourners, and then continued a little further. A tannaitic tradition reports: 'Formerly, they never stood and sat less than seven times at a funeral, (saying) for instance: 'Rise, friends, rise!, sit, friends, sit!'[4] The crowd did not finally disperse until the mourner or mourners informed them, or hinted, that they could go home, having fulfilled their obligations of going to the funeral and sharing in the mourning.[5]

Mourning practices were numerous and complex, some lasting thirty days, others for an entire year.[6] The first seven days of mourning were the most serious: men and women sat shoeless on the ground or on low supports, and they were forbidden to work, wash, anoint themselves or engage in sexual intercourse; even the study of Torah was prohibited.[7] Beds remained in their lowered positions during the entire week of mourning. Mention should be made of another custom, which eventually fell into disuse: the mourner kept his head covered, removing the covering only when guests came to offer consolation.[8] During the first three days of mourning, even the poor were forbidden to work.[9] Some texts claim that during the first three days a mourner was also forbidden to put on phylacteries, for the impact of his bereavement came during those days, and, according to some opinions,

---

[1] *T. B. Sanhedrin* 19a; cf. *P. T. Berakoth* III, 6b.
[2] *M. Sanhedrin* 2:1; *T. B. Sanhedrin* 19a.
[3] *M. Moed Katan* 3:7; *M. Berakoth* 3:2; *Semahoth* 10:8; 11:3.
[4] *T. B. Baba Bathra* 100b; cf. *P. T. Megillah* IV, 75a (end).
[5] This is implied in *M. Moed Katan* 3:7.
[6] *T. B. Moed Katan* 21a-b; *P. T. Moed Katan* III, 82a-83a.
[7] *P T. Moed Katan* III, 82d; *T. B. Moed Katan* 21a.
[8] *Semahoth* 10:8-9; *Aboth de Rabbi Nathan*, Version A, 1. (p. 4); *T. B. Moed Katan* 15a.
[9] *P. T. Moed Katan* III, 82b; *Gen. Rabba* 100 (p. 1290); *T. B. Moed Katan* 21a.

during the remaining days of the week a mourner was to remove his phylacteries whenever guests came to console him.[1]

Visitation and comforting the bereaved was very important during the first week of mourning: people came from near and far, and in the larger settlements the city council (חבר עיר) or, more probably, a delegation of its members, also came. The consolers brought food and drink with them, and meals were served at which not insignificant amounts of wine were consumed; in the presence of a quorum of ten men special blessings of condolence were also recited.[2] A baraita relates[3]: 'We have learned, ten cups of wine are to be consumed in a house of mourning: two before the meal, five during the meal, and three after the meal. Which are the three after the meal? One for the grace over meals, one for "acts of kindness" (גמילות חסדים), and one for comforting the mourners. But when Rabban (Simeon ben)[4] Gamaliel died, three more were added: one each for the *hazzan*, the head of the synagogue, and Rabban Gamaliel. But when the court saw that people were continuously becoming drunk, they decreed a return to the former practice.' The entire ceremony, including the condolences and the blessings, is frequently mentioned in our literature. There were special charitable societies in Jerusalem which provided for the consolation of mourners. The above-mentioned baraita dealing with the differences between the burial practices of rich and poor also reports:

'Formerly, rich visiting the mourner's house were served drinks in white glass cups, while the poor were served with cups of coloured glass, and the poor felt shamed; out of respect for the poor it was therefore ruled that all should be served with cups of coloured glass.'[5]

All the practices of mourning and consolation were the same whether the deceased was male or female. The sole difference between men and women in this regard was that some formal ceremonies, such as the visit by city councillors, occurred only after the death of men.[6] If one spouse was in mourning for one of his or her relatives, the other was not obliged by the laws of mourning, but the rule was: 'If his mother-in-law or father-in-law or another of his wife's close relations

---

[1] Cf. preceding note and *P. T. Berakoth* III, 5d.
[2] *T. Berakoth* 3:24; *Semahoth* 14:13-14; *M. Megillah* 4:3.
[3] *P. T. Berakoth* III, 6a; *T. B. Ketuboth* 8b; *Semahoth* 14:14.
[4] These words, contained in the Palestinian Talmud, are not in the continuation of the parallels and are certainly corrupt.
[5] *T. Niddah* 9:17; *T. B. Moed Katan* 27a; *Semahoth* 12.
[6] *Semahoth* 11:2.

(e.g., her brother or sister) dies, a husband cannot compel his wife to paint her eyes or put on rouge, but must rather act as she does; similarly, if her mother-in-law or father-in-law or another of her husband's close relations dies, she may not paint her eyes or put on rouge, but must act as he does.'[1] Only a young woman living at home was exempted from mourning customs which would impair her appearance: 'An adolescent girl is not allowed to make herself ugly (even) on account of her father's death.'[2]

In all the discussions of burial practices, including the blessings, nothing suggests that they were performed in order to atone for the deceased or aid him after his death. There are scattered statements which suggest that the living can atone for the dead,[3] but these beliefs were not widespread, nor did they find any expression in the blessings or early burial practices. The blessings stress the justice of divine judgement and belief in immortality and resurrection; they also include prayers for the welfare of the mourners and those who engage in 'acts of kindness' and consolation. Nothing is said, however, regarding the dead, atonement for him, or salvation of his soul.[4] The later Jewish practices, according to which the son or other relatives of the deceased could help the latter's soul by saying such prayers as *borehu* and the *kaddish*, are mentioned only in much later sources. The stories which report that some of the early sages, such as Rabban Johannan ben Zakkai and Rabbi Akiba, instructed the sons of sinners to say the *kaddish* and thus save their fathers from being sentenced to Gehenna, are most likely late traditions projected back to the ancients.[5]

The beginning of the eighth chapter of *Semahoth* states: 'One should go to the cemetery to check the dead within three days and not fear that such smacks of pagan practices; it once happened that a [buried] man was visited and went on to live another twenty-five years.'[6] This

---

[1] *P. T. Moed Katan* III, 83a; *T. B. Moed Katan* 20a; *Semahoth* 11:8.
[2] *T. B. Taanith* 13b. This passage has no Palestinian parallels and its date is unknown.
[3] 2 Macc. 12:44-45; *Sifre Deut.* 210 (p. 244).
[4] See G. Alon, *Studies in the History of Israel* (1957, in Hebrew) II, pp. 99-105; L. Ginzburg, *A commentary on the Palestinian Talmud* II (1941), pp. 69-76.
[5] *Pseudo Seder Eliyahu Zuta* (pp. 22-3); *Kallah Rabbati* II (p. 202).
[6] Semahoth (ed. Higger, p. 148, ed. Zlotnick, p. 19). Both Higger and Zlotnick read: 'thirty days,' but this reading is found only in one manuscript. The other manuscripts read 'three days', which reading also appears in ancient commentaries and is confirmed by various tannaitic sources. See J. N. Epstein, *Introduction to the Text of the Mishnah* (1948; in Hebrew), pp. 469-71); cf. esp. p. 471, n. 2. See also V. Aptowitzer, *Sefer ha-Ravia* III (1964), p. 565.

baraita shows that it was customary to go and verify that the buried person was really dead, for as burial followed death so quickly, errors might sometimes occur. The baraita bolsters its ruling with the story of a man who was in fact discovered to be alive after his burial, which we should understand in view of the fact that graves were not filled with dirt, but only blocked with moveable boulders. The women who came to visit Jesus' grave were following the Jewish custom of rolling back the entrance boulder in order to make sure that he was really dead.[1] It is not impossible that the practice became customary even when the fact of death was known with complete certainty, although, as our baraita testifies, the practice of visiting graves within the first three days after burial originated in the need to allay all doubt that there had not been only apparent death, and that the buried person in the meantime had not returned to life.

The principal practices of mourning terminated with the first week, but some continued for thirty days: these were mainly the prohibitions of cutting one's hair, wearing pressed clothes, marrying, and visiting public taverns. Following a parent's death, some of the mourning practices lasted a full twelve months. Although the customs of mourning were thus numerous and prolonged, the Talmud still saw a need to enjoin people against increasing their mourning beyond the requirements of the Halakah.[2]

Upon the conclusion of the first week of bereavement, the mourners were considered to be impure, as were most of their household vessels; apart from pottery, however, all vessels could be purified. Even those who did not carefully observe all the strict laws of purity in accordance with Pharisaic tradition apparently followed the practice of purifying themselves from the pollution of death, which is explicitly detailed in the Torah (Num. 18). Josephus, at any rate, reports that following mourning both the house and its inhabitants must be purified,[3] and talmudic traditions report that several sages, feeling death at hand, ordered vessels to be removed from the house, to prevent their incurring impurity.[4]

---

[1] Matt. 28:1; Mark 16:1-4; Luke 24:1; John 20:1.
[2] *M. Moed Katan* 3:5; *P. T. Moed Katan* III, 82a; *T. B. Moed Katan* 23a; 27a; *Semahoth* chaps. 7, 9, 10.
[3] Jos. *Against Apion* II, 205.
[4] *P. T. Sotah* IX, 24c; *P. T. Abodah Zarah* III, 42c; *T. B. Berakoth* 28b. The Halakah knows no purification of the house itself, as the house cannot become unclean; perhaps Josephus is referring to the purification of those household articles which are susceptible to pollution.

The interment we have described was not, as a rule, the final burial. During the last two centuries of the Temple era, it became customary to place the coffin in a niche in the burial cave and, after a considerable time, to collect the bones, from which all the flesh had rotted away and place them in a chest which was then set in a niche, thus completing the interment.[1] The practice of collecting the bones (*ossilegium*) is quite frequently mentioned in our sources, and many customs and traditions were linked to it.[2] Many of the burial caves of Jerusalem and its environs give clear evidence of this practice, as the small chests contained in their crypts could not possibly contain whole bodies, but only collections of bones.[3] Of this type of burial we read: 'Formerly, they buried them first in mounds, but after the flesh was consumed the bones were collected and re-interred in coffins.'[4] Rabbi Eliezer ben Zadok, who lived in the generation following the destruction of the Temple, once spoke of his father's burial: 'Before his death my father said: "Son, first bury me in a fosse, and then collect my bones and put them in a chest, but don't you yourself collect them." And this is what I did: Johanan went and collected the bones and spread a sheet over them, whereupon I entered, rent my garments over them, and sprinkled over them dry herbs. Just as he attended his father, so I attended him.'[5] Many burial caves in Israel contain a sort of large trough which temporarily held the whole corpses until such time as the bones were gathered and re-interred.

From the above statement by Rabbi Eleazar it is obvious that not all followed the custom of collecting the bones, and we also have clear archaeological evidence that alongside the widespread practice of double burials, some were accustomed to bury their dead only once. This latter custom spread in the period after 70 and eventually caused the former, i.e. burying the corpse and then later collecting the bones for re-interment, to sink into oblivion. Where it was customary, the final interment of the bones was not always at the site of the first burial, as the family might have moved about during the interval, and for this reason there are various laws dealing with problems arising from the transfer of bones from place to place.[6] The day the bones were gathered was apparently similar to a day of

---

[1] *Midrash Tanhuma*, Lev. 8.
[2] *M. Sanhedrin* 6:6; *M. Moed Katan* 1:5; *Semahoth* ch. 12; *T. Megillah* 4:15.
[3] See Meyers, *passim*.
[4] *P. T. Moed Katan* I, 90c; *P. T. Sanhedrin* VI, 23d.
[5] *Semahoth* 12:9.
[6] *P. T. Berakoth* III, 6a; *T. B. Berakoth* 18a.

mourning, although some saw it as a day of rejoicing, as only then did the bones of their late relatives reach a final resting place; in any case the mourning lasted only that single day.[1]

Talmudic tradition taught that one need not put tombstones on the graves of the righteous, 'for their words are their memorials,' and Josephus too claims that the Torah does not require ornate tombstones.[2] The sources mention the existence of tombstones, however, from the time of the Hasmonaeans until the late Temple period,[3] and tombstones of our period or their remains, some very ornate, may still be found today in the environs of Jerusalem and elsewhere. According to later Jewish practice, the annual anniversary of the death of a member of the family was celebrated by visiting the grave, reciting the *kaddish*, lighting a memorial lamp, and keeping the day as a fast. The attempts of some scholars to find indications of these practices in our period, however, are not convincing.[4] In the amoraic period we find cemetery visits, but only for the purpose of asking the dead to intercede for the living.[5]

Widowhood, levirate marriage, and divorce

Marriage contracts from Galilee and Jerusalem stated that in case the husband died, his widow could remain in his house and support herself from his property.[6] Many reports, from various periods, testify to the fact that widows both young and old remained in their husbands' houses.[7] A passage in the Mishnah gives the two options which custom offered the widow: the widow could go from her husband's grave to her father's house, or she could return to the house of her in-laws.[8] Formal law and accepted custom beyond any doubt agreed that a widow's remarriage was both permissible and desirable, and she was

---

[1] *M. Moed Katan* 1:5; *Semahoth* 12:4.

[2] *P. T. Shekalim* ii, 47a; Jos. *Against Apion* ii, 205.

[3] 1 Macc. 13:27-29; Jos. *Ant.* xvi, 182: *T. Ohiloth* 17:4; *P. T. Erubin* v, 22a.

[4] See Y. Avida, 'Chapters Regarding Memorials (Jahrzeit)', *Sinai* (1957), pp. 55-68.

[5] *T. B. Taanith* 16a; *T. B. Sotah* 34b.

[6] *M. Ketuboth* 4:12; cf. *T. Ketuboth* 11:5. This right is made explicit in a marriage contract published in *DJD* ii, no. 21, and is apparently also a basic assumption of other marriage contracts discovered in the caves of the Judaean desert.

[7] Judith 8:4; see also the testament of Rabbi Judah the Patriarch in *T. B. Ketuboth* 103a.

[8] *M. Ketuboth* 9:6; 12:3 and many other passages.

only required to wait long enough for it to be ascertained that she was not already pregnant at the time of the second marriage, thereby avoiding uncertainty as to the paternity of a future child; in any case, a widow had to wait at least until the end of the first thirty days of mourning.[1] After waiting the required period, widows usually did not disdain any opportunity to marry a suitable partner, and talmudic literature is replete with laws and incidents relating to the second marriages of widows. The sages made every effort to find ways to allow second marriages for women whose husbands had disappeared without proper testimony as to their death being available, that is, without the two witnesses required by the standard procedures of Jewish law.[2] The principal reason for these efforts was the desire to allow the widows to remarry. In one report, we read that basing his decision solely on the testimony of a lone witness to the death of some men in Tel Arza, Rabban Gamaliel the Elder allowed all the widows to remarry.[3] We have also the testimony of the latter's great-grandson, Simeon ben Gamaliel who said: 'It once happened that a party of men went to Antioch, and when they returned one of them, a Gentile, reported that of us all, only so-and-so, a Jew, was killed, and when the case came before the sages they permitted his wife to remarry.'[4] For the purpose of allowing a widow to remarry, the sages were willing to accept the testimony of a lone witness, man or woman, Gentile, male or female slave. Even the widow was allowed to testify to her husband's death, not to mention other witnesses whose testimony in other cases no sage or judge would even consider accepting.[5]

Alongside of this practice, however, there were some groups which considered a widow's abstention from remarriage to be a pious and proper act. This is emphasized in the Pauline epistles,[6] but this idea was apparently also known in Jewish circles. The widowed Judith, we are told, remained unmarried despite her many suitors, and Luke reports that Anna, the daughter of Phanuel, of Jerusalem, remained single despite the fact that she was widowed after only seven years of marriage.[7] Jewish inscriptions in Rome praise two women for marrying only one husband each in the course of their lives (μόνανδρος), and of

[1] M. Yebamoth 4:10; T. Yebamoth 6:6.
[2] M. Yebamoth chaps. 15 and 16 and many other passages.
[3] M. Yebamoth 16:7.
[4] T. Yebamoth 14:7.
[5] M. Yebamoth 15:1; T. Yebamoth 14:7.
[6] 1 Tim. 5:9; 1 Cor. 7:39-40.
[7] Judith 8:4; 16:22; Luke 2:36-38.

one it is emphasized that she remained a widow all her life.[1] According to the Targum, when Naomi praised her two widowed daughters-in-law for dealing kindly with the dead, she was referring to their not re-marrying.[2] It may thus be concluded that at least some circles considered it to be particularly praiseworthy for a widow to remain faithful to the memory of her late husband, and not remarry. If a man died without leaving any male or female descendants, one of his brothers was required to marry the widow (cf. Deut. 25:5ff.). Various sources show that this practice was actually carried out during the Second Temple period and afterward.[3] The practice of levirate marriage entailed some very complicated problems, particularly in cases of marriage within the family, and the tractate *Yebamoth* includes many laws and historical traditions dealing with the difficult problems which arose in connection with the practice. Many controversies, some very early, developed regarding the actual application of the levirate. One of the arguments, for example, dealt with the proper procedure in case the deceased brother had been married to two wives.[4]

According to the Torah, a man could refuse to marry his childless brother's widow. To do so, however, he had to be summoned to court and undergo a ceremony called *halitzah* (חליצה cf. Deut. 25:9), the original purpose of which was to degrade him for his refusal to 'build up his brother's house;' this ceremony released the widow from all connection with her brother-in-law. In tannaitic tradition, however, *halitzah* does not appear as a punishment intended to degrade the obstinate brother-in-law, but as a legitimate alternative to marrying one's widowed sister-in-law. There was even an opinion that, because of those whose intentions were not 'for the sake of the commandment,' it would be better if they did not marry their widowed sisters-in-law, as the commandment of *halitzah* takes precedence over the 'commandment of levirate marriage.'[5] The sages even went so far as to 'give him appropriate advice: if he is young and she old, or he old and she young, they should say to him: "What would you do with a young

---

[1] *CII* 81; 392. See also H. Leon, *The Jews in Ancient Rome* (1960), pp. 129-30.
[2] *Targum Ruth* 1:8; the midrash gives another explanation of the 'kindness' referred to.
[3] Salome, the wife of Aristobulus I, married his brother Jannaeus (Jos. *Ant.* XIII, 320). In *T. Yebamoth* 1:10 Rabbi Joshua reports that certain priestly families descended from the offspring of levirate marriages.
[4] *M. Yebamoth* ch. 1; *T. Yebamoth* 1:9; and the two Talmuds ad loc.
[5] *M. Bekhoroth* 1:7.

woman?" or "What would you do with an old woman?". And to a man already married, they would suggest, "Go to one whose age is as your own, and create no strife in your house."[1] Another passage reads: 'If either [the widow or her brother-in-law] opposes [the leviratical marriage], we comply [and require *halitzah* instead].'[2] It seems that cases of *halitzah* were very numerous, especially when the brother on whom the leviratical duty devolved was already married.

In a well-known controversy between the schools of Shammai and Hillel, the former held that divorce was permissible only if the wife was guilty of unchastity or some similar offence, while the latter school allowed divorce for any reason at all.[3] Although as a rule the Shammaites stood for the older law while the Hillelites represented more progressive views, it seems that in the present case the ancient view was approximately that of the school of Hillel. Not only do Philo's and Josephus' accounts of divorce matters agree with the Hillelite view,[4] but even the ancient regulation requiring marriage contracts was based, at least according to its formulation in our sources, on the assumption that a man is permitted to divorce his wife at any time. The stipulation of a sum of money to be paid in case of divorce was, therefore, ordained so that 'he would not lightly consider divorcing her.'[5] From Ben Sira as well, who comes out against arbitrary divorce, we may deduce that a man could divorce his wife even without claiming she had committed adultery.[6]

In theory a bill of divorce (גט) had not to be written in court: it could be signed and transmitted by any two men. The formula, in the Mishnah and the bills of divorce found in caves in the Judaean desert, include no hint that they were written or executed by a court. The bill of divorce was really no more than the husband's announcement that he had divorced his wife and that she was therefore free to marry any other man.[7] It would seem, however, that they were in fact written and executed in court, when the husband's reason for the divorce was a charge of adultery against his wife, which if true would exempt him from the obligation of paying the *ketubah*. If a husband was unable to fulfil his marital obligations, or if she found him loath-

[1] *M. Yebamoth* 12:6; *P. T. Yebamoth* XII, 12d; *T. B. Yebamoth* 44a.
[2] *P. T. Yebamoth* XII, 12d.
[3] *M. Gittin* 9:10; *M. Ketuboth* 7:6; *P. T. Gittin* IX, 50d; *P. T. Sotah* I, 16b.
[4] Philo, *Spec. Leg.* III, 30; Jos. *Ant.* IV, 253.
[5] *T. Ketuboth* 12:1; see Sirach 7:19, 26; 25:25-26.
[6] See Sir. 7:19, 26; 25:25-26.
[7] *M. Gittin* 9:3; *DJD* II, no. 19.

some, the wife could herself demand that he grant her a divorce and, if necessary, she could demand that the court compel him to do so.[1] Palestinian sources, from the second century C.E. indicate that at times it was part of the marriage contract that if one of the couple began to hate the other, a husband would pay a stated sum, and divorce would follow, and that when the wife demanded a divorce, a husband could either grant the divorce willingly or be compelled to do so by the court.[2]

The failure of a marriage to produce children was occasionally the reason for divorce. Mishnaic law ruled that if a man married and after ten years remained without children, he was no longer permitted to neglect his obligation to be fruitful and multiply; the wife had a similar right to divorce so that she could marry another and bear children.[3] Priests were forbidden to marry divorcees, even their own. Diverse sources mention the frequency with which men remarried their divorced wives,[4] the Torah forbidding such remarriages only if the woman had in the meantime been married to a second husband (who had then divorced her or died). Although a divorcee could marry anyone other than a priest, her social status was far from respectable, and to be a 'son of a divorcee' carried with it a certain stigma; the very fact of divorce was a tragedy over which 'even the altar sheds tears.'[5]

BIBLIOGRAPHY

For a general discussion of town and village, courtyard and house in the Land of Israel, see S. KRAUSS, *Talmudische Archäologie* I, 1910, repr. 1966; the Hebrew version, *Kadmoniot ha-Talmud* I, 1910, is more extensive. The reader should be warned that Krauss does not distinguish sufficiently between early and late sources nor Palestinian and Babylonian traditions. On Jewish towns in the Land of Israel, see S. SAFRAI, 'The Jewish Town in Mishaic and Talmudic Times', in

---

[1] *T. B. Gittin* 57a. The practice of executing divorces in court is also mentioned in the Elephantine papyri: cf. ed. Kraeling, nos. 2, 7 and ed. Cowley, no. 15. In the *Document of Damascus* 13:17 and *Targum Ps. Jonathan* on Deut. 24:1 also it is required that divorces be executed in a court. On divorce upon the demand of the wife, see *M. Ketuboth* 5:6; *M. Nedarim* 11:12; *M. Arakhin* 5:6; *T. B. Ketuboth* 63b.
[2] *P. T. Ketuboth* v, 30b; *P. T. Baba Bathra* VIII, 9c; cf. Jos. *Ant.* xv, 259.
[3] *M. Yebamoth* 6:6; *T. Yebamoth* 6:4; *T. B. Yebamoth* 64a.
[4] *M. Moed Katan* 1:7; *T. B. Pesahim* 113b.
[5] *M. Nedarim* 9:9; *T. B. Gittin*, end.

Collected Papers of the Israel Historical Society (1967), pp. 227-36 (in Hebrew). For a detailed examination of ten archaeological excavations of towns in Galilee and the Golan, see z. YEIVIN, *Survey of Settlements in Galilee and Golan from the Period of the Mishnah in the Light of the Sources*, unpublished dissert. Jerusalem 1971. On several aspects of household articles see Y. YADIN, *The Finds from the Bar Kokhba Period in the Cave of Letters*, 1963. On pottery see Y. BRAND, *Ceramics in the Talmudic Literature*, 1963 (in Hebrew).

On family life see the books of L. M. EPSTEIN, *Marriage Laws in the Bible and the Talmud*, 1942; and *Sex in the Jewish Law*, 1959.

On customs of betrothal and marriage, see HERSHBERG, 'Customs of Betrothal and Marriage in Talmudic Times', in he-Atid (1923), pp. 104-75. Pregnancy and childbirth are treated by J. PREUSS, 'Schwangerschaft, Geburt und Wochenbett nach Bibel und Talmud', in *Zeitschrift für Geburts-Hilfe und Gynäkologie* LIII, pp. 1-47.

The two modern editions of *Tractate Semahot* discuss mourning and burial customs: M. HIGGER *Treatise Semahot*, 1931, and D. ZLOTNICK, *The Tractate Mourning*, 1966. On customs of reburial see: E. M. MEYERS, *Jewish Ossuaries: Reburial and Rebirth*, 1971, and P. FIGUERAS, *Jewish and Christian Beliefs in Life after Death*, unpublished dissert. Jerusalem 1974.

Chapter Fifteen
Religion in Everyday Life

The most striking characteristic of the Jewish people in the period of
the Second Temple was the observance of the Law of the one God, as
revealed in the written Torah and the oral tradition. That the whole
life of the Jewish people, from hour to hour of its working days as well
as on the solemn moments of sabbath and feast-day, was dominated
by the Law is evident from talmudic tradition,[1] Josephus[2] and the
New Testament, especially the writings of Paul.[3]

The Torah, the Law of Moses as contained in the Pentateuch, was the
primary source of Law. Even in the written Torah, little was left
outside the scope of the commandments (*mitzwot*). Personal and
social ethics, family relationships, property, agriculture and even
food and dress were catered for, almost as much as strictly religious
behaviour, like the observance of sabbaths and feast-days or the
offerings to be made to priests and Levites. Many topics, however,
which were dealt with only vaguely or in general in the written Law
were expanded and given detailed application in the oral tradition of
the Second Temple period.[4] The development in oral law was so full
and systematic that the whole style of life was changed for individual,
family and nation. However, up to the early tannaitic period, laws
had not yet acquired the formal structure of the talmudic period and
later, nor was the legislation so closely scrutinized for possible implications.

Multitudinous though the precepts were, they were carefully observed,
it seems, by most people. But there were exceptions. The Sadducees

---

[1] Rabbi Johanan ben Torta, a Tanna of the first generation after the Destruction
of the Temple relates that he knew people during the Temple period who were
'careful in their observances of the commandments and the tithe' (*P. T. Yoma* I,
38c and parallels). Likewise, Rabbi Joshua ben Hananiah boasts of this in
presence of the emperor Hadrian (*Ruth Rabba* 3 and parallels).

[2] *Against Apion* I, 38-46; II, 277.

[3] Cf. Paul's discussion on righteousness in the epistle to the Romans, chapter 10.

[4] *M. Aboth* 1:1 'and make a fence around the Law.' See also *Aboth de Rabbi
Nathan* 1 (version A and B); *T. B. Moed Katan* 5b, etc.

rejected the whole of the oral law, obeying only the written Torah. The *am-ha-aretz*, an ill-defined section of the common people, were lax, if not indifferent to the laws of the tithing and ritual purity, and, at least by the Pharisees, always held to be suspect in such matters. But the judicial system, for instance, functioned according to the written Torah (especially Deuteronomy), and even oral tradition was in fact widely honoured as regards the system developed for the offerings and the tithes.

Only in a few cases the Halakah was not carried out fully such as the laws concerning the jubilee year and those concerning Hebrew bonds-men.[1] The oral law was not fully uniform. The laws of the sabbath and tithing were sometimes a matter for debate among Pharisees, whose construction of them was complicated and rigorous, and gave rise to divergent traditions. The calendar of feasts differed among certain groups, whose exclusivity merits them the term of 'sects.'

Tannaitic practice, in which the written and oral law of the earlier period is to some extent reflected, might well appear burdensome at first sight. But certain groups adopted even a more stringent system of Halakah, as may be seen from such literature as the *Book of Jubilees* and that of Qumran. And in fact, observance of the precepts was a joyous matter, since they were regarded as so many privileged opportunities bestowed by divine favour. A tannaitic source, for instance, tells how a certain man forgot to take in a sheaf of corn from his field. He then ordered his son to make a burnt-offering and a peace offering. 'Why,' asked the son, 'did you think fit to rejoice more at this commandment than at the others of the Torah?' The answer was: 'Our maker ordained that all the commandments of the Torah should be deliberately fulfilled. But this one demands our indeliberate participation.'[2] By this he meant that it was a command-ment which could not have been fulfilled by deliberate intent, since it could only be done when one had forgotten something, that is, on the occasion of an indeliberate act. He offered sacrifice because he was glad to have 'chanced upon' the occasion of leaving a forgotten sheaf for the poor, as the law ordained. The story deals with a 'pious' man, but such joyful observance was the general rule, if one may go by the sages of the second century C.E., who listed the commandments which the people received 'joyfully'.[3] The *Midrash on the Psalms*,

---

[1] See below p. 822.
[2] *T. Peah* 3:8; *Ruth Zuta* 2.
[3] *Sifre Deut.* 76 (p. 141); *T. B. Sabbath* 130a.

ch. 112, reads, ''Blessed is the man who fears the Lord' (Psalm 112:1). Why is he blessed? Because he did not perform this commandment as though he were doing forced labour (*angaria*)'.[1] The same joy is vouched for in the common custom of reciting a blessing before performing a commandment. Many versions even of particular blessings of this nature are preserved in tannaitic writings which echo the days of the Second Temple. One type was, 'Blessed be thou, o Lord, who hast sanctified us with thy commandments and has commended us.' Another frequent type was, 'Blessed be he who has enabled us to reach this time,' i.e. of praising the Lord for his sanctifying the people, for his giving them the privilege and opportunity of observing the commandments.[2]

Even variations in observance are instructive here. Individuals, families or associations could apply their own measure of rigour, or stress one particular commandment, or take on works of supererogation.[3] These differences, which could be found all over society, from Pharisees to *am ha-aretz*, did not always stem from differences of biblical exegesis or tradition. They were the spontaneous outcome of a religious vitality on the lookout for new ways of expressing itself. The ultimate source of all observance was the conviction that the Torah was the word of God and the manifestation of his will. This faith was basically its own reward. Obedience was not just to gain merit or avoid punishment, though these motives are stressed in the ancient writings. From the earliest sages on, one of the major themes was rather that one should serve God for his own sake, 'not for the sake of receiving a bounty.'[4] Another motive was that observance of one precept provided the chance of obeying another, while a contravention opened up the way for further offences. So a sage could say: 'Better one hour of repentance and good works in this life than [the reward of] the whole life of the world to come.'[5] Another ennobling motive was that observance counted with God in his estimation of all mankind. 'Blessed is he who has fulfilled a commandment. He has

---

[1] This is the version found in Ms. Vat. and in *Jalkut Shimoni*.
[2] *T. Berakoth* 5:22; *T. Berakoth* 7:10; *P. T. Berakoth* VI, beginning; *T. B. Pesahim* 7b. Apparently the obligation to precede the fulfilment of a commandment with a blessing is a later development.
[3] *M. Peah* 1:2; *M. Pesahim* 4; *T. Pesahim* 2:14-21; *P. T. Pesahim* IV, 30c-d; *P. T. Taanith* IV, 69b; *M. Hagigah* 2:7; *T. B. Shabbath* 130a etc.
[4] *M. Aboth* 1:3, according to the traditional reading. The better reading presented by the more important manuscripts is: 'for the sake *not* to receive a bounty.'
[5] *M. Aboth* 4:17.

tipped the scales of justice not only in his own favour but in favour of the whole world. Woe to him who has transgressed. He has tipped the scales towards his own condemnation and towards that of the whole world.'[1]

In the following exposition of the concrete forms of religious life, matters dealt with elsewhere such as the Temple, the synagogue and study of the Torah will be presupposed; see chapters seventeen, eighteen and nineteen.

The mezuzah

As early as the first century B.C.E., the commandment of Deuteronomium 'And you shall write them on the doorposts of your house and on your gates,'[2] was taken to be an obligation to write the commandments on a small piece of parchment (the *mezuzah*, literally, doorpost) and fix it on the righthand upright of each door or city gate.[3] Even the inside rooms of dwelling-houses had their *mezuzoth*, but not such minor offices as bath-houses, lavatories or stables, while tannaitic tradition varied as to barns or depots. Buildings serving religious purposes were exempt, except the Nicanor gate of the Temple, according to tannaitic tradition. This was the entrance into the high priest's room, which was regarded as his second residence.[4]

That parchment was used is known from the *Letter of Aristeas*, Josephus and later writings, and seems to have been the general custom,[5] as in the Qumran community.[6] But the Samaritans seems to have engraved their version on stone, some examples of which, dating from Muslim times, have been found in the Land of Israel. It also seems to have been their custom earlier, since in reaction, tannaitic tradition rules out stone.[7] In tannaitic tradition, the *mezuzah* contained Deut. 6:4-9 and 11:12-21.[8] The Samaritan version contained either the decalogue or the ten divine words of creation[9] or various biblical texts in praise of God. In the Second Temple period, the Jewish *mezuzah* may also

---

[1] *T. Kiddushin* 1:14.
[2] Deut. 6:9; 11:20.
[3] *The letter of Aristeas* 158-61; Jos. *Ant.* IV, 213; *Sifre Deut.* 36 (pp. 65-8).
[4] *Sifre Deut.* ibid.; *P. T. Yoma* I, 38c.
[5] See above n. 3; *T. B. Menahoth* 34a etc.
[6] *DJD* II, pp. 85-6; 158-9.
[7] Y. Ben Zvi, in *Jediot* III (1935), pp. 3-6 (in Hebrew); ibid. XVIII (1954) pp. 223-9.
[8] *M. Menahoth* 3:7 etc.
[9] Gen. 1:3-30.

have contained the decalogue, which was then also part of the *shema* and the phylacteries,[1] and which may have disappeared from the *mezuzah* at the same time as it disappeared from *shema* and phylactery.[2] In inns and soldiers' camps, the *mezuzah* was often tied to a stick and left at the entrance. This was also the practice in some families, including the proselytes of the royal house of Adiabene. But tannaitic tradition did not regard this custom as the complete fulfilment of the commandment.[3] Writings from the Temple era regard the *mezuzah* as an acknowledgement of God's omnipresence and providence, and as a way of being encompassed by the commandments. It was only much later, in the amoraic period, that one finds the *mezuzah* regarded as a sort of protective amulet.[4]

Tzitzit

Jews dressed like the rest of the Hellenistic world, with a tunic and cloak (*talit*) above the underwear. The tunic was usually of linen and the cloak of wool, though the latter could also be of linen.[5] Only a woven mixture of wool and linen was prohibited. Fringes (ציצית) were attached to the four corners of a rectangular cloak, though not to one round in a shape like the Roman toga; they were actually tassels, because each set of strings had to be folded and knotted, making a total of eight tassels.[6] One of these was the 'thread of blue,' dyed with the blood of a snail found on the northern part of the coast. This 'thread of blue' gradually disappeared[7] since the dyeing process was expensive and the dye itself rare. The appearance of substitutes obliged people to go only to tried and trusty dealers.[8] The dyes from the time of the Bar Cochba revolt, which have been found in the caves of the Judaean desert, have been proved to be substitutes.[9] In later times, at least when they were exported, the dyes carried a guarantee,

---

[1] See below p. 798.
[2] See A. M. Habermann, 'The Phylacteries in Antiquity,' in *Eretz Israel* III (1953), pp. 174-97.
[3] *T. Megillah* 3:30; *P. T. Megillah* IV, 75c; *T. B. Menahoth* 32b.
[4] See *P. T. Peah* I, 15d; *T. B. Menahoth* 33b.
[5] *P. T. Sanhedrin* II, 20c.
[6] Num. 15:37-41; Deut. 22:12; *Sifre Deut.* 234; *M. Menahoth* 3:7-4:1.
[7] *T. B. Menahoth* 40a; *Sifre Deut.* 354; *T. B. Shabbath* 26a; *Tanhuma, Shelach* 15.
[8] *Sifre Deut.* 354; *Sifre Num.* 115 (p. 127); *T. B. Menahoth* 42a.
[9] Y. Yadin, *Judean Desert Studies, The Finds from the Bar-Kokhba Period in the Cave of the Letters* (1963), pp. 182-7.

often attached to the official document notifying Jews abroad of leap year.[1]

Women were not obliged to have the tassels, as we know from a sage of c. 70 C.E., who said: 'The sages abrogated the custom whereby a woman's shawl should have tassels,' but she had to have them on her cloak, because her husband might use it occasionally.[2] The length of the tassels was not fixed, as both the schools of Shammai and Hillel admitted. Those of the strict observance—or who pretended to be, as Jesus complained—favoured long tassels.[3]

The cloak was not the prayer shawl of later times, which was worn only on special occasions. It was the ordinary overgarment, taken off in the house or at work, but resumed after work or when guests arrived. The tassels were important as symbols of God's reign and commandments, and as warnings against sin.[4] The *hasidim* attached tassels as soon as a cloak had been cut to the minimum length for tassels.[5] But the rule was not universally kept. According to a tannaitic source the tassels distinguished a *haver* from a *am ha-aretz*.[6] In any case, the obligation went with the cloak, not the person; or so it was generally believed.

Tefillin

The *tefillin* or phylacteries, were pieces of parchment containing certain verses from the Torah, and attached to the head and arms. They were part of ordinary dress, not just for prayer, as a later custom had it, and were removed for work or upon entry into a ritually impure place, to be replaced as soon as possible.[7] Often only the

---

[1] *T. B. Menahoth* 40a-b as interpreted in *Sefer ha-Eshkol* I (p. 214) in the name of Gaon and in the commentary of Rabbenu Gershom which appears in the Talmud (ed. Vilna). The text of this document is found in *T. B. Sanhedrin* 12a.

[2] *Sifre Num.* 115 (beginning).

[3] *Sifre Num.* ibid.; cf. *T. B. Menahoth* 41b-42a. *T. B. Gittin* 56b tells of a wealthy inhabitant of Jerusalem who received a nickname because of his long fringes. The words of Jesus are found only in Matt. 23:5.

[4] *Letter of Aristeas* 158; *Sifre Num.* 115 (end); *T. B. Menahoth* 39a; 43b-44a.

[5] See especially *T. B. Menahoth* 43a; *Sifre Num.* 115 (end) etc.

[6] *T. B. Menahoth* 43a; *T. B. Berakoth* 47b; *T. B. Sotah* 22a. The words of Rabbi Meir in *T. Berakoth* (end), that 'there is not a man in Israel whom the commandments do not encircle and the phylacteries on his head and the four fringes encircle him,' did not actually apply to everyone, but, rather to the *haberim* and those who sympathized with them.

[7] *Tractate Tefillin* 16 (end); *T. B. Erubin* 98b; *P. T. Berakoth* II, 4c.

phylacteries on the head were removed[1] as was demanded later for normal meals.[2]

From the second century B.C.E. onwards, the words of Exodus 'It shall be to you a sign on your hand and as a memorial between your eyes',[3] were seen as obliging Jews to write certain texts on parchment and tie them to the head and arm.[4] Shammai the Elder (c. 50 B.C.E.) or Hillel, according to another tradition, had phylacteries which he had inherited from his grandfather.[5] In recent years, parchments containing the required texts and, separately, fragments of the rectangular leather boxes which contained such parchments have been found at Qumran and in the caves occupied by refugees at the time of Bar Cochba's revolt.[6] The order of the texts, the positioning of the straps and the shape of the boxes correspond in the main to descriptions given in tannaitic and later writings. There are some differences, however (see below).

Women, according to the general legal opinion, had not to wear phylacteries.[7] Since these were to be worn only in the daytime, some people, to make doubly sure, removed them as evening approached.[8] Since they were a 'sign', they were not worn on the sabbath or on festivals, these days being themselves 'sign' enough.[9] They could only be worn by those in a state of strict ritual purity, and minors were given them only when it was certain that they would take good care of them.[10] Jesus reproached the Pharisees for enlarging their phylacteries to demonstrate their piety.[11] Those of Qumran are quite small, and the capsule containing them only 13 by 20 mm.[12]

The texts used are Exodus 13:1-10, 11-16; Deut. 6:4-9; 11:13-21.[13] One complete capsule from Qumran and some fragmentary parchments

---

[1] *P. T. Berakoth* ii, 4c. Perhaps it is not a coincidence that the *Letter of Aristeas* 158, mentions only the phylacteries of the hand.
[2] *T. B. Berakoth* 23b; *P. T. Berakoth* iv, 4c.
[3] Exod. 13:9; 13:16; Deut. 6:8; 12:18.
[4] *Letter of Aristeas* 158. Jos. *Ant.* iv,213 emphasized the phylacteries of the hand.
[5] *Mekhilta* 17 end (p. 69).
[6] Y. Yadin, *Tefillin from Qumran* (1969), p. 7, with bibliography. See also Y. Yadin and S. Goren, 'The Phylacteries from the Judean Desert in the Light of the Halacha', in *Mahanajim* LXII (1962), pp. 5-15 (in Hebrew).
[7] *M. Berakoth* 3:3; *T. Kiddushin* 1:10; *Mekhilta* 17.
[8] *Mekhilta* 17; *P. T. Berakoth* ii, 4c; *T. B. Menahoth* 36a.
[9] *Mekhilta* 17; *P. T. Berakoth* ii, 4c; *M. Shabbath* 6:2; *T. B. Sanhedrin* 68b.
[10] *Mekhilta* 17; *P. T. Berakoth* ii, 4c; *T. B. Hullin* 110a.
[11] Matt. 23:5.
[12] Yadin, *Tefillin*, op.cit. p. 9.
[13] *M. Menahoth* 3:7; *M. Sanhedrin* 11:3.

have the decalogue as well, which was customary in the Temple era and still later, in Jerome's time, in Babylonia.[1] The *shema* and the *mezuzah* also included the decalogue at that time, but since some 'apostates' (מינים) exaggerated the power of the decalogue it was eliminated in the Jabneh period.[2] The preservation of the older custom in Babylonia was due to the fact that the 'apostates' did not constitute a problem there.[3]

Though the phylacteries, as symbols of the commandments, are highly praised in the Talmud, tannaitic tradition shows that they were worn only by the very devout.[4] Like the tassels, they could be the criterion of a *haver* as distinct from the *am ha-aretz*.[5] The demand for simultaneous ritual purity certainly restricted their use. And during the religious persecutions following the Bar Cochba revolt, the wearing of phylacteries was banned and so could not be worn in public. According to tannaitic writings, since people were not ready for martyrdom for this particular precept, it remained 'weak in their hands', and was so even when persecution had ceased.[6]

The recitation of the shema and daily prayers

In the period of the Second Temple and the Tannaim the recitation of the *shema* was not regarded as part of the daily prayer service (*tefillah*) but as a separate commandment. The precept of the *shema* was based on Deut. 6:7, and the *shema* had therefore to be recited in the morning and evening: 'when you lie down and when you rise.' The *shema* itself consisted of Deut. 6:4-9 (beginning with 'Hear, o Israel' (שמע ישראל, whence the title), Deut. 11:3-21 and Numbers

---

[1] Jerome on Ezek 24:15 (17) and the author of the *Quaestiones* on 2 Chron. 23:11.
[2] *M. Tamid* 5:1; *P. T. Berakoth* II, 3c; *T. B. Berakoth* 12a. It is not certain that the *minim* referred to Christians. See G. Vermes, 'The Decalogue and the Minim,' in *In Memoriam Paul Kahle* (1968), pp. 232-40.
[3] *T. B. Berakoth* 12a tells of attempts to reintroduce the ten commandments in Babylonia. On another custom which was abolished because of the 'minim' but which was continued to be observed in Babylonia see *T. B. Pesahim* 56a. A papyrus found in Egypt among the Nash papyri contains the ten commandments in the recitation of the *shema*. It is not certain whether the papyrus represents the period before the ten commandments were removed or represents a later attempt to preserve an ancient custom. See V. Tcherikover in *CPJ* I (1957), pp. 197-8.
[4] *T. B. Shabbath* 130a; *P. T. Berakoth* IV, 4c. See Ginzberg I, pp. 253-63.
[5] *T. B. Berakoth* 47b; *T. B. Sotah* 22a.
[6] *P. T. Berakoth* II, 4a; *T. B. Hullin* 110; *M. Megillah* 4:8; *T. B. Shabbath* 130a.

15:36-41. During the Second Temple period, however, it began with
the decalogue, which was afterwards omitted (see above, p. 799). The
recitation was done at home, and in the synagogue. But while the
Temple stood, it was also done there, by the priests who came together
during an interval in the morning services.[1] The time for the household
shema was before starting the day's work, at sunrise therefore, and
after the working day was over, at sunset. There was a dispute at one
time about the posture to be adopted. The school of Shammai held
that the morning *shema* was to be said standing, the evening lying
down. The school of Hillel, however, maintained that the text
appealed to referred only to the time, not to the posture of recitation.[2]
The prayer (*tefillah*) consisted of a series of benedictions (*shemone esre*)[3]
and was said three times a day as is suggested by Daniel,[4] the *Slavonic
Book of Enoch*[5] and some Christian writers.[6] But the Essenes and
Therapeuts prayed only twice a day,[7] and no text from the period just
before 70 C.E. mentions evening prayers.[8] There was, of course, the
evening *shema*, said at home even after it had been said in the
synagogue—and only at home, by the Jews of the south.[9] The afternoon prayer (*minhah*) was usually said at the 10th hour (3.30 p.m.),
which was also the time of the afternoon daily whole-offering in the
Temple. It contained the *shemone esre* in a form retained long after
70 C.E.[10]
Special rules made provision for travellers and others in difficult
situations, and sages from the second part of the first century C.E.
report traditions of shorter versions which could be used by a traveller
if he were passing through danger zones.[11]

Grace and other rites at meals

Two meals were usually taken each day, a light breakfast and the
main meal in the evening, after work. They were preceded by a ritual

[1] *M. Tamid* 5:1.
[2] *M. Berakoth* 1:3; *T. Berakoth* 1:6.
[3] See chapter eighteen, pp. 926ff.
[4] Dan. 6:11.
[5] 51:4. Here it is written: 'morning, midnoon and evening.'
[6] *Didache* 8 (end).
[7] Jos. *War* II, 128-31.
[8] *P. T. Berakoth* IV, 7c-d; *T. B. Berakoth* 27b-28a.
[9] Ginzberg I, pp. 68-74.
[10] *M. Berakoth* 4:1. See Ginzberg III, pp. 150-7.
[11] *M. Berakoth* 4:4; *T. Berakoth* 3:7.

washing of hands. 'The Pharisees, and all the Jews, do not eat unless they wash their hands, observing the tradition of the elders.'[1] This may be too sweeping a statement for the Temple era, but in the main, it is confirmed by many other traditions of the time.[2] Scholars who see in Mark a reflection only of later traditions undoubtedly make too much of a report about a sage 'who questioned purity of the hands' and another about someone who never washed his hands before eating.[3] A tannaitic source says that such ablutions were the minimum, and could be the requisite, qualification for admission into a group of *haberim*.[4] The Essenes took baths before meals.[5] For further discussion of the universality of the custom, see below, on ritual purity (p. 828).

The meal itself started with a blessing, of the type: 'Blessed art thou who bringst forth bread from the earth.' The bread stood for the whole meal and an extra blessing was required only if wine was served.[6] One person in each group pronounced the blessing for all.[7] Then the bread was 'broken'—the invariable order when the New Testament describes a meal,[8] as in the Talmud.[9] But we hear of an ancient custom in which the order was reversed, and at the meal on the eve of the Passover, the rite (*seder*) was complicated. First a piece of (unleavened) bread was placed between two other pieces, then the blessings were pronounced, following which the rest of the bread was divided.[10]

After the meals came a grace, for which there was no set form. Even as late as the amoraic period, the shepherd's simple 'Blessed be the master of this bread' was enough.[11] In the period after the destruction of the Temple, there were often three blessings, one for the food, another for the covenant, the Torah and the Land, and a third for the

---

[1] Mark 7:3; cf. Matt. 15:1-2; Luke 11:38.

[2] *M. Hagigah* 2:5; *T. B. Shabbath* 13b-14a; *P. T. Sabbath* I, 3d; *T. B. Yoma* 87b etc.

[3] *M. Eduyoth* 5:6; *P. T. Berakoth* VIII, 12a. See A. Büchler, *Der Galiläische Am ha-Ares des zweiten Jahrh.* (1906). pp. 96-138. For an opposing view see Alon, *Studies* I, pp. 121-76.

[4] *T. Demai* 2:11; see S. Liebermann, *Tosefta ki-Fshutah* ad loc. pp. 214-5.

[5] Jos. *War* II, 129. No mention is made of the washing of the hands.

[6] *M. Berakoth* 6:1-6.

[7] *M. Berakoth* 6:6; *T. Berakoth* 4:8.

[8] Matt. 15:36; 26:26; Mark 6:41; 8:6; Luke 9:16; 22:19; Acts 27:35; 1 Cor. 11:24.

[9] *T. B. Berakoth* 39b. Cf. *P. T. Berakoth* VI, 10a.

[10] *T. B. Berakoth* 39b. The *Didache* 19 prescribes the blessing on sliced bread.

[11] *T. B. Berakoth* 40b.

re-building of Jerusalem. These could be reduced to two by people who ate during their work, according to a tannaitic text.[1] The spokesman of a group invited the others to join him in praising God, and asked their leave to begin.[2] Blessings were also pronounced over any food or drink that might be taken outside meal-times. The rule that it was forbidden to 'enjoy anything in the world without a blessing' occurs constantly in tradition.[3] So too the *Sibylline Oracles:* 'Happy are they all over the earth who truly love the mighty God, blessing him before eating or drinking'.[4] But there were many other occasions for blessings. Ben Sira could say: 'Behold the rainbow and bless its maker'.[5] Tannaitic writings give the blessing for such occasions as the building of a house, the acquisition of new objects, the building of a *sukkah,* the donning of phylacteries and the ritual slaughter of animals.[6] Eventually a series of blessings was composed, to be said on waking in the morning, to express the joy of being enabled to keep the commandments. A text from shortly after Bar Cochba said that three blessings were required each day: 'Blessed art thou ... for not having made me a pagan ... for not having made me a woman ... for not having made me an *am ha-aretz'*,[7] Later, the blessings were said to amount to one hundred a day, including those accompanying the *shema*, the eighteen blessings (*shemone esre*), said three times a day, and those going with the observance of a commandment.[8] But probably only circles close to the sages went to such extremes. Thus when Rabbi Meir says that there is not a Jew who is not constantly surrounded by the commandments, each of which would require a blessing, he was referring to the phylacteries. And these, as has been seen, were not always worn.

There were also communal meals, for groups of *haberim,*[9] held as a rule only on the eve of the sabbath, but sometimes also on working-day nights. They featured in particular the study of the Torah, and sometimes continued late into the night when they warmed to their

---

[1] *T. Berakoth* 4:25. The three blessings are found in the *Didache* 10 in a Christian form and in a different order: covenant, food, and the redemption of the community which corresponds to the building of Jerusalem.
[2] *M. Berakoth* 7:1-3.
[3] *T. B. Berakoth* 35a, etc.
[4] *Oracula Sibyllina* IV, 24-6. Cf. *Sifra, Kedoshim* 3; *T. B. Berakoth* 6 beginning.
[5] Sir. 43:11.
[6] *M. Berakoth* 9; *T. Berakoth* 7 etc.
[7] *T. B. Menahoth* 43b; *T. B. Berakoth* 60b.
[8] *T. Berakoth* 7:24 cf. *T. B. Menahoth* 43b.
[9] *M. Berakoth* 1:1 and the commentary in *T.B.* and *P.T.*

discussions, or when there was a lecture from their teacher or a visiting sage. It was the custom at Qumran to 'keep vigil in common for a third of the night each night of the year, to read in the Book, to study its decree and to bless God in common', which was just a highly developed form of the *haberim*'s meals.[1]

The sabbath

The sabbath was so characteristic that hardly any text, Jewish or non-Jewish, omits to mention it when speaking of the Jews in our period. The main features of the sabbath were abstention from work, attendance at the synagogue and common meals, in the family or in other groups.

The Torah forbade all work on this day of rest.[2] The Prophets and the Writings added further details, by which business transactions, burden-carrying outside the house and travelling were excluded.[3] Tannaitic rulings went further, since we find in the mishnaic tractate *Shabbath* (7:2ff.) thirty-nine classes of forbidden work, such as ploughing or planting, and going with each class, a set of accessory or corollary labours which were also forbidden. So many of these restrictions had no real basis in the Torah that an early mishnaic text could say: 'The rules for the sabbath are like mountains hanging by a hair, for Scripture is scanty and the rules many.'[4] Apart then from the 'main labours and corollaries' (lit. 'fathers and descendants'), a large number of things were forbidden which might interfere with the sabbath rest, according to the sages, not by virtue of the Torah but as providing the harmonious setting for the sabbath.[5] So too prohibitions came in by reason of the 'unavailable' (מוקצה). It was forbidden to move anything which had been excluded from use on the sabbath, or anything not prepared on the previous evening for sabbath use if necessary. Thus the transport of tools used on working-days was forbidden.[6]

All this more or less tannaitic law was less stringent than some earlier approaches, such as that of the *Book of Jubilees* (see first and last chapter of the book), that of the Damascus Covenant and that of the

[1] *Damascus Document* 6:7-8.
[2] Exod. 16:22-26; 16:29-30; 34:21; 23:12; 31:12-17; 34:12; 35:2-3; Lev. 23:3; Num. 15:32-36; Deut. 5:12-15.
[3] Is. 58:13-14; Jer. 17:21-22; Am. 8:5; Neh. 10:32; 13:15-19.
[4] *M. Hagigah* 1:8; *T. Hagigah* 1:9.
[5] *Mekhilta* 9.
[6] *M. Shabbath* 17; *T. Shabbath* 14; *Damascus Document* 10:22.

Essenes in general, as Josephus noted.[1] In the time of the Maccabean revolt the *hasidim* would not fight even a defensive battle on the sabbath, and even after the time of Mattathias Maccabee Jews refrained from combat on the sabbath.[2] Tannaitic law, however, allowed for self-defense, and the continuation of an offensive begun three days earlier at least, which latter was allowed even by the rigorist Shammai.[3] So the Zealots found that they could carry on with their attacks on the sabbath.[4] Then, the *hasidim* forbade marital relations on the sabbath, and even remained continent from the preceding Wednesday, so that the woman need not be ritually impure on the sabbath eve by reason of some residues from intercourse.[5] But the more general view was that marital relations on the sabbath eve were an integral part of family life.[6] Even some of the actions of Jesus' disciples which vexed the Pharisees, such as the plucking or rubbing of a handful of corn, were still a matter for debate in tannaitic times.[7] Jesus' sabbath healings which angered the head of the synagogue were permitted by tannaitic law.[8] Torah study on the sabbath occupied such a major place that one of the greatest sages of the amoraic period could say: 'Sabbaths and feasts were given only for study of the Torah'—an attitude already discernible in Philo and Josephus.[9] Various mishnaic texts speak of people gathering in the courtyard of the synagogue to hear a well-known sage on a sabbath.[10] Another great feature of the sabbath was the family or group dinner. Groups of *haberim* ate together, and it seems to have been the custom in the Diaspora to collect money to provide for such meals, all the

[1] Jos. *War* II, 147.

[2] I Macc. 2:35-41; Jos. *War* I, 145-6; II, 391-2; II, 634. For an earlier period see Jos. *Against Apion* I, 210-1. For the problem of engaging in warfare on the sabbath see Mann, pp. 502-10 and M. D. Herr, 'Concerning the Problem of War on the Sabbath during the Second Temple Period,' in *Tarbiz* XXX (1961), pp. 242-56; 336-41 (in Hebrew).

[3] *Sifre Deut.* 203-4; *T. Erubin* 3:7; *Midrash Tannaim* (p. 123) etc.

[4] See Jos. *War* II, 456.

[5] *T. B. Niddah* 38a. See L. Finkelstein in *MGWJ* LXXVI (1932), p. 530.

[6] *M. Ketuboth* 5:9.

[7] See S. Pines, *The Jewish Christians of the Early Centuries of Christianity according to a New Source* (1966), p. 63, n. 257.

[8] J. Epstein, *Prolegomena ad Litteras Tannaiticas* (1952), pp. 280-1.

[9] *P. T. Shabbath* xv, 15a; Philo, *Quod omnis probus* 81; *Vita Mosis* II, 211; Jos. *Against Apion* II, 75.

[10] *M. Shabbath* 16:1; 18:1; 3:5; *M. Erubin* 3:5. On public services in the synagogue on the sabbath see chapter eighteen, pp. 927ff.

more important because they were the occasion for Torah study.[1] Thus the sabbath could be summed up as 'half for God and half for oneself,' partly for religious services and Torah study, partly for relaxation and meals in common.[2] Indeed, as was already observed by a scholar in the nineteenth century,[3] the main reason for the *erub* was to enable food to be carried from house to house for such meals.[4] The meal, taken just after the synagogue service, was accompanied by wine, which was sanctified by the recitation of the *kiddush* over it before the meal. The head of the household or the chairman of the group lifted up the cup of wine and said the blessing, which took in both the sabbath and the wine. This was the tannaitic interpretation of the commandment, 'Remember the sabbath day to keep it holy.'[5] The tradition of the *kiddush* was very ancient, and ascribed to the 'great synagogue', supposedly of Ezra's time, by the Talmud.[6]

Sabbath observance was so highly prized that it had repercussions on the rest of the week, apart of course from the days being numbered in relation to the sabbath. The special food for the sabbath had to be provided for beforehand. The food was bought on the Thursday, and clothes were laundered, and mended if necessary.[7] So much had to be done on Friday that it was known as the day of preparation, the parasceve of the New Testament and Josephus.[8] Hence such sayings as, 'If one does not prepare food on Friday, what will one eat on the sabbath?'[9] Foreign rulers realized the importance of Friday and exempted Jews from attendance at court on the afternoon.[10] It was the time for the last household tasks, such as folding blankets and making beds.[11] The cooking had been done in the morning, and the food was then kept warm on a stove or the like, which had of course to be lit before the sabbath. The evening meal on Friday was usually taken later than usual, so that it could last into the sabbath. One

---

[1] Jos. *Ant.* XIV, 213-6: *CPJ* 139. Concerning the relationship of these meals with the Christian εὐχαριστία and the ἀγάπη see Alon, *Studies* I, pp. 286-91.
[2] See *Sifre Deut.* 135 and *P. T. Sabbath* xv, 15a. Cf. *T. B. Betzah* 15b.
[3] A. Geiger, *Urschrift und Übersetzung der Bibel* (2nd ed. 1928), p. 124.
[4] Chapter fourteen, p. 1.
[5] Exod. 20:8; *Mekhilta, Behodesh* 7.
[6] *M. Berakoth* 8:1; *T. B. Berakoth* 33a.
[7] *M. Taanith* 1:16; 2:7; *P. T. Megillah* IV, 75; *T. B. Baba Kamma* 82a.
[8] Matt. 27:62; Mark 15:42; Luke 23:54; John 19:31; Jos. *Ant.* XVI, 163. Cf. S. Zeitlin in *JQR* XLII (1951)-2), p. 252, n. 3.
[9] *Ruth Rabba* 3; *Eccl. Rabba* I.
[10] Jos. *Ant.* XVI, 163; cf. XVI, 168.
[11] *T. B. Shabbath* 119b.

tannaitic text says that the right time for the evening *shema* was 'when people come home for the meal on the sabbath eve.'[1] Some even held that this meal could not be eaten till after sunset on Friday.[2] From Josephus and various tannaitic sources we learn of the custom to sound three blasts of the *shofar* at the Temple before the sabbath eve in order to inform the people that all work should be stopped. Three additional blasts were then sounded to announce the official arrival of the sabbath. Josephus also relates that the *shofar* was sounded at the conclusion of the sabbath.[3] Tannaitic sources state that this custom was followed in all cities. The *hazzan* of the synagogue or of the town (see chapter eighteen, p. 935) went to the roof of some tall building and blew the horn once to stop work in the fields and summon people home. He blew again to signal closing time for shops. When he blew for the third time, all household work stopped, and the sabbath lights were lit, just before sunset. A little later, the horn was sounded several times in succession, fortissimo, to announce the start of the sabbath.[4] (Later ,indeed, some demanded that the sabbath rest should have begun by the *minhah*, c. 3.30 p.m.).[5] The sabbath lights were so characteristic that they were imitated by people who felt akin to the Jews, as we know also from non-Jewish sources.[6] They were usually the responsibility of a woman. One tradition has it that a would-be convert was specially urged to be careful 'about the commandments for her periods and the lighting of the sabbath candles.'[7] The Mishnah says that there were three things a man must say: 'Have you tithed? Have you prepared the *Erub*? and, Light the lamp.'[8]

---

[1] *T. Berakoth* 1:1; *P. T. Berakoth* 1, 2a; *T. B. Berakoth* 2b.

[2] *T. Berakoth* 5 (beginning); *P. T. Pesahim* x, 37b; *T. B. Pesahim* 99b.

[3] In recent excavations carried out at the Southern Wall, a stone was found with an inscription in Hebrew saying that this was the 'corner of blowing to announce.' See *Qadmoniot* v (1973), p. 75.

[4] Jos. *War* iv, 582; *T. Sukkah* 4:11-12; *T. B. Shabbath* 35b. For the sounding of the shofar on Saturday night after the sabbath see *M. Hullin* 1:7; *T. Hullin* 1:2; *T. B. Shabbath* 114b.

[5] *T. B. Pesahim* 50b.

[6] Tertullian, *Ad Nationes* I, 13 and see B. M. Levin, 'Concerning the History of the Sabbath Candle', in *Essays and Studies in Memory of Linda R. Miller* (1938), pp. 45-68 (in Hebrew).

[7] *Tractate Gerim* 1.

[8] *M. Shabbath* 2:7; see *M. Shabbath* 3 and 4; *T. Shabbath* 3 and 4 and the commentary in *P.T.* and *T.B.* ad loc.

New moon

The celebration of the new moon was of more consequence in the Temple era than later. Though not strictly a feast, the new moon is mentioned along with sabbaths and feast-days in the major sources for those times, including official documents conferring certain privileges on the Jews.[1] Work was not forbidden, except to women, but there were certain restrictions, as on the days within the octaves of Passover and Tabernacles (חול המועד).[2] The date was fixed by the tribunal which sat in the court of the Temple at Jerusalem, and the announcement was passed on by a series of torches used as beacons throughout the country. Efforts were made to abolish the torches as early as in the Temple era, but were effective only in the Diaspora, and the custom was preserved around Tiberias even after the intervention of Rabbi Judah the patriarch, c. 200 C.E.[3] The arrival of emissaries announcing the date of the new moon was fêted with banquets, according to the Mishnah. Later, groups of *haberim* are said to have celebrated the new moon by dining together, even borrowing money for this occasion. The synagogue or its annexes were often used for this celebration of the new moon.[4]

Passover

We shall consider here only the celebration of the feast outside Jerusalem, leaving the rest to chapter seventeen on the Temple.

The Passover, the passage from bondage of Egypt to the freedom of the promised land, was a memorial and re-enactment of one of Israel's greatest days, when it passed from the old to the new, to the new world of Israel's blessings and hopes. The celebration centred on a meal taken in common on the night before the 15th Nisan. Preparations began well in advance, with the removal of all *hametz*, that is, leavened bread and anything such as beer which had required fermentation, as well as all flour mixed with other food or fermentation agent.[5] Up to the early tannaitic period, *hametz* had not to be destroyed,

---

[1] Judith 8:6; 1 Macc. 10:34; Col. 2:16; Gal. 4:10 etc.
[2] *T. B. Megillah* 22b; *T. B. Rosh ha-Shanah* 23a; *P. T. Pesahim* IV, 30d.
[3] *M. Rosh ha-Shanah* 2:2-4; *P. T. Rosh ha-Shanah* II, 58b.
[4] *M. Rosh ha-Shanah* 2:5; *P. T. Moed Katan* II, 816; *P. T. Pesahim* I, 27b; (concerning this last source, see Lieberman, *Ha-Jerushalmi ki-Fshutah* I (1935) p. 371; *Tractate Soferim* 19.
[5] *M. Pesahim* 3:1-2; *T. Pesahim* 2:1-2.

but merely hidden till after the Passover.[1] But according to the accepted Halakah, it had been burnt or sold to non-Jews.[2] Before the eve of the Passover, that is, during the night of the 13th Nisan, a thorough search was made for any remnants of *hametz* in store-houses or courtyards, with the help of lights. Any that was found was eaten early in the morning, if possible. This was to avoid further searches.[3] The eve itself was a sort of feast, because the paschal sacrifice was offered that afternoon. Mishnaic texts dealing with the Second Temple period say that heavy work was usually suspended after midday, and in some places, such as Galilee, all work stopped, except the necessary preparations for the feast, such as the work done by tailors or barbers. The people of Jericho continued the grafting of palms on the 14th, but as this seasonal work was necessary, they were not condemned by the sages.[4]

By midday of the 14th, no more *hametz* could be eaten.[5] The great moment came that night, with the Passover meal. Sources from the Temple era, when the meal actually followed a sacrifice,[6] and later texts describing the *seder*, from the end of the first century C.E. and onwards,[7] all suggest that the essential accompaniments of the meal were the 'sanctification' of the day, the drinking of four cups of wine, the recitation of the *hallel* (Psalms 115-8) and the eating of the bitter herbs and *haroset*, a mixture of apples, nuts and wine. This seems to have been done everywhere, not merely in Jerusalem. But it seems that the telling of the story of the Exodus (the *haggadah*) only became customary after 70 C.E.

The whole family gathered for the meal, and children were encouraged to ask questions about the rites, so that the *seder* could be fully meaningful, as a recall and a sort of revival of the beginnings of the nation, of the first taste of liberation and of the profound hope then awakened of final redemption. Family, national and religious feeling reached its acme.[8] Hellenistic customs affected the actual course of

---

[1] This satisfied Hananiah, one of the leaders of Persian Jewry as is seen from his letter to the Jews of Elephantine in 419 B.C.E. See A. Cowley, *Aramaic Papyri* (1967), no. 21, l.9. This is also the opinion of Rabbi Jose ha-Galili and of other sages. See *T. B. Pesahim* 28b; *Sifre Deut.* 130.

[2] *M. Pesahim* 2:1; 1:5; *T. Pesahim* 1:4. etc.

[3] *M. Pesahim* 1:1-3; *T. Pesahim* 1:1-3.

[4] *M. Pesahim* 4:1; 4:5-6; 4:8; *T. Pesahim* 2:18-19.

[5] *M. Pesahim* 1:4-5; *T. Pesahim* 1:7.

[6] *Jubilees* 49:6; *De Spec. Leg.* II, 148; Matt. 26:27-30 and parallels.

[7] *M. Pesahim* 10.

[8] The *seder* is described in *M. Pesahim* 10. On the appropriate time of the *seder*

the meal, which resembled to some extent the symposium of the Greeks: it was eaten in a reclining position, and was the setting for important discourses on a set theme. The ceremony began with a cup of wine and the vegetables. Then a second cup of wine was drunk and the main meal eaten, with which came then the *haggadah* and the *hallel*. Much of the rite symbolized the ancient bondage: the bitter herbs were dipped in the *haroset* in memory of the mud on which the Israelites had to work in Egypt to make bricks. The exodus was recalled in the biblical texts, and later in the *haggadah*, which was developed in response to the queries of the young people.[1]

On the second day of the feast, a sheaf (עומר) of barley was offered, as the first fruits of the new crops.[2] Then the new corn could be eaten. As the Mishnah says: 'After the *omer* had been offered, they used to go out and find the market of Jerusalem full of meal and parched corn.'[3] The new corn was also eaten outside Jerusalem after midday, since it could be supposed that the offering had been made in the Temple at the proper time.

Pentecost

Fifty days later came the feast of Pentecost (שבועות). 'You shall count from the morrow after sabbath, from the day that you brought the sheaf of the wave offering; seven full weeks shall they be, counting fifty days to the morrow of the seventh sabbath; then you shall present a cereal offering of new grain to the Lord.'[4] The counting was everybody's duty, not just that of the Temple tribunal.[5] The count was part, very probably, of the public ceremony attached to the harvesting of the sheaf on the night before the 16th Nisan. Pentecost centred mainly on the Temple service, and the offering of the first fruits.[6] There were no special customs otherwise, just the ordinary elements of a feast-day: the *kiddush* or blessing, and the appropriate prayers and Torah reading.

---

see *M. Pesahim* 5 etc. On the *seder* in general see J. Baneth, *Der Sederabend* (1904).

[1] See S. Stein, in *JJS* VIII (1959), pp. 13-44.
[2] See chapter seventeen, p. 893.
[3] *M. Menahoth* 10:5; *Sifra, Emor* 11 (end).
[4] Lev. 23:15-16.
[5] *T. B. Menahoth* 65b; *Sifra, Emor* 12 (beginning).
[6] See chapter seventeen, pp. 893-4.

New Year

The Bible and texts from the Second Temple period treat Nisan (March-April) as the first month of the year, and various practices in the Temple are based on this supposition.[1] Josephus says that it was only the start of the religious year, while Tishri (September-October) began the secular year.[2] But in ordinary life, outside the Temple, Tishri began the new year, and the term 'new year,' without further qualification, means Tishri. Tishri is only one of four New Years mentioned in the Mishnah.[3]

The New Year service used today was already in use in the Temple era. It stresses God's sovereignty and providence, as creator and judge. The special prayers are the מלכייות (kingship prayers), the זכרונות (remembrance prayers) and the שופרות (texts mentioning the blowing of horns or trumpets). The basic theme of the texts chosen was that all living things are judged at the New Year. 'They used to say: recite before him the *malkujot* to acknowledge his kingship over all his works, the *zikronot* to have him remember you with favour, the *shofarot* to make your prayers fly up to him like the notes of a horn.'[4] The Torah says that the first day of the seventh month (here meaning Tishri) is 'a day for you to blow the trumpets.'[5] The ancient texts stress the connection with the Temple service, and Philo seems to imply that the horn was sounded only in the Temple, during the sacrifices.[6] But the sounding of the horn had become part of the synagogue ceremonies even before the destruction of the Temple.[7]

The New Year was celebrated on the first Tishri, and there was always some doubt as to whether the new moon would actually be seen that evening or only the next day, and hence whether the projected day of observance was correctly timed. Outside the Land of Israel, therefore, and apart from places which had been officially notified elsewhere, the custom came in of celebrating the feast on the evening both of the

---

[1] *M. Shekalim* 1:1. See esp. *P. T. Shekalim* (beginning); *M. Taanith* 4:5. Cf. chapter sixteen, pp. 834ff.

[2] *M. Rosh ha-Shanah* 4:5-6; *T. Rosh ha-Shanah* (end). Jos. *Ant.* 1, 81.

[3] *M. Rosh ha-Shanah* 1:1.

[4] *M. Rosh ha-Shanah* 1:2; *T. Rosh ha-Shanah* 1:12 cf. Philo, *De Spec. Leg.* II, 198.

[5] Numb. 29:1; Lev. 23:24.

[6] *P. T. Rosh ha-Shanah* IV, 59b; *De Spec. Leg.* II, 188. Cf. Alon, *Studies* I, pp. 106-11.

[7] *M. Rosh ha-Shanah* 1:4; *P. T. Rosh ha-Shanah* ad loc. etc. Cf. Alon, *Studies* I, p. 110.

29th and the 30th day of the month. No texts say so earlier than Bar Cochba's revolt,[1] but the custom may have been in force in the temple era.

Day of Atonement

The next feature of Tishri was on the 10th, the Day of Atonement (יום כיפורים). Most of our information is concerned with the Temple, especially the high priests' rôle.[2] But the special prayers were recited by all and the fast was observed by all. Philo says that even those who were otherwise indifferent sanctified the Day of Atonement.[3] The usual sabbath and feast-day practices were supplemented, at the end of the day, by the closing service (תפלת נעילה). The main theme was repentance and atonement for sin. Tannaitic texts, as well as enjoining the fast, forbade washing, the use of unguents, the waring of leather shoes and sexual intercourse—matters discussed in detail even in the earliest of such writings.[4] Nonetheless, contrary to the impression given by the *Book of Jubilees*,[5] the Day of Atonement was not a gloomy one. It was a festival, celebrating Israel's repentance and the expiation of its sins. The liturgy makes this quite clear, as Philo already saw.[6] One particularly joyful note was struck by the young girls. When the feast was over, they dressed in white and went out to the vineyards to dance, in the hope of attracting one of the young men who had gathered there on the look out for a suitable bride. One tannaitic writer from Usha, telling of olden times, says that 'there were no happier days for Israel than the 15th Ab and the Day of Atonement'.[7]

Feast of Tabernacles

This feast, called Tabernacles, (סוכות) the σκηνοπηγία of the Septuagint, was celebrated on the 15th Tishri. It was a major feast in the Temple era, and most of the special ceremonies are connected with the people's

---

[1] *T. Rosh ha-Shanah* 4:5 and parallels.
[2] *M.* and *T. Yoma.*
[3] *De Spec. Leg.* I, 186.
[4] *M. Yebamoth* 8:1.
[5] *Jubilees* 34:18-19.
[6] Philo, *De Spec. Leg.* II, 193.
[7] *M. Taanith* 4:8; *P. T. Taanith* IV, 69d; *T. B. Taanith* 31a.

presence in the Temple.[1] In Jerusalem, the custom was to carry in procession the 'four kinds of trees' (Leviticus 23:40) each of the seven days of the feast. Elsewhere this was done only on the first day. After the fall of Jerusalem, Rabbi Johanan ben Zakkai ruled that the 'four kinds' (the cluster of lulab, a palm branch, a willow and myrtle, and the ethrog, a citron) were to be carried all seven days.[2] One element of the feast, however, the sitting in leafy huts, had nothing to do with the Temple service. The hut and roof, according to tannaitic tradition, were to be things growing from the earth, but not manufactured or finished articles, or, in tannaitic terms, not of anything 'susceptible of impurity.' Cut branches and leaves or planks were to be used,[3] but not standing trees, say, with their branches bent over and tied together.[4] One tannaitic tradition, already suggested in Nehemiah, forbade the use of any but the greenery of the 'four kinds' mentioned above.[5]

Dwelling in booths is often mentioned in writings from the Second Temple period[6] and the precept was observed sometimes even when travelling, though travellers were exempt. But they could build a booth on a ship, for instance.[7] Women too were exempt, but the writings of the period often describe them as dwelling in booths, alone or with their husbands. The booths could be a modest structure, in the courtyard or on the roof.[8] But sometimes larger and more elegant ones were built, like that of Queen Helena of Adiabene in Jerusalem.[9] Very often the booth was made to cover the whole courtyard, from the roof of one porch, say, to another, so that it surrounded all the entrances to the house.[10]

---

[1] See chapter seventeen, pp. 894ff.
[2] *M. Sukkah* 3:12 and Alon, *Studies* I, pp. 112-214.
[3] *M. Sukkah* 1:4.
[4] *M. Sukkah* 1:2; 1:4.
[5] *Sifra, Emor* 17; *T. B. Sukkah* 36b; *P. T. Pesahim* II, 28d. Cf. Neh. 8:14-18.
[6] The *sukkah* of Shammai the Elder (*M. Sukkah* 2:8); of Rabbi Johanan ben ha-Horani and the elders of the House of Shammai (ibid. 2:7); of Queen Helene (*T. Sukkah* 1—beginning); of the men of Jerusalem (ibid 2:3); the two *Sukkot* of the guardians of Agrippa in Tiberias and Sepphoris etc.
[7] *T. Sukkah* 2:3; *T. B. Sukkah* 23a; *P. T. Sukkah* I, 52d; *P. T. Erubin* I, 19a.
[8] Generally it is mentioned that one ascends to and descends from the *sukkah* since they were built on roofs. See the commentary of Rashi to *T. B. Shabbath* 154b.
[9] *T. Sukkah* 1 (beginning) and parallels.
[10] *M. Sukkah* 1:10.

Fasts

Fasting (תענית) played an important part in Jewish life. In the post-exile period, the prophet Zechariah was asked whether the fast of the fifth month (Ab) should be continued as was done 'for so many years'.[1] Though the answer is not clear, tannaitic texts affirm that it was continued, on the 9th of Ab. The destruction of the First Temple was still being mourned, and the return of the divine presence to Jerusalem prayed for, till the end of the Second Temple period, since it was thought that Jewish life was not what it used to be. The mishnaic tractate *Rosh ha-Shanah*, listing the months in which emissaries were sent to announce the date of the New Year, mentions Ab because of its fast-day.[2] Other tannaitic sources also mention the 17th of Tammuz, the 3rd of Tishri and the 10th of Teveth as days of fasting (the fourth, seventh and tenth months respectively, in Zechariah 8:19). But the proofs are not convincing, and it is possible that such fast-days were not kept.[3] However, after the destruction of the Second Temple in 70 C.E., fasting on the 17th of Tammuz and on the 9th of Ab were observed in memory of the First and Second Temple.[4] There were special prayers, and readings from the Bible which stressed retribution and repentance, and the whole Book of Lamentations was read on the 9th of Ab.[5]

Other occasions for fasts, according to the Mishnah, were a plague of locusts, such as that mentioned in the Book of Joel,[6] or the outbreak of war, as in Maccabees,[7] or blight on the corn as at Ascalon in the Second Temple period,[8] and 'any public calamity.' The fasts, especially on the occasion of a drought, were on a Monday, Thursday and the following Monday, as a rule. They were first undertaken by individual sages, on their own initiative. If rain did not fall, the *bet din* proclaimed 'three days of fasting to be observed by all'. They started at the beginning of Kislev (9th month, November-December) and additional three-day fasts were ordered if necessary, though thirteen fast days

---

[1] Zech. 7:3-5 cf. 8:19.
[2] *M. Rosh ha-Shanah* 1:3 and see Epstein, *Prolegomena*, pp. 1012-4.
[3] The words of Rabbi Hanania, prefect of the priests in *P. T. Betzah* II, 61b and parallels and the words of Rabbi Eliezer ben Zadok in *T. Taanith* 4:10, and parallels. Cf. Epstein loc.cit.
[4] *M. Taanith* 4:6.
[5] *Tractate Soferim* 18; cf. *P. T. Sabbath* XI, 15c.
[6] *M. Taanith* 3:5; Joel 1 and 2.
[7] *M. Taanith* 3:5; 1 Macc. 3:46-54. Cf. 1 Macc. 4:39ff.; 2 Macc. 20:25; Judith 4:9.
[8] *M. Taanith* 3:6.

were the maximum in a given drought.[1] The tractate *Taanith* records the accompanying prayers. Some mishnaic customs go back to the Second Temple period, as we know from Josephus,[2] but they mostly date from the tannaitic period. One such tradition says that the ark containing the sacred books was brought into the town square, where ashes of wood were placed upon it, and on the heads of the *nasi* and the *av bet din*. Then each of the townsfolk put ashes on his own head. Some texts from after 70 c.e. say that sages were sent to supervise the ceremony. Their main function was to exhort the people to repentance, stressing that without repentance and good works, sackcloth and fasting were not enough. The sages then read from the Bible and recited the prayers. Six extra blessings were pronounced, according to the Mishnah, after which the priests blew the horns. In the days of the Temple, the people gathered at the Mount of the Temple, while the priest stood at the eastern gate,[3] and after the fall of the Temple the custom of the priests blowing the horn was kept up, as earlier even outside Jerusalem. Normally, the fast was kept from sunrise to sunset, but at the second three days of fasts on the occasion of a drought, the fast was from the evening of the day before till sunset of the fast day, as was the custom on the 9th of Ab and the Day of Atonement.[4]

Individuals also fasted privately to avert an impending evil, to mourn a personal or national disaster or to express their faith in God, and so on. Tradition has it that Rabbi Zadok fasted for forty years to avert the destruction of the Temple.[5] Judith fasted all the years that she was a widow.[6] According to the *Testaments of the Twelve Patriarchs*, the patriarchs fasted for longer or shorter periods, and Joseph for seven years, to be able to withstand the temptations of his master's wife.[7] Certain tannaitic sages fasted as a penance, for instance for losing their temper in the heat of argument or for boasting of their successful study of the Torah ('their crown').[8] The Book of Tobit urges prayer, fasting and good works, and the *Psalms of Solomon*

[1] See *M. Taanith* 1 and *T. B. Taanith* 14a; *T. B. Taanith* 25b.
[2] *M. Taanith* 2; *T. Taanith* 1:3-14; *Jos. Life* 290-3.
[3] *M. Taanith* 2:1-5; *B. T. Taanith* 12b-13a. Concerning the custom of sages to go out on public fast days see *T. Taanith* 1 (end); *P. T. Taanith* III, 66c-d; *P. T. Taanith* II, 65a-b; *T. B. Taanith* 25a-b; *P. T. Berakoth* I, 3d.
[4] *M. Taanith* 1:5-6.
[5] *T. B. Gittin* 56a; *Lam. Rabba* I.
[6] Judith 8:6.
[7] *Testament of Reuben* 1:10; *Simeon* 3:5; *Judah* 15:4; *Joseph* 3:4; 9:10.
[8] *T. B. Hagigah* 22b; *T. Ohiloth* 5:11; *P. T. Shebiith* IV, 35b; cf. Sir. 34:26.

speak of a pious man who expiates his faults by fasting. The various stories of people who fasted freely, wishing to lift up their souls to God, in the New Testament, such as Anna the daughter of Phanuel, and Paul, are in keeping with general Jewish custom.[1] The 'men of the deputation' who went up to Jerusalem to represent their district and who stood by the priests at the service[2] are said to have fasted most of the week, as did the members of the sanhedrin from the same district.[3] The statement that the disciples of John and of the Pharisees fasted while those of Jesus did not represents a real situation.[4] Fasting and ascetic practices were widespread though warnings against them are evidenced in talmudic literature.[5]

Mondays and Thursdays, which were synagogue days, when country-folk came to town and the courts sat and the Torah was read, were the favoured days for public and private fasts.[6] People would assemble for prayer, and mention the reason for the fast, as follows from a baraita in the Babylonian Talmud.[7] Most texts which mention fasting on Mondays and Thursdays are later than 70 C.E. though some are definitely earlier.[8] Epiphanius says that these were the days of the Pharisees' fasts in Jesus' time[9] and the *Didache* warns against fasting 'along with the hypocrites' (the Pharisees) on these days, urging Wednesday and Friday instead.[10] The Pharisee in Luke who boasted of his twice-weekly fasts must have meant Mondays and Thursdays.[11] But the custom was confined to certain circles among the Pharisees and their disciples.[12] The boasts of the Pharisee in Luke would explain the advice given in Matthew, not to flaunt one's fasting openly.[13] But private fasting was an individual matter, practised only by those groups or individuals who desired greater union with God.[14]

[1] Luke 2:36-38; 2 Cor. 11:27.
[2] See chapter seventeen, p. 873.
[3] *M. Taanith* 4:3; *P. T. Taanith* IV, 68b; *T. B. Taanith* 27b.
[4] Mark 2:18-19; Luke 5:33-5.
[5] See especially *T. B. Taanith* 11a-b.
[6] See *M. Megillah* 1:1-2; *T. Megillah* 1:2-3, *T. B. Megillah* 2a; *M. Ketuboth* 1:1 and see Alon, *Studies* II, pp. 120-7.
[7] *T. B. Shabbath* 24a; Alon, ibid.
[8] Baraita to *Megillath Taanith*, end (p. 95).
[9] *Haer.*, I, 15.
[10] *Didache* 8:1.
[11] Luke 18:12.
[12] *Tractate Soferim* 21.
[13] Matt. 6:16-8.
[14] Concerning the attainment of visions through fasting see P. R. Arbesmann, 'Das Fasten'...*RGVV* 21 (1929), pp. 97ff. and M. Hengel, *Judentum und Hellenismus* (1969), p. 376.

Precepts appertaining to agriculture

Much was done, in the Second Temple period and afterwards, to regulate country life and the gifts to be offered by countryfolk. The precepts affected both producer and consumer. If, for instance, the wave offerings or the tithes had not been set aside, the food in question was also forbidden to the guests of the producer and the buyers. Thus the precepts gave rise to many social as well as economic problems, all the more so since many producers were anything but strict in their observance.

We begin with the prohibition of *mixing two kinds of seed* (כלאים). On the basis of Deut. 22:9, 'You shall not sow your vineyard with two kinds of seed, lest the whole yield be forfeited to the sanctuary, the crop which you have sown and the yield of the vineyard',[1] the sages forbade the sowing of two types of seed in every field, and the grafting of one tree on to another type. They also forbade the planting of corn or vegetables in a vineyard, unless they were at least four cubits from the vines. Since this prohibition was in the Torah, it was considered much graver. Once sown, mixed produce of ordinary fields could in the end be eaten but such mixtures in a vineyard could entail forfeiture of the whole crop and its burning.[2] The mishnaic tractate *Shekalim* says that in the Second Temple period, emissaries were sent to check the vineyards on the 15th of Adar (February-March), when the corn had started to show. Rabbi Judah's comment was: 'At first the corn was uprooted and thrown at the owner's feet. But when transgressions multiplied, the corn was uprooted and thrown by the wayside. Later the rule was to declare the whole field ownerless.'[3]

The *corn in the 'corner' of the field* (פאה) i.e. near the edges, had to be left for the poor. The Torah only laid this down for wheat[4] but the tannaitic sages extended the rule to take in other crops, and also pulse, and trees whose crops were picked completely at one time.[5] The rule held only for crops that had to be stored away, not therefore for greens, though there were people who left the gleanings of the latter, according to tradition. So the men of Jericho, in the Second

---

[1] See also Lev. 19:19.
[2] See especially *M. Temurah* 7:5.
[3] *M. Shekalim* 1:1-2; *T. Shekalim* 1:3; *M. Moed Katan* 1:2.
[4] Lev. 19:20; ibid. 23:22.
[5] *Sifra, Kedoshim* 1; *Sifre Deut.* 284; *M. Peah* 1:4-5.

Temple era.[1] On the basis of biblical and tannaitic law, the rule was that even ears of corn which fell from the arms of the harvesters had to be left for the poor, apart from the gleanings on the edges. A forgotten sheaf had likewise to be left for them. In a vineyard, the odd grapes left on the vine by mistake could not be gleaned by the owner. The grapes which were not ripe for picking had also to be left.[2] Numerous traditions speak of such gleanings,[3] which could also benefit non-Jews.[4] The Jewish poor were not obliged to give wave offerings or tithes from what they had gleaned.[5]

Wave offerings and tithes (תרומות–מעשרות) were regulated by oral law according to a precise system, based on biblical texts.[6] Wave offerings had to be given to the priests not only from the corn, wine and oil mentioned in the Torah, but also from other produce.[7] The 'first tithe,' or the tithe in general, had to be given to the Levites, who then gave the priests one tenth, called the wave offering or tithe of the tithes.[8] When a producer had given the offering and tithe in the first, second and fifth years of the seven year cycle, he had to set aside a tenth of the remainder of his produce, the 'second tithe' (מעשר שני). Then, from the produce of the third and sixth years came the 'poor man's tithe' (מעשר עני).[9] The second tithe was brought to Jerusalem and had to be consumed there in a state of ritual purity (see below). If the trip was impossible, the tithe could be sold and the money used to buy food, which was to be eaten as before.[10] There was nothing 'sacred' about the poor man's tithe, which was simply given to the poor.[11] During the sabbatical year (see below), the produce was exempt, and neither the owner or anyone else who gathered it were obliged to set aside offerings or tithes.

[1] *M. Peah* 1:4; *M. Pesahim* 4:8; *T. Pesahim* 2:19-20; *P.T. Pesahim* IV, 31b; *T.B. Pesahim* 56b-57a.
[2] Lev. 19:9-10; ibid. 23:22; Deut. 24:19-22; *M. Peah* 5:7; ibid. 4:1-4.
[3] See above p. 818, n. 1; *M. Peah* 2:7. See especially *P.T. Peah* VIII (beginning) etc.
[4] *M. Gittin* 5:8; *P.T. Demai* II, 24a; etc.
[5] *M. Terumoth* 1:5; *M. Hagigah* 1:3; *Sifre Num.* 110.
[6] Num. 18:5; 18:11-12; 18:21-32; Deut. 18:4; Lev. 22:10-14; Deut. 12:6; 14:22-27; Deut. 26:12-15; Lev. 27:30-31; Lev. 19:23-25.
[7] *M. Maaseroth* 1:1. The use of the word tithe in the Mishnah in many cases also includes the weave-offering.
[8] *M. Terumoth* 4:5etc. *T.B. Berumoth* 47a etc.
[9] See especially the discussion in *M. Yadaim* 4:3.
[10] *M. Maaser Sheni.* 1:4.
[11] *M. Peah* 5:5-6.

Offerings and tithes had not to be handed over immediately and could be stored at home. But the latest time for their 'payment' (בעור, 'elimination') was the last day of passover week, in the fourth and seventh years.[1] At such times, the solemn protestation had to be made, in keeping with the Torah, Deut. 26:13-15, to the effect that the laws of offerings and tithes had been observed.[2]

The wave offering was considered sacred, and could be consumed only by priests and their households, and then only in a state of ritual purity. The amount of the offerings was not defined by the Torah, which merely said, 'the first fruits of your grain, of your wine and of your oil, and the first of the fleece of your sheep, you shall give him' (Deut. 18:4). According to the school of Hillel, a generous man would give a fortieth, while the school of Shammai demanded a thirtieth. The latter said that a fortieth or fiftieth denoted the average type of man, while a sixtieth or less showed 'the evil eye' (envy and avarice).[3] There are many texts, from Hasmonaean to tannaitic times, to show that the wave offering was made even by the *am ha-aretz*, who were suspect as to tithing.[4] The laws of all periods dealing with such offerings suppose that the practice was universal.[5] Tithes could be consumed under any circumstances, but the sacredness of the wave offering was respected even by tax-collectors.[6] General observance was furthered by the fact that the demands of the offering were moderate. Possibly some gave less than prescribed in the Mishnah, but even so they would have fulfilled their obligation. Some amoraic sages even held that a single grain from a crop of corn satisfied the law.[7] One tradition, upheld most strongly in Palestinian texts, was that one per cent was the minimum to satisfy the Torah.[8]

The Mishnah describes the final stage of production at which the wave offering from the given article was to be set aside. As a rule, this

---

[1] *M. Maaser Sheni* 5:6-9. Our version reads on the eve of the 'first' feast-day. All the major versions read on the eve of the last feast-day.
[2] *Ibid.* 5:10-13.
[3] *M. Terumoth* 4:3; *T. Terumoth* 5:3.
[4] *T. Sotah* 13:10. *P. T. Maaser Sheni* v, 56d and *T. B. Sotah* 48a mention that Johanan the high priest (either Hyrcanus I or II) checked all the cities in Israel and found that the people were setting aside only the wave offering. The first tithe and the second tithe were set aside by some but not by others.
[5] This is the major assumption of the *Mishnah* and *Tosefta Demai*.
[6] *M. Nedarim* 3:3; *T. Nedarim* 2:2.
[7] *T. B. Kiddushin* 58b; *P. T. Terumoth* IV, 44d.
[8] *P. T. Terumoth* IV, 44d. This is found also in certain tannaitic sources. See V. Aptowitzer, 'Heker Halachah' *Sinai* VI (1940), pp. 292-319.

was when it was stacked in barns, ready to be sent to market.[1] If this stage had not been reached, produce could be eaten at an informal meal, even if the dues had not been deducted. They could of course be handed over in the fields, but as a rule, this happened only with wave offerings, while the tithes were dealt with at home.[2] According to the Mishnah, Rabban Gamaliel was making a sea voyage once when the offerings and tithes fell due, so he gave the 'first tithe' to a Levite who was with him, and the poor man's tithe to someone else, to be passed on to the poor. Nothing is said about his setting aside the wave offering.[3]

Often enough, according to tannaitic texts, such offerings were set aside in the barns, where the priests and Levites came for them. The tannaitic sages had sharp words for the priests who came to help the producer in his barn, in the hope of having their offerings at once. The practice was forbidden, and the offerings thus acquired were declared to be profane.[4] Josephus also affirms that the dues could be set aside in the barns.[5] He says that high priests, in the time of Ishmael ben Phiabi and Ananias (15-16 and 47-55 C.E.) sent their servants to the barns to collect their dues.[6]

Produce found scattered in the fields after the barns were cleared could be eaten, according to a baraita in the Palestinian Talmud. This was not considered stealing, and the presumption was that the offering had been deducted in the barns, though not the tithes.[7] The wave offering was set aside from dried grain, pulse and other dry produce, and could also be set aside from liquids, as was commonly done in the case of oil and wine or with their raw materials. But the wave offerings from such liquids or their raw material sometimes caused difficulties in the matter of ritual purity. Those of the strict observance could not buy them from the lax. Only the *haberim*, as will be seen, were held to be fully reliable. A halakah from the Temple era says that even the *am ha-aretz* were considered reliable as regards the purity of the

---

[1] *M. Maaseroth* 1:5-7. Although the Mishnah only mentions tithes, wave offerings are also implied.
[2] *M. Peah* 8:5-6; *M. Yebamoth* 11:5; *T. Peah* 4:3-6; *T. Demai* 5:4; *T. Demai* 6:5 etc.
[3] *M. Maaser Sheni* 5:9.
[4] *T. Demai* 5:17; *Sifre Zuta* (p. 299); *P. T. Demai* VI, 25b etc.
[5] Jos. *Ant.* XX, 181; 206.
[6] Although Josephus mentions only tithes, as in Talmudic sources the wave offering is implied.
[7] *P. T. Maaseroth* III, 50c cf. *T. Terumoth* 1:7.

wave offering while the wine and olive presses were actually working,[1] and hence priests who were *haberim* could accept dues from them in this particular case. Rabban Johanan ben Zakkai, with whom Rabbi Tarphon, himself a priest, concurred, held that the *am ha-aretz* were reliable at all times as regards the purity of their wave offerings.[2]

Such offerings, for the priest and his household to eat, could also be eaten by their non-Jewish servant, and could even be given to animals if suitable as fodder.[3] The oil was often used by the priests as an unguent.[4] Evening was the usual time for such a meal, before which the priests took a bath. They then waited till after sunset, before eating. The first item in the Mishnah runs: 'When may the *shema* be recited in the evening? As soon as the priests go in to eat their offerings'. The bath had nothing to do with ritual impurity, but was the custom for all, men, women and children, before the offerings were eaten; so all tannaitic and amoraic texts, as scholars agree.[5] The laws of the offerings and tithes remained in force after the destruction of the Temple, while the meal made of them was regarded by the priests as a sort of liturgical rite surviving from the Temple.[6]

The tithe, an obligation from the Torah, was a major item, and was in fact paid by the strict. The Book of Numbers says that the Levites were the intermediaries through whom the priests received their dues,[7] but various texts, ranging from soon after the exile to amoraic times, suggest that the tithes were given directly to the priests. The covenant described in Nehemiah obliged the people to give the tithes to the Levites,[8] from which it would follow that the priests got only the tenth of a tenth. But is appears from the rest of the book that the priests usually got the actual tithe.[9] Tannaitic opinions differ as to whether priests or Levites should get the 'first tithe'.[10] One explanation was that the Levites who returned under Ezra were so few that the whole

---

[1] *M. Hagigah* 3:4. Concerning the application of this law to all parts of Israel see *T. B. Hagigah* 25a.
[2] *T. Hagigah* 3:36 (p. 393, ed. Lieberman).
[3] Lev. 22:11; *M. Yebamoth* 7:1-3; *Sifra, Emor* 5 (beginning) etc.
[4] *M. Terumoth* 11:9; *M. Shebuoth* 8:2.
[5] *T. Yoma* 5:5; *P. T. Pesahim* I, 27b; *T. B. Ketuboth* 26a. See J. N. Epstein, *Prolegomena* p. 1013; L. Ginzberg I, p. 7; Ch. Albeck, *Order Zeraim*, p. 235.
[6] *T. B. Pesahim* 72b (the parallel in *Sifre Num.* 116 does not mention 'last night.' The version in the *T.B.*, however, is the more authoritative.
[7] Num. 18:21-32.
[8] Neh. 10:35-40.
[9] Neh. 13:4-13. Cf. Neh. 12:44.
[10] *M. Yebamoth* 6:1-2; *T. B. Ketuboth* 26a; *T. B. Baba Bathra* 816; *T. B. Hullin* 131b. See *T. Peah* 4:5 and *T. Ketuboth* 3:1 and variant readings.

class of Levites lost their prerogative, which was then transferred to the priests. The Books of Judith and of *Jubilees* also seem to say that the tithe went to the priests,[1] Philo is obscure on the point.[2] Josephus, when speaking of biblical law, says that both priests and Levites received the tithe, but when speaking of his own times says that it went to the priests.[3]

It seems that during Hasmonaean times the priests gained control of the tithe, which had to be brought to the Temple. According to the Mishnah, 'Johanan the high priest (Hyrcanus I?) abolished the protestation concerning the tithe',[4] and the Talmud goes into great detail on the matter. One gathers finally that this was part of Hyrcanus' effort to make the Temple the central agency for the collection of the tithes, and to assign them to the priests.[5] Possibly the mishnaic tradition refers to Hyrcanus II, who along with his sons was authorized to receive the tithes by Julius Caesar, according to Josephus.[6] The tithes, then, had to go to the high priest in Jerusalem, who was to have them distributed among the priests. During the Second Temple period, the priests usually received the tithes, though sometimes Levites received them, as biblical law laid down. One source affirms that until John Hyrcanus' time, the tithes were divided into three parts, one of which went to friends of priests or Levites.[7] After the destruction of the Temple, the tithe was only occasionally given to the Levites,[8] and the sages made unsuccessful efforts to restore the ancient custom.[9] The dues could be paid to priests and Levites in any place, according to tannaitic law,[10] which lists the wave offering among the gifts which can be made 'within the frontiers', that is, not just in Jerusalem but anywhere in the Land of Israel.[11] And in the last years of the Temple, this was certainly the case. The Talmud often has such expressions as 'the priests and Levites who

[1] Judith 11:13; *Jubilees* 13:24-47.
[2] *De Virtut.* 95; *De Spec. Leg.* I, 156.
[3] Jos. *Ant.* IV, 240-5; 68; XX, 181; 206-7; *Life* 12 and 15.
[4] *M. Maaser Sheni* 5:15; *M. Sotah* 9:10.
[5] See *P. T. Maaser Sheni* V, 56d; *P. T. Sotah* IX, 24a; *T. B. Sotah* 47a-b. Cf. Alon, *Studies* I, pp. 83-92.
[6] Jos. *Ant.* XIV, 203. See Alon loc.cit. A. Oppenheimer, 'The Separation of First Tithes during the Second Temple Period' in the *Benjamin de Vries Memorial Volume* (1962), pp. 70-83.
[7] *P. T. Maaser Sheni* V, 56d; *P. T. Sotah* IX, 24a.
[8] *M. Maaser Sheni* 5:9.
[9] *P. T. Maaser Sheni* V, 56b.
[10] *M. Betzah* 1:6; *T. Peah* 4:7 etc.
[11] *T. Hallah* 2:9 and parallels.

were standing in the barns'.[1] Josephus says that his friends Joezer and Judah, priests who were sent to Galilee with him at the beginning of the revolt, made so much money from their tithes that they wanted to do nothing but go home. He then congratulates himself for not having accepted the tithes that he was offered.[2] He adds that some high priests used to send their men to the barns to take the tithes by force.[3] It seems strange that at this time priests or Levites received their dues directly, since the accepted custom, from the exile down to Hasmonaean times, was to bring them to the Temple for distribution by the authorities there.[4] Philo still knew of the ancient custom, which had disappeared in his day, and gave it his own peculiar interpretation.[5]

The second tithe remained the property of the householder, but had to be brought to Jerusalem, where it was eaten in a state of ritual purity. People living near the city could themselves bring the produce in question to Jerusalem, but if they lived too far away, they could sell it, and bring the money to Jerusalem to buy food there or to furnish peace offerings, which could be eaten almost in their entirety.[6] The trip was generally made at the time of the great feasts.[7] If all the tithe or the equivalent money was not used, the rest went to the poor of Jerusalem, since it could not be taken out.[8] The 'second tithe' was one of the few precepts which could not be fully carried out after the destruction of the Temple. The food in question could not be eaten in Jerusalem, according to the Halakah, except while the Temple was in existence, so it was sold and the money put away, in the hope that the Temple would soon be re-built.[9] The Talmud has much to say about such savings, and it was not till long after 70 C.E. that the tithe was bought in for merely a token sum.[10] In the third and sixth years

[1] *T. Peah* 4:3 cf. *T. Demai* 5:17; *T. B. Bekhoroth* 26b etc.
[2] *Life* 12 and 15.
[3] Jos. *Ant.* xx, 181; 206-7.
[4] See Mal. 3:10; Neh. 12:44; 2 Chron. 31:5ff.; Tob. 1:6-7; Judith 11:13; 1 Macc. 3:49-50; 10:31 etc.
[5] *De Spec. Leg.* I, 132-50.
[6] Thus the law explains the verses in Deut. 14:12-15. See *Sifre Deut.* 105-8; *M. Maaser Sheni* 1-2.
[7] See S. Safrai, *Pilgrimage at the Time of the Second Temple* (1965) in Hebrew, pp. 126-7.
[8] *M. Maaser Sheni* 3:5 and in *P. T.* ad loc.
[9] *Sifre Deut.* 106; *T. B. Makkoth* 19a; *T. B. Zebahim* 60a.
[10] *M. Maaser Sheni* 2:7; *T. Maaser Sheni* 3:18; 4:5. Concerning the amoraic period see *Ha-Hilluxim. The Differences between Babylonian and Palestinian Jews*, ed. M. Margaliot, (1938) p. 141.

of the cycle, the poor man's tithe took the place of the second tithe, in tannaitic law. This meant that there were never more than two tithes in any given year. The tannaitic practice can be traced back as early as the Septuagint version of Deut 26:12. Other traditions however, especially those of the *Book of Jubilees*, Josephus and the *Targum Pseudo Jonathan* on Deut. 26:1-13, held that all three tithes had to be paid in the third and sixth years, including the poor man's tithe.[1] In contrast to the wave offering and other precepts, tithing, as has been noted, was often neglected, as early as the time of Hyrcanus I, according to tannaitic traditions.[2] This was possibly due to the fact that there were so many other demands on people's resources. The tithe was the most exacting of the dues. Further, the original reason for tithing, as given in the Torah, was that the Levite for whom it was levied owned no land and was entirely dedicated to divine service.[3] In the Second Temple period, however, the distribution of land did not accord with biblical provisions. Priests and Levites could be well-to-do landowners. Tithing then seemed pointless and many people felt that they were excused. And the priests belonged on the whole to the upper classes, with a proportion of landowners among them higher than among the rest of the population. Any given division of priests or Levites functioned in the Temple only twice a year, for a week at a time, and not all the members of the division on duty actually went to Jerusalem. Some were in the public service, functioning as teachers of the Torah, or in the administration. Levites could be policemen or law officers. All this militated against tithing.

The Pharisees were of course very strict in the matter. It was one of the great ways of distinguishing a *haber* from one of the *am ha-aretz*. One of the *haber's* main obligations was strict tithing.[4] A vendor who was not a *haber* was always suspect of marketing 'dubious produce' (דמאי). It was presumed that the wave offering had been deducted, but not the tithe. But the tithe was not 'sacred', so the buyer could himself set aside the 'tithe from the tithe', and enjoy the other ninetynine-hundredths of his purchase. So too with the poor man's tithe, and the second tithe, when obligatory. The custom of setting

---

[1] *Jubilees* 32:11; Jos. *Ant.* IV, 240-1. Apparently this approach is also found in Tobit. See the short version 1:7-8 and the longer version ibid.

[2] *T. Sotah* 13 (end); *P. T. Maaser Sheni* v, 56d; *T. B. Sotah* 48ff.

[3] Num. 18:21-4.

[4] *M. Demai* 2:3; *T. Demai* 2:2.

aside the fraction of the dubious produce is well attested, even after the destruction of the Temple.[1]

Tithes were levied on grain, wine and oil, according to the written Torah,[2] a law which was echoed in other parts of the Bible and in the Apocrypha.[3] But in tannaitic times the law was extended to take in 'anything used as food, anything stored, anything that grows from the soil'.[4] The custom of tithing non-agricultural products was, however, already known in the Temple era, and can be detected with some certainty behind *Jubilees*,[5] and the *Damascus Document*,[6] while it is definitely attested in later writings, tannaitic[7] and amoraic.[8] This is what is behind Luke 18:12, where the Pharisee boasts of giving tithes from all that he gets. The *Didache*, which reflects many Jewish traditions, also says that the offering must be levied on 'money and clothes and all possessions', as well as on wine and corn.[9] But the custom was never really widespread, and was confined to those who were particularly strict.

The law of the *sabbatical year*, (שביעית) as interpreted both in biblical and oral law, was undoubtedly one of the most difficult to observe, since it should cause real hardship in an agricultural society. The Torah forbade in that year the planting and reaping of corn, and the pruning and cropping of fruit trees.[10] Tannaitic law added such prohibitions as that against eating the 'aftergrowth', grain or fruit which ripened in the seventh year as an aftergrowth of the sixth.[11] Fields could not be worked in the sixth year except for that year's crop, not for longterm results, least of all in the seventh year. The field then lay fallow, neither ploughed nor sown, though orchards could be tended as far

---

[1] See *Mishnah* and *Tosefta Demai*.
[2] Lev. 27:30; Num. 18:27; Deut. 12:17; 14:13.
[3] Neh. 10:38; 13:5; 2 Chron. 31:5; Tob. 1:1; Judith 11:13.
[4] *M. Maaseroth* 1:1.
[5] *Jubilees* 32:2. Levi dreams that he has been appointed a priest and that Jacob set aside a tithe from all his property, from his gold and utensils and give it to Levi.
[6] *Damascus Document* 14:11-15.
[7] Thus the Tosaphists (*T. B. Taanith* 9a) cite a lost section of *Sifre*.
[8] *Pesikta de Rav Kahana* 10 (p. 173).
[9] *Didache* 13:3.
[10] Exod. 23:10-11; Lev. 25:1-7.
[11] *Sifra, Behar* (108a). There is no reason to see the prohibition of aftergrowth as a later prohibition. See S. Safrai, 'The Practical Implementation of the Sabbatical Year After the Destruction of the Second Temple,' in *Tarbiz* xxxv (1966), p. 304.

as was necessary for their bare survival. But the fruit was considered ownerless and anyone could pick the fruit for personal use. The general practice was to let fields lie fallow some year, in any case, and this could be planned so as to coincide with the sabbatical year. Nonetheless, hardships resulted, as may be seen from the following instance. According to oral law, agricultural laws were in force only in the Land of Israel, but other duties could be discharged anywhere.[1] In fact, during the Temple era, Diaspora Jews gave wave offerings and tithes: so in Ammon, Moab, Egypt and Babylonia, as discussion at Jabneh shows. But there is not the least suggestion that they also undertook to keep the sabbatical year.[2] Now no halakic or haggadic distinction can be adduced to differentiate the sabbatical year from the dues, as regards their obligatory force. And since dues were paid, though not explicitly demanded of them by the Torah, the only possible reason for Diaspora Jews not keeping the sabbatical year was that it involved too great economic hardships. This is confirmed by third century sermons which describe the anxieties and burdens of the sabbatical year.[3]

In contrast to the jubilee year, which in Pharisaic tradition was only to be celebrated when the Land of Israel was duly divided among the tribes, according to biblical standards, the sabbatical year was obligatory throughout the Second Temple period. The fields, except for the minimum required for survival, were left fallow and the fruit trees free for all. Our earliest attestation comes from Josephus, who says that Alexander exempted the Jews from taxation in the sabbatical year.[4] Julius Caesar did the same,[5] and the exemption was probably still granted after the destruction of the Temple. But it was abrogated after Bar Cochba's revolt, and then observance became more sporadic.[6] It was particularly difficult in wartime, when food was scarce, as when Lysias marched from the south via Beth Zur against the Maccabees, in a sabbatical year (c. 162 B.C.). Both sides suffered great hardships,[7]

---

[1] *M. Kiddushin* 1:9; *Sifre Deut.* 44, 59.

[2] *M. Yadaim* 4:3.

[3] *Lev. Rabba* 1; *Lam. Rabba* 17 (proem), etc.

[4] Jos. *Ant.* XI, 338. Numerous scholars doubt the authenticity of this tradition and claim it is merely a projection to the time of Julius Caesar.

[5] Jos. *Ant.* XIV, 202; 320-8.

[6] See Safrai loc.cit., pp. 320-8.

[7] 1 Macc. 6:49-57. The parallel in 2 Macc. 13:19-22 does not mention the sabbatical year nor does Josephus. There is no reason, however, not to accept the paucity of food because of the sabbatical year as do some scholars.

as did Jerusalem in 37 B.C.E., when Herod besieged and took the city.[1]
Leases from Bar Cochba's time show that land was often rented out
only till the end of the last working year in the cycle, the sixth.[2]
Another example of the hardships involved may be deduced from the
rule about wild endives. Ordinarily they were not eaten, but they
were in the sabbatical year. Thus, when many of the restrictions were
lifted in the time of Rabbi Judah the patriarch, the wild endive was
declared unfit for human consumption, since there was no longer any
need to eat it.[3] Third century texts tell how non-Jews jeered at the
people for eating wild vegetables in the sabbatical year and how skits
were played about it in the theatre of Caesarea.[4]

The *offering of some of the dough or bread* (חלה) was a precept universally
observed in the Land of Israel and elsewhere during the Second Temple
period. The Book of Numbers commands that some 'of the first of
the coarse meal' was to be offered to the Lord,[5] which was re-affirmed
by Ezekiel and accepted once more by the people under Nehemiah.[6]
It was generally taken to mean that some bread should be offered,
though some people held that a particularly pleasing offering could be
made from the dough, basing themselves on the words, 'of the first of
the coarse meal'.[7] Only a notable quantity of dough or bread came
under the rule, and it was finally agreed that the offering had to be
made only if the bread contained at least 2 1/2 liters of flour.[8] The
offering was considered sacred, to be eaten only by a priest in a state
of purity. Though all cooked foods were regarded as ritually impure
in the Diaspora, a small offering was still set aside and then burned,
which was the rule for a defiled offering. Then a second piece of due
proportions was set aside, as a memorial of the offering, and given
to the priest.[9] The amount is not specified in the Bible, but in tannaitic
texts it is one twenty-fourth for the householder and one forty-eighth

[1] Jos. *Ant.* XIV, 475, XV, 7.
[2] *DJD* II, 24A-F. Concerning the chronology of the sabbatical year see B.
Wacholder, 'The Calendar of Sabbatical Cycles During the Second Temple', in
HUCA XLVI (1973), pp. 153-96.
[3] *P. T. Shebiith* VI, 37a; 37b; *P. T. Nedarim* IX, 39d.
[4] *Lam. Rabba* 17 (Proem); ibid. chapter 3 in the name of Rabbi Abahu of
Caesarea.
[5] Num. 15:17-28.
[6] Ezek. 44:30; Neh. 12:38.
[7] Thus it would seem based on the Septuagint and thus Philo says in *De Spec.
Leg.* I, 132. *M. Hallah* 3:6; cf. *M. Hallah* 3:1 and *Sifre Zuta* (p. 283).
[8] *M. Eduyoth* 1:2; *Sifre Zuta* ibid.
[9] *M. Hallah* 4:8; *T. B. Ketuboth* 25a.

for the baker.[1] While the wave offering and the tithe were incumbent on men, the woman who made the bread had to set aside this offering. The 'dough offering' was regarded as truly biblical. Even people who in the Temple era and afterwards disqualified the wave offering, the tithe and the sabbatical year as non-biblical, accepted the law of the dough offering. So too even the *am ha-aretz*, who had little time for precepts which they thought were merely thought out by the sages.[2]

Ritual purity

The question of the ritual purity and impurity (טומאה – טהרה) was a major issue in the Temple era and in tannaitic times. But most of the laws in question affected only the priests. Other Jews came under them only when assembling in the Temple or eating 'sacred' foods. Maimonides summed up the situation when he said: 'All that is written in the Torah about the laws of purity concern only the Temple and its holy things, the wave offering and the second tithe...'[3] However, as we know from many regulations, especially those dealing with practical matters, and as we learn from Josephus, Philo and the New Testament, the laws of purity were widely observed. Some tried to restrict their ambit, but others to enlarge it, aiming at raising all Israel to the same level of holiness as the priests. The Sadducees maintained that purity was only for the latter, while some at least of the Pharisees held that it should be preserved by all who were willing to accept the obligation, though not necessarily incumbent on all Israel.[4] The Essenes insisted on the full rigour of the law for all their groups, and ritual purity was one of their priorities. We list here the main grounds for ritual impurity, starting with the least serious.

1. The male sexual act. This affected both the man and the woman after intercourse. They had to take a bath and were only purified at sunset.[5]
2. The carcase of animals, except 'pure' animals killed by men and forming lawful food. This impurity also lasted till sunset.[6]

---

[1] *M. Hallah* 3:1; 2:3; 4:1; *T. Hallah* 1:11, cf. *M. Shabbath* 2:6.
[2] *T. B. Ketuboth* 25a; *P. T. Shebiith* IX (end).
[3] *Laws of Uncleanness of Foodstuffs*, chapter 15.
[4] *M. Demai* 2:3; *T. Demai* 2:3; *Aboth de Rabbi Nathan*, version A, 41 etc. For the position of the Sadducees on ritual purity see A. Geiger, *Urschrift*, 223.
[5] Lev. 15:16-18; Deut. 22:10-12.
[6] Lev. 11:24-8.

3. A flux from man or woman, a woman during her period and during childbirth. The impurity lasted seven days after the disappearance of the symptoms. The purification, except in the case of the woman's period, demanded the offering of sacrifice, the minimum being two doves.[1]

4. Contact with leprosy. This rendered a person impure for seven days, and a sacrifice had to be offered after the priest had verified the cleansing. The Torah gives details of the rite of purification, which included sprinkling with various liquids.[2]

5. A corpse. This impurity was cleansed by the water with which the ashes of the red heifer had been mingled.[3]

These are in the Torah. Oral law added: the non-Jew,[4] his main residence,[5] land outside the Land of Israel[6] and idolatry.[7] These were sources of impurity because of their connection with paganism, though other reasons are given in later sources. The notion of impurity in a less strict sense, that of impurity which affected only the hands, also came in. Such a limitation of impurity to a single member of the body was unknown to the Torah, but oral law held that the hands were impure as a rule because they thouched things automatically and so came under suspicion. This meant that even a person in a state of purity could not touch food or anything else for which purity was required, without first purifying his hands. The Talmud gives various dates for the establishment of this rule, but in any case, the *Letter of Aristeas* already says thatthe elders washed their hands before prayer.[8] Anyone who came into contact with a major impurity incurred a minor impurity. All could be cleansed by a ritual bath (מקוה) containing the forty *seahs* required for total immersion. It could hold rain-water or water from a spring or a stream, but not water which had been drawn or pumped. A river or the sea were of course valid.

[1] Lev. 15:1-32; 12:1-8.
[2] Lev. 13-14.
[3] Num. 19:11-19.
[4] Concerning the impurity of Gentiles during early times see *M. Pesahim* 8:8; *M. Shekalim* 8:1; *T. Yom ha-Kippurim* 4:20; Jos. *Ant.* XVIII, 90; Acts 10:28 etc. For a list of early sources see Alon, *Studies* I, pp. 121-41 against the opinion of those who see the institution as a later one.
[5] *M. Oholoth* 18:7, 9; John 18:28 etc.
[6] The enactment is ascribed to the time of the first 'pair' or to the time of Hillel and Shammai (*T. B. Shabbath* 14b; *P. T. Shabbath* I, 3c). Some sources, however, even ascribe it to earlier periods (*T. Parah* 3:10).
[7] *M. Shabbath* 9:1; *M. Abodah Zarah* 3:6; *P. T. Pesahim* II, 36c.
[8] *Letter of Aristeas* 304-6; *T. B. Shabbath* 13b-14b; *P. T. Shabbath* I, 3d. *Mishnah Yadaim* is devoted to the ritual cleanness and uncleanness of the hands.

The hands could be purified by having water poured on them from a vessel.[1] The ritual bath is the main reason for the many cisterns found throughout the Land of Israel, especially near the Temple and the synagogues. They are often mentioned in the texts, and excavations have discovered hand-basins in synagogue courtyards and entrances.[2] Such hand-basins still exist, as the custom of washing the hands has persisted among Jews, though technically the whole body is considered impure. According to the Torah, clothes, wooden utensils, leather receptacles and sacks were susceptible to impurity; so too pottery, if contaminated by a dead reptile, for instance.[3] Oral law extended the possible impurity to take in utensils made of bone.[4] Only stone utensils were immune.[5] When one utensil defiled another, or when a utensil defiled food, the ritual of purification was the same as for human beings. But if pottery was defiled, there was no way of purifying it. It could only be broken, or used for impure foods.[6] A rule from the time of the *Zugoth* (c. 50 B.C.E.) held that glass was the same as earthenware, which meant that any glass vessel which had been defiled even in a minor degree was barred to a large section of the community.[7]

Food was also included in the rules. According to the Torah and the oral law, produce actually growing from the soil was immune, like standing corn, but ceased to be so once it was detached. It was defiled by contact with any of the seven liquids which favoured impurity.[8] Anyone eating impure food was himself defiled. Liquids were the worst, because they constituted 'first degree defilement in all circumstances, defiling both the person and the food'. Contact with them turned second degree into first degree impurity.[9]

[1] *Sifra, Shemini* chap. 8; *Sifra, Mezora, Zabim* chap. 6. *Tractate Mikvaoth* deals with this topic.
[2] See L. Robert, in *Revue de Philologie* XXXII (1958), pp. 43-5; J. B. Frey, *Corpus Inscriptionum Judaicarum* no. 751; *P. T. Megillah* III, 74a (end). In the Palestinian fragments in the *genizah* published recently by M. Margaliot in 'The Laws of Eretz Israel from the Genizah' (1973; in Hebrew), p. 132 one reads: 'Therefore the men of old set up in the courtyards of synagogues whole sinks to sanctify the hands and the feet'.
[3] Lev. 11:32-5.
[4] *Sifra, Shemini* 9; *T. B. Hullin* 25b; *M. Hullin* 9:1.
[5] *M. Betzah* 2:3; *M. Oholoth* 5:5 etc.
[6] Lev. 11:33. This law did not restrict the use of earthenware lamps which did not have an interior (*Sifra* ad loc.).
[7] *P. T. Shabbath* I, 2d; *T. B. Sabbath* 14b and *T. Kelim Baba Bathra* 7:7.
[8] Lev. 11:34-8. *Tractate Makshirin* deals with this topic.
[9] *T. Tebul Yom* 1:5-6. Liquids also attracted additional strictures in the law of the Dead Sea Sect. See *Rule of the Community* 6:20-1; Jos. *War* II, 137-8.

In the Second Temple era, the wider ambit of the purity laws had notable effects on ordinary life. It was generally accepted, as a ruling laid down by Ezra, that the ejaculation of the male seed, even in marital intercourse, rendered one unfit for Torah study or prayer before purification by a bath. However, many still claimed that 'the words of the Torah were not susceptible to impurity' and that the obligation of bathing arose anyway. Thus the Palestinian Talmud says: 'The real reason for this rule is that Israel should not be like cocks and hens that couple and go on at once to eat'.[1]

The Talmud says that many of the ordinary people were strict about this, while some abstained from forbidden intercourse when they saw that there was not enough water for a bath.[2] Some, like the Hemerobaptists, bathed every morning for fear of having suffered an ejaculation. And tannaitic tradition which goes back to the Temple era reports how the Pharisees were in dispute about the matter with the group in question.[3]

It was quite common to wash the hands before eating[4] and before prayer. The custom is attested as early as the *Letter of Aristeas* and the third book of the *Sibylline Oracles*. Judith's custom of leaving Holofernes' camp every day to bathe was probably her way of keeping up the custom, since washing the hands was really a token bath.[5] The strict purified all utensils bought in the market, and since earthenware could not be purified, it was bought only from *haberim*; so too with liquids or any food in which liquid had been an ingredient, like bread, though dry foods could be bought anywhere.[6] An instance which illustrates the general prudence with regard to purity is the peopling of Tiberias. Herod Antipas had gone to great expense to build the new town but he had to bring in settlers from all classes, including slaves, since the Jews in general were more than reluctant, Tiberias being on the site of a cemetery. The Halakah declared such settlers impure for seven days.[7] Hence the great care taken not to

---

[1] *T. B. Baba Kamma* 82a; *T. B. Berakoth* 22a; *P. T. Berakoth* II, 6c etc.
[2] *T. B.* and *P. T. Berakoth* ibid. See W. Brandt, *Die jüdischen Baptismen* (1910) pp. 39-41, 124-5.
[3] *T Yadaim* 2:20 (the full version found in the explanation of Rabbi Samson of Sens near the end of the Mishnah). Eusebius citing Hegesippus includes among the Jewish sects of old 'Ημεροβαπτίσται (*Eccles. History* IV, 22).
[4] See above p. 801.
[5] *Letter of Aristeas* 305-6; *Sibylline Oracles* III, 591-4; Judith 12:5-8; *T. B. Berakoth* 14b-15a; *T. B. Pesahim* 46a; *T. B. Hullin* 122b.
[6] *M. Demai* 2:3 and *T. Demai* 2 and 3.
[7] Jos. *Ant.* XVIII, 36-8. Only in the second century C.E. was the city purified.

touch a corpse or enter a cemetery except in case of necessity. Many instances of this have been recorded, as have the many regulations bearing on the matter.[1]

The greatest care was taken of purity coming up to the sabbath or a feast-day, e.g. 'Judas (Maccabee) took his army into the town of Adullam, where, as the seventh day was coming on, they purified themselves according to the custom and kept the sabbath'.[2] The practice was often urged in the Midrashim and amoraic writings and the purification of utensils is often mentioned in the Mishnah.[3] With the destruction of the Temple, the *fons et origo* of ritual purity, the laws became even more strict. 'The priests preserved their status by not passing on to everyone the rules of purity,' and 'purity spread' among the ordinary people.[4] This was partly in reparation for the ruin of the Temple, partly to fill the vacuum left in religious life by its destruction.

But then purity began to be neglected, both in theory and in practice, first and almost necessarily the impurities contracted by living abroad and coming into constant contact with non-Jews.[5] And then all the rules began to be neglected towards the end of the tannaitic period. The Temple and its holy things were only a distant memory; the ashes of the red heifer, the main if not the sole source of purity according to the Torah, ceased to be available. But insofar and as long as the rules of purity were obeyed, they were always considered an end in themselves, not just the preparation for a good deed like study of Torah. They were held to be the best way of avoiding sin and attaining the heights of sanctity, as all texts affirm, from Philo to the tannaitic period.[6]

BIBLIOGRAPHY

On the observance of the commandments during the Second Temple period generally, see S. SAFRAI, 'Tora und Gebote in der Tannaitischen

---

[1] *T. Abodah Zarah* 3:10; *T. B. Gittin* 61b. Those who eat in a state of ritual cleanness are called 'members of the congregation' as in *M. Zabim* 3:2.

[2] 2 Macc. 12:38; cf. *P. T. Shabbath* 1, 3c.

[3] *Sifra, Shemini* 4; *M. Shabbath* 7:7; *M. Betzah* 2:2 etc.

[4] *T. B. Bekhoroth* 30b; *P. T. Shabbath* 1, 3b-c and parallels.

[5] See Alon, *Studies* I, pp. 121-41.

[6] The baraita describing the spiritual elevation of man teaches: purity leads to abstinence and abstinence leads to holiness (*Mishnah Sotah*, end, and parallels). See *De Spec. Leg.* II, 205-6; III, 63; Jos. *Against Apion* II, 205.

Literatur', in *Juden und Christen lesen dieselbe Bibel*, ed. H. Kremers (1973), pp. 88-101. On the *mezuzah* see V. APTOWITZER, 'Les noms de Dieu et des Anges dans la Mesuza', *REJ* (1910), pp. 39-52. Customs of *erub* are discussed in the introduction and commentary of CH. ALBECK on M. ERUBIN, *Seder Moed* (1953), pp. 77-81ff. The subject of phylacteries is discussed by A. COWEN, *Tefillin* (1960). On the *shema*, blessings, and prayers, see I. ELBOGEN, *Der jüdische Gottesdienst in seiner geschichtlichen Entwicklung* (1931), repr. 1962), pp. 14-279. On the *shema* see L. BLAU, 'Origine et histoire de la lecture Schema', in *REJ* (1895), pp. 179-201; V. APTOWITZER in *MGWJ* LXXIII (1929), pp. 93-118. On the eighteen benedictions see K. KOHLER, 'The Origin and Composition of the Eighteen Benedictions' in *HUCA* I (1924), pp. 387-425. For the relation between the *shema* and the eighteen benedictions see L. J. LIEBREICH, 'The Benediction immediately preceeding and following the Recital of the *Shema*' in *REJ* CV (1966), pp. 151-65. On the blessing after meals see L. FINKELSTEIN, 'The *Birkat Ha-Mazon*' in *JQR* XIX (1929), pp. 211-62. L. GINZBERG, *A Commentary of the Palestinian Talmud*, 4 vols (1941-61; in Hebrew) is a rich source of information on blessings and prayers. A general view of customs and practices related to the sabbath and festivals is presented by J. MANN, 'The Observance of the Sabat and the Festivals in the First Two Centuries' in *Jewish Review* IV (1911), pp. 502-10. On fasts see G. ALON, *Studies in the History of the Jewish People* I (1957; in Hebrew). p. 291ff. Much material upon those commandments directly related to the Land of Israel is contained in the introduction to individual tractates in *Order Zeraim* of the Mishnah, ed. CH. ALBECK. On the sabbatical year see *Kobetz Shmitah*, ed. Z. Admonit (1973). For the laws of ritual purity and impurity see J. NEUSNER, *A History of the Mishnaic Law of Purity*, 1974ff.

Chapter Sixteen

The Calendar

The biblical calendar

We have very little information regarding the calendar of the ancient Hebrews. The obscurity of our sources has occasioned various and strange suppositions: it is very instructive to note the contrast between the poverty of our sources and the abundance and wealth of details of the theories. It will suffice to mention only one of the more popular theories of modern scholarship, according to which the calendar of the biblical Hebrews was purely solar, similar to the ancient Egyptian, which took account neither of the moon nor of the fact that the length of the solar year is approximately $365\frac{1}{4}$ days. The ancient calendar year is thus said to have been based on a solar year of 365 days, which means that every four years, approximately, each date would have retrograded one day in relation to the sun. According to a very popular variant of this theory, the solar calendar of the ancient Hebrews was that of the *Book of Jubilees* (and the Qumran sect), i.e., a calendar with a 364-day solar year, which means that every seventy years each date would retrograde about three months, and a springtime festival would fall in midwinter.

This entire theory, with its variants, is based on unsubstantiated conjecture. In the ancient Near East, a purely solar calendar was followed only in Egypt, and it is unwarranted to assume that the ancient Israelites adopted the Egyptian practice. Further, even according to the first variant of the theory, and still more according to the second, we are asked to assume that during the period of the First Temple, a period of several hundred years, the Passover festival wandered backwards through the seasons, so that this festival of unleavened bread, dated by the Torah to the 'spring (Abib) month',[1] fell eventually in the autumn or winter, while Tabernacles, the harvest festival 'at the year's end'[2] would have come in the summer or spring. Such assumptions are too preposterous to be seriously considered.

As against such theories, the Bible explicitly affirms that the calendar

[1] Exod. 23:15.
[2] Exod. 34:22.

is to be regulated according to the moon: 'Thou hast made the moon to mark the seasons.'[1] The ancient Israelites celebrated not only the new moon but probably also, under Canaanite influence, the day of the full moon.[2] Even the ancient term *yerah* for month derived from *yareah*, moon, a term common to many Semitic languages and frequently appearing in the Bible,[3] indicates the reasonableness of the assumption that the ancient Israelite calendar was lunisolar, similar to that of the ancient Babylonians, although we do not know the details of methods of lunisolar harmonization and intercalation.[4]

More is known regarding the division of the year into months, of which there were twelve,[5] but we do not know whether the Israelites of the First Temple period had their own names for the months. In other parts of the ancient Near East, some cities had their own names for the months. The list of the months, with the farm-work to be done in each, as preserved in the famous Gezer calendar, does not seem to have been official. And even the identities of the months it mentions and the meaning of the various agricultural labours remain matters of dispute among scholars.[6]

Another unsolved riddle is the meaning of the term 'month of Abib,' which appears in Exodus and Deuteronomy as a name for the first month, that of the Passover festival.[7] This name does not appear at all in Canaanite sources, nor is it part of any other ancient list of months. It probably should be viewed as an informal term which derived from the fact that the ripening (אביב) of barley takes place in this month.[8] The exodus from Egypt also occurred in this month, which was counted as the first of the year,[9] as in Babylonia. Although some scholars claim that during the period of the First Temple there was also an official agricultural calendar, which began in the autumn,

---

[1] Ps. 104:19.
[2] כסה: Ps. 81:3; Prov. 7:20; cf. the Phoenician inscription on the pedestal from Lapethos, in H. Donner and W. Röllig, *Kanaanäische und Aramäische Inschriften* I (1962), no. 43, line 12: *UVKSAM*.
[3] See, for example, Exod. 2:2; Deut. 21:13; Zech. 11:8; Job 29:2.
[4] There is no need to prove the calendar's additional linkage to the solar year, without which the holidays (and all other dates) would retrogress about eleven days yearly, relative to the seasons (cf. below, p. 838, n. 5). The lunisolar intercalation of years is proved by Ezek. 1:1f.; 3:15f.; 4:4ff.; 8:1.
[5] 1 Kings 4:7; 1 Chron. 27:1-15.
[6] The problems with this calendar have been well summarized by M. D. Cassuto, in *Encyclopedia Mikrait* II (1954), pp. 471-4.
[7] Exod. 13:4; 23:15; 34:18; Deut. 16:1.
[8] Exod. 9:31.
[9] Exod. 12:2 and frequently elsewhere.

the evidence is insufficient.[1] It is very possible, however, that with the division of the monarchy, the practice of counting years from the autumn was instituted in the northern kingdom of Israel.[2]

The Bible uses three systems for designating the months. Most frequently, it simply gives the ordinal number of the month, and no more, e.g.: 'in the first month,'[3] 'in the fifth month,'[4] 'in the twelfth month,'[5] or simply 'in the first.'[6] This system was apparently used throughout the First Temple period, and was not entirely discarded during the Second Commonwealth. A second terminology is reflected in the report of the building of Solomon's Temple in the First Book of Kings, which mentions 'the month of Ziv,'[7] 'the month of Ethanim,'[8] and 'the month of Bul.'[9] These names are also found in Phoenician inscriptions, and are part of a longer Phoenician list.[10] Only a few of the names have been explained, such as *KRR*, which is the name of a god, and the identification and sequence of the months are not known at all. Neither is it clear whether this list of names, in part or *in toto*, was widely used in ancient Israel; it is possible that these names were rather taken into the First Book of Kings from some source or document of the time of Solomon, where their use was occasioned by the participation of Tyrians in the building of the Temple. The latter possibility seems more likely, particularly as in three of the four cases in which the Bible uses these names, it prefaces them with the term *yerah*, as do the Phoenician inscriptions. Elsewhere, the Bible always uses *hodesh*,[11] with the number or the name of the month.

The third system is Babylonian. Originating in the city of Babylon itself, it was adopted by the Jews during their exile and hence came into Judaea, according to the ancient sages: 'They carried the names of the months back with them from Babylonia.'[12] Most of these names were also adopted by the Nabataeans, the Palmyreans, and the

---

[1] The Gezer Calendar offers no conclusive evidence (see above).
[2] The relevant conjectures have been summarized by H. Tadmor in his exhaustive discussion of chronology in *Encyclopedia Mikrait* IV (1962), pp. 264-7.
[3] Exod. 40:17. [4] Jer. 1:3.
[5] 2 Kings 25:27. [6] Gen. 8:13.
[7] 6:37, cf. 1 Kings 6:1, 'in the month of Ziv, which is the second month.'
[8] 8:2, 'which is the seventh month.'
[9] 6:38, 'which is the eighth month.'
[10] ZBḤŠŠM, HJR, KRR, MP', MRP', MRP'M (intercalated in leap years?), and P'LT. The series has not been entirely preserved.
[11] Cf. the usage of *hodesh* in the Arad inscriptions. See Y. Aharoni, *Arad Inscriptions* (1975; in Hebrew).
[12] *P. T. Rosh ha-Shanah* 1, 56d.

Syrians.[1] As in the case of the Phoenician terminology, the meaning of only a few of the names is known, e.g., Tammuz, the name of a god,[2] Marheshvan (= [w]árah šamna), 'the eighth month'. Nor do all biblical books of the exilic period or later use this third system: Ezekiel, Haggai, Chronicles, and Daniel still use ordinals. The Babylonian names first appear in Zechariah, accompanied by the number of the month: 'the eleventh month, which is the month of Shebat,' 'the ninth month, which is Kislev.'[3] This is the usual terminology in Esther as well.[4] Without accompanying ordinals, the Babylonian names appear in the Aramaic portions of Ezra,[5] and a few times in Nehemiah and Esther.[6] But even in books which use the Babylonian names, months are also indicated simply by ordinals: so very frequently in Zechariah,[7] always in the Hebrew portions of Ezra[8] and in those parts of Nehemiah which deal with Ezra's activities,[9] and once in Esther.[10] (It would thus be unjustified to consider the use of an unaccompanied ordinal in Daniel 10:4 as anachronistic, as this might be only a matter of chance usage).

The Bible mentions seven Babylonian names of months: Nisan, Sivan, Elul, Kislev, Tebeth, Shebat, Adar. The others occur in the Elephantine papyri,[11] in the Samaritan papyri from Wadi Daliyah and in an inscription from Jason's Tomb,[12] in Jewish literature of the Second Temple period (Apocrypha and Pseudepigrapha, Josephus), *Megillath Taanith*, the documents from the Bar Cochba period found in the Judaean Desert, and in talmudic literature. The Apocrypha generally

---

[1] The names are: Nisan (nisánu), Iyar (ayáru), Sivan (simánu), Tammuz (du'úzu), Ab (abu), Elul (elúlu), Tishri (tešrítu), Marheshavn ([w]árah šamna), Kislev (Kislimu), Tebeth (tebítu), Shebat (šabátu), Adar (ad[d]áru). Tishri is also mentioned in the texts from Ugarit: 'yrh tšrt.'

[2] See Ezek. 8:14.

[3] Zech. 1:7; 7:1.

[4] Esther 2:16; 3:7, 13; 8:9, 12; 9:1.

[5] Ezra 6:15.

[6] Neh. 1:1; 2:1; 6:15; Esther 9:15, 17, 19, 21.

[7] Zech. 1:1; 7:3,5; 8:19.

[8] Ezra 3:1, 6, 8; and frequently elsewhere.

[9] Neh. 7:73; 8:2, 14.

[10] Esther 3:12.

[11] Here Babylonian names of months usually accompany the Egyptian; at times, however, only the Egyptian names appear (Cowley, *Aramaic Papyri of the Fifth Century* B.C. (1923), 1, 1; 7, 1; 11, 8; 22, 1; Kraeling, *The Brooklyn Museum Aramaic Papyri* (1953), 11, 1; 12, 1, 10). Babylonian names alone appear in the documents regarding Passover (Cowley 21, 8) and in the epistles regarding the Temple (*ibid.* 30, 4, 19, 30; 31, 29).

[12] See N. Avigad, *IEJ* XVII (1967), p. 109.

use the Babylonian names, sometimes with ordinals[1] but usually un-accompanied.[2] At times, however, we still find unaccompanied ordinals,[3] while some books, such as Third Maccabees, use only non-Jewish dates. Josephus usually uses the Macedonian names, sometimes accompanied by the name of the corresponding Hebrew (Babylonian) month, most probably indicating the parallel Jewish month.[4]

As the length of the lunar month (the period between two successive new moons) is 29 days-12 hours-44 minutes-2.8 seconds, it seems that the length of successive months must always have alternated between twenty-nine and thirty days. We have no real evidence that the regulation of months during the First Commonwealth was dependent upon visual sighting of the new moon; regarding this question, as well as that of intercalation,[5] it is doubtful whether comparison with other cultures will meaningfully illuminate the details of ancient Israelite practice. The ancient Babylonians apparently always used a mixed lunisolar calendar, intercalating at first when necessary without any fixed cycle. In the sixth century B.C.E., however, Babylonia saw the introduction of an eight-year cycle, consisting of five ordinary years and three leap years. The ancient Greeks at first used a purely lunar calendar, also with an eight-year cycle (five years of 354 days and three years of 355) without any harmonization with the solar year, but later, approximately in the seventh century B.C.E., this was replaced by a lunisolar calendar, still with an eight-year cycle. Neither Babylonia nor Greece remained satisfied with an eight-year cycle. In the fifth century B.C.E. the Athenian Meton discovered the nineteen-year cycle which bears his name: consisting of twelve ordinary years and seven leap years, it allowed a degree of exactitude incomparably greater than that of the eight-year cycle it replaced.

---

[1] 1 Macc. 4:52; 16:14; 2 Macc. 15:36; Additions to Esther (LXX) 2:6 (13:6).
[2] 1 Macc. 1:54; 4:59; 7:43, 49; 14:27; 2 Macc. 1:9, 18; 10:5; Additions to Esther (LXX) 1:1 (11:2); Baruch 1:8; 1 Esdras 5:6.
[3] 1 Macc. 9:3; 10:21; 13:51; Jud. 2:1; *Syriac Baruch* 72, 18; *Liber Antiquitatum Biblicarum* XIX, 7; XXIII, 2-8. This latter book uses the ordinal system only, perhaps as an archaizing technique. On the 'Enoch circle' see below.
[4] See Schürer—Vermes—Millar I, pp. 587, 595-9.
[5] As the length of the lunar year is 12 times 29 days—12 hours—44 minutes—3 seconds = 354 days—8 hours—48 minutes—36 seconds, while the present length of the solar year is 365 days—5 hours—48 minutes—46 seconds (this loses about five seconds every thousand years; i.e., about three thousand years ago the length of the solar year was approximately 365 days—5 hours—49 minutes), the gap between the two amounts to about 10 days—21 hours. This means that about once every three years, or even biennially if necessary, an extra ('leap') month was inserted in order to harmonize the lunar and solar years.

The Metonic cycle was also adopted in Babylonia at about this time, perhaps independently.

The calendar of the 'Enoch circle' and the Dead Sea sect

It seems that there can be no real doubt that the Judaean calendar of the Second Temple period was lunisolar; we need only refer to the impressive testimony of BenSira: 'Moreover, the moon prescribeth the seasons, a [rule of period and for an everlasting sign]. His the appointed season, and from him feast [...]. New moon as its name (betokens) rene[weth. How awe-inspiring is it in its changing].'[1]
A different, solar, calendar is described in the writings of a very small circle within Second Temple Judaism, the so-called Enoch circle.[2] According to the *Book of Jubilees* (apparently written during the reign of John Hyrcanus, last third of the second century B.C.E.), the year consists of 364 days, or fifty-two full weeks which are divided into four equal periods of thirteen weeks each. The author does not explain just how the fifty-two weeks are divided into twelve months. He does tell us explicitly, however, that most of the Jewish people did not follow this calendar, for they follow 'the feasts of the Gentiles after their error and after their ignorance. For there will be those who will assuredly make observations of the moon—now it disturbs the seasons and comes in from year to year ten (sic!)[3] days too soon;'[4] hence, he says, their calendar and the dates of their feasts are all erroneous.
This solar system based on a year of 364 days also appears in the *Ethiopian Book of Enoch*.[5] The author does give various bits of information regarding the relationship of the lunar and solar years, which may possibly indicate his familiarity with an eight-year or other cycles, but his information is very inexact.[6] Here we also learn that according to this particular calendar, the beginning of each

[1] Sir. 43:6-8, according to Y. Yadin, *The Ben Sira Scroll from Massada* (1965), pp. 29ff., 46.
[2] This appellation was given by Ch. Albeck (*Das Buch der Jubiläen und die Halacha*, 1930) to the group which produced the *Book of Jubilees*, the *Ethiopian and Slavonic Books of Enoch*, and the *Testaments of the Twelve Patriarchs*; we may now add the *Genesis Apocryphon* from Qumran.
[3] As the solar year, according to the author's reckoning, is only 364 days long (instead of 365¼).
[4] *Jub.* 6:23-38.
[5] Chapters 72-82. ('The Book of the Courses of the Luminaries of the Heaven').
[6] See especially chapter 74; cf. chapter 78 (on the moon and the length of the lunar month).

quarter came at the astronomical start of each season, i.e., the vernal equinox, the summer solstice, the autumnal equinox and the winter solstice. The *Slavonic Book of Enoch*, however, is more exact about the lengths of the solar and lunar years, $365\frac{1}{4}$ and 354 days, respectively,[1] and about the difference between the two, eleven days. The author of this book already knew the nineteen-year Metonic cycle,[2] and even the system of solar leap years, i.e., three years of 365 days followed by a fourth of 366.[3] In another passage,[4] however, the book still mentions a solar year of 364 days, similar to that of *Jubilees* and *Ethiopian Enoch*.

This 'Enoch circle' calendar, the strict observance of which is forcefully enjoined by the *Book of Jubilees*, was accepted as obligatory by the Qumran sect, which was greatly influenced by 'Enoch circle' literature and ideas.[5] In fact, thanks to discoveries in the Judaean desert of the past thirty years, the details of the calendar of *Jubilees* have become clear. It is now known that the year comprised four seasons—the season of reaping (spring), the summer, the season of sowing (autumn) and the season of vegetation (winter), each beginning on a Wednesday and lasting three months[6] making thirteen weeks (= ninety-one days). The first two months of each season had thirty days each, the third thirty-one. Thus according to this calendar, every date of the year, and even every date in each of the four seasons, would always fall on the same day of the week each year. Passover and Tabernacles fall on Wednesdays, so too the 'day of the sounding of the *shofar*,' also known as the 'day of remembrance,' i.e., the first day of the seventh month. The Day of Atonement always fell on a Friday, the eve of the sabbath (an occurrence which the later rabbis, for their part, tried hard to avoid because of the inconvenience which it caused; their efforts found expression in the later rule of the calendar, that the first day of the seventh month could not be a Wednesday or a Friday, so that the Day of Atonement would neither immediately precede or follow the sabbath). Pentecost, which the Torah puts on the fiftieth day, the morrow of the seventh sabbath following the

---

[1] 14:1; 16:1; both passages are found only in the longer version.
[2] 16:8, as above.
[3] 16:6, as above. This system was instituted in Egypt only in the Ptolemaic period, and later in Rome as part of Caesar's reform of the calendar, replacing the faulty older lunisolar calendar by a purely solar one.
[4] 48:1f., again, only in the longer version.
[5] The *Damascus Document* (16:3f.) refers explicitly to the *Book of Jubilees*.
[6] *Rule of the Community* 10:7.

'raising of the *omer*,' which itself was on 'the morrow of the sabbath', was always on a Sunday, i.e., 'the morrow of the sabbath,'[1] and just as Passover and Tabernacles always fell on the fifteenth of their respective months, so too this Pentecost Sunday was always on the fifteenth of the third month. This is due to the assumption in this calendar that Leviticus' 'morrow of the sabbath' date for the 'raising of the *omer*' refers to the morrow of the first sabbath following the end of the Feast of Unleavened Bread: Passover spanned the fifteenth to the twenty-first of the first month, Wednesday to Tuesday. The first succeeding sabbath would fall on the twenty-fifth of the month, and the *omer* would thus be sacrificed on the twenty-sixth. Following this, there remain five days of the first month, thirty of the second, and the first fourteen days of the third month which bring us to forty-nine days; 'the morrow,' the fifteenth day of the third month, was Pentecost.[2]

Two major problems have been raised concerning this calendar, and they have already been hinted at above. It is true that many scholars have assumed that it actually represents the original ancient biblical calendar prior to the 'revisions' and 'innovations' of the lunisolar calendar, and that it was current throughout Israel during all or at least most of the First Temple period and still in wide use during the Second Commonwealth as well. According to this view, it was thus precisely the 'Enoch circle' and the Qumran sect which were the preservers of the original, ancient, and 'legitimate' calendar, while the rabbis were reformers and schismatics. Many other scholars have already shown, however, that such suppositions are completely unfounded and highly improbable as well. From everything we know of the Qumran sect, we are justified in concluding that they tried in every possible way to cut themselves off from the rest of the people. In following the calendar of the deviant and schismatic 'Enoch circle', it thus acted no differently than it did in forbidding marriage with the daughter of one's brother or sister—matches which were not only allowed but considered particularly meritorious throughout the periods of the Second Temple, the Mishnah, and the Talmud. As for the 'Enoch circle' itself, the halakah of its writings reflects not only some early practices, but also strange sectarian laws, clearly

---

[1] Lev. 23: 11-16.
[2] *Jubilees'* dating of Pentecost was unclear to scholars before the discoveries at Qumran, despite the fact that the book clearly fixes the feast in the middle of the third month.

innovations (e.g., the number of holiday and festive sacrifices, different from that laid down by the Bible, and the view that the Day of Atonement is a day of mourning, grief, and tears, a day of obligatory sorrow—in contrast to the otherwise universally accepted concept of this day as one of great joy). It is true that both the 'Enoch circle' and the Qumran sect energetically demanded the strict observance of their solar calendar, claiming that all the rest of Israel was in error. But this is no proof that they were in fact conservatives and the others innovators. Very frequently it is the innovator who attempts to pass himself off as a conservative follower of the 'legitimate' line. The Qumran sectarians were well aware that claims such as they made for their calendar involved difficulties, and they resorted to various pretexts in order to overcome them.[1] Furthermore, it is relevant to note that the books of the 'Enoch circle' avoid using the Babylonian names of the months, although these were widespread in Israel since the exile (see above); these books use ordinals only.[2] This fact seems to indicate that their authors saw clearly that the Babylonian nomenclature was meant to be used with a calendar very different from their own.

Another question, also hinted at above, is to what extent this calendar could ever have actually been in operation. The size of the 'Enoch circle' and the extent of its actual influence are not clear, but the Qumran sect apparently existed for at least close to five generations. We have already seen that because of the disparity of about one and a quarter days between the true (tropical) solar year and that of the strange calendar of *Jubilees*, which was followed by the Qumran sect, every seventy years or so each date of the year would retrogress about one season (one quarter). Thus, had this calendar been adopted by the sect, after about seventy years Passover would have come at the beginning of winter, the Day of Atonement and Tabernacles at the beginning of summer. This would not only have deepened the rift between the sect and the rest of Israel, but would also have made a mockery of their own calendar, according to which feast days were to

[1] See, for example, *Damascus Document* 5:2ff., which claims that the Torah had been unknown in Israel since the beginning of the period of the Judges.
[2] E.g., *Jubilees* 1:1; 3:32; 49:1; *Eth. Enoch* 72:6f; *Testament of Naphtali* 1:2; *Slav. Enoch* 1:2. The latter book is an exception to this rule, however, as it also gives names of months: see 48:2 (the names are corrupt but it is clear that a 364-day solar year is contemplated!); 68:1, 3 (apparently Sivan), and also in the additional section on Nir and Zofonima, where the Babylonian-Hebrew names appear along with the names of the corresponding Egyptian months.

be regulated according to the sun. In reality, the disruptive nature of this calendar would have been realized after only a few years of actual use; in particular, the gap between the beginning of the seasons and their respective solstices and equinoxes would have been noticed within four or five years at the most. There is no evidence at all that the sect ever intercalated a leap year (e.g. five additional days every fourth year) in order to correct its calendar. Thus we may also conclude that this was an original calendar, uninfluenced, for example, by the ancient Egyptian or Roman-Julian calendars, as these were all much more accurate.

The calendar of the first century C.E.

Except for some material from the writings of Philo and Josephus, most of our information regarding the Jewish calendar in the first century C.E. comes from rabbinic sources, particularly from the early strata of tannaitic literature; it is often very difficult, however, to distinguish these strata from later accretions.

It was during our period that the biblical 'day of remembrance' or 'day of the sounding of the shofar,' the first of Tishri, came to be defined as the New Year.[1] Philo, who terms it the 'opening of the sacred month'[2] and the 'trumpet feast'[3] describes it as the New Year,[4] although elsewhere he emphasizes that Nisan, the seventh month of the solar year, is the first month of the calendar year.[5] Josephus claims that 'Moses appointed Nisan, that is to say Xanthicus,[6] as the first month for the festivals, because it was in this month that he brought the Hebrews out of Egypt; he also reckoned this month as the commencement of the year for everything relating to worship, but for selling and buying and other affairs he preserved the ancient order.'[7] Josephus' reference to 'the ancient order' is not historical

---

[1] The designation 'day of remembrance' was preserved in the writings of the Qumran sect, as well as in the prayerbook of 'normative' Judaism, which also preserved the terms 'day of the sounding of the shofar' and 'day of the remembrance of shofar blowing.'

[2] De Dec. 159; De Spec. Leg. I, 180, 186; II, 188 (ἱερομηνία).

[3] Ibid. I, 186; II, 188 (σαλπίγγων).

[4] Ibid. I, 180; cf. II, 150 ff.

[5] Ibid. II, 150-4; cf. Quaest. in Exod. 12:2; I, 186; II, 188; De vita Mosis II, 229 ff.

[6] On such equivalences, see above p. 838, n. 4.

[7] Ant. I, 81. Just prior to this (80), Josephus says that 'the second month' in which Gen. 7:11 reports that the flood began was Marheshvan (not Iyar).

testimony that the months were originally counted from Tishri, but rather a reflection of the view, later expressed in rabbinic literature by R. Eliezer ben Hyrcanus (latter half of first century c.e.), that the creation was in Tishri and the months of the flood story are counted from Tishri.[1]

Like Josephus, the Mishnah lays it down that 'on the first of Tishri is the New Year for the reckoning of the years, of the years of release and jubilee years, for the planting of trees and for vegetables,'[2] while 'the first of Nisan is the New Year for kings and feasts.'[3] The first of Nisan thus remained, in the words of the Tosefta, 'the New Year for kings, feast days, months, and the contribution of shekels; some say even for the leasing of houses.'[4] Thus, according to this baraita, not only regnal years, feast-days[5] and contributions of shekels[6] are counted from Nisan, but even the months themselves. And such, in fact, is their order (from Nisan to Adar) in *Megillath Taanith* (which seems to have been composed in the latter part of 66 c.e.) and in early passages of the Mishnah.[7] Only later, in the second century, were the months counted according to the new reckoning, from Tishri.[8] Further, since First and Second Maccabees (sometimes), and *Liber Antiquitatum Biblicarum* (always) utilize the ordinal system (with or without the corresponding names of the months), running from Nisan to Adar,[9] we may combine their evidence with that of *Megillath Taanith*, the early portions of the Mishnah, and both Philo and Josephus, to conclude that the turning point in the reckoning of the New Year came at about the destruction of the Temple.[10] It is

Similarly, and in contrast to both Philo and the Torah, Josephus begins the list of the festivals with Tishri (Pentecost ending the list), and this despite the fact that he terms Nisan 'the New Year' and gives no name whatsoever to the first of Tishri (*Ant.* III, 239-53, especially 239 and 248).

[1] *Seder Olam Rabba* 4; *T. B. Rosh ha-Shanah* 11b-12a. So too according to *Targum Ps. Jonathan* on Gen. 7:11 (and cf. *ibid.* 8:4f., 13f.); also cf. *Targum Jonathan* on 1 Kings 8:2; *T. Rosh ha-Shanah* 1:3 (ed. Lieberman, p. 305); *Mekhilta, Pisha* I (p. 7); *Mekhilta de R. Simeon ben Yohai* 12:2 (pp. 8f.).

[2] *M. Rosh ha-Shanah* 1:1; *Mekhilta Pisha* I (p. 7); cf. the more extended version in *T. Rosh ha-Shanah* 1:7 (p. 306).

[3] *M. Rosh ha-Shanah* 1:1.

[4] *T. Rosh ha-Shanah* 1:1 (ed. Liebermann, p. 305 and pp. 2-5).

[5] This is an early law; see J. N. Epstein, *Prolegomena ad Litteras Tannaiticas* (1957; in Hebrew), p. 367.

[6] Cf. *M. Shekalim* 1:1, 3; this too, is undoubtedly an ancient law.

[7] *M. Rosh ha-Shanah* 1:3; *M. Taanith* 4:5; cf. *T. Sotah* 6:11; *T. B. Pesahim* 94b.

[8] See, for example, the baraita in *T. B. Baba Metzia* 106b.

[9] See the sources listed above, p. 838, n. 1 and 3.

[10] Coins of the first revolt apparently count the years from Nisan.

probable that the transition was neither total nor clean-cut at first,[1] a supposition bolstered, *inter alia*, by the varying customs regarding leases.[2] In any case, however, the first of Tishri came to be universally accepted as 'the New Year for the reckoning of the years, the years of release and jubilee years, for the planting of trees and for vegetables, for tithes and for vows.'[3]

It is generally accepted that the calendar of this period was lunisolar *par excellence*; being thus based upon the lunar month, whose length, as already noted, is about $29\frac{1}{2}$ days, it was always necessary to decide whether a given month was to have twenty-nine or thirty days. The decision was made by a court of three,[4] on the basis of the testimony of witnesses who reported sighting the new moon, as to whether each past month had had twenty-nine or thirty days. That is, if witnesses came on the thirtieth of a month and testified that they had seen the new moon the previous evening, that day was declared to be the start of the new month (*rosh hodesh*), the previous month having been 'deficient'; if, on the other hand, no witnesses came forward on the thirtieth, the morrow was declared *rosh hodesh*, the outgoing month having been 'full'. 'There was a large courtyard in Jerusalem called Beth Yaazek, where all the witnesses assembled, and there the court examined them. And they prepared large meals for them so that they might make it their habit to come. Before time they might not stir thence the whole day [i.e., on a sabbath]; but Rabban Gamaliel the Elder ordained that they might walk within two thousand cubits in any direction.'[5] This enactment of Rabban Gamaliel the Elder referred to those who came from without the sabbath limits to testify on that holy day, a violation allowed while the Temple stood, 'so as to determine aright the time of the [additional new moon] offering.'[6]

---

[1] Cf. G. Alon, 'Studies in Philonic Halakah,' in *Studies in Jewish History in the Times of the Second Temple, the Mishna and the Talmud* 1 (1957; in Hebrew), pp. 109-12, particularly n. 91. We must note, however, that there is no necessity to link the questions of the identity of 'the day of the sounding of the shofar' with 'the day of judgement,' on the one hand, and with the New Year, on the other.

[2] Also cf. *Mekhilta, Pisha* 1 (p. 7).

[3] *T. Rosh ha-Shanah* 1:7 (ed. Liebermann, p. 306 and pp. 8-10).

[4] *M. Sanhedrin* 1:2.

[5] *M. Rosh ha-Shanah* 2:5. Rabban Gamaliel the Elder was active c. 30-50 C.E.

[6] *M. Rosh ha-Shanah* 1:4, 9 ('If a man saw the new moon but could not walk, he may be taken on an ass (on the sabbath) or even on a bed, and if any lie in wait for them they may take staves in their hands. If it was a far journey they may take food in their hands, since for a journey enduring a night and a day they may profane the sabbath and go forth to bear witness about the new moon...').

Similarly, 'if the witness was not known to the judges, another was sent with him [by the local court] to testify of him,'[1] even on the sabbath. The latter provision is explained in the following report: 'Beforetime, they used to admit evidence about the new moon from any man. Once, however, the Boethusians hired two witnesses to mislead the sages, for the Boethusians do not agree that Pentecost fall other than on a Sunday. The first witness came, testified, and departed, but the second came and said: 'I was going up the ascent of Adumim, and I saw it [i.e., the moon] couched between two rocks, its head like a young goat, its horns like those of a deer, and its tail between its legs. Upon seeing it, I fell backwards, afrightened, and lo!—there were two hundred zuzzim tied in my cloak.' The sages told him: 'The two hundred zuzzim are yours as a gift, and he who gave it to you will be pilloried for it. But why did you act this way?' He replied, 'I heard that the Boethusians were attempting to mislead the sages, and told myself that it would be better if I notified them.''[2] From that time on, 'they ruled that evidence will be admitted only from those whom they knew.'[3] The above baraita seems to substantiate the Mishnah's explanation that this new caution followed 'the evildoing of the heretics';[4] the 'heretics' here were none other than the Boethusians who obviously wished to move up the beginning of Nisan (not Sivan!) so that the 'raising of the *omer*,' the sixteenth of Nisan, would fall on a Sunday instead of Monday.[5]

R. Jose ben Halafta, who preserved some early historical traditions although he lived in the mid-second century, reported that 'Once Tobiah the Physician saw the new moon in Jerusalem, together with his son and his freed slave; and the priests accepted him and his son but pronounced his freed slave ineligible [to testify]. And when they came before the court they accepted him and his slave but declared his son ineligible'.[6] The priests allowed the testimony of close relations regarding the new moon,[7] but they excluded the testimony of

---

[1] M. *Rosh ha-Shanah* 2:1; T. *Rosh ha-Shanah* 1:16. Cf. M. *Rosh ha-Shanah* 1:5: 'Whether the new moon was manifestly visible or not, they may profane the sabbath because of it.'
[2] T. *Rosh ha-Shanah* 1:15; cf. P. T. *Rosh ha-Shanah* ii, 57d; T. B. *Rosh ha-Shanah* 22b.
[3] M. *Rosh ha-Shanah* 2:1.
[4] *Ibid.*
[5] On the sectarian dispute regarding the date of Pentecost, see below on Pentecost.
[6] M. *Rosh ha-Shanah* 1:7.
[7] This is also the opinion of R. Simeon ben Yohai (*ibid.*).

former slaves, as the priests were very scrupulous in matters of birth and social status. The rabbinical court, however, in contrast with the priests but in accordance with the Halakah, refused the joint testimony of father and son but admitted that of the former slave.

Many witnesses came to Jerusalem, and to Jabneh following the destruction of the temple. One tradition reports that 'once more than forty pairs of witnesses came forward' (on the sabbath), but they were restrained in Lydda by Rabbi Akiba, or, according to another report, by Shizpar, the mayor of Gezer; in any case, Rabban Gamaliel of Jabneh opposed the move, arguing that such restraint is forbidden, lest in the future it discourage potential witnesses.[1] Witnesses had to undergo the usual thorough examination,[2] following which, if their testimony was accepted, 'the chief of the court says 'It is hallowed' and all the people answer after him, 'It is hallowed, it is hallowed.' '[3] The Mishnah reports a disagreement, however, as to whether the new moon is to be hallowed 'whether or not it appeared at its proper time;' according to R. Eleazar ben Zadok, 'if it did not appear at its proper time, they need not acclaim it as hallowed, since Heaven has hallowed it already.'[4]

The hallowing of the new moon had to be completed during the daytime; it was forbidden at night and any nighttime announcements were invalid. Even if the examination of witnesses had been concluded before nightfall and only the formal proclamation, 'It is hallowed,' was lacking, the day just past was *not* considered the start of the new month.[5] It is thus clear that the thirtieth day of each month was of doubtful status, as before nightfall the court might perhaps proclaim that it was really the first of the next month (see Appendix II). A festive meal accompanied the proclamation of a new month.[6] In practice, these decisions were generally handled by the court of the *nasi*. According to R. Joshua ben Korha, 'Rabban Johanan ben

[1] M. Rosh ha-Shanah 1:6; P.T. Rosh ha-Shanah 1, 57b; T.B. Rosh ha-Shanah 22a.
[2] M. Rosh ha-Shanah 2:6; cf. 2:8: 'Rabban Gamaliel had pictures of the shapes of the moon on a tablet and on the wall of his upper chamber. These he used to show to the unskilled and say, 'Didst thou see it on this wise or on that?''
[3] M. Rosh ha-Shanah 2:7.
[4] Ibid.; T. Rosh ha-Shanah 1:17; 2:9 (p. 311 and 315).
[5] Ibid. 2:1; T. Sanhedrin 2:14; T.B. Sanhedrin 11b; Mekhilta de R. Simeon ben Yohai 13:10 (p. 42); M. Rosh ha-Shanah 3:1.
[6] T. Megillah 3:15, according to the reading of the London and Erfurt manuscripts; M. Sanhedrin 8:2. Later sources stipulate that these festive meals were to be held in the company of a quorum of ten (minyan), and detailed descriptions of such gatherings have been preserved from the end of the Byzantine period.

Zakkai ordained that wheresoever the chief of the court might be, witnesses should go only to the place of assembly.'[1] When the chief was present, he governed the proceedings,[2] but even he was not allowed to make rulings on his own.[3] There are some traditions dealing with cases in which some rabbis expressed doubts as to the reliability of witnesses according to whose testimony the court had ruled the passing month deficient.[4] These stories serve to emphasize the authority and sovereignty which was ascribed to the court—its decisions were taken to constitute facts. In the same spirit, the Tosefta rules that 'if they hallowed the new moon, and then the witnesses were found to have been in conspiracy, it is still hallowed; if they were forced to hallow it, or erred, whether deliberately or unwittingly, it is still hallowed.'[5]

There is another potential problem, however, of which we learn from the following *baraita*: 'Once the heavens were covered with clouds, and the likeness of the moon was seen on the twenty-ninth of the month. The public wished to declare new moon, and the court wanted to hallow it, but Rabban Gamaliel said to them: I have it on the authority of my father's father that the renewal of the month takes place after not less than twenty-nine and one half days...[6] On that day the mother of Ben Zaza died, and Rabban Gamaliel made a great funeral oration over her, not because she had merited it, but so that the public should know that the court had not hallowed the month.'[7] This story,

---

[1] *M. Rosh ha-Shanah* 4:4.

[2] Cf. *ibid.* 1:6; 2:5, 8-9; *T. B. Rosh ha-Shanah* 25a. See Alon, *History* I, pp. 66, 126.

[3] *M. Rosh ha-Shanah* 3:1.

[4] *Ibid.* 2:8ff.; cf. also *P. T. Rosh ha-Shanah* II, 58b; *T. B. Rosh ha-Shanah* 25a.

[5] *T. Rosh ha-Shanah* 2:1; *Sifra, Emor,* 10, 2f.

[6] The text here continues 'and two-thirds of an hour and seventy-three *halakim*' (the hour, according to this system, was divided into 1080 'parts', eighteen per minute). This is apparently an interpolation by Babylonian Amoraim or Saboraim, as such precision was unknown in the first century. This exact reckoning of the lunar month was first achieved by Claudius Ptolemaeus, in the first half of the second century c.e., too late for Rabban Gamaliel (see Slonimski, p. 34). The previous calculation of the length of the lunar month by Hyparchus (second century b.c.e.), however, was much more inexact: 29 days—12 hours—two-thirds of an hour and sixty-nine *halakim*.

[7] *T. B. Rosh ha-Shanah* 25a. Cf. *T. Rosh ha-Shanah* 2(3):1f.: 'If they hallowed it too early... after less than thirty days, or more than thirty [one] days, is it hallowed? No. For as the Bible repeats the word 'month' (Num. 28:14), we infer from this emphasis that it may not be less than thirty days long.' On the emendations of this text, see Lieberman's commentary ad loc. *Tosefta Kifshutah* p. 1037. Cf. *Sifra, Emor,* 10, 4, 6; *Mekhilta, Pisha* 2 (p. 8).

and a few similar hints,[1] have led some scholars to believe that as early as the first century, if not earlier, calculations were the real basis of the regulation of months, with the testimony of witnesses remaining a mere legal formality.[2] Such a belief is nowhere near the truth: not only were the Tannaim ignorant of some of the details of calendar calculations,[3] but even some of the earliest calendar rules propounded by the Amoraim were clearly not in force in the mishnaic period.[4] Thus, as far as tannaitic literature is concerned, every date could fall on any day of the week, the Day of Atonement could fall on a Friday or Sunday[5] and the New Year could still fall on Sunday (making Hoshanah Rabbah, the seventh day of Sukkoth, i.e., the twenty-first of Tishri, fall on the sabbath);[6] the *omer* was sacrificed on the sabbath and so Pentecost too came on that day.[7] All these were excluded by the later calendar rules.

However, there is no doubt that there were some calculations, however imprecise, regarding the length of the lunar year, as is indicated by tannaitic sources: 'There must not be less than four full months in the year, and it never appeared necessary to the sages to intercalate more than eight;' and 'never did [it appear necessary to make] six full months follow one another.'[8] But from these same sources we may see that at times five full months did follow one another, and that there were sometimes years of only four full or only four deficient months. This implies in turn that each month was at times full and at times deficient,[9] and so Pentecost could fall on the fifth, sixth, or seventh of

---

[1] See, for example, *T. B. Rosh ha-Shanah* 25a: 'It has been taught: Rabban Gamaliel said to the sages: It has been handed down to me from the house of my father's father, that sometimes the moon comes by a long course and sometimes by a shorter route.' Cf. *P. T. Rosh ha-Shanah* II, 58b.

[2] See e.g. Alon, *History* I, p. 66f.

[3] This was noticed by Slonimski, pp. 33ff.

[4] So, e.g., the claim that 'From the days of Ezra onwards we have had no instance of Elul being full' (*T. B. Rosh ha-Shanah* 19b, 32a; *T. B. Betzah* 6a, 22b) is contradicted not only by the speculative amoraic discussion in which it appears, but also by instances to the contrary (*T. B. Rosh ha-Shanah* 20a, 21a; cf. *P. T. Rosh ha-Shanah* I, 57b. Cf. *M. Erubin* 3:7; *M. Sheviith* 10:2).

[5] *M. Menahot* 11:7, 9; *M. Shabbath* 15:3; cf. *M. Keritoth* 4:2; *T. Keritoth* 2:15; *T. B. Shabbath* 114b.

[6] *M. Sukkah* 4:3, 6; *T. Sukkah* 3:1.

[7] *M. Menahot* 10:1, 3; *T. Menahot* 10:19-20, 23.

[8] *M. Arakhin* 2:2; *T. Arakhin* 1:7.

[9] Including Elul and Adar (or both Adars, in a leap year); see *T. B. Rosh ha-Shanah* 19b, and cf. *P. T. Rosh ha-Shanah* III, 58c.

Sivan.[1] Furthermore, the rule of a slightly later period, that 'the New Year must fall either on the same day of the week as the 'raising of the *omer*' or on its morrow,'[2] is admittedly based upon a more or less regular alternation of full and deficient months, but only more or less, as is indicated by the uncertainty: 'the raising of the *omer* or on its morrow' (i.e., the sixteenth or seventeenth of Nisan).[3] For the former to occur, that is, for the New Year and the sixteenth of Nisan to fall on the same day of the week, only two of the six intervening months could be full. As similar conclusions may be reached via other routes as well, we must reject the conjecture that there were fixed calculations regulating months and years.[4]

Following the court's proclamation of a new month, the nation had to be notified. This was first done by a relay system of flares: 'After what fashion did they kindle the flares? They used to take long cedar-wood sticks and rushes and oleaster-wood and flax-tow, and a man bound these up with a rope and went up to the top of the hill and set a light to them; he waved them to and fro and up and down until he could see his fellow doing the like atop the next hill. And so, too, on the top of the third hill. And from what place did they kindle the flares? From the Mount of Anointment they signalled to Sarteba, and from Sarteba to Agrippina, and from Agrippina to Hauran, and from Hauran to Beth Biltin. They did not go beyond Beth Biltin, but there the flare was waved to and fro and up and down until a man could see the whole exile (i.e., Babylon) before him like a sea of fire.'[5] Other sources give differing lists: 'At first, they used to wave the flares from the tops of high mountains: the Mount of Anointment, Sarteba, Agrippina, Tabor, Hauran, Beth Biltin; R. Simeon ben Eleazar

---

[1] See *T. Arakhin* 1:9 and below pp. 859-60.
[2] *T. Arakhin* 1:11. Cf. *T. B. Arakhin* 9b.
[3] For the use of *jom ibburo* in the sense of 'morrow', see the commentary attributed to Rabbenu Gershom, on *T. B. Arakhin* 9b; cf. the article by H. J. Bornstein, in *A. Harkavy Festschrift* (1908), Hebrew section, p. 93 n. 1.
[4] And there is consequently no real chance of success for the efforts of those well-meaning scholars who try to determine the Roman equivalents of the Jewish dates found in the documents from Wadi Murabaat, or in the Books of Maccabees, etc. The same may be said of efforts to link a given Jewish date to a day of the week, e.g., Jesus' last supper, trial and execution. The rule, dating from the mid-second century C.E., that 'from year to year, Pentecost and the New Year will fall on days of the week differing by only four from those of their respective counterparts the previous year, five if it was a leap year' (*T. Arakhin* 1:11), does not imply a fixed calendar, but only refers to the number of days left over after all the full weeks of any lunar year, ordinary or intercalated.
[5] *M. Rosh ha-Shanah* 2:2ff.

says even in the mountains of Machaerus, Gedor, and its environs.'[1] Only some of these places can be positively identified, e.g., the 'Mount of Anointment' (= the Mount of Olives); the locations of most are unclear, and in some cases we do not even know on which side of the Jordan we should look.

'Flares were waved at the start of every month',[2] during the night following the proclamation,[3] but only if the passing month had been deficient. Thanks to the latter provision, even if the new moon was declared on a Friday and the waving of flares necessarily postponed until Saturday night, there was no cause for confusion, as all knew that had the sabbath been the start of the new month, making the previous month full, there would have been no flares at all.[4]

At a later time, however, 'after the evildoings of the Samaritans, they enacted that messengers should go forth'.[5] The beginning of the month according to the Samaritans' reckoning did not always coincide with that of the Jews, at times preceding (or following)[6] it by a day; in such cases, when the Samaritans innocently waved their flares, it misled the Jews into believing, for instance, that the previous month had been deficient when in reality it had been full. These 'evildoings' by the Samaritans occurred prior to the destruction of the Temple, and in that early period the new enactment did not replace the former procedure,[7] but supplemented it. 'Messengers were sent out to announce the start of six months: Nisan, to determine the time of Passover; Ab, to determine the time of the Fast; Elul, to determine the New Year; Tishri, to determine aright the set feasts; Kislev, to determine aright the time of Hannukah; and Adar, to determine the time of Purim. And while the Temple still stood they went forth also for Iyar, to determine the time of the Lesser Passover';[8] i.e., messengers were despatched only for the beginning of those months which included

---

[1] *T. Rosh ha-Shanah* 1:17 (p. 309ff.). Cf. *P. T. Rosh ha-Shanah* II, 58a; *T. B. Rosh ha-Shanah* 23b. Cf. also *T. Shebiith* 7:11 (p. 197).
[2] *T. Rosh ha-Shanah* 1:17.
[3] *Ibid.* = *T. Megillah* 3:15 (p. 357).
[4] See the sources referred to in the previous note, also *P. T. Rosh ha-Shanah* II, 58a; *T. B. Rosh ha-Shanah* 22b. Cf. Lieberman, *Tosefta Kifshuta* V, pp. 1031ff.
[5] *M. Rosh ha-Shanah* 2:2.
[6] *T. Pesahim* 2:2 (p. 145).
[7] See Alon, *History* I, p. 149f., and Lieberman's commentary on *T. Rosh ha-Shanah* 1:17 in *Tosefta Kifshutah*, pp. 1029f. There were apparently two types of flares, one for use across short distances, within Palestine, and another long-distance system for the Diaspora.
[8] *M. Rosh ha-Shanah* 1:3; cf. J. N. Epstein, *Mavo le-Nusah ha-Mishnah*, pp. 1012ff.

festivals or led up to them. With the destruction of the Temple, there was no longer any justification for the dispensation which allowed witnesses of the new moon to violate the sabbath, if necessary, in order to give their testimony (see above, p. 845): 'Rabban Johanan ben Zakkai said to them, 'Are there now any offerings?' They therefore enacted that the sabbath may be profaned on account of Nisan and Tishri alone',[1] 'for on them messengers used to go forth to Syria, and by them the set feasts were determined.'[2] According to R. Eliezer ben Zadok, 'Messengers may not go forth to Syria until the court so instructs them on the morrow',[3] and all agreed that in any case the messengers were not allowed to violate the sabbath, just as flares were not waved on the sabbath.[4]

Although these messengers reached distant lands,[5] it still frequently happened that some people did not know the exact beginning of the month (i.e., they did not know if the previous month had been declared full or deficient). This could be the case not only during the first part of the month,[6] but even later on as well: 'In a place where the true date of the new moon is unknown, one should proceed according to an assumed alternation of full and deficient months; in the Diaspora, similarly, the practice is to assume an alternation of full and deficient months. But if while they are in the course of such a progression, e.g. Tammuz deficient, Ab full, it becomes known that Ab had been declared deficient, they should abandon the previous progression and begin the alternation anew, starting with Ab being deficient.'[7] Furthermore, as in the Diaspora the messengers often did not arrive in time for Passover or Tabernacles (much less for the Day of Atonement),[8] an enactment required the observance there of second (additional) festive days, in ordei to provide for doubts.[9]

Intercalation of the year, like the fixing of the beginning of months,[10]

---

[1] *T. B. Rosh ha-Shanah* 21b.
[2] *M. Rosh ha-Shanah* 1:4.
[3] *T. Rosh ha-Shanah* 1:17 (p. 311). See also Lieberman's *Tosefta Kifshutah*, pp. 1028ff., 1035, unlike Epstein, op.cit. (above p. 844, n. 5), pp. 364f.
[4] *Sifra, Emor* 10, 7.
[5] See *P. T. Ketuboth* 11, 26d: 'to Nimrin' (in Syria; cf. *P. T. Rosh ha-Shanah* 1, 57b); *T. Peah* 4:6 (p. 56f.); *T. Ketuboth* 3:1 (p. 62); *T. B. Ketuboth* 25a.
[6] *M. Sanhedrin* 5:3; cf. *T. Sanhedrin* 9:1.
[7] *T. Arakhin* 1:8.
[8] *T. B. Rosh ha-Shanah* 21a.
[9] Originally this was not so everywhere in the Diaspora, but only where the messengers did not, or could not, arrive before the festivals.
[10] There was one clear distinction between the two: the year was intercalated if necessary, when circumstances required it (see below); not so the month,

was done by courts of three;[1] actually, this was usually reserved for the court of the *nasi*,[2] first in Jerusalem[3] and later in Jabneh; often a court of seven would be summoned for the purpose.[4]

A year was intercalated, that is, a thirteenth month (second Adar, see below) was added, if circumstances required it. 'Years are intercalated according to three criteria: the ripening of crops,[5] and of fruits,[6] and according to the season.[7] Years are to be intercalated if two criteria call for it, but not on account of only one, but if a year was intercalated (even on account of only one) it is valid; if the ripening of crops was one of the two signs, they were joyful.'[8] That is, if two of the three criteria were met, e.g. barley not ripe in time for Passover, or first fruits in time for Pentecost, or Passover before the spring equinox—the year was intercalated. Furthermore, 'Years are intercalated according to [the situation of] three regions: Judaea, Transjordan, and Galilee. Years are to be intercalated if that is called for in two regions, but if a year was intercalated (even according to the needs of one region alone) it is valid; if Judaea was one of the two regions they were joyful, because of the ripe [barley] which it supplies.'[9] Thus, as the agricultural circumstances referred to by the first two criteria of intercalation could differ in the various parts of Palestine, the three regions of Palestine, Judaea, Transjordan, and Galilee,[10] were considered separately: if in two of them the situation called for it, the year was inter-

---

however, which was not intercalated, even when desirable for various possible reasons, if the new moon had been on the eve of the twenty-ninth day (*Sifra, Emor* 10, 5; *P. T. Rosh ha-Shanah* III, 58c).

[1] *M. Sanhedrin* 1:2.

[2] See *M. Eduyot* 7:7; *T. B. Sanhedrin* 11a. Cf. pp. 856f.

[3] *Mekhilta, Pisha* 2 (p. 9), cf. *T. Sanhedrin* 2:13; *P. T. Sanhedrin* 1, 18d-19a.

[4] *M. Sanhedrin* 1:2; *T. B. Sanhedrin* 11a; *P. T. Sanhedrin* 1, 18c.

[5] Particularly of barley, which was required for the 'raising of the *omer*' on the sixteenth of Nisan.

[6] Which would be needed for the first fruits ceremony on Pentecost.

[7] As Passover must fall in the 'spring month', not in winter, it could not precede the spring equinox (see below). Cf. *Mekhilta, Pisha* 2 (p. 8); *Mekhilta, Kaspa* 20 (p. 333); *Sifre Num.* 66 (p. 62); *Sifre Deut.* 127 (p. 185); the *Palestinian Targum* on Deut. 16:1.

[8] *T. Sanhedrin* 2:2; *P. T. Sanhedrin* 1, 18d; *T. B. Sanhedrin* 11b. The joy referred to was due to the fact that if the year was intercalated without this being one of the two signs, it would mean that even though the crops were ripe, they would still be prohibited during the additional month (until the sixteenth of Nisan, see below p. 858, n. 3).

[9] *T. Sanhedrin* 2:3; *P. T. Sanhedrin* 1, 18a; *T. B. Sanhedrin* 11b.

[10] Cf. *M. Sheviith* 9:2; *M. Ketuboth* 13:10; *M. Baba Bathra* 3:2; *T. Shebiith* 7:10.

calated, with special joy if Judaea was one of the two, as the *omer* was brought from Judaea.[1] And the barley, fruits, and equinox were not the only criteria which called for the addition of a thirteenth month: 'Years should not be intercalated without need. They may be intercalated, however, on account of needs, ovens, and on behalf of Jews of the Diaspora who have not yet left their homes, but not on account of cold or snow or Diaspora Jews who have already set out for Palestine (but not yet arrived). All these reasons, however, are considered auxiliary grounds for intercalation, and, in any case, if a year is intercalated, it is valid.'[2] Years were thus also intercalated if the roads and bridges used by pilgrims were in bad condition or if the winter rains would ruin the Passover ovens. Mere rain, cold, or snow, however, were not enough to warrant intercalation; and as for the difficulties encountered by pilgrims from the Diaspora, it depended on whether or not they had already begun their journey.[3] But even these latter non-valid criteria could be considered as 'auxiliary' reasons which along with one of the three main considerations (first grain, fruit, equinox) were enough to allow intercalation. Similarly, 'Years should not be intercalated on account of young goats or lambs or fledglings which have not come (of age), but they are all considered auxiliary grounds for intercalation and, in any case, if a year is inter-calated, it is valid.'[4] These reasons are reflected in surviving epistles announcing intercalations (see below). Again, 'Years are not to be intercalated due to impurity':[5] even if in late Adar the majority of the nation was ritually unclean due to contact with corpses, there being no available ashes of a red heifer (see Num. 19), still the year was not to be intercalated, as paschal sacrifices could be offered even by an unclean community. 'Years of famine may not be intercalated,'[6] so that the produce of the new season could be enjoyed as soon as possible. In such years it would be very difficult to wait another month for the sixteenth of Nisan. For the same reason, 'sabbatical years and their immediate successors may not be intercalated. What

---

[1] *M. Menahot* 10:2; *T. Menahot* 10:21; *M. Menahot* 8:1 and *T. Menahot* 9:2.
[2] *T. Sanhedrin* 2:12. Cf. *T. B. Sanhedrin* 11a. Also cf. *Sifra, Emor* 9, 5.
[3] The Tosefta (just quoted in text) and the Babylonian Talmud give contradictory versions of the baraita ruling regarding pilgrims from the Diaspora. Cf. *Sifra, Emor* 9, 1 according to MS. Rome, ed. Finkelstein (1956), p. 443 = *P. T. Sanhedrin* 118d and parallels.
[4] *T. Sanhedrin* 2:4; *P. T. Sanhedrin* 1, 18d; *T. B. Sanhedrin* 11a.
[5] *T. Sanhedrin* 2:10; *P. T. Sanhedrin* 1, 18d; *T. B. Sanhedrin* 12a; *Sifra, Emor* 9, 6.
[6] *T. B. Sanhedrin* 11b-12a; *T. Sanhedrin* 2:9.

year is usually intercalated? That preceding the sabbatical year.'[1] The prohibition of intercalating the seventh year stemmed from the desire to avoid prolonging the ban on agricultural labour and also from the fear of a shortage of food; the latter consideration held good for the eighth year as well.

The extra month, when decreed, could only be inserted after Adar,[2] because Adar was the last month of the year according to the ancient scheme.[3] In general, the court would convene during Adar itself, very close to the last possible date.[4] The decision was frequently made after Purim. 'If they had read the Scroll in First Adar, and the year was intercalated, they must read it again in Second Adar.'[5]

Which Adar was added, the first or the second? On the face of it the answer seems obvious: the second. The latter is indeed the answer of the ancient tradition, which we find represented by R. Zechariah the butcher's son, who disagreed with the ruling just cited, claiming instead that 'they do not have to read it in the second Adar, as all the laws pertaining to the second Adar pertain to the first as well'[6] (i.e., this tradition knew no difference between the two Adars). Only later was it ruled that the reading of the Scroll of Esther and the donation of gifts to the poor (see Est. 9:22), and perhaps other observances related to Purim, as well as those practices listed in *M. Shekalim* 1:1, relating to the last month of the year or to preparations for Passover, should be performed in the second Adar, not the first.[7]

The decision to intercalate could of course be made prior to Adar. It was stipulated, however, that 'a court may not decide on intercalation prior to the New Year, and if it did, its ruling is not valid. In cases of urgent need, however, the decision may be made immediately after New Year, but even then the additional month may be inserted only after Adar.'[8] Actually, however, the court usually dealt with intercalation during the winter, for only then was it possible to

[1] *Ibid.*; *P. T. Sanhedrin* 1, 18d; *P. T. Shekalim* 1, 46a.

[2] *T. B. Rosh ha-Shanah* 7a; *Mekhilta, Pisha* 2 (p. 8).

[3] *Mekhilta, Pisha* 2; *T. Sanhedrin* 2:7, 11; *T. Pesahim* 8:5 (p. 184 and the par. noted there); cf. *M. Pesahim* 4:9.

[4] *T. Sanhedrin* 2:13; *T. Eduyot* 3:1; *M. Eduyot* 7:7.

[5] *M. Megillah* 1:4; *T. Megillah* 1:6 (p. 345).

[6] *T. Megillah* 1:6; *T. B. Megillah* 6b (according to all the MSS).

[7] See the references of the previous note, also *P. T. Megillah* 1, 71a; *P. T. Shekalim* 1, 45d; *T. B. Rosh ha-Shanah* 19b. Moreover, by the ancient custom regarding documents, the first month was simply Adar, while the second was designated 'the second' (*T. Megillah* 1:6; cf. *T. Nedarim* 4:7; *M. Nedarim* 8:5; *T. Baba Metzia* 8:31).

[8] *T. Sanhedrin* 2:7; *P. T. Sanhedrin* 1, 18d; *T. B. Rosh ha-Shanah* 7a.

properly consider the relevant criteria.[1] Again, 'A court may not, during one year, intercalate the next, and if it did, its ruling is invalid; nor may two successive years be intercalated.'[2] On the other hand, apart from the latter restrictions, an intercalation was valid as long as a court decided upon it, even if it did so 'conditionally', mistakenly, under constraint, or because it did not realize that 'the year did not require intercalation'.[3] If, however, 'the year did require intercalation, and the court convened and debated the matter, and decided indeed to intercalate, but was not able to proclaim 'It is intercalated' before it happened (i.e., the end of Adar)—the year is not intercalated.'[4] In another ruling similar to those regarding the intercalation of months, it is stated that the intercalating court must sit during the daytime, its decision otherwise having no effect[5] (cf. *supra*, p. 847). Finally, it is emphasized that a year could only be lengthened: there was no possibility of shortening a year, even if the spring came early: only a complete month could be inserted, no more and no less,[6] but, according to the ancient practice, this additional month, like all other months, could be either 'full' or 'deficient'.[7]

Our sources have preserved some epistles announcing intercalations, such as those sent by the court of Rabban Gamaliel the Elder, which clearly illustrate the measures the court took to publicize its decisions: 'It once happened that Rabban Gamaliel and the elders were sitting on steps on the Temple Mount, and that the scribe Johanan was sitting before them. He bade him write: 'To our brethren in Upper Galilee and to those in Lower Galilee: May your peace be great. We beg to inform you that the time of removal has arrived for setting aside

---

[1] Cf. *Mekhilta de R. Simeon ben Johai* 13:10 (p. 42). This is obvious regarding the status of crops and fruits, as well as regarding the roads and bridges, etc. It was also true, however, of the third main criterion, the equinox, as here the need to intercalate might depend on a difference of only one or two days (i.e., without intercalation, Passover might precede the spring equinox by one or two days; cf. *T. Sanhedrin* 2:7: 'One should not intercalate unless otherwise the equinox would come after the greater part of the month is out. How much is 'the greater part of the month'? Sixteen days'). In a period when the beginning of months was fixed by eyewitnesses alone, it is obvious that such close predictions could not be made before Adar.

[2] *T. Sanhedrin* 2:8; *T. B. Sanhedrin* 12a; *Sifra, Emor* 9, 4.

[3] See *M. Eduyot* 7:7; *Sifra, Emor* 9, 3.

[4] *Sifra, Emor* 9, 2.

[5] *Sifra, Emor* 9, 4; *T. Sanhedrin* 2:13; *T. B. Sanhedrin* 11b.

[6] *T. Sanhedrin* 2:8; *Mekhilta, Pisha* 2 (p. 8f.); *Sifre Deut.* 123 (p. 185). Cf. *Mekhilta de R. Simeon ben Johai* 12:2; *Midrash Tannaim* 16:1 (p. 89f.).

[7] *T. B. Rosh ha-Shanah* 19b.

the tithes from the olive heaps' (see Deut. 27:13). And: 'To our brethren throughout the South: May your peace be great. We beg to inform you that the time of removal has arrived for setting aside the tithes from the corn sheaves.' And: 'To our brethren the exiles in Babylonia and to those in Media, and to all the other exiles of Israel: May your peace be great. We beg to inform you that the doves are still tender and the lambs too young and the crops not yet ripe. To me and my colleagues it seems right to add thirty days to this year'.'[1] This story indicates that the court sat in Jerusalem under the direction of the *nasi*, as previously mentioned; it also illustrates how two subsidiary, 'auxiliary' reasons—the excessive youth of the doves and the small livestock—were drafted (and added to the lateness of the crops) in order to swing the decision in favour of intercalation.

During the early second century C.E., while Rabban Gamaliel was still living, Rabbi Akiba is said to have intercalated in the Diaspora; in his own words, 'When I went down to Nehardea (in Babylonia) to intercalate the year...'[2] It is improbable, however, that these words should be taken too literally, for that would mean that Rabbi Akiba acted contrary to some explicit regulations regarding intercalation, e.g., that it must be proclaimed in Judaea, in the court of the *nasi*, etc. It thus seems that Rabbi Akiba really meant that he went to Nehardea in order to investigate the need for intercalating a year, i.e., in order to see how the seasonal conditions in Babylonia should be considered in the Palestinian debates regarding intercalation (e.g., whether or not the barley had ripened there yet, the prohibition on the consumption of new produce prior to the sixteenth of Nisan applying even outside the Land of Israel, as is well known).[3]

The rabbis were well aware that the solar year averages 365 days, the lunar, 354, leaving an annual gap of about eleven days.[4] Despite that knowledge, however, and despite the fact that their contemporaries in some other lands were following regular intercalatory cycles (see *supra*, pp. 838f.), the Jews of our period followed no such cycle.

[1] T. *Sanhedrin* 2:6; *P. T. Sanhedrin* I, 18d; *P. T. Maaser Sheni* V, 56c; *T. B. Sanhedrin* 11b. Similar epistles, which were sent in the name of Rabban Simeon ben Gamaliel (1), whose career was roughly between the years 50-70 C.E., and Rabbi Johanan ben Zakkai, from the Dung Gate in the Upper Market of Jerusalem to Galilee and the South regarding the removal of tithes, have been preserved in *Midrash Tannaim* 26:13 (p. 175f.).
[2] M. *Yebamot* 16:7. Cf. *T. B. Berakoth* 63a; *P. T. Sanhedrin* I, 19a.
[3] See Alon, *History* I, pp. 151-6, *pace* Graetz, *Geschichte* IV (4th ed. 1908), pp. 442f., and Halevy, *Dorot* II, p. 191ff.
[4] *Seder Olam Rabba* 4; *T. Nezirot* 1:5 (p. 124).

Appendix I: The date of Pentecost

The Torah designates the date of this festival as the fiftieth day, that is, the morrow of the seventh sabbath, following 'the day that you brought the *omer* (sheaf) of the wave-offering';[1] the *omer* itself was also to be brought 'on the morrow of the sabbath'.[2] These stipulations appear following the discussion of Passover, the Feast of Unleavened Bread, but there is no explicit specification as to what 'sabbath' is referred to in these laws. From the Book of Joshua,[3] however, we may conclude that 'the morrow of the sabbath' was actually the morrow of the first day of Passover,[4] and this is supported by the Septuagint[5] and by the descriptions of Philo[6] and Josephus.[7]

The *Book of Jubilees* (and the *Ethiopian Enoch*), however, whose calendar was followed by the Qumran sect as well, took the 'morrow of the sabbath' to refer to the morrow of the first sabbath (Saturday) following the end of Passover. As the latter festival always began on Wednesday, the fifteenth of the first month, and ended the following Tuesday, according to this calendar, the 'morrow of the sabbath' would always fall on the twenty-sixth, and Pentecost would thus also come, on a Sunday fifty days later, on the fifteenth of the third month.[8] The Boethusians followed yet another reckoning. Like the *Book of Jubilees*, they held that the specified 'morrow of the sabbath' meant a Sunday (and not the morrow of the first day of Passover), but they held that the reference was to the morrow of the sabbath within the feast itself.[9] This sabbath could fall in the intermediate days (*hol*

[1] Lev. 23:15f. Cf. also Deut. 16:9ff.; Ex. 23:16; 34:22; Num. 28:26.
[2] Lev. 23:11.
[3] Jos. 5:11: 'And on the morrow after the Passover, on that very day, they ate of the produce of the land, unleavened cakes and parched grain,' corresponding to the law of Lev. 23:14: 'And you shall eat neither bread nor grain parched or fresh until this same day,' i.e., the day of the 'raising of the *omer*.'
[4] One could claim, as did the Karaites, that the verse in Joshua actually refers to the morrow of the Paschal sacrifice (fourteenth of Nisan), which would thus place the 'raising of the *omer*' on the fifteenth of Nisan instead of the sixteenth, but as the language used in Joshua is clearly reminiscent of Leviticus, it is clear that no different date was intended. See Ch. Albeck's supplementary note on *M. Menahot* 10:3 in his commentary of the Mishnah (1957; in Hebrew), pp. 369ff.
[5] Lev. 23:15f.
[6] *De Spec. Leg.* 2, 175.
[7] *Ant.* III, 250-2.
[8] *Jubilees* 15:1; 16:13; 44:1-4.
[9] *T. Rosh ha-Shanah* 1:15 (p. 309); *M. Menahot* 10:3; *T. Menahot* 10:23; Scholion to *Megillat Taanith* 1 (pp. 324f.); *T. B. Menahot* 65a-66a.

ha-moed) of Passover, the last day of the festival, or on its first day; in the latter case, the Boethusians' date for Pentecost would be identical with that of the rest of Israel. For this reason, the sages ruled that if Pentecost fell on a sabbath, and 'the day of slaughtering'[1] is after the sabbath, the high priest may not put on his high priestly vestments, and mourning and fasting are permitted, so as to lend no support to the words of them that say: 'Pentecost must fall on Sunday.'[2] Therefore, there is no substance to the theory of Y. M. Grintz,[3] who identified the Boethusians with the Qumran sect, and both with the Essenes. For, according to the Dead Sea sect, Pentecost must fall on the fifteenth of the third month, while the Tosefta reports that the Boethusians attempted, through the use of suborned testimony, to make the 'raising of the *omer*' fall on Sunday instead of Monday, so that the Pentecost of all Israel would fall on the same day as it would according to their own reckoning. That would be possible, however, only if the Boethusians basically followed the calendar of the majority, unlike the Qumran sectarians who had a completely different calendar; the Boethusians' only dispute here was as to the interpretation of Leviticus' 'morrow of the sabbath'.[4]

In contrast to the *Book of Jubilees*, which gave a fixed date for Pentecost, the date of the 'normative' Pentecost, was subject to slight variations from year to year. This is because it was fixed only as fifty days after the first day of Passover, while the intervening months could be either both full, both deficient, or one each. The result, in the words of the tannaitic rule, was that 'Pentecost may fall on the fifth, sixth, or seventh (of Sivan)—not before and not after.'[5]

When did Pentecost come to be considered the anniversary of the giving of the Torah at Sinai? It is quite likely that the *Book of Jubilees* is hinting at such an identification when it claims that the celebration of Pentecost, which had fallen into disuse since the period of the Patriarchs, was renewed at Mount Sinai.[6] *Jubilees* also refers

---

[1] I.e., the day of the slaughtering of the 'pilgrim's sacrifice' (*reijjah*) and 'peace-offerings' (*Shalmei hagigah*), which were postponed until Sunday when a festival fell on the sabbath.
[2] *M. Hagigah* 2:4.
[3] Y. M. Grintz, 'The Yahad Sectarians, Essenes, Beth(e)sin', *Sinai* xxxii (1952-3), pp. 11-43 (in Hebrew).
[4] *T. Rosh ha-Shanah* 1:15. See above p. 846.
[5] *T. Arakhin* 1:9; *T. B. Rosh ha-Shanah* 6b.
[6] *Jubilees* 6:19.

to the 'two-fold' nature of this festival,[1] and the date which it sets for it, is the same as that it gives for the giving of the Torah.[2] It is still an open question whether such an identification is also behind Acts 2:1ff. Among the rabbis, however, there was disagreement regarding the date the Torah was given: some favoured the sixth of Sivan,[3] others the seventh.[4] It thus seems clear that these rabbis could not have considered Pentecost to be the anniversary of the giving of the Torah, for they agreed that Pentecost could fall on the fifth, sixth, or seventh of Sivan (see above) while their disagreement regarding Revelation concerned only the sixth and the seventh.[5] Yet the rabbinic identification of Pentecost as the anniversary of the giving of the Torah appears not later than the beginning of the third cent. C.E.[6]

Appendix II: The two days of rosh hodesh and rosh ha-shanah

The Mishnah relates that 'Beforetime they used to admit evidence about the new moon throughout the day. Once the witnesses tarried so long in coming that the Levites were disordered in their singing, so it was ordained that evidence could be admitted only until the afternoon offering. And if witnesses came from the time of the afternoon offering onwards, that day was kept holy and also the morrow was kept holy. After the Temple was destroyed, Rabban Johanan ben Zakkai ordained that they might admit evidence about the new moon throughout the day.'[7] The earliest commentators already encountered difficulties in this report: does it refer to the start of every month (rosh hodesh) or only to the start of Tishri, i.e., the New Year (rosh-ha-shanah)?[8] Be that as it may, it is probable that when the month just past was 'full', even the early practice was to celebrate two days

---

[1] *Jubilees* 6:21; 22:1.   [2] *Jubilees* 1:1.

[3] *Mekhilta, Vayissa* 1 (p. 159); *Seder Olam Rabba* 5; *T. B. Shabbath* 86b.

[4] *T. B. Shabbath* 86b; *T. B. Yoma* 4b; *T. B. Taanith* 28b.

[5] Had they held Pentecost to be the anniversary of the giving of the Torah on Mount Sinai, anyone who held that the latter occurred on the sixth could not have tolerated the festival's falling on the seventh, and vice versa, and no one would have tolerated the falling of Pentecost on the fifth. Cf. the statement by R. Judah in *T. Arakhin* 1:9. Regarding the whole question cf. also Alon, *Studies* I, pp. 111-2, n. 91. Cf. B. Noack, *ASTI* 1 (1962), pp. 73-95.

[6] *T. Megillah* 3:5; *T. B. Megillah* 31a; *P. T. Megillah* III, 74b. Cf. *T. B. Pesahim* 68b and the *amidah* prayer of Pentecost.

[7] *M. Rosh ha-Shanah* 4:4 (on the psalms sung daily by the Levites in the Temple, see *M. Tamid* 7:3f.).

[8] See the discussions of the two Talmuds on this mishnah: *P. T. Rosh ha-Shanah*

as *rosh hodesh*: the thirtieth of the outgoing month and the first of the new.[1] (This may have already been true in the period of the First Temple, although we have no clear proof).[2] The earliest attestation of this practice is in the baraita describing R. Dosa's customs regarding the prayers of *rosh hodesh* (see below); we may assume the practice *a fortiori* for *rosh ha-shanah* as well. The Mishnah explicitly refers to the 'two festival days of the New Year',[3] and reports that 'R. Dosa b. Harkinas says: 'He that goes before the ark (to recite prayers) on the first festival-day of the New Year says: Give us strength, O Lord our God, this first day of the month, whether it be today or tomorrow, and on the morrow he says, ...whether it be today or yesterday. But the sages did not agree with him.'[4]

We may therefore conclude that two days of *rosh ha-shanah* were observed as early as the late first century C.E., and probably two days of *rosh hodesh* as well. However, when it was clear that Elul was not full, the New Year was observed only one day.[5]

Appendix III: The day (and the night)

In our discussion of this weighty and involved subject, we deal only with aspects related to the calendar. Various peoples reckon the beginning of the day from different points; that the days of the ancient Israelites ran from evening to evening, we find most conclusively illustrated in the laws regarding the Day of Atonement: 'In the tenth of this seventh month is the Day of Atonement; it shall be for you a time of holy convocation... It shall be to you a sabbath of solemn rest, and you shall afflict yourselves; on the ninth day of the month

---

[1] See Lieberman's comprehensive commentary on *T. Megillah* 3:15, pp. 1184-6, and on *T. Taaniyoth* 3:4, pp. 1106f.

[2] This assumption would explain some difficult verses in 1 Sam.: 'But on the morrow of the second new moon...' (20:27); '...and he ate no food the second new moon day' (20:34).

[3] *M. Shabbath* 19:5; *M. Menahot* 11:9; *M. Arakhin* 2:5. Cf. *M. Erubin* 3:7; *T. Erubin* 4(5):2f.

[4] *M. Erubin* 3:9. Cf. *T. B. Erubin* 40a, regarding R. Dosa's similar custom on any *rosh hodesh*.

[5] See *T. B. Megillah* 31a. Cf. S. Gandz, *JQR* XL (1949-50), pp. 157-72; 251-77; M. Margaliot, *Ha-Hillukim. The Differences between Babylonian and Palestinian Jews*, pp. 161ff.

beginning at evening, from evening to evening'.[1] That is, this festival, whose date is the tenth of Tishri, began with the evening of the ninth and continued until the next evening, which ushered in the eleventh. The same conception may be inferred from Isaiah's prophecy: 'You shall have a song as in the night when a holy feast is kept',[2] i.e., festivals began at night; similar evidence from the post-exilic period may be found in Nehemiah's report: 'When it began to be dark at the gates of Jerusalem before the sabbath, I commanded that the doors should be shut.... Then the merchants and sellers ... passed the night outside of Jerusalem...'.[3]—The sabbath too began with the evening. For the rabbis too, this was self-evident; a day began with nightfall and ended prior to the start of the next night. However, the point of transition between two days was not clear and unambiguous: separating two successive days was a period called 'twilight' (בין השמשות)[4] or 'perhaps darkness, perhaps not.'[5] The rabbis were uncertain whether this period should be considered part of the day or part of the night, and they thus did not know to which of the two days it should be attributed[6] (and, consequently, for some halakic purposes they considered this period as if it were part of both).[7] Further, there were conflicting opinions as to the length of this 'twilight' period.[8]

The calendar of the *Book of Jubilees* and the Qumran sect is another matter; the Dead Sea Scrolls contain not a few indications that the sect considered sunrise the start of the day. The matter, however, is still not completely settled (see bibliography).

BIBLIOGRAPHY

Much has been written on the calendar of the biblical period. See A.-G. BARROIS, *Manuel d'archéologie biblique* II (1953), pp. 171ff.; R. DE VAUX, *Les institutions de l'Ancien Testament* I (2nd ed. 1961), pp. 271ff. (with bibliography, pp. 346ff.). Regarding the theory of a

---

[1] Lev. 23:27-32.   [2] Is. 30:29.
[3] Neh. 13:19f. Cf. Ps. 55:18(17). It seems, however, that there were other traditions and practices as well; see M. D. Cassuto, *From Adam to Noah* I (1961), pp. 28-30.
[4] *M. Shabbath* 19:5;   *M. Keritoth* 4:2;   *M. Zavim* 1:6;   *M. Niddah* 6:14; *T. Shabbath* 2:9; *T. Zavim* 1:13.
[5] *M. Shabbath* 2:7.
[6] See above n. 4.
[7] See, for example, *T. Keritoth* 2:15.
[8] See, for example, *T. B. Shabbath* 34b; *P. T. Ber.* 1, 2b-c; cf. L. Ginzberg, *Commentary on the Palestinian Talmud* I (1941; in Hebrew), pp. 3-37.

solar calendar, we confine ourselves to some of the many studies by J. MORGENSTERN (which are at times tendentious): 'The Three Calendars of Ancient Israel', *HUCA* I (1924), pp. 13-78; 'Additional Notes on 'The Three Calendars of Ancient Israel' ', *HUCA* III (1926), pp. 77-107; 'The Gates of Righteousness', *HUCA* VI (1929), pp. 1-38; 'Supplementary Studies in the Calendars of Ancient Israel', *HUCA* X (1935), pp. 1-148; 'The Chanukkah Festival and the Calendar of Ancient Israel', *HUCA* XX (1947), pp. 1-136; XXI (1948), pp. 365-496; 'The Calendar of the Book of Jubilees, its Origin and its Character', *Vetus Testamentum* V (1955), pp. 34-76. On New Year see R. DE VAUX, *op.cit.* II (2nd ed. 1967), p. 469.

Regarding the theory which identifies the supposedly solar calendar of the Bible with that of the *Book of Jubilees*, see the recent summaries by A. JAUBERT, *La date de la Cène* (1957), and J. VAN GOUDOEVER, *Biblical Calendars* (2nd ed. 1961). Other opinions have been expressed by J. B. SEGAL, 'Intercalation and the Hebrew Calendar', *Vetus Testamentum* VII (1957), pp. 250-307, and by J. M. BAUMGARTEN, 'The Calendar of the Book of Jubilees and the Bible', *Tarbiz* XXXII (1962-3), pp. 317-28 (in Hebrew). The calendar of *Jubilees* has itself been the subject of frequent studies, particularly since the discoveries in the Judaean Desert. Particularly noteworthy are the studies of S. TALMON, 'Yom ha-Kippurim in the Habakkuk Scroll', *Biblica* XXXII (1951), pp. 549-63; 'The Calendrical Reckoning of the Judaean Desert Sect', in *Studies in the Judaean Desert Scrolls* (1957), pp. 24-39 (in Hebrew); 'The Calendar Reckoning of the Sect from the Judaean Desert', *Scripta Hierosolymitana* IV (1958), pp. 162-99; as well as those of A. JAUBERT, 'Le calendrier des Jubilés et de la secte de Qumrân', *Vetus Testamentum* III (1953), pp. 250-64; 'Le calendrier des Jubilés et les jours liturgiques de la semaine', *Vetus Testamentum* VII (1957), pp. 35-61; 'Jésus et le calendrier de Qumrân', *NTS* VII (1960-1), pp. 1-22. See also E. R. LEACH, 'A Possible Method of Intercalation for the Calendar of the Book of Jubilees', *Vetus Testamentum* VII (1957), pp. 391-7; E. WIESENBERG, 'The Jubilee of Jubilees', *Revue de Qumran* III (1961), pp. 3ff.; J. M. BAUMGARTEN, *JJS* (1976), pp. 36-46.

For a short informative survey of the problems of the calendar in the Second Temple period, with bibliography, see SCHÜRER-VERMES-MILLAR I, pp. 17-19, 587-609. Many important questions are discussed in several studies by S. GANDZ, 'The Calendar of Ancient Israel', in *Homenaje a Millás-Vallicrosa* I (1954), pp. 623-46; 'Studies in the Hebrew Calendar', *JQR* XXXIX (1948-9), pp. 259-80; XL (1949-50), pp. 157-72; 'The Problem of the Molad', *PAAJR* XX (1951), pp. 235ff.; 'The Calendar of Seder Olam', *JQR* XLIII (1952-3), pp. 177-92; 249-70. See also E. WIESENBERG, 'Elements of Lunar Theory in the Mishnah, Rosh Hashanah 2:6, and the Talmudic Complements thereto', *HUCA* XXXIII (1962), pp. 153-96.

Pioneers in the study of the mathematical bases of the hebrew calendar were B. ZUCKERMANN, *Materialien zur Entwicklung der altjüdischen Zeitrechnung im Talmud* (1882); H. S. SLONIMSKI, *Jesode ha-Ibbur* (3rd ed. 1889; in Hebrew), and particularly H. J. BORNSTEIN, who was the author of several excellent and comprehensive articles in Hebrew, including: 'The Controversy Between Rav Saadia Gaon and Ben Meir' (1904); 'The Latter Days of Intercalation', *Ha-Tekufah* XIV-XV (1922), pp. 321-72; XVI (1922), pp. 228-92; 'Intercalation and Cycles', *Ibid.* XX (1923), pp. 285-330. The astronomical foundations of the calendar calculations were discussed by D. SIDERSKY, 'Etude sur l'origine astronomique de la chronologie juive', *Mémoires de l'Académie des Inscriptions et Belles Lettres* XII,2 (1914), pp. 595-683.

An original work of research as well as a summary of the subject was produced by Z. H. JAFFE, *Korot Heshbon ha-Ibbur* (1931; in Hebrew). More recent surveys are provided by A. H. FRAENKEL, in *Encyclopedia Hebraica* XXI, pp. 341ff. s.v. *Luah*, and E. J. WIESENBERG in *Encyclopedia Judaica* V (1971), pp. 43-50, s.v. Calendar.

Problems relating to the calendar of the first and second centuries C.E. are also treated to some extent by G. ALON, *History* I (1967; in Hebrew), pp. 66ff., 126, 149-56. On the question of a supposedly second Elul, see B. COHN, *ZDMG* LIX (1905), pp. 622-4; D. SIDERSKY, *REJ* LVIII (1909), pp. 293ff.; B. Z. WACHOLDER and D. B. WEISBERG, *HUCA* XLII (1971), pp. 227-42.

Regarding the day see the excellent article by H. J. BORNSTEIN, 'The Jewish Calendar and its Development', *Ha-Tekufah* VI (1920), pp. 247-313 (in Hebrew). On the beginning of the day at Qumran, see J. M. BAUMGARTEN, 'The Beginning of the Day in the Calendar of Jubilees', *JBL* LXXVII (1958), pp. 355ff.; S. TALMON, in *Scripta Hierosolymitana* IV (1958), pp. 162-99; 'The Manual of Benedictions of the Sect of the Judaean Desert', *Revue de Qumran* II (1959-60), pp. 475-500. On the day in the Bible, see R. DE VAUX, *op.cit.* I, p. 347.

Chapter Seventeen

The Temple

The Temple and the courts

The Second Temple, particularly in the last years of its existence, differed in its structure and functioning from the First Temple. Worship was conducted by twenty-four priestly courses in turn each week; in addition, there were twenty-four deputations composed of priests, Levites and Israelites. The people as a whole evinced great attachment to the Temple and participated in various ways in divine worship. The public administrative institutions were located in the Temple courtyards. Within the Temple area there was a synagogue, or quasi-synagogue, and the sages taught the Law in the courtyards. All these developments necessitated changes in the Temple structure and in the use of its courts and chambers.

The outermost precinct of the Temple, the Temple Mount, measured, according to the Mishnah, 500 cubits by 500 cubits (approximately 62,500 sq.metres).[1] These figures refer to the temenos, or to the area as it was before its extension by Herod. The precinct of the Temple Mount as enlarged by Herod can be seen today in the walled area of the Temple Mount.[2] The current excavations in the area of the southern and western walls indicate that to the south there was a large square from which stairs ascended to the two sourthern gates of the Temple Mount, serving as the main entrance for the people.[3] Access to the Mount was also permitted to ritually unclean Israelites and to God-fearing Gentiles. None of the Temple ritual was performed on the Temple Mount; rather, its colonnades served as a gathering place for the people before and after worship, or for those who ascended the Temple Mount to hear the words of the Law.[4] The *bet midrash* was also located on the Temple Mount, and the sanhedrin, which on sabbath and holidays convened as an academic rather than as a judicial body,

---

[1] *M. Middoth* 2:1.
[2] See chapter twenty, pp. 978-83.
[3] *M. Middoth* 1:3. See B. Mazar, 'Excavations near the Temple Mount,' *Qadmoniot* v (1972), pp. 74-90, and the illustration pp. 981-2.
[4] *M. Pesahim* 5:10; John 10:23.

met 'in the *bet midrash* on the Temple Mount.'[1] Business transactions relating to the Temple, as for example the purchase of sacrificial doves, oils, wines, and even the money changing, were not conducted in the inner courts but rather on the outer court of the Temple Mount, or perhaps on the above mentioned square outside the southern wall.[2] Pilgrims to the Temple entered through one of the southern gates, turned right and customarily circled the inner walls before prostrating themselves thirteen times in front of the gates which led to the inner courts.[3] The gates of the western wall led to bridges which connected the Temple with the Upper City and served mainly the aristocracy; the other gates apparently served only the various activities related to Temple ritual and, as a rule, were not used by the people.

A stepped ascent led from the area of the Temple Mount to a wide platform which surrounded the Temple courts; in Hebrew tradition it is known as the Rampart (חיל). The sanctity of this area surpassed that of the Temple Mount and access to it was forbidden to Gentiles and to those defiled by the dead. In front of the steps was a low wall with a latticed railing to which were affixed slabs bearing Greek and Latin inscriptions warning Gentiles of the death penalty for entering. These inscriptions are mentioned by Josephus and two of them, in Greek, have been recovered.[4] A court also convened in the Rampart area. Several gates led from the Rampart to the third and holier region, the court of the women, access to which was forbidden until sundown to those who had had to take a ritual bath that day.[5]

In contrast to the Temple Mount and the Rampart which surrounded the Temple on all four sides, the court of the women extended only along the eastern side of the Temple and served as a sort of secondary or outer court for the inner court. It was smaller than the inner court and measured 135 cubits by 135 cubits. All the communal functions relating to divine worship in the Temple period were conducted in the court of the women. It was here that, upon the completion of the sacrificial rites on the Day of Atonement, the high priest read the Torah before the people;[6] here also, once in seven years on the Feast of Tabernacles, either the high priest or the king read the Torah to the

---

[1] *T. Sanhedrin* 7:1; *T. Hagigah* 2:9. In *M. Yoma* 7:1 and *M. Sotah* 7:7-8 a synagogue is mentioned.
[2] See above p. 865, n. 2.
[3] *M. Shekalim* 6:1-3.
[4] *M. Kelim* 1:8; Jos. *Ant.* xv, 417; *War* v, 194; *CII* 1400.
[5] *M. Kelim* 1:8.
[6] *T. B. Yoma* 69b.

assembled multitude;[1] and here too the public gathered for the procession of the pouring of water during the Feast of Tabernacles.[2] The court of the women also housed the chambers frequented by the people: the 'house of oils,' the chamber of wood for sacrifices, the nazirites' and lepers' chambers for the offering of their respective sacrifices. Adjacent to the lepers' chamber was one of the famous ritual baths in which it was customary to bathe before entering the inner court.[3] The name 'court of the women' is found in talmudic literature and in the description by Josephus of the rebuilding of the Temple by Herod. It does not derive from the fact that this court accommodated only women, for all visitors to the Temple passed through it and often spent some time there; it stems, rather, from the fact that for the most part women did not advance beyond it, although during the offering of the sacrifices they were not forbidden access even to the inner court.[4] It is also possible that the name arose because, during the evening libations of the Feast of Tabernacles, the women mounted the gallery and watched the men dancing in the court. The inner court, called simply 'the court' (העזרה) towered above the court of the women and passage to it was through one gate alone, the Nicanor gate, on the western side of the court of the women. Fifteen steps 'rounded like the half of a round threshing-floor' led from the court of the women; the Levites stood on them with their musical instruments during the libations of water.[5] Lepers and other ritually unclean persons were placed near the entrance to the Nicanor gate in order to be cleansed, just as the suspected adultress was placed before the high priest at the same gate.[6] The bronze doors of the Nicanor gate were exceptionally beautiful and they were the only ones which remained ungilded later on.[7]

The inner court measured 135 cubits by 185 cubits; it was divided into the court of the Israelites, from which they watched the ritual, and the slightly elevated court of the priests where most of the worship was conducted. The Israelites did not have access to it save when ritual rendered it necessary, as for example the wavings of the offerings or the procession round the altar with palm-branches (לולב)

[1] *T. B. Sotah* 41b.
[2] *M. Sukkah* 5:1-4.
[3] *M. Middoth* 2:5; *T. Negaim* 8:9.
[4] *T. Arakhin* 2:1.
[5] *T. Sukkah* 4:1; *M. Middoth* 2:5.
[6] *T. Negaim* 8:9; *M. Tamid* 5:6; *M. Sotah* 1:5.
[7] *M. Middoth* 2:3; Jos. *War* v, 201-204.

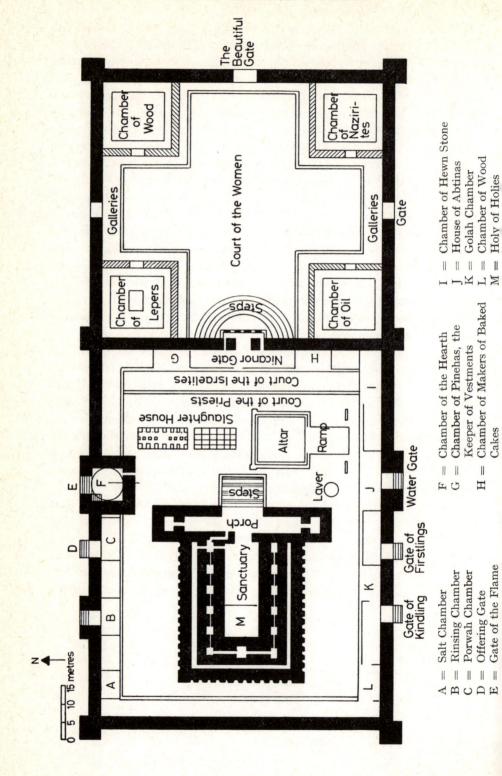

A = Salt Chamber
B = Rinsing Chamber
C = Porwah Chamber
D = Offering Gate
E = Gate of the Flame

F = Chamber of the Hearth
G = Chamber of Pinehas, the Keeper of Vestments
H = Chamber of Makers of Baked Cakes

I = Chamber of Hewn Stone
J = House of Abtinas
K = Golah Chamber
L = Chamber of Wood
M = Holy of Holies

on the Feast of Tabernacles. The court of the Israelites, a narrow strip measuring eleven cubits on the eastern side of the inner court, was separated from the court of the priests by a low partition. The Levites stood on a raised platform connected to this partition while they sang.[1] The major part of the Temple worship was conducted in the open court of the priests. In its centre stood the sacrificial altar, to the north the slaughter-house, and to the south the laver. All sacrifices were offered on the altar; the priests stood on steps leading to the sanctuary (היכל) as they blessed the people.[2] The entire inner court was surrounded by colonnades; along the walls were the various chambers relating to worship, reserved to the priests. Among these chambers was the chamber of hewn stone, which lay partly in the court of the priests and partly in the court of the Israelites.[3]

To the west of the inner court stood the sanctuary. In front of it was an open structure called the porch (אולם); its façade had four columns, two on either side of the entrance to the sanctuary. The shape of the façade can be seen on the coins of Bar Cochba and in the synagogue of Dura-Europus.[4] The sanctuary was a rectangular structure, one hundred cubits long, seventy cubits wide and one hundred cubits high. It was divided into a forward section called 'the holy' (קודש) and an inner section called Adytum or 'holy of holies' (דביר; קודש קדשים). In the centre of the sanctuary stood the golden altar for the burning of incense, to the north the golden table upon which the shewbread was placed, and to the south the golden candelabrum. We are familiar with the shape of the vessels from detailed descriptions in tannaitic sources as well as from the relief on the arch of Titus in Rome.[5]

The sanctuary was separated from the holy of holies by a curtain (פרוכת), and the Mishnah states: 'After the ark was taken away a stone remained there from the time of the early prophets, and it was called *shetijah*. It was higher than the ground by three fingerbreadths.'[6] Access to the holy of holies was forbidden to all save the high priest, who entered once a year on the Day of Atonement.

The Temple was very impressive, particularly after its reconstruction by Herod and the subsequent embellishments. Even talmudic tradition, which looks unfavourably upon Herod, states: 'He who has

[1] *M. Middoth* 2:6; Jos. *War* v, 226.
[2] *M. Middoth* chap. 3: *M. Tamid* 1:4.
[3] Jos. *War* v, 200; *M. Middoth* chap. 1.
[4] *M. Middoth* 3:7; Jos. *War* v, 208.
[5] *M. Middoth* chap. 4.
[6] *M. Yoma* 5:2.

not seen the Temple of Herod has never in his life seen a beautiful structure.'[1] Echoes of the vivid impression created by the Temple can be heard also in the words of Jesus' disciples to their teacher upon visiting the Temple.[2]

Priests

The daily Temple ritual was performed mainly by the priests, who had sole access to the altar and the sanctuary. They offered both communal and individual sacrifices, burned incense and kindled the candelabrum in the sanctuary, and bestowed the priestly benediction on the people. The priests participated also in the rites conducted mainly by the Levites, such as singing and sentry duty, but they emphasized their privileged position in relation to the Levites. They sounded the trumpets at the beginning and conclusion of songs, and where both priests and Levites kept watch together, the former were stationed 'above,' the latter 'below.'[3]

The priests were divided into twenty-four divisions (משמרות), each of which served for one week. The divisions were divided in turn into fathers' houses (בית אבות) each of which served on a prescribed day. The number of fathers' houses in each division was not equal: some divisions had four, others as many as nine, and these were proportionally divided according to the days of the week. The priestly divisions had their own internal organization. Each was presided over by the head of the division (ראש המשמר) who was assisted by the head of the fathers' house (ראש בית אב). It is related that the elders of fathers' houses (זקני בית אב) were entrusted with the keys to the Temple, which were handed on in turn to the elders of the succeeding division.[4] Most of the priests, particularly the ordinary priests, did not live in Jerusalem. During this period we find families and larger groups of priests living in Sepphoris, Jericho, in a town in the Judaean Hills, and elsewhere.[5] The priests went up to Jerusalem for their period of service and returned home at its conclusion. During their sojourn in Jerusalem, they slept within the Temple precincts.

We cannot determine the exact number of priests in each of the

---

[1] *T. B. Baba Bathra* 4a.
[2] Mark 13:1; Luke 21:5.
[3] *M. Tamid* 7:3; *M. Middoth* 1:5.
[4] *T. Taanith* 2:2; *T. Horayoth* 2:10; *M. Middoth* 1:8; Jos. *Against Apion* II, 108.
[5] *T. Yoma* 1:4; *P. T. Taanith* IV, 68a; Luke 1:39.

various divisions. The diverse figures which appear in the literature of the Second Temple period are not very helpful, since they are exaggerated or simply unreliable, all the more so since we do not know who were included. Approximately twenty priests were chosen by lot for the daily whole-offering. In addition, a large number of priests officiated during the offering of the individual sacrifices, but we are unable to determine their number.[1] And we do not know to what extent Diaspora priests participated. The latter were permitted to officiate except for those who had served in the Temple of Onias (בית חניו) in Egypt, who were barred by the injunction against priests who officiated in the high places.[2]

One mishnaic source speaks of the participation of Babylonian or Alexandrian priests in the partaking of the offerings for the Day of Atonement. The feast-day offerings were divided among the priests who made the pilgrimage, although we cannot infer from this the extent to which they took part in the feast-day or daily offerings.[3] According to Leviticus 21:17 only those who were without blemish were qualified for Temple service. Nevertheless, those with a blemish were not excluded from the Temple activities; they went up with their division to the Temple and enjoyed the right to partake of the 'holy things' from individual and communal offerings, and they took part in their distribution. Evidence from various sources indicates that the tradition of distributing the 'holy things' to priests having blemishes was actually in force. These priests were not entirely barred from Temple service, and several of the rites which were not directly connected with the sacrifices, such as the sounding of the trumpets in certain instances, the bestowal of the priestly benediction, and the preparation of the sacrificial wood were performed by priests with blemishes.[4]

The sources frequently speak of the loyalty of the priests to the Temple, their diligence in normal times and their great devotion during the difficult times which came upon the Temple.[5] All traditions in talmudic literature which protest against the priests' contempt for worship and the Temple, refer only to the office of the high priest.

---

[1] *M. Yoma* chap. 2; *M. Tamid* chap. 3.
[2] *M. Menahoth* 13:10.
[3] *M. Menahoth* 11:7; *T. B. Menahoth* 100a; *M. Sukkah* 5:7.
[4] *M. Sukkah* 4:3; *Sifre* Num. 75 (p. 70); *T. Sotah* 7:8; *M. Middoth* 2:5.
[5] Jos. *Ant.* XIV, 65-67; III, 321.

Levites

The Levites who officiated alongside the priests enjoyed a lesser status; the sources clearly indicate that at least from the Hellenistic period onward, they were deprived of their former position. While the Levites are frequently mentioned in the descriptions of the dedication of the Temple in the books of Ezra, Nehemiah and in Chronicles,[1] they are completely ignored in description of worship and the dedication of the altar in Maccabees and Ben Sira.[2] In the first century the Levites were removed from all contact with the altar and sacrifices and are not mentioned in the sources except as singers and gatekeepers and then only as enjoying an inferior status to that of the priests.[3] In I Chronicles chapter 9, the Levites are divided according to families into singers and gatekeepers, a division strictly enforced until the last days of the Temple.[4] The gatekeepers were responsible for opening and closing the gates, guarding the Temple area by day and night, and ensuring that no visitors were ritually unclean. They were also responsible for the cleanliness of the Temple.[5] In many practical regulations relating to the Temple, the Levites were discriminated against by the priests. At the end of the Second Temple period they fought for their right to wear fine linen during their ministrations; the sources provide contradictory information regarding this privilege. Apparently, conflicting traditions existed and it was not until the last days of the Temple that the matter was resolved in favour of the Levites by a decision of the sanhedrin specially convened by King Agrippa II.[6]

The Levites, like the priests, were divided into twenty-four divisions, each serving one week, but the sources do not indicate a specific division into father's houses as in the case of the priests.

The watch

The divisions did not simply guard the entrances to the Temple: they served as guard of honour as well. The watch were stationed in twenty-four places: at the five Temple gates, at the four inner corners, at the five gates of the Temple court, at the latter's four exterior

---

[1] E.g. Ezra 6:16-18; Neh. 12:44.
[2] I Mac. 4:36-57; cf. esp. v. 42; Ben Sira 50:12-13.
[3] *M. Middoth* 1:1-2; *M. Tamid* 7:3.
[4] *T. B. Arakhin* 11b; Jos. *Ant.* xx, 216-218.
[5] Philo, *De Spec. Leg.* I, 156.
[6] Jos. *Ant.* xx, 216-218; cf. viii, 94.

corners, behind the holy of holies, and in five chambers.[1] Josephus tells us that at least two hundred gate-keepers closed the Temple gates, and it would appear that these were the men who afterwards remained at their posts.[2] At one point he writes that, during the time of the governor Coponius (6-9 C.E.) the Temple was defiled with bones at night apparently by the Samaritans; following this the watch was re-inforced.[3] The guards were reviewed by an officer of the Temple Mount (איש הר הבית) who 'would make the rounds of every watch preceded by kindled torches.' Philo tells of the existence of Levite watchmen who made rounds day and night in order to ensure the purity of the Temple and of its visitors.[4]

Israelites

The participation of the Israelites in the ritual of the sacrifices was by deputations (מעמד). The Mishnah states: 'What are the deputations? In that it is written: 'Command the children of Israel and say unto them: my obligation, my food' how can a man's offering be offered while he does not stand by it? Therefore the First Prophets ordained twenty-four courses, and for every course there was a deputation in Jerusalem made up of priests, Levites and Israelites.'[5] The idea here is that communal sacrifices were not the concern of the officiating priests but of the entire nation, for 'the individual does not volunteer a communal offering' and the priests only represented the people.[6] The division into deputations was based upon the geographical constitution of the twenty-four districts; the terms deputation and district were interchangeable in talmudic literature. The men of the deputations stood beside the priests during their ministrations and, after the completion of the sacrifices, gathered for the daily reading of the Torah and for the prescribed prayers. Throughout most of their week they fasted.[7] We are unable to determine how each deputation was composed.

---

[1] The order of the watch is described in *M. Middoth* chap. 1 and *M. Tamid* 1:1.
[2] Jos. *Against Apion* II, 119.
[3] Jos. *Ant.* XVIII, 29-30.
[4] *M. Middoth* 1:2; Philo, *De Spec. Leg.* I, 156; cf. *P. Oxy.* V, 840.
[5] *M. Taanith* 4:2.
[6] *Sifre Num.* 107 (p. 106).
[7] *T. B. Taanith* 27b; *P. T. Taanith* IV, 67d-68a.

The Temple officers

A permanent staff of officers supervised and counselled the priests in their ministrations and presided over the daily worship and procedures and over the weekly divisions of priests. These officers allotted the various priestly duties, announced the rites, and discharged the administrative duties connected with the Temple and the public. *Mishnah Shekalim* chapter 5 contains a list of officials such as those in charge of bird-offerings, allotments, libations, clothing and such items. Additional officials are mentioned in the descriptions of the ritual in the tractate *Tamid*, and in *Tosefta Shekalim* there is a list of secondary duties, particularly those related to the work of the Levites. It appears that these officials were also Levites; they included those responsible for locking the gates, for the keys, for the wood, and so on. The duties were generally passed on as an inheritance from father to son, and complaints are found in the sources against such families as that of Garmu which was responsible for the shew-bread, and against the family of Avtinas which was responsible for the incense. They are blamed for their reluctance to divulge their secrets to anyone other than their sons.[1]

The high priest

The distribution of duties among the twenty-four divisions relieved the high priest and his family of much of the daily Temple ritual. He stood out in permanent contrast to all the division priests, including the heads and the elders, who alternated in weekly shifts. All the communal institutions concentrated on the Temple were more or less subordinate to his authority. The high priest's privileged status is reflected in his position at the head of Temple hierarchy, and several traditions and customs relating to divine worship rendered his status unique. A daily cake-offering was sacrificed in the name of the high priest, together with the daily whole-offerings, while the prescribed rite for the Day of Atonement, the only day on which the high priest entered the holy of holies to burn incense, was valid only when offered by the high priest himself. In addition to the white garment worn by all his fellow-priests, the high priest wore a splendid gold vestment composed of eight pieces of clothing, in keeping with the description in Exodus 28. Only the oracle mentioned there did not exist during the period of the Second Temple.

[1] *T. Shekalim* 2:14; *M. Yoma* 3:11; *T. Yoma* 2:5-8.

The cake-offering was part of the daily whole-offering and responsibility for this rite was distributed by lot along with the other rites of this. This meal-offering was the 'individual offering' of the high priest; a special officer and a special chamber were set aside for it.[1]

The high priest had not to follow the divisional distribution of the ritual duties: he was permitted to sacrifice the daily whole-offering or to burn incense at will. But, either because of the infringement of the rights of the priests, or because he was occupied with communal and political matters, the high priest did not serve on a daily basis. His estrangement from daily Temple worship should not, however, be exaggerated, for both talmudic tradition and Josephus note that the high priest customarily participated in the worship on sabbaths and festivals.[2] In particular, the sources stress the activities of the high priest during the Feast of Tabernacles when the crowds gathered in the Temple court and the ritual was performed with great festivity and pomp.[3] Either in deference to ancient tradition, or because of his interest in serving at such events, the high priest took part in the ritual on special occasions. Thus, the high priest participated in the infrequent rite of burning the red heifer although it need not necessarily have been performed by the high priest, at least according to tannaitic tradition. In the communal gathering once in seven years on the Feast of Tabernacles for the reading of the Torah, it was the high priest who read to the people.[4]

The prefect

Second in command to the high priest in Temple worship was the prefect (הסגן), whose full title was prefect of the priests, or head of the priests.[5] The prefect took the place of the high priest when the latter was deemed invalid to officiate, accompanied the high priest during his ministrations, and also presided over the daily whole-offering. The prefect noted in talmudic sources is probably identical with the στρατηγός or στρατηγὸς τοῦ ἱεροῦ in Josephus and the New Testament.[6] Not only does the Septuagint render the biblical prefect as στρατηγός but the duties of this officer in rabbinic literature,

---

[1] T. Shekalim 2:14; M. Tamid 1:3.
[2] P. T. Hagigah II, 78b; Jos. War V, 230.
[3] I Macc. 10:15-21; Jos. Ant. XIII, 372: XV, 50-51.
[4] M. and T. Parah chap. 3; Sifre Num. 123 (p. 153); Jos Ant. IV, 209.
[5] T. B. Yoma 39a; M. Tamid 7:3; M. Yoma 7:1; 4:1; P. T. Yoma III, 41a.
[6] Acts 4:1; 5:24-26; Jos. War VI, 294.

Josephus and the New Testament are similar. According to the Greek sources the prefect presided over the daily administration of the Temple and was responsible not only for the ritual procedures but also for the maintenance of order and discipline. When the revolt broke out, it was the prefect Eleazar son of Ananias who issued the order to stop the sacrifice for the Roman empire.[1] It seems that towards the last days of the Temple the prefecture was held by Pharisees; the prefect who accompanied the high priest made certain that the latter observed Pharisaic tradition during his ministrations.[2] The two Pharisaic prefects known to us by name are Rabbi Hananiah, 'prefect of the priests', and Eleazar son of Ananias, a political opponent of the Sadducean high priesthood. It is reasonable to assume that Eleazar did not share the Sadducees' religious or social standpoint. He may be identified with the Tanna Eleazar ben Hananiah, the follower of the school of Shammai, who is mentioned in talmudic literature in relation to the Temple.[3]

The worshippers

The Israelites came to the Temple for various reasons: a) to fulfil their obligations, such as the offering of the first fruits, the tithes and the wave-offerings and obligatory sacrifices, b) to worship and pray during the liturgy and at other times, or to pose questions on legal tradition and to study the Torah, c) to participate in Temple worship alongside the priests, especially in the form of deputations (see above). Aside from his pilgrimage, to be considered below, there were numerous occasions on which the Israelite ascended to the Temple to offer either the obligatory sacrifices or those which he volunteered as thanks-offering or as whole-offering. Many came to the Temple to cleanse themselves of severe impurities such as defilement by the dead, which required sprinkling with 'cleansing water' (מי חטאת) on the fourth and seventh day.[4] There was, indeed, cleansing water in the twenty-four districts of the country established for this specific purpose, and after the destruction of the Temple we find cleansing water in Judaea, Galilee, Transjordan and Etzion-Gaver (Assia) in the south.[5] Never-

---

[1] Jos. *War* II, 409.
[2] *M. Yoma* 4:1; *T. Yoma* 3:2.
[3] Jos. *War* II, 409; Scholion to *Megillath Taanith* (beginning); *Semahoth* 6:11.
[4] *M. Parah* 3:3.
[5] *T. Parah* 3:14; 10:2: 5:6; 7:4.

theless, it was not found in all areas, and many people came to the Temple to cleanse themselves ritually, particularly before the festivals. For Diaspora Jews this visit was almost the only means of purification, and a specific time and place were allotted for the cleansing of the ritually unclean.[1] Many Jews would go up daily to the Temple in order to be present at the worship, to receive the priestly benediction bestowed up- on the people at the end, to pray during the burning of the incense, and to prostrate themselves before God upon hearing the singing of the Levites. Others would go up to hear or to teach the Torah; or they would combine several such activities.[2]

Everyone, priest or layman, took a ritual bath, even if he were clean, before entering the Temple. He could do so in any one of the numerous ritual baths located in the Temple courts.[3] It was customary for visitors to the Temple to wear white rather than coloured clothing, for the former was held to indicate modesty and piety: pious people were careful always to wear white.[4] Before entering the Temple courts they removed their shoes, and laid aside their staffs, their money belts, their cloaks and bundles.[5]

Women too from all parts of the land of Israel and the Diaspora went up to the Temple. We have already mentioned the galleries set up in the court of the women so that they could watch the dancers during the Feast of Tabernacles. Legal tradition specifies that women were not bound to make the pilgrimage; yet women frequently accompanied their husbands to the Temple. Tannaitic tradition considers them obliged to participate in the rejoicing as expressed primarily in the peace-offering meals.[6] Numerous legends reflect the attachment of the women of Judaea and Galilee to the Temple and their diligence in visiting it at appointed times, despite their domestic obligations.[7] Of five or six Nazirites known to us by name in the last years of the Second Temple, three were women; Queen Helena, Berenice, sister of Agrippa II, and an unknown woman named Miriam the Tadmorite.[8] When men had to bring an offering, women had to do also; in addition, women were obliged to bring an offering after childbirth. Tombstones

[1] Jos. *War* I, 229; Acts 21:24; John 11:55; *M. Tamid* 5:6.
[2] *M. Tamid* 7:2; Ben Sira chap. 50; Luke 1:10.
[3] *P. T. Yoma* III, 40b; *T. Negaim* 8:9. This also appears in the apocryphal gospel from *P. Oxy.* v, 840.
[4] Jos. *War* II, 1; *Ant.* XI, 327; Eusebius, *Hist. eccles.* II, 23; *P. Oxy.* v, 840.
[5] *M. Berakoth* 9:5; *T. Berakoth* 7:19; Jos. *War* IV, 150.
[6] *T. B. Hagigah* 2b-3a; *T. B. Pesahim* 89a.
[7] *P. T. Maaser Sheni* v, 56a; *Lam. Rabba* 3.
[8] *M. Nazir* 3:6; Jos. *War* II, 313; *T. Nazir* 3:10.

in Jerusalem record the names of many women from the Land of Israel and the Diaspora.[1] We are familiar with the role of women from various sources: they wove the curtains and renewed them each year: 'The women would weave the curtains... and received their payment from the contributions to the chamber'.[2]

It was not exaggeration when the high priest, Jesus of Gamala, said to the Edomites, during the siege, that the Temple in Jerusalem was a house of prayer for all nations of the world.[3] In chapter four we noted the various pieces of evidence pointing to pilgrimages by Gentiles from outside Palestine. Even the impurity which Jews imputed to their heathenism and the injunctions against their partaking of food did not deter Gentiles from making the pilgrimage to the Temple or from having sacrifices offered there. Tradition and practice rendered Gentile sacrifices acceptable; often, particularly on feast-days, Gentiles could be seen in the Temple. They came to prostrate themselves before God, to hear the Torah and to bring their offerings. A pilgrimage hymn in the book of Psalms reads: 'Who shall ascend the hill of the Lord? And who shall stand in his holy place? He who has clean hands and a pure heart, who does not lift up his soul to what is false, and does not swear deceitfully.'[4] Josephus and the sages teach us that it was not only physical purification which was required of visitors to the Temple and those bringing offerings but also undefiled hands. First fruits of doubtful origin were not accepted as offerings, while those who had acted against the accepted rules of conduct were barred from the Temple precincts.[5] Josephus relates that Simon, who was considered learned in legal tradition, demanded that King Agrippa be barred from entering the Temple because he had attended the theatre at Caesarea, which was a violation of the injunction against idolatry and the spilling of blood. The king summoned Simon to the theatre to persuade him that the act did not constitute an infraction of the Law.[6] The sages stressed that one who was placed under a ban was forbidden to come to the Temple and that the ban merely served to indicate that he had transgressed against accepted standards of conduct.[7]

---

[1] *CII* 1226; 1390; 1372-4; 1383-4.
[2] *T. Shekalim* 2:6; *II Baruch* 10:19; *Protoevangelium Jacobi* 10:1.
[3] Jos. *War* IV, 262.   [4] Ps. 24:3-4; cf. Ps. 15.
[5] *M. Bikkurim* 1:1-2.
[6] Jos. *Ant.* XIX, 332-4.
[7] *T. B. Moed Katan* 7b; *M. Eduyoth* 5:6. Cf. also *Targum Ps. Jonathan* on 2 Sam. 5:8.

The Temple treasury and its officers

The Temple treasury was composed of a number of rooms. They had several sources of income. The one fixed source was the 'contribution to the chamber' which derived from the half-shekel. The tractate *Shekalim* mentions the chamber of utensils, to which all contributions in kind were brought; the chamber of secrets, for secret charity, and the chamber of the Temple, which received contributions for construction and repair of the Temple.[1] The Mishnah mentions thirteen shofar-chests, money chests in the form of ram's horns, whose lower portion resembled a barrel and which tapered gradually towards the top. These chests held the half-shekel coins and the money for specific offerings, both obligatory and free-will. If a man vowed or freely offered a dove's nest, he contributed the value of the nest to the chest; the priests then sacrificed a number of bird-offerings in accordance with the sum contributed. A man could proffer a certain sum for a specific offering; sacrifices were paid for with this money. One might also make a contribution of wood and frankincense or gold for use in the Adytum.[2]

The Temple revenues were undoubtedly great since nearly every Jew sent his fixed contributions. Various other contributions were sent by Jews and Gentiles. Tannaitic sources continually speak of a surplus rather than a dearth of funds.[3] It was customary to dedicate a field, a house or a servant to the Temple. Of course, in lieu of the dedicated property the monetary value was paid to the Temple treasurers. The sources do not contain the slightest suggestion that the Temple owned either slaves, houses, fields or any property whose revenues went to the Temple, as was not unusual in other ancient civilizations.[4] The Temple treasury had great responsibilities. It had to finance not only sacrifices and direct Temple expenses but also the expenses of various bodies connected with the Temple. The correctors of books and the judges were paid by the treasury. In addition it paid for all the communal needs of Jerusalem, including the upkeep of the water-works, the city walls and towers. The fund for these came from the shekel chamber.[5]

Three treasurers (גזבר) headed the administration. They distributed

---

[1] *M. Shekalim* 5:6.
[2] *M. Shekalim* 6:5-6; *T. Shekalim* 3:1-8.
[3] *M. Shekalim* chap. 4; Philo, *De Spec. Leg.* 1, 70-76.
[4] *T. Shekalim* 3:15; cf. also *M.* and *T. Arakhin* chap. 5.
[5] *M. Shekalim* 4:1-2; *P. T. Shekalim* IV, 48a; *T. B. Ketuboth* 105a-106a.

Temple funds, inspected purchases, supervised the redemption of vows and the gifts and contributions to the Temple. They were the agents of a sevenman council of supervisors (אמרכל), who were in overall charge. The treasurers and supervisors appear as the administrators who acted for the high priests inside and outside the Temple.[1] In addition to these men, a baraita mentions two officials of a somewhat higher rank: the controllers (קתליקוס). The hierarchy of Temple administration consisted of high priests, controller, supervisor, and treasurer.[2] We do not have much information about the office of controller; it is possible that this position was identical to that of one of the types of supervisors mentioned above, such as the prefect or the head of a division.

The half-shekel

According to tannaitic tradition all adult males had to contribute yearly a half-shekel; moreover, a minor whose father had begun to make this payment for him could not desist. Women were not obliged to contribute, but various sources indicate that it was a widespread custom for them to do so. Contributions from Gentiles were not acceptable, since they could only bring free-will, not obligatory offerings. According to certain sages, priests were also obliged to contribute the half-shekel: however, the priests, or at least certain circles within the priesthood, were opposed to this. We cannot ascertain whether the priests did, in fact, make this contribution. In any event, the Mishnah states that one does not take a pledge from the priests when these fail to pay, 'because of consideration of concord' or 'because of considerations of respect.'[3]

The half-shekel was worth two Roman dinars. The contribution was called for on the first day of the month of Adar so that on the first day of Nisan, with the start of the year in the Temple, the new contributions might be used for the daily whole-offerings; surplus money was transferred to other needs of the Temple. On the fifteenth day of Adar, money-changing tables were set up throughout the country to change and receive coins. Levies were imposed according to the lists in the hands of the money-changers. Traditions speak of various Galilean cities which gathered the lists in order to transfer them to

---

[1] M. Shekalim 5:2; 2:1; T. Shekalim 2:15; M. Menahoth 8:7; T. Menahoth 13:21.
[2] P. T. Shekalim V, 49a.
[3] M. Shekalim 1:3-5; P. T. Shekalim I, 46a.

Jerusalem. On the twenty-fifth of Adar, the money-changers terminated their activities in the cities and continued operations only in the Temple. From that time on, they took pledges from those who did not bring a contribution.[1]

Even groups and factions which expressed reservations about the Temple or its sacrifices sent their contributions to the Temple, voluntarily or under duress. We find that the Essenes sent their contributions to Jerusalem. Jesus and his disciples as well gave their contribution to the collectors of the half-shekel.[2]

It appears from the sources that the collectors in the cities of the Land of Israel were dispatched under the aegis of the Temple supervisors; in the Diaspora, however, local residents were engaged in the levying and collecting of the contributions.

The needs of the Temple and their supply

It was the duty of the Temple treasurers to supply the Temple with not only communal sacrifices but also those individual sacrifices which it was difficult or impossible for the worshippers to bring with them. Animals could be brought by the worshipper or bought from the merchants in the vicinity of the city. Meal-offerings, fine flours and oils, however, because of their susceptibility to impurity were often bought from the treasurers; not everyone who brought sacrifices was able to bring in addition wine, fine flour and oil. This was especially difficult for those who came from the Diaspora, and impossible for a Gentile who brought his offering to the Temple. Doves in large numbers were supplied to the Temple by the treasurers, for the occasions on which they were required were numerous. Although everyone was permitted to bring doves with him, he could save himself the trouble. 'If any wished for drink-offerings he would go to Johanan who was over the seals and give him money and receive from him a seal; he would then go to Ahijah who was over the drink-offerings and give him the seal and from him receive drink-offerings.[3] Mishnah and Tosefta *Menahoth* contain detailed traditions regarding the sources of communal sacrifices and supplies for the Temple. Certain localities were chosen because they were known for their choice produce or because their fruits ripened in the appropriate season

---

[1] *M. Shekalim* 1:3; 2:1; *P. T. Taanith* IV, 69a.
[2] Jos. *Ant.* VIII, 19; Matt. 17:24-27.
[3] *M. Shekalim* 5:3-4.

of the year. Flour and wine were brought mainly from the area of Judaea (Mihmash, Zencha, Hapharajjim), oil from Galilee (Tekoa, Gush Halav), rams from Moab, calves from the Sharon, and sheep from Hebron. The doves were bred on the Mount of Anointing near Jerusalem.[1]

A large quantity of salt was required for the sacrificial rites, for the Law commanded: 'with all thine offerings thou shalt offer salt' (Lev. 1:13). Salt was assigned an important place in the life of the Temple, and a special chamber was set aside for it within the inner court, in contrast to the other supplies whose chambers were located in the women's court. According to legal tradition a man could not bring salt with his sacrifice; rather, the priests were to sprinkle the sacrifice with salt from the Temple. For the most part, Sodom salt was used, that is, salt from the traditional site of Sodom, near Zoar.[2]

The Temple also needed much wood. Faggots were arranged on the altar every morning, and two logs were added when sacrifices and incense were burned in the evening, to keep the perpetual flame alive on the altar. A fire was kept burning perpetually in the chamber of the hearth, so that the altar-fire could be rekindled from it. Wood for individual sacrifices was also supplied from the wood-treasury. The priests cooked their offerings over a templewood fire before eating them. One might proffer a wood offering and sacrifice it on the altar, but, rather than bring wood from home, the worshipper paid its value and the priests offered up two logs of wood.[3]

Wood was not purchased as were other articles for the altar: certain families in Israel traditionally brought wood for the altar at appointed times during the year. The origin of this custom is mentioned in Nehemiah 10:3 in the account of the casting of lots for bringing wood: 'at appointed times, year by year' each family in turn. This custom was perpetuated until the end of the Second Temple period. *Mishnah Taanith* 4:5 contains a list of the families who traditionally brought wood to the altar at set times: 'on the first day of Nisan, by the family of Arah of the tribe of Judah, on the 20th day of Tammuz, by the family of David of the tribe of Judah, ...' All the families in this list are mentioned among the families of returning exiles in Ezra and Nehemiah, except the family of the pestlesmugglers and that of the fig-pressers.

[1] *M. Menahoth* chap. 8; *T. Menahoth* chap. 9; *P. T. Taanith* IV, 69a; Jos. *War* V, 505.
[2] *Sifra* Lev. 14 (p. 12a-c); *T. B. Menahoth* 21b; *T. Menahoth* 9:15.
[3] *T. B. Menahoth* 21b; *M. Shekalim* 7:7; *T. Shekalim* 3:4.

The latter did not, however, have an appointed time, but brought their wood on the fifteenth day of Ab, which was the general day for the people to bring wood,[1] and the ninth of Ab was set aside as a general day 'for the priests and the people.'[2] At the beginning of the Second Temple period, a levy was imposed to provide wood, because of the difficult financial situation of the Temple, but in the later period it was a matter of established family privilege and of popular desire to participate in the commandment, 'even if the chamber were filled with wood'.[3]

The wood was brought with great ceremony, and the services of the weekly deputation of Israelites in the afternoon service or at the closing of the gates were cancelled on the day wood was brought. Those who brought wood were forbidden to work on that day, and they were received ceremoniously, as were the caravans of bearers of first-fruits; they are mentioned together in tannaitic sources. The halakah which required bearers of first-fruits to spend the night in Jerusalem, returning only in the morning to their homes, also applied to those who brought wood. Even after the destruction of the Temple, the descendants of these families observed the custom on its day.[4] Haggadic tradition tells of attempts to prevent the bringing of wood, and of families' perseverance even in face of danger to their lives.[5] The Mishnah has preserved information on the types of acceptable trees for the altar wood, but it considers 'all trees to be acceptable faggots except grapevine and olive wood.'[6] Yet the *Book of Jubilees* and the *Testament of Levi* are more exacting and give detailed lists of only twelve trees which are suitable. The *Testament of Levi* adds that they must be brought with leaves upon them.[7]

The daily morning and evening whole-offerings were accompanied by the burning of incense upon the golden altar within the sanctuary. The incense served only as a communal offering, and might not be offered by an individual. The Torah mentions only four ingredients

---

[1] Jos. *War* II, 430 mentions the 14th of Ab as the holiday on which wood was brought, but it is possible that he already mentioned the eve of the holiday. See H. Lichtenstein, HUCA VIII-IX (1931), p. 270.
[2] *T. Bikkurim* 2:9 (accordings to the superior reading); cf. also *M. Taanith* 4:5. See S. Lieberman, *Tosefta Kifshutah, Zeraim*, p. 848.
[3] *T. Taanith* 4:5.
[4] *M. Taanith* 4:4; *T. Bikkurim* 2:9; *P. T. Pesahim* IV, 30c; *T. Taanith* 4:6.
[5] *T. Taanith* 4:7-8.
[6] *M. Tamid* 2:3.
[7] *Jubilees* 21:12-14; *Testament of Levi* 9:12 and the Aramaic version (Charles, *Apocrypha and Pseudepigrapha* II, p. 364).

of incense: stacte, onycha, galbanum, and frankincense (Exodus 30:34), while a tannaitic source specifies seven more ingredients to which were added Sodom salt, ingredients designed to send up the smoke, and *anasthatico hierochuntino* (a flower not yet identified).[1] Later haggadic traditions mention the environs of Jerusalem as the area in which spice plants grew.[2]

The incense was prepared once a year and divided into 365 minas: half of each was burned in the morning, half in the afternoon. Josephus relates that Pompey, upon bursting into the Temple, saw the accumulated incense. Twice a year, the incense was sent to the mills.[3]

The water supply

The Siloam spring at the foot of the hill upon which the City of David was built did not serve as a water source in the Second Temple period. Its waters were used for the libation during the Feast of Tabernacles but the waters required for immersion, sacrificial worships and washing the courts were drawn from two other sources: stone cisterns in which the considerable amounts of rainwater in the Temple Mount area were stored and aqueducts, partly on the surface and partly in the form of tunnels which brought water from distant southern springs. Thirty-four hewn cisterns have been excavated in the area of the Temple Mount; the capacity of some of these is as much as 8,000-12,000 cubic metres. Two cisterns are mentioned in the Mishnah, the 'Golah cistern' located under the 'Golah chamber', 'over which a wheel was set; from which water enough for the whole Temple court was drawn'. In another place, the 'large cistern' is mentioned.[4] We have no way of identifying them with any of the known cisterns on the Temple Mount. As the number of visitors to the Temple increased at the end of the Hasmonaean period, and particularly during the Roman period, there was a need for additional water and a project was initiated for bringing water from a distance by aqueduct. The project necessitated elaborate planning and a great deal of work, for not only were the wells with an abundant water supply more than twenty kilometres from Jerusalem but, in addition, the minimal difference in height from Jerusalem posed problems. The first reservoir was not more than

---

[1] *T. B. Kerithoth* 6b.
[2] *Midrash Canticles* 4:13 (p. 90) and *Targum Cant.* 1:14.
[3] Jos. *War* I, 152; *T. B. Kerithoth* 6a.
[4] *M. Middoth* 5:4; *M. Erubin* 10:14.

eighty metres above the area of the Temple Mount, and because of the limited incline, it was necessary to maintain carefully the serpentine canals and aqueducts connecting the various valleys and pools in which the water was gathered, including the reservoirs known as 'Solomon's Pools', south of Bethlehem. The channels extended for sixty-eight kilometres, and their average incline was between 0.9 and 1 degree. It is difficult to comprehend how water could effectively be directed through so limited an angle of descent in their extensive channels. The water reached not only the Temple Mount area, but also the loftier Temple court and at least one of the ritual baths located near the gates.[1] Tannaitic tradition relates that in order to clean the inner court after the slaughter of the paschal lamb, the free flow of water was blocked, so that the marble floor of the court could be flooded.[2]

Daily worship in the Temple

Daily worship in the Temple consisted basically of the whole-offering of two lambs, one opening the worship in the morning and another concluding it in the afternoon. Free-will offerings and obligatory offerings were sacrificed between the daily whole-offerings: the former consisting of burnt-offerings, peace-offerings, thanks-offerings and various categories of meal-offerings, the latter including sin-offerings, guilt-offerings, and purification-offerings for both men and women.

The Torah does not mention prayers accompanying the offerings, nor are the times and occasions for the priestly benediction specified. The link between the priestly benediction and the Temple is not even mentioned. During the Second Temple period prayers and the reading of the Torah were added to the Temple service. The singing of psalms, already included in the order of service in the First Temple, was developed and expanded by the Levites during the Second Temple period. Hymns were sung daily at the time of the libation and on every feast-day.

On sabbaths, new moons, and feast-days an additional offering was sacrificed after the morning whole-offering; its precise composition varied according to the day or feast. On each feast the prescribed rites for that particular day were performed at this additional whole-offering. Examples of this include the waving of barley sheaves in the

[1] *T. B. Yoma* 31a.
[2] *T. Pesahim* 3:12.

period between Passover and Pentecost, the offering of the two loaves at Pentecost, and the libation at the Feast of Tabernacles. Some were closely associated with the altar ritual itself, while others, such as the sounding of the ram's horn at New Year and the shaking of the palm-branch during Tabernacles, had only a tenuous link with it. The prescribed festival rites, whether they were mentioned in the Torah or were introduced only during the time of the Second Temple, were related for the most part to the natural cycle of the year. 'Rabbi Akiba said: The Torah states: Bring barley at Passover, since that is the time of ripening barley, so that the grain crop may be blessed; and bring the first fruits of wheat at Pentecost, since it falls in the time of wheat when the fruits of the tree may be blessed; and bring the water libation at Tabernacles since it falls in the season of the rains, in order that you may be blessed with rains.'[1] Daily and feast-day sacrifices were accompanied by singing and music. The music was played on lyres, harps and cymbals; in addition the priests sounded two trumpets which began and concluded the singing. Later biblical sources mention all the musical instruments with which the Levites accompanied the worship; it is doubtful, however, that they were used daily during the morning and afternoon whole-offerings. Ben Sira, chapter 50 describes the procedure of the daily whole-offering and, although singing is noted, there is no mention of musical accompaniment. The baraita appended to the end of the Mishnah, tractate *Tamid*, lists the psalms which were sung each day of the week. Psalm 92 is attested to as early as the Masoretic text: 'A Psalm—A Song for the Sabbath'. Various baraitas contain evidence for particular days, some of which are verified by the Psalm superscriptions in the Septuagint. Apart from the daily chapters recited on weekdays and feast-days, the Hallel comprising psalms 113-118 was sung on feast-days. It was sung during the offering of the people's sacrifices and was accompanied by the flute, as was customary at all communal gatherings and pilgrimages.[2] Isaiah 30:29 states: 'You shall have a song as in the night when a holy feast is kept; and gladness of heart, as when one sets out to the sound of the flute to go to the mountain of the Lord, to the Rock of Israel'. The Mishnah stipulates that there should not be fewer than twelve Levites on the platform, while an unlimited number might be added. Children of the noble families of Jerusalem joined in to enhance the music. There was also a fixed number of instruments:

[1] *T. Sukkah* 3:18.
[2] *T. B. Rosh ha-Shanah* 31a; *P. T. Megillah* III, 74b; *T. B. Sukkah* 55a.

not fewer than nine lyres, two harps and one cymbal.[1] Many of the psalms which were sung by the Levites were not only hymns of praise but also meditations making for piety and good behaviour. 'Lord, who shall abide in thy tabernacle? Who shall dwell on thy holy hill? He that worketh in righteousness and speaketh the truth in his heart... (he that) putteth not out his money for usury, nor taketh reward against the innocent. He that doeth these things shall never be moved' (Ps. 15:1, 5).

Daily whole-offerings

Daily worship commenced near dawn with the resounding call of the Temple crier: 'Priests to worship, Levites to the platform, and Israelites to deputations.'[2] The priests who had slept in the chamber of the hearth, at one of the northern gates, got up and awaited the arrival of the officer responsible for the first lots by which duties relating to the daily whole-offering were distributed. Following the arrival and entry of the officer, who was a resident of Jerusalem, the first lot was cast for the task of removal of the ashes of the sacrifices consumed on the altar during the night. The officer than opened the wicket between the chamber of the hearth and the court; the priests, divided into two groups, went in the various directions of the colonnades to see that the vessels were in their appointed places, and to ascertain that the court had not been defiled. These inspections began during the time of the procurator Coponius (6-9 C.E.) following the discovery of the bones, for which the samaritans were made responsible.[3] The inspectors met again at the house of the cake makers by the Nicanor gate.

After removing the ashes and arranging the faggots of wood on the altar, the priests gathered in the chamber of hewn stone for the distribution of the main sacrificial duties. Those whose lot came up washed and sanctified their hands and feet and awaited daybreak to begin the daily worship. When the supervising officer announced that daylight had arrived, worship commenced; those to whose lot fell the preparation of the sanctuary for worship, the trimming of the candelabrum and the removal of ashes from the altar of incense went to

---

[1] M. Arakhin 2:5-6.
[2] P. T. Shekalim v, 48d.
[3] Jos. Ant. xv, 29-30. For textual corrections see S. Safrai, Pilgrimage at the Time of the Second Temple (1965; in Hebrew) p. 100.

open the gates of the sanctuary; the others went to bring the sacrificial lamb. The opening of the sanctuary gates signalled the start of the day's worship when the whole-offering was slaughtered; the locking of the gates signalled its conclusion. Any offering slaughtered while the gates were closed was invalid.[1] The gates of the sanctuary remained open the entire day, but the curtain was drawn back only on feast-days and other special days, in order that visitors might see the sanctuary.[2] Following the slaughter of the whole-offering and the arrangement of its members so that they could be brought to the altar, the priests gathered in the chamber of hewn stone and recited a prayer, the ten commandments, the *shema* and its benediction, and other prayers together with the people who had meanwhile begun to arrive.[3] After this, the priests cast lots for offering the incense. Only priests who had never burned incense participated in this lottery: 'He said to them: Ye that are new to the incense preparation come and cast lots.'[4] Since it was performed within the sanctuary and by special lottery, this was considered to be the most important of the day's rituals. Afterwards the last lot was cast for the duty of bringing the dismembered sacrifices to the altar.[5] Numerous preparations preceded the incense-offering. When the officiating priest and his deputy drew near their approach was announced; the other priests arrived to enter the sanctuary and prostrate themselves after the incense was burned while the Levites began their singing. At the same time the unclean stood before the Nicanor gate in order to be cleansed. Before the offering of the incense the people left the area in front of the entrance hall; the deputy priest entered first and scattered coals on the inner altar. 'He who offered the incense did not offer it until the officer said to him: Offer the incense. When all were gone away he offered the incense and prostrated himself and came away.'[6] During the incense-offering, the people gathered for prayer in the court. Outside the Temple people also said prayers, at this time, particularly during the afternoon incense-offering.[7]

[1] *P. T. Shekalim* v, 48d; *M. Tamid* chaps 1-3; *M. Yoma* chap. 2; *T. B. Zebahim* 55b.
[2] Jos. *Ant.* III, 128-9; *T. B. Zebahim* 55b.
[3] *M. Tamid* 5:1; *T. B. Yoma* 37b.
[4] *M. Tamid* 5:2.
[5] *M. Yoma* 2:3.
[6] *M. Kelim* 1:9; *M. Tamid* chaps. 5-6.
[7] Luke 1:10; Judith 9:1; cf. also the prayers in Acts 3:1 and *Protoevangelium Jacobi* 2:4.

After the incense-offering was completed, all the priests entered the sanctuary, prostrated themselves, came out and stood upon the porch steps in order to bestow upon the people the priestly benediction. Those priests who had participated in the incense-offering stood in the centre.[1] The priestly benediction was followed by the last parts of the ritual: the offering of the members of the sacrificed animal as a meal-offering, and the cake-offering as the sacrifice of the high priest; the wine libation on the altar marked the conclusion of the worship. Before the libation two priests blew a prolonged, a staccato and again a prolonged blast; when the priest was about to perform the libation, the prefect waved a scarf as a signal and the Levites began to sing to the accompaniment of musical instruments. There was a prescribed chapter from the Psalms for each day of the week. The daily psalm was divided into two or three parts; priests sounded the horn for each portion, and at each blast the people prostrated themselves. The end of the singing marked the conclusion of the morning whole-offering ritual.[2]

Following the completion of the morning whole-offering, the men of the deputation turned to prayer and the reading of the Torah while the priests offered the individual sacrifices of the people. At approximately three in the afternoon the afternoon whole-offering commenced. With the exception of a few changes, it resembled that of the morning. The clearing of the ashes pertained only to the morning worship; in the afternoon an additional two faggots of wood were brought to the altar in order to maintain the perpetual fire, and all seven candles of the candelabrum were lit, having only been but trimmed in the morning when one was left kindled.[3] All those whose lot had come up in the morning served in the afternoon as well; only the incense-offering was allotted anew.[4]

Following the afternoon whole-offering, the gates of the sanctuary, and probably those of the inner court as well, were locked. But the divisional priests remained in order to offer the members and the portions which they had not been able to offer during the day and which were consumed on the altar fire during the night. It was also their duty to see that the altar fire did not go out.[5] Towards evening

[1] *M. Tamid* 7:1-2.
[2] *M. Tamid* 7:3-4. For details of the order of the songs, see above.
[3] *M. Pesahim* 5:1; *M. Tamid* 6:1; *M. Yoma* 3:4.
[4] *Sifre Zuta* on Num. 30:2-3 (p. 325); but cf. *P. T. Yoma* II, 39d and *T. B. Yoma* 26a.
[5] *M. Zebahim* 9:6; *M. Berakoth* 1:1.

the priests gathered for their meals of 'holy things': the lesser 'holy things' such as peace-offerings could be eaten in any part of Jerusalem, but the 'most holy things' were eaten only in the inner court. A priest could bring home with him from his period of service only the hides of the sacrifices. The sages inveighed against the exploitation of the ordinary priests in the distribution of the hides.[1]

The morning and afternoon whole-offerings constituted the essence of the divine service and the main function of the altar. Extreme importance was attributed to the daily whole-offering; its possible cessation was viewed with great concern. The whole nation was anxious that it should continue without interruption, even during times of calamity and when the city was besieged.[2]

The sabbath

The performance of all duties pertaining to the altar was permitted on the sabbath. The altar fire was kindled, the whole-offering was slaughtered, the incense was burned and the candles were lit. On the sabbath the twelve loaves of shewbread were laid out on the golden table in the sanctuary, although the rites relating to their preparation had been performed the previous evening.[3]

Individual sacrifices were not offered on the sabbath, only the communal whole-offerings and the additional whole-offerings. The priestly division changed on the sabbath and during their morning prayer along with the people, following the slaughter of the whole-offering, a benediction was added for the outgoing division. According to another tradition, the outgoing division blessed the incoming one: 'Let him whose name dwells in this House cause to dwell amongst you love and fraternity, peace and comradeship'.[4]

Following the morning offering, the additional whole-offering of two lambs was sacrificed; the accompanying hymn prescribed was the 'Song of Moses' (Deut. 32).[5] The twelve loaves of shewbread were then laid out on the golden table in the sanctuary and the previous week's bread was removed; the frankincense which was with the new loaves was burned, thus rendering permissible the partaking of the

---

[1] *T. Menahoth* 13:18-19.
[2] Cf. the baraita at the end of *T. B. Sotah* 49b and Jos. *Ant.* III, 318-321.
[3] Sabbath customs in the Temple and the procedures involving the shewbread are found in *M.* and *T. Menahoth* chap. 11.
[4] *M. Tamid* 5:1; *T. B. Berakoth* 12a; *P. T. Berakoth* I, 3c.
[5] *T. B. Rosh ha-Shanah* 31a.

bread from the last sabbath. The laying out of the bread was done by the new division and marked the beginning of its service. The twelve loaves were equally distributed between the two divisions, although at times only a morsel was apportioned to each priest. 'Once one grabbed his portion as well as that of his fellow, wherefore they would call him grasper until his dying day'.[1]

Passover, Pentecost and Tabernacles

Temple procedures were different on the three feasts of Passover, Pentecost and Tabernacles. Aside from the additional whole-offerings and the prescribed rites of the day, sufficient time had to be allowed for offering the sacrifices of pilgrims; on these feasts, unlike sabbaths, individual sacrifices were also offered.[2] In order to ensure sufficient time for these, the daily worship commenced earlier and the removal of the ashes began at the first night watch. At midnight the Temple gates were opened to the people, and before dawn the Temple court was already filled with Israelites.[3] It seemed at times as though on these feast-days authority over the Temple passed from the jurisdiction of the priests and the Sadducean high priests, to the people, who adhered to the teaching of their Pharisaic sages and leaders. In an effort to facilitate contact between those in the city and those in the Temple, and to ease the difficulty of pilgrimage to the Temple, laws regarding uncleaness were relaxed on these feasts in Jerusalem generally and even within the Temple.[4] We have mentioned the custom of drawing back the curtain at the entrance to the sanctuary gates. This, however, was deemed insufficient and, so, the holy vessels were taken out to the Temple court in order that the people might draw near and gaze upon them.[5] On the three feasts all the priests from all the divisions could make the pilgrimage, and all of them were entitled to the festal offerings, whether brought for sacrifice or to be distributed.[6] The special feature of Passover in the Temple was the slaughter of the

---

[1] *T. Menahoth* 11:12-13; *T. B. Yoma* 39a.
[2] *M. Betzah* 2:4 records a controversy between the schools of Hillel and Shammai concerning which individual sacrifices can be offered on a feast-day. At the time of Hillel the practice of sacrificing peace-offerings, eaten on the feast-day, and whole-offerings, completely burnt on the altar, was established; cf. *P. T. Betzah* II, 61b-c and *T. B. Betzah* 20a.
[3] *M. Yoma* 1:8; Jos. *Ant.* XVIII, 29-30.
[4] *M. Hagigah* 3:6-7; *P. T. Hagigah* III, 79c; *M. Oholoth* 18:4.
[5] *M. Hagigah* 3:8; *P. Oxy.* V, 840.
[6] *M. Sukkah* 5:7.

paschal lamb by all worshippers, inhabitants of Jerusalem and pilgrims alike. Those who wished to offer a sacrifice formed groups, each of which slaughtered one paschal lamb. There were even some who thought that the paschal lamb could not be slaughtered by an individual, and that a quorum of ten was required. In any event, they formed groups which generally consisted of at least ten men.[1] We have found in the Mishnah groups including women, slaves and, of course, priests; the latter also offered their sacrifices together with the people.[2] The paschal lamb was eaten, at least during this period in households and courtyards throughout the city; as was customary, however, in all peace-offerings, it was offered in the inner court and its blood tossed on the altar. Unlike the usual animal-offerings, the paschal lamb was sacrificed by the Israelites themselves, as attested in talmudic sources and Philo, the latter with particular emphasis.[3] The lamb was sacrificed on the fourteenth day of Nisan, on the eve of Passover, at the ninth hour of the day. The sacrificial procedure is described in detail in chapter five of the mishnaic tractate, *Pesahim*. The people filled the court three times; when one group completed the slaughter, the doors were opened and the second group entered, and so forth. When the eve of Passover fell on the sabbath, the paschal lamb was similarly offered. From tannaitic sources we know that in the time of Hillel a legal decision was made that the paschal lamb could be slaughtered on the sabbath.[4]

At the close of the first festival-day, the people participated in the harvesting of the barley sheaves; these generally came from Beth Makleh beside the Kidron brook, but if, due to the late arrival of winter, it proved difficult to find ripe barley nearby, and the sheaves thus could not be harvested in this area, they were brought from afar. Tradition relates that, on one occasion, they were brought from the gardens of Zarifin in the Lydda lowland.[5] There was a dispute between Sadducees and Pharisees regarding the appropriate time for bringing the barley sheaves. The Torah states, after the laws concerning Passover, that the barley should be waved 'the morrow after the sabbath' and that a count should be made for seven weeks until 'the

---

[1] *M. Pesahim* 8:7; *Targum Ps. Jonathan* on Exodus 12:4. Cf. also Jos. *War* VI, 423-433 and *T. Pesahim* 4:3.
[2] *M. Pesahim* 8:7; 9:8.
[3] *M. Pesahim* 5:6; *P. T. Pesahim* VI, 33a. Philo, *De Spec. Leg.* II, 145; *Quaest. in Ex.* I; 10.
[4] *T. Pesahim* 4:1-2; *P. T. Pesahim* VI, 33a; *T. B. Pesahim* 66a-b.
[5] *T. Menahoth* 10:21; *M. Menahoth* 10:2.

morrow after the seventh sabbath;' when the Feast of Pentecost was to be celebrated.[1] The Sadducees interpreted 'the morrow after the sabbath' as signifying literally the day after the sabbath, the first sabbath after Passover, i.e. the very next Sunday. The Pharisees, on the other hand, interpreted the term sabbath as festival and maintained that the sheaves should be brought on the morrow of the first day of Passover, the sixteenth day of Nisan.[2] Unquestionably, at least in the time immediately before the destruction of the Temple, Pharasaic tradition prevailed and was carried out 'with much pomp' because of the Boethusians, who used to say: 'The *omer* may not be reaped at the close of a festival-day'.[3] The offering of the sheaves rendered the new crop permissible for eating.

Ancient sources do not explicitly connect Pentecost with the giving of the Torah. Acts, chapter 2 speaks of the Holy Spirit with which the Twelve Apostles were imbued on Pentecost. Recently some scholars have tried to relate this incident to the tradition linking Pentecost with the bestowal of the Torah. It may, indeed, be reasonably assumed that the tradition which saw Pentecost as the festival on which the Torah was given was known, but insofar as daily Temple worship was concerned, Pentecost was but a wheat-harvesting festival whose prescribed rite entailed bringing two wheat-loaves as a food-offering.[4] The two loaves on Pentecost rendered permissible the use of the new crop on the altar.[5] Pentecost lasted only one day, but the pilgrim was permitted to bring the obligatory sacrifices during the six days following the festival. If on Passover or Tabernacles some one did not manage to bring his sacrifices at the appointed time, or was prevented from doing so by the abundance of the sacrifices, he could bring them during the six or seven remaining days; six days of payment were therefore added to the feast of Pentecost.[6] The prescribed rite for the day involving the participation of the people was not performed on Pentecost; but from the time of the festival and including the festival day itself, the first fruits were brought. Probably some whose first fruits had ripened combined one rite with another and thus mitigated the burdens of their journey.

[1] Lev. 23:11-16.
[2] The Septuagint ad loc.; Jos. *Ant.* III, 250; Philo, *De Spec. Leg.* II, 162; *Targum Onkelos* and *Targum Ps. Jonathan* ad loc.
[3] *M. Menahoth* 10:3.
[4] Lev. 23:15-22.
[5] *M. Menahoth* 10:6.
[6] *M. Hagigah* 1:6; *T. B. Hagigah* 17a.

The bearers of first fruits brought them when their fruit ripened. For the most part they brought their fruits in caravans, all the communities of each district gathering in the city of the assembly (deputation) whence they set out on the pilgrimage. The Mishnah describes in detail how the pilgrims having baskets on their shoulders were welcomed to Jerusalem. They arrived at the Temple and read the chapter on first fruits in Deuteronomy chapter 26. The Mishnah states that, at the beginning, 'all that could recite [the prescribed words] recited them, and all that could not recite them repeated the words [after the priest]; but when these refrained from bringing [their first fruits] it was ordained that both they that could recite them and they that could not should repeat the words [after the priest].'[1] The Mishnah also notes the participation of King Agrippa in the procession of bearers of first fruits and states that he also 'would take his basket on his shoulder.'

Tannaitic literature refers to the *Feast of Tabernacles* simply as 'the Feast' and both Jewish and non-Jewish sources stress that it was celebrated with special pomp.[2] Additional sacrifices were much more numerous on Tabernacles than on other festivals, as appears in detail in the Torah. Furthermore, it was only on Tabernacles that the *Hallel* was sung on all eight days of the feast to the accompaniment of the flute.[3] The prescribed rites for Tabernacles were numerous. The Torah mentions only the rite of the palm-branch, but in the Mishnah we find a list of rites performed in the Temple. Aside from the willow-branch which formed part of the palm-branch, the willow itself was carried and lifted up around the altar and was shaken the last day of the feast. The wine-libation ceremony throughout the year was accompanied by a water-libation, not mentioned in the Torah, and the water-libation ceremonies performed throughout the festival nights in the court of women. The distinctive feature of this festival was its spirit of rejoicing: the waving of the palm-branch served as an expression of the people's joy during the procession, just as it did on other occasions of communal rejoicing.[4] The people participated in all the rites of the Feast of Tabernacles and, with the exception of the water-libation which was performed by a priest or the high priest,

---

[1] *M. Bikkurim* 1:6; *T. Sotah* 15:12. Descriptions of the bringing of first fruits appear in *M. Bikkurim* chap. 3 and Philo, *De Spec. Leg.* II, 215-222.

[2] 2 Macc. 10:6-9; Jos. *Ant.* VIII, 100; Plutarch, *Quaestiones Convivales* IV, 6,2.

[3] *M. Arakhin* 2:3; *P. T. Sukkah* V, 55a.

[4] *M. Sukkah* chaps. 4-5; 2 Macc. 10:7; cf. also John 12:13.

their role in Temple rites and customs was equal to that of the priests. They surrounded the altar with palm-branches and with willow, which is, of course, the essence of the water-libation ceremonies. During Tabernacles in particular it seemed as if Temple authority passed from the hands of its appointed officers and was invested in the people. When a Sadducean high priest seemed inclined to evade or mock the water-libation ceremony—which the Sadducees did not recognize—and poured the libation over his feet, the multitude pelted him with the citrons they held in their hands.[1] When the Sadducees tried to prevent the lifting up of the willow branch on the sabbath—an action likewise unacceptable to the Boethusians—and weighted the branches of the willow from the eve of the sabbath with large stones the people dragged the branches from under the stones and lifted them up.[2] All the people participated in the procession around the altar, (from which they were barred during the rest of the year) with the palm-branch.[3]

The water-libation ceremonies commenced at the conclusion of the first festival-day and continued throughout the mid-festival nights. Bonfires were kindled in the Temple courtyard and the people danced all night in the court of the women, while the women looked down from the galleries on three sides of the court. The Levites stood on the steps leading up to the Nicanor gate, and sang the fifteen 'Songs of Ascent' from the Book of Psalms to the accompaniment of numerous musical instruments. The people and the 'men of piety and good deeds' also sang songs and praises in addition to the psalms; some of them danced with torches in their hands. Various traditions note the dancing and singing of great sages such as Hillel the Elder and Rabban Simeon ben Gamaliel, and of others unknown to us from other sources. Tradition has even preserved the parting words customarily uttered at the conclusion of the ceremonies. The dancing continued through the night and, at dawn there was a descent *en masse* to draw water from Siloam for a libation on the altar. The expressive cries of the people during this procession, stating that they were only attached to God and no longer to the idols as their ancestors were, have also been preserved.[4]

[1] *M. Sukkah* 4:9; *T. Sukkah* 3:16.
[2] *T. Sukkah* 3:1.
[3] In *Mishnah Sukkah* 4:5 the identity of the encirclers is not given, but it is understood in this way in *P.T.* See Safrai, *Pilgrimage*, p. 191.
[4] *M. Sukkah* chap. 5; *T. Sukkah* chap. 4 and the *sugijot* in both Talmuds.

Once in seven years, after the sabbatical year, at the conclusion of the last day of the feast, a communal assembly was convened; at it chapters from the Torah, particularly from Deuteronomy, were read to the people.[1] For the Torah states: 'At the end of every seven years, at the set time of the year of release, at the feast of booths, when all Israel comes to appear before the Lord your God at the place which he will choose, you shall read this law before all Israel in their hearing'.[2] During the period of the Second Temple this assembly was not the sole occasion for reading the Torah before the people, but the Assembly met as prescribed in the Torah.

The Mishnah and Tosefta have preserved details of the rules and procedures for this assembly. A wooden platform was placed in the inner court and the king seated upon it. The scroll of the Torah was then passed from hand to hand, starting with the head of the synagogue, until it reached the high priest who presented it to the king. Upon receiving it the king read several portions and concluded with a series of blessings. Mishnah and Tosefta also describe the last 'reading assembly', which took place in the autumn of the year 63, when Agrippa II read from the Torah.[3] While the Torah does not say who was to read to the people at this assembly, the Mishnah not only attributes the reading to Agrippa but also calls the assembly 'the king's reading'. According to Josephus, however, the reader was the high priest.[4] This is quite probable, in view of the fact that during the Second Temple period, for the most part, no monarchy existed. It is possible that Josephus' emphasis upon this fact stems from his tendency to stress the importance of the priesthood in the governing of the people. According to mishnaic tradition the assembly took place 'in the court,' the reference being, probably to the spacious court of the women.[5] But a Tanna contemporaneous with the destruction of the Temple related that the assembly took place in the outer court of the Temple Mount.[6] All the sources stress the participation of women and children in the 'reading assembly.'

---

[1] *M. Sotah* 7:8 (the best mss. read 'last', not 'first').
[2] Deut. 31:10-13.
[3] *M. Sotah* 7:8; *T. Sotah* 7:13-17. In the Tosefta the flattering of Agrippa II is connected with the destruction of the Temple.
[4] Jos. *Ant.* IV, 209-211.
[5] *T. B. Sotah* 41b.
[6] *T. Sotah* 7:13.

The Day of Atonement

The unique element of this day in the Temple worship was the offering by the high priest, in atonement for the sins of the people, once a year. The liturgy, which consisted of the daily whole-offering, the additional offerings, and the prescribed rite for the day (including the annual entry into the holy of holies for the burning of incense), was performed by the high priest alone. A few auxiliary rites outside the Temple, such as the burning of the high priest's heifer and the ejection of the scapegoat, were performed by other priests or even by Israelites. The people gathered at the Temple in order to watch the liturgy conducted by the high priest, and observed in awe his entry to and exit from the sanctuary. There were some residents of Jerusalem who kept vigil all night in the Temple, along with the high priest who was forbidden to go asleep. Even before dawn, the inner court was filled with people. They did not participate in the ritual, but only observed silently the actions of the high priest. Only when the crowds heard him pronounce the name of God during his blessings and prayers did the people prostrate themselves and say: 'Blessed be the name of the glory of his kingdom.'[1]

Seven days prior to the Day of Atonement, it was customary to transfer the high priest from his house to a special chamber wherein he prepared himself and practised the ritual. Throughout the night preceding the Day of Atonement he had to remain awake to avoid being contaminated by a pollution. The people of Jerusalem came to divert him and prevent him from falling asleep; they read to him from the Scriptures or he read to them. This custom of reading the Scriptures on that evening was practised outside Jerusalem, and was continued even after the destruction of the Temple in commemoration of the Temple.[2] The high priest commenced the worship at midnight in order to have sufficient time in which to complete all the prescribed rites. The daily whole-offering and the additional whole-offerings, which took place, as did most of the other rites, in the Temple court and to a far lesser extent in the sanctuary, were made by him while clothed in special golden garments. The prescribed rites of the day, such as that of the two goats and the burning of incense in the holy of holies, were performed in white garments; from these he changed back again to golden ones for the afternoon whole-offering. Each

[1] The order of worship on the Day of Atonement is described in Mishnah and Tosefta *Yoma*. See *M. Yoma* 1:5-8; 3:3-8; 6:2-3.
[2] *M. Yoma* 1:6-7; *T. Yoma* 1:9; *T. B. Yoma* 19b.

change of garments was accompanied by an immersion and sanctification of hands and feet before and after the performance of each rite. After the whole-offering and the additional offerings, the high priest began the prescribed rite for the day with a blessing; afterwards he entered the holy of holies to burn incense. While burning the incense he said a brief prayer, preserved in various versions. The announcement of the ejection of the scapegoat into the Judaean Desert ushered in the final stage of the worship: the reading of the Torah to the people, and the concluding benedictions for the Law, for Temple-service, for thanksgiving, for the forgiveness of sin, for the Temple, for Israel, for Jerusalem, and for the priests. A prayer for all Israel completed the worship. The people then took out their books from under their garments and read from them.[1]

The high priest's worship on the Day of Atonement and his entry into the holy of holies made a great impression upon the people. Even in the time of the Temple numerous traditions and legends circulated among the people concerning the assembly. After the destruction of the Temple the legends were combined with yearnings for lost grandeur. The day's activities were given a variety of literary expressions. One of these is found in Mishnah tractate *Yoma*. During the amorite period, there already existed variants which were customarily read during the prayers for the Day of Atonement; some of the papyri discovered in Egypt from the second and third centuries contain fragments from the ritual of the Day of Atonement. In the early days of liturgical composition, various hymns were composed which served in place of the ritual.[2]

The pilgrimage

One activity which reflected clearly the people's relationship to the Temple and to Jerusalem, and their mutual influence, was the pilgrimage made on the three feasts of Passover, Pentecost and Tabernacles. At each of these feasts, tens of thousands of pilgrims from Judaea, Galilee and the Diaspora went up to the Temple. This practice had a great impact on the Jews who prepared themselves, sometimes

---

[1] *M. Yoma* 7:1; *T. Yoma* 4:18; *T. B. Yoma* 70a.
[2] *T. B. Yoma* 36b. Fragments of papyri, containing orders of worship and ritual procedures, were published by A. Cowley in *JEA* II (1917), pp. 209ff. See also I. Elbogen, *Studien zur Geschichte des jüdischen Gottesdienstes* (1907), pp. 181, 152.

during a period of years, for the day when they would visit the Temple courts; they were obliged to provide themselves with a substantial amount of money to defray the expenses of the journey and of the prescribed sacrifices of the pilgrimage. The pilgrim was still affected by his experience when he returned home, an experience reflected not only in his stories of the grandeur of the Temple and of the elevation of spirit he had experienced in the Temple and in the schools of the city, but also, at times, by his renewed devotion to the study of the Torah.[1] The pilgrimage exerted a considerable influence on the life of the city. First of all, the economic influence of the pilgrimage was notable: the pilgrims spent a great deal of money during their sojourn in the city for their expenses as well as for charity. The city had prepared to provide accomodation for the pilgrims, many of whom, particularly those from the Diaspora, remained in the city for a lengthy period. It was especially during the pilgrimages that Jerusalem was the centre of Jewish life; in its streets could be heard the many languages and dialects of Diaspora Jews and their various currencies were used in commerce.[2]

Josephus relates that the riots against the Roman government often erupted during the feasts.[3] It was not only the fact that tens of thousands converged upon Jerusalem which made possible the riots and rebellions; the very gathering of the masses in Jerusalem heightened religious and national fervour which sharpened the resentment against foreign rule. Teachers of the Law, preachers, and prophets were attracted to Jerusalem throughout the year, and they invariably found a ready audience among those who had made the pilgrimage to Jerusalem. The feasts afforded an unusual opportunity for anyone who had some message to the people, not only because there was a large audience in the city, but because the pilgrimage, the purification before visiting the Temple, and the prostrations before God gave rise to an exaltation of the spirit and a heightening of religious fervour.

The Torah says: 'Three times in the year shall all your males appear before the Lord.'[4] However, this biblical injunction was not interpreted as obliging every male to go up to the Temple three times a year in the Second Temple period. Nowhere in tannaitic literature is mention made of such an obligation. The commandment to make a

---

[1] See esp. Hoffmann, *Midrash Tannaim*, p. 78.
[2] Acts chap. 2; *T. Shekalim* 2:13.
[3] Jos. *War* I, 88; II, 224.
[4] Exod. 23:17; 34:23; Deut. 16:16.

pilgrimage fell in the category of 'a command which has no limit', i.e. a positive action to be encouraged but not demanded.[1] These biblical verses were interpreted to mean when a man makes a pilgrimage, he has certain obligations. These obligations are listed in the Babylonian Talmud. They include: an appearance before God in the Temple, festal celebration and rejoicing. In fact, each of these obligations involved making a sacrifice. 'Appearance' (ראיה) meant also a burnt-offering because of another biblical verse which reads 'and they shall not appear before the Lord empty handed.'[2] The two other commands were also understood as sacrifices, in this case peace-offerings. Many legends show us that even exemplary sages and scrupulous observers of the Law did not regard the pilgrimage as an obligation to be fulfilled thrice yearly. In mishnaic tradition it was seen as no more than one of the 'immeasurable things'.[3] People went up to Jerusalem every year or once in several years, or even only once in their lifetimes. This reality is reflected in Luke chapter two, stating that Jesus' parents went every year to Jerusalem, and suggesting that they followed the general rule. The gospel of John mentions several visits of Jesus to Jerusalem, but there is no evidence that Jesus was following an established halakah, obliging a pilgrimage three times a year. The Synoptics mention only one visit of Jesus to Jerusalem on Passover.

Even if there were no obligation to make the pilgrimage on each feast, it is certain that thousands from the Land of Israel and from the Diaspora did go to Jerusalem and it is probably safe to assume that there was hardly a community in Palestine or the Diaspora from which some members did not go up, either in large or small numbers.

In chapter four we gave some references to the pilgrimage from the various parts of the Diaspora,[4] but of course the greatest number of pilgrims were from Palestine. Of these the largest number came from nearby Judaea and Edom. The sundry testimonies and traditions which tell of whole cities going, refer primarily to Judaea.[5] There is a dearth of information on pilgrimages from Transjordan, but in general we have little information about its Jewish communities. In his description of the War of Varus, Josephus affirms that, for the feast

---

[1] *T. B. Pesahim* 70b; *Midrash Tanhuma* on Ex. 29:1 (p. 102), *M. Peah* 1:1.
[2] *T. B. Hagigah* 6a-b.
[3] Ibid.
[4] See chapter four, pp. 191-8.
[5] Jos. *War* II, 43; 515; *Cant. Rabba* 7.

of Pentecost, a countless number of pilgrims came from Galilee, Edom, Jericho as well as Transjordan.[1]

There is abundant evidence of pilgrimages from Galilee, and of the great devotion of Galileans in general to the Temple. The Palestinian Talmud and the Palestinian midrashim give accounts of legends and miracles which touched both the simple and the wise on their pilgrimages to Jerusalem. Such stories are told about a minister of the synagogue in Migdal Zabaaia, the women of Sepphoris, and Rabbi Hanina ben Dosa, a pious sage of the city of Araba of Lower Galilee.[2] Various halakic traditions also connect legal decisions with such incidents as happened with a man from Meron on his visit to Jerusalem[3] or with a man who spent the Day of Atonement in Jerusalem.[4] The Gospel according to Luke speaks at length of the pilgrimage undertaken by Jesus and his parents together with acquaintances and friends, and others from Galilee.[5] Luke 13:1 tells of Galileans whose blood Pontius Pilate mixed with the blood of their sacrifices. Most probably they made the pilgrimage on one of the feasts and were killed in the Temple while offering their sacrifices. Josephus, too, frequently mentions pilgrims from Galilee and even notes the roads they were wont to travel. We learn from his description that for the most part they went through Samaria, Ginaea and Sychar, on their three-day journey from Galilee to Jerusalem. This route is not only the shortest possible one; it also eliminates the climbs and descents otherwise necessary, and passes through populated districts supplied with water. However, this route crossed the land of the Samaritans, a fact which led to violent confrontations and consequently caused many to prefer other routes. An alternative route followed the Jordan Valley to Jericho and from there the ascent would be made to Jerusalem. A third way went through the foothills of Mount Ephraim from Kefar Othnai to Antipatris and thence to Jerusalem.[6] How many pilgrims came? Our sources speak of the numerous pilgrims who filled the city and its environs. But can their number be estimated? Several scholars have attempted to do so on the basis

[1] E.g. Jos. *War* II, 43; cf. S. Klein, *Jewish Transjordan* (1925; in Hebrew), pp. 25-31.
[2] *P. T. Maaser Sheni* V, 56a; *Eccles. Rabba* I.
[3] *T. Baba Bathra* 10:12.
[4] *M. Yoma* 6:3.
[5] Luke 2:41ff.
[6] Jos. *Life* 269; Jos. *War* II, 223-232; *Ant.* XX, 118. See G. H. Dalman, *Orte und Wege Jesu* (1924), p. 167; 222-56; D. Chwolson, *Das Letzte Passamahl Christi* (1892); J. Jeremias, *Jerusalem zur Zeit Jesu* (3rd ed. 1963), pp. 90-7.

of the description in tractate *Pesahim*, chapter 5, which says that, during the slaughter of the Paschal lamb, the court was filled three times with sacrifices, and that, at the third time, it was not filled to capacity. They calculated the area of the court, estimated the density of the crowd, and multiplied the number of sacrifices by ten, for both Josephus and the Talmud relate that each sacrifice was offered by at least ten individuals. According to these calculations, Chwolson set the number of pilgrims from outside the city at 100,000, while Jeremias suggested 125,000, after subtracting 55,000 Jerusalemites. It seems, however, impossible to determine the extent of the area in which the celebrants congregated. We do not know which areas outside the court of the Israelites, whose area was only 11 × 135 cubits, the celebrants were permitted to enter, nor do we know what buildings in it limited its area. Most important of all, we cannot determine the density of the crowd; the quota ten persons for each sacrifice is certainly inadequate even for guesswork, for it is quite possible that the participants offering each sacrifice were only seven or eight in number, or yet as many as fifteen. Calculations on the basis of the rabbinic reports are as high as about twelve million,[1] and Josephus gives the more modest figure of nearly three million.[2] However, such estimates cannot be reconciled with the area of Jerusalem, nor with the description of the procedures at Passover in the Temple, as found in the Mishnah.

In chapter three of the tractate *Bikkurim*, the Mishnah discussed the procedure of bringing the first fruits: 'all the smaller towns that belonged to the deputation (district in the Tosefta) gathered in the town of the deputation and spent the night in the street of the town,' and while singing hymns of pilgrimage from the book of psalms and other books of the Bible, to the accompaniment of the flute, they went up to Jerusalem preceded by a decorated ox. The Mishnah describes the bearers of first fruits, but the description is mainly that of pilgrims in general and portions of the same description are found in shortened portrayals of pilgrims in various sources, as early as Jeremiah and also in talmudic literature.[3] Pilgrimage in caravans, both from the Land of Israel and the Diaspora, did not prevent individuals or families going by themselves.[4] Women also participated in the

---

[1] *T. Pesahim* 4:3.
[2] Jos. *War* VI, 423-426 (see the variant readings).
[3] Jer. 31:6; *Agadath Cant.* (pp. 28; 108); *Lam. Rabba* I (pp. 80-1).
[4] *T. Bikkurim* 2:12.

pilgrimage, as did the entire family including sons and daughters. Women were not obliged to offer sacrifices at the pilgrimage, but brought their own personal sacrifices when it was incumbent upon them. They also participated in the family offerings for they too were obliged to join in the festal rejoicing.[1]

Many pilgrims arrived before the feast, particularly those from outside Palestine who had to ritually cleanse themselves of the impurity of the Diaspora for a period of seven days. Several days before the feast the city was already full of pilgrims who were cleansing themselves or who came early in order to spend extra time in Jerusalem.[2]

Those who came to adore had to offer two sacrifices: a vision-sacrifice and a peace-offering as a happy obligation. This traditional practice is stressed numerous times in tannaitic literature and is the main concern of tractate *Hagigah*. But there was also a tradition which interpreted 'and they shall not appear before the Lord empty handed', part of the precept of pilgrimage, not only as an obligation to offer sacrifice but also as an obligation to bring alms, or primarily the latter. Some midrashim and targums interpret this verse as 'empty of alms' or 'also empty of alms.'[3] In any event, in the accounts of the pilgrimage undertaken by Jesus and his entourage the act of alms-giving is noted to the exclusion of sacrificial offerings.

The pilgrims slept in the city itself, in the nearby villages and in tents around the city.[4] The sources show that one of the aims of the pilgrimage was to make friends when brother believers met. And both custom and legal tradition stressed this aim. During the feast, legal tradition regarding laws of impurity was relaxed both inside the Temple and outside it, in order that the strict customs relating to purity would not prevent people from meeting each other. House-holders in Jerusalem were forbidden to take rent from the pilgrims, and they received as a gift only the skins from the sacrifices. The pleasant atmosphere pervading the city, among the pilgrims and inhabitants alike, found expression in the tannaitic traditions which tells of miracles which happened 'to our forefathers in Jerusalem... A man did not say to another, I have not found a bed to sleep upon in Jerusalem; a man never said to another the place is too small for me

---

[1] *T. B. Hagigah* 6b; *T. B. Pesahim* 89a; Jos. *Ant.* XI, 109.
[2] Jos. *War* VI, 290; I, 229; John 11:55; Acts 21:26-27.
[3] *Sifre Deut.* 143 (p. 196); *Midrash Tannaim*, p. 158; *Targum Ps. Jonathan* on Deut. 16:16.
[4] Jos. *Ant.* XVII, 213-217; *T. B. Pesahim* 80a.

to sojourn in Jerusalem.'[1] The worshippers could spend the night outside the city, but on the day they brought the paschal lamb or offered their sacrifice they had to remain in Jerusalem through the night. Before the feast Jesus stays outside Jerusalem, but with the approach of Passover he commands his disciples to go to one of the inhabitants of the city and fix a place for their meal. The townsman is not necessarily a follower of Jesus but they are welcomed to his house as a matter of course.[2]

We have not found any clear legal tradition which shows that pilgrims were obliged to remain throughout the seven days of Passover and the eight days of Tabernacles, but many traditions from the time of the Temple take it for granted that a pilgrim remained until the end of the feast-days. The words 'and thou shalt turn in the morning and go unto thy tent' (Deuteronomy 16:7) were interpreted as indicating an obligation on the part of the pilgrim to remain throughout all the feast and return 'to his tent' only when the week was over.[3] The Gospel according to Luke (2:43) speaks of the return of Jesus' parents from Jerusalem 'when they had fulfilled the days', in the plural.

During their sojourn in Jerusalem the pilgrims could avail themselves of the public and juridical institutions of Jerusalem, which functioned during the week to attend to their needs.

The rôle of the Temple in the life of the people

The Jewish community which grew up with the return to Jerusalem, was formed for the construction of the altar and the Temple. The spiritual and communal life of subsequent times were rooted in the Temple and its divine worship.

In the Second Temple period, worship in the form of sacrificial rites did not constitute the sole element in the religious life of Israel. The synagogue and the *bet midrash* played an important role and communal leadership was not solely in the hands of the priests. Rather, these institutions, communal leadership and social activities became associated with the Temple and drew their authority from it. There were synagogues and schools in Jerusalem and in the Temple courtyards. During weekdays and feasts the ritual of the daily whole-

---

[1] Jos. *Ant.* IV, 203-204; *M. Hagigah* 3:6-7; *P. T. Hagigah* III, 79d; *T. B. Hagigah* 26a-b; *T. B. Megillah* 26a; *Aboth de Rabbi Nathan* Version A, 35 (p. 104).
[2] *Sifre Num.* 151; *Sifre Deut.* 134; Matt. 26:17-18.
[3] *M. Zebahim* 11:7 as understood in *T. B. Zebahim* 97a; *T. Sukkah* 4:17; *Targum Ps. Jonathan* on Deut. 16:7. See Safrai, *Pilgrimage*, pp. 200-1.

offering was linked with the divine service of the synagogue, with the gathering of the priests for prayer and the recitation of the *shema* or with the reading of the Torah by the high priest and the deputations. The origin of the synagogue should be seen in the gatherings of the people in the Temple courtyards during the time of Ezra and Nehemiah, when the Torah was read to them. Synagogue worship did not replace the sacrifices; rather it complemented them and added new dimensions to religious and social experience. At any rate, the prayers were linked to the Temple service and were timed to coincide with the sacrifices; worshippers turned to face Jerusalem and the Temple.[1]

The other liturgical elements of the synagogue which existed during the time of the Second Temple also have their origin in the Temple service; only later did they spread to the synagogues. The origin of the priestly benediction is certainly linked with the Temple and was recited at the completion of the daily whole-offering. The same applies to the sounding of the horn, the waving of the palm-branch, and the reading of the *hallel*, all of which we found to be part of the sacrificial offerings and whose original function was limited to the sacrifices.[2]

The study of the Torah was also largely related to the life of the Temple. We have seen that there was a *bet midrash* within the courtyards of the Temple. Tradition relates that Rabbi Johanan ben Zakkai used to 'sit and teach in the shadow of the sanctuary'.[3] The Gospels note that Jesus taught daily in the Temple and that after his death the people of the Jewish Christian community gathered in the Temple, where some of them taught the people.[4]

The Temple is variously depicted as a place for the cultivation, preservation and dissemination of the holy scriptures and of historical narratives and genealogies. Problems related to the transmission of the text and authenticity of various books of the Bible were examined in the Temple; copyists and correctors sat in the Temple and worked to supply books to those who needed them in the Land of Israel and in the Diaspora.[5] There was a bible in the Temple called 'the book of the court' on the basis of which books were corrected. It was read on festal occasions and was among the booty which Titus took to Rome.

[1] See *M. Berakoth* 4:5-6.
[2] See also Alon, *Studies the History of Israel* I (1967; in Hebrew), pp. 106-14.
[3] *T. B. Pesahim* 26a.
[4] Luke 21:37; Acts chaps. 2-4.
[5] Jos. *Against Apion* I, 33; *Ant.* V, 61; III, 38; IV, 303; *Sifre Deut.* 356 (p. 423); *P. T. Shekalim* IV, 48a; II Macc. 2:13-15.

When Titus burst into the Temple, not only the 'book of the court' but other books were also carried off; Josephus subsequently succeeded in acquiring some of them.[1]

In chapter seven we saw to what extent law and communal life were related to the Temple. The Temple encompassed numerous spheres of activity but in the eyes of the people it constituted primarily the divine dwelling-place of the God of Israel which set them apart from other nations. The religious and social values and institutions which became linked to the Temple, did not detract from the image of the Temple as the only all-embracing place for divine worship in the form of sacrificial offerings in the name of the nation and for the welfare of all mankind. But even in the religious realm of the individual, a large place was set aside for Temple worship. The offering of the sacrifices and the ritual cleansing involved atoned for the individual's transgressions and served as a framework for his spiritual elevation and purification.

The Temple, its vessels and even the high priest's vestments were depicted as representing the entire universe and the heavenly hosts;[2] and the Temple constituted a blessing for all the nations of the world.[3] It was firmly believed that the Temple was destined to exist eternally, just like heaven and earth. The Temple's long existence during more than 600 years and its established procedures strengthened and intensified this feeling. Viewed within this context, it is possible to understand the devotion to the Temple which the people evinced during times of peace, and the fervour with which they defended it during the war which led to its destruction, as well as the agony and despair and spritual vacuum which was created within the nation when the Temple was burned down. With the destruction of the Temple the image of the universe was rendered defective, the established framework of the nation was undermined and a wall of steel formed a barrier between Israel and its heavenly Father.[4]

BIBLIOGRAPHY

A description of the Temple of Herod according to the archeological findings has been given by F. J. HOLLIS, *The Archaeology of Herod's Temple*, 1934. The material from the Mishnah on the Temple of Herod

[1] *M. Moed Katan* 3:4; *P. T. Sanhedrin* II, 20c; Jos. *War* VII, 150; 162.
[2] Philo, *Vita Mosis* II, 117-126; Jos. *Ant.* III, 179-87; *War* V, 117-8; *T.B. Sukkah* 55b.
[3] *T. B. Sukkah* 55b. [4] *T. B. Berakoth* 32b.

is discussed by L. H. VINCENT, 'Le Temple Hérodien d'après la Michna' in *RB* LXI (1954), pp. 5-35, 398-418. The talmudic material is found in O. HOLTZMANN, *Die Mischna Middot*, 1913, and in the article, 'Beth Mikdash' of *Encyclopaedia Talmudit* III, 1951, pp. 224-241. A survey of modern research is presented by M. AVI-YONAH, 'The Second Temple' in *Sefer Jerushalajim* (1956), pp. 392-418. On the place of the Temple in the life of the people see S. SAFRAI, *The Temple in the Second Temple Period* (1959; in Hebrew). On the earlier part of this period see J. W. DOEWE, 'Le domaine du temple de Jérusalem' in *La literature Juive entre Tenach et Michna*, ed. by W. C. VAN UNNIK (1974), pp. 118-63. On priests and Levites and the Temple services during the last years of its existence see A. BÜCHLER, *Die Priester und der Cultus im letzten Jahrzehnt des jerusalemischen Tempels* (1895). For the role of women and the women's court in the Temple see the unconvincing article by A. BÜCHLER, 'The Fore-Court of Women and the Brass Gate in the Temple of Jerusalem' in *JQR*, Old Series X (1898), pp. 678-718. On the question of the relationship between 24 districts in the Land of Israel and the 24 deputations see S. KLEIN; *Land of Judah*, (1939; in Hebrew), pp. 202-19.

On the Temple worship and its rejection in early Christianity, see S. LOWE, 'The confutation of Judaism in the Epistle of Barnabas' in *JJS* XI, 1960, pp. 1-33. On the Temple treasury see A. SCHWARZ, 'Die Schatzkammer des Tempels in Jerusalem', in *MGWJ* LXIII (1919), pp. 227-252. On the daily worship in the Temple, see S. SAFRAI 'The Ritual in the Second Temple' in *Sefer Jerushalajim* (1956), pp. 369-91. On the division of duties in the daily worship see A. BÜCHLER, 'Zur Geschichte des Tempelkultus in Jerusalem' in *Chwolson-Festschrift* (1899), pp. 1-41; id. 'Zur Geschichte der Tempelmusik und der Tempel psalmen' in *ZAW* XIX (1899), pp. 96-133, 329-44; XX (1900), pp. 97-135 discusses the Temple singing, and L. J. LIEBREICH, 'The Hymns of the Levites for the Days of the Week' in *Eretz-Israel* III (1954), pp. 170-3. On the water supplies see M. HEEKER, 'Water Supply of Jerusalem in Ancient Times' in *Jedioth* IV-VI (1937-9) and his survey in *Sefer Jerushalajim*, pp. 191-218. On the wood sacrifices see J. N. EPSTEIN, 'Die Zeiten des Holzopfers' in *MGWJ* LXXVIII (1934), pp. 97-103; and against his view, S. SAFRAI, *Pilgrimage at the Time of the Second Temple* (1965; in Hebrew), pp. 220-4; 238-9. On pilgrimage see S. SAFRAI, 'Pilgrimage to Jerusalem at the End of the Second Temple Period' in *Studies of the Jewish Background of the New Testament* (1969), pp. 10-21.

Chapter Eighteen
The Synagogue

The synagogue was one of the most stabilizing institutions in Jewish society in the Land of Israel and in the Diaspora during the era of the Second Temple and afterwards. It was where townsfolk or villagers assembled for divine service, and the centre towards which all religious, cultural and social life gravitated. This was primarily due to the special character of divine service in the synagogue. The worshippers were actively involved in large numbers, since they took it in turn to recite the prayers and read Scripture, and on all such occasions there had to be a quorum of at least ten men. Another notable characteristic was that the synagogue service took place frequently, at fixed, regular intervals. Men, women and children came to the synagogue every sabbath, as well as on feast-days and special occasions. Later, many were to come there every day, and sometimes up to three times a day. On the sabbath, the congregation stayed for hours, praying, listening to Scripture reading and the explanations given by a sage or by some member of the public. People also came to listen to Scripture reading outside the fixed time of prayer on sabbaths and working-days. The synagogue also served as a town hall for such community affairs as fund-raising or deciding matters of public interest. Very often public institutions such as schools, tribunals and guest-houses were attached to it, not from any intrinsic need, but because in fact it provided facilities either in the building itself or in some neighbouring rooms.[1]

But the main factor in the significance of the synagogue was that it was regarded as the assembly of the local Jewish community, giving expression to the civic and communal spirit of the people. The word synagogue should not be taken as meaning just 'meeting-house.' It stands for the people, the community, the congregation and the place where they assembled. Anyone wishing to speak of three members of the Jewish community, spoke of them as 'three members of the synagogue.'[2] When people met for prayer and Scripture reading, this

---

[1] See chapter nineteen, pp. 938ff. and the end of this chapter.
[2] *T. Sanhedrin* 1:2; *T. Bekhoroth* 3:8 and elsewhere. The LXX usually translates

too was 'public business,' a matter of significance for public order. Tannaim at the end of the first century C.E. did not agree on the question of the additional prayers to be said on the sabbath, the new moon and feast-days. Some held that only the congregation was competent to say these prayers. Others held that where there was a local congregation, the individuals were not obliged to say the additional prayers.[1] Just as the Temple had been the centre of national life, so too the synagogue was the rallying-point for community life in the towns and villages of the Land of Israel and the Diaspora.

Origins

By the beginning of the first century C.E., synagogues existed in great numbers throughout the whole of the Land of Israel and the Diaspora, and even in Jerusalem itself. The Gospels refer to synagogues in Nazareth and Capernaum and in Galilee in general.[2] Josephus then tells us that there were synagogues in Tiberias, Dor and Caesaraea Maritima.[3] Other literary sources make it clear that there were synagogues in all parts of the Diaspora. Philo, for instance, says that there were many in various quarters of Alexandria and Rome.[4] Paul's travels are very instructive on the matter of synagogues throughout the Hellenistic or Roman world. The Acts of the Apostles speak of synagogues in Damascus and in Salamis, a town in Cyprus (in the plural both times), and of others in Antioch, Iconium and Ephesus in Asia Minor, and in Thessalonica, Beroea, Athens and Corinth on the Greek mainland.[5] First century statements refer to synagogue customs in Jerusalem,[6] and a long list of the synagogues there belonging to Diaspora Jews can be drawn up on the basis of the Acts of the Apostles and rabbinic sources.[7] There is also an inscription in Greek from Mount Ophel, which records the building of a synagogue there for the

---

community (עדה) by συναγωγή. Hellenistic Jewish inscriptions in the Land of Israel and the Diaspora utilize the blessing, εἰρήνη τῆ συναγωγῆ, in place of 'peace upon Israel', found in Hebrew and Aramaic inscriptions: so in *CII* no. 867 (Gerasa).

[1] *M. Berakoth* 4:7.
[2] Matt. 4:23; 13:54; Mark 1:21; Luke 4:44; 7:5; 8:41; 13:10; John 6:59.
[3] Jos. *Life* 277; *Ant.* XIX, 300; *War* II, 285.
[4] *Legatio ad Gaium* 132, 156, 311; *In Flaccum* 47.
[5] Acts 9:2; 13:5, 14; 14:1; 17:1, 10, 16-17; 18:4-7, 19-26; 19:8.
[6] *T. Sukkah* 2:10 and parallels.
[7] *T. Megillah* 3:6; *T. B. Megillah* 26a; Acts 6:9.

use of pilgrims from abroad.[1] In the hyperbolic haggadic style, the Palestinian Talmud speaks of a multitude of synagogues in Jerusalem.[2] Then there is the archaeological evidence from the period before and shortly after 70 C.E. And many halakoth, some from the earlier period, deal with the obligation of building and equipping a synagogue. From all this, it might well be argued that there was a synagogue wherever an appreciable number of Jews were living, even in towns or villages where the majority of the population was non-Jewish, as could happen in the Land of Israel as well as in the Diaspora. The same impression is given by the passage in the Acts of the Apostles where the discussion on the obligation of Gentile converts to keep the Law is reported: 'For from early generations Moses has had in every city those who preach him, for he is read every sabbath in the synagogues' (Acts 15:21).

When did the synagogue originate as an institution? The Talmud speaks of synagogues during the Babylonian exile, and says that the first group of exiles, under Jehoachin, brought stones from Jerusalem, which were then incorporated into the buildings.[3] This tradition implies that the synagogue was a substitute for the Temple and had its origin during the first exile. This view was expressly stated in the ancient interpretation of a text in Ezekiel, 'Though I removed them far off among the nations, and though I scattered them among the countries, yet I have been a sanctuary to them for a while in the countries where they have gone' (Ezek. 11:16), which was taken to refer to synagogues and houses of study in Babylon.[4] This view is echoed in various forms even in modern research, but remains completely devoid of foundation.[5] There is no proof at all for the existence of any institution for divine service during the Babylonian exile or at the beginning of the Second Temple period, and we know of no arrangements which would have provided the fundamentals of such a service. As will be explained later, such forms of divine worship as were retained were not meant to fill the vacuum created by the destruction of the Temple and the cessation of sacrificial rites.

There is likewise no reason to think that the expression 'the house of the people' (בית העם), in Jeremiah 39:8, has anything to do with the

---

[1] R. Weill, *La cité de David* I (1920), pp. 1ff; T. Reinach, 'L'inscription de Theodotos' in *REJ* LXXI (1920), pp. 46-56; *CII* no. 1404.

[2] *P. T. Megillah* III, 73d and parallels.

[3] *T. B. Megillah* 29a; *Igeret Sherira Gaon* (ed. Lewin), pp. 72-3.

[4] *T. B. Megillah* 29a; this is also the understanding of the Targum ad loc.

[5] J. Wellhausen, *Israelitische und jüdische Geschichte* (1901), pp. 149ff.; 196ff.

origin of the synagogue, though this is held by some scholars.[1] The term was used to refer to the synagogue in later times, and the verse came to be interpreted then as referring to the synagogue.[2] But this meaning is not in the text, which is not speaking of a place of divine worship and is totally silent on the form of worship offered in the synagogue.

It seems to have been the general opinion of Jews in the first century C.E. that the synagogue and its discipline was a very ancient institution, dating from the time of Moses, who according to talmudic tradition, established the institution of reading Scripture on sabbaths and feast-days.[3] Philo and Josephus also affirm that the practice of meeting in the synagogue each sabbath for the reading of Scripture was instituted by Moses.[4] The Acts of the Apostles, (15:21, quoted above), speaks to more or less the same effect. The earliest archaeological evidence for the existence of the synagogue comes from Egypt, about 250 B.C.E., where several inscriptions have been found.[5] One from Lower Egypt is particularly interesting.[6] Though its exact provenance is unknown, and its date is later, it is clear that it replaced an earlier one from the time of Ptolemy Euergetes, apparently Ptolemy III, 246—221 B.C.E., who granted the synagogue the right to afford asylum.[7] The granting of such a right in this early period shows that the institution of the synagogue existed some time before the date even of the earlier inscription.

One can readily understand how some scholars could assume that Diaspora Jews who were living far away from the Temple were responsible for the establishment of the synagogue system.[8] But it is very doubtful whether the fact that the earliest archaeological evidence is from the Diaspora suffices to settle the question, since the absence of evidence elsewhere may be accidental. Synagogues were opened in the Diaspora in the last centuries of the Second Temple, but synagogues were also set up in the Land of Israel and in Jerusalem

---

[1] L. Löw, 'Der synagogale Ritus' in *Gesammelte Schriften* IV (1899), pp. 1-71.
[2] *T. B. Shabbath* 32a; Rashi and David Kimchi cite this explanation from a midrash now lost.
[3] *M. Megillah* 3:6; *P. T. Megillah* IV, 75a.
[4] *De Vita Mosis* II, 215-6; *De opificio mundi* 128; Jos. *Against Apion* II, 175.
[5] The list of these inscriptions is found in Schürer, II, pp. 499-500. and in Krauss. pp. 263-265.
[6] *CII* no. 1449.
[7] This is the interpretation of Schürer, ibid. See also the bibliography in *CII* no. 1449.
[8] See esp. M. Friedländer, *Synagoge und Kirche in ihren Anfängen* (1908).

itself. It is thought that there was a synagogue even within the precincts of the Temple. In any case, along with the sacrificial rites of the Temple, there were arrangements for divine service along the lines of what was done in the synagogue, with prayers and Scripture reading.[1] The primary and seminal element in the synagogue was not prayer but Scripture reading. When the synagogue and its functioning are mentioned in tannaitic sources, they highlight Scripture reading and do not mention prayer. We hear that the synagogue is a place from which all frivolity is excluded. It is not to be used as a shelter from the heat or the cold or from rain. People may not eat, drink, sleep or walk about in it, and they may not use it to do business. The synagogue is for the reading, studying and expounding of Scripture, and the place where funeral orations over important people are delivered.[2] As reflected in the Gospel stories about Jesus in the synagogue or those of the Acts of the Apostles about Paul, the synagogue was a place for reading and expounding Scripture. We get the same impression from the Mount Ophel inscription mentioned above: 'Theodotus the son of Vettenus, priest and *archisynagogus*, son of the *archisynagogus* and grandson of an *archisynagogus* built the synagogue for the reading of the Torah and the study of the commandments ...'.[3] It must be noted on the other hand that Scripture reading was not part of the services in the Temple before the Babylonian exile. It was only introduced in the era of the Second Temple, and even when it had become customary on certain occasions, it was not an essential part of the Temple services. In other words, Scripture reading was not intended to be some sort of substitute for the Temple liturgy and its sacrificial rites. It was a supplement to the worship paid in the Temple, and corresponded to a deepening of religious feelings.

We may not be far out if we see the initial stages of the institution of the synagogue in the public assemblies under Ezra, where the main purpose was the reading of the Torah, though there is also mention of prayer.[4] From such assemblies, which were only convoked for special purposes and for brief periods, with nothing of a regular fixture about them, the synagogue may well have developed, that is, a place was appointed where the community should meet for Scripture reading

[1] *M. Taanith* 4:1-2; *M. Tamid* 5:1; *M. Yoma* 7:1; but cf. S. Zeitlin in *JQR* LIII (1962-3), pp. 168ff.
[2] *T. Megillah* 3:7 and parallels.
[3] See p. 910, n. 1.
[4] See Neh. chaps. 8, 9, 13. For the combining of prayer with readings in the Torah, see Neh. 9:3.

and prayer, at first on feast-days and sabbaths, and later on working-days. If our surmise is correct, the institution did not begin in the Diaspora but in the very precincts of the Temple and in Jerusalem itself.[1] This is not to affirm that Ezra founded the synagogue, but merely that the elements on which it was based and from which it developed may be traced back to certain activities of Ezra.

Nomenclature

In the Hebrew of the Talmud, the synagogue nearly always appears as 'the place of assembly' (בית הכנסת), with the corresponding plural.[2] Very often it is simply designated as 'assembly' (כנסת) without 'place' or 'house of' before it.[3] The Talmud also speaks of the 'head of the synagogue' and the '*hazzan* of the synagogue', and it is hard to say whether the officials in question have to do with the synagogue itself, or rather with municipal and community affairs.[4] In Aramaic the term בי כנישתא appears, and more often, simply כנישתא (place of assembly, assembly).[5] The Greek word is συναγωγή, which the Septuagint uses for the עדה and קהל (assembly, congregation) of the Hebrew Bible. The New Testament practically always says συναγωγή whether referring to the Land of Israel or the Diaspora.[6] Josephus always calls the place of worship 'the synagogue'.[7] In the Acts of the Apostles (twice), in Hellenistic Judaism and in papyri and inscriptions a further term occurs, προσευχή, meaning 'prayer' and then 'place of prayer'. This is the term mostly used by the Jews of Egypt, almost exclusively in their early inscriptions and papyri, from c. 250 B.C.E. on[8], and predominantly in such writings as 3 Maccabees and the works of Philo.[9] But the term is not

[1] Cf. M. Rosenmann, *Der Ursprung der Synagoge und ihre allmählige Entwicklung* (1902).
[2] In the singular: *M. Berakoth* 7:3; *M. Bikkurim* 1:4; *M. Nedarim* 5:5; in the plural: *M. Terumoth* 11:10; *M. Pesahim* 4:4; *T. Taanith* 2:4; *T. Megillah* 4:22, etc.
[3] *P. T. Nazir* VII, 56a; *T. B. Megillah* 25a.
[4] *T. Megillah* 4:21; *T. B. Yoma* 11a; *Semahoth* 14:14; cf. *M. Yoma* 7:1.
[5] *P. T. Peah* VIII, 21b; *Lev. Rabba* 22 (p. 511); *T. B. Yebamoth* 65b, etc.
[6] Matt. 4:23; Luke 7:5; Acts 6:9 (in Jerusalem); 13:5 (Cyprus); 14:1 (Iconium) and others.
[7] Jos. *Ant.* XIX, 300; *War* II, 285; for the Diaspora, *War* III, 44.
[8] For the papyri, see *CPJ* nos. 129, 134, 138, 432; the inscriptions appear also in *CPJ* III, Appendix I, nos. 1434, 1440-4, 1449.
[9] 3 Macc. 7:20. Philo uses the term *proseuche* except when referring to the Essenes: see *In Flaccum* 41, 45, 122; *Legatio ad Gaium* 152. The exception is found in *Quod omnis probus liber sit* 81.

confined to Egypt. It is also found in Palestinian sources and in
various sources referring to the Diaspora, including the Acts of the
Apostles.[1] Doubt attaches to all efforts to explain the different
usages, as for instance by trying to indicate different types of
synagogue. Originally perhaps the words had distinct meanings, or
varied according to the locality. But as things stand, it is impossible
to tell. In some inscriptions, 'place of prayer' means the synagogue,
and 'synagogue' means the congregation and the public in general.

No Jewish community was without this important institution, and so
it is not surprising that it should be called by various names, in Jewish
and other writings.[2] But only two special usages need be mentioned.
In one text, Josephus calls the synagogue in Antioch τὸ ἱερόν (temple,
sanctuary) as well as συναγωγή (synagogue).[3] More interesting is
another term, σαββατεῖον (the sabbath house), found in an edict of
Augustus dealing with the rights of the Jews and the status of the
synagogue.[4] The term comes, it would seem, from the custom which
was in vogue before 70 C.E., when the congregation assembled mainly
on the sabbath, or perhaps only on that day, as will be discussed later.

Characteristics of the synagogue and its divine service

There are some distinctive marks attaching to the synagogue in the
religious and the social sphere. In contrast to the Temple, which was
in the hands of the priesthood, especially the high priests, the
synagogue was run by the congregation and the community in general.
When the rites of the desert tabernacle and the later Temple are
described, the role of the people is practically confined to being the
bearers of the gifts which the priests were to offer. Only the priests
could approach the altar, and they performed all the rites, practically
none of which were valid otherwise. The chief places in the priesthood
were occupied by noble families, and the succession was hereditary.
No outsider could attain the rank of priesthood, which was reserved
to the descendants of Aaron, and then only if there were no blemishes
in the lineage of the persons in question. The people were deeply

[1] Thus in Jos. *Life* 280; Acts 16:13-16; see *CII*, nos. 682-684; 690; 726.
[2] An incomplete list appears in Krauss, pp. 2-29.
[3] Jos. *War* VII, 44-45.
[4] Jos. Ant. XVI, 164. It is mentioned again on a sarcophagus inscription (*CII*
no. 752), but its Jewishness is in doubt. In Syriac sources this name appears as
'sabbathhouse of the Jews'; cf. J. S. Assemani in *Bibliotheca Orientalis* I (1719),
p. 272.

attached to the worship offered in the Temple, but that such worship could be offered at all depended on the presence of the priests.

In the synagogue, on the other hand, divine service depended on the congregation, and not on the priests. If priests happened to be there, they were just part of the public and had no special function. Indeed, the whole institution was based on public participation, and it was this communal character which gave it its special status. The ark in which the books of the Bible were kept was not always a permanent feature of the synagogue. During the era of the Second Temple and for a long time after, the chest with the books was brought in when required from an adjoining room and brought back there afterwards. The essential feature of the synagogue was the assembly of at least ten adult males for Scripture reading and prayer. Hence, when a sage was proving from Scripture that 'the Holy One, blessed be He, is found in the synagogue', he quoted from Psalm 82:1, 'God has taken his place in the congregation of God'. The person who led the prayers was not appointed to do so permanently. He was a member of the public who was asked on the occasion to come forward and recite the prayers. Even the reading of Scripture was not the province of a specialist. Different people were invited, and each read a short section from the Torah and the prophetic books, while someone stood beside him and translated from the Hebrew, so that all could understand. It was only some time after the talmudic era that Scripture reading became the task of a specialist. During the earlier period, the Halakah was that there should be three readers for working-days, and five or more on sabbaths and feast-days.[1] On these latter days, it was usual to invite a sage to comment on the topics of the day or on the Scripture reading, but this was not obligatory, and any member of the public was entitled to have his say.[2]

So much for the social role of the synagogue. Still more noteworthy, however, is the new note which it struck in religious history. In the synagogue, divine worship consisted of Scripture reading and prayer, with no trace of any sacrificial rite. And then, prayer in the synagogue was definitely orientated to divine worship as such, whereas the prayers mentioned in the Bible, whether connected with sacrifice and Temple or not, were mostly petitions for some definite human need. The psalms chanted in the synagogue were undoubtedly, to some extent, the psalms chanted in the Temple. But the chanting of

[1] *T. B. Berakoth* 6a; *M. Megillah* 4:1-2, 3, 6.
[2] See *M. Taanith* 1:1-2.

psalms as an accompaniment of the sacrificial rites probably only became a standard element in Temple worship during the period when the synagogue came into existence, and may be regarded as inspired by the idea of divine service as it took shape above all in the synagogue. The final version of the synagogue prayers in present-day use is later than the period with which we are dealing. But many elements of this version can be shown to go back much earlier. According to tannaitic tradition, it was during the Jabneh period, thanks to Rabban Gamaliel, that the prayer known as 'the eighteen benedictions' (*shemone esre*) was given the set form in which it was recited two or three times a day.[1] 'Simeon Pekoli (or: the cotton dealer) arranged the eighteen benedictions in their order, in the presence of Rabban Gamaliel at Jabneh.'[2] There are many traditions which refer the arrangement of the benedictions to the early days of the Second Temple or even to a period further back, such as 'one hundred and twenty elders, including some prophets, drew up the eighteen benedictions in their order,' or, 'the men of the great synagogue drew up for Israel blessings, prayers, benedictions of *kiddush* and *habdalah*' or, 'the eighteen benedictions which the early prophets instituted, to be pronounced by Israel every day.'[3] There can be no question of trying to reduce these traditions to some unifying formula. But obviously, they all stem from the conviction that the main outline of the eighteen benedictions was already established during the Second Temple era, at least to some extent.

The blessings in question are echoed in Ben Sira 51:21-35.[4] The Mishnah, when describing the daily service in the Temple, says that after the killing of the victim, before it was offered in sacrifice, the priests gathered in the chamber of hewn stone to recite the *shema* with its accompanying blessings and some of the eighteen.[5] In a dispute between the followers of Shammai and those of Hillel, the question arose as to what the ritual of the blessings should be if a feast-day fell on a sabbath; Honi the Younger, it is said, acting as

---

[1] See the view of Rabban Gamaliel that the eighteen benedictions must be recited fully thrice daily, in contrast to the view of other sages who were not so consistent in demanding this. *M. Berakoth* 4:3-4; *P. T. Berakoth* IV, 7c-d; *T. B. Berakoth* 27b-28a.

[2] *T. B. Berakoth* 28b; *T. B. Megillah* 17b.

[3] *T. B. Megillah* 18a; *T. B. Berakoth* 33a; *Sifre Deut.* 343 (p. 395).

[4] These blessings appear only in the Hebrew mss. from the Cairo Genizah; cf. Charles, *The Apocrypha and Pseudepigrapha of the Old Testament* I, pp. 514-5.

[5] *M. Tamid* 4:3; 5:1.

precentor in the presence of all the sages of the school of Shammai, pronounced only seven blessings.[1] Most of the disputes between these schools took place before 70 C.E., so the general outline and the number of the blessings must have been already fixed at that time. From the dispute just mentioned and from other sources, it can be deduced that in the prayers to be said daily, including sabbaths and feast-days, the three first and the three last blessings were a fixture, while on working-days six more were added, before the three first and the three last respectively. On sabbaths and feast-days, a blessing was inserted in the middle, making a total of seven, and this blessing summed up the extra twelve of working-days and took their place.

The first three blessings are praises, where the fundamental and perpetual beliefs and hopes of Judaism also stand out. They begin with the greatness of God, the election of the patriarchs and the resurrection of the dead. The last three blessings are thanksgivings, and they also speak of the fundamentals of Israel's faith. The prayer for peace and the blessing of God as the peace-maker form the conclusion. As will be seen later, the benedictions were still fluid in form at our period, being only given a set form later. The officiant was free to adapt them as he wished, adding sayings and verses from the Bible. This was true above all when the blessings and their prayers were prolonged, on such special occasions as the New Year, the Day of Atonement and public fasts.[2] Nonetheless, for all the freedom granted to the officiant, the benedictions came to have a set form, especially the opening and concluding ones. The formulas of the working-day blessings became a fixed element in piety, the worship of the heart, as it was called, corresponding to the perpetual regularity of the former sacrificial worship. 'Prayer is called worship, just as the service of the altar is called worship'.[3] But whereas sacrifice was offered only in the Temple, the prayers could be recited by anyone, or by any group, great or small, in the synagogue.

Scripture reading was much more closely linked to the life of the synagogue than was prayer. Prayer could be offered in private as the individual chose, though public prayer had its own special form and expressions. But Scripture reading could only be done in public, in the synagogue. As the Mishnah says, 'If fewer than ten are present... neither the Torah may be read, nor a passage from the Prophets in

---

[1] *T. Rosh ha-Shanah* 4:11.
[2] *M. Rosh ha-Shanah* 4:6; *T. Rosh ha-Shanah* 4:6-7; *M. Taanith* 2:2-5.
[3] *T. B. Taanith* 2a and parallels; *Sifre* Deut. 41 (pp. 87-88).

conclusion.'[1] Scripture reading, done by one of the congregation with another translating, constituted divine worship.

The obligation of praying two or three times a day is alluded to frequently in writings from the Second Temple period. The Apocrypha often speak of morning prayers, though not about obligatory prayers at other times.[2] The Qumran community prayed twice a day,[3] and the Talmud also speaks of the obligation of praying twice a day.[4] Some taught that prayer was obligatory three times a day, as was the practice of the prophet Daniel. There is something similar in the *Slavonic Enoch*, which says, 'Morning, noon and night it is well to go to the house of God to praise the creator of all.'[5] Early Christian tradition also urges prayer three times a day. There are also various pointers to the practice of prayer in the afternoon.[6]

In the first century C.E., however, synagogue-going was probably confined to sabbaths and feast-days. All the relevant tradition, from Palestine and the Diaspora, seems to point this way. As has been noted above, one of the names for the synagogue was *Sabbateion*, no doubt because it was open mostly on the sabbath. The Gospels speak several times of Jesus' visiting the synagogues of Galilee. One cannot always determine which day of the week it was, but when the actual day is mentioned it is always the sabbath.[7] Paul's travels, which took him far and wide throughout the Diaspora, tell the same story. He visited synagogues 'on the sabbath', 'on three successive sabbaths' or 'every sabbath'.[8] Philo says that his Therapeuts met in their synagogue or holy place only once a week.[9] Josephus says in one place that the people gathered in the great synagogue of Tiberias on the sabbath.[10]

[1] *M. Megillah* 4:3.
[2] Wisdom 16:28; *Ps. Sol.* 6:4-5; *Orac. Sib.* III, 591-593; *Aristeas* 305. This situation is also reflected in Judith 12:5-6.
[3] *Rule* 10:11; *Hymns* 12:5; *War of the Sons of light* 14:13-14. Jos. *War* II, 128 mentions only the morning prayer; cf. Philo, *De Vita Contemplativa* 3 concerning the Therapeutae.
[4] The question whether the evening prayer was obligatory or voluntary was debated for generations; cf. *M. Berakoth* 4:1; *P. T. Berakoth* IV, 7b-c; *T. B. Berakoth* 27b; L. Ginzberg, *A Commentary on the Palestinian Talmud* III (1941), pp. 28-29, 170-174.
[5] Dan. 6:11; *Slavonic Enoch* 51:4.
[6] *Didache* 8:3; *Didascalia Apostolorum* (ed. Gibson p. 20); Judith 9:1; Acts 10:9, 30.
[7] Matt. 12:1-12; Mark 1:21; 6:2; Luke 4:15, 31; 6:6; 13:10.
[8] Acts 13:14 (Antioch of Pisidia); Acts 17:1-2 (Thessalonica); Acts 18:4 (Corinth).
[9] *De Vita Contemplativa* 30-32.
[10] Jos. *Life* 276-279.

Tannaitic tradition affirms that the custom of reading Scripture on Mondays and Thursdays, as well as the sabbath, was an ancient one, and some Tannaim attribute it to the 'prophets and elders', others to Ezra.[1] In any case, the custom was certainly in existence before 70 C.E. Mondays and Thursdays were market days, when villagers gathered in town, and it seems that this was the occasion for Scripture reading. These were also the days on which tribunals sat, till the time of the revolt of Bar Cochba. We are told in so many words that villagers could put off the reading of the Book of Esther to the Thursday or Monday nearest to Purim, if they had no one to read for them in the village.[2] Mondays and Thursdays were also marked, in some circles, by being observed as fast-days. The *Megillath Taanith*, which goes back in the main to the time of the Second Temple, contains a discussion about 'a person who was resolved to fast on Mondays and Thursdays'.[3] Early Christian writings speak of this as the custom of the Pharisees, 'the hypocrites'. The *Didache* warns against fasting 'along with the hypocrites' and says that it should be done on Wednesdays and Fridays. Epiphanius also affirms that in the time of Jesus the Pharisees fasted on Mondays and Thursdays.[4] The custom undoubtedly points to the fact that these were days when people assembled in the synagogue, just as in biblical times we find that fasts are connected with public assemblies. Hence villagers who were strict in their observance of the commandments came to the synagogue on Mondays and Thursdays, if they were in town. There may also have been others who followed this custom, but in general the people came to the synagogue only on the sabbath.

The presence of women and children in the synagogue at the appropriate times is attested in many sources. Tannaitic Halakah makes prayer obligatory for women. 'Women and slaves and minors are not obliged to recite the *shema* or wear phylacteries. But they are obliged to pray, to put up the *mezuzah* and to join in the blessing after food'.[5] Many halakoth suppose that women were normally at the synagogue service. There was a rule that Jews were forbidden to eat food cooked by a non-Jew. A baraita supplements this by saying, 'An Israelite need not hesitate to leave meat on the fire and let a Gentile

---

[1] *Mekhilta, Vayissa* I (p. 154); *P. T. Megillah* IV, 75a.
[2] *M. Megillah* 1:2; *T. Megillah* 1:3; *T. B. Megillah* 2a.
[3] *Megillath Taanith*, end; *P. T. Pesahim* IV, 30c; *Soferim* 21; see Alon, *Studies* II, pp. 120-2.
[4] Epiphanius, *Adv. Haereses* XV, 1; *Didache* 8:1.
[5] *M. Berakoth* 3:3.

turn it till he comes back from the synagogue or the *bet midrash*. A woman need not hesitate to put a pot on the stove and let a Gentile woman stir it, till she herself comes back from the baths or the synagogue'.[1] So this baraita regards the synagogue, like the baths, as one of the ordinary places where women go as often as men. Another halakah says, 'In a town where all are priests, they must give the blessing. Whom do they bless? Their brethren in the north, in the south, in the east and in the west. And who say Amen after the priests? The women and children'.[2] In a midrash on the text, 'You stand this day...your children, your wives ...' (Deut. 29:9-10), we read, 'your wives, even though they do not understand, are to come and listen and receive their reward'.[3] A later talmudic text, reflecting no doubt, at least in general, what was always the custom, has this to say: 'Thus it is correct to say that after every passage from the Torah and the Prophets read on the sabbath, the translation should be given, for the benefit of the people, including the women and the children. This is what is meant by the saying, 'Early to come and late to go on the sabbath.' Good people are early to arrive, to join in the recitation of the *shema*, before sunrise. They leave late, so as to hear the Scripture reading explained. But on feast-days they come late, because the food has to be prepared for the feast-day'.[4] The Halakah explains that they come early on the sabbath because cooking is forbidden, but late on feast-days because the women can prepare the food, cooking being permitted on feast-days.

All the evidence about the presence of women in the synagogue which can be found in tannaitic sources seems to be later than 70 C.E. But the Acts of the Apostles points clearly to the presence of women. When Paul and Timothy reached Philippi on the frontier of Macedonia, Paul went to a synagogue outside the town and addressed the women, who included a 'God-fearer' who was not a Jew. So too at Thessalonica, he converted some of the leading women when he spoke in the synagogue.[5]

Undoubtedly, the congregation was mostly male, but it is equally certain that it included women and children. But women took no active part in the conduct of divine service, either as officiants or as

---

[1] *T. B. Abodah Zarah* 38b-39a.
[2] *P. T. Berakoth* v, 9d; cf. *T. B. Sotah* 38b.
[3] *Midrash ha-Gadol* on Deut. 29:10 (p. 639).
[4] *Soferim* 18:6.
[5] Acts 16:13; 17:4.

readers of Scripture. This is clear from a halakah which runs: 'All may come forward to make up the quorum of seven, even women and minors. But the sages say that a woman should not read Scripture, out of respect for the congregation'.[1] This may well be compared with the passage in Paul's Epistle to the Corinthians, 'Women should keep silence in the churches. For they are not to speak, but should be subordinate, as the law says. If there is anything they desire to know, let them ask their husbands at home. For it is shameful for a woman to speak in church'.[2]

There were non-Jews, 'God-fearers', as they were called, in the synagogue, as there had been in the Temple. This is quite clear from Paul's travels. When he and his companions came to Antioch in Pisidia, he went to the synagogues and addressed 'the Jews and the 'God-fearers'.[3] At Thessalonica, where he spoke in the synagogue on a number of sabbaths, he made converts there among Jews and devout Greeks, and they then joined him and Silas.[4] At Athens he spoke in the synagogue to 'Jews and devout persons', and to others in the market place.[5] The presence of non-Jews is also evident from the midrashim, which interpret several texts of Scripture in terms of this situation. The Song of Solomon 1:15, 'Behold, you are beautiful, my love; behold, you are beautiful; your eyes are doves', is explained as follows: 'There is a kind of dove which serves as food, and her companions are drawn by her fragrance and come to her nest. So too when the sage takes his seat to expound doctrine, many strangers become proselytes'.[6] Another midrash runs as follows: 'The verse, 'Then I saw the wicked buried; they used to go in and out of the holy place' (Eccles. 8:10), speaks of proselytes who go and repent; 'they come out of the holy place' means that this is the result of walking in a holy place, that is, in synagogues and houses of study'.[7]

In the period which we are studying, the custom of meeting in the synagogue on the eve of the sabbath did not yet exist.[8] The service

---

[1] *T. B. Megillah* 23a; *T. Megillah* 4:11.
[2] 1 Cor. 14:34-35.
[3] Acts 13:14-16.
[4] Acts 17:1-4.
[5] Acts 17:16-17.
[6] *Cant. Rabba* ad 1:15; cf. *Cant. Rabba* ad 4:2 and 1:3.
[7] *Eccles. Rabba* 5 and parallel in *Midrash Tanhuma* on Exod. 18 (p. 69).
[8] At the end of the first century c.e. it was not yet customary to meet on the evening of the sabbath: *T. Berakoth* 3:7; *T. B. Pesahim* 100a; cf. Geiger, *Urschrift und Übersetzungen der Bibel* (1928), p. 124; Elbogen, p. 197; Ginzberg, I, p. 89.

was held in the early hours of the sabbath morning, though the very devout came earlier, to have the *shema* recited before sunrise.[1] The service was very long, as it included reading from Scripture, translation of the Hebrew text and the commentary or exhortation which followed.[2] It ended in time for the main meal of the day, which was taken before midday.[3]

When tannaitic tradition speaks of prayers, that is, of the obligatory prayers to be said in private or in public, it always means the eighteen benedictions, or the smaller number recited on sabbaths and feast-days. The prayers of the Jewish believer, in the Second Temple era, mainly took the form of blessings, as we know from many sources. They usually began with the formula, 'Blessed art thou, O Lord', or the like, though sometimes this formula came only at the end.[4] This pattern of one or more blessings became standard for all 'liturgical' occasions, such as Scripture reading, the recitation of the *shema*, the *kiddush* and the *habdalah*. There were two blessings before the *shema* and one at the end. But the commonest pattern was three in succession, as at grace after meals.

The Mishnah, tractate *Berakoth*, 4:3, says that Rabban Gamaliel held that 'the eighteen' were to be recited every day. Both the Babylonian and the Palestinian Talmud assume that the eighteen benedictions (or seventeen before the 'benediction' on apostates etc. was inserted) existed in main outline before Rabban Gamaliel's time (end of the first century C.E.). This view was based on a tradition which said that the eighteen benedictions were instituted by the authorities at the beginning of the Second Temple period.[5] It is still held by many scholars today, and many efforts have been made, by a comparison of the various extant forms of the blessings, to determine their original form and date of origin, or to date various groups of the blessings.[6]

A definite structure for the public prayers had emerged, it seems safe to say, before 70. C.E. But that any original version can be determined is highly improbable, not only because source material is lacking, but

---

[1] *M. Berakoth* 1:2.
[2] Acts 13:14 ff.; *T. B. Berakoth* 28b.
[3] *T. B. Betzah* 15b; Jos. *Life* 279; *P. T. Taanith* III, 67a.
[4] See Heineman, pp. 52-66; 30-1.
[5] *P. T. Berakoth* IV, 8c; *T. B. Berakoth* 28b.
[6] L. Zunz, *Die gottesdienstlichen Vorträge der Juden* (2nd ed. 1892), p. 369ff advocated this approach, as did L. Finkelstein in 'The Development of the Amida', *JQR* XVI (1925-6) p. 211f. The reconstructions of Zunz and Finkelstein are rejected by Elbogen, p. 11 and Heineman, p. 32ff.

simply because there was never any such single original which through various modifications gave rise to the different versions now extant. Even the number of eighteen, which tannaitic sources already regard as having been established in the early days of the Second Temple, is highly doubtful for the early period. Tannaitic tradition affirms that a disciple once recited a short version in the presence of Rabbi Eleazar. He was jeered by the other students, but Rabbi Eleazar calmed them by saying that Moses had also prayed briefly, according to Num. 12:13, 'Heal her, O God, I beseech thee'. The tradition goes on to say that on another occasion a disciple prolonged the prayers, and that the others complained of the length. Rabbi Eleazar again re-assured them, by reminding them of Moses, who according to Deut. 9:25, prayed before the Lord forty days and forty nights.[1] The sayings of the Tannaim, and the many disputes which still went on among their successors, the Amoraim, show that the text was fluid. The officiant had only to keep to the main outline and the general regulations. 'Whether he was an *am ha-aretz* or a sage could be seen from the way he gave out the blessings'.[2] The Talmuds contain fragmentary prayers which have been preserved by chance. Some of these fragments show the standard text, or at least some version of it, in a more or less modified form. But there are fragments which do not coincide with any known version.[3] Some prayers have reached us in so many versions and with so little in common that they can only be remnants of alternative versions.[4] The version of the eighteen benedictions now in general use among Jews is the Babylonian one. Variations as between different communities are slight, being confined to single words. But the Babylonian version hardly coincides at all, either in phraseology or in single words, with the 'Palestinian', which was found in the Cairo Geniza.[5] It is quite unbelievable that the Jews of Babylon should have changed all the blessings so completely if they had come to them from Palestine. Different independent versions must have therefore existed.

---

[1] *Mekhilta, Vayissa* 1 (p. 155) and parallels.
[2] *T. Berakoth* 1:6; *P. T. Berakoth* 1, 3c; *T. B. Berakoth* 50a.
[3] *M. Erubin* 3:9 mentions the text of a prayer: 'Give us strength, O Lord our God the first day of the month.' This version has not been preserved in any of the received traditions.
[4] See the many different versions of the prayer: 'Who rebuilds Jerusalem' in the appendix to Heineman p. 48 and the many versions of the sabbath prayer in Heineman, p. 35.
[5] Cf. the Genizah versions published by J. Mann, in *HUCA* 11 (1925), pp. 306-11.

Historical research has been able to point out remnants of lists of blessings from the Second Temple period. Ben Sira ch. 51 has already been noted above, and to this may be added 36:1-17,[1] which echo the high priest's blessings after Scripture reading on the Day of Atonement.[2] Notable parallels to the petitions contained in the eighteen benedictions can be found in the Psalms of Solomon.[3] The Mishnah, tractate *Tamid* 5:1, lists the blessings to be recited at the *shema*, and the items from the eighteen to be said by the priests at an interval during the offering of the morning sacrifice.

We shall not discuss the relevance of all these parallels. A few points may be noted, however. Though there are similaiities, there is never any actual coincidence with the eighteen benedictions. And no two of the sources here alluded to, nor indeed any of the others, show the same blessings or petitions in the same order as the eighteen. Chapter 51 of Ben Sira comes closest. Many of its thanksgivings and petitions are like the last part of the eighteen benedictions. They have e.g. the same 'redeemer of Israel', 'He who gathers the dispersed children of Israel', 'He who upholds and strengthens the house of David'.[4] But these epithets do not occur in the same sequence as in the eighteen, and they have a different structure. In Ben Sira, the people are addressed with the imperative, that of the 'Praise the Lord', whereas in the eighteen, in tannaitic sources, God is addressed directly, 'Blessed art thou O Lord…'

Similar reflections may be made on that part of the prayers which is known as 'the sanctification' (קדושה), mentioned in the later tannaitic period.[5] This is the proclamation of the 'trisagion' by the congregation: before the *shema*, in the eighteen benedictions and, at a much later period, after the Scripture reading of the day (קדושה דסדרא), which followed the eighteen benedictions. It was basically a congregational hymn, meant to correspond with that of the angels (Isaiah 6:3), and was mostly heard in public worship. It also appears in early Christian writings.[6]

---

[1] Cf. K. Kohler, 'The Origin and Composition of the Eighteen Benedictions' in *HUCA* I (1924), pp. 393-403.

[2] *M. Yoma* 7:1; *T. Yoma* 3:18; cf. Kohler, op. cit., p. 393; Lieberman, *Tosefta Ki-Fshutah, Order Moed*, p. 801.

[3] Cf. J. Levi in *REJ* XXXII (1896), p. 161-78.

[4] Ben Sira 51:12.

[5] *T. Berakoth* 1:9; this is also mentioned in the amoraic period (*P. T. Berakoth* v, 9c), but only infrequently in the talmudic literature.

[6] The decisive source for this is *Constitutiones Apostolorum* VIII, 12, a fourth century Christian source which preserves much ancient material.

It is not found in the blessings before the *shema* in any of the Palestinian versions, or in early Palestinian poetry,[1] but it may have been current already in the first century C.E. in certain circles which were more interested in angelology. It was only at a later date that it was adopted into the version of the prayers used by all levels of the population.

One should not therefore speak of an original or early version of the eighteen benedictions at the start. There was a variety of versions, which were elaborated in various circles and gradually took on a fixed structure, where blessings, introductions and conclusions were given set form, and were adopted into the prayers. The institutional authorities to whom the prayers are attributed were responsible, in the main, only for settling the order and deciding how a prayer should be structured and formulated. In particular, they were responsible for the structure of the regular public prayer, by laying down such rules as, 'All blessings must open with, Blessed be ...' (ברוך), except such blessings as follow another blessing'; 'Any blessing which does not include the divine name is invalid'; 'Any blessing which does not include the [divine] kingship is invalid'.[2] At Jabneh the number of the benedictions was fixed at eighteen, but earlier, we find only seven used at public worship.[3]

Tannaitic tradition about the customs of the Temple records a series of eight blessings, along with some of their formulae, as recited by the high priest after Scripture reading on the Day of Atonement. After Scripture reading on the Feast of Tabernacles, the king did likewise for the ceremonial assembly, but only once every seven years.[4] These blessings qualify as complete prayers, uttered for the Torah, for the worship in the Temple, for the thanksgiving, for the forgiveness of sin and for 'thy people Israel, as needing deliverance in thy presence'. Scholars have noted that these are materially and formally very like the blessings after Scripture reading which are mentioned in the tractate *Soferim* and are in use at the present day. These blessings too do more than round off Scripture reading. They offer thanksgiving and prayer for Jerusalem and for the kingship of the house of David, and they also take in the affairs of the day.[5] One may well

---

[1] Cf. J. Mann in *HUCA* II (1925), pp. 289-290.
[2] *T. Berakoth* 1:9; *T. B. Berakoth* 40b.
[3] *T. Rosh ha-Shanah* 4:11; see above p. 917.
[4] *M. Yoma* 7:1; *M. Sotah* 7:7. The contents of the blessings and their patterns are found in *T. Yoma* 4:18 and *P. T. Yoma* IV, 44b.
[5] *Soferim* 13:7-14.

regard these groups of blessings as having the structure of the synagogue prayers, that of the eighteen benedictions or the seven after Scripture reading (though not of those before it), which existed at least as early as the tannaitic era.[1] Scripture was also read before the blessings at the public assemblies on fast days.[2]

The public prayers were led by the officiant, so much so, that even when they had for the most part crystallized into fixed forms, he was the main spokesman. In the earlier period when the prayers (blessings) could to some extent be improvised, they were entirely at the discretion of the officiant, with the congregation only saying Amen at the end of the blessings.[3] The only restriction was that the prayers should be in accord with some more or less current version, so when the officiant was chosen from among the congregation, he had to be at least of average education in order to qualify. On the less frequent occasions of public fasts, however, when a series of blessings was added to the prayers, the choice of officiant was more restricted. 'They sent down before the ark an elder, a man of experience.'[4]

The next main item of the liturgy, after the eighteen benedictions, was the recitation of the *shema*, morning and evening. During the Temple era it comprised the ten commandments as well as the 'Hear, O Israel' (Deut. 6:4-9), 'And if you will obey' (ibid. 11:13-21), and 'The Lord said' (Num. 15:37-41), with one or two blessings before and after.[5] In ancient times the recitation was mainly a private affair: 'when you lie down and when you wake up', at night and in the morning.[6] But as early as the Temple era, the *shema* seems to have been combined with the prayer when the congregation assembled for the morning office.[7] It was then recited antiphonally, the verses being divided among officiant and congregation.[8] And in such public recitation, after the 'Hear O Israel' verse a response was introduced, like that used in the Temple, 'Blessed be God, whose glorious kingdom is for ever and ever.' It is still in current usage today, even in the

[1] See Heinemann, pp. 143-144.
[2] *M. Taanith* 2:1-2; *T. B. Taanith* 13b.
[3] *M. Rosh ha-Shanah* 4:9 and both Talmuds ad loc.; cf. L. Ginzburg, *A commentary on the Palestinian Talmud* III, p. 395.
[4] *M. Taanith* 2:2; *M. Megillah* 4:5.
[5] *M. Tamid* 5:1.
[6] Cf. *Letter of Aristeas* 160; Jos. *Ant.* IV, 213; *M. Berakoth* 1:3.
[7] *M. Tamid* 5:1; *M. Megillah* 4:3; *M. Pesahim* 4:8.
[8] *M. Megillah* 4:6; *T. Megillah* 6:3.

private recitation of the *shema*, but in all probability it was first used in the public prayers. There is a tradition from the Temple era to the effect that the response in question was not inserted in the *shema* by the people of Jericho.[1] The added blessings (above) were the custom both in the private and the public *shema*, and some, if not all, appear to have been part of the priestly prayer in the Temple.[2]

Scripture reading

Scripture reading was the next great rite which the synagogue featured. It took place on sabbaths, feast-days and public fasts. We know from amoraic and later sources, including midrashim and liturgical poetry, that there were two main approaches of reading through the whole of the Torah. There was a cycle of three years in Palestine, while it was completed in one year in Babylon, which may have been once also a Palestinian custom.[3] But whether either cycle was in use in the first century C.E. or even in early tannaitic times may be doubted. Tannaitic sources, in the Mishnah and the baraitas, only speak of the number of readers on sabbaths and feast-days or of the minimum number of verses to be read either by each reader or in the whole lesson.[4] There is nothing to say when or if the cycle was completed.

But there was a normal sequence of readings to be followed, according to tannaitic sources, which was interrupted on many occasions, such as the special sabbaths before the new moon, Hanukkah, Purim, and the four sabbaths before the Passover. And on feast-days, the appropriate text could be read, which is still the custom today.[5] But then again, tannaitic and amoraic sources show that the actual sequence was in dispute. Were the texts read on the sabbath afternoon, the Monday and the Thursday to be repeated on the next sabbath, at the morning service? Or was the reading to be continuous, starting each time where it had left off on the previous occasion? These and similar disputes show that there was no fixed traditional sequence.[6] Many variations turn up in the Palestinian tradition, and

[1] *T. Taanith* 1:13; *M. Yoma* 6:1; *M. Pesahim* 4:8.
[2] *M. Berakoth* 1:4; *M. Tamid* 5:1.
[3] The earliest explicit mention of the contrasting Palestinian and Babylonian customs is in *T. B. Megillah* 29b.
[4] See esp. *M. Megillah* 3:4-6; *T. Megillah* 4:1-12; *T. B. Megillah* 29b.
[5] *M. Megillah* 3:4. For its interpretation see L. Ginzberg. op. cit., III, pp. 132-9 and *Mishnah, Order Moed* (ed. Ch. Albeck), p. 501.
[6] *T. Megillah* 4:10.

the divisions given in the Midrashim, which are based on Palestinian customs, are again different.[1] All this shows that the sequence was not fixed, but gradually crystallized into the two cycles, over a long period, covering the Temple era and later. All that can be concluded from tannaitic literature is that the sabbath morning readings formed a continuity, while on feast-days a relevant passage was read.

Only the reading of the Torah is mentioned in the early rabbinic sources, but that the Prophets were normally read both in Palestine and the Diaspora in the first century c.e. may be gathered from the story of Jesus' visit to the synagogue at Nazareth and of Paul's at Pisidian Antioch.[2] The reading from the Prophets was called the *haftarah* (הפטרה), the ending or completion (of the Torah reading). 'He ended with the prophet' and 'he completed it from the prophet' were common expressions.[3] The term *haftarah* also implies the dismissal of the people, since the *haftarah* ended the service, as will be seen later. The Prophets were read by one person only, who also read, or perhaps merely repeated, the last part of the Torah reading. This overlap, however, is only vouched for in later documents.[4] The Prophets were not read in continuity. There was either a standard anthology, or a passage was selected each week. Different texts could even be combined: 'They may skip in the Prophets, but not in the Torah'.[5] If the tradition about Torah reading is compared to that about the Prophets, including early or late lists of the readings, it appears at once that the latter tradition was more fluid, with a much freer choice of readings. The custom of reading from the Prophets was not universal. But on the whole it may be said that the Prophets were read after the longer Torah readings on fast-days, sabbath mornings and feast-days, but not after the shorter readings on Mondays, Thursdays and sabbath afternoons.[6]

---

[1] See the articles of J. Theodor in *MGWJ* xxxiv-xxxvi (1885-87); J. Heineman, 'Chapters of Doubtful Authenticity in Leviticus Rabba' in *Tarbiz* xxxvii (1968), pp. 339-54.

[2] Luke 4:17; Acts 13:15.

[3] *P. T. Sanhedrin* i, 19a; Rabbi Nathan rose and supplemented (ואשלים) the reading of the prophet. The expression to supplement in the prophet (בנביא השלים) is found frequently in *Pesikta Rabbati* (i.e. 1b; 42a). For the expression הפטיר with the meaning to send away the congregation at the end of an assembly, see *P. T. Berakoth* iv, 7d; there the meeting of sages was concluded and they were dismissed after reading appropriate verses.

[4] *T. B. Megillah* 23a; *P. T. Megillah* iv, 75c.

[5] *M. Megillah* 4:4; *T. Megillah* 4:4.

[6] The custom in Babylon and elsewhere of reading a concluding lesson on

Late talmudic sources say that on feast-days there were readings from the 'scrolls' (*megilloth*), such as the Song of Solomon at the Passover, Ruth at Pentecost, Lamentations on the ninth of Ab and Ecclesiastes at Tabernacles. For the 'five scrolls', which included also Esther, we have midrashim along the lines of the midrashim on the five books of the Torah.[1] Some of them contain much tannaitic material, which provides earlier proof of their being read in public than do the sources where this is explicitly mentioned. But it is highly doubtful that they were read in the Temple era or for some time after, except the Book of Esther on the Feast of Purim, as mentioned in the Mishnah and other tannaitic sources.[2] The second of these books to qualify for public reading was Lamentations. The tannaitic Halakah does not say that this was obligatory, but there are various proofs that it was read on the 9th of Ab, from about 150 C.E. on.[3]

The reading from the Torah was divided among several officiants. There were at least five on feast-days, six on the Day of Atonement and seven on the sabbath.[4] But since not all synagogues had several qualified readers, there was a halakah to the effect that if only one was available, he was to read a portion, stop, and then continue, even if this meant six breaks in the lesson.[5] The Talmud adds that the 'foreigners' (Jews living in the Hellenistic world) did not have the custom of calling on 'three, five or seven' readers, but had only one. This is confirmed by Philo, who says that the Pentateuch was read on the sabbath by one person only.[6] But this does not seem to have been a universal custom in the Diaspora, where sometimes one reader began and ended with the Hebrew, while in between others used the vernacular.[7] There is every reason to think that when the tannaitic

Saturday afternoon from the Hagiographa is apparently late. See *T. B. Shabbath* 24a and *Ozar ha-Geonim* II (1930), pp. 26-27.

[1] *Soferim* 14; Ecclesiastes is not mentioned in the mss. but is contained in citations of this work. See *Tractate Soferim* (p. 250).

[2] *M. Megillah chaps.* 1-2; *T. Megillah chaps.* 1-2, esp. 2:5.

[3] *P. T. Shabbath* XVI, 15c.

[4] *M. Megillah* 3:2; *T. Megillah* 4:11.

[5] *T. Megillah* 4:12; *P. T. Megillah* IV, 75a.

[6] This is stated explicitly in *P. T. Megillah* IV, 25a; 'Those speaking foreign tongues did not so conduct themselves, but read the whole section'. See the explanation of this passage by Rabbi Hananel in his commentary to *T. B. Megillah* 23a. This is also stated in *T. Megillah* 4:13, but only as an exceptional circumstance: 'if they have only one person to read for them'. See also Philo in Eusebius, *Praeparatio Evangelica* VIII, 7, 13 and Schürer II, p. 531.

[7] *T. Megillah* 4:13 and the explanation of Lieberman, *Tosefta Ki-Fshutah, Order Moed*, p. 1179; *Novella Justiniani* 146 from a still later period.

sources speak of the vernacular, they mean the Greek of the Septuagint, or the later Greek version by Aquila, from about the beginning of the 2nd century C.E.[1]

No duty, and above all no public duty, was discharged without a prior blessing, so there was one before the reading of the Scripture. The reader first turned to the congregation and cried out, 'Bless!', to which they responded, 'Blessed be God who is worthy of all praise!' He then recited the appropriate blessing.[2] The last of the readers ended with a blessing, as is already recorded in the Mishnah. It may be assumed that the opening blessing came in earlier than the concluding one, though the addition at the end was already made in the Temple era, at least on public feast-days. This conclusion could take the form of a series of blessings, the first of which was for the Torah.[3] The first reader was a priest, the second a Levite and the others members of the public; so according to the Mishnah. But this sequence did not affect the significance of the service and was followed merely 'for the sake of peace', as again the Mishnah says, and was possibly not customary in the Temple era. In any case, a distinguished sage was invited first in later times even if a priest was present.[4] Philo too leaves the choice open as between an elder and a priest.[5] The reader had to be invited by the head of the synagogue or the *hazzan*, and according to the Tosefta, neither of the latter read unless invited by others, while if the *hazzan* read, someone else stood beside him and took over his duties for the moment.[6]

Scripture reading was accompanied by a translation from the Hebrew. This was done by someone who stood beside the reader and gave out the translation, which he had already memorized, after each verse.[7] In Palestine and other Aramaic-speaking countries, the translation was in Aramaic, elsewhere in Greek or some other living language. The Talmud also mentions Coptic, Elamitic and Median, but where it simply speaks of translation, it means Aramaic.[8] One should not think that a translation was provided merely for the sake of the

[1] See *M. Megillah* 1:8.
[2] *M. Megillah* 4:1; *P. T. Berakoth* VII, 11c; *T. B. Berakoth* 11b.
[3] *M. Yoma* 7:1, at the reading of the High Priest on the Day of Atonement; *M. Sotah* 7:8, at the reading in the presence of the whole community during Tabernacles every seventh year.
[4] *M. Gittin* 5:8; *T. B. Megillah* 22b; cf the discussion in *P. T. Gittin* v, 47b.
[5] See above p. 929, n. 6.
[6] *T. Megillah* 4:21; *Gen. Rabba* 79 (pp. 949-50); cf. Luke 4:20.
[7] *M. Megillah* 4:4, 10; *T. Megillah* 4:20-41.
[8] *M. Megillah* 2:1; *T. B. Shabbath* 115a.

uneducated or the women and children, who understood Hebrew not at all or at best imperfectly.[1] But there were other reasons for it, since it was a sort of commentary, and ensured that the transmission of the Bible was done in accord with oral tradition. Hence the saying: 'Anyone who translates a verse literally is a traitor.'[2] Translation was also justified on other grounds. 'Since the Scripture was given through a mediator, we too must deal with it through a mediator.'[3] The gift of Scripture was being made anew, as it were, when it was read, and so had to come indirectly. And since the translation was regarded as oral law, it could not be read out, at least in public, but had to be delivered from memory.[4] The translation was usually given out by someone who ranked lower than the reader, and anything else was held to be unsuitable. The disciple translated for the sage or the inferior for his superior.[5] The Torah was translated more exactly than the Prophets. The translation was given after each verse of the Torah, while the Prophets could be done three verses at a time. Sometimes the passage from the Prophet was only given a rough translation, and could even, according to later testimonies, be read without a translation.[6]

The Aramaic translations, which took many years to reach their final form, were committed to writing, and such translations of the whole of the Torah and the Prophets survive in the form of our Targums. But there is evidence from tannaitic times that parts of some verses in the Torah and the Prophets were skipped in the reading of the original text, and above all, in the translation, 'out of respect' or because they were felt to be indelicate. So for instance, 'the story of Reuben (Genesis 35:22) is read out but not interpreted'.[7] And so we hear, 'It happened that Rabbi Hananiah ben Gamaliel read out [in the synagogue of] Cabul, 'Reuben went and lay with Bilhah. Now the sons of Jacob were twelve', and said to the translator, 'Only translate the last part''.[8]

The service ended with the blessings after the reading of the Prophets. The custom of reciting an additional prayer was not widespread. In

---

[1] See *Soferim* 18:5.
[2] *T. Megillah* 3:41.
[3] *P. T. Megillah* III, 74d; on this reading see B. Ratner, *Sefer Ahavat Tsion*.
[4] *P. T. Megillah* IV, 74d.
[5] *T. Megillah* 4:21.
[6] *M. Megillah* 4:4; *P. T. Megillah* IV, 75a; *T. B. Megillah* 23b.
[7] *M. Megillah* 4:10.
[8] *T. Megillah* 4:31.

the opinion of a sage who lived in the second half of the first century C.E., it was said only when the town council (חבר עיר) came.[1] The reading from the Prophets was therefore a sort of conclusion and the signal for the dismissal of the congregation.[2]

The service in the synagogue also came to take in the sermon preached on the sabbath, which was a common practice in both Palestine and the Diaspora in the second half of the first century C.E., as we know from many sources. But the sermon was not really part of the synagogue service. Basically, the sermon was study of Torah, which was a duty at all appropriate times and was not tied to any particular time, or any particular part of the liturgy or the sabbath. The sabbath, as the day of rest, with the people assembled in the synagogue, was an obvious time for it. The passage read and translated was comparatively short, and so called for fuller explanation, which was all the more welcome because the congregation was familiar with the text, as part of their explicit beliefs. There are two instances in the New Testament of the sermon being given immediately after the Scripture reading,[3] which is also abundantly attested in tannaitic and amoraic traditions. We know therefore that there was a sermon before the congregation broke up for the midday meal.[4] But such study of Torah could be done at other times on the sabbath, and also could go on till late at night on the eve of the sabbath, though not running on till the time of the liturgy proper.[5]

If there was a sage in the synagogue, it was he, no doubt, who addressed the people, but this was not necessarily the case. Anyone who had a message for the public could be asked, if the head of the synagogue considered him fitted for the role. A baraitha giving the order of the day on public fasts says that the people should be exhorted to repent: 'if there is an elder (a member of the sanhedrin) there, it is he who exhorts the people to repent, otherwise a sage, and failing that, some distinguished person'.[6] But that all synagogues provided a sermon

---

[1] See *M. Berakoth* 4:7 and both Talmuds ad loc.; cf. chapter seven p. 415.

[2] An additional prayer was said during the feast of Tabernacles in the time of Rabbi Joshua, *T. Sukkah* 4:4; but this is lacking in the better mss., cf. Lieberman, *Tosefta Ki-Fshutah, Order Moed*, pp. 888-9.

[3] Luke 4:16-22; Acts 13:15.

[4] *T. B. Betzah* 15b for the end of the first century; *T. B. Betzah* 4a for a later period.

[5] *P. T. Sotah* 1, 16d: R. Meir was wont to preach in the synagogue of Hammath every sabbath evening. The story implies that he prolonged his sermon and that women as well as men participated in the service.

[6] *T. B. Taanith* 16a. Cf. Acts 13:14-15.

every sabbath may be doubted. There is indeed evidence from the era of the Second Temple to the effect that the synagogue was described as a place for studying the word of God, but this need only mean that Scripture was read and translated there. And it cannot be assumed that there was a capable sage everywhere, since a synagogue could be founded and be run from day to day independently of the sages.[1]

Administration

As we know from sources prior to and after 70 C.E., there were synagogues which catered for certain groups, such as fellow-countrymen who were in Jerusalem as pilgrims or as permanent settlers.[2] There were also synagogues for craftsmen's guilds and other associations,[3] while some were the property of individuals.[4] But the synagogue normally belonged to the local community as a whole, and was counted as part of municipal property.[5] It could be sold, if necessary, by the regular municipal authorities, the seven aldermen.[6]

As has already been remarked, local government is constantly identified in our sources with synagogue government.[7] But this could not be the case in localities extensive enough to have a number of synagogues, or where Jews were a small minority. Local government was in fact in the hands of a larger body.[8] The town councillors numbered seven, while the representatives of the synagogue numbered only three, as we know from the various descriptions given in the Palestinian Talmud.[9] There was a president at the head of the latter body, who was known as ראש הכנסת,[10] corresponding to the ἀρχισυνάγωγος so often mentioned in the writings of Hellenistic Judaism, the New

[1] In a late Palestinian source we find: 'And if on the sabbath there was a translator or sermon, the reader of the prophetic lesson says...'. This would imply that a translator for the prophetic portion or someone to deliver a sermon was not always available. See J. Mann in *Tarbiz* III (1932) p. 6 and a similar saying in *Soferim* 12:10.

[2] A long list of these synagogues in Jerusalem appears in Acts 6:9; this can be supplemented from the talmudic literature. Moreover after 70 C.E. the same situation existed elsewhere; see *T. Megillah* 3:6; *Genesis R.* 33 (p. 305).

[3] For Jerusalem see *T. B. Megillah* 26a (but the meaning is uncertain). For post 70 see *P. T. Shekalim* II, 47a and VII, 50c.

[4] *P. T. Megillah* III, 74.

[5] *M. Nedarim* 5:5.

[6] *T. B. Megillah* 26a-b.

[7] See above pp. 908-9.

[8] See above chapter seven, pp. 415ff.

[9] *P. T. Megillah* III, 74a.

[10] *M. Sotah* 7:7; *T. Megillah* 4:20; *T. Terumoth* 2:13. *Semahoth* 12:14.

933

Testament and in inscriptions from synagogues and Jewish graves.[1] Our sources range widely in time and space, but they remain random samples, so it is hard to say how the head of the synagogue stood with regard to local government, or to what extent his office coincided with that of the archon (ἄρχων) which is one of the commonest titles in local government in the Diaspora. Some inscriptions suggest that there were a number of archons in a given community,[2] and possibly the head of the synagogue was one of their number. From later Roman law it appears that the head of the synagogue was regarded as the leader and representative of the Jewish community,[3] but this may not have been the case at an earlier period.[4] An inscription from Rome, in Latin and Greek, says that a certain person was both archon and head of the synagogue, but the Acts of the Apostles, according to one witness to the text, puts archons and heads of synagogues into separate groups.[5] The Talmud, when enumerating the grades in Jewish society, speaks only of heads of synagogues and not of archons. This may mean that they were regarded as identical, but it might also mean that they were different but of equal rank.[6]

Little is known about the process of nomination: how the head of the synagogue was selected, and whether he was elected to serve a term, or for life, or whether the office was hereditary. In the Mount Ophel inscription quoted above (p. 909) the father and grandfather of the office-holder had been in the same positions. But this was not necessarily standard procedure, and the case may be rare. The synagogue in question had been built by the ancestors of the office-holder, as the inscription says, and their descendants were the obvious people to be elected as heads of the synagogue. And they may have held office merely to keep up a family tradition and not because of any hereditary principle. An inscription from Acmonia in Phrygia mentions the head of a synagogue who held office for life: ὁ διὰ βίου ἀρχισυνάγωγος, and another about whom nothing special is noted. Both took part in re-building the synagogue.[7] But again we cannot say whether the

---

[1] See Schürer II, p. 510, nn. 23-29. To these sources should be added many recently published inscriptions; cf. *CII* I, pp. 97-99.

[2] In Cyrenaica their number was seven in 24-13 B.C.E., nine in 8 B.C.E. and ten in 56 C.E. See *CIG* III, 5361; *SEG* XVII, 823; 5362.

[3] *Codex Theodosianus* XVI, 8, 13, 14.

[4] *CII* no. 265.

[5] 14:2 according to Codex D and other mss.

[6] *T. B. Gittin* 60a; *T. B. Pesahim* 49b.

[7] CII no. 766; this inscription has been extensively discussed. The latest discussion is in Lifschitz, *Beth Shearim* II (1967), p. 33.

office was by appointment or by heredity, or whether the inscription is noting the exceptional fact that someone had the privilege of holding office for life. As mentioned above, talmudic sources say that the synagogue was represented by three delegates. But the question remains as to whether the 'head of the synagogue' was the sole president, or whether two or three persons held office at the same time. In most cases, the term is used in the singular, and no doubt only one person at a time was engaged in the ordinary running of the synagogue. But the term is also found in the plural both in Palestine and the Diaspora.[1]

The head of the synagogue was not necessarily a distinguished sage, but he was definitely an educated man, who was familiar with the rites and could judge the competence of those who were invited to read the Scriptures, translate, or address the people. No distinction was made between the management of religious and financial affairs. The head of the synagogue ran its finances, as may be gathered from many inscriptions, over a long period, coming from buildings in Palestine and in the Diaspora. As to his other functions, it may be remarked that Luke once mentions a head of the synagogue who was angry with Jesus for healing a woman on the sabbath, and who also found fault with people who looked for cures on such a day.[2] Does this mean that one of his traditional duties was to ensure correct behaviour? Or was his action simply inspired by the fact that he was more familiar with the Law and the precepts, and that he was used to being obeyed?

The head of the synagogue had an adjutant the *hazzan* (חזן), undoubtedly the ὑπηρέτης of Luke 4:20,[3] who acted as executive officer in the practical details of running the synagogue. He also acted as executive officer for the town, the tribunals and other public bodies.[4] Officers with similar functions had been attached to the Temple.[5] In contrast to the head of the synagogue, who gave his services gratis, the *hazzan* was a paid employee of the community and synagogue. Some

---

[1] Mark 5:20; Acts 13:15; see the inscription in the previous note.
[2] 13:14.
[3] Cf. Epiphanius, *Adv. Haereses* XXX, 11. It is the *hazzanim* who execute the flogging imposed by the court (*M. Makkoth* 3:2) and who call upon the judges for their sentence (*T. Sanhedrin* 9:1).
[4] *T. B. Sanhedrin* 17b mentions two *hazzanim* among the requirements of a town.
[5] *Hazzanim* are mentioned in the arrangements of the sacrificial service in the Temple (*M. Tamid* 5:3); there also a *hazzan* of the synagogue is twice mentioned in the Mishnah (*M. Yoma* 7:1; *M. Sotah* 7:8).

synagogues even provided him with housing.[1] The *hazzan* acted in fact as master of ceremonies throughout the whole liturgy. Having prepared the scrolls of the Bible which were to be read, it was he who brought them into the hall and gave the actual invitation to the nominees who were to be the community's spokesmen in the prayers and the readers of Scripture.[2] In a synagogue of Alexandria which was still in existence up to the Jewish revolt under Trajan (115-118 C.E.), the *hazzan* waved a scarf to signal for the Amen at the end of the blessings, since the speaker's voice could not reach the whole congregation.[3] The *hazzan* recited the priestly blessing, word by word, while the priests repeated it after him. At the service on public fasts, the *hazzan* gave the signal for the sounding of the horn and the trumpet at the end of the blessings.[4] He gave out the prayers and read the Scriptures when there was no one else to do so.[5] And he had various other duties, such as to announce the total collected after an appeal for funds in the synagogue.[6] Since the school-room was usually in the synagogue or a nearby room, he was to be found there helping with the children when the master was absent.[7] He sounded the trumpet on the Friday and the sabbath evening, to announce the beginning and the end of the day of rest. This duty may be regarded perhaps as part of the work he did as town *hazzan*.[8] In thinly-populated localities he could also function as judge, public speaker (preacher) or schoolmaster.[9]

A number of *hazzanim* were provided for in the Temple regulations. Two are mentioned for local government, but only one, as a rule, for the synagogue, which may be supposed to have been the general practice. The *hazzan* was certainly not classed among the sages, but he had more standing than the rest of the population, since he was well educated and familiar with the procedures of the synagogue and the rites of the liturgy. Traditions from the end of the first century C.E. rank him below the schoolmaster but above the rest of the population.[10] According to tannaitic tradition, the townspeople were obliged to

---

[1] *Seder Eliahu Rabba* II (p. 54 and n. 18); *T. B. Erubin* 55b; *T. B. Yoma* 11b.
[2] *P. T. Megillah* IV, 75b; *Midrash Tanhuma, Yitro* 15; *P. T. Berakoth* I, 9c.
[3] *T. Sukkah* 4:6 and parallels.
[4] *Sifre* Num. 39 (p. 43); *T. Megillah* 4:21; *T. Taanith* 1:13.
[5] *P. T. Berakoth* IX, 12d; *P. T. Megillah* IV, 74b; *T. B. Megillah* 25b.
[6] *Lev. Rabba* 16 (p. 357); *Eccles. Rabba* 5;
[7] *M. Shabbath* 1:3.
[8] *T. Sukkah* 4:12.
[9] *P. T. Yebamoth* XII, 13a.
[10] *M. Sotah* 9:15.

build themselves a synagogue, just as they had to provide for other public institutions and buildings.[1] But as we know from inscriptions of various dates, the cost of building, repairing or re-building a synagogue could be borne by one or more individuals instead of the community.[2] Donations, of course, came mainly from Jews, but there is evidence from Palestine and the Diaspora that non-Jews sometimes paid for the building or provided some of its accoutrements, such as the candelabrum.[3] It seems that maintenance and running costs were mainly provided for by the donations of individuals, who guaranteed to pay for the lighting and other charges.

Location and structure

Tannaitic tradition lays down two rules for the siting of synagogues. 'They must not be built except at the highest point of the town', and, 'They must not have their door pointing anywhere but east'.[4] And in fact many synagogues in Palestine were built on the heights, as at Gerasa, Eshtemoa (As–Samu) and Baram (Kefir Bir'im). A late Palestinian midrash says, 'Synagogues were built on the heights of the town in earlier times'.[5] Efforts were also made in the Diaspora to follow this principle.[6] But of course this was not always feasible, since sites were private property and it was impossible to requisition them. At all events, a large proportion of the synagogues discovered in the Land of Israel were not built on the heights, which is also true in many cases of the Diaspora.

The second rule, about the orientation, seems to have been kept only in Judaea, where there are examples from the Temple era at Masada and Herodium, and from such places as Eshtemoa and Susia at a later period. The rule was far from being rigorously kept in Galilee.[7]

In the Diaspora, synagogues were often outside built-up areas. Various passages in the Babylonian Talmud suppose that this was the usual practice, or at least a common one, in Babylonia.[8] In the

---

[1] T. Baba Metzia 11:23.
[2] P. T. Peah VIII, 21b; CII no. 1404 (Jerusalem); CII no. 694 (Stobi in Macedonia) CPJ no. 1444 (Egypt). One instance (CPJ no. 1443) of an individual together with the whole community building a synagogue is recorded.
[3] Luke 7:1-5; CII no. 766; P. T. Megillah III, 74a.
[4] T. Megillah 3:22-23.
[5] Midrash Tanhuma, Behukotai 3.
[6] T. B. Shabbath 11a.
[7] See S. Safrai in Immanuel III (1974), pp. 44-50.
[8] T. B. Erubin 21a; T. B. Kiddushin 73b.

Hellenistic Diaspora, synagogues were also built outside the towns, or by the sea or the like, as may be gathered from various sources. Josephus says that the authorities of Halicarnassus, apparently in the time of Julius Caesar, decreed that the Jews could follow their ancestral customs, which gave them, *inter alia*, the right 'to perform their liturgy' or 'build a house of prayer, by the sea, according to ancestral custom'.[1] Philo also speaks of the Jews of Alexandria assembling for prayer by the sea.[2] And when Paul came to Philippi in Macedonia, he made for the river outside the city on the sabbath, supposing that he would find the synagogue there.[3] What inspired the Jews to build outside the towns or at a waterside site is hard to say. Tannaitic sources say that outside the Land of Israel the Shekina did not rest upon the prophets, as for instance Ezekiel and Daniel, 'except in pure places, by the waters', and that Moses only prayed outside cities, as God did not speak to him in a place 'which was full of abominations and idols'.[4] One cannot say, however, how far such ideas influenced the choice of site in tannaitic times. It is certain, at any rate, that they were not followed out consistently or regarded as a matter of principle. Synagogues were built in towns all through the ancient period and in much later times.

Another halakah which had much more practical influence at all times was the one which ruled that the synagogue was to be orientated towards Jerusalem and the Temple. 'When they recited their prayers in foreign lands, they turned towards the Land of Israel... in the Land of Israel, they turned towards Jerusalem ... in Jerusalem, they turned towards the Temple Mount'.[5] The principle of facing towards Jerusalem at the time of prayer is already found in late biblical books.[6] From the first century B.C.E. on, synagogues in Palestine and elsewhere began to be built in accordance with this notion.[7] In synagogues from the fourth to the sixth century C.E., when the ark was already a permanent fixture, the wall to which it was attached was on the side facing

---

[1] Jos. *Ant.* XIV, 256-258. The expression καὶ τὰς προσευχὰς ποιεῖσθαι may be translated in either way.

[2] *In Flaccum* 122-123. However, at that moment the synagogues of Alexandria were destroyed.

[3] Acts 16:12-13.

[4] *Mekhilta, Pisha* I (pp. 2-3).

[5] *P. T. Berakoth* IV, 8b-c and parallels; cf. *M. Berakoth* 4:5.

[6] I Kings 8:44 and the parallel in 2 Chron. 6:34; I Kings 8:48 and its parallel 2 Chron. 6:38; Dan. 6:11.

[7] The earlier view that synagogues were not build in definite directions has now been refuted. See E. L. Sukenik in *Tarbiz* I (1929), p. 147.

Jerusalem. Sometimes it was set in a shallow niche, or decorated in a special way. In the earlier synagogues of Galilee, when the ark was not yet a permanent fixture, the main portal faced towards Jerusalem, and when the ark was carried into the hall, it was probably set down opposite the portal and the officiant stood in front of it.[1] The synagogues whose structure can be determined mostly date from the end of the second century C.E. and after, and little is known of their structure in the first century. But the principle of orientation towards Jerusalem seems to have been generally accepted even then.[2] The custom of facing towards Jerusalem when praying also prevailed among the various Jewish-Christian sects.[3]

The synagogues which have been discovered in Galilee, like many of those in the Diaspora, had an esplanade in front. Inside, they often had a balcony resting on three rows of pillars, but it cannot be affirmed that this was the women's gallery since the custom of having such a place only came in in the Middle Ages. Women frequented the synagogue, as we have seen, but there is no justification for saying that there was any segregation there, and no ancient source calls for segregation. Many discussions in the Talmud and other writings are only intelligible on the supposition that men and women were together in the synagogue. In many synagogues in Palestine and the Diaspora, either there is no trace of a balcony, or there is positive proof that none existed. And likewise, there is no trace of any partition in the hall. Similarly, in the Court of the Women, in the temple precincts, there was no such thing as a partition. Men and women entered together. It was only on the Feast of Tabernacles, when dancing went on all night, that there was any segregation. Women watched the dancing from the galleries round the Women's Court. Possibly, in the synagogue, women sat on the back benches or along the walls, but there is no reason to believe that the balcony was designed for them. Various uses are assigned to the upper rooms of synagogues, but they are never said to have been for the use of women. Various distinctions made in the literature of Hellenistic Judaism and early Christianity also imply that no provision was made in the architecture for any segregation. Inscriptions mention the building of various parts of the synagogue, but none mention the construction of a women's gallery.[4]

[1] L. Ginzberg, *A Commentary on the Palestinian Talmud* III (1941), pp. 394-5.
[2] E.g. the synagogues at Masada and in the Herodium.
[3] Irenaeus, *Adversus Haereses* I. 26; see also S. Pines, *The Jewish Christians of Early Centuries of Christianity according to a New Source* (1966), p. 11.
[4] See S. Safrai in *Tarbiz* XXXII (1963), pp. 329-338.

Further, no provision was made for segregation in the buildings of the early Christian Church. If a separate women's section had been a permanent feature of the synagogue, it is hard to imagine that the Christian Church would have so quickly abolished such an installation. The main piece of furniture in the synagogue was the ark containing the sacred scrolls, which, as has been noted, had no fixed place in our period. Sometimes it was carried in for the service, but sometimes only the books were brought. It may be assumed that the small room found in many ancient synagogues was designed to house the ark. The room seems to have been curtained off, but in some synagogues there may have been only a curtain to mark off a special corner for the ark. The scrolls, of rolled-up parchment, were wrapped in cloths which covered them from top to bottom. The cloths were sometimes embroidered with figures and had small bells attached.[1] Early tannaitic sources, speaking of the townspeople's duty of having rolls penned for use in the synagogue, speak only of the Torah and the Prophets. The Hagiographa were not yet read in public, but only came in later, at a date which cannot be determined.[2] But we are told that they were to be found in the synagogue.[3]

Though archaeological research has not turned up any traces of a platform, most synagogues must have had some sort of dais where the reader stood, along with the head of the synagogue, the *hazzan* and the translators. The platform was probably of wood, hence its total disappearance. The great synagogue of Alexandria had one, as tannaitic tradition says explicitly.[4] The platform was furnished with a wooden stand (ἀναλογεῖον) for the books of Scripture.[5] There were wooden benches, sometimes perhaps running the length of the walls, for the worshippers.[6] The benches were sometimes built in the form of a series of rising steps, as at Masada, Dura Europos and elsewhere. As well as the benches, the synagogue usually had a special chair, called 'the chair of Moses', for the sage who delivered the sermon. Matthew 23:2, as we know, speaks of the Scripture teachers and the Pharisees 'sitting on the chair of Moses'. The term is also found in the Midrash. Such chairs have been found in a considerable number of

---

[1] *P. T. Megillah* IV, 75b; *M. Megillah* 3:1; *M. Kelim* 28:3; *T. Kelim Baba Metzia* 1:13; *T. B. Shabbath* 58b.
[2] *T. Baba Metzia* 11:23 according to the superior reading.
[3] *P. T. Megillah* III, 73d.
[4] *T. Sukkah* 4:6 and parallels.
[5] *P. T. Megillah* III, 73d.
[6] Wooden benches are probably intended in *P. T. Megillah* III, 73d.

synagogues from the first century B.C.E., such as those of Delos, Chorazin and Hammath-Tiberias.[1] On the seating arrangements, the Tosefta has this to say: 'How were the elders seated? They sat facing the people, with their backs towards the holy place (Jerusalem and the Temple). The ark was set down with its front towards the people and its back towards the holy place. When the priests raised their hands to give the blessing, they faced the people, with their backs towards the holy place. The *hazzan* of the synagogue and the whole congregation faced towards the holy place'.[2]

This fits in very well with the tradition already mentioned, that the entrance was on the east, and this rule is inculcated in the Tosefta which follows the passage just cited. It is also borne out by the synagogues to the south and east of Jerusalem, where the wall facing Jerusalem was left blank, and could have had benches along it. It is difficult to say how the seating was arranged in Galilee, where the entrance was on the south, facing Jerusalem. The permanent equipment also included a large number of lamps and candelabra, for which there is plenty of evidence from all periods.[3] A horn too was required for the rites, and was kept in the synagogue.[4] The customs dealing with ritual purity and impurity were not intrinsically connected with the synagogue, but there are many traditions which linked such states with the reading of Scripture and the prayers,[5] and even with entering the synagogue.[6] Impurity, of itself, could not be cleansed without bathing, but for the minor types, or when there was merely a suspicion that impure objects had been handled, washing the hands sufficed. Only the Amoraim held that the hands had to be washed before prayer. But there is much to indicate that this was an ancient custom, dating from the period of the Second Temple.[7] There were in fact two customs prevailing at the time. Purity before prayer was ensured either by washing the hands or by total immersion.[8] To facilitate the worshippers,

---

[1] See Sukenik in *Tarbiz* I (1929), pp. 145-151 and the remarks of J. N. Epstein, ibid., p. 152.
[2] *T. Megillah* 4:21.
[3] See e.g. *M. Pesahim* 4:4; *T. Megillah* 3:3.
[4] *P. T. Rosh ha-Shanah* III, 58d; *T. Taanith* 1:14; *T. Sukkah* 4:11-13; cf. Jos. *War* IV, 252.
[5] *T. Berakoth* 2:13; *T. B. Shabbath* 127b.
[6] *Baraitha of Niddah*, 3, 33, 17.
[7] *T. B. Berakoth* 14b; *T. B. Hullin* 122b.
[8] *Letter of Aristeas* 305-306 (the washing of hands is treated in an allegorical manner); *Sibylline Oracles* III, 591-594 (although an optional reading mentions washing the whole body); cf. *T. B. Berakoth* 53b.

there were pools or cisterns where they could bathe near the synagogues,[1] or special installations for washing the hands or the feet.[2]

Utilization

Since the synagogue was the chief public building, it was used not just for the liturgy proper, as described above, but on many other communal and religious occasions. But this secondary utilization, temporary or permanent, was by no means obligatory. Schools, for instance, or the cisterns used for ritual washing, could be away from the synagogue and completely independent. In practice, however, whether for convenience or for economy, or simply because developments took that turn, many institutions came to be linked with the synagogue. Some of the more notable examples follow.

First and foremost, it served as the town hall, where the people met to transact municipal business, since it was the largest public building, and sometimes the largest building in town. Josephus relates that a public meeting, on the sabbath, was held in the great synagogue of Tiberias.[3] And there is a passage in the Talmud which says that meetings could be held in the synagogue on the sabbath, to discuss matters of public interest, just as in the theatre or the forum.[4]

Various collections, especially for charitable purposes, were made in the synagogue, for which there is evidence from the era of the Temple and throughout the whole of antiquity.[5] Then there were the schools, which in many places were housed in the hall of the synagogue or a nearby room,[6] though they could be found elsewhere (see chapter nineteen). It was also very common for the tribunals to sit in the synagogue. The Mishnah says that it was the *hazzan* of the synagogue who gave the flogging when this penalty was imposed by the judges. There is ample proof that the tribunals delivered judgment in the synagogues, though from much later times.[7] Early Christian writings

[1] Judith bathed each morning before praying (Jud. 12:5-8).
[2] Bathing pools are often found near ancient synagogues in Palestine; cf. also *CII* no. 1404; *CPJ* no. 432; *P. T. Megillah* III, 74a and E. L. Sukenik, 'The Ancient Synagogue in Jaffa near Nazareth' in *Bulletin of the L. M. Rabinowitz Fund* II (1951), p. 15.
[3] Jos. *Life* 276-277.
[4] *T. B. Shabbath* 150a.
[5] *P. T. Demai* III, 23a; *P. T. Horayoth* III, 48a; *Eccles. Rabba* 5; *T. Shabbath* 16:12; cf. Matt. 6:1-4.
[6] See below, p. 953.
[7] *M. Makkoth* 3:12; *M. Shebuoth* 4:10; *T. B. Yebamoth* 65b; *T. B. Ketuboth* 63b; *P. T. Gittin* I, 43b.

affirm repeatedly that floggings were usually given in the synagogue, both in Palestine and in the Diaspora, and the assertion is repeated in later writings.[1] An inscription from a synagogue not much later than the first century C.E. includes an indication of the place where the judge or arbitrator sat in the synagogue.[2]

Besides judgments, various other announcements were made in the synagogue, such as descriptions of property which had been lost, found or stolen, or requests for information if such property had been noticed.[3] Similarly, it was the custom in Panticapaeum on the Cimmerian Bosporus, to put up a notice in the synagogue about the freeing of slaves.[4] We have an inscription of this type from 80 C.E.

One notable feature was the use of the synagogue as a dininghall. Club dinners were an important institution in Jewish society before 70 C.E. and for many years after. They were a setting in which study of Torah could be pursued and traditions preserved informally. On many occasions, the dinners were held at the home of one of the members, but the clubs also used to dine in the synagogue or one of its adjoining rooms. The evidence is particularly clear for dinners held on the occasion of the new moon or on the night of the sabbath (Saturday evening). The evidence is from the amoraic period, but the custom was presumably carried over from earlier times.[5]

In many places, rooms adjoining the synagogue provided lodgings for travellers.[6] The custom of lodging travellers and their mounts in the precincts of the synagogue was widespread, and there are many indications of it.[7] The annexes discovered in many excavations probably served to some extent as lodgings for travellers.

The *kiddush* of the wine at the ending of sabbaths and feast-days was usually pronounced in the synagogue as well as at home. Our sources indicate that this double practice was mainly on the occasion of

---

[1] Matt. 10:17; Acts 22:19; Eusebius, *Historia Eccles.* v, 16, 12; Epiphanius, *Adv. Haereses* xxx, 2.

[2] M. Schwabe—B. Lifschitz, *Beth Shearim* ii (1967), no. 204; an alternative interpretation of this inscription has recently been proposed. See the literature cited by Schwabe and Lifschitz.

[3] *M. Baba Metzia* 2:6; *Lev. Rabba* i (p. 30).

[4] CII nos. 683, 684; see S. Krauss, 'Sklavenbefreiung in den jüdisch-griechischen Inschriften aus Sudrussland' in *Festschrift A. Harkavy* (1908) pp. 52-67.

[5] *P. T. Sanhedrin* viii, 26b; *P. T. Berakoth* ii, 5d.

[6] See p. 910, n. 1.

[7] The Palestinian Talmud expresses surprise that those bringing first fruits sleep in the town square and not in the synagogue. For other sources, see *Gen. Rabba* 92 (pp. 1144-1145); *P. T. Megillah* iii, 74d.

lodging travellers overnight in the precincts of the synagogue.[1] But
the custom was hardly an early one. The legality of night-time
assemblies was considered dubious in the Temple era.

BIBLIOGRAPHY

The secondary literature on Synagogue is large because of the many
sources and aspects and because of the interest of Jewish and Christian
readers. From the general books, mention should be made of S. KRAUSS,
Synagogale Altertümer, (1922; repr. 1966). This book deals principally
with the organizational and physical structures of ancient synagogues
in the Land of Israel and the Diaspora. Although slightly dated now,
because of recent discoveries, it is still useful. A more current discussion is found in E. R. GOODENOUGH, *Jewish Symbols in the Greco-
Roman Period* I, pp. 178-263. (for synagogues in the Land of Israel)
and II, pp. 70-100 (for Diaspora synagogues). A list of excavations of
synagogues in the Land of Israel and its environs with bibliographical
details is to be found in S. J. SALLER, *A Revised Catalogue of the Ancient
Synagogues of the Holy Land* (1969) (not comprehensive). For an over-
view of the archaeological difficulties concerning synagogues, see E. L.
SUKENIK, *Ancient Synagogues in Palestine and Greece* (1934). Another
general work is K. HRUBY, *Die Synagoge: Geschichtliche Entwicklung
einer Institution* (1971).

On synagogal worship and services the standard work is that of I.
ELBOGEN, *Der jüdische Gottesdienst in seiner geschichtlichen Entwicklung*
(1931; repr. 1967); a Hebrew translation including additions appeared
in 1972 by J. HEINEMAN and others.

On prayer in the ancient period, see J. HEINEMAN, *Prayer in the Period
of the Tannaim and Amoraim* (1964; in Hebrew). On prayers related
to the Christian liturgical practices, see G. ALON, *Studies in the History
of Israel* I (1957), pp. 283-294 and D. FLUSSER, 'Sanctus und Gloria' in
Abraham unser Vater, Festschrift Otto Michel (1963), pp. 129ff.

On the cycles of liturgical readings in the Pentateuch and Prophets,
see A. BÜCHLER, 'The Reading of the Law and Prophets in a Triennial
Cycle', *JQR* (1893) pp. 426-68; (1894), pp. 1-73; J. MANN, *The Bible
as Read and Preached in the Old Synagogue*, 2 vols (1940-66). For the
influence of Jewish liturgical readings upon early Christianity, see A.
GUILDING, *The Fourth Gospel and Jewish Worship* (1960), and L. CROCKET,
'Luke 4; 16-30 and the Jewish Lectionary Cycle' *JJS* (1966), pp. 13-46.

[1] *T. B. Pesahim* 101a; *P. T. Pesahim* X, 37c.

Chapter Nineteen
Education and the Study of the Torah

The main component of Jewish education in the first century c.e. is the study of the Torah. In order to understand education we must first see what place the Torah occupied in the life and thought of the Jewish people. The nation's return to the God of Israel after the Babylonian captivity was expressed principally by its acceptance of the Law of Moses as the Law of God. In the course of the Second Temple period different sects and movements came into being, which developed their own ways of interpretation of the written and oral Law, but they all accepted the Torah as the fundamental law of existence and as teacher and guide of the Jewish nation for all times. The Torah was the basis of the entire social and legal system and of the way of life of the community and of the individual. The Torah established a man's place within the nation and the nation's place among the other nations; it established the rules for every-day life and provided the ideals to strive after.

The study of the Torah, however, was not only done to learn proper conduct and action; it was also an act of worship, which brought the student closer to God. The study of the Torah was a holy duty, the fulfilment of which became a religious experience. It was cultivated in public worship in the synagogue (in the readings from the Torah on sabbaths, mondays, thursdays and during the festivals), and in the Temple, at all public meetings and in individual and group study. Almost all the literature from the Second Temple period manifests this religious aim of Torah study. This is most powerfully expressed in Psalm 119, which is a paean to the Torah. All stages of education are centred around the study of the Torah. Even the initial learning of the letters of the alphabet was understood as a religious act, as was children's further study. This is the background of the wellknown sayings: 'Schoolchildren may not be made to neglect their studies even for the building of the Temple' and 'The world endures only for the sake of the breath of schoolchildren.'[1] ;Though these statements

[1] *T. B. Shabbath* 119b.

945

are from a later date (about the third century), they admirably express the atmosphere and views which prevailed earlier as well.

The duty of education and the establishment of schools

The national assemblies in the days of Ezra and Nehemiah were definitely orientated to public instruction: 'And he read from it from early morning until midday, in the presence of the men and the women and those who could understand; and the ears of all the people were attentive to the book of the Law' (Neh. 8:3). During the Second Temple period and even more after the destruction of Jerusalem and the Temple in 70 C.E. the entire Jewish community, from its public institutions to the individual families, developed into an education-centred society, which paid particular attention to the education of children. An illustration of this is found in the Passover *seder*, in which questions for the children are incorporated into the service to encourage their interest and participation. It states that 'Here the son asks his father and if the son lacks intelligence, his father instructs him.'[1] Numerous laws were enacted and formulated so that 'the children...should be educated...so that they will be familiar with the commandments.'[2] We are ignorant of the way of life among the Sadducaeans, but this characteristic is conspicuous among the Pharisees and it also emerges from the various descriptions of the Essene way of life and especially from the Dead Sea scrolls. Torah study was not confined to the legal experts and the priests, but became a general community matter. Everyone who had gained a knowledge of the Torah was obliged to teach others, and he who studied Torah and did not teach it 'hath despised the Word of the Lord' (Num. 15:31).[3] After the Bar Cochba revolt when a Roman decree demanded apostasy, the sages met and announced: 'Everyone who has studied shall come and teach, and everyone who has not studied shall come and learn.'[4]

As early as the first century C.E. and perhaps even earlier, the majority of the children received education at school. A baraita from the end of the first century counted the school among the institutions which a town is obliged to maintain.[5] When talmudic tradition described the

[1] *M. Pesahim* 10:4 and the Haggadah of Passover.
[2] *M. Yoma* 8:4.
[3] *T. B. Sanhedrin* 99a.
[4] *Canticles Rabba* 2.
[5] *T. B. Sanhedrin* 17b.

greatness and prosperity of a town, it gave the number of schools and schoolchildren. Of pre-70 Jerusalem we read: 'Four hundred and eighty synagogues were in Jerusalem each of which had a "house of reading" (בית ספר) and a "house of learning" (בית תלמוד), the 'house of reading' for the written Law and the 'house of learning' for the oral Law.'[1] So too when the town of Beitar was expanding after 70 C.E. it was said: 'There were five hundred schools in Beitar and in the smallest of them there were no less than five hundred children.'[2] The regular upkeep of the schools was considered to be the secret of the existence and the strength of the nation as a whole and of every single settlement. In a midrash transmitted by Abba ben Kahana, a third century sage, the 'nations' consult Abnomos of Gadara concerning the best time to destroy Israel. He advises them, 'Go round to their synagogues and schools, and if you find there children with voices uplifted you cannot subjugate them; if not, you can, for thus did their father assure them, saying: 'The voice is the voice of Jacob (Gen. 27:22): when the voice of Yacob rings out in the synagogues, Esau has no hands.''[3] A town which did not employ teachers of the written and oral Law had no right to exist, and this sin of omission, according to Rabbi Simeon ben Johai, led to the destruction of the place.[4]

According to tannaitic law the responsibility for education fell upon the father: 'What is the father's duty towards his son? ... and he shall teach him the Law.'[5] Philo and Josephus also emphasize the educational effort made by the parents to furnish the children with a knowledge of the Torah from a tender age.[6] Beginning at the end of the second century we hear of instances of tutors staying in the house of the parents;[7] there were probably such instances also in the first century but, as a rule, children went to school.

The Talmuds contain two traditions concerning the regulation of school attendance and the establishment of schools. The Palestinian Talmud says of Simeon ben Shetah, who was president of the sanhedrin during the reign of Alexander Jannaeus and Salome (103-76 B.C.E.), that he ordained 'that children go to school'.[8] The Babylonian Talmud

---

[1] P. T. Megillah III, 73d; P. T. Ketuboth XIII, 35c. For the explanation of the terms bet sefer and bet talmud see below.
[2] P. T. Taanith IV, 69a; in a more exaggerated form T. B. Gittin 58a.
[3] Gen. Rabba 65 (pp. 734-5) and parallels.
[4] P. T. Hagigah I, 76c.
[5] T. Kiddushin I:11; Sifre Deut. 46.
[6] Jos. Against Apion II, 178; Philo, Legatio ad Gaium 210.
[7] P. T. Peah (end); T. B. Ketuboth 111b.
[8] P. T. Ketuboth VIII, 32c.

contains another, more detailed tradition: 'Rabbi Judah has told us in the name of Rab to wit: Verily the name of that man is to be blessed, Joshua ben Gamala, for but for him the Torah would have been forgotten from Israel. For at first if a child had a father, his father taught him, and if he had no father he did not learn at all... They then made an ordinance that teachers of children should be appointed in Jerusalem ... Even so, however, if a child had a father, the father would take him up to Jerusalem and have him taught there; and if not, he would not go up to learn there. They, therefore, ordained that teachers should be appointed in each prefecture, and that boys should enter school at the age of sixteen or seventeen. They did so; and if the teacher punished them, they used to rebel and leave the school. At length Joshua ben Gamala came and ordained that teachers of young children should be appointed in each district and each town and that children should enter school at the age of six or seven.'[1]

It is difficult to know whether a contradiction exists between the tradition about the earlier regulation of Simeon ben Shetah and the tradition about the regulation of Joshua ben Gamala, who officiated during the last years of the Temple (63-65 C.E.) or if they complement each other. The Babylonian tradition contains in its present form some literary embellishments and should not be seen as strictly historical in every detail. But basically it has to be accepted as historical. It is transmitted by the Amora Rab who lived in Palestine for many years and who took numerous reliable traditions with him to Babylonia. In general talmudic tradition does not tend to overpraise the high priests of the end of the Temple period, and it does not exaggerate their contribution to legislation. It is apparently a historical fact that during Joshua ben Gamala's period of office, shortly before the destruction of the Temple, great progress was made in the establishment of a network of schools in every town. One definitely has also to accept the tradition given in the Palestinian Talmud, which states that as early as the days of Simeon ben Shetah action was taken to establish schools for children. What precisely was done by each of them cannot be determined. From the two traditions mentioned, which are confirmed by many other sources, we are entitled to state that in the first century not only a basic knowledge of Jewish culture was widespread, but also that schools existed in all towns and even in the smaller settlements.

Of course, there existed settlements which were not organized accord-

[1] *T. B. Baba Bathra* 21a.

ing to the Halakah, which had no proper schools and 'which did not employ teachers of the written and oral Law,' as we hear from the complaints of sages at later times.[1] There were children who did not study at all during their childhood. Rabbi Akiba, who came from a poor family, did not study as a child, but received his education only as an adult. Even Rabbi Eliezer ben Hyrcanus (before 70 C.E.) who belonged to a well-to-do family, went up to Jerusalem to study only at the age of twenty-one.[2] The Halakah envisages the possibility of a group sitting down to the Passover meal and no one among them able to recite the *hallel*.[3] A tradition from the Second Temple period relates that during the offering of the first-fruits it was customary that someone able to recite the passages of the first-fruits would do so, 'and all that could not recite them repeated the words [after the priests]; but when these refrained from bringing [their first-fruits] it was ordained that both those that could recite the words and those that could not should repeat them [after the priests].'[4] Halakoth of this type are also found in connection with other cases.[5] But as a rule, children did attend school, learned to read the books of the Bible and acquired the basic knowledge which enabled them to participate in Jewish life.

The reading from the Torah in the synagogue was generally done by ordinary members of the congregation, who were invited to do so. On the sabbath there were at least seven who read from the Torah and one from the Prophets and also at least one who translated these readings. Among a group of people eating together one recited the grace after the meal. The sermon in the synagogue was directed to the whole congregation, which had to know not only the contents of the portion that was being read from the Torah but also other Scripture passages, to which the preacher related the reading. We possess a vivid picture of the study of the Law in the Qumran sect, whose members obviously had a thorough knowledge of the Bible and at least some knowledge of the oral Law. Their knowledge presumably did not exceed that of Pharisaic circles.

We find several approaches in the Second Temple period towards the teaching of the Law to adults. Some wanted to teach the Law only

---

[1] *P. T. Hagigah* 1, 76c.
[2] *Aboth de Rabbi Nathan*, Version A, 6; Version B, 12-13.
[3] *T. Pesahim* 10:8.
[4] *M. Bikkurim* 3:7. Philo, *De Spec. leg.* 11, 216 relates to the situation before the decision that all should repeat the words after the priest.
[5] Cf. *M. Sukkah* 3:10.

to apt and deserving pupils and trained disciples only from among those whose 'inside was as their outside', but others taught everyone and trained anyone who came to them, without examining who it was that came to study the Torah.[1] But when it came to instructing children and accepting them into school, it was clear to all that every single child, the rich man's as the poor man's had to be accepted, the son of the *haver* and of the respected citizens as well as the son of the ignorant and the despised, even the sons of sinners and criminals.

The structure of the schools and the methods of teaching

Many talmudic sources, both early and late, and particularly the Palestinian ones, mention the division between the *bet sefer*, the 'house of the book', in which the reading of the written Law was taught, and the *bet talmud*, the 'house of learning', which taught Mishnah or oral Law. The sources differentiate also systematically between the *sofer*, the teacher of the written Law, corresponding to the *bet sefer*, and the *mashneh*, the teacher of the oral Law, corresponding to the *bet talmud*.[2] In the *bet sefer* the child learned the alphabet and reading. The teacher taught the letters by writing them on a small wax tablet with a stylus, and the children recited them. From the tablet the children passed to the *megillah*, a small scroll on which passages from the Torah were written and from the *megillah* they graduated to the 'book' of the Torah.[3]

Since in our period Hebrew was not vocalized, reading could only be learned by repeating the reading of the teacher and auditive memory. A child or adult who had not received from his teacher the tradition for the reading of a given passage did not know how to read it correctly.[4] Absolute precision was, therefore, required from the teacher for the exact transmission of the reading tradition. We are told of a teacher who was dismissed for excessive punishment of the children; but in the end he was re-instated because no one so precise as he could be found.[5] I tend to accept the view of some scholars, who hold that written vocalization was first practised by the teachers of

---

[1] *Aboth de Rabbi Nathan*, Version B, 4 (p. 14) and *T. B. Berakoth* 28a.
[2] *P. T. Maaseroth* III, 50d; *P. T. Megillah* III, 73d; *Cant. Rabba* 5; *T. B. Ketuboth* 105a.
[3] *Aboth de R. Nathan*, Version A, 6; *Deut. Rabba* 8; *Midrash ha-Gadol* on Exodus 31:18 (p. 675) from an unknown source.
[4] *T. B. Kiddushin* 33a; *T. B. Pesahim* 117a.
[5] *T. B. Gittin* 36a.

young children as a teaching aid.[1] In order to facilitate memorization, the teachers divided up long verses. We possess evidence from the amoraic period of conflicts between teachers and sages, who did not allow division of the verses of the Torah, similar to the conflict between fathers and strict teachers, who did not allow themselves this division.[2] The Halakah forbids the writing of parts of the Torah on small scrolls; however, it was permitted to write passages from Creation to the Flood in Genesis and from the section on sacrifices, Leviticus 1-8, on small scrolls for the sake of children.[3] Several tannaitic and amoraic sources say that children began their studies with Leviticus and that Genesis was studied afterwards. That seems to be the reason why the beginning of Leviticus was included in the permission to write on small scrolls. The fact that Leviticus was chosen is difficult to explain, as the Torah does not begin there; moreover, the material in this book—halakic details of sacrifices—is not really suitable for introducing a young child to the study of the Torah. A midrash gives the following reason for it: 'Why do children begin with the Book of Leviticus and not with Genesis? Because children are pure and the sacrifices are pure, so the pure deal with the pure.'[4] This is possibly only a secondary reason, although it is extremely dubious whether those scholars are correct who think that this custom goes back to an early period when instruction was mainly in the hands of the priests, who taught their sons the reading of the Torah in view of their future function in the Temple service. Information relating to this custom only goes back as far as the time of R. Akiba and even if it could be presumed to go back to several generations preceding him, we are still not justified in attributing this custom to such an early period in Jewish history as when instruction centred around the Temple service and its priests. It is even doubtful if such a condition ever actually existed.

No passages were left out in the study of the Torah and the Prophets;[5] and all the books of the Bible were studied in their order. With regard to the public readings of the Torah we find different opinions and customs concerning the omission of certain passages which were read but not translated such as the stories of Amnon and Tamar and of David and Bathsheva, yet the 'teacher instructs in his usual way'.[6]

[1] Cf. Bacher.
[2] *T. B. Megillah* 22a and *P. T. Megillah* IV, 75b.
[3] *P. T. Megillah* III, 74a.
[4] *Lev. Rabba* 7 (p. 156) and parallels; *Aboth de R. Nathan*, Version A, 6 (p. 29).
[5] *M. Megillah* 4:10; *T. Megillah* 4:31-38; *T. B. Megillah* 25a-b.
[6] *T. Megillah* 4:38.

Education in reading and training for writing were not connected; the sources do not mention the teaching of writing in schools. Writing was a professional skill acquired separately. Yet the ability to write was fairly widespread as can be proved by the various samples found in the manuscripts which date from our period. There is also a considerable amount of evidence concerning the method and actual process of learning to write. The ability to write was less widespread than that of reading which everyone possessed. We know that some of the most famous Amoraim were unable to engage in correspondence. The Amora Rab states that a true sage has to learn three things: Writing, ritual slaughter and circumcision.[1] The ability to write was a means of serving the needs of the public just as was the knowledge of ritual slaughter and circumcision, and it was proper for a sage to acquire them, though not as part of the school curriculum. The schools taught pupils how to read the books of the Torah and the Prophets, to translate them, to recite the *shema* and grace after meals and so on, which prepared a student to play his part in the life of the family and the community.[2]

Mishnah Aboth 5:21 fixes the age for school attendance: At five the age is reached for the study of Scripture, at ten for the study of Mishnah. Other sources mention six to seven years as the suitable age. Rab (beginning of the third century) instructs a well-known contemporary teacher of children as follows: 'Before the age of six do not accept pupils; from that age you can accept them and stuff them like an ox.'[3] After about five years of Bible study the boy was promoted to the oral Law, i.e. Mishnah, though the Halakah obliges a father to teach his son only the Bible.[4] From amoraic literature we learn that it was usual to send boys to school up to the age of twelve or thirteen. We are told that in Usha during the second half of the second century it was decreed that a man was obliged to provide for instruction for his son until the age of twelve and then to begin to teach him a craft and slowly to introduce him to work.[5]

In the first century C.E. the oral Law was still studied in oral form, even though various written collections existed of halakic and similar material. The teacher explained the halakic item or the Midrash and

[1] *T. B. Hullin* 9a.
[2] *Aboth de R. Nathan*, Version B, 13.
[3] *T. B. Baba Bathra* 21a; *T. B. Ketuboth* 50a.
[4] *T. B. Kiddushin* 30a.
[5] *Gen. Rabba* 63 (p. 692); *T. B. Ketuboth* 50a (according to the explanation of Nathan of Rome in *Aruk ha-Shalem* s.v. 77).

encouraged the student to participate actively in asking questions and explaining them, but he also demanded memory-work and a constant effort to remember the actual text of the Halakah or Midrash. Individual and group study of the Bible, repetition of the passages, etc. were often done by chanting them aloud. There is the frequent expression 'the chirping of children', which was heard by people passing close by a synagogue as the children were reciting a verse. Adults too, in individual and in group study, often read aloud; for it was frequently advised not to learn in a whisper, but aloud. This was the only way to overcome the danger of forgetting.[1]

At the age of twelve or thirteen a boy finished his studies at school. If he was gifted and so inclined he went on to a *bet midrash* to sit at the feet of teachers of the Law with other adults who studied Torah in their spare time. If the boy showed further ability and willingness he might even after some years go to one of the famous sages and stay with him for a number of years. A formal, continuous educational framework after the age of twelve or thirteen seems to have been unknown in Israel at this time.

The school was connected with the synagogue according to most Second Temple and later sources.[2] The instruction took place in the prayer hall or in a room adjoining the synagogue; in smaller towns the *hazzan* also acted as teacher or assisted the teacher.[3] But this was by no means a matter of principle for we find teachers holding classes in the courtyard of their houses and consequently becoming involved in quarrels with their neighbours who tried to prevent the opening of such schools. Rules were therefore formulated concerning the rights of the neighbours, the rights of the teacher and the priority of the school.[4] The main equipment in the school consisted of benches for the teachers which were often collapsible.[5] Perhaps such benches were used in the synagogue, since they had to be dismantled upon the conclusion of the study period, to prepare the place for the prayers due to begin. While the Temple existed, the presence of a school in a synagogue, even inside the prayer-hall itself, did not constitute a serious nuisance either for the school or for the synagogue because the latter was open principally on the sabbath.

[1] *Pesikta de R. Kahana* 15 (p. 255); *Midrash Psalms* 93 (p. 416); *T. B. Erubin* 53b-54a and elsewhere.
[2] *P. T. Megillah* II, 73d.
[3] *P. T. Yebamoth* XII, 13a; *M. Shabbath* 1:3.
[4] *M. Baba Bathra* 2:3; *T. Baba Bathra* 1:4; *T. B. Baba Bathra* 21a-b.
[5] *T. Kelim Baba Bathra* 1:1.

The school started early in the morning. A certain midrash has preserved the story of how the mother rises early and stands and washes the faces of her sons 'so that they would go before the teacher. And at the sixth hour, noon, she would stand and receive her sons who returned from school.'[1] We are expressly told that the *bet talmud* held two sessions a day, one in the morning and another in the evening.[2] Probably only the boys who studied at the more advanced level and not the young ones returned to school towards evening. Small children who had to walk some distance to school were, of course, accompanied by their parents. Here and there we hear of children being taken by their fathers but it usually fell to the mother's lot, the women even being encouraged to be punctillious and not to say: 'If he is destined to learn, he will learn'. They should make an effort to bring him to the synagogue, to the children's teacher.[3] The fact that women were accustomed to take their children to school is the basis of the rule that a bachelor is forbidden to be a teacher of children because the mothers bring their children.[4]

Lessons took place on all the days of the week including the sabbath when they would, however, read no new material, but repeat earlier lessons. We even find the children going over their lessons on Friday evenings in the synagogue.[5] In the amoraic period we find the rule that during the twenty-one days from the seventeenth of Tammuz to the ninth of Ab (July-August) the children were to be dismissed at the fourth hour, probably because those are the hottest days of the year. On the ninth of Ab they were released from study altogether and the boys returned to their villages.[6]

Discipline was quite strict. It was mainly based on respect for the Law and for the teacher who transmitted the word of God. But the strap was permitted and was an accepted means of enforcing discipline. The Halakah recognizes the teacher's right to beat his pupils.[7] We read in a parable: 'This may be compared to a school-teacher who comes to school with a strap in his hand. Who becomes apprehensive? He who is accustomed to be punished daily.'[8] On the other hand, at

[1] *Pesikta Rabbati* 43 (18b).
[2] *Pesikta Rabbati* 41 (p. 174a); *Ex. Rabba* 47.
[3] *T. B. Berakoth* 17a; *P. T. Hallah* 1, 57b.
[4] *M. Kiddushin* 4:13; *P. T. Kiddushin* iv, 66b.
[5] *M. Shabbath* 1:3; *T. Shabbath* 1:12.
[6] *Lam. Rabba* 1; *P. T. Taanith* iv, 68d.
[7] *M. Makkoth* 2:2.
[8] *T. B. Sukkah* 29a.

least from the beginning of the amoraic period onward, excessive punishment was frowned upon. There are detailed and clear instructions on how to cut down on corporal punishment as much as possible and a teacher could be dismissed or other disciplinary action could be taken against him for excessive beating.[1] It was certainly considered ideal for a teacher to conquer the hearts of his pupils not by external disciplinary measures, but by friendly treatment and efficient teaching. Many early and late sayings extol the virtues of the teacher who in his guidance and support shows understanding for his pupils' problems and difficulties.[2]

Tannaitic literature only makes learning the Torah obligatory for boys and not for girls. This view is also expressed in the later books of the Bible, the apocryphal literature and in the works of Philo and Josephus. We find a dispute in the Jabneh period among the Tannaim with Ben Azzai saying that a man is obliged to teach his daughter the Torah and R. Eliezer maintaining that teaching a girl the Torah would encourage too much intimacy between the sexes,[3] and that 'there is no wisdom for a woman except at the spindle'.[4] Whether as a result of the prevailing conditions or because the decision went according to R. Eliezer, his point of view became widespread and girls did not generally attend school. Women were, however, obliged to utter blessings and recite grace after meals; and from the place they occupied in the life of the family, including the occupation with the children's education, it would appear that the girls too were given some education. We frequently find women present in the synagogue at times of prayer and sermons, though mainly as passive listeners.[5] We know of several women from the tannaitic and amoraic periods who were Torah scholars. The most outstanding example is Beruryah the daughter of R. Hananiah ben Teradyon from Siknin in Galilee and the wife of R. Meir, who had received her education before the Bar Cochba revolt. Beruryah disagreed with the rabbis on a halakah and they actually accepted her viewpoint. There are also stories of her outstanding knowledge of the Law,[6] but she and the few similar women probably constitute exceptions.

[1] *T. B. Baba Bathra* 21a; *P. T. Moed Katan* III, 81d.
[2] *M. Aboth* 2:5; *T. B. Berakoth* 63b and elsewhere.
[3] *M. Sotah* 3:4. R. Eliezer's words should be understood as follows: 'If a man gives his daughter a knowledge of the Law, it is as though he taught her lechery.'
[4] *P. T. Sotah* III, 19a.
[5] *T. Sotah* 7:9 and parallels.
[6] *T. Kelim Baba Kamma* 4:17; *T. Kelim Baba Metzia* 1:6; *T. B. Pesahim* 62b.

From the beginning of the amoraic period we possess ample information about the public concern for and supervision of the schools, about the number of children to a class, the time they had to be sent home, the methods of instruction, the division of the text into verses, punishment of the pupils, etc.[1] It is not impossible that in this period the rule of the patriarch was established and many public institutions were founded, but it seems more likely that it is merely accidental that we possess no earlier detailed information of public supervision of schools. From the amoraic period onwards information becomes in general more abundant. Many aspects of practical and intellectual life are documented only from the amoraic period, though from internal evidence their origin must be dated earlier. We know for certain that in tannaitic times public concern was not limited to the establishment of schools in every locality, but that it included also the care for payment of the teachers. Tannaitic halakoth deal with the problems involved in levying taxes for educational expenses, just as tannaitic traditions give as the reason for the destruction of Palestinian towns 'that they did not keep salaried teachers of written and oral Law.'[2]

Tannaitic literature repeatedly affirms the principle that teaching the Law like the other public services ought to be performed without financial reward. They explained the verse: 'Behold, I have taught you statutes and ordinances' (Deut. 4:5) as: 'What I do for nothing you too do for nothing.'[3] In one place we read: 'Let your teaching of the Torah be free and do not accept payment for it, for one does not accept payment for the words of the Law'.[4] This ideal was in fact extensively practised in teaching Torah to adults. As a matter of principle this rule also applied to the teachers of children, but there is no doubt that the latter received payment. We are told of a school teacher who did not differentiate between rich and poor and who did not demand tuition fees from a child unable to pay.[5] But we know for certain that in general the teacher received a salary for his work. Various explanations are given of this permission: The teacher would accept indemnification for idleness, that is to say, compensation for the time he was losing from work he might be doing, but not for the actual teaching of the Torah, or he would receive a salary for teaching

---

[1] Cf. *P. T. Hagigah* I, 76c; *P. T. Megillah* IV, 75b; *T. B. Megillah* 22a; *Lam. Rabba* I; *P. T. Megillah* III, 74a etc.

[2] *P. T. Peah* VIII, 21a; *P. T. Hagigah* I, 76c.

[3] *P. T. Nedarim* IV, 38c; *T. B. Bekhoroth* 29a.

[4] *Derek Eretz Zuta* 4; cf. Matt. 10:8.

[5] *T. B. Taanith* 24a.

punctuation and accents which are not an integral part of the Torah, or for looking after the children.[1]

Tannaitic and amoraic sources discuss the collection of taxes for 'the salaries of teachers of written and oral Law' and they praise bachelors who contribute their share.[2] On the other hand, the sources also mention the paying of tuition fees by fathers and even bargaining with teachers. These negotiations between parents and teacher were permitted, according to the school of Hillel, even on the sabbath because it was a 'heavenly affair'.[3] It seems likely that the maintenance of the teacher was divided between the town and the fathers. One source in the Babylonian Talmud states that if the number of students rises above twenty-five—when the Halakah obliges the teacher to engage an assistant—the town will help him with the assistant's salary.[4] It is fairly certain that children from poor families were not deprived of schooling, and we find no complaint on this account from any sage.

Because of his special attitude to the Law and its teaching it seems hardly feasible that the teacher should have been a servant on the lines of the *paidagogos* in the Graeco-Roman world. Tradition considers the teacher of the Torah and the oral Law to be engaged in God's work. Numerous passages in tannaitic and amoraic literature praise teachers for the faithful performance of their work and compare them with those 'who turn many to righteousness, like the stars for ever and ever' (Dan. 12:3) and to other such verses which they interpreted in their praise.[5] Even so, in the social hierarchy the teachers come last, the order being: sages, the 'leaders of the generation', the heads of synagogues and finally the teachers, though many sources also count the teachers among the spiritual élite of the society.[6]

With regards to the study of Greek in the Second Temple period it is certain, that at least in the Land of Israel no Greek was taught in the *bet sefer* and the *bet talmud*. There was even a prohibition against teaching children Greek.[7] The entire school curriculum was oriented

---

[1] *P. T. Nedarim* IV, 38c; *T. B. Nedarim* 37a-b; *Pesikta de R. Kahana* 27 (p. 402).
[2] *P. T. Peah* VIII, 21a; *Lev. Rabba* 27 (p. 624).
[3] *T. B. Betzah* 16a; *T. B. Shabbath* 12a and 150a.
[4] *T. B. Baba Bathra* 21a according to the better reading.
[5] *Semahoth de R. Hiyya* 3:8 (p. 224); *Esther Rabba* 6; *Lev. Rabba* 9 (p. 175); *Cant. Rabba* 1.
[6] Cf. *Lev. Rabba* 30 (p. 693); *Eccles. Zuta* 2 (p. 116).
[7] Cf. S. Lieberman, 'The Alleged Ban on Greek Wisdom' in *Hellenism in Jewish Palestine*, pp. 100-14.

towards the teaching of Torah and its commandments. Among the ruling classes, however, and also in the aristocratic-priestly circles many knew Greek. Even some Pharisaic leaders knew Greek for the purpose of maintaining contact with the Diaspora. After 70 C.E. Greek was also learned by those who intended to take part in public affairs and who had to deal with the cities of mixed population in the Land of Israel, the Diaspora and the foreign authorities.[1] Greek was taught outside the traditional school system by both Jewish and non-Jewish teachers. This phenomenon was already known for Jerusalem before 70 C.E.

An early baraita, enumerating the obligations a father has towards his son, specifically includes 'to teach him the Torah and to teach him a craft.'[2] The reason for this rule is not only care for the boy's future, but also the considerable importance ascribed to work and crafts. Second Temple sages not only taught: 'Love work, hate lordship',[3] but they considered work as a means for attaining spiritual elevation.[4] Very often the son would take up his father's profession, and we even find sayings which praised this practice;[5] otherwise the boy was apprenticed to another craftsman and occasionally even went to live in his house for a number of years. According to the school of Hillel negotiations for a son's apprenticeship, as well as for his education in Scripture, could be conducted on a Sabbath.[6]

The study of Torah by adults

The study of Torah did not terminate when a boy finished school. Those, who were preparing to be scribes, teachers, judges or heads of the synagogue continued their studies, and larger numbers of others were also involved in Torah study in groups or as disciples of a sage and even more attended at least the sermons given on the Sabbath and festivals in the synagogue.

What subjects were studied by these groups, by the disciples of a sage and by the general public? Of course, the Bible played an important role in their studies, but not in the same way as the Bible is studied today. Specific study of the Bible was undertaken by specialists

---

[1] *T. Sotah* 15:8; *T. B. Baba Kamma* 83a.
[2] *T. Kiddushin* 1:11.
[3] *M. Aboth* 1:10.
[4] Cf. *Aboth de R. Nathan*, Version A, 11 (pp. 44f.).
[5] *P. T. Rosh ha-Shanah* 1, 57b; *T. B. Arakhin* 16b.
[6] *Lam. Rabba* 3; *T. B. Shabbath* 12a.

(בעלי מקרא) who were mostly associated with the sanhedrin and who dealt with textual problems, exact readings, and similar subjects. However, the main subject of study was the oral Law according to its different disciplines: Halakah, Midrash and Haggadah. Halakah was the study and formulation of the Law in mishnaic form without any direct connection with the text of the Bible. Midrash was the study of the biblical text for the purpose of drawing from it according to certain rules, new legal precepts. Or new scriptural bases were sought for existing Halakah. Through Midrash new halakoth were created and ancient halakoth were adapted to contemporary situations. The third discipline, Haggadah, is hard to define precisely since it ranges over a number of areas: theology, religious philosophy, ethics, practical wisdom, historical legend, biblical non-halakic exegesis, speculations on messianic times, etc. In general, it comprises all aspects of the oral Law which are not Halakah. In general public instruction the subject was mostly Haggadah, but halakic items were explained as well. In the smaller more advanced groups and in the case of the sage with his disciples the discussion of Halakah constituted the main object. When Haggadah was studied in those groups, the form was more technical than that used by the general teacher or preacher, who made greater use of parables and images, trying to make his teaching more lively and attractive. Not every teacher or sage dealt with all the disciplines in equal measure. The great well known sages have left their imprint on all three disciplines, yet there were sages and teachers who specialized in Halakah and did not deal with Midrash at all. On those who devoted themselves solely to the collection and preservation of ancient halakic traditions without inquiring into their (biblical) roots, the sages said: 'The *tannaim* (those who repeat) bring destruction upon the world.'[1] There are sages who are remembered mainly for halakic matters while the greatness of others lay in Midrash.

In addition to these three main disciplines there existed two other associated disciplines: 1. Astronomy, with which went mathematics, which served the calculation of time and the determination of the months and the years. Great sages were praised for their knowledge of these subjects and anyone able to learn them was obliged to do so. Astronomy and mathematics, or as they were frequently called *gemetria*, merely constituted a kind of 'after-course of wisdom' as a sage of the Jabneh period defined them.[1] 2. Mystical and philosophical

[1] *T. B. Sotah* 22a.
[2] *M. Aboth* 3:18; *T. B. Sukkah* 28a; *T. B. Shabbath* 75a.

959

speculation. This focused upon the interpretation of two biblical passages: the creation of the universe in Genesis chap. I (מעשה בראשית) and the divine chariot in Ezekiel chap. I (מעשה מרכבה). Around these two subjects metaphysical and mystical theories, and ideas on the angels and the heavens, were developed. Detailed traditions are known about Johanan ben Zakkai and his pupils and about a group of the Jabneh sages involved in this study. They are called 'the four who entered the Garden' which means esoteric thought.[1] But this study was only done by a few sages, being handed down in secret and in private meetings.[2]

Characteristic of the teaching of the great sages in all fields are the innovations and new creations brought about in their method of teaching and in the contents. It occasionally appears as though the sages only tried to transmit the traditions they had themselves heard from their teachers. In fact they established new interpretations in all their teachings. R. Eliezer ben Hyrcanus says of himself: 'Nor have I ever in my life said a thing I did not hear from my teachers.'[3] No doubt, he represents the conservative trend which tended to abstain from innovations, but even his teachings contain many new elements, both in the field of Haggadah and Halakah.

The various settings for teaching and studying the Law among adults may be divided conveniently into three main categories: 1. The *bet midrash* whose members young and old devoted most or all their time to study. 2. The synagogue, where the wider public was instructed in the course of the liturgy. 3. Other meetings of groups for meals and other occasions, in which study and instruction took place.

Bet midrash as an appellation for the institution of education already occurs in Ben Sira 51:23. The term applies here to the school of Ben Sira in Jerusalem at the beginning of the second century B.C.E. which dealt rather with the wisdom literature than with the traditional sources such as the Torah and Prophets. The students of Ben Sira were sons of aristocratic families, who prepared themselves for leading functions in politics and the economy. The *midrash* schools of the Scribes, mentioned in tannaitic literature and whose presence is felt in the New Testament and in Josephus' works, considered themselves to be the successors of the schools of the Prophets in transmitting and fostering the written and oral Law. In these schools of the scribes

[1] *T. Hagigah* 2:3; *P. T. Hagigah* II, 77a-b; *T. B. Hagigah* 14b.
[2] *M. Hagigah* 2:1; and *T. Hagigah* 2:1-2.
[3] *T. B. Sukkah* 28a.

wide circles of young people and adults, in Jerusalem and in the country, were taught. In the course of the Second Temple period the schools of the scribes became the most common institution of study in the Land of Israel and in the Diaspora, and transmitted and studied the written and oral Law.

Early evidence for the existence of the *bet midrash* of the scribes is linked to the central institution of the sanhedrin in Jerusalem. Within the sanhedrin, the scribes and Pharisees constituted a *bet midrash*, which was centred on the leaders of the Pharisees, such as Shemaiah and Abtalion, Hillel and Shammai and afterwards the descendants of Hillel. After the brief interval of Rabban Johanan ben Zakkai, the descendants of Hillel returned to head the sanhedrin and the *bet midrash* until the end of the second century when the division took place between the offices of the patriarchate and the leadership of the *bet midrash*.

After the destruction of the Temple all members of the sanhedrin were sages and belonged to the *bet midrash*. In the Tosefta it is said that the sanhedrin, on the sabbath and on festivals, 'would only enter the *bet midrash* on the Temple Mount.'[1] Even when the sanhedrin sat as a council after 70 C.E. and dealt with specific questions concerning public administration or with halakic questions brought before it, it would at the same time function as a *bet midrash* dealing also with the theoretical side of the questions concerned. The Mishnah describes the sanhedrin deciding in a capital case: before the court sat three rows of sages, from which judges were selected for the case when necessary; moreover, all the members, even those not sitting in the three rows who had a contribution to make in favour of the accused could do so.[2] A baraita from the time after 70 C.E. describes the seating order in the sanhedrin and the precedence of the questioners: 'If one person asks on the matter in hand and another on another matter, reply is given to the one who has asked on the matter in hand. If there is a choice between the matter in hand and some other matter, the matter in hand is dealt with. If there is a choice between an actual case and something else, the actual case is dealt with.'[3] These halakic details might reflect the sessions of the sanhedrin in Jabneh or in Usha, but in principle this is also how they were conducted during the Second Temple period in Jerusalem.

[1] *T. Sanhedrin* 7:1.
[2] *M. Sanhedrin* 4:4; cf. also the baraita in *T. B. Sanhedrin* 42a.
[3] *T. Sanhedrin* 7:7.

The *bet midrash* which was connected to the institutions of the Temple was a kind of great *bet midrash*, but other midrash schools existed in various places in the country. There is a great deal of evidence for the post-70 period, but we also possess evidence for the existence of schools of sages during the Second Temple period. Before he came to Jerusalem, R. Johanan ben Zakkai lived in Araba (= Gabara) in lower Galilee, and had in his school R. Hanina ben Dosa, who was also a native of that city.[1] Just before and after the destruction of the Temple we hear of Galilean sages such as Abba Jose Holikufri of Tibeon[2] and R. Zadok from the same place.[3] R. Halaphta and R. Hananiah ben Teradyon had magnificent law courts, the former in Sepphoris and the latter in Siknin.[4] Also the social and religious movements in Galilee and their customs which were praised in the tradition, are doubtlessly connected with Galilean midrash schools in one form or another.[5] A passage of *Sifre Zuta* from the Genizah mentions 'Edomite pupils of the house of Shammai,'[6] i.e. a group of disciples belonging to the school of Shammai who lived in the south. Discussion between the schools of Shammai and Hillel belong, of course, to the pre-70 period, and the group of Edomites appears to date from the same period. There are various early pre-70 collections embedded in the Mishnah just as there are compilers of *mishnayoth* who lived during the Second Temple period. The work of the compilers of the Mishnah collections was not done at once but it formed part of the activities of the midrash schools in transmitting the Halakah.

As said above, a great deal of information exists about the schools of sages from the end of the first and from the second century. Tradition mentions the distinguished school at Lydda kept by R. Eliezer ben Hyrcanus.[7] Rabbi Akiba headed another in Benei Beraq,[8] Rabbi Joshua (ben Hananiah) in Pekiin[9] and Rabbi Ishmael taught at Kefar Aziz south of Hebron.[10] At this time there were other schools

---

[1] *P. T. Shabbath* xvi, 15d (end); *T. B. Berakoth* 34b.
[2] *M. Makshirim* 1:3.
[3] *T. Niddah* 4:3-4.
[4] *T. B. Sanhedrin* 32b; *T. Taanith* 1:14.
[5] *M. Pesahim* 4:5; *M. Ketuboth* 4:12; *P. T. Ketuboth* iv, 29b.
[6] J. N. Epstein, *Tarbiz* (1930), p. 70, l. 17 and the discussion, pp. 52-53.
[7] *T. B. Sanhedrin* 32b; *T. Sukkoth* 2:1; *Cant. Rabba* 1.
[8] *T. B. Sanhedrin* 32b; *Gen. Rabba* 95 (p. 232).
[9] *T. B. Sanhedrin* 32b; *T. Berakoth* 4:16.
[10] *M. Kilaim* 6:4.

in Tiberias[1] and at Beth Shearim.[2] The sources mention various buildings which were called by the name of the school of this or that sage. Recently an inscription was found in the Golan dating from the end of the second to the beginning of the third century, which reads as follows: 'This is the school of Rabbi Eliezer ha-Kappar.' This school was apparently also mentioned in the Palestinian Talmud.[3] Apart from the great *bet midrash*, which was headed by several generations of sages, all other schools depended upon the personality of the sage, and upon his death his pupils gathered round some other sage or one of his disciples who continued to teach in the same spirit.[4] Frequently, and in particular after 70 C.E., the sage and his school were involved in public administration and works of charity. The school functioned as a law court and the sage participated in public administration, though there were sages who withdrew from public affairs and even thanked the Almighty for not knowing how to administer justice, just as there were sages who regretted not having discharged their obligation in the matter of charity because they had been taken up entirely with the teaching of the Torah.[5] The schools were divided in their approach to practical affairs. Some thought that these were part of the special duties of the sage and his disciples, while others held that a sage's main task was the Torah and the instruction of the disciples and the public.

The major task of the sages consisted of teaching the Torah, which was the means by which to gain spiritual advancement and perform meritorious deeds. Just as he was expected to be erudite in the Torah, the sage was required to perform good deeds; and his conduct had to be highly moral. In short, he was expected to be the kind of person whose example the pupils would wish to follow. 'If the teacher is like an angel of the Lord of hosts, they should seek the Law at his mouth.'

---

[1] R. Jose ben Kisma lived there at the end of the first century (cf. *T. B. Yebamoth* 96b). He described its sages in *M. Aboth* 6:10.

[2] *T. Terumoth* 7:14; *T. Sukkah* 2:2; *T. Parah* 5 (4):6.

[3] The inscription was published by D. Urman in *Tarbiz* (1971), pp. 406-8; cf. *P. T. Shabbath* VI, 8a.

[4] *P. T. Kiddushin* II, 63a; *T. B. Kiddushin* 52b; *T. B. Nazir* 49b.

[5] R. Akiba charged his son not to live in a town, headed by a sage (*T. B. Pesahim* 112a). R. Simeon ben Yohai regretted having occupied himself with a poor man who had been extremely arrogant; he justifies the divine punishment which he himself received for neglecting the study of the Law in order to deal with transitory matters (*Aboth de R. Nathan*, Version A, 41 (p. 130). Cf. also his saying in *P. T. Sanhedrin* I, 18a. The opposite position is taken by R. Hananiah ben Teradyon in *T. B. Abodah Zarah* 17b.

The same applied to the students of whom it was demanded that they should devote themselves wholly to the study of the Torah, according to the principle that study precedes action, as was decided in the teaching of the sages of Jabneh, though on the understanding that study led to action.[1] In addition there was the requirement of 'attending the sages' which was already mentioned by Hillel the Elder and which was repeated in different forms in every age.[2] Learning by itself did not make a pupil, and he did not grasp the full significance of his teacher's learning in all its nuances except through prolonged intimacy with his teacher, through close association with his rich and profound mind. The disciples accompanied their sage as he went to teach, when he sat in the law court, when he was engaged in the performance of meritorious deeds such as helping the poor, redeeming slaves, collecting dowries for poor brides, burying the dead, etc. The pupil took his turn in preparing the common meal and catering for the general needs of the group. He performed personal services for his teacher, observed his conduct and was his respectful, loving, humble companion.[3] Some laws could not be studied theoretically or merely discussed, but could only be learned by serving the teacher.

The groups which consisted of a sage and his disciples had property in common, or a common fund from which food was brought. At times this only applied when the sage moved from place to place accompanied by his disciples. In some instances these arrangements became permanent. We possess tannaitic regulations which deal with the relationship between the sage and the pupil. They see them as 'the brothers who did not divide their estate' or as 'a father and his son.'[4] In the first century sages did not earn their livelihood by teaching the Law. Regular arrangements, such as tax exemptions for supporting sages entirely pre-occupied with the Torah, were not as yet current. A number of sages being priests received tithes, and were thus able to devote most of their time to the study of the Law. Some sages were even supported by their pupils. But it was most common for the sage to practice a trade part of the time and to devote all the rest of his time to the study of the Law. This explains the many traditions

---

[1] T. B. Hagigah 15b; Sifre Deut. 41 (pp. 84ff.) and parallels.
[2] P. T. Nazir VII, 56b; Aboth de R. Nathan, Version A 12 (p. 55); 36 (p. 109).
[3] T. Negaim 8:2; T. B. Pesahim 36a.
[4] T. B. Erubin 73a.

which tell of the gathering of disciples in the evenings, on the sabbath and on festivals.[1]

Like their teachers the disciples supported themselves by their work and studied in their free time, occasionally under serious pressure. Others left home for a place of learning, and studied under their teacher for a number of years, sometimes while they were still single, but if married with the permission of their wives. There are many instances of wives being praised for enabling their husbands to study. Some men were given financial assistance from their families or received irregular support in some way.[2] They were called students (תלמידים), even at an advanced stage and when they were old. Everyone who was not ordained (נסמך) was considered a student; ordination was not given at the conclusion of studies, but upon appointment to a public office. Some chose to remain students all their life and a number of them were counted among the greatest scholars of their age, for example Simeon ben Azzai and Simeon ben Zoma of the Jabneh period. Study was not confined to the school or the synagogue, but was also carried on in the vineyard, in the shade of a dove-cote, in fields, on paths under fig-trees and olives and in the market. It was not uncommon for a sage to conduct discourses and discussions with his pupils in the town-square or in the market place, with the towns-people gathering around them and listening, irrespective of whether they were able to understand all or only part of the discussion.[3] At the end of the second century R. Judah the Patriarch tried to prohibit the study of the Torah outside the walls of the school, but the practice did not completely cease even then.[4]

Many sages were not content to teach at their local school, but wandered from town to town to teach the Law. As early as the time of the 'pairs' (זוגות), e.g. Hillel and Shammai, we read of appeals addressed to the people to accommodate these wandering sages: 'Let your house be a meeting house for the sages' (*Aboth* 1:4). The public were invited to attend such gatherings: 'Sit amidst the dust of their feet' (ibid.). Many regulations deal with such occasions when on sabbaths and festivals sages found accommodation in another town, where they taught the Law. The nucleus of the listeners consisted of the

---

[1] For the period before 70 c.e., cf. *T. Yom Tob* 3:8. For the period after 70, cf. *T. B. Betzah* 15b; *Sifre Num.* 148.
[2] *Aboth de R. Nathan*, Version A, 6 (pp. 28ff); *T. B. Ketuboth* 62b.
[3] *T. Berakoth* 4:16; *P. T. Berakoth* II, 5c.
[4] *T. B. Moed Katan* 16a-b.

sage's close adherents, but many others also came.[1] The sage, generally accompanied by a few of his pupils, was received and housed by some members of the local community who looked after their needs during their stay. Even scholars who were meticulous in refusing payment for teaching the Law, permitted themselves to be accommodated while on the move, as is illustrated by Jesus who told his disciples: 'Take no gold, nor silver, nor copper in your belts, no bag for your journey, nor two tunics, nor sandals, nor a staff; for the labourer deserves his food. And whatever town or village you enter, find out who is worthy in it, and stay with him until you depart'.[2]

The teaching in schools of the sages was entirely oral. The various notebooks and lists of halakoth only served the personal use of the sage or his disciple. The sage directed the lesson, and the pupils could ask questions. In fact, the entire teaching was directed towards encouraging their participation. Some sages were in the habit of putting questions to their students. R. Johanan ben Zakkai is said to have told his pupils: 'Go forth and see which is the good way to which a man should cleave'.[3] It is told of R. Tarphon: 'He sat in the shade of a dove-cote on a sabbath in the afternoon, and they brought him a bucket of cool [water]. He asked his pupils: 'He who drinks water to quench his thirst, what blessing does he recite?'' Later on he asked them the meaning of a verse, etc.[4] To a large extent the teaching took the form of question and answer.

Another setting for study was the worship in the synagogue with its public reading of the Targum to the Pentateuch and Prophets and the sermon. The Aramaic Targum as we possess it today is not only a translation of the biblical text, but also an explanation by midrashic, legal and didactic interpretation. It is true that the Targum as we have it contains late strata, yet it is clear that basically the Targum did not differ in the early periods and that it constituted one of the principal means by which the public was educated in the Bible. During the Second Temple period the synagogue was open mainly on sabbaths and feast-days, participation was general and included women and children: 'And every portion of the Torah and prophetic

---

[1] M. Aboth 1:4 and its explanation in Aboth de R. Nathan A, 6 and B, 11 (pp. 27ff). Cf. also M. Erubin 3:5; T. Sukkah 1:9; T. B. Sukkah 28a; T. B. Erubin 54b; T. B. Betzah 15b.
[2] Matt. 10:9-11 and parallels; Sifre Deut. 1 (p. 6).
[3] M. Aboth 2:9.
[4] T. Berakoth 4:16.

lesson of the Sabbath reading should be translated for the people, the women and the children.'[1] As early as the first century sermons were regularly delivered on the sabbath and on feast-days in the Land of Israel and in the Diaspora as is clear from the analysis of the midrashic collections and from other sources.[2] This discourse was based on the lesson from the Torah read in the synagogue on that particular sabbath or feast-day, or on the chapter from the Prophets. The place of the discourse in divine worship was not as closely defined as the reading from the Torah; some sages gave their public sermons immediately after the prayer or the reading from the Torah or even as an introduction to the lesson, while others gave it only later in the day.[3]

The sermon, which was normally haggadic, constituted the link between intellectual developments in the schools and the general public. Many of the discussions between the sages and their pupils reached the public through the discourses. Morals were inculcated in sermons, and words of consolation and hope uttered. In fact, sermons were a basic element of education. The expositors considered their sermons to be a means of public education in the written and oral Torah, they explained their subject in a simple and interesting way, without neglecting practical obligations and major questions. Apart from the sermons in the synagogue, there were others on the sabbaths and feast-days in the schools in Jerusalem and Jabneh and in other towns. These sermons were not only addressed to the students, but to the wider public which included women and children, irrespective of whether they took an active part or only came to listen.[4] The discourse was based upon Haggadah, but occasionally also on the Halakah. In a certain tradition we read: 'He (Moses) said to them: "The Passover laws should be studied on the Passover, the Pentecost laws on Pentecost, and on Tabernacles the laws for Tabernacles"'. This led them to say that Moses admonished the Israelites to study the rules for the occasion

---

[1] *Tractate Soferim* 18 (p. 317).

[2] Philo, *Legatio ad Gaium* 156; Jos. *Against Apion* II, 175; Mark 1:21; Luke ch. 4; 13:10; Acts 13-14 and elsewhere.

[3] Acts 13:15; *T. B. Betzah* 15b; *Midrash Proverbs* 31 (p. 108). For the use of the introduction in midrashic works in the discourse before the reading of the Law, cf. J. Heinemann, 'The *Petichtot* in Aggadic Midrashim, their Origin and Function', *Fourth World Congress of Jewish Studies* II (1968) pp. 43-7.

[4] *T. Sotah* 7:9; *P. T. Sotah* I, 16d. A baraita in *Midrash ha-Gadol* on Deut. 29:10 reads: 'Your wives—even though they do not know, they come to hear and to receive a reward. This teaches that every one who enters a synagogue and hears words of Torah, even if he does not know, attains merit and acquires reward'.

and to discourse upon them. And further on in this same tradition: 'In the synagogue they ask concerning Passover thirty days before the festival.'[1]

The sage who taught sat either on a pillow or a chair (*cathedra*), or like his disciples on the floor or on mats.[2] At the public discourses in the schools a *meturgeman* or *amora* was put at the disposal of the sage. The latter, while sitting down, would briefly explain the matter to the *meturgeman* who then repeated it and explained it aloud. Questions were addressed to the *meturgeman* and after having received a brief reply from the sage he gave the answer to the questioner; he, in fact, conducted the meeting. Placing a *meturgeman* before the sage was done not only for the purpose of assisting him, but also out of respect for the study and transmission of the Written Torah. Complaints were occasionally voiced of a *meturgeman* who raised his voice and declaimed in an exaggerated and artificial way and who by his theatrical behaviour obscured the words of the sage. But in general we hear only praise of the *meturgeman*, some of whom were known as men of great learning and esteemed for their work in spreading the Law. We have no explicit evidence for the institution of the *meturgeman* before 70 C.E., but since we find it as a fixed and well known institution at Jabneh, it can be assumed to have existed before 70 C.E.[3]

Torah study was a remarkable feature in Jewish life at the time of the Second Temple and during the period following it. It was not restricted to the formal setting of schools and synagogue, nor to sages only, but became an integral part of ordinary Jewish life. The Torah was studied at all possible times, even if only a little at a time, one or two halakoth or a haggadic story during attendance at the synagogue for the morning or evening prayer, or at home in the evening. Some people formed groups of varying sizes and studied together on weekday nights or on the sabbath. One of the first of the 'pairs' teaches that a man should provide himself with a teacher, adding 'and get thee a fellow-disciple', 'that he eat with him and drink with him and read with him and learn with him'.[4] Torah study was the main feature of the

---

[1] *Sifre Deut.* 127 (pp. 185-6); *T. Megillah* 4:5.
[2] For the custom of sitting on a cathedra, cf. Matt. 23:2. For the existence of such cathedras in ancient synagogues, cf. E. L. Sukenik, *Tarbiz* (1930) pp. 145-151. Concerning the demand for equality of seating, cf. *T. B. Megillah* 21a.
[3] *Eccles. Rabba* 9, 7. One of the early *Meturgemanim* was R. Huspith the *Meturgeman* in Jabneh who was one of the Ten Martyrs executed by the Romans, cf. *P. T. Berakoth* iv, 7c-d; *T. B. Berakoth* 27b.
[4] *M. Aboth* 1:6; *Aboth de R. Nathan* A, 8 (p. 36).

group meals which were common in the Land of Israel as well as in the Diaspora. A certain sage taught: 'If three have eaten at one table and have not spoken over it words of the Law, it is as though they had eaten of the sacrifices of the dead... But if three have eaten at one table and have spoken over it words of the Law, it is as if they had eaten from the table of God.'[1] The sound of Torah learning issuing from houses at night was a common phenomenon. When people assembled for a joyous occasion such as a circumcision or wedding, a group might withdraw to engage in study of the Law. People learned Torah while walking, and some sages warn against the interruption of Torah study by the diversion of gazing at nature.

Torah study was mainly oral and because of the very real fear of forgetting what had been acquired there were constant repetitions to ensure that the Halakah was practised and developed.[2]

BIBLIOGRAPHY

Most works on education in ancient Israel focus on school education for children, paying little or no attention to the structure and methods of the *bet midrash*. For school education the following general works should be mentioned: I. WISEN, *Geschichte und Methodik des Schulwesens im Altertum* (1892); F. H. SWIFT, *Education in Ancient Israel from Earliest Times to the Year* 500 (1937); N. DRAZIN, *History of Jewish Education from* 515 B.C.E. *to* 226 C.E. (1940); S. TCHERNA, *History of Education in Israel* II (1939; in Hebrew); E. EBNER, *Elementary Education in Ancient Israel* (1956); N. MORRIS, *History of Education of the Jewish people* I (1960; in Hebrew). See also the following articles: W. BACHER, 'Das altjüdische Schulwesen,' in *Jahrbuch für jüdische Geschichte und Literatur* (1903), pp. 48-82; S. SAFRAI, 'Elementary education, its religious and social significance in the talmudic period,' in *Cahiers d'histoire mondiale* (1968), pp. 148-99.

For adult education see: A. SCHWARZ, 'Die Hochschulen in Palästina,' in *Jahrbuch für jüdische Geschichte und Literatur* (1899); A. BÜCHLER, 'Learning and Teaching in the Open Air in Palestine,' in *JQR* (1914), pp. 485-91.

The classical work on sermons is L. ZUNZ, *Die gottesdienstlichen Vorträge der Juden historisch entwickelt* (2nd ed. 1892). See also: CH. ALBECK, *The Sermon in Israel and its Historical Development*, revised and

[1] *M. Aboth* 3:3; *T. B. Erubin* 18b; 54a.
[2] *P. T. Hagigah* II, 77b; *M. Aboth* 3:7-8.

enlarged Hebrew translation of Zunz's work (1947); S. MAYBAUM, *Die ältesten Phasen in der Entwicklung der jüdischen Predigt*, (1901); J. MANN, *The Bible as Read and Preached in the Old Synagogue*, 2 vls. (1940-66); J. HEINEMAN, *Sermons in the Talmudic Period*, (1970; in Hebrew).

Chapter Twenty

Art and Architecture in Palestine

The art of Palestine during the Second Temple period is characterized by a pronounced combination of local tradition and artistic influences from the surrounding world. The country's position at important crossroads between the great Hellenistic kingdoms and subsequently at the centre of the Roman empire of the east naturally contributed to this peculiar fusion. The Hellenistic and Roman influences on art and architecture, which found their expression mainly after the time of Alexander the Great and even earlier, over vast areas extending from Afghanistan on the east to Spain in the west, to Egypt and Nubia in the south and to Britain in the north, did not fail to affect Palestine also.

The religious limitations imposed upon the Jews by the second commandment[1] to some extent restricted the variety of Jewish creative art. This peculiar and well-marked phenomenon found its chief expression in the period of the First and more especially of the Second Temple, when the aniconic trend was prominent. In the period of the First Temple, it would seem that there were numerous infringements of the prohibition to represent living figures;[2] such find their most striking expression in the detailed biblical accounts of Solomon's Temple, which witness that the latter's ornamental work differed little from contemporary Canaanite and Phoenician iconography, the figured decorations of which were executed both in relief and in the round.[3] The aniconic trend of the Second Temple period practically ended

---

[1] Exod. 20:3-5; Deut. 5:8-9.
[2] The first aberration is the worship of the golden calf at the foot of Mount Sinai by the Israelites after the exodus from Egypt (Exod. 32:1-4). Then comes the surprising story of the 'serpent of brass' fashioned according to the Lord's command, which accompanied the Israelites throughout their wanderings in the desert and survived until the reign of Hezekiah. Archaeological excavations have brought to light evidence, such as ivories, minor art objects and the like, which shows that the kings of Israel made use of Canaanite-Phoenician iconography, much as it was used in the Temple. Other finds indicate Egyptian influence, e.g. the winged scarab found on royal stamp impressions on jar handles.
[3] 1 Kings 7:23-26.

after the war of Bar Cochba. Great historical changes revived among Jews a more liberal attitude to the art of the living figure. This changed attitude is most dramatically expressed in the decoration of synagogues and tombs, now adorned not only with simple geometric and plant designs, but also with figures partly derived from a decidedly pagan iconography. Contemporary Jewish sources too are imbued with this liberal approach, which was apparently now accepted by most of the Jewish nation.[1]

The first contacts with Greek culture in the artistic sphere are to be found in pottery of the proto-geometric and geometric periods recovered in various excavations in this country,[2] and these links persisted in the Second Temple period.[3] In the period after the return from Babylon, trade with Greece was intensified and Attic black-figure wares bearing representations of animals and plants are found at various sites in the country such as Samaria, Shechem, Athlith, En Geddi, Mizpah, Tell Jemmeh, Tell el Far'a and elsewhere.[4] Coins of the Persian province of 'Yahud' inspired by Athenian coinage and by governmental cartouches issued by the local authorities of the priestly group bore human and animal figures.[5]

The conquest of Judaea by Alexander the Great and his successors brought in its wake the intensive penetration of every aspect of Hellenistic culture: one of the major signs of this penetration was the foundation of a series of cities by both the Ptolemaic rulers and by the Seleucids. These cities were usually founded in areas where the non-Jewish inhabitants of the country were a considerable majority, and mostly in localities where cities had previously existed. Among them we may mention: Accho-Ptolemais, Beth Shean-Scythopolis, Philoteria, Dor, Straton's Tower, Jaffa-Joppa, Ascalon, Ashdod-Azotus, Gaza, Raphia and, across the Jordan, the Decapolis cities of Gadara, Hippos (Susitha), Pella, Dion and Gerasa.[6]

The Hellenistic age in Palestine can be divided into two periods, the pre-Hasmonaean and the Hasmonaean. Our knowledge of the art and architecture of the first is derived, so far as it goes, chiefly from

---

[1] This approach to figurative representational art can be compared to some extent to that in the period of the First Temple. Cf. Urbach; Avigad, 'Figurative art.'
[2] See Clairmont.
[3] See Naveh.
[4] See Iliffe, 'Pre-Hellenistic Greek Pottery'; Weinberg, 'Post-exilic Palestine.'
[5] See Stern, pp. 215 ff.
[6] See M. Avi-Yonah, *The Holy Land from the Persian to the Arab Conquest* (1966).

the non-Jewish centres. The most important excavated site of the period is the townlet of Marissa in the Idumaean region, founded in the third century B.C.E. and evidently an administrative centre of that area; it was destroyed in 40 B.C.E. by the Parthian allies of Antigonus. The plan of this fortified town, which is nearly square, was executed on the Hellenistic model with chessboard streets; it contained two centres, one the temenos and the other a civic centre. The meagre finds included various figurines, pottery and metal objects, most of a Hellenistic type.[1] The chief discoveries of artistic interest come from the cemetery; two series of rock-cut tombs yielded fine coloured wall-paintings in the realist Hellenistic style, incorporating local motifs, among which were pictures of hunting and musicians in Hellenistic garb.[2] These gallery-tombs, which belonged in part to the Sidonian community of Marissa, as we learn from their Greek inscriptions, were executed in a style which had developed in Alexandria in the same period. This type of tomb is also common later in the Hasmonaean period and under the Herods. Another small Hellenistic towncentre has been excavated in recent years, at Tell Anafa in Upper Galilee.[3] This town seems to have been founded by the Seleucids at the beginning of the second century B.C.E. and was destroyed by Alexander Jannaeus about a century later. Its ancient name has not yet been identified. It has yielded a very rich collection of finds, among which prominence should be accorded to the moulded glassware, and to the delicate pottery which exhibits Hellenistic influence. Of special significance is the painted and gilded moulded stucco which covered the walls of some of the buildings, often in the form of Doric friezes or of Ionic and Corinthian capitals, in the best Hellenistic tradition; these techniques and styles were apparently utilized in the Hasmonaean palaces and chiefly in the Herodian mansions and villas. Parts of buildings and streets have been exposed at Azotus, and according to the excavators the agora can also be made out.[4] Various remains of the period have been found at Straton's Tower, but none is architectural.[5] We know contemporary sculpture mainly from the fine clay statuette of Aphrodite in the Praxitelean style found in one of the caves of Mount Carmel where it was perhaps part of a local cult.[6]

[1] See Bliss and Macalister, pp. 52-61; 67-70; 124-34; 238-54.
[2] See Peters and Thiersch.
[3] See Weinberg, 'Tel Anafa.'
[4] See the report of Dothan and Freedman, pp. 17-20.
[5] See Avi-Yonah and Negev, in *IEJ* XIII (1963), pp. 146-8.
[6] See Iliffe, 'A nude terra-cotta statuette of Aphrodite'; Applebaum.

Considerable artistic and architectural importance attaches to the temple or fortified palace of Araq el-Amir in Transjordan, known as Qasr el-Abd.[1] This structure is apparently the one referred to by Josephus as the fortress built by Hyrcanus grandson of Tobiah on his estate.[2] Its dimensions are 37 by 18.50 metres and it is built of huge carefully dressed blocks measuring as much as 5.36 by 2.50 metres. The wall is crowned by a frieze on which a procession of lions is portrayed in a markedly oriental fashion. The oriental elements are associated with capitals adorned with the heads of oxen and eagles. Hellenistic influence, on the other hand, finds expression in various architectural embellishments such as the columns, Corinthian capitals, and a Doric frieze on the façade. This peculiar mingling of artistic styles is instructive evidence of the style which had developed in Palestine following the Greek conquest. It is doubly interesting that this building should have been built according to the instructions of an aristocratic Jewish family known for its assimilation to Greek culture, and connected with the high priests of Jerusalem.

Remains of pre-Hasmonaean fortifications have been found at Samaria; these include round towers, one of which is built of ashlar blocks with convex bosses in a pronounced Hellenistic style. This tower, which is 13 metres in diameter, is preserved to a height of 8.50 metres.[3] Fragments of walls and round and square towers of this period have been disclosed at Accho-Ptolemais[4] and at Beth Yerah (Philoteria?) south of the Sea of Galilee.[5] At Jaffa (Joppa) the remains of a Hellenistic citadel have been found, built of dressed headers and stretchers.[6] More recently an attempt has been made to locate the Seleucid acropolis (the Acra) in the Temple Mount area, part of its eastern wall being apparently incorporated in the east wall of the Temple Mount.[7] Our information about the art and architecture of the Hasmonaean period is derived in the main from fortifications and funerary art. Something can be learnt of minor arts from Hasmonaean coinage, which was without the images of the rulers, but was otherwise largely tributary to contemporary Seleucid minting. Some notion of private building is obtainable now the remains of the Hasmonaean palace at

[1] See Lapp; Brett.
[2] *Ant.* XII, 230-1.
[3] Crowfoot, pp. 24-31, plates 36-38.
[4] *Hadashot Archeologiot* LI-LII (1974), pp. 9-10.
[5] See Mazar and Bar-Adon.
[6] See Kaplan.
[7] See Tsafrir.

Jericho have been found.[1] Remains of this structure, whose plan has not yet been elucidated, were found buried beneath the remains of the Herodian palace. Some of the rooms were adorned with wall-paintings in the 'masonry style,' possessing panels imitating veined marble slabs, but also white stucco. Attached to the building was a large pool (perhaps the one in which the high priest Aristobulus was drowned), as well as other structures whose nature is still to be established. We therefore now possess for the first time evidence of the character of the Hasmonaean palaces, and it would seem that they too were clearly tributary to the art and architecture of the epoch. The Hasmonaean citadel at Beth Zur (Hirbet et-Tubeiqa) is planned after the fashion of a typical oriental courtyard house, measuring 41 by 33 metres.[2] Another Hasmonaean citadel is that of the Alexandrium, built by Alexander Jannaeus as part of the defensive systems of Judaea; it was undoubtedly one of the important strongholds of the Hasmonaeans and subsequently of Herod.[3] The site has not yet been excavated, hence its plan is obscure, but its drafted masonry with rusticated bosses is regarded as an example of Hasmonaean work (see below). Similar work is also to be found in various sectors of the 'first wall' of Jerusalem, exposed by excavations inside the present citadel-area and belonging to that epoch.[4] But it should also be remarked that instances of smooth dressing of the entire block are also common, as in the Joppa citadel and in the tomb of Jason (see below). Very interesting literary evidence relating to the tombs of the period is to be found in 1 Macc. 13:26-29 and in Josephus' *Ant.* XIII, 211-12, which describe the monument raised by Simeon to his ancestors and brothers at Modiin. This was made, according to the accounts, of dressed masonry, and over it were set seven pyramids surrounded by porticoes adorned with friezes on which weapons and ships were carved, perhaps to commemorate a naval victory. Monuments in this style, combining oriental and classical elements, were common in the same period in Judaea and in the Hellenistic world. Two groups of tombs and splendid funerary monuments of this time are known in Jerusalem: the first is the tomb of the priestly family of Hezir in the Kidron Valley;[5] it consists of the tomb and the *nefesh* (to use the language of the inscription on the architrave of the rock-cut façade of the tomb).

[1] See Netzer, 'The Hasmonaean and Herodian Winter Palaces at Jericho.'
[2] See Sellers.
[3] See Plöger, pp. 142-8.
[4] See the preliminary report by Amiran and Eitan.
[5] See Avigad, *Ancient monuments*, pp. 37-78.

The façade is modelled in the Doric style; by it is the *nefesh*, rock-cut and likewise probably once crowned by a masonry pyramid. This plan is unconventional, and Avigad holds that it drew on ancient traditions precise parallels with which are to be found in Egypt. Another monument with pyramidal *nefesh* of the Second Temple period has been exposed in western Jerusalem; this tomb, known as the tomb of Jason, is rock-cut except for its front, which is of masonry in the Doric style, and superior in quality to that of the tomb of Hezir; it was surmounted by a pyramid.[1] On the walls of the tomb-complex, which were partly plastered, three warships, a merchant-man and a vessel with ram engaged in pursuit, have been drawn in charcoal. A number of seven-branched candelabra are also incised on the walls of the chamber. Rahmani thinks that the complex belonged to a Sadducee family of Alexander Jannaeus' time, and that the representations of the ships are perhaps to be viewed in connection with the Maccabean family-monument at Modiin.

The processes which set their stamp on the art and architecture of the reign of Herod and his heirs down to the destruction of the Temple are no more than a natural continuation of processes marking the Hellenistic age in Palestine. The artists, whether they were Jews or merely working for Jews, used artistic styles and architectural elements current in the Hellenistic world, adapting them to local taste. It should nevertheless be stressed that there is a nearly complete avoidance of the representation of human or animal figures, in painting and in sculpture, both of which formed an integral part of contemporary art and architecture. This is the picture furnished by the archeological finds, and also by what Josephus writes of the Jewish attitude to figurative art in his period. We nevertheless learn from the historian himself of deviations as in the palace of Herod Antipas at Tiberias, decorated with animal figures. Particularly instructive is the fact that Herod placed a golden eagle over the central entrance to the Temple of Jerusalem. As against such exceptions it must be emphasized that Herod's coins bore no image of the sovereign, although some of his successors did not hesitate to offend their Jewish subjects' susceptibilities in this respect. Naturally the same general artistic trends which were developing in pronouncedly Jewish areas were not common in the Gentile regions or in the cities of Gentile or mixed population.

Rich archaeological discoveries combined with the detailed and unique testimony of Josephus concerning the building projects of Herod and

[1] See Rahmani, 'Jason's Tomb.'

his family, enable us to obtain a fairly complete picture of the various aspects of the country's art and architecture in the century after Herod's ascent to power down to the destruction of the Temple. The extent of Herod's building projects in Palestine and other countries in the Roman empire, as they are described by Josephus and confirmed, on the whole, by archaeological research, undoubtedly places him among the great builder-sovereigns of the ancient world. Herod's building works in Palestine included city-foundations, the chief of which were Caesarea and Sebaste. Here and elsewhere he erected public buildings such as temples, theatres, amphitheatres and hippo- dromes, and installed up-to-date aqueducts leading to the cities concerned. The palaces erected by Herod for himself and his family in various parts of his kingdom constitute a distinguished chapter in the history of art and architecture in Palestine and throughout the Roman world. Fortifications and fortresses also occupied an important place in his architectural activity, a fact which is easily explained by his precarious political position among his own people and also by his bad relations with his eastern neighbours, the Nabataeans. The crowning jewel of his massive work was the doubling of the area of the Temple Mount and the rebuilding of the Temple. This flourishing period of art and architecture, hitherto unparalleled in the country, found expression not only in royal construction, but also in the build- ings of such residential quarters as that in the upper city of Jerusalem. Funerary art also flowered and found its principal expression in Jerusalem.

In the eighteenth year of his reign (19/20 B.C.E.) Herod commenced the rebuilding of the Temple, which ended officially nine and a half years later. Eight years were occupied in the enlargement of the area of the Temple Mount, and in the building of the walls of the valley and the porticoes, the most difficult part of the project, and eighteen months in the reconstruction of the Temple itself. But in reality the work ended, according to Josephus, only under the procurator Albinus, who functioned from 62 to 64. When it was concluded, 18,000 labourers were left without employment.[1]

The temenos including the esplanade or outer court of the Temple formed a trapeze measuring on the west 480 metres, on the east 470 metres, on the north 315 metres, and on the south 280 metres, its total area being some 150,000 square metres.[2] A temenos of this size

[1] *Ant.* xv, 380-402; xx, 219.
[2] Simons, pp. 344-81; Vincent and Stève II-III, pp. 526-95. See illustration p. 979.

was without precedent or peer in the Roman world; the sanctuaries approximating to it in area were those of Damascus and Palmyra. The preparation and levelling of the enclosure involved two apparently contrary activities owing to the conditions of the terrain; in the north of the enclosure the rock had to be quarried away, whereas in the south it was necessary to raise the natural surface by several dozen metres. This latter was achieved by a complicated and elaborate system of vaults now known as 'Solomon's stables.' They have undergone numerous repairs in the course of years, but there is no doubt that fundamentally the floor of the temenos was laid over a similar system of vaults. For this reason the retaining walls surviving in the south-east rise to a height of 45 metres. They had to be very strong and they are carried up with a moderate batter from where they rest on the rock. Their walls were built of carefully dressed blocks some of which weigh up to 120 tons apiece. The stone courses average 1.02—1.20 metres in height, while one in the south wall was 1.85 metres high. The normal length of the blocks varied from 1—3 metres, but could be as much as 14 metres. The walls were 4.60 metres thick where they could be examined. The blocks were beautifully drafted, and the bosses carefully smoothed, but not worked in the lower courses which were invisible from the outside. The southern and western walls of the enclosure are those which survive as originally built, the latter being known as the 'wailing wall.' They were adorned with flat counterforts crowned by capitals projecting over the level of the enclosing wall of the court like the temenos walls at Hebron and those at Damascus, Palmyra and elsewhere.[1] Josephus, in his account of the work of construction, dwells on such general items as the topography of the area, but also describes such building details as the clamping of the stones with iron and lead, a fact not yet verified, although it was a common practice in the Roman world. The measurements given by Josephus for the temenos do not stand up to the test of reality, but approximate to it, differing little from those given by the Mishnah.

No remains have been found of the courts on the Temple Mount, but many details are known from Josephus and the Mishnah. The outer court was surrounded on three sides by double porticoes, except the southerly, where the 'royal stoa' stood. The width of the double porticoes, which contained two rows of columns, was 15 metres, their

[1] Ibid. and the excavations since 1968 in Mazar, *The Excavations*, pp. 1-36; Mazar and Ben Dov, 'Finds.'

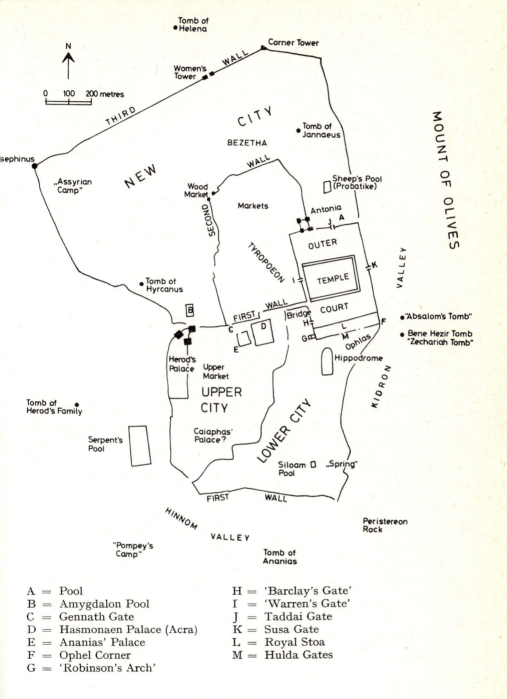

A = Pool
B = Amygdalon Pool
C = Gennath Gate
D = Hasmonaen Palace (Acra)
E = Ananias' Palace
F = Ophel Corner
G = 'Robinson's Arch'

H = 'Barclay's Gate'
I = 'Warren's Gate'
J = Taddai Gate
K = Susa Gate
L = Royal Stoa
M = Hulda Gates

height 13 metres. The 'royal stoa', described by Josephus as 'a structure more noteworthy than any under the sun,' was 39 metres broad, but the other measurements given by Josephus appear to be corrupt. The stoa contained two aisles and a nave which was carried up as a clerestory. The capitals of the colonnades were Corinthian. In the centre of temenos, on an elevation, where 'the dome of the rock' is now situated, apparently stood the Temple, separated from the surrounding area by a barrier of trellises and slabs which prevented Gentiles approaching it.[1] Despite the detailed character of the accounts of Josephus and the Mishnah, not a few difficulties attend the reconstruction of the Temple and its ornamentation, owing to the complete absence of archaeological data, but it may be supposed that its plan and ornamentation were akin to those of various other oriental temples.[2] The plan of the entire ensemble of the Temple Mount is especially reminiscent of the *caesareum* of the Roman world, which originated in the *caesareum* erected in Alexandria.[3] If this was Herod's intention, it is additional evidence of his utter subjection to Augustus and of the impact of Hellenistic Roman styles on the character of his buildings even in his people's most sacred places. Perhaps it could be interpreted as a deliberate slight to the nation.

The extensive excavations carried out continuously since 1968 at the foot of the southern and western retaining walls of the Temple Mount have produced important and interesting results relating to the layout of the area at the foot of the Mount.[4] The excavations have also furnished the first data on the architectural ornamentation of the porticoes and perhaps of the Temple itself.[5] According to Josephus there were a number of entrances to the Mount, four on the west and an undefined number on the south.[6] The Mishnah (*Middoth* 1:3) speaks of a gate on the west, that of Ciponus, and two entrances on the south, the gates of Huldah; one on the east, the Susa gate, and one on the north, the Taddai gate. So far four have been identified on the west, and two on the south.[7] The foundation of the 'golden gate' on the east may also date from Herod's reign. Remains of a bridge exist at the southern corner of the eastern wall, leading in all probability to some

---

[1] See chapter seventeen, p. 866.
[2] See the plan of the Temple on p. 868.
[3] See Sjöqvist.
[4] See Mazar, 'The Excavations in the Old City'; Mazar and Ben Dov, *Finds*;
[5] See illustrations Mazar, 'The Excavations near the Temple Mount,' on pp. 76-77.
[6] *Ant.* xv, 410.
[7] Simons, pp. 526-95.

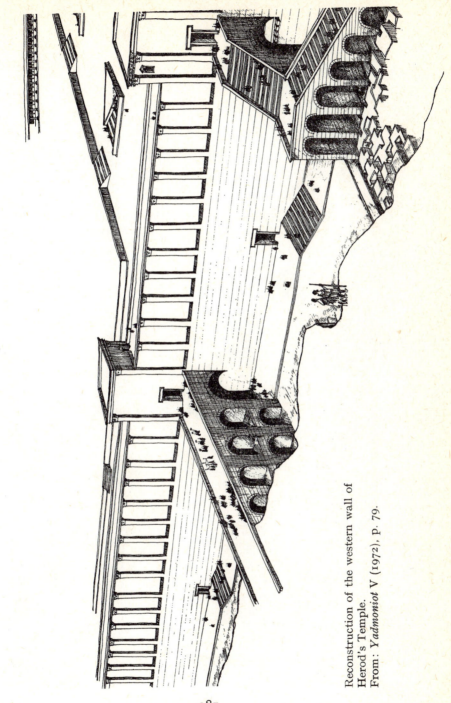

Reconstruction of the western wall of
Herod's Temple.
From: *Yadmoniot* V (1972). p. 79.

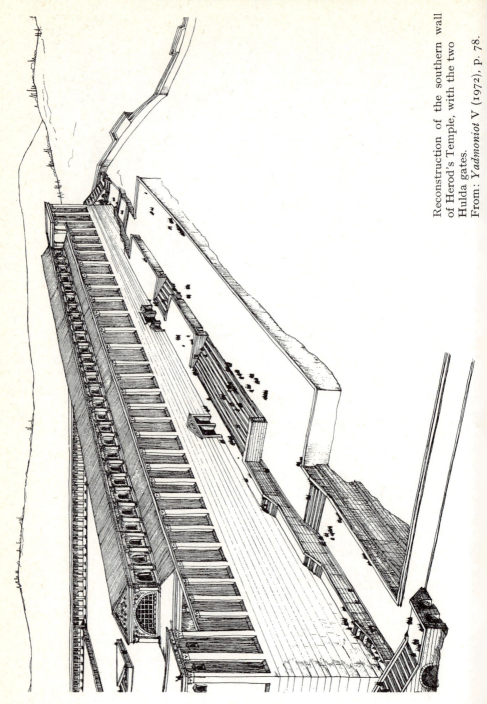

Reconstruction of the southern wall of Herod's Temple, with the two Hulda gates.
From: *Yadmoniot* V (1972), p. 78.

entrance or other. Two of the western entrances were at a high level; one gave access over the bridge today known as 'Wilson's arch' (partly built over the remains of the Herodian bridge); the other entrance leading to the 'royal stoa' was reached by a flight of steps discovered in part by the recent excavations.[1] Two subterranean entrances led from the street-level into the sanctuary. Access to the outer court on the south was through the Huldah gates by a similar thoroughfare. The excavations have uncovered a well-paved Herodian street 12.50 metres wide and running close beside the Temple wall. It descends by steps to the southern corner and there turns to ascend eastward with a width of 6.40 metres along the southern wall towards the Huldah Gates. The street on the west is built over a series of rock-foundation vaults; into the same rock an aqueduct or drainage canal was hewn and constructed. The street was spanned by an arch whose remains still project from the wall. To westward this arch, 15.20 metres in length, rests on a large pier containing a number of shops. The arch is not part of a bridge, as previously thought, but of a large flight of steps whereby the ascent was effected from the Tyropoeon valley to the royal stoa. These would seem to be identifiable with the steps described by Josephus as leading from the lower city to the royal stoa and to the upper city.

South of the Temple Mount a well-paved piazza, 23 metres broad, was cleared, rising eastward past the Huldah Gates. To its north lay shops built below the level of the street, which was higher than the piazza. The square itself was supported on the south by retaining walls. In its centre were two ranges of steps, one leading to the western, the other to the eastern Huldah gate. The western flight is largely preserved; it is 64 metres broad and contains thirty rock-cut steps faced with stone slabs. These lead to the level of the southern street, and to the gate. The eastern flight has been destroyed but the vaults which carried the steps survive.

The architectural features revealed by the excavations include friezes and panels adorned with rosettes of various types, acanthus leaves, variations of the intertwined leaf-scroll and geometric elements such as meanders and the guilloche. The carving on the whole is excellent, but flat, differing in no way from the style so popular in Jerusalem at the end of the Second Temple period. Corinthian capitals with gilded leaves have also been found, reminding us of what Josephus

[1] Mazar, 'The Archaeological Excavations.' See illustration on pp. 26-27.

writes of the gilded decoration of the Temple.[1] No adornments deriving from figurative art have been discovered.

About a decade before the commencement of Herod's extensive work on the Temple Mount, and before the battle of Actium, he had erected the citadel of Antonia in honour of his friend Antony. This splendid citadel commanded the Temple Mount and the Temple. The Herodian splendour with which it was built is described in detail by Josephus, who writes that it looked like a fortress externally but was planned internally as a palace.[2] The absence of clear archaeological remains makes a final solution of the problem of the exact site and area of the fortress impossible; it was situated, according to Josephus, in the north-western corner of the Temple Mount. The writer inclines to Benoit's surmise that the Antonia was within the area of the present hill, at the north-west angle on a massive piece of rock south of the accepted spot, and that its dimensions were therefore smaller than hitherto supposed.[3] It would further seem that the Roman *praetorium* was not at the Antonia but in Herod's palace in the north-west of the upper city. Herod's palace was another impressive undertaking, in Josephus' view.[4] It was surrounded by a wall and contained banqueting halls, bedrooms, porticoes and gardens, decorated, it seems, much as the other palaces at Jericho, Masada and Herodium, whose details are known to us from archaeological excavations. Unfortunately it would seem that in the area where the palace is thought to have been built, no remains of superstructures have been found, and they would appear to have been destroyed when the camp of the tenth legion was erected. Digging has however located indications of an area raised by means of supporting walls to a height of 3.5 metres. The palace's conjectured area, on the evidence derived from excavation, was therefore a square measuring some 350 metres.[5] We learn from Josephus that north of the palace rose Herod's three royal towers which were incorporated in the city-wall; one called by him after his brother Phasael, the second after his wife Mariamme, and the third after his friend Hippicus.[6] The base of one of these, perhaps Phasael, has been identified in the citadel area; this is the one known as the 'tower of David,' and extensive excavations have been carried out in its vicinity.[7]

[1] Ibid.   [2] *War* v, 238-45.
[3] See Benoit.   [4] *War* v, 177-83.
[5] See Bahat and Broshi, pp. 55-56.
[6] *War* v, 161-76.
[7] See Amiran and Eitan.

The tower, built of tooled drafted blocks, measures 21.4 by 17 metres, and is preserved to a height of 20 metres. According to Josephus' account the measurements of the tower-bases were 40 cubits and their height 90 cubits, nor is the identity of these data to be ignored; apart from the exterior outline of the tower generally identified as that of Phasael, archaeological details of its plan are entirely lacking.

Contemporarily with the Herodian palaces rose the palaces of the Judaizing kings of Adiabene in the lower city;[1] their remains have not yet been identified. This part of the city also contained such public buildings as the public records office and the *bouleuterion* or council house[2] whose remains are also as yet unknown. Herod also erected buildings for entertainment in Jerusalem as in the other localities where he was active; these include, according to Josephus, a theatre decorated with trophies celebrating the victories of Augustus, and an amphitheatre erected, as Josephus emphasizes, on lower ground;[3] a hippodrome is also ascribed to him[4] but none of these has yet been discovered. Something of the character of the upper city in which were situated the palace of the Hasmonaeans and the town's residential quarters, may be learnt from the intensive excavations carried out in the north-west of the city within the present-day Jewish quarter and on the Hill of Zion.[5] These have disclosed remains of the sonte-built houses of the well-to-do, embellished with frescoes in the 'masonry style,' which is decoratively architectural rather than pictorial. The frescoes nevertheless incorporated elements found in the west in the second, third, and even the fourth styles, and among them representations of birds occurred.[6] These structures were built under the Herods, and were demolished in 70. In them were found mosaics of remarkable beauty adorned with geometric patterns whose chief colours were black, red and white.[7] Architectural details such as Corinthian and Ionic capitals were also found.[8] These elements recur in Herodian buildings in various parts of the country.

Besides these investigations various test-digs have been carried out to ascertain the course and construction of Jerusalem's fortifications at the end of the Second Temple period as indicated by archaeological finds[9]

[1] Josephus, *War* IV, 567; V, 252; VI, 355.   [2] *War* VI, 354.
[3] *Ant.* XV, 268. 272.   [4] *Ant.* XVII, 255.
[5] See the reports of Avigad, 'Excavations'; Broshi, pp. 57-60, plate 3.
[6] Broshi, plate 3.
[7] Avigad, *Archaeological Discoveries*.
[8] Ibid.
[9] See Avi-Yonah, 'The Third and Second Walls'; Amiran.

and the literary sources, predominantly by Josephus.[1] This historian enumerates three walls, Jerusalem's area being expanded northward. While the course of the first wall is fairly clear to us, and some of its sections have been laid bare, chiefly to south of the citadel, it is extremely difficult to locate the line of the second wall, which appears to lie entirely within 'the old city' of today. The remains of the fine Roman gate and its towers uncovered under the present Bab el Amou (Shechem) gate, may however lie on the line of this wall.[2] Impressive remains of the third wall, the construction of which was begun by Herod Agrippa but not completed, have been identified for several hundred metres north of the Ottoman city-wall.[3]

Jerusalem's water-supply was ensured by means of an elaborate and efficient system of aqueducts which brought spring-water over several dozen kilometres from the area south of the city. This system is mentioned in the Talmud and by Josephus.[4] The aqueducts were partly built and partly rock-cut to form channels or tunnels in conformity with the conditions of the terrain.[5]

The cemeteries of Jerusalem at the end of the Second Temple period constitute a very rich source of information on the art and architecture of the epoch, and will be discussed at the end of the present chapter.

The development and building projects of the Herods, whose greatest achievements were in Jerusalem, also found expression in the founding of a number of important cities, and of an extensive system of royal fortresses. We shall see that the archaeological and literary testimony present an impressive picture of energetic and novel construction, combining oriental Hellenistic taste with the technology of the Roman west.

The harbour-city of Caesarea, completed between 12 and 9 B.C.E., on a coast possessing no natural bays, contained, beside a large royal harbour 'larger than Peiraeus' according to Josephus, palaces, temples, a theatre, an amphitheatre and a hippodrome.[6] The city, apparently planned and built orthogonally, was provided with an efficient sewage system not inferior aesthetically, in Josephus' words, to the city above ground. The many investigations carried out of the remains of Caesarea have encountered numerous difficulties owing to the con-

---

[1] *War* v, 142-75.
[2] See Hennessy.
[3] See Sukenik and Mayer; Hamrick; Ben Arieh and Netzer.
[4] *T. B. Yoma* 41a; Josephus, *War* ii, 175. Cf. chapter five, p. 257.
[5] See Mazar, 'The Aqueducts.'
[6] *Ant.* xv, 331-41; *War* i, 408-15.

tinuous occupation characterizing this important city down to modern times. These difficulties have been caused by the need to remove the deep occupation-strata accumulated over the remains of the Second Temple period. Despite all these, some of the remains of the town of Herod and his successors have been excavated, chiefly below the remains of the crusader town, but also in other areas. Remains of the temple dedicated to Augustus, mainly the podium on which it stood overlooking the harbour, and to its east, as described by Josephus, have been identified in the artificial hill near the present anchorage. The podium was composed of a system of walls, vaults and fillings which rose to a height of at least 15 metres over the surrounding area. Little remained of the temple, but it is clear from Josephus' account that it was seen by those entering the port.[1] The west side of the podium was near the port and the sea may have reached it. The great royal harbour was already practically silted up in the Roman period, like other artificial harbours of the Roman world. The port has been explored by a submarine archaeological expedition which successfully located its limits. It was surrounded by the breakwaters partly built of huge blocks tied and reinforced by metal clamps. Its area was some 35 acres (14 hectares), the entrance being on the north, as Josephus describes it. According to the same account two towers flanked the entry, their foundations being found by the survey. The port of Caesarea, which was without doubt one of Herod's most important and novel projects, was erected in a place where no natural bay existed, as Josephus stresses, and was made possible, moreover, only by the Roman technology adopted by the Herodian builders. The closest example to the port of Caesarea is that of Leptis Magna, constructed 200 years later. To the west of the podium were found the remains of internal jetties and complexes of rectangular vaulted chambers, which seem to have been used as the warehouses of the port and perhaps also to dock ships.[2]

The Jewish quarter was located in the north-west of the city where Straton's Tower is thought to have been, but the remains found there are mainly of the Byzantine period.[3] The positions of the theatre, the amphitheatre and the hippodrome have been identified and excavations have been carried out in two of these edifices. The theatre, which embodies various periods, was built under Herod and its *cavea*

---

[1] See Levine, pp. 18-19.
[2] Ibid. pp. 13-18.
[3] Ibid. pp. 40-45.

and *scaenae frons* were discovered. The floor of the orchestra was found to have been decorated with fifteen successive layers of colour and was meant to imitate an *opus sectile* floor.[1] The hippodrome has not yet been excavated but a number of test-holes have been dug and a survey has been conducted; in its state of preservation this is one of the most interesting buildings of its class. The measurements of the arena are 320 by 80 metres; remains of the *spina* have been cleared in the centre, including an obelisk and *metae* (turning marks) of red granite.[2] The street-plan of Caesarea, which was founded on a level area, as described by Josephus, receives apparent confirmation from air-photographs, which also reveal an orthogonal plan. The fortifications of the Herodian city are not sufficiently clear, but some notion can be gained from a wall-section and gate found in the north of the town. The gate was flanked by round towers like the Herodian gates of Sebaste. The wall continues down to the sea but its eastern and southern extensions have not yet been clarified. Subsequently, it would seem in the late Roman period, the city was enclosed by a semicircular wall. The water supply was also one of the most efficient in the country. It is interesting to note that it is not referred to Josephus any more than the city-wall. Two aqueducts brought spring and river water from the southern slopes of the Carmel over a distance of 10 kilometres. They were carried partly on arches, and partly quarried as rock-cut tunnels. Sections were repaired in the course of years by Roman legionary units whose inscriptions have been discovered affixed to the aqueduct, also by various rulers in later periods.[3]

Sebaste (Samaria) was another city founded and rebuilt under Herod.[4] Many remains have been disclosed by excavation. At the city's centre, at its highest point, over the remains of the Israelite palaces and the Hellenistic fort, a temple of Augustus was built facing northward over a large temenos measuring 80 by 20 metres. Access to the temple was gained by a magnificent flight of steps reminiscent of that leading to the Huldah Gates on the Temple Mount. The great temple of Sebaste, which is but poorly preserved, seems to have been prostyle octostyle, and an altar survives in front of it. Attached to all sides of the temple were various structures connected, the excavators believed, with the priests and soldiers who conducted a cult of Augustus here. A marble statue of Augustus was found in the area, which reinforces

---

[1] Ibid. pp. 23-26.　[2] Ibid. pp. 27-29.　[3] Ibid. pp. 30-36.
[4] Josephus, *Ant.* xv, 292-8. Cf. chapter five, pp. 257-8.

the validity of the identification of the temple's cult.[1] To the north of
the temple of Augustus were found the foundations of another sacred
enclosure originating in the Hellenistic period with a cult of Sarapis and
Isis, and continuing as a cult of Kore in the second and third centuries
C.E.[2] Besides the temple of Augustus, Josephus alludes to the city's
fortifications; the Herodian gate has been exposed by excavation,
flanked by round towers like the north gate of Caesarea and the
south gate of Tiberias. Considerable sectors of the contemporary
city-wall, strengthened by towers, have also been disclosed and
surveyed.[3] A colonnaded street which began at the west gate ran
eastward, parallel with another colonnaded thoroughfare coming
from the north-east and reaching the forum. The latter, erected at the
end of the second century C.E., was a rectangle measuring 128 by 72
metres, surrounded on three sides by porticoes; on the fourth side to
west stood a basilica. The *forum* was similar in plan to imperial *fora*
in various places in the Roman world. The colonnaded street in its
present state is also dated to this epoch, although it is probable that
it was planned when the city was rebuilt under Herod.[4] Sebaste also
possessed those buildings of entertainment which formed an integral
part of Hellenistic and Roman culture, such as the theatre, built in
the second century; here no proof has been found of an early building
date like that established at Caesarea.[5] The stadium, measuring
194.45 by 29.5 metres, is the only one of its kind in the country; it was
of the Doric order, and was decorated in fresco in the 'masonry style,'
and could be dated to the Herodian period. The stadium was restored
in the second century C.E.[6] The city's water was supplied by an
aqueduct from springs east of the city as early as the reign of Herod.
This consisted partly of a rock-cut tunnel, partly of freestanding
masonry.[7]

Beside the three cities of Jerusalem, Caesarea and Sebaste, to which
Herod devoted his main building efforts, other urban centres enjoyed
the contributions of the royal builder and his house, but the excavations carried out in them and the information furnished by Josephus
are somewhat limited. Gaza, Gadara and Susitha (Hippos) may be
mentioned as having been granted to him by Augustus, also Joppa,
Apollonia, Jabneh, Caesarea-Panion, Antipatris and Agrippias (Anthe-

---

[1] See Reisner, pp. 171-80.
[2] See Crowfoot, pp. 62-67.
[3] Ibid. pp. 39-41; Reisner, pp. 198-205.
[4] Crowfoot, pp. 50-57.
[5] Ibid. pp. 57-62. [6] Ibid. pp. 41-50. [7] Ibid. pp. 74-81.

don). We should add Tiberias, Sepphoris and Tarichaeae. Susitha's eastern gate has been uncovered, as well as sections possibly belonging to the first century c.e., as the gates can be paralleled in the towns of Herod and his dynasty. Most of the other remains disclosed at Susitha belong to the late Roman and Byzantine periods, and suggest the great wealth which was acquired by the city.[1] In recent excavations at Ashdod and Antipatris remains of the Herodian period have been found but are not such as to provide a complete and continuous picture.[2] Extensive digging has been carried out at Sepphoris, which according to Josephus contained a palace of Herod, but the remains exposed belong mainly to the second and third century c.e., the most important being the theatre of that period.[3] At Ascalon, which was outside Herod's kingdom, he built a palace whose remains have not yet been discovered. Important remains of the Roman imperial epoch exist there, including those of a very large basilica.[4] Tiberias, founded by Herod Antipas ca. 20 c.e., offers a political model of the city-structure of the period in this country, thanks to Josephus' detailed description.[5] The historian is also a very important source for the plan and buildings of this Jewish city, which became the centre of Palestinian Jewry in the third century. In Josephus' day it contained, *inter alia*, a large synagogue, the palaces of the rulers, and a stadium.[6] Excavations have cleared sectors of the fortifications and the south gate whence the *cardo* proceeded to the *agora*; the markets were situated here also in the Byzantine and Arab periods. The date of the city-walls, of which parts have been uncovered, while others remain above ground, is not known for certain.[7] They occupied the steep cliffs to west of the town and enclosed it on all sides. The water supply was furnished by an aqueduct bringing water from the springs of the Yavniel gorge south of the Sea of Galilee, 15 kilometres away.[8] As a link between the royal fortresses and splendid palaces built by the Herods in various places, mainly in Judaea, frequently on the sites of the Hasmonaean fortresses and palaces, and his urban centres, may be noted the economic, administrative and strategic centre established

---

[1] See Schumacher, pp. 194 ff.; Anati.
[2] See the reports of Dothan and Freedman, pp. 27-32; M. Kokhavi (1975), p. 40.
[3] See Waterman.
[4] See Garstang.
[5] *Ant.* XVIII, 36-38; *War* II, 638.
[6] *Life* 65; 276.
[7] G. Foerster, in *RB* LXXXII (1975) pp. 105-109.
[8] See F. M. Abel, *Géographie de la Palestine* I (1933), pp. 447.

by him at Jericho. The oasis in the southern Jordan rift, focused on Jericho, was chiefly renowned for its peculiar plants and first and foremost for the opobalsam, a medicinal and perfume plant which grew only in the Jordan valley. Due to its special significance the oasis was a royal estate of the various rulers of Judaea, while first-class strategic importance attached to Jericho as the eastern approach of Jerusalem. On account of all these factors it became an urban centre and the headquarters of a toparchy. The town was located at modern Jericho; Josephus writes that it held a theatre, an amphitheatre and a hippodrome, whose position has only recently been identified.[1] The splendid winter-palace of the Hasmonaean and Herodian dynasties have also been partly excavated. A series of palaces was erected on both sides of Wadi Qelt south-west of the town near the wadi-exit; the wadi when in winter spate was a natural centre which was planned in full harmony with its surroundings. The two wings of the palace, north and south of the stream respectively, and linked by a bridge, were surrounded by ornamental gardens whose remains have been discovered, partly to the point where it has become possible to reconstruct them and perhaps even to identify the plants grown there. The two wings of the palace, which were not built at the same time, were nevertheless erected on a similar coordinated plan, the northern wing being more pretentious, more spacious and more complex. The measurements of the southern wing were 81 by 46 metres; it included living quarters, a bath, a central courtyard and of course a resplendent hall where the rulers gave audience. The structure was adorned with stucco and frescoes in the 'masonry style'. The northern wing was much larger, but possessed the same architectural elements, being built with *opus reticulatum*, a style doubtless introduced into the country by a group of Italian builders. Its floors were decorated in various *opus sectile* patterns partly composed of imported marble, in an intensive manner otherwise unknown in this period in Judaea. Some of the rooms of the palace were floored with geometric mosaics, mostly in black, white and red. The colours of the frescoes, painted in the 'masonry style', comprised red, white, black, green, blue and yellow. Along the southern front of the wing a splendid garden was laid out also in *opus reticulatum*. Looking out upon the bed of the stream, it was embellished with a series of niches and exedrae with pools and fountains in the centre, and to its east lay a large pond whose use has not yet been ascertained. Opposite, in the

[1] *Ant.* XVII, 161.193; *War* I, 407.659; II, 57.

northern wing, the palace front facing the stream was adorned with a row of impressive colonnades.[1] In general planning and many details these and other palaces can be paralleled by the descriptions of Italian *villae rusticae* in ancient literature, and by archaeological discoveries. Jericho's water supply was furnished by means of a ramified system of aqueducts deriving their water from springs to the north and west. The Herodian estates at Phasaelis and Archelais to the north of Jericho, whose existence is known to us from Josephus,[2] have not yet been explored and our information on their planned agriculture is still deficient. Jericho and the important oasis of which it formed the centre, were protected by a series of fortresses originating in the Hasmonean epoch and continuing under Herod. These were situated on the hill crests to west of Jericho; they were Threx and Taurus, destroyed by Pompey[3] and the fortress of Doc where Simeon the Hasmonean was assassinated.[4] Cypros was another stronghold built to take the place of one of the Hasmonean fortresses,[5] and although excavations were carried out here recently, they are not yet fully published and our knowledge of these fortresses is still scanty.[6] A fortress of primary strategic importance was the Alexandrium, built by the Hasmoneans rulers (see above), and a focal royal stronghold under Herod. It was sited on the top of a high mountain in eastern Samaria and looked out over the central Jordan valley, protecting the north-eastern approaches to Judaea.[7] The place has been surveyed and considerable sections of its impressive structure, composed of dressed and drafted masonry, can be seen by the visitor. Like the royal strongholds already mentioned, Herod's other fortresses were built on the sites of Hasmonean strong points, as is made clear by Josephus and in a large measure also by archaeological excavation. These additional works, designed principally to safeguard the internal security of Herod's kingdom, and referred to by Josephus in great detail, are Masada, Herodium, Hyrcania in the wilderness of Judaea, and Machaerus in Transjordan east of the Dead Sea.

Extensive digging has been carried out at Masada in the eastern Judaean desert and at Herodium south of Jerusalem, and this has

[1] See Baramki; Pritchard; Netzer, 'The Hasmonaean and Herodian Palaces'.
[2] *Ant.* XVI, 145; XVII, 340.
[3] Strabo XVI, 2, 40.
[4] Josephus, *Ant.* XIII, 230. See Harder pp. 49-69.
[5] *War* I, 417.
[6] See Netzer, 'Cypros', pp. 54-61.
[7] See Abel.

to a large extent filled in and verified the detailed and sometimes apparently exaggerated accounts of Josephus. The royal fortress of Herod built in 30 B.C.E. on the site of the former Hasmonaean strong point on the rock of Masada, would have been an exceptional natural stronghold even without artificial fortification.[1] Apart from two paths, one to the west of the rock and one to its east, called by Josephus 'the snake path', the crag is cut off from its surroundings by steep cliffs which prevent all access. A series of palaces, administrative buildings, soldiers' barracks, an extensive series of magazines and a well-appointed set of baths were erected in the upper area of the rock. The whole was surrounded by a casemate wall strengthened by towers. As the only important source of water near Masada is at Engeddi, some thirty kilometres to the north, an efficient system of water supply and water storage was prepared, both enabling the place to withstand a prolonged siege and making possible a supply of running water for the inhabitants and for the well-appointed baths.[2] Two principal palaces were exposed by the Masada excavations and beside them three smaller palaces, designed, presumably, to house Herod's numerous family in time of need. The northern palace described in detail by Josephus[3] was the finest achievement of the Masada building projects; it was established at the northern end of the rock on three natural rock-terraces prepared and widened to enable extensive construction. This was carried out by means of a most impressive series of retaining walls which literally overhung an abyss. The uppermost terrace received four living rooms arranged around an internal court, with a semicircular verandah at the edge of the rock to north; this was surrounded by a double colonnade facing the awe-inspiring landscape of the Judaean wilderness. A flight of steps led down from the upper to the middle terrace which was 20 metres lower. On this a circular structure was erected, of which only the foundations remains. It seems to have been adorned with two rows of columns and was designed as a resplendent place of retreat and repose for the inmates of the palace, and as an integral part of the artistic and architectural fabric of this unique residence. A further flight of steps, partly preserved, led down to the lowest terrace, about 15 metres below the middle one; overlooking the expanses of the Judaean wilderness, it held a splendid reception hall measuring 15 by

[1] *War* VII, 280-406.
[2] Yadin, pp. 26-33; 75-86.
[3] *War* VII, 288-90.

15 metres, embellished with pilasters and surrounded by a Corinthian peripteros. To its east, on the edge of the cliff, was built a small bathhouse with a hypocaust. This inspiring palace was adorned with mosaic pavements in black and white, and its walls with stucco and fresco in the 'masonry style'.[1] The second palace is located on the west of the rock near the west gate, being the largest residential building at Masada, with an area of 4,000 square metres. It comprises three parts: the residential wing, a service block and workshops, and a block of storerooms. The living rooms are built round a central court on a pronouncedly Hellenistic plan. The entrance to the throne-room and *triclinia* is at the south corner of the court, through two successive pairs of columns *in antis*. A well-appointed bathroom and other service-rooms flank the living rooms. The workshops, which include a potter's shop, were also built around a central yard. The storage block included *inter alia* a storeroom 70 metres in length. The residential wing comprised two storeys.

The walls of the western palace were also plastered with stucco in the 'masonry style'. The *triclinium* was decorated with a coloured mosaic floor with geometric borders and plant-motifs such as vines, grape clusters, fig-leaves and pomegranates. Another geometric pavement was located in the service wing.[2] Beside the northern and western palaces, three additional smaller palaces were built to plans identical with that of the residential wing of the western edifice. A well executed swimming pool was constructed beside this palace.

Large and splendid baths were built near the northern palace, planned in the usual fashion to contain *apodyterium, frigidarium, tepidarium,* and a particularly up-to-date *calidarium*. The external court was surrounded by a portico adorned with black and white mosaics, possessing at their centres *emblemata* which had been subsequently defaced. The remaining rooms of the bath range had also been decorated with mosaics in their first phase, but they had been later replaced by *opus sectile* floors. The walls were, as usual, decorated with stucco in the 'masonry style'.[3] A large block of public storerooms lay near the bath; it contained fifteen storerooms averaging 30 by 4 metres; the walls and floors of these storerooms, which are described by Josephus, were covered with mud plaster.[4] On their west side rose an administrative building, to the south of which was a structure quartering the garrison commandant and his staff. A masonry

[1] Yadin, pp. 40-73.   [2] Ibid. pp. 116-33.
[3] Ibid. pp. 75-86.   [4] Ibid. pp. 87-106.

columbarium discovered in the southern area of the fortress was probably for the use of the non-Jewish troops of the garrison.[1] The stronghold was enclosed by a casemate wall 1,400 metres long and with an overall thickness of four metres; these measurements correspond to those given by Josephus. The casemate chambers comprise rooms of varying length up to 35 metres; here were quartered, it would seem, most of the garrison under Herod and subsequently, during the Zealot occupation in 66 C.E., the Zealot families lived in them. The wall contained 70 rooms in all and possessed 30 towers whose positions were selected on tactical and constructional grounds. The wall was pierced by four gates on the east and west, commanding the main approaches; on the south a gate overlooked the path leading to groups of cisterns, another on the north the path to the principal cisterns. These gates are built to one pattern: a square gatehouse, with benches along the walls, which were stuccoed in the 'masonry style'; exceptional was the south gate, which lacked these elements.[2] It should be emphasized that the northern palace was excluded from the enceinte for tactical and constructional reasons, and thus once again Josephus' account conforms to archaeological reality.

Water was supplied from the flood runoff down the Masada gorge from the west, diverted by a dam and aqueducts to two groups of rock-cut cisterns at the north-west end of the rock. These dozen cisterns were well plastered with hydraulic plaster and had a capacity of 40,000 cubic metres. Thence the water was carried by beasts of burden and by water-carriers to the top of the cliff and stored in cisterns within the fortress. Additional cisterns existed in the east and south cliffs, being fed by rainwater collected from the citadel area by means of a network of canals.[3] After the Zealot occupation of Masada few alterations were made; they included the conversion of a small east-west orientated hall in the north-west sector of the wall to a synagogue, by the addition of rows of stone benches along the walls.[4] In addition two ritual immersion baths (מקוה) were found, constructed by the Zealots in accordance with halakic prescription.[5] As the number of belligerents who made Masada their stronghold grew, additional lean-to structures were added to |the quarters in the casemates.[6] The entire stronghold was constructed of the hard dolomite rock quarried on the summit of Masada, and one of the

[1] Ibid. pp. 134-9.　　[2] Ibid. pp. 102 ff. (phot.)
[3] Ibid. pp. 26-33.　　[4] Ibid. pp. 181-6.
[5] Ibid. pp. 164-7.　　[6] Ibid. pp. 141-63.

quarries so used has been discovered. The more easily carved sandstone quarried at the foot of the cliff was used for various architectural details such as columns, column-capitals and parts of the entablatures. Of special interest are the Roman siege-works put up in the year 73 C.E. including a huge ramp on the west of the rock, designed to enable the building of the tower with which the Roman legions succeeded in breaching the wall and entering the fortress. The timber lacing with the help of which the ramp was erected was well preserved thanks to the dryness of local conditions. A siege dyke was also built round Masada, strengthened by eight camps serving the troops of the Tenth Legion and its auxiliary units who were investing the fortress. Other sectors of this dyke were reinforced at regular intervals by watch-towers. The entire Roman siege works are well-preserved and have been surveyed, but little digging has been carried out in connection with them.[1]

The fortress and the royal centre of the Herodium, which was also the burial place of the builder ruler, is without doubt one of the peak points of building in his time. Herodium is 12 kilometres south of Jerusalem, its centre being on a hill rising 758 metres above sea level. At the centre of the royal ensemble rose a circular structure composed of two concentric masonry rings, with an over-all diameter of 62 metres. The point of departure of the two rings is in the round tower on the east, 18 metres in diameter. The corridor formed between the two rings is 3.5 metres broad. In addition to the eastern tower, three semi-circular towers projected from the outer wall northward, westward and southward. The circular walls and towers were partly built over a system of vaults which helped to extend the area of the hill; over them conditions were created favourable to the superimposition of strong and lofty walls. The building so uniquely planned appears to have been covered to its entire height of 12 metres by an earth and stone mound in order to give it the appearance of a huge tumulus, the Mausoleum of Herod. The covered entrance-passage was set within the artificial mound, ascending from the foot of the hill to the enclosed area within the circular structure, the palace. This area is divided into two equal parts: in its eastern half, at the foot of the great tower, a garden was laid out, surrounded by a Corinthian peristyle and enhanced by niches and exedrae. Its western half contained a *triclinium* measuring 15 by 11 metres, more rooms, and well-appointed baths to northward. Of special interest here, in view of the construction

[1] See Schulten.

of the Herodium in the thirties B.C.E., is the dome covering the *frigidarium*. The location of Herod's burial place is still unknown, but there are grounds for assuming that it was within the circular structure, perhaps in the eastern tower, which has yet to be adequately explored.[1] A small portion of a complex of palaces, colonnades and other structures has been uncovered at the foot of the hill to northward; Josephus speaks of these in his detailed account of Herodium, which he calls 'a complete town within a royal palace'.[2] Worthy of note among these buildings is a huge edifice, only the outline of which is known at present, its measurements being 130 by 55 metres; this was an audience hall adorned with pilasters and niches overlooking a long terrace–perhaps a hippodrome–and not yet properly investigated. The centre of the lower area was occupied by a great pool with fountains in the middle; this acted as a focal point in the architectural design of the area, which, though deep in the desert, was covered with gardens.[3] Construction at Herodium was generally in dressed blocks quarried in the vicinity. The walls were stuccoed and painted in the 'masonry style', the floors adorned with mosaics and *opus sectile*, nor was this unconventional. A special aqueduct led from Artas south of Jerusalem to Herodium, supplying the great pool at its foot and the complex of cisterns quarried in the hill itself.[4] Herodium was captured by the Zealots during the first war with Rome and was one of the last fortresses remaining in the hands of the insurgents when Jerusalem was about to fall; it was taken by the Romans before Machaerus and Masada. This event left its traces in the marks of a great configuration found during the excavations. During the second war against Rome, Herodium was the headquarters of one of Bar Cochba's units, as we learn from a contemporary document. Various finds of this period have been made at Herodium, especially noteworthy being a system of quarry-tunnels under the hill which rendered the cisterns useless for water-storage and shed a special light on Dio Cassius' description of the tactics of Bar Cochba's fighters and their use of underground bunkers. A number of surveys and some excavations have been conducted at Hyrcania and Machaerus, but the material at our disposal does not furnish a picture of its art and architecture.[5]

[1] See Corbo, pp. 74-76.
[2] *War* I, 421.
[3] See Netzer, 'Recent investigations.'
[4] See G. Foerster's short report in *RB* LXXVII (1970), pp. 400-1.
[5] See Wright, 'The Archaeological Remains'; Vardmann; Rainey.

The Nabataean towns constitute a chapter of peculiar importance in the country's history in the period under discussion. Central among them was Petra, whose offshots were the caravan-towns of the Negev along the trade-routes to Gaza and Rhinocorura (el-Arish): Avdat, Subeita, Elusa and Nessana. Nabataean art and architecture, which reached their acme in the last third of the first century c.e., constitute an original fusion of the oriental cultures, beginning with Mesopotamia and Egypt and ending with Persia, Parthia, and Hellenistic-Roman culture. The town of Petra was established along each side of a narrow valley. In excavations carried out recently, following surveys made at the beginning of the century, three large markets and two temples have been discovered.[1] One temple, standing in the middle of a large enclosure measuring 160 by 53 metres, is Corinthian peripteral with two basilicas in front of it. The second temple, known as the Qasr bint Farun, one of the most impressive monuments of Petra, is situated within an enclosure 105 by 75 metres in area. Embodying ancient oriental traditions, it was built on the model of the Nabataean temples of Edom, the original heartland of the Nabataean kingdom. The temple's ornamentation was Hellenistic-Doric and the building was faced with painted and moulded stucco[2]. Additionally the city possesses a rock-cut theatre, a gymnasium, a palace, *nymphaea* and well-appointed baths.[3] Qasr bint Farun is approached by a colonnaded street containing a triumphal arch set up, apparently, after the annexation of the Nabataean kingdom to the Roman empire in 106.[4] The town is surrounded by hundreds of rock-cut funerary monuments in the oriental Hellenistic Roman style. Amongst these Khaznat Farun ed-Deir and the tomb of Sextus Florentinus, one of the Roman governors of Petra under Hadrian, are prominent. This last monument is the only one at Petra dated by an inscription. The façade of the Khazne is rock-cut like all the other funerary monuments, being 25 metres in width and 39 metres in height. The façade is enhanced by a two-storeyed structure; the lower embodies columns crowned by a Corinthian entablature and pediment with 'Baroque' deviations. The upper storey is similar, but the entablature is broken at the centre by a carved tholos with conical roof within a colonnaded surround. The frieze of the lower storey is enriched by griffins,

---

[1] See the very useful summary and bibliography by Starcky.
[2] See Kohl; Parr, *Découvertes*.
[3] See Bachmann; Parr, 'Excavations.'
[4] See Wright, 'Petra. The Arched Gate'; Kohl, pp. 25-40.

alternating with amphorae and plant-ornamentation. The *tympanum* was also adorned with plant elements and crowned with the 'crown of Isis'; figures of the Dioscuri were carved in the intercolumniations. The friezes of the upper part of the monument were adorned with bucrania. The intercolumniations of the colonnades contained carvings of Amazons and Nikai (Victories); in those of the tholos, Tyche is apparently portrayed bearing the cornucopia, and eagles were carved at the ends of the pediment. This resplendent monument is dated by various scholars between 50 B.C.E. and 150 C.E., and the former date seems the more likely.[1] The ed-Deir monument differs little from those preceding it, but is larger and its decoration is restrained and distinguished by greater simplicity.

Unlike Petra, the Nabataean towns of the Negev were also densely populated in the Byzantine period, hence their Nabataean remains are but slightly known. Excavations have been carried out so far at 'Avdat, Subeita, Nessana, Kurnub and Halutzah, and in all of them characteristic architectural remains have been found. Two gates and a portico of the Nabataean period have been discovered at 'Avdat, also parts of a temple of the reign of Aretas IV.[2] The interesting potter's plant belongs to the first half of the first century C.E.[3] Contemporary remains are rare at Subeita and Nessana, but on the other hand remains of a theatre of this period have recently been disclosed at Halutzah with other remains of the Nabataean epoch.[4]

Notable among the most impressive remains of art and architecture of the end of the Second Temple period is the rich necropolis of Jerusalem, which surrounded the city on all sides except the north-western. The tombs comprise both freestanding rock-cut monuments and the façades of tomb-complexes themselves rock-cut. In addition there are a number of subterranean tomb-complexes parts of which are of masonry construction. Stone sarcophagi, ossuaries and small coffins were sometimes richly decorated with plant and geometric motifs.[5]

The most splendid of these tombs was built by the royal family of Adiabene which had adopted Judaism and fixed their family burial-place at Jerusalem in the middle of the first century C.E. Its location

---

[1] See Wright, 'The Khazne at Petra.'
[2] See Negev, 'Avdat a Caravan Halt'.
[3] Negev, *The Nabataean Potter's Workshop*.
[4] Negev, *RB* LXXXII (1975), pp. 109-113.
[5] See Galling, pp. 73-101; Vincent I, pp. 313-71.

is given by Josephus, who describes the three pyramids set over it.[1] Pausanias in his enthusiastic account compares the monument, perhaps with some exaggeration, with the Mausoleum of Halicarnassus, but the comparison is highly significant.[2] Remains of the tombs have been identified in the fine tomb-complex today known as 'the tombs of the kings'.[3] The approach is by a monumental flight of steps fronted by a gate descending to a large square court cut, like the steps, in the rock; it measures 27.50 by 25.70 metres and is 8 metres below ground-level. The façade of the monument, which looks eastward, takes the form of two columns *in antis*, but the spaces between the columns and the *antae* was closed by a wall and a door was placed between the columns. The doors were worked by a mechanical device enthusiastically described by Pausanias. The upper part of the façade was decorated by two friezes one above the other. The lower was composed of moderately naturalistic representations of acanthus leaves and clusters of fruit, including etrogs and pine-cones. The upper frieze was Doric with a grape cluster in the centre, flanked by garlands represented in a naturalistic fashion. Slight traces of the pyramids described in the ancient sources are to be found over the rock-cut façade. They were of masonry, with conical superstructures like those found in other tombs in the east and west. The tomb-complex itself, which was closed by a rolling stone, was composed of burial chambers in which sarcophagi were found, adorned with rich plant and geometric motifs, and galleries (*kukhim*) in which the bodies of the dead were laid.[4] Besides this royal monument a number of fine monuments are to be found in the Kidron Valley and in other areas of Jerusalem. The oldest group is the tomb of Hezir, the identity of whose occupants is established by a Hebrew inscription on the front of the complex, and dated to the Hasmonaean period, perhaps to the second half of the second century B.C.E. The façade of this rock-cut group is two columns *in antis* in the Hellenistic-Doric style; the entablature was carved in the same style. Beside the façade is the base of a monument, a rock-cut *nefesh*, whose upper part, which seems to have been a masonry pyramid, has not survived (see above).[5] Another monument in the Kidron valley is that known as 'the tomb of Zechariah', a cube measuring 5.60 by 5.60 metres, entirely rock-hewn. It is composed of two

---

[1] *Ant.* XX, 95.
[2] Pausanias VIII, 16.
[3] See Kon.
[4] Ibid. fig. 14.
[5] See Avigad, *Ancient Monuments*, pp. 74-79.

parts, the corners of the lower being decorated with angle-pilasters and attached quarter-columns, with two columns between each pair, all in the Ionic style. The upper part is separated from the lower by an Egyptian cavetto moulding and is crowned with a pyramid. This interpenetration of oriental and Hellenistic styles is characteristic of the period not only in Palestine but also throughout the Roman empire.[1] The most complex monument in the Kidron valley is that known as 'Absalom's tomb'.[2] This, like the previous example, is composed of two principal parts, the lower being the square rock-cut base, measuring 6.40 by 6.55 metres, adorned with Ionic pilasters and columns like the Tomb of Zechariah, but crowned with a Doric frieze. This fusion of styles is also very common in the Hellenistic period and at the beginning of the Roman era. Here too the separation between the upper and lower part was effected by means of an Egyptian cavetto band. The upper part was built as a square base upon which a circular structure was erected terminating in a concave conical dome. This circular structure is to be conceived as a tholos whose columns were deliberately omitted by the architect, perhaps because he wished to avoid figuring statues and reliefs in the intercolumniations. Many architectural parallels to this columned tholos can be found in both the west and the east, for example in the Khaznat Farun at Petra, also in the wall-paintings of Pompei and Herculaneum. The Kidron monument contains a burial chamber and by it a group of tombs the façade of which is adorned with a pediment typical of the other tomb-façades of Jerusalem; this one contains acanthus scrolls in somewhat shallow relief. Other resplendent funerary façades decorated with architectural and plant elements as already described are to be found in Jerusalem in 'the tombs of the sanhedrin', in the 'tomb of the columns' and 'the tomb of the grape clusters'.[3] A further group of tomb-complexes may be noted which are masonry-built; such are the 'tomb of Herod' and the tombs of Nicanor and the Nazirite on Mount Scopus.[4]

Sarcophagi were made of hard, ossuaries generally of soft limestone. The former were adorned with plant-motifs such as acanthus scrolls, vines and grape-clusters, similar to those on the tomb-façades, only rarely with geometric or architectural motifs. The carving is some-

[1] Ibid. pp. 79-90.
[2] Ibid. pp. 91-133.
[3] See Avigad, 'The rock carved façades'; Rahmani, 'Jewish rock-cut tombs.'
[4] See Vincent and Stève I, pp. 342-46.

what shallow and lacking in plasticity, instead of which the craftsmen depended rather on the technique of contrast between light and shade.[1] This technique finds additional expression and emphasis in the decoration of the ossuaries, hundreds of which have been discovered in Jerusalem and to a lesser extent elsewhere in the country. The decoration is executed by incision in the soft stone in a manner resembling woodcarving or the Kerbschnitt technique. The decoration is generally divided into metopes by means of plant motifs. Less often, various architectural representations appear, such as tomb-buildings, façades and entrances, which impart to the ossuaries a houselike appearance.[2]

The art and architecture of the Hellenistic and early Roman period in Palestine were, as we have seen, a complete fusion of local traditions and contemporary external influences, without noticeable eclecticism, if we except the almost complete and deliberate omission of figurative representation. Exceptional in this respect were pronouncedly pagan cities such as Samaria, Caesarea and Ascalon. For the most part the trend which rejected such forms ended in the second century, after the war of Bar Cochba. This change of attitude to figurative art found its chief expression in synagogues and at Beth Shearim, the central necropolis of the Jews of the Land of Israel in the period of the Mishnah and the Talmud. In this respect greater expression was afforded to the combining of local Jewish art with the art and architecture of the time.

BIBLIOGRAPHY

ABEL, F. M. 'De l'ovadi Faraa a Fasail—l'Alexandrion,' in *RB* XXII (1913), pp. 227-34.

AMIRAN, R. 'The First and Second Walls of Jerusalem Reconsidered in the Light of the New Wall,' in *IEJ* XXI (1971), pp. 166-7.

— and A. EITAN, 'Excavations in the Courtyard of the Citadel, Jerusalem 1968-9. Preliminary Report,' in *IEJ* XX (1970), pp. 9-17.

ANATI, E. 'Susita,' in *Bulletin of the Department of Antiquities of the State of Israel* V-VI (1951), pp. 31-3 (in Hebrew).

APPLEBAUM, S. 'A Greek Statue from Scythopolis,' in *Bulletin Museum Ha-Aretz* XIII (1971), pp. 14ff.

[1] See Avi-Yonah.
[2] See Rahmani, 'Jerusalem's Tomb Monuments.'

AVIGAD, N. 'The Rock-Carved Façades of the Jerusalem Necropolis,' in *IEJ* I (1950-1), pp. 96-106.

— *Ancient Monuments in the Kidron Valley* (1954, in Hebrew).

— 'Excavations in the Jewish Quarter of the Old City of Jerusalem 1969-71,' in *IEJ* XX (1970), pp. 1-8; 41-51; 129-40.

— 'Figurative Art of the Jews,' in *Beth Shearim* III (1971), pp. 202-8.

— 'The Burial Vault of a Nazirite Family on Mount Scopus,' in *IEJ* XXI (1971).

— *Archaeological Discoveries in the Jewish Quarter of Jerusalem in the Second Temple Period* (1976).

AVI-YONAH, M. *Oriental Art in Roman Palestine* (1961).

— 'The Third and Second Walls of Jerusalem,' in *IEJ* XVIII (1968), pp. 98-125.

BACHMANN, W. and others, *Petra* (1921).

BAHAT, D. and M. BROSHI, 'Excavations in the Armenian Gardens', in *Jerusalem Revealed*, ed. by Y. Yadin (1975).

BARAMKI, D. C. 'Excavations at New Testament Jericho and Khirbet en-Nitla,' in *AASOR* XXIX-XXX (1949-51).

BEN ARIEH, S. and E. NETZER, 'Excavations along the Third Wall of Jerusalem, 1972-4,' in *IEJ* XXIV (1974), pp. 97-107.

BENOIT, P. 'L'Antonia d'Hérode le Grand et le Forum Oriental d'Aelia Capitolina,' in *HTR* LXIV (1971), pp. 135-67.

BLISS, F. J. and R. A. S. MACALISTER, *Excavations in Palestine during the Years 1898-1900* (1902).

BRETT, M. J. B. 'The Qasr el Abd: a Proposed Reconstruction,' in *BASOR* CLXXI (1963), pp. 45-55.

BROSHI, M. 'Excavations in the House of Caiaphas, Mount Zion', in *Jerusalem Revealed*, ed. by Y. Yadin (1975).

CLAIRMONT, C. 'Greek Pottery from the Near East,' in *Berytus* XI (1954-5), pp. 85-141; XII (1955-7), pp. 1-34.

CORBO, V. 'L'Herodion di Gebel Fureidis,' in *Liber Annuus St.Bibl. Franc.* XIII, pp. 219-77; XVII, pp. 65-121.

CROWFOOT, J. W. and others, *The Buildings at Samaria* (1942).

DOTHAN, M., *IEJ* XXIV (1974), pp. 276-9.

— and D. R. FREEDMAN, 'Ashdod I. The First Season of Excavations 1962,' in *Atiqot*, English Series VII (1967).

GALLING, K. 'Die Nekropole von Jerusalem,' in *PJB* 32 (1936), pp. 73-101.

GARSTANG, J. 'The Funds Excavations of Askalon,' in *PEQ* (1921), pp. 12-16; (1922), pp. 112-7; (1924), pp. 24-35.

HAMRICK, E. W. 'New Excavations at Sukenik's Third Wall,' in *BASOR* CLXXXIII (1966), pp. 19-26.

HARDER, G. 'Herodes Burgen und Herodes Städte im Jordangraben,' in *ZDPV* LXXVIII (1962), pp. 49-69.

HENNESSY, J. B. 'Preliminary Report on Excavations at the Damascus Gate, Jerusalem 1964-6,' in *Levant* II (1970), pp. 22-7.

ILIFFE, J. H. 'Pre-Hellenistic Greek Pottery in Palestine,' in *QDAP* II (1933), pp. 15-26.

— 'A Nude Terra-cotta Statuette of Aphrodite,' in *QDAP* III (1934), pp. 106-11.

KAPLAN, J. 'Jaffa's History Revealed by the Spade,' in *Archaeology* XVII (1964), pp. 270-6.

KOHL, H. *Kasr Firaoun in Petra* (1910).

KON, M. *The Tombs of the Kings* (1947; in Hebrew).

LAPP, P. W. 'Soundings at Arak el-Emir,' in *BASOR* CLXV (1962), pp. 16-34; CLXXI (1963), pp. 8-39.

LEVINE, L. I. *Roman Caesarea* (1975).

MAZAR, A. 'The Aquaducts of Jerusalem,' in *Jerusalem Revealed*, pp. 79-84.

MAZAR, B. *The Excavations in the Old City of Jerusalem near the Temple Mount. Preliminary Report of the Second and Third Seasons 1969-70* (1971).

— 'The Archaeological Excavations near the Temple Mount' in *Jerusalem Revealed*, ed. by Y. Yadin (1975), pp. 25-7, fig. 26-27.

— 'The Excavations near the Temple Mount,' in *Qadmoniot* V (1972), pp. 74-90 (in Hebrew).

— and P. BAR-ADON, 'Excavations at Beth-Yerah,' in *IEJ* II (1952), pp. 166-7; III (1953), p. 132; V (1955), pp. 273.

— and M. BEN DOV, *Finds from the Archeological Excavation near the Temple Mount* (1973).

NAVEH, J. 'The Excavations at Mesad Hashavyahu. Preliminary Report,' in *IEJ* XII (1962), pp. 89-113.

NEGEV, A. 'Avdat a Caravan Halt in the Negev,' in *Archaeology* XIV (1961), pp. 122-30.

— *The Nabatean Potter's Workshop at Oboda* (1974).

NETZER, E. 'Recent Investigations at Lower Herodium,' in *Qadmoniot* VI (1973), pp. 107-10 (in Hebrew).

— 'The Hasmonaean and Herodian Palaces at Jericho,' in *IEJ* XXV (1975), pp. 89-100.

— 'Cypros,' in *Qadmoniot* VIII (1975), pp. 54-61.

PARR, P. J. 'Découvertes récentes au sanctuaire du Qasr à Pétra,' in *Syria* XLV (1968), pp. 1-24.

— 'Excavations at Petra 1958-9,' in *PEQ* XCII (1961), pp. 124-35.

PETERS, J. P. and H. THIERSCH, *Painted Tombs in the Necropolis of Marisa* (1905).

PLÖGER, O. 'Die makkabäischen Burgen,' in *ZDPV* LXXI, 2 (1955).

PRITCHARD, J. B. 'The Excavations at Herodion Jericho 1951,' in *AASOR* XXXII-XXXIII (1952-4; publ. 1958).

RAHMANI, L. Y. 'Jerusalem's Tomb on Jewish Ossuaries,' in *IEJ* XVIII (1968), pp. 220-5.

— 'Jewish Rock-cut Tombs in Jerusalem,' in *Atiqot* III (1961), pp. 93-120.

— 'Jason's Tomb, in *IEJ* XVII (1967), pp. 61-100.

RAINEY, A. F. 'Surface Remains Pertaining to the Fall of Macherus,' in *Eretz Israel* X (1971), pp. 276-9.

REISNER, G. A. and others, *Harvard Excavations at Samaria 1908-10* (1924).

SCHICK, C. 'Der Frankenberg,' in *ZDPV* III (1880), pp. 88-99.

SCHULTEN, A. 'Masada, die Burg des Herodes, und die römischen Lager,' in *ZDPV* LVI (1933), pp. 1-179.

SELLERS, O. R. *The Citadel of Beth-Zur* (1933); 'The 1957 Campaign at Beth-Zur,' in *AASOR* XXXVIII (1968).

SIMONS, J. *Jerusalem in the Old Testament* (1952).

SJÖQVIST, E. 'Kaisareion,' in *Opuscula Romana* I (1954), pp. 86-108.

STARCKY, J. 'Pètra et la Nabatène,' in *Dictionnaire de la Bible*, Supplément VII, pp. 886-1017.

STERN, E. *The Material Culture of the Land of the Bible in the Persian Period* (1975; in Hebrew).

STROBEL, A. 'Machärus-Geschichte und Ende einer Festung im Lichte archäologisch-topographischer Beobachtungen, in *Bibel und Qumran, Festschrift A. Bardtke* (1968), pp. 198-225.

SUKENIK, E. L. and L. A. MAYER, *The Third Wall. An Account of the Excavations* (1930).

TSAFRIR, Y. 'The Location of the Seleucid Akra in Jerusalem,' in *Jerus. Revealed*, pp. 85-86.

URBACH, E. E. 'The Rabbinical Laws of Idolatry in the Second and Third Centuries in the Light of Archaeological and Historical Facts,' in *IEJ* IX (1959), pp. 149-65.

VARDMANN, J. *Preliminary Report on the 1968 Excavations at Machaerus* (1968).

VINCENT, L. H. and A. M. STÈVE, *Jérusalem de l'Ancien Testament* 3 vols. (1956).

WATERMAN, L. and others, *Preliminary Report of the University of Michigan Excavations at Sepphoris* (1937).

WEINBERG, S. S. 'Post-exilic Palestine. An Archaeological Report,' in *Proceedings of the Israel Academy* IV (1969), pp. 78-97.

— 'Tel Anafa. The Hellenistic Town,' in *IEJ* XXI (1971), pp. 86-109.

WRIGHT, G. R. H. 'Petra. The Arched Gate 1959-60,' in *PEQ* XCIII (1961), pp. 124-35;

— CII (1970), pp. 111-5.

— 'The Archaeological Remains at el Mird in the Wilderness of Judea,' in *Biblica* XLII (1961), pp. 1-21.

— 'The Khazne at Petra. A Review,' in *Syria* XLV (1968), pp. 1-24.

YADIN, Y. Masada. *Herod's Fortress and the Zealots' Last Stand* (1966).

Chapter Twenty One
Hebrew and Aramaic in the First Century

In the first century C.E., Palestine was a country of many languages, as were most countries of the Middle East. Owing to its chequered history, and being a centre of transit trade, it was perhaps more so than neighbouring countries. A special element of multilingualism was provided by members of the Jewish Diaspora, who visited the land of their fathers and centre of their religion for pilgrimages or in order to study, and stayed for a while or perhaps permanently, forming their own separate communities and synagogues in which at least part of the liturgy and readings were in the language of their country of residence.[1] Not only were there speakers of many languages, but the same individuals often spoke more than one language, a feature which is still common in the Middle East of our own days. In this matter we have to distinguish several patterns. The first is common bilingualism (or multilingualism) caused by the personal circumstances of the individual: a man may pick up the language of his neighbours, a merchant that of his suppliers or customers, in a mixed marriage both parents and children may currently use both languages, etc. The second pattern is that of the *lingua franca*:[2] people with different home languages living within a certain area use for inter-communication one and the same language, which may be one of the home-languages of their area or a language from outside (and in some cases is a language that came into being as a *lingua franca* and is not spoken by anyone in his own circle).[3] Such languages, whatever their origin, may gradually replace the other languages in the home and among friends and become

---

[1] *T. Megillah* 4:13: 'a synagogue of Greek speakers (לעוזות)'; *P. T. Sotah* VII, 21b; *M. Megillah* 2:1.

[2] The name originates from the language, based mainly on Italian, which was spoken from the middle ages until the nineteenth century around eastern Mediterranean ports. 'Frankish' is the Arabic word for European.

[3] Such languages are often called *pidgin* languages, and normally contain elements of different languages in vocabulary and grammar. *Pidgin* is the way English 'business' is pronounced in the Chinese-English *lingua franca* of the Far East.

areal standard languages. As long as they only serve inter-group communication, they are likely to be known only to adult men, and tend to be known functionally and imperfectly, and to be simplified in course of time. The third pattern has in recent times come to be called *diglossia*;[1] in it, the same community uses two different languages in its innercommunity activities, their use being regulated by social conventions. In most cases, one language is spoken in ordinary, everyday life by everybody, and the other is employed in formal speech, on formal occasions, in writing, in religious activities, and the like. We refer to the more formal language as the upper language of the diglossia, to the less formal one as the lower. *Diglossia* situations are extremely common. They exist in many European countries as between local dialect and standard educated language. In a *diglossia*, too, not everyone is able to handle the upper language. In most cases, it is imparted by some process of formal education. The number of those who understand it to some extent will be larger than of those who can speak it and write it. In contrast to the *lingua franca*, anyone who handles such a prestige language will aspire to do so perfectly, without mistakes, even though perhaps not elegantly. Local standards may, however, develop as a kind of compromise between the local lower language and the upper language, and may for a time enjoy all the prestige of the upper language in its pure form.[2]

The term 'language' in this context is impossible to define. Matters are easy for the linguist when the two languages used within one society are unrelated, or very different from each other. Where they are related and similar, degrees of difference which in one society characterize distinct languages are in others reckoned as dialects and vice versa. Our modern ideas on the difference between language and dialect are taken from the modern western state, where one variety is taught in schools and used officially, while all others are dialects or *patois*, but in the ancient world languages were not connected with states in the same way. The Achaemenid Persian empire carried out its business in Aramaic, Rome used Greek as its administrative language in the East. The naming of languages was haphazard: the same language might be called by different names in different districts,

---

[1] The term was created by C. A. Ferguson, 'Diglossia,' in *Word* xv (1959), pp. 325-40. In its original use, the term applied to cases where both the upper and the lower language belong to the same historical language, e.g. literary and colloquial Arabic. A case in point is mixed literary Hebrew versus spoken mishnaic Hebrew, discussed in this chapter.

[2] An example of this may be New Testament Greek.

or two languages might be called by one name. A case in point is the name ʿΕβραϊστί, which apparently was used indifferently of Hebrew and of Jewish Aramaic.[1] In fact, it is doubtful whether we can at that time, with few exceptions, speak of names of languages as distinct from names of peoples or designations of use (in languages which form part of a *diglossia*).[2]

The type of languages which we have called 'home-languages' often enjoy among their speakers great affection and tenacious loyalty, but no social prestige. They are not written—though they may possess an oral literature—and therefore do not turn up amongst epigraphic material found in the area. Sometimes they make their appearance in personal names,[3] but in most cases the greater prestige of religion or culture leads also to the adoption of names in the languages associated with the latter. It is therefore impossible to get a clear picture of the variety of languages actually spoken in any country in ancient times. All we can do is to make inferences on the basis of our knowledge about the origin of the populations mentioned in the sources as living there, and to some extent upon data concerning languages attested as having been used in the area previously or beginning to appear in writing some time after the period under discussion. The justification for such inferences is provided by observation of the history of languages: before dying, languages may pass through a long period of gradual diminution in use; on the other hand a language may be spoken in an area for a long time before it begins to be used in writing. The active use of the three major languages of Palestine in the first century C.E., Hebrew, Aramaic, and Greek, is well attested by written documents. In the northern mountain areas (Ituraea) and in southern Transjordan and in the Negev, there were populations of Arab stock, shown to be so by historians' statements and by their personal names. The Nabataeans, in the South, put up numerous inscriptions in Aramaic, in a special Nabataean ductus and with certain grammatical peculiarities, containing also a small number of Arabic words.[4] Inscriptions in Thamudic, a language belonging to the so-called proto-Arabian sub-group and written in a script originating in the Arabian

---

[1] Cf. e.g. Dalman, p. 5.

[2] E.g. the name לשון הקודש ('holy tongue', perhaps originally meant as 'language of the Temple') used by Jews for Hebrew in the first century C.E.

[3] E.g. the Arabic names in Greek and Aramaic inscriptions in the first century C.E. People often had two names, one in their home language, the other in the language of prestige.

[4] Cf. J. Cantineau, *Le Nabatéen* (1930-2).

Peninsula, have been found in Transjordan,[1] and while most of these are probably later, some may go back to our period. The same applies to the numerous Arabic names found in Greek and Latin inscriptions in south-east Syria and Transjordan.[2] We can thus say, with some confidence, that early Arabic dialects, probably rather different from the later classical Arabic, were spoken in marginal areas of Palestine, and probably known to some Jews. The Babylonian and Palestinian Talmuds and the midrashim occasionally mention Arabic words, though some of the words quoted as being used in 'Arabia' prove to be Aramaic.[3] This seems to indicate that such Jews as lived in the Arabian Peninsula[4] spoke Aramaic with some local admixture, though by the sixth century C.E., after the emergence of classical Arabic, they took some part in Arabic poetry.[5]

It is difficult to come to any conclusions concerning the problem, which, if any, of the languages of the non-Israelite peoples of Canaan survived into our period. The Philistine language was non-Semitic, possibly Indo-European. Already for the time when the Philistines were a powerful factor in the country, we have curiously little evidence for the use of their language, and the surmise has been put forward that they had given up their own language soon after their settlement in Canaan and adopted the speech of the Semitic Canaanites,[6] probably with an admixture of words from their former language. In Neh. 13:24, however, a language called Ashdodian is mentioned as being

---

[1] J. L. Harding and E. Littman, *Some Thamudic Inscriptions from the Hashemite Kingdom of Jordan* (1952).

[2] H. Wuthnow, *Die semitischen Menschennamen in griechischen Inschriften und Papyri* (1950), largely based on Ph. le Bas and W. H. Waddington, *Inscriptions grecques et latines recueillies en Grèce et Asie Mineure* (1870).

[3] A. Cohen, 'Arabisms in Rabbinic Literature,' in *JQR*, Old Series III (1912-13), pp. 221-33; A. Brüll, *Fremdsprachliche Redensarten und ausdrücklich als fremdsprachlich bezeichnete Wörter in den Talmuden und Midraschim* (1869), p. 41; D. S. Margoliouth, *The Relations between Arabs and Jews prior to the Rise of Islam* (1924), pp. 58-9.

[4] Cf. H. Z. Hirschberg, *Israel in Arabia* (1946; in Hebrew); I. Ben-Zeev, *The Jews in Arabia* (2nd ed. 1957; in Hebrew). It is probable that Josephus, *War* I, 6: 'the most remote Arabs,' refers to Jews, as few heathen Arabs can have been able to read Aramaic.

[5] E.g. Samaual ibn Adiya. The *Quran* 16:103, counters the claim that Muhammad had a human teacher by saying 'the language of the man to whom they allude is foreign, while this (the language of the revelations) is intelligible Arabic.' This may well indicate that Arabian Jews still spoke a foreign language in the seventh century (though the Muslim commentators think the person meant was a Greek). Cf. also C. Rabin, *Qumran Studies* (1957), pp. 112-30.

[6] Even their chief god, Dagon, bears a Semitic name.

distinct from both Hebrew and Aramaic, and not being intelligible to speakers of Hebrew. It is thus possible that even in the first century C.E. some of the population of south-west Palestine still spoke a different language. Likewise, the northern part of the coastline of Palestine had been of Phoenician culture and language. Phoenician, a Semitic language closely related to Hebrew, survived at Carthage until about the fourth century C.E., but inscriptions in the Asiatic motherland cease in the second century B.C.E., no doubt because the language was being displaced by Aramaic and Greek. Yet is is not unlikely that islands of Phoenician speech persisted into the early centuries C.E., as may have done Canaanite dialects spoken in various other parts of the country. Scholars have noted numerous words from Canaanite and Hebrew which are still used in the Arabic speech of the Christian and Moslem population of Lebanon, Syria, and Palestine.[1] While these may have passed into spoken Arabic via Aramaic, even in cases where their use is not attested by Aramaic sources, the possibility exists that they were taken over directly by Arabic speakers in contact with villagers speaking some form of Canaanite, or spread from villages whose Canaanite-speaking inhabitants had adopted Arabic while keeping terms from their previous language.

There may even have been written literature in some of the remnant languages we have discussed. Such literature, if it existed, would have been written on perishable materials, and with the decay of the languages and the coming of Christianity, for whom such writings were of no interest, ceased to be copied. Of what was probably a good-sized Phoenician literature, we have only some scanty notices in Sanchuniathon's works as excerpted by Philo of Byblos, and some possible quotations in Josephus. But for the finds in the Nahal Hever cave, we would not have known that the Nabataean language was used for documents on papyrus. As against this, the literary products of the period in Hebrew, Aramaic, and Greek have been preserved by the religious zeal of Jews, Samaritans, and Christians; it is possible, even likely, that at the same time pagan literature or profane literature was being written in Palestine in these three languages and has disappeared without trace. We thus know these major languages, as far as Palestine is concerned, in such registers as were

---

[1] M. T. Feghali, *Etudes sur les emprunts syriaques dans les parlers arabes du Liban* (1918); G. R. Driver, in *JTS* XLVII (1946), p. 210; J. Blau, in *Vetus Testamentum* v (1955), pp. 337-44. The leader of the Hebrew revival, E. Ben-Yehuda, is said to have discovered 400 such words, cf. D. Yellin, in *JPOS* III (1929), p. 107.

found suitable for religious writings by educated members of these three communities.

Hebrew

In the literature produced and read in the first century C.E., the Hebrew language appears in several distinct forms. These are representatives of different stages in the historical development of the language, but in their active use at the same time functioned as registers on the one hand and as sectarian variants on the other.

In order to understand their historical relation to each other, we have to throw a brief glance at the history of Hebrew. In the period of the monarchy, ca. 1000-587 B.C.E., all formal prose was in classical biblical Hebrew, which we find, apart from biblical books of the period, also in the Lachish letters. For poetry a distinct form of Hebrew was used, which incorporated all the classical language and in addition a set of grammatical forms and of vocabulary peculiar to poetry, and in part at least archaic and held in common with other Semitic languages. In contrast to modern western usage, the speeches of the Hebrew prophets were couched in the language of poetry and also to some extent in its forms. These two language forms remained pretty constant throughout those four centuries, probably owing to the teaching of scribal schools, though there were changing stylistic fashions. It is highly probable that from the beginning this standardized court language differed from the spoken Hebrew of regions distant from the capital Jerusalem. As for Jerusalem itself, it was not an Israelite town before the monarchy, and the Israelite population drawn into it by David and Solomon was a mixture from different tribes. We cannot say anything about the spoken language of the common people of the city during the united monarchy, nor do we know what was the relation of either the spoken language or of classical Hebrew to the language of the tribe of Judah, to whose area Jerusalem now belonged.[1] Whatever may have been the relation between spoken Hebrew and the classical written language at the outset, there can be no doubt that by the sixth century B.C.E. the spoken forms had changed, and thus the distance between the spoken and written language had become greater. The destruction of Jerusalem was accompanied by the decimation

---

[1] C. Rabin, *A Short History of the Hebrew Language* (1973), pp. 29-30. Classical Hebrew is equated with the dialect of Jerusalem by Z. S. Harris, *Development of the Canaanite Dialects* (1939), pp. 22-3.

and deportation of the educated classes, leaving in the country only 'vintners and ploughmen' (2 Kings 24:14, 25:12). During the exile, no doubt, the popular language changed more rapidly (as language often does in times of social upheaval), and the educated classes in Babylonia learnt to speak Aramaic, which by then had replaced Babylonian (Akkadian) as the spoken language of Mesopotamia. This, and the disturbance of life and education, impaired the stability of the written language, as we can observe in the peculiarities of the book of Ezekiel. In 721 the Assyrians had introduced into the former kingdom of Israel exiles from southern Mesopotamia (Kutha, Avva, Sepharvaim = Sippar, 2 Kings 17:24) and northern Syria (Hamath), and these, if they did not already speak Aramaic at home,[1] certainly spoke this *lingua franca* in their new seats in Palestine, thus aiding its spread to that country. With the return of the exiles from Babylonia, a new Aramaic-speaking element was introduced. Most important, however, imperial Aramaic (see below, p. 1026) became an administrative language, and thus had to be learnt by the local upper classes. While in 701 it could be assumed that the population of the city of Jerusalem would not understand Aramaic (2 Kings 18:26 = Is. 36:13), wide circles now spoke the language, so much so that many scholars believe, following the *Babylonian Talmud* (*Megillah* 3a), that the term *mephorash* (interpreted) in the description of the public reading of the Torah by Ezra (Neh. 8:8) means that the reading was accompanied by an Aramaic translation.[2] On the other hand, we learn from Neh. 13:24 that Judaean, i.e. Hebrew, was still spoken, and the complaint that many of the sons of mixed marriages 'could not speak Judaean' implies that it was thought normal for Jews to be able to do so.

The religious literature of the Jewish population of Judaea, however, continued to be written in Hebrew. The Aramaic portions of Daniel and Ezra are no evidence that Aramaic had become a Jewish literary language. The book of Daniel describes happenings at the court of the king of Babylon, and the Aramaic portions of Ezra consist largely of official documents to and by functionaries of the Achaemenid Persian empire. Readers of that period were of course aware that both the later Babylonians and the Persian officials had used Aramaic, and

[1] The region of Hamath, modern Hama, produced Aramaic inscriptions, but an inscription by king Zakir, found in the town itself, has peculiarities which some scholars take as evidence of a local language different from Aramaic. There are in northern Syria also Neo-Hittite (Luvian) inscriptions, thus there was also a non-Semitic population.

[2] H. H. Schaeder, *Iranische Beiträge* I (1930), pp. 190-212.

the Aramaic in those two books was therefore part of the *milieu*, something abnormal and therefore significant. Of greater weight are the arguments of various scholars, that the present Hebrew parts of Daniel, the Books of Chronicles, or Ecclesiastes were originally written in Aramaic and the Hebrew text in our Bible is a translation.[1] The arguments, partly based on the language of those books (on which see below, p. 1016), have not found wide acceptance, but even if we were to grant that any of those books were originally composed in Aramaic, there remains the fact that Hebrew translations were made at a period early enough for them to be canonized. Such labour would hardly have been undertaken unless the masses had found Hebrew easier to read than Aramaic.

In intention, the Hebrew of the post-exilic books of the Bible was classical Hebrew. Indeed, it proclaims this intention by re-employing phrases from pre-exilic books, a result both of the practice of all ancient and medieval school systems of teaching the language through following the example of the ancients and of the deep religious significance attributed to many of these phrases, which in their new context carried the connotations of their original contexts. However, re-employment of ancient linguistic material betrays itself by the abolition of the former division between prose and poetry: poetical vocabulary, and to some extent poetical grammar, are freely employed in prose contexts. The post-exilic poetry, while sometimes prosy in style, makes up for this by excessive use of grammatical archaisms. Yet not all is imitation of the old. Post-exilic prose has a number of new words, which recur in various books, as well as in the Dead Sea Scrolls. Moreover, the author of Chronicles, while using either the Books of Samuel and Kings or their sources, frequently changed their language without any change in meaning. This suggests that he was conscious that his time required a different form of expression, of sufficient value to allow introducing it into an ancient text.[2] Finally, we can discern grammatical features that resemble Aramaic and

---

[1] H. H. Howorth, 'Some Unconventional Views on the Text of the Bible, VII: Daniel and Chronicles,' in *Proceedings of the Society of Biblical Archaeology* XXIX (1907), pp. 31-8; 61-9; F. Zimmermann, 'The Aramaic Provenance of Qohelet,' in *JQR*, New Series XXXVI (1945), pp. 17-45, 'Chronicles as a Partially Translated Book,' in *JQR*, New Series XLII (1951-2), pp. 165-82, 387-412; H. L. Ginsberg, *Studies in Daniel* (1948); *Studies in Kohelet* (1950).

[2] For these changes we have for the time being only a partial description by A. Kropat, *Die Syntax des Autors der Chronik* (1909). See however also A. Hurvitz, *The Transition Period in Biblical Hebrew* (1972; in Hebrew); E. Y. Kutscher, *The Language and Linguistic Background of the Isaiah Scroll* (1959; in Hebrew).

mishnaic Hebrew rather than classical Hebrew,[1] as well as a number of Aramaic words[2] and loan-translations, Hebrew words or combinations of words with the meaning that the corresponding words would have in Aramaic. This language can thus be distinguished as late biblical Hebrew.

Late biblical Hebrew persisted in use for a period as long as that of its predecessor, from ca. 500 until the latter part of the first century B.C.E., when we find it used in the Dead Sea Scrolls. In the intervening period it is attested outside the Bible by Ben Sirach and by the Hebrew fragments of *Jubilees* and the *Testaments of the Patriarchs* found in the Qumran caves. It is likely that large parts of the Apocrypha and Pseudepigrapha existed in this language form. Late biblical Hebrew must have been widely understood and read in circles close to nascent Christianity, as well as by the early Christians themselves. As is well known, the Apocrypha and Pseudepigrapha were preserved by the Church alone, having been rejected by official pharisaic and rabbinic Judaism. Along with those books, pharisaic Judaism also at one stage abandoned the active use of late biblical Hebrew, since we have no works in this language preserved by rabbinic Jewry apart from the Bible itself.[3] The present author suggested that the Pharisees abandoned the use of biblical Hebrew in order to set off their own teaching clearly from that of the sectarians.[4]

A rival to late biblical Hebrew appears to have come into being in the second half of the second century B.C.E. This was a form of language in which the grammar and syntax was largely mishnaic Hebrew, while the vocabulary was an admixture of mishnaic and biblical vocabulary. We shall discuss later the basis of mishnaic Hebrew, and will at this stage merely state our opinion that it was the spoken language of the Judaean population. The mixed style was therefore

---

[1] Such as the use of the simple perfect and imperfect tenses in cases where biblical Hebrew of the classical period would use the consecutive (conversive) tenses.

[2] Cf. M. Wagner, *Die lexikalischen und grammatischen Aramaismen im alttestamentlichen Hebräisch* (1966). Wagner does not separate Aramaic intrusions into late Biblical Hebrew from those (often doubtful) in classical Hebrew, but his references to chapter and verse enable the reader to sort out the material.

[3] In the ninth cent. C.E., Jews began again to use biblical Hebrew, almost exclusively for poetry and *belles lettres*. This 'revived biblical Hebrew' took its materials impartially from classical and late biblical Hebrew. It remained in use until 1885, when modern Hebrew came into being, cf. C. Rabin, *Short History*, p. 65.

[4] C. Rabin, *Qumran Studies* (1957) p. 67 and in C. Rabin and Y. Yadin, eds., *Aspects of the Dead Sea Scrolls* (1958), pp. 160-1.

a far-reaching concession to the language habits of the less educated reader, but enriched his limited everyday vocabulary from the rich reservoir of the Bible, with which the reader could be assumed to be reasonably familiar, and which provided also the emotional overtones and associations which make up a literary language.[1] The biblical component of the mixed language is not late biblical Hebrew, but the vocabulary of the entire Bible, prose and poetry, with special attention to rare words. Another important difference is that late biblical Hebrew drew from the text as understood in the fifth century B.C.E. as well as from a living educational tradition; the mixed language, on the other hand, drew only from the text, having rejected the tradition of late biblical Hebrew and did so on the basis of the manner in which the same text was understood in the second century B.C.E., when it had become the object of the type of interpretation which was later on called midrash. Moreover, this was the period of the intensive evolution of midrashic exegesis, and texts in the mixed language may exhibit different interpretations of the same word or phrase in the manner in which they employ it.

The mixed language was used for historical works relating to the Hasmonaean period. These works have been lost, but fragments from them have been preserved in the Mishnah and in talmudic literature, where they stand out clearly by their biblicizing language and their narrative technique.[2] The main genre in which we are able to observe the mixed language is the liturgy, in those parts which are not chapters from the Psalms and other biblical books or *catenae* of Bible verses.[3] These prayers were originally fixed only in the sequence of the blessing formulas, and it was left to each prayer-leader to make up his own

---

[1] English did the same when it began to be used for purposes for which Latin had served before. It absorbed large numbers of Latin words directly, and created loan-translations for others.

[2] Three such texts are the story of King Jannaeus, *T. B. Kiddushin* 66a, the story of Simeon the Just, *Sifre* on Num. 22, the story of the Sons of Levi at Zoar, *M. Yebamoth* 16:7, cf. C. Rabin, in *Aspects of the Dead Sea Scrolls* (1965), p. 155; full text in the Hebrew version of that article, M. Bar-Asher, ed., *Reader on the Language of the Sages* (1972; in Hebrew), pp. 371-3. It is possible that historical works and historical romances continued to be written in this language, as we have in it two medieval works which antedate the revival of biblical Hebrew (cf. above p. 1015, n. 3), viz. *Sefer ha-Jashar* and *Josippon*.

[3] Note that the various versions of the daily and festival prayer books contain many later additions, a large part of which, however, is couched in the same mixed language. Cf. I. Elbogen, *Der jüdische Gottesdienst in seiner geschichtlichen Entwicklung*, passim. Samaritan and Karaite prayer books are quite different in their language.

text; all the more significant that the different versions which finally emerged are so homogeneous in their language type. Here we find a basically mishnaic sentence construction, with some biblical accretions in the syntax, a largely biblical inflection system (but with rare use of the 'consecutive' tenses), and a vocabulary composed of mishnaic and biblical words, with some hebraized Aramaic words and a number of new creations, in fact the 'open' vocabulary of natural poetry (as opposed to formalized, restricted poetry). This openness was to increase spectacularly in the following centuries, when the poetical forms became more elaborate in the so-called *piyyut*,[1] and thousands of new words were created.

We cannot know how widely historical works of the variety described were read in the first century, but it is clear that the early Christians were familiar with synagogal prayer, as this provided the model for some features of Christian prayer. The use of biblical imagery in New Testament prayers and in early Christian liturgies is thus likely to be the adaptation of a register already well established in the cultural background.

Quotation of Bible verses, with or without the introduction 'as it is said', etc., is a well-known feature of New Testament style. But attention has also been drawn to the frequent use of biblical phraseology worked into the fabric of the narrative itself.[2] The question might well be asked whether this is not a further piece of evidence of Christian acquaintance with the mixed language.

Our earliest datable written documents in mishnaic Hebrew are some letters of Bar Cochba written in the years 132-5 C.E. and found at Wadi Murabbaat.[3] Probably a good deal earlier, but not datable with any confidence, is the *Copper Scroll* from Qumran.[4] While the letters

---

[1] From Greek ποιητής. Cf. L. Zunz, *Die Synagogale Poesie des Mittelalters* (2nd ed. 1920) with much linguistic material in the *Beilagen*; M. Wallenstein, *Some Unpublished Piyyutim* etc. (1956) with linguistic analyses; and the first grammatical description by J. Yahalom, *Syntax of the Early Pijjutim* (unpublished dissertation, Jerusalem 1973; in Hebrew). J. Schirmann, 'Hebrew Liturgical Poetry and Christian Hymnology,' in *JQR* New Series XLIV (1953), pp. 123-61, places the beginnings of the *piyyut* in the third century C.E., while E. Fleischer, in *Tarbiz* XL (1970-1), pp. 41-63, places it into the fifth or early sixth century. Such poetry was written till the eleventh century, and in France and Germany in a modified form until the fourteenth.

[2] Cf. especially W. Dittmar, *Vetus Testamentum in Novo* (1903).

[3] J. T. Milik, 'Une lettre de Siméon bar Kokheba,' in *RB* LX (1953), pp. 276-94; R. de Vaux, 'Quelques textes hébreux de Murabbaat,' ibid., pp. 268-75. On the language, E. Y. Kutscher, in *Leshonenu* XXVI (1961-2), pp. 7-23.

[4] M. Baillet, J. T. Milik, R. de Vaux, *Les Petites Grottes de Qumran* I (1962);

suggest that mishnaic Hebrew was used for private correspondence, it is not clear why the *Copper Scroll* is not in the late biblical Hebrew generally found at Qumran, or indeed what genre of writing it is. In the present writer's opinion, it is a form of witnesses' deposition, whether real or pretended, and its language is meant to represent the *ipsissima verba* of those who gave the evidence. However, when we think of mishnaic Hebrew, it is not as the vehicle of occasional letters or reports, but as the language of a large halakic and midrashic literature, as is indicated by its very name, which connects it with the most esteemed of those works, the Mishnah. The latter is the work of scholars who lived around the year 200 C.E. The problem is when the first of these works were written down. Early rabbinic literature stresses the prohibition of writing down any part of the oral Law—to which all halakic works of this group belong—and implies that they were handed down orally for centuries, and only written after 300 C.E. It is still a matter of debate among scholars whether these statements are theoretical only, or correspond to reality. It has also been pointed out that *megilloth*, private recordings of groups of *halakoth*, may have been in existence long before the full collections were put into writing.[1] For these reasons it must be left open whether in the first century C.E. mishnaic Hebrew was a written or an oral literary language. In any case, if it was at that time written, it certainly was also still used in oral literary activities, such as midrashic sermons, halakic teaching, and legal discussions. We can also say with confidence that these oral uses preceded its written use. When exactly they began, is a question of the history of the Jewish sects: in all probability the Pharisee sect used these methods of oral teaching, and therefore also mishnaic Hebrew, from its beginning. Again, we cannot say whether other groups, contemporary with the Pharisees or preceding them, such as the Maccabean *hasidim*, used mishnaic Hebrew in their teaching. With regard to the Qumran sect, it has been suggested by the present author that references to a 'halting', 'uncircumcised', and 'blasphemous' language in which the sect's opponents speak to God's people,[2] are to be

J. T. Milik, 'Le rouleau de cuivre de Qumran', in *RB* LXVI (1959), pp. 321-57; J. M. Allegro, *The Treasure of the Copper Scroll* (1960).

[1] The oral preservation of such large texts is not a physical impossibility. Partly through the writings of M. McLuhan, we are now familiar with the nature of oral culture and its feats of memory. The Indian Vedas, for instance, were handed down orally for many centuries.

[2] *Hymns* II, 18-19; IV, 16-17; *Damascus Document* V, 11-12. Cf. *Qumran Studies*, pp. 68-9.

taken as allusions to the use of mishnaic Hebrew by the Pharisees in their public teaching. This would imply that the Qumran sect did not use mishnaic Hebrew, but conducted also their oral teaching in late biblical Hebrew (or possibly in colloquial Aramaic). Acceptance of this suggestion would also provide a valuable synchronism for the use of mishnaic Hebrew in oral literature, apart from the argument from probability, that a sect such as the Pharisees would not have made a sudden change in its habits of instruction. A further confirmation for the assumption that mishnaic Hebrew was in use for a long period may be found in the observation of Epstein that the language of early *halakoth* differs from that of later ones, especially in having more biblical words[1]—which is what we would expect in a literary idiom gradually establishing its independence of the mixed language with its use of biblical vocabulary.

It could be argued that the fact that the sermons and legal teaching of the sages were written down in mishnaic Hebrew does not prove that in its oral form this material was put out in the same language. The sages might have taught the people in Aramaic, for instance, but what they said was recorded in mishnaic Hebrew. Indeed, we find some midrash statements in Aramaic in earlier midrash collections, and in Hebrew in later collections, so that they must have been translated at some time. However, the Hebrew versions of these items appear after 500 c.e., at a time when there was already a Hebrew linguistic nationalism.[2] Apart from one isolated statement relating to spoken usage,[3] we find no such opposition to Aramaic in the tannaitic period, and indeed one can observe that some teachers, such as the Babylonian Hillel, are quoted in Aramaic in the Mishnah,

---

[1] J. N. Epstein, *Introduction into the Text of the Mishnah* (1948; in Hebrew), p. 1129.

[2] As can be concluded from the *piyyut* and from the manifestations castigated in Justinian's *Novella* 146, of the year 553 c.e.

[3] Cf. the quotation on p. 1032, n. 3. This is immediately followed by a statement ascribed to the Babylonian Amora R. Joseph, condemning Aramaic (*lashon arami*) in Babylonia, where mishnaic Hebrew was never spoken (it is, however, possible that *arami* means here 'Roman', as it sometimes does, and that this is a reaction to Roman attempts to conquer Babylonia). Curious is also the statement *P. T. Megillah* iv, 71b: 'Four languages have come into the world to be used, Greek for singing, Latin for warfare, Aramaic (*sursi*) for lamentation, Hebrew (*ivri*) for speaking'; but *ivri* may also mean Jewish Aramaic (cf. above p. 1009, note 1), and 'speaking' (*dibbur*) may mean divine pronouncements. Nor do we know what to make of the statement quoted in *T. B. Shabbath* 12b, that 'the ministering angels do not understand (or: recognize) Aramaic (*aramit*)', i.e. do not carry Aramaic prayers to the divine throne.

and we find parts of the oldest midrashim in Aramaic. The quotations from Hillel are an instance of the tannaitic principle 'one must hand down statements in the language (i.e. exact words) of one's teacher',[1] and we may conclude from this that statements recorded in mishnaic Hebrew were handed down orally in that language. There may have been deviations from this rule for various reasons, but then the cases where possibly statements in other languages were recorded (or re-recorded) in Hebrew, would be additional evidence that normally oral statements were in that language.

The question whether the oral material recorded in tannaitic literature was originally taught in mishnaic Hebrew, is quite distinct from the question whether mishnaic Hebrew was a 'natural' language spoken by the people, or an artificial mixture of biblical Hebrew and Aramaic made up by the sages for their purposes. Even if it was the latter, it could have been used in spoken instruction and discussion, and not only in writing. Many languages, amongst them medieval Latin and late biblical Hebrew, were used orally at times when they were not spoken by the people, and we shall see below in the case of targumic Aramaic a language that was probably artificial and was used in oral instruction. The discussion whether mishnaic Hebrew was 'natural' or 'artificial' affects the question why it came to be used by the sages, as well as the character of late biblical Hebrew and the mixed language, and it is for those reasons that we now have to turn to it.

Mishnaic Hebrew differs from biblical Hebrew in the following respects: it does not have the 'consecutive' tenses in the verb; where biblical Hebrew has only two tenses, which express mainly 'aspect' (completed action and ongoing activity), mishnaic Hebrew has three tenses, having turned the active participle into a present tense, and its tenses express time; it probably expressed aspect (single action and repeated actions) by adding forms of the verb 'to be' to the participle, even imperative, and infinitive; it expressed the passive by different means than biblical Hebrew; while biblical Hebrew distinguished gender in all pronouns of the second and third person, mishnaic Hebrew did so only in the third singular; instead of the biblical Hebrew general subordinating conjunction *asher*, mishnaic Hebrew used *she-*, and it uses it practically always before subordinated clauses, while biblical Hebrew also used other conjunctions and often had no conjunction; it has a regular way of forming verbal nouns, while in

[1] *M. Eduyot* 1:3; discussion in M. Z. Segal, *Mishnaic Hebrew Grammar* (1927), p. 19.

biblical Hebrew these were irregular in formation, and the verbal nouns take over functions allotted in biblical Hebrew to the infinitives; it has many more adjectives than biblical Hebrew; in the combination noun + adjective both had to have the article in biblical Hebrew when the noun was definite, in mishnaic Hebrew often only the adjective has the article; the typical older Semitic 'construct' for the genitive[1] is often replaced by a circumlocution with של (she-l-, 'that which is of'). There are also many grammatical forms which differ, as well as a number of phonetic features, especially the weakening of the glottal stop (aleph) and the confusion of final m and n and tendency to add n to words that end in -a.[2] The vocabulary differs considerably,[3] and the style is much less elaborate than biblical Hebrew prose, but we cannot say how much of the difference in these two respects is due to the stylistic conventions of the Bible, and would be less noticeable if we possessed texts in spoken biblical Hebrew. There are a large number of Aramaic, Greek, and to a much lesser extent, Latin loan-words.[4]

Several of the grammatical developments mentioned are common to mishnaic Hebrew and to Aramaic, some of them more specifically to the Jewish Aramaic of Palestine known as Galilaean Aramaic. In most cases they are features that did not exist in the earliest documented stages of Aramaic, but developments which emerged in Aramaic about the same time that we find their parallels in mishnaic Hebrew. This also applies to some extent to the words which exist in mishnaic Hebrew and in Aramaic, but not in biblical Hebrew. Our knowledge of the vocabulary of the older stages of Aramaic is rather limited, and we often cannot be certain whether a word found in mishnaic Hebrew and in Palestinian Aramaic only, and not in other dialects of

---

[1] I.e. changing the form of the word 'house' (the headword) in a phrase like 'the house of the Lord' rather than the form of the word in the genitive.

[2] The phonetic differences are largely obscured by the consonantal character of the Hebrew script. The vowel signs were added many centuries later, and it is quite likely that the way our Hebrew Bibles are pointed reflects in some respects mishnaic rather than biblical pronunciation. In addition the printed Mishnah is pointed according to biblical rules and thus ignores the differences between mishnaic and biblical grammar preserved in ancient vocalized manuscripts and in oriental traditions. No printed grammar of mishnaic Hebrew has yet appeared incorporating that information.

[3] Cf. Segal op. cit. pp. 54-57.

[4] Ch. Albeck, *Introduction in the Mishnah* (1959; in Hebrew), pp. 134-215. See also S. Krauss, *Griechische und Lateinische Lehnwörter im Talmud, Midrasch und Targum* (1898-1900), to be used with caution; S. Liebermann, *Hellenism in Jewish Palestine* (1950); id. *Greek in Jewish Palestine* (1942).

Aramaic, is of Aramaic or of Hebrew origin. But even where a word is also found in Aramaic dialects outside Palestine, this cannot be absolute proof that it could only have reached mishnaic Hebrew from Aramaic, because both the older stages of Aramaic and its later local developments were under the influence of Canaanite and other West-Semitic languages, and later under that of Hebrew via Christian and Jewish cultural diffusion. Even words exhibiting the typical Aramaic sound-laws[1] could have reached mishnaic Hebrew from Hebrew, rather than Aramaic dialects, since we have evidence that at the time of the Judges similar sound-laws operated in North-Palestinian Israelite speech. Indeed, the earliest attestation of the 'Aramaic' change of common Semitic *th* to *t* comes from the Song of Deborah, Judges 5:11, centuries before the same change is found in Aramaic inscriptions.[2] In spite of all these reasons for caution, there cannot be any doubt that mishnaic Hebrew shows signs of Aramaic influence.

A number of nineteenth-century scholars advanced the theory that mishnaic Hebrew was not a real language at all, but the attempt of Aramaic-speaking scholars to express themselves in biblical Hebrew.[3] They believed that Hebrew had ceased to be spoken after the Babylonian Exile, and only Aramaic was spoken by the Palestinian Jews. One of the main planks in their argument is the Targum, the Aramaic translations of the Pentateuch and other parts of the Bible, which we know to have been recited in the Synagogues in close connection with the reading of the Law and the Prophets. These are taken as proof that the people did no longer understand Hebrew. In spite of this, the rabbinic scholars wished their teaching to be recorded in the Holy Tongue, but being ignorant of its grammar and syntax, they used Aramaic forms and constructions, and where they did not know the Hebrew word, they employed an Aramaic one.

This theory is still held by many scholars and given in handbooks as statement of fact. It has been used to account for the deviations from classical biblical Hebrew in the post-Exilic books of the Bible, for the Aramaic parts of the Bible, for Aramaic prayers, and for the Aramaic utterances of Jesus as recorded in the New Testament. Already in the nineteenth century, however, some scholars noted that mishnaic

---

[1] These are Aramaic ת for Hebrew שׁ when it corresponds to proto-Semitic *th*; ד for ז when it corresponds to *dh*; ע(ק) or ט for Hebrew צ when it corresponds respectively to *ḍ* or *ẓ*.

[2] In the Old Aramaic inscriptions (approximately ninth - fifth century B.C.E.) this sound is written *sh* (שׁ), which probably represents the pronunciation *th*.

[3] See especially A. Geiger, *Lehrbuch zur Sprache der Mischnah* (1845).

Hebrew did not make the impression of a learned artefact, but rather looked like a natural language.[1] In the beginning of the twentieth century, a student of S. R. Driver of Oxford, Segal, demonstrated in detail that some of the distinct features of mishnaic Hebrew could not be accounted for by interaction of biblical Hebrew and Aramaic.[2] He suggested that mishnaic Hebrew arose out of the situation after the Exile through the spread of one spoken dialect or the mixture of several dialects. To Segal's grammatical evidence may be added that mishnaic Hebrew (as distinct from Aramaic) traces can be found in involuntary deviations from biblical Hebrew grammar and idiom in the Dead Sea Scrolls; Mishnaisms exist in the Christian Palestinian Aramaic written by a Melkite community in southern Judaea in the sixth-ninth centuries c.e., who knew no Hebrew and translated their entire literature from the Greek; and the way the Septuagint translates some Hebrew words shows that the translators understood them in mishnaic Hebrew senses rather than biblical ones.[3] Also the way in which the Samaritans wrote and understood biblical Hebrew shows some similarities with mishnaic Hebrew.[4] All this would make no sense if mishnaic Hebrew was an artificial jargon restricted to rabbinic academies. We can go further, however. The theory of mishnaic Hebrew as a mixture represents a nineteenth-century attitude (even then not held by professional linguists) which saw languages as monolithic structures and any deviation from such structures as corruption, for which reasons had to be sought. Today, especially since the rise of sociolinguistics, we know that a language is a conglomerate of many language varieties, amongst which the literary standard of a given time is one. Changes in literary usage are often due to shifts in status of existing varieties (e.g. greater prestige of some form of the spoken language); and foreign influence, the *bête-noire* of the traditional normative linguist, should be held responsible for a change in standards only in cases where this can be proved beyond doubt. Moreover, the nature of influence of one language on another, or 'interference', as the phenomenon is called nowadays, has

---

[1] For references see C. Rabin, in *Current Trends in Linguistics*, ed. T. A. Sebeok, VI (1970), p. 317, note 71. Of special importance is the opinion of Th. Nöldeke, the most outstanding Semitist of the nineteenth century.
[2] M. H. Segal, 'Mishnaic Hebrew and its Relation to Biblical Hebrew and to Aramaic,' in *JQR* Old Series xx (1908-9), pp. 647-737.
[3] Cf. C. Rabin, in *Aspects of the Dead Sea Scrolls*, pp. 145-8.
[4] Z. Ben Hayyim, 'Traditions in the Hebrew Language etc.,' in *Aspects*, op.cit., pp. 200-14.

been much investigated in recent years, in connection with language learning and bilingualism. In the particular case of the theory here discussed, this would correspond to the situation of an educated person (for such the rabbinic scholars undoubtedly were) handling a foreign language which he knows only from reading. Such a person would transfer to the acquired language mainly features of his mother-tongue that are not too obvious or not easily analyzed, such as sentence structure or the meaning of the tenses. On the other hand he would take great care to get right the obvious and frequent features, the common words, and the set phrases. It is quite unthinkable that such a person should fail to realise that biblical Hebrew uses as subordinating particle *asher*, that its plural ending is *-im* (and not the mishnaic *-in*), or to use the consecutive tenses, albeit wrongly. The use of פרצוף for פנים (face), ממון for כסף (money), כיצד for איך (how?), and the like is almost proof that there was no pretence to use biblical Hebrew, for such common words would be known not only to the scholars who used the language, but also to their audience. As it happens, we can test our hypothesis on an actual attempt to write biblical Hebrew by people who spoke Yiddish: the novels of writers of the Haskalah period 1750-1880. In those texts all the obvious details of biblical Hebrew are right, but the tenses express time, not aspect, the sentences have a European cast, and some biblical words are used in senses they acquired in mishnaic Hebrew or in Yiddish. There remain, as possible proofs for Aramaic 'interference', such features as the employment of the tenses to express time in mishnaic Hebrew. However, while this also occurs in contemporary Aramaic, it is also a prominent feature of Greek, and since Palestine seems to have been a centre of diffusion for the new function of the tenses, it is very likely that it was in fact Greek which influenced both Hebrew and Aramaic in this matter. Of course it would be absurd to suggest that the sages really spoke Greek and transferred their Greek speech habits to mishnaic Hebrew. We have here a genuine case of the influence of a foreign prestige language, coupled no doubt with changes in mental attitudes that favoured unambiguous expression of time relations.

There is no intention of denying that mishnaic Hebrew was influenced by Aramaic in various ways. It would have been strange if this had not happened with two languages so closely interwoven in the life of the country and so many bilingual speakers. But this is influence of Aramaic on an existing, spoken mishnaic Hebrew, just as there was a strong influence of Greek on spoken mishnaic Hebrew,

which led to the borrowing of such basic words as פרצוף (face) from
πρόσωπον, or קנטר (the annoyed) from κέντρον (sting).

If mishnaic Hebrew was a spoken language in the first century C.E.,
we are entitled to assume that it must have been spoken, in some form
or other, for some centuries previously, and can thus make it, and not
Aramaic, the factor responsible for some of the non-biblical-Hebrew
features of late biblical Hebrew and the basic component of the mixed
language. Needless to say, the recognition that mishnaic Hebrew was
a living language does not imply that there was no Aramaic spoken
in Palestine in the Second Temple period. We shall now turn to a
sketch of the history of Aramaic and of the varieties that one was
likely to meet with in first century Palestine.

Aramaic

The first inscriptions in Aramaic known today were put up in northern
Syria in the ninth and eighth centuries B.C.E.[1] It is likely that the
kingdom of Aram with its centre at Damascus, founded a little earlier,
also used the Aramaic language in its official business, though we
have no visible evidence of this. In the eighth century we also begin
to find evidence of the use of Aramaic in Assyria, which went so far
that we have Aramaic summaries or filing directions on cuneiform
Assyrian clay tablets, a letter on political matters in Aramaic from
one official to another, and a tablet with magical formulas in Aramaic
in cuneiform script. It is now well established that both Assyria and
Babylonia gradually acquired large numbers of Aramaic speakers,
whether by immigration or by the spread of the language. It is assumed
that during the last stage of the Babylonian empire the Babylonian
language was only written, while Aramaic was in fact the language of
the country. When in 539 Cyrus conquered Babylon and set up a

---

[1] G. Garbini, *L'Aramaico antico* (1956); R. Degen, *Altaramäische Grammatik*
(1969); E. Y. Kutscher, *History of the Aramaic Language* (1971-2; in Hebrew);
S. Segert, *Altaramäische Grammatik* (1973); I. N. Vinnikov, 'Slovar' arameyskich
nadpisey,' in *Palestinski Sbornik* III (1958) - XIII (1965); E. Y. Kutscher, in
Current Trends in Linguistics VI, pp. 348-60. For the historical background, see
now A. Malamat, 'The Aramaeans,' in *Peoples of Old Testament Times*, ed. D. J.
Wiseman (1973), pp. 134-55; add to his bibliography: S. Moscati, 'Sugli origini
degli Aramei', in *Rivista degli Studi Orientali* XXVI (1951), pp. 16-22; M.
McNamara, 'De populi Aramaeorum primordiis', in *Verbum Domini* XXXV
(1957), pp. 129-42. There seems to be no link between the earliest Aramaic
inscriptions and the Aramaic empire of Aram-Zobah, which was destroyed by
David about 1000 B.C.E.

Persian empire on the ruins of the Babylonian one, Aramaic was made the language of administration for the whole empire, except the Persian homeland, and became the *lingua franca* used between its many-tongued population. This language, now referred to as imperial Aramaic, was cultivated by scribal schools and seems to have enjoyed great prestige.[1] This lasted a long time beyond the existence of the Persian empire. Inscriptions in it were put up outside the boundaries of the former Persian empire, e.g. by King Ashoka of India in the third century B.C.E. in his north-western provinces, and by local rulers in Armenia and in the Caucasus. Its use penetrated Persia itself, and Persian scribes were so used to it that when, early in the Christian era, Persian began to be written in an Aramaic script, many words continued to be written in Aramaic, though they were pronounced in Persian when reading out the document. Its most lasting influence, of course, imperial Aramaic had in those areas where Aramaic was spoken, viz. Mesopotamia, Syria, and Palestine. Both the local populations and the Arabs, which in those centuries increasingly penetrated into the Fertile Crescent and set up small states,[2] used it for inscriptions in forms which were all to some extent influenced by the changes which were affecting spoken Aramaic and leading to its break-up into the various languages that make up middle Aramaic:[3] Syriac,[4] Mandaean, Jewish Babylonian (talmudic) Aramaic, Galilaean Aramaic, Samaritan, and Christian Palestinian Aramaic. All these middle Aramaic languages began to be written from about 200 C.E. onwards, and therefore lie outside the scope of our account of Aramaic, except for comparison. The first century C.E. exhibits the later stage of the transition from imperial Aramaic

[1] Imperial Aramaic was first identified by H. H. Schaeder, op. cit. (p. 1013), and by H. L. Ginsberg, 'Aramaic Dialect Problems', in *American Journal of Semitic Languages and Literatures* L (1933), pp. 1-9; LII (1936), pp. 95-103. Cf. F. Rosenthal, *Die aramaistische Forschung* (1939), pp. 24-71; E. Y. Kutscher, in *Current Trends in Linguistics* VI, pp. 361-93. There is no grammar of imperial Aramaic as such; the nearest to one is P. Leander, *Laut- und Formenlehre des Aegyptisch-Aramäischen* (1928).
[2] Cf. F. Altheim & R. Stiehl, *Die Araber in der alten Welt* (1964-67), *passim*.
[3] J. A. Fitzmyer, *The Genesis Apocryphon* (1966), p. 19, note 60, suggested the name 'middle Aramaic' for the dialects influenced by imperial (or as he calls it, official) Aramaic, and calls Syriac and the other literary languages 'late Aramaic' (instead of the present designation middle Aramaic). This nomenclature was accepted by Kutscher in: *Current Trends in Linguistics* VI, pp. 347-8.
[4] The oldest Syriac inscriptions still show imperial Aramaic influence, cf. E. Jenni, 'Die altsyrischen Inschriften', in *Theologische Zeitschrift* XXI (1965), pp. 377-82.

to middle Aramaic, in other words, the stage when the written language was in intention still imperial Aramaic. We have in fact what was described above, p. 1008 as a local standard of the upper language of a *diglossia*. The lower languages of the Aramaic *diglossia* were, according to the locality, various forms of dialect tending towards middle Aramaic, or dialects belonging to proto-Arabic, the predecessors of classical literary Arabic. It is not to be excluded that there were also places with an Aramaic-Hebrew diglossia in which Aramaic played the role of the upper, and mishnaic Hebrew that of the lower language.

In and around Palestine there were several of these local standards of transitional Aramaic. We have already discussed Nabataean (p. 1009), a language which was probably better known amongst Palestinian Jews than was hitherto believed. As we have no knowledge of a pre-third century Aramaic literary activity of the Samaritans, all other forms of Aramaic used at the time and known to us are Jewish. This may not be a true picture of the Aramaic written activity of the period: some pagan groups are likely to have had even literatures of their own (see above, p. 1011).[1]

The oldest of the Jewish transitional dialects is biblical Aramaic, the language of the Aramaic passages in Ezra and Daniel (as well as one verse in Jeremiah and two words in Genesis 31:47). This has been the subject of much scientific controversy, largely concerned with the question whether its position within the development of Aramaic shows it to fit the time of the events described or proves a much later date of composition.[2] The question is still undecided. In its grammar

---

[1] If R. Macuch, 'Anfänge der Mandäer' in: F. Altheim & R. Stiehl, *Araber in der alten Welt* II (1965), pp. 76-191 is right in his contention that the Mandaean sect came originally from Palestine and their literature partly was brought from there, we would have some echoes of such a pagan Aramaic literature.

[2] F. Rosenthal, op.cit. pp. 60-71; E. Y. Kutscher, in *Current Trends*, op.cit. pp. 399-403 give the history of the problem. For a late dating argue mainly R. H. Charles, *A Critical and Exegetical Commentary of the Book of Daniel* (1929), pp. LXXVI-CVIII; H. H. Rowley, *The Aramaic of the Old Testament* (1929); id., *Review of Kitchen*, in *JSS* XI (1966), pp. 112-16. For an early dating see K. A. Kitchen, 'The Aramaic of Daniel', in D. J. Wiseman et al., *Notes on some Problems in the Book of Daniel* (1965), pp. 31-79. The principal grammar of biblical Aramaic is still H. Bauer and P. Leander, *Grammatik des Biblisch-Aramäischen* (1927); of importance also F. Rosenthal, *A Grammar of Biblical Aramaic* (1961). Neither takes full account of what can be learnt from manuscripts with 'Babylonian' vocalization, on which cf. S. Morag 'Biblical Aramaic in Geonic Babylonia', in *Studies in Egyptology and Linguistics in Honour of H. J. Polotsky* (1964), pp. 117-31; id., *The Book of Daniel. A Babylonian Yemenite Manuscript* (1973).

and syntax, biblical Aramaic is still very close to imperial Aramaic, and especially to the Aramaic of Elephantine, but its spelling is in most respects already middle Aramaic: common Semitic *dh* is represented by *d* (and not *z*), *th* by *t* (not *sh*), *ẓ* by *ṭ* (not *ṣ*), *ḍ* as *ayyin* (not *q*). The old *ś* is mostly still written with the *sh* sign (and not *s*), but this may be under Hebrew influence. This, however, is typical for all Jewish Aramaic dialects, and it may be that Jews introduced the middle Aramaic spellings earlier than others because they spoke the language most similar to Aramaic, and there were many words identical in their consonants in the two languages except for the ones mentioned, e.g. Hebrew זהב (gold), Aramaic דהבא, spelled in imperial Aramaic זהבא, a rather irksome situation which could be resolved by spelling phonetically, and thus the result was achieved that all letters had the same value in Hebrew and Aramaic.

The language of the *Genesis Apocryphon* and other Aramaic fragments from the Dead Sea Scrolls is somewhat closer to the western type of middle Aramaic.[1] There are also other Aramaic documents going back to roughly that period, such as the *Scroll of Fasts*,[2] the traditional texts of the marriage document (*ketubbah*), the divorce document (*get*) and other legal formularies, and some inscriptions in the neighbourhood of Jerusalem.[3] This language, which Kutscher named Jerusalem Aramaic, is of major importance for our period, because it is the only type of Aramaic of which we can say with full confidence that it existed in the first century C.E.

The *Genesis Apocryphon* is also important in Jewish language history as evidence that there was in pre-mishnaic times a Palestinian Jewish Aramaic literature. The question seems not to have been asked for whom such a literature was intended. This problem does not exist with the legal formularies, as it is likely that they are a continuation of the practice of the Persian period, when documents of public validity were in Aramaic, the *lingua franca*. The same desire to be understood by all comers may be the cause for the Aramaic inscrip-

[1] Cf. E. Y. Kutscher, 'The Language of the Genesis Apocryphon; a Preliminary Study', in *Aspects of the Dead Sea Scrolls* (1958), pp. 1-35; A. Dammron, 'A Sketch of Qumran Aramaic' in J. A. Fitzmyer, *The Genesis Apocryphon of Qumran Cave I* (1966), pp. 173-206.

[2] A list of joyous days, on which no fasting is permitted, according to *T. B. Shabbath* 13b compiled originally by Hananiah ben Garon, a teacher who lived before 70 C.E. The early character of its language was recognized by G. Dalman, *Grammatik des jüdisch-palästinischen Aramäisch* (2nd ed., 1905), pp. 8-9.

[3] These are the inscriptions on bone-casks (*glusqema'ot*, from γλωσσοκομεῖον), many of which are believed to be pre-70 and even pre-Christian.

tions. It seems difficult to assume that the Judaean Jewish community was bilingual in literature, and literary works could be produced at will in either language, Hebrew or Aramaic. A possible explanation would be the existence of an uneducated class, who could read Aramaic but not Hebrew. However, such people would probably have been illiterate, and unable to understand the elegant archaizing language of the *Apocryphon* or its many learned allusions. Here we may take our clue from an Aramaic work known to have existed at the time, though not preserved, the Aramaic original of Josephus's *War*. That he wrote Aramaic, not Hebrew, is generally accepted to be proved by the many Aramaic forms of Jewish religious terms occurring in the Greek text of his works. Josephus states that he wrote the *War* 'in his ancestral tongue' (1, 3) for, amongst others, 'our fellow-nationals beyond the Euphrates and the inhabitants of Adiabene' (1, 6), i.e. Jews outside Palestine. We may thus assume that Palestinian Jews produced literature for those who could not be expected to know enough Hebrew to read a 'modern' work. Such Jews also came to settle in Jerusalem, where they had their own synagogues, and although there were different opinions as to whether parts of the Bible might be written or read out in any foreign language, with the exception of Greek,[1] there could be no reason for refraining from writing books of religious or national instructive value in languages such people understood. It might even be argued that the *Genesis Apocryphon*, with its stress on the wider boundaries of the Land of Israel[2] was thought suitable reading for the eastern Diaspora.

If we accept the idea that parts of the New Testament were originally written in Aramaic, it is in this Aramaic we must imagine them to be written. We have no evidence of any form of fully-fledged middle Aramaic being written in the first or early second century.

This also applies to the other large body of Aramaic writings connected with this period, the targums. The problem of the targums is twofold: a sociolinguistic one and one of language history. The first one is the question: for whom were the targums made? If we are right in our view that mishnaic Hebrew was spoken during the Second Temple period, there seems to be no *raison d'être* for targums in Judaea at that period. Yet we find in the Mishnah the targum accompanying the reading of the Law and the Prophets in the Synagogue as a well-established institution, regulated by Halakah in greatest detail.[3] In

[1] *M. Megillah* 1:8; 2:1.
[2] *Genesis Apocryphon* 21, 10-18.   [3] *M. Megillah* 4:5-6.

the whole of early rabbinic literature, we are never told that the Aramaic Targum is to be recited only to those who speak no Hebrew (as is done where reading in Greek is mentioned) or that it is properly an institution to be used outside Judaea or the Land of Israel.[1] We thus find that an Aramaic translation was obligatory for communities which knew Hebrew.

Closer examination, however, does provide some possible reasons why the Aramaic rendering was found to be a religious advantage, worthy to be institutionalized. Being able to speak mishnaic Hebrew was no guarantee for understanding all the vocabulary or constructions of an archaic and rich literature in the Hebrew language. The Hellenistic Greeks needed dictionaries of difficult words in their classical literature, and in the time of Augustus one Verius Flaccus produced a dictionary in which he explains 'ancient' words. The differences between the ancient Bible versions show that by then there were already different interpretations of some words. Moreover, there were ways of interpreting certain passages which the Pharisee teachers favoured, and others which they rejected. How was the communication gap to be bridged? In the case of the initiated (in the Qumran sect) or of the studious pupils of the sages, this could be done by systematic instruction in the forms of a *pesher* or a midrashic lecture. The wider public could be reached in the synagogue, where the regular readings from the Pentateuch and the Prophets were meant to serve as instruction and as a means to enable them to observe the commandment of studying the Torah. In the synagogue, explanations had to be brief and clear, and closely linked to each verse; they also had to be complete, as no dialogue between teacher and taught was possible. A paraphrase into Hebrew was impossible, because the uninstructed could easily take the paraphrase as part of the sacred text. The difference between the mixed language and pure biblical Hebrew was hardly such that it would assure the clear distinction, at speaking speed, between the two kinds of text. It was therefore an almost ideal way out of the difficulty to provide the explanations in a literary language, transitional Aramaic, which was no doubt widely understood, resembling both spoken mishnaic Hebrew and spoken Aramaic, but almost word for word clearly set off from its Hebrew equivalents. There may even have existed, at the very beginning of targumic activity, some memory of the way in which official documents in the

[1] For a summary of information to be gleaned from rabbinic sources about the targums, cf. R. le Déaut, *Introduction à la littérature targumique* I (1966), pp. 52-5.

Persian period were written down in Aramaic from dictation in any language that the sender of the message happened to speak, and read out to the recipient in his own language.[1] The *meturgeman*, standing next to the reader and 'reading out' the Hebrew text in Aramaic, presented the same image, though the roles of the languages were reversed.

For the theory here presented, it is immaterial whether we accept the theory that the more midrashic and discursive Palestinian targums were earlier, or think that the less expanded *Targum Onkelos* preceded the midrashic type. The *Targum to Job* from Qumran, dated by M. Sokoloff on linguistic grounds late in the second century B.C.E.,[2] shows that non-expanded Aramaic translations existed even before the date assigned to the Palestinian targums by these who hold the view that they preceded, although probably the translation of Job, a book not read as part of the liturgy, was made for Jews abroad for private reading. It is not impossible that such translations provided a pattern for the Onqelos type targums. While *Onkelos* is couched in a controlled and standardized type of transitional Aramaic, the Palestinian targums exhibit a far larger quota of middle-Aramaic forms and words (including many Greek words) and are less consistent in their language. It is generally accepted that this, in the same way as some references to late historical events, is due to unhindered evolution of the text, while the Onkelos text was early fixed and provided with a massorah, and that it gives no clues as to the date of the original text of either targum type.

Neither type of targum has a vocabulary which can be entirely accounted for by what we know of the original imperial Aramaic plus middle Aramaic as known from other sources. Many words are simply transpositions of Hebrew words into Aramaic phonology and morphology; others are unparalleled from any other Semitic language. Whatever their origin, such words when used in the Targum no doubt belonged to a special register of sacred translation[3] and were hardly

---

[1] Cf. H. H. Schaeder, *Iranische Beiträge* I (1930), pp. 202-3; H. J. Polotsky, 'Aramäisch *prs* und das Huzvaresch,' in *Le Muséon* XLV (1932), pp. 273-83; and cf. C. Rabin, in *Textus* VI (1968), pp. 17-18.

[2] *The Targum to Job from Qumran Cave XI* (1974), p. 25.

[3] Such special words were used in the Yiddish literal translation employed in teaching the Pentateuch to children, and in other traditional renderings. Note that the famous German Bible translation by M. Buber and F. Rosenzweig took up this method as a matter of principle (cf. also their book: *Die Schrift und ihre Verdeutschung* (1936), and especially Buber's article 'Ueber die Wortwahl in einer Verdeutschung der Schrift', pp. 135-67).

understood without explanation. Both these words and the Hebraisms deprived the Targum to some extent of its value as a translation, since explanation of the Hebrew words would have been equally effective, and in any event was still needed. The same may be said of the midrashic expansions of the Palestinian targums, which for their full appreciation really presuppose a good grasp of the Hebrew original. All this points to a conception of the Targum more as a guide to the correct understanding of a Hebrew text for those who already understood the words than as a means of giving the meaning of an otherwise unintelligible text.[1] The fact that its language differed greatly from the spoken Aramaic of those whom it served, that it was artificial and bristled with semantic difficulties, did therefore not matter.

Attention must be drawn to another feature of Aramaic. Normally, a language is also the bearer of a culture. If this is evidently true of national languages, it applies with even greater force to the upper language of a *diglossia* situation. In the context of the first century C.E., both Greek and biblical Hebrew stood for a rich cultural content, each in its own way. Mishnaic Hebrew stood for the values and folklore of Judaean Jewry. But neither literary nor spoken Aramaic carried in the world of first century Palestine any cultural message. This was before the time of cultural resistance of the East to Roman-Hellenistic civilization[2] and the emergence of national literary languages out of middle Aramaic. Aramaic was a means of communication, no more. It commanded no loyalty. This is forcefully put in a saying attributed to R. Judah the Prince, the compiler of the Mishnah: 'In the Land of Israel, why the Aramaic tongue? Either the Holy Tongue (Hebrew) or the Greek tongue!'[3] What is remarkable about that statement, is that it was made at a time when Hebrew had practically ceased to be spoken, and its place as a home language had been taken by Aramaic, to be followed, within less than a hundred years, by the use of Aramaic also as a language of halakic discussion and literature, as exhibited in the Palestinian Talmud.[4]

[1] It is a a guide to correct understanding that the targums are quoted in the Talmuds, as well as in the medieval commentaries, which were written at a time when Aramaic was understood less well than Hebrew.
[2] Cf. J. Oberdick, *Die römerfeindlichen Bewegungen im Orient während der letzten Hälfte des 3. Jahrhunderts n. Chr.* (1869); S. K. Eddy, *The King is Dead. Studies in Near-Eastern Resistance to Hellenism 334-31 B.C.* (1961).
[3] *T. B. Sotah* 49b. The word used for Aramaic is here *sursi* = συριστί.
[4] In general, sayings of Amoraim in the Palestinian Talmud are in Aramaic, while sayings of Tannaim are quoted in Hebrew even where these sayings are not otherwise recorded in the older halakic works (baraita). In this, the

The spoken languages of first-century Palestine

We have so far dealt with the written languages of the first century
C.E. in Palestine. Questions of spoken language have been discussed
only in so far as they threw light on the origins and character of a
written form of language. It is of course natural for anyone interested
in the period to wish to know in which language the personages
mentioned in the literature of this period spoke and taught, even
without considering the importance the identification of that language
may have for the understanding of their thought in general and of
certain statements reported of them in particular. 'The language of
Jesus' has proved to be a problem which has generated much discussion, and can be considered as being still unsolved. Before discussing what we know of the languages current in speech at that time,
we have to mention certain difficulties met with in dealing with
spoken languages in history.

The first is that historical sources rarely mention what language is
spoken in a certain place or milieu. However, if they do so, the information given may be difficult to interpret. Language names are
vague, and often depend on the nationality of the reporter, who may
have been accustomed to call a language by a different name or may
have been unable to distinguish between languages which are kept
apart by other sources or by us. Where there was a *lingua franca* or a
diglossia situation, the observer may often have believed that the
language he heard was the language usually spoken. There are many
cases where people are shy to let a stranger know what language they
speak at home, or they may like to mystify the unwary traveller.
Many groups themselves hold ideas about their own language which
are evidently erroneous.

When we say that someone speaks a language, this has two distinct
meanings: one that he speaks it habitually, which again may be
exclusively or in certain circumstances, the other that he is able to
speak it. In many societies it is considered an accomplishment to be
able to speak a certain language, though no one in that society uses it

Palestinian Talmud corresponds to its contemporary, the Babylonian Talmud.
It is important to note, however, that this does not mean that the Amoraim
did not know Hebrew. Their close exegesis shows that they had full mastery in
the understanding of biblical Hebrew and mishnaic Hebrew, but some of them
also wrote poetry and prayers, and many are quoted with Hebrew midrash
statements. There are also Hebrew sayings by Amoraim in both Talmuds, cf.
E. Margalioth, in *Leshonenu* XXVII (1962-63), pp. 20-33.

for any purposes of normal communication. A special and not infrequent case of this is where a language is near the point of dying out in a given society (even if it may still be fully alive elsewhere, e.g. in immigrant groups). Parents will often go to great lengths to see that their children are able to speak a language which they themselves do not normally use. This may well be the implication of the passage, often quoted as evidence that Hebrew was still spoken, in *Sifre on Deuteronomy* 26:4. 'And you shall teach them to your sons'[1] (Deut. 11:19): your sons and not your daughters, according to R. Jose ben Akiba. Hence it has been said: when the toddler begins to speak, his father shall talk to him in the Holy Tongue and teach him the Law. And if he does not speak to him in the Holy Tongue and does not teach him the Law, it is as if he had buried him.[2] The statement shows clearly that the child is assumed to have started speaking in another language, and that it is only the father who can talk to him in the Holy Tongue. On the other hand the separate mention of talking in the Holy Tongue and of teaching the Law shows that the intention is not merely to enable the child to repeat and understand the biblical verses, but that this is what would today be called by sociolinguists 'language loyalty' or 'language preservation'. Such a passage proves that there was still a living tradition of speaking the language, in this case no doubt mishnaic Hebrew. Since this is a social ideal, the members of a society engaged in language preservation will mostly themselves believe and claim before outsiders that they speak the language in question, and that this is their 'real' or 'only' language, while the language they actually communicate in is shrugged away as something unimportant or accidental.

Moreover, a spoken language at a given time and place may often be something quite different from the norm with which we associate it, such as the written form or the spoken form used at a place or time where this language enjoys or enjoyed prestige. It may, for instance, have undergone deep influence of another language, and may in some cases have replaced almost its entire vocabulary by borrowings and/or have adopted the pronunciation, grammar, and syntax of that other language to varying degrees, but still retain some distinctive features enabling its users to feel that they speak their own language and not

[1] This is the literal meaning. The Revised Standard Version and others rightly translate by sense 'your children'. Rabbi Issi ben Akavia (sic) belongs to the second half of the second century.
[2] *Sifre Deut.* 46.

the other one. Or, where two languages border on each other and are of the same stock, speakers of a dialect close to the standard form of language A may claim that their dialect belongs to language B, which is their language of culture. Again these things are likely to happen where one language is declining and another one is on the upgrade.

There can be little doubt that this was the nature of the relation between Hebrew and Aramaic at the time we are discussing. For the sake of argument, we may assume that mishnaic Hebrew was a fully living spoken language in Judaea at the time of the Maccabean revolt, and that it ceased to be spoken sometime in the third century C.E.; both datings may be too narrow, i.e. the decline may have started earlier, and pockets of living Hebrew speech may well have existed generations later. The first century C.E. is somewhere upon that line. Mishnaic Hebrew was still spoken, but was already both displaced to some extent by Aramaic as home language and Aramaicized to some extent. The following historical details may enable us to define this a little more.

It may be assumed that immediately after the beginning of the Maccabean revolt, Hebrew was in a very healthy state. Being an important symbol in the struggle against Greek influence, it may possibly have made good some previous losses. However, in 165 or 164 B.C.E. Simeon and Judas went out to Galilee and Transjordan and led the Jews living there to Judaea,[1] thus sharply reducing the area where Hebrew was spoken, and possibly importing to the centre elements already speaking Aramaic. When in 104-103 Aristobulus conquered Galilee and part of the land of the Arab Ituraeans, and John Hyrcanus between 135 and 104 conquered Idumaea, and in both cases the local inhabitants were forced to accept Judaism, large numbers of Aramaic speakers were incorporated into the community, and some of those who took their new religion seriously would come and settle in Jerusalem. Indeed, the very splendour of the Temple attracted Jews from the eastern, Aramaic-speaking countries, and thus further increased both the percentage of Aramaic speakers in Judaea and the reward to merchants and craftsmen for being able to speak fluent Aramaic. Priests and Pharisaic teachers, who came into constant contact with such Aramaic-speaking Jews, were probably completely bilingual, and as we see from the remnants of pre-mishnaic Aramaic literature, such as the *Job Targum* and the *Genesis Apocryphon*, some sages wielded an elegant Aramaic pen.

[1] I Macc. 5:23; Jos. *Ant.* XII, 332-49.

While we may assume that in Jerusalem and Judaea mishnaic Hebrew was still the ruling language, and Aramaic took the second place, the situation must have been reversed in areas such as the coastal plain and Galilee. There Aramaic, and possibly Greek, were the dominant languages spoken by people from all classes, while Hebrew mainly functioned as a literary language. The important point to remember is, however, that prestige and loyalty were accorded to Hebrew, and perhaps to Greek, but not to Aramaic, and that therefore many of those who habitually spoke Aramaic, but had acquired a certain facility in Hebrew, would count themselves as Hebrew speakers. Those who, like Jesus, took part in the discussions in the synagogues (Mark 1:21) and in the Temple of Jerusalem (Mark 11:17) and disputed on Halakah (Matthew 19:3) no doubt did so in mishnaic Hebrew. In other words, while in Jerusalem mishnaic Hebrew was a home language and probably already also a literary language, and Aramaic a *lingua franca*, in Galilee Aramaic was a home language and mishnaic Hebrew the upper language of a diglossia.

After 70 C.E. the situation changed, owing to the destruction of Jerusalem and the shift of the centres of learning to the coastal plain. Speakers of mishnaic Hebrew now lived as a minority amongst speakers of Aramaic and Greek; their wives and children moved in largely Aramaic surroundings, and the very pupils, and soon also the teachers, of the academies were Aramaic speakers who had acquired mishnaic Hebrew as part of their education only. A rapid process of erosion must have set in, speeded up in the tension following the Bar Cochba revolt and the further shift of the centres of learning to Galilee. Already the letters Bar Cochba writes to his lieutenants are mostly in Aramaic, and only two are in mishnaic Hebrew. Mishnaic Hebrew is retained as a language of learning, and indeed continued in this role for centuries after the probable date of cessation of Hebrew speaking, but speaking in it must have become progressively less common, even in the academies, so that by ca. 250 we find teachers whose sayings are recorded in Aramaic. At the same time the active use of imperial Aramaic, however, debased, seems to have come to an end, and middle Aramaic penetrates even into the targums.

It thus emerges that, while the events described in the New Testament took place in a time when Hebrew was still strong and dominant, the descriptions of those events were finally formulated in circumstances where Aramaic had gained the ascendancy, and speaking Hebrew outside halakic discussions or midrashic lectures had become an anomaly, perhaps something that ordinary people might never experience. It is remarkable that in the whole of early rabbinic literature there is not one passage deploring the decline of Hebrew speaking, and we can only ascribe this to the fact that people seem to be relatively insensitive to sociolinguistic (and linguistic) changes in their own time.[1] It is therefore quite likely that the authors and redactors of the Gospels unwittingly described, in the few references to language in their account, conditions of the post-70 period rather than those of the time of the events.[2]

BIBLIOGRAPHY ON THE LANGUAGE OF JESUS

J. VORSTIUS, *De hebraismis Novi Testamenti* (1665, 2nd ed. 1778); DOMINICUS DEODATUS, *De Christo graece loquente exercitatio* (1767); G. de ROSSI, *Della lingua propria di Christo e degli Ebrei nazionali della Palestina da tempi de' Maccabei* (1772): Jesus spoke Hebrew; J. F. FISCHER, *Supplementorum commentarii Ioh. Vorstii* etc. (1791); G. de ROSSI and H. F. PFANNKUCHE, *Language of Palestine in the Age of Christ and the Apostles*, transl. by T. G. Rapp, (1833); A. ROBERTS, *Inquiry into the Original Language of St. Matthew's Gospel, with Relative Discussions on the Language of Palestine in the Time of Christ* (1859); id., *Greek the language of Christ and His Apostles* (1888); T. K. ABBOTT, *Essays Chiefly on the Original Texts of the Old and New Testaments* (1891): Jesus spoke Greek; A. NEUBAUER, 'On the Dialects Spoken in Palestine in the Time of Christ' in *Studia Biblica* I (1895), pp. 39-74: History of research; A. MEYER, *Jesu Muttersprache. Das galiläische Aramäisch* (1896); F. ZORELL, 'Das Magnificat ein Kunstwerk hebräischer oder aramäischer Poesie?', in *Zeitschrift für Katholische Theologie* XXIX (1905), pp. 754-8; J. YOUNG, 'The Language of Christ', in *Dictionary of Christ and the Gospels* II (1908), pp. 2-5 'evidence ... is decisive for Aramaic'; FR. SCHULTHESS, *Das Problem der Sprache Jesu* (1917); G. DALMAN, *Die Worte Jesu* (1898, 2nd ed. 1930); id., *Jesus-Jeschua* (1922, English tr. by P. Levertoff, 1929); S. GREIJDANUS, *Het gebruik van het Grieksch door den Heere en zijne apostelen in Palestina* (1932); D. W. RIDDLE, 'The logic of the Theory of Translation Greek', in *JBL*

---

[1] As a parallel we may mention that the beginnings of Hebrew speaking in Palestine in the 1880s were hardly mentioned by writers of the period. Today, Israeli children refuse to believe that Hebrew was not spoken less than three generations ago.
[2] Cf. the bibliographical appendix.

LI (1932), pp. 13-30; I. ZOLLI, *Il Nazareno. Studi di esegesi neotestamentaria alla luce dell' aramaico e del pensiero rabbinico* (1938); F. ROSENTHAL, *Die aramaistische Forschung* (1939), pp. 106-14; R. O. P. TAYLOR, 'Did Jesus speak Aramaic?', in *Expository Times* LVI (1944-5), pp. 95-7: Jesus spoke mainly Greek; S. M. PATTERSON, 'What language did Jesus speak?', in *Classical Outlook* XXII (1946), pp. 65-7; E. STAUFFER, *Teaching of Jesus* (2nd edn. 1948), p. 49: Jesus spoke Hebrew; P. KAHLE, 'Das zur Zeit Jesu in Palästina gesprochene Aramäisch', in *Theologische Rundschau* N.F. XVII (1949), pp. 201-16: Jesus spoke the language of the Palestinian Targum published by Kahle; H. BIRKELAND, *Språk og religion hos Jøder og Arabere* (1949), pp. 25-29; id., *The language of Jesus* (1954): Jesus spoke Mishnaic Hebrew; A. S. KAPELRUD, Review of Birkeland, in *Norsk Teologisk Tidsskrift* LV (1954), p. 251; S. AALEN, 'Jesu morsmål', in *Tidsskrift for Teologi og Kirke* XXVI (1955), pp. 45-61; J. CANTINEAU, 'Quelle langue parlait le peuple en Palestine au premier siècle de notre ère?' in *Semitica* V (1955), pp. 99-101; review of Birkeland; H. LJUNGMANN, Review of Birkeland, in *Svensk Teologisk Kvartalskrift* XXXI (1955), pp. 122-3: 'shows how complicated the language situation was in Jesus's time'; J. RICHTER, *Ani hu und Ego eimi* (Dissert. Erlangen 1956).

Discussion on whether Jesus could speak Greek: A. W. ARGYLE, in *Expository Times* LXVII (1955-6), pp. 92-93; J. K. RUSSELL, ibid. p. 246; H. M. DRAPER, ibid. p. 317; A. W. ARGYLE, ibid. p. 383; R. MCL. WILSON, ibid. LXVIII (1957), pp. 121-2.

W. EISS, 'Zur gegenwärtigen aramaistischen Forschung', in *Evangelische Theologie* XVI (1956), pp. 170-81: against Birkeland; M. BLACK, 'Die Erforschung der Muttersprache Jesu', in *Theologische Literatur-Zeitung* LXXXI (1956), pp. 653-68; P. JEREMIAS, in *Götting. Gelehrte Anzeigen* (1956), p. 7: words at Last Supper in Hebrew; M.BLACK, 'The recovery of the language of Jesus', in *New Testament Studies* III (1956-7), pp. 310-3; R. MEYER, review of Birkeland, in *Orientalistische Literatur-zeitung* LII (1957), pp. 47-50; S. SEGERT, 'Zur Verbreitung des Aramäischen in Palästina zur Zeit Jesu', in *Archiv Orientalní* XXV (1957), pp. 21-37; Aramaic and mishnaic Hebrew were at the time very similar, and their reflexions in translation are hard to distinguish; P. NEPPER-CHRISTENSEN, *Das Matthäusevangelium, ein judenchrist-liches Evangelium* (1958), p. 105: history of problem; pp. 117-120:

'Hebrew' in sources may mean mishnaic Hebrew, Aramaic, or Judaeo-Greek indiscriminately; P. KAHLE, 'Das palästinische Pentateuchtargum und das zur Zeit Jesu gesprochene Aramäisch', in *ZNW* XLIX (1958), pp. 100-116; E. G. KUTSCHER, ibid. LI (1960), pp. 46-54; P. KAHLE, ibid. pp. 55ff.; J. A. EMERTON, 'Did Jesus speak Hebrew?' in *JTS* New Series (1961), pp. 189-202: Jesus usually spoke Aramaic; I. RABINOWITZ, 'Be Opened = Εφφαθα: Did Jesus speak Hebrew?', in *ZNW* LIII (1962), pp. 229-238; M. BLACK in: *Mélanges bibliques, Béda Rigaux* (1970), pp. 57-60; J. A. EMERTON, in *JTS*, New Series XVIII (1967), pp. 427-31; I. RABINOWITZ, in *JSS* XVI (1971), pp. 151-156; S. MORAG, in *JSS* XVII (1972), pp. 198-202; A. DÍEZ MACHO, 'La lengua hablada por Jesucristo', in *Oriens Antiquus* II (1963), pp. 95-132; K. HRUBY, 'La survivance de la langue hébraique pendant la période post-exilique' in *Memorial du Cinquanténaire, Écoles des langues orientales de l'Institut catholique de Paris* (1964), pp. 109-120; R. H. GUNDRY, 'The language milieu of first-century Palestine', in *JBL* LXXXIII (1964), pp. 404-8: Hebrew, Aramaic, and Greek were spoken; M. BLACK, 'Second Thoughts IX: The Semitic Element in the New Testament', in *Expository Times* LXXVII (1965), pp. 20-23; H. OTT, 'Um die Muttersprache Jesu: Forschungen seit Gustaf Dalman', in *Novum Testamentum* IX (1967), pp. 1-25; J. N. SEVENSTER, *Do you know Greek? How much Greek could the first Jewish Christians have known?* (1968): Full summary of the history of the question. M. BLACK, 'Aramaic Studies and the Language of Jesus', in *In Memoriam Paul Kahle, Beihefte zur Zeitschrift für Alttestamentliche Wissenschaft* CIII (1968), pp. 17-28; J. A. EMERTON, 'The Problem of Vernacular Hebrew in the First Century A.D. and the Language of Jesus', *Journal of Theological Studies*, New Series XXIV (1973), pp. 1-23; note also: P. JOÜON, *L'Évangile de notre seigneur Jésus-Christ* (1930), 'the most brilliant contribution ever written on the problem of the mother-tongue of Jesus' (P. Jeremias, 1956).

Chapter Twenty Two
Greek in Palestine and the Diaspora

By 'Greek in Palestine and the Diaspora' we understand the Greek used in Jewish and early Christian sources in the Second Temple period and in the first centuries C.E. It is part of Koine Greek, by which we mean all the varieties of post-classical Attic Greek, that is of the Attic dialect used between roughly 325 B.C.E. and 550 C.E. We apply this term not only to what are regarded as the more colloquial and popular, or even vulgar and solecistic types of language, but also to the chancellery style of the legal documents and the more literary uses of language, including the archaizing style that came into vogue from the reign of Augustus on ('Atticism'). The term Koine Greek, therefore, is the equivalent of Hellenistic Greek and covers the language of such highly Atticizing authors as Aelius Aristides and Lucian of Samosata, as well as the clumsy patois of the letters and petitions of Egyptian peasants. The *terminus a quo* of 325 B.C.E. marks the occupation of the Persian Empire by the Macedonians and the subsequent rise of independent Hellenistic kingdoms on its soil, which meant that Attic Greek, the language of the Macedonian court, was now forced to spread over a huge area and definitely became a world language. The year 325 B.C.E. also closes the period of Attic Greek which was later considered to be the literary standard and called 'classical'.

Our sources for Jewish and early Christian Greek may be divided as follows: inscriptions on stone and graffiti; numismatic inscriptions; papyri, ostraca and parchments; literary works; Greek loan words in Hebrew and Aramaic works; Greek names borne by Jews, and contemporary testimonies on the use of Greek by Jews.

In accordance with the title of this chapter we may draw a further distinction between Palestine and the Diaspora, but this distinction is not always relevant or feasible, and may at times be artificial or even misleading. The place of origin of the inscriptions is in the majority of cases the only clue we have. If we base ourselves only on this, we should be hopelessly misled. Only a few of them contain information about the origin of the persons referred to, and none say how and where these gained their knowledge of Greek. We learn only that an inscription found outside Palestine had been commissioned by a Jew who had emigrated from his country, while some of the inscribed ossuaries found near Jerusalem tell us that the deceased had come from abroad.[1] Obviously the inscriptions which do not contain such geographical indications may cover similar cases. Moreover, we should bear in mind that in the case of many inscriptions, if not all, we do not know whether the Greek is that of the deceased person's relatives or that of the stone-mason, who may or may not have been Jewish.

A comparable situation arises in Jewish and early Christian Greek literature. It is precisely the questions of authorship, dating and milieu which the disciplines devoted to this literature try to solve, and also, as a rule the question of the original language of a work. Only in few cases, such as the Greek Esther and Sirach and the works of Josephus, are we exactly informed with regard to the place of origin, and here again we perceive that the background may be more complicated than the simple distinction between Palestine and Diaspora would suggest. Josephus, for instance, wrote first in Aramaic or Hebrew, probably while still in Palestine. He translated his *War* into Greek at Rome, and had the result revised by professional correctors. Books may have been written outside Palestine by persons who had been taught Greek in that country (so, very probably, Revelation) while others were composed in Palestine by authors who had achieved their command of Greek abroad (so possibly Luke). Of the majority of works one cannot say definitely where, when and by whom they were composed and translated. Moreover, the presence of a large number of Hellenistic centres in Palestine itself blurs still further the distinction between Palestine and Diaspora. Nevertheless, we shall retain it for practical reasons, mainly in our survey of the inscriptions and papyri, which are generally labelled after their location. A further reason for singling out Palestine is that we have to pay attention also to the use of Greek by the non-Jews in that country, so as to shed as much light as possible on the linguistic situation there, since it plays such a pivotal role in the discussion of authorship and milieu of the New Testament writings. In the following pages we give a survey of the available sources according to the above division. In the final section on testimonies to the use of Greek by Jews, we pay special attention to the situation in the first century C.E. After giving the contemporary testimonies we shall sum up the

[1] *CII* 1233; 1284.

situation as regards the use of Greek by Jews at this period. It may be useful, therefore, to describe here in outline how the Greek language stood in the first century C.E.:

Phonology. Evening out of vowel quantities and disappearance of circumflex accent, resulting in one series of vowels of indifferent length; disappearance of diphthongs: αι becoming [ε], οι becoming [ü], ει becoming [i]; loss of 'iota adscript' in pronunciation; in the second century C.E., η became [i], and υ became [i].

Morphology. Loss of the dual number in the substantive and adjective, loss of the dual in the verb; increasing obsolescence of the superlative except in its 'elative' aspect ('very...'); obsolescence of optative, middle future and aorist, future participle and infinitive; after 100 C.E. gradual disappearance of the perfect indicative which was merged with the aorist, and of the dative case which was merged with the genitive; second aorists generally adopt α vocalization e.g. εἶπον > εἶπα.

Syntax. Tendency towards elimination of the dative case; towards 'predicative' position of the adjective or participle (e.g. 1 Cor. 11:5 ἀκατακαλύπτῳ τῇ κεφαλῇ), or towards omission of the article with substantive when an adjective is present (type ἀνὴρ ὁ ἀγαθός e.g. in Luke 23:49); shifts in the use of cases with some prepositions: ἐπί often used indiscriminately with all oblique cases; εἰς and ἐν merged; εἰς with accusative does not necessarily imply movement (e.g. Acts 8:40: εὑρέθη εἰς Ἄζωτον).

All the tendencies mentioned are present in various degrees in works written from the first century C.E. on, depending on how far the authors succeeded in suppressing such tendencies by the substitution of archaizing Attic usage. Often enough old and new occur side by side.

Inscriptions on stone and graffiti

In Palestine proper (excluding Transjordan) a total of 440 Jewish inscriptions in Greek have been found.[1] These inscriptions are mainly located in three places: 69 in the cemeteries of Joppa (2nd-3rd cent.), 196 in Beth-Shearim (1st-4th cent.) and 90 on the ossuaries of Jerusalem (2nd cent. B.C.E. - 2nd cent. C.E.). Among them we find two metrical inscriptions,[2] but these are exceptions: the greater part are naturally only short ones, bearing no date and containing little more

---

[1] According to Frey's *CII* the number then amounted to 326, and from the later publications of *SEG* XI ff. we have counted 114 more items.
[2] *SEG* XIV, 847; XVI, 829.

than a traditional formula and the names of the deceased. Besides the usual itacizing spelling, such as κιτε for κεῖται,[1] ανυξε for ἀνοῖξαι,[2] some of them also show a remarkable lack of proper agreement in appositions: Ἀντωνίνου καὶ Κύρου, τέκνα Σαμουήλου instead of τέκνων,[3] and so Ἰεσούου Ἰαμουρίτης;[4] cf. Rev. 1:5: ἀπὸ Ἰησοῦ Χριστοῦ ὁ μάρτυς ὁ πιστός. Further peculiarities are: Γληγορίας for Γρηγορίας,[5] Ἀτιγόνα for Ἀντιγόνα,[6] Σαπίρα for Σαπφίρα,[7] φροτιτῶν for φροντιστῶν,[8] the double comparative μιζοτέρας.[9]

Outside Palestine 683 Jewish Greek inscriptions have been found. Here again the majority are located in a restricted number of places: 262 in the catacombs of Rome (1st-3rd cent.), 31 in the catacomb of Venosa in Apulia, 65 in the cemetery at Tokra in Cyrenaica (ancient Teucheira-Arsinoe (1st cent. B.C.E. - 1st cent. C.E., most of them dated), and 80 in the cemetery at Tell el-Yehudieh in Egypt (ancient Leontopolis in the Heliopolite nome (2nd cent. B.C.E. - 1st. cent. C.E.). In these four places only a few Hebrew or Aramaic inscriptions occur (7 at Rome, 6 at Venosa). The 245 Jewish Greek inscriptions that remain are scattered all around the Mediterranean, but until now none have come to light in France, Britain and Germany. Eight of the Egyptian inscriptions are in hexameters or pentameters, one of them in the Doric dialect;[10] we give here the translation of the most complete funerary poem, the one inscribed on the tomb of a certain Jesus:[11]

'Traveller, my name is Jesus, and my father's name Phameis; when descending into Hades I was 60 years of age. All of you should weep together for this man, who went at once to the hiding place of ages, to abide there in the dark.

[1] *CII* 948, 1008, etc. [2] *SEG* XX, 439.
[3] *CII* 970 (Caesarea Maritima).
[4] *SEG* XX, 422, but 427 Ἰεσοῦος Ἰαμουρίτης, both from Beth Shearim.
[5] *CII* 927, Jaffa.
[6] *CII* 1382, Jerusalem.
[7] *CII* 1272, Jerusalem; for this name, cf. Acts 5:1.
[8] *CII* 919, Jaffa.
[9] *SEG* XVIII, 624, Beth Shearim; cf. μειζοτέραν in 3 John 4.
[10] *CII* 1530.
[11] Εἰμεὶ ἐγὼ Ἰησοῦς, ὁ φὺς δὲ Φαμεῖς, παροδεῖτα,
ΞL (i.e. ἑξηκονταέτης) ἦλθον δ'εἰς Ἀείδαν;
κλαύσατε δὴ ἄμα πάντας (for πάντες) τὸν ἐξαπίνης μεταβάντα
εἰς μυχὸν αἰώνων ἐν σκοτίᾳ διάγειν.
καὶ σὺ δὲ Δωσίθεε, κατάκλαέ με· σοὶ γὰρ ἀνάνκη
δάκρισι πικροτάτοις τύμβῳ ἐμῷ προχέειν.
τέκνον ἐμοὶ εἴ σ[ύ], ἐγὼ γὰρ ἀπῆλθεν ἄτεκ[ν]ος
κλαύσατε παντες ὁμοῦ Ἰησο[ῦ]ν δυσμενέα (*CII* 1511).

Will you please also bewail me, dear Dosítheos, because
you are in the need of shedding bitter tears upon my tomb.
When I died I had no offspring, you will be my child instead.
All of you, therefore, bewail me, Jesus the unhappy man.'

Linguistically all these inscriptions are hardly different from those
found in Palestine.[1]

Numismatic inscriptions

In a few Hellenistic towns of Palestine such as Ascalon and Gaza,
Greek or bilingual coins had been struck since the time of Alexander
the Great. By the first century c.e., many other towns issued coinage
with Greek legends: Joppa, Neapolis, Nysa-Scythopolis, Sebaste,
Tiberias, Caesarea Maritima, Dora, and in the Decapolis: Canat(h)a,
Antiochia ad Hippum, Gadara, Gaba (?), and in Arabia Petraea:
Eboda.

The inscriptions on the Jewish coins struck by the Hasmoneans were
exclusively Hebrew until Alexander Jannaeus, who started to issue
bilingual (Hebrew-Greek) coins as well; his grandson Antigonus
Mattathias did likewise, but he was the first Jewish king to issue also
coins which had only a Greek legend. After him the Herodian princes
and the Roman procurators issued Greek coins only, whereas the last
king, Agrippa II, also struck bilingual Graeco-Latin ones.

As might be expected, foreign languages were banned from the coins
of the first and second revolt against the Romans, but as the cor-

---

[1] Compare ἀσύκριτος for ἀσύγκριτος (*CII* 130, Rome) with Ἀτιγόνα (*CII* 1382),
ἱέρισα for ἱέρισσα (*CII* 315, Rome and 1514 Tell el-Yehudieh) with Σαπίρα
(*CII* 1272) and with Σύμαχος (*CII* 986, El-Hammâm, Palestine). Peculiar to
Rome and Venosa is, as far as we can see, the value [j] of γ, especially in the
word, γερουσιάρχης, which is spelled: γιερ- (*CII* 95), ιερ- (*CII* 355 and 408), in
Latin: *iervsiarcontis* (*CII* 613), compare also *Gesva* for *Iesva* (*CII* 614). The
curious mixture of alphabets is also typical: Greek letters in Latin words
RHBEKA (*CII* 261), TRHNVS (*CII* 611), Hebrew letters in Greek words
ΒΑΡѾΕΟΔΑ (*CII* 108); Greek is twice written in the Latin alphabet (*CII* 224
and 284), the former one reading: EN IRENE AE CVMESIS SV, i.e. the
stereotype formula ἐν εἰρήνη ἡ κοίμησίς σου; at Venosa there is even a Greek inscription in Hebrew letters (*CII* 595), which contains the numeral אוגדואטא,
i.e. ὀγδοήνται (for -ηκοντα) as in modern Greek, cf. in *CII* 596 πεντήντα 'fifty'
(modern Greek πενήντα). A Latinism is probably the use of τις as a relative
pronoun in Rome (*CII* 99; 148; 152; 159; 377): in Vulgar Latin *qui* served as
both relative and interrogative pronoun, but τις for ὅς is also found in Cnidus
and Egypt.

respondence of Bar-Cochba has proved, this did not mean that Greek
was no longer used. Some of these coins, however, show traces of Latin
or Greek, but these are pieces that have been re-minted.

Papyri, ostraca and parchments

As compared with the immense amount of papyri unearthed in Upper
Egypt, the few found in Palestine may seem negligible, but it is
precisely the scarcity of any documents which makes the few that we
have so important, more important perhaps than comparable pieces
from Egypt. Here they are listed with the places where they were
found: Qumran cave 7: two Septuagint fragments from Exodus and
the Epistle of Jeremiah and 16 scraps of papyrus;[1] Qumran cave 4:
3 Septuagint fragments as yet unpublished: found together with
88 Hebrew and Aramaic documents; Murabbat: 70 documents,
mainly lists, contracts and accounts from the second century C.E.;[2]
Nahal Hever: two letters to Jonathan, forming part of the Bar-Cochba
archive, found together with 5 Hebrew and 8 Aramaic letters;[3] Nahal
Seelim and Nahal Mishmar: 9 small fragments, two of them containing
names:[4] Cave of the Letters: the so-called Babatha archive consisting
of 26 legal documents, with 3 Aramaic and 6 Nabataean documents,
all still unpublished;[5] Masada: a personal letter from 'Αβάσκαντος to
'Ιούδας;[6] Cave of Horror: one unreadable letter and 9 very small
biblical fragments on parchment,[7] and probably also from this cave:
a parchment scroll of the Minor Prophets, showing a type of text
which is more akin to that of Symmachus and Justin Martyr (Micah
4:1-7 in *Dialogus* (119) than to the LXX, and possibly identical with
Origen's *Quinta*.[8] Of all these documents only the biblical fragments
from Qumran and the Cave of Horror and the Masada letter may
safely be ascribed to the first century C.E.[9] To the above list we should

---

[1] *DJD* III, pp. 142-3.
[2] *DJD* II.
[3] *IEJ* XI (1961), pp. 40ff. According to some, one of the two letters was written
by Bar Cochba himself, but this is doubtful. Cf. *Aegyptus* XLII (1962), pp. 240
ff., and *IEJ* XXIII (1973), pp. 101 ff.
[4] *IEJ* XI (1961), pp. 53 ff.
[5] *IEJ* XII (1962), pp. 227ff. and pp. 258ff.
[6] *IEJ* XV (1965), p. 110.
[7] *IEJ* XII (1962), pp. 201ff.
[8] *RB* LX (1953), pp. 18ff.
[9] See Sevenster, pp. 149-173.

add, however, a number of papyri found in Egypt, but drawn up in or dispatched from Palestine.[1]

The papyri and ostraca written by Jews or bearing on Jews and Jewish matters in the Diaspora have been collected in the *Corpus Papyrorum Judaicarum*, altogether 520 items, almost exclusively of Egyptian provenance. The third volume, which contains documents later than 117 C.E., lies outside our present scope. Of the remaining 450 documents only twelve have certainly been drawn up by Jews themselves, or contain portions in the first person, representing language actually spoken by Jews. In the rest of them Jews either appear as witnesses, as parties in business transactions, loans, etc., or are simply mentioned in other connections (lists, etc.). This latter group of documents may, strictly speaking, signify only a certain understanding of Greek in the persons concerned, but from the very variety of these documents which include deeds of mortgage as well as simple receipts, it is clear that they must also have been able to speak or write some Greek. Nevertheless, we concentrate in particular on the former group, the personal letters, petitions, and the like.[2]

Of the character of the language we may say that it shows the signs of the well-known phonetic and morphological development of the Hellenistic period. Only a few peculiarities are to be mentioned here:

CPJ 12 line 11 τηνεῖ 'here' Doric for the more usual ἐνθάδε (reign of Philadelphus).

CPJ 13 line 11 καταφθειρώμεσθα old-fashioned for -μεθα (same period as no. 12).

CPJ 46 is curious because of its incorrect case usage, a phenomenon which we have already met elsewhere. It is a deed of agreement between two Jews about the joint use of a pottery. Being analphabetic, they had the document written by a scribe with the Greek name Χαιρήμων son of Καλλικράτης. He was far from correct. We find in it a genitive for a nominative (line 1), a dative for a nominative (line 2), nominatives for datives (line 4), an accusative plural for a nominative singular (line 13), and in line 5 ὁμολογοῦμεν συνμετέχομεν (for συνμετέχειν, or has ὅτι been omitted?).

---

[1] *CPJ* nos. 4 (257 B.C.E.) and 5 (257 B.C.E.), which were sent to the secretary of the landowner Zeno by Tobias, a member of the famous Tobiad family (see *IEJ* VII (1957), pp. 137ff. and 229ff.). The remaining pieces date from the Byzantine period and can for that reason be left out of consideration here (P. Nessana 13.306 and 14; S.B. 7011 and 7012).

[2] *CPJ* 12; 13; 14; 19; 43; 46; 133; 141; 151; 417; 424. They date from 241 B.C.E. to 87 C.E.

CPJ 424, a personal letter from one Johanna to a certain Epagathus, dated 15 December 87 C.E., may illustrate an illiterate woman's more or less phonetic spelling: Ἐπαγάθο for -ῳ (line 1), εἰδίο for ἰδίῳ (line 1), and so θαυμάζο (line 6), θέλο (line 8), οὔπο (line 12), γίνοσκε (line 16), ἴχσεσσθαι for ἴσχεσθαι (line 6), ἐρῖς for ἐρεῖς (line 11), and so θέλις (line 12), ἰσφέριν (line 20); ν for γ in ἀνανκάσης (line 7), ἐνένκα[ι] (line 15). For the accusative τοὺς αὐτοῦ πάντες (line 26) cf. Rev. 4:4 (A) θρόνους εἴκοσι τέσσαρες.

From Egypt, papyri and ostraca in Aramaic are available for the third and second century B.C.E. up to *c.* 150; after that Greek seems to have gained the upper hand. From the fourth century C.E. on, however, two small fragments of Hebrew letters show that the Semitic languages could be revived; one of them contains a Greek loan word: פרוסטטי προστάται.[1]

Literature

The main division of the literary sources is based on their relationship to the Hebrew or Aramaic language. A first group are translations from the Hebrew or Aramaic or works markedly influenced by those languages, as opposed to a second group of non-Semitizing writings (i.e. which have not, or have hardly been influenced by Hebrew or Aramaic). A further distinction is the extent to which the latter have been under the influence of classical Greek, and show archaizing ('Atticistic') features or not. If possible a distinction will also be made between works from Palestine and the Diaspora. As Semitizing works we class first of all the translations from Hebrew or Aramaic, of which the originals are extant or are known to have existed. The primary instance is the Septuagint translation of the Hebrew Bible, which according to the legendary Epistle of Aristeas was done by 72 Jews within 72 days during the reign of Ptolemy II. In reality translation went on for at least a century. And the original reason at first for the translation may have been other than Aristeas says. He may be correct when he depicts an Egyptian king as having instigated the translation, but the actual motive was not so much this king's love of books nor his interest in Jewish religion as a juridical one. A reliable copy was needed of the law which prevailed in the country conquered from Macedonian opponents.[2] We have also to mention here Eccle-

---

[1] See *JEA* 11 (1915), pp. 209 ff.
[2] For this I would like to acknowledge the unpublished theory of J. W. Doeve.

siasticus or the Wisdom of Sirach, of which the Hebrew original is not contained in the Hebrew Bible, but has been discovered in the Geniza of Cairo and in Masada. We may also add the Gospel of Matthew, which, if Papias is to be trusted, was originally composed in 'Hebrew',[1] and the Enoch literature of which Hebrew fragments were found in Qumran.

It may be useful to append here a summary of what we consider to be the more important characteristics of translation Greek, because it is from the presence of identical phenomena in other works that the latter are supposed to have been translated from Semitic originals.

1) High frequency of καὶ at the beginning of sentences and elsewhere, for instance Gen. 1:1-31 (cf. I Mac. 1:1-64).

2) High frequency of (καὶ) ἰδού e.g. Am. 7:1, 4, 7, 8.

3) High frequency of genitive pronouns immediately following substantives e.g. Judg. 1:3 (cf. Jud. 2:2), and also of dative and accusative pronouns with verbs.

4) Omission of the article with a substantive which is itself followed by a genitive e.g. Nah. 1:1 βιβλίον ὁράσεως Ναουμ (cf. Tob. 1:1 βίβλος λόγων Τωβίτ).

5) The tendency not to separate the article from the substantive, and to have the substantive followed by (article plus) adjective e.g. Jon. 1:2 Νινευη τὴν πόλιν τὴν μεγάλην.

6) Use of the nominative preceded by the article 'as a vocative' e.g. Ps. 41:2; 42:1; 43:2; 44:7 (cf. Jud. 9:5); much more frequent than in non-biblical Greek.

7) Use of the dative instead of a possessive genitive e.g. 4(2) Kings 13:1 ἐν ἔτει εἰκοστῷ καὶ τρίτῳ ἔτει τῷ Ιωας and ψαλμὸς τῷ Δαυιδ in Ps. 97; 98; 100; 102; 103, etc.

8) Use of εἷς with the meaning of πρῶτος e.g. Est. 1:1 τῇ μιᾷ τοῦ Νισα.

9) The use of paronomastic datives or accusatives with verbs e.g. Gen. 2:17 θανάτῳ ἀποθανεῖσθε, and of a participle with a verb 'of the same stem' e.g. Gen. 16:10 πληθύνων πληθυνῶ τὸ σπέρμα σου, (cf. Ps. Philo Lib. Ant. VI, 14, frangentes fregerunt). These constructions render the Hebrew infinitive absolute and have therefore an emphatic value: 'you shall certainly die' and 'I will greatly multiply your seed'.

10) Frequent occurence of nominal sentences e.g. 4(2) Kings 14:2 καὶ ὄνομα τῆς μητρὸς αὐτοῦ Ιωιαδιν.

[1] Ed. Funk-Bihlmeyer, fragment II, 16.

11) Frequent occurence of participles in nominal sentences ('ptc. used as finite verb') e.g. 1 Chron. 12:1 καὶ οὗτοι ἐν τοῖς δυνατοῖς... βοηθοῦντες.

12) Participle coordinated with a finite verb e.g. 2 Esdras 2:1 καὶ οὗτοι οἱ υἱοὶ τῆς χώρας οἱ ἀναβαίνοντες ἀπὸ τῆς αἰχμαλωσίας... καὶ ἐπέστρεψαν.

13) καὶ ἐγένετο followed by (καὶ plus) finite verb e.g. 2 Chron. 12:1 καὶ ἐγένετο ὡς ἡτοιμάσθη ἡ βασιλεία Ροβοαμ... ἐγκατέλιπεν τὰς ἐντολὰς κυρίου (cf. 2 Esdras 11:1 and 1 Mac. 1:1).

14) Frequency of the order: verb - subject - object (see Rife's art. below).

15) The *parallelismus membrorum* in poetical portions and books: e.g. Judg. 3:3 (A) Deborah's Song
ἀκούσατε βασιλεῖς, ἐνωτίζεσθε σατράπαι δυνατοί·
ἐγὼ τῷ κυρίῳ ᾄσομαι, ψαλῶ τῷ θεῷ 'Ισραήλ.
(cf. Sir. 3:21; Ps. Sol. 11:1; Wisdom of Solomon 1:10-12).

The group of Semitizing works also comprises a number of writings of which no Hebrew of Aramaic originals are extant. They are often considered translations, but some of them may equally well be original Greek compositions, containing Semitisms simply because the authors were Jews or Jewish-Christians. In our opinion no sharp dividing line can here be drawn, less so because this Semitizing Greek, the spontaneous product of bilingual Jews, was imitated in later apocryphal literature, growing into some kind of genre-language.[1]

The works to be mentioned here are the following apocryphal books from the Septuagint: Wisdom of Solomon, Psalms of Solomon, Baruch, Letter of Jeremiah, Susanna, Bel and the Dragon, 2 Esdras or Greek Ezra, Judith, Tobit, 1 Maccabees: and the following Pseudepigrapha: Testaments of the XII Patriarchs, Testament of Job, Apocalypse of Baruch, Testament of Abraham, Martyrdom of Isaiah, Joseph and Aseneth, Apocalypse of Moses, Ascension of Isaiah (Greek fragments only). We could add a few works which have not been preserved in Greek but which are supposed to have been translated from it. The more important ones are the Slavonic Apocalypse of Enoch and the Latin Apocalypse of Ezra (4 Esdras), chapters 3-14,

[1] This may be the case in the *Testament of Abraham*, dating from the second century C.E. See N. Turner, 'The Testament of Abraham. Problems in biblical Greek,' in *NTS* 1 (1954), pp. 219-223. Other examples probably include the *Narratio Zosimi* (5th-6th cent.) and the *Apocalypse of Sedrach* (10th-11th cent.), and certainly the *Apocalypse of the Virgin* (9th cent.).

written in Hebraizing Latin but not free of Graecisms, such as the genitive of comparison in 11:1 *et medium caput erat maius aliorum capitum*. From the New Testament we should add the Gospels of Mark, Luke and John, Acts and Revelation.

To the category of Atticizing literature belong the following works: 3 and 4 Maccabees and the works of Philo and Flavius Josephus.[1] In addition there are the following poetical works: Philo the Elder, Theodotus, Pseudo-Phocylides and the Sibylline Oracles (hexametric) and Ezekiel Poeta (iambic trimeters). Lacking both clearly Semitizing and Atticizing features are the following works: Pseudo-Hecataeus, Aristobulus, the Letter of Aristeas (Pseudo-Aristeas) to Philocrates, 2 Maccabees, the Pauline Letters, the Epistle to the Hebrews, the Epistles of James, Peter, John and Jude, and of the Apostolic Fathers the Epistle of Barnabas.

Greek loan words

In the later books of the Hebrew Bible we encounter the first Greek loan words,[2] and Hillel is supposed to have used the Greek legal term προσβολή.[3] In the Hebrew text of Jesus ben Sirach and in the Qumran documents no loan words from Greek appear, except for the Copper Scroll, in which there are a number of Greek architectural terms.[4]

That there are many Greek words and phrases in talmudic literature is well known. They have been collected by Samuel Krauss whose book lists over two thousand words, but Immanuel Löw, who drew up the indexes at the end of the book, expressed his doubts with regard to some 800 of them. Such borrowings sometimes no doubt ephemeral do not in the strict sense testify to the actual use of Greek in Palestine. But they do show that in the second century and later the language was heard or read so much among the Jews, that (omitting the international words for foreign products and instruments or clothes

---

[1] We can only guess at the linguistic character of the Jewish or Samaritan authors Demetrius, Eupolemus and Pseudo-Eupolemus, Artapanus, Cleodemus alias Malchus, Thallus and Justus of Tiberias. The fragments which we possess are all paraphrases, worded in Alexander Polyhistor's style.

[2] Cant. 3:9 אפריון = φορεῖον, litter, and Dan. 3:5, 7, 10, 15 for the musical instruments קיתרוס = κιθάρις, סבכא = σαμβύκη, פסנתרין = ψαλτήριον, סומפניה = συμφωνία. Cf. LXX 3:5 and Theodotion 3:5, 7, 10, 15.

[3] פרוזבול, M. *Shebiith* 10:3ff.

[4] *DJD* III, pp. 246ff., nos. 84, 88, 104, 128, 149; from Murabbaʿat: *DJD* II no. 21 (1-3, l.11).

hitherto unknown, like περιστύλι(ο)ν we can only conclude that the Greek language played the same role as English does nowadays in many countries outside Britain. It makes people intersperse their native tongue with foreign words or expressions, sometimes without actual need, for instance out of snobbishness, but usually when a satisfactory equivalent has not yet been found or does not present itself immediately to the speaker's mind. This happens especially when the topic under discussion belongs to a sector of life where it is the foreign language which is used, as a rule. For the second and third century in Palestine, such sectors were undoubtedly those of government and legislation.

Greek names borne by Jews

Greeks visited Palestine long before Alexander the Great and the Hellenistic period. The first known to have done so are probably Yamani *i.e.* 'the Ionian', a man who for some time held the throne of Philistine Ashdod (712 B.C.E.), and Antimenidas, the brother of the poet Alcaeus, who in all likelihood fought as a mercenary at the siege of Ascalon in 604 B.C.E.[1] Although international trade undoubtedly brought many Greeks to the Palestinian coasts we do not know of any Greek names taken over by Jews in Palestine before Hellenistic times. The first are the names of Ἀντίγονος of Socho[2] and the envoys sent to Sparta and Rome: Νουμήνιος Ἀντιόχου and Ἀντίπατρος Ἰάσονος.[3] That we have no older examples may be due to our incomplete knowledge of this period; the first examples of non-Jewish Palestinians bearing Greek names date from about a century earlier.[4]

Outside Palestine we first meet Jews with Greek names about the middle of the third century B.C.E.[5] The adoption of foreign names by Diaspora Jews, we believe, implies only a superficial adjustment to new circumstances meant only to facilitate social contacts. In Dan. 1:6-7 Jews are represented as receiving Babylonian names along with their Hebrew ones; so in Esther 2:5 Mordecai is a Babylonian name,

---

[1] J. D. Quinn, 'Alcaeus 48 (B 16) and the Fall of Ascalon' *BASOR* 164 (1961), pp. 19-20.
[2] Third or second century B.C.E.
[3] Both circa 150 B.C.E. Their fathers were born about 200 B.C.E. (I Macc. 12:16).
[4] Νικασώ, circa 325 B.C.E., daughter of Sanballat III, governor of Samaria (Jos. *Ant.* XI, 303) and Μένιππος, the comedian of Gadara, circa 275 B.C.E.
[5] *CPJ* 18: Ἀνδρόνικος, 260 B.C.E.; *CPJ* 8: Ἀντιγόνης, 256 B.C.E.; *CPJ* 126: Ἀπολλώνιος (ὃς καὶ Συριστὶ Ἰωναθᾶς καλεῖται), 238/7 B.C.E.

derived from the deity Marduk. In Egypt Jews incidentally also had Egyptian names[1] and even Persian ones.[2]

Within Palestine the bearing of Greek names may imply at first some spread of Hellenistic culture, particularly in aristocratic circles, but when this novelty was taken over by people of all social levels, no conclusions with regard to an actual command of Greek may be drawn from that fact only. We think it even conceivable that some took an extra name as soon as they had to do with government affairs; often these names were simple translations or phonetic echoes of the native ones: Ἐτητος (i.e. Αἴτητος for Sha'ul;[3] Θεόδωρος, Θεόδοτος, Θεοδόσιος, Δοσίθεος for Jonathan, Nathanjah,[4] Παρηγόριος for Menahem,[5] Γελάσιος for Isaac.[6] Examples of phonetic resemblance are: Ἰάσων for Jeshua, Ἄλκιμος for Eljakim, Μουσαῖος for Moses,[7] Σίμων for Shimeon (but also: Ἰησοῦς, Μωϋσῆς, Συμεών). On the whole there was not much objection to pagan theophoric names, particularly not to names composed with Zeus: Ζήνων,[8] Ζηνοβία,[9] but other gods occurred as well: Ἰσίδωρος,[10] Διονυσία,[11] Σεραπίων (reminiscent of the seraphim?),[12] Ἀρτεμίδωρος.[13]

Testimonies and final survey

As far as the first century C.E. is concerned, it cannot be doubted that in the major centres where Diaspora Jews had settled, Greek was written and spoken. This is amply proved by the numerous funeral inscriptions in Rome and Cyrenaica, and the personal letters which they wrote to each other in Egypt. It is also implied by the fact that Paul wrote in Greek to the churches in Asia Minor, which at first partly coincided with the local Jewish congregations. The quality of the Greek naturally depended entirely on the social status of the

---

[1] E.g. *CPJ* 9: Πᾶσις Ἰουδαῖος, 253 B.C.E.
[2] E.g. Artapanus, the author, circa 100 B.C.E. Cf. in Palestine Arsamos, a priest (*Aristeas* 50), Hyrcanus, circa 185 B.C.E., one of the Tobiads.
[3] *CII* 325, Rome.
[4] *Aristeas* 47-50. *CII* 922, Joppa; 1358-9, Jerusalem.
[5] *CII* 926, Jaffa.
[6] *CII* 991, Sepphoris.
[7] *CPJ* 20.
[8] *CII* 903, Jaffa.
[9] *CII* 1035, Beth Shearim.
[10] *CII* 985, El-Hammâm.
[11] *CII* 1063, Beth Shearim.
[12] *SEG* XVI, 910, Cyrenaica.
[13] *CPJ* 30, Egypt.

person: Philo wrote his immense oeuvre in excellent Greek and usually in a good style as well, his vocabulary having much in common with that of Plato. On the other hand we have also seen instances of bad Greek, and it is due to such examples that the mathematician Cleomedes (? 50 B.C.E.) may have come to consider 'Jewish Greek' as the instance of bad style.[1]

Our interest, therefore, is mainly centred on the linguistic situation in Palestine. It has been the subject of numerous studies, and was most recently treated by J. N. Sevenster and also by H. Ott, who surveys the Semitistic work done in this field between 1930 and 1965. If we restrict ourselves to first century Palestine with Jesus and the New Testament particularly in mind, we believe that from among the material displayed in the preceding paragraphs the following items are especially relevant: the inscriptions of the Jerusalem ossuaries,[2] the inscription on Jason's tomb,[3] the Mt. Ophel inscription of a synagogue ruler,[4] the temple inscription,[5] and the decree on tomb robbery from Nazareth;[6] the Scroll of the Minor Prophets from Qumran, the Masada letter, and the following books: Wisdom of Solomon, Baruch, Apocalypse of Baruch, Enoch *ch.* 37-71, Martyrdom of Isaiah, New Testament, Barnabas, Josephus, Justus of Tiberias, 4 Maccabees, Apocalypse of Moses. We include Paul, because he probably spent his youth in Jerusalem,[7] and may, therefore, have learned his Greek there, rather than in Cilicia or Syria after his conversion (his nephew, too, could make himself understood by a Roman officer in Jerusalem: Acts 23:16-22).

Greek had been the language of the Ptolemaic and Seleucid governments. The Maccabean revolt may have caused a temporary break but Hasmonean princes could correspond with the council of Sparta, while their later coins show that Greek certainly regained its position by the side of Hebrew; the Herodians probably used Greek only, the Roman government Greek and Latin.[8] That this situation did not

---

[1] τὰ δὲ ἀπὸ μέσης τῆς προσευχῆς... Ἰουδαϊκά τινα καὶ παρακεχαραγμένα καὶ κατὰ πολὺ τῶν ἑρπετῶν ταπεινότερα. (II, 1 ed. Ziegler). He uses, however, the comparison to criticize the style of Epicurus!

[2] *CII* 1210-1387, from the second century B.C.E. to the third century C.E.

[3] *IEJ* XVII (1967), pp. 112ff., from the first century B.C.E.

[4] *CII* 1404, first century C.E.

[5] *OGIS* 598.

[6] *RH* CLXIII (1930), pp. 241ff.

[7] Cf. W. C. van Unnik, *Tarsus or Jerusalem, the City of Paul's Youth*, 1962.

[8] Cf. the Temple inscription according to Josephus: *War* V, 193-4; VI, 124-126,

change is shown by Hillel's use of the legal term προσβολή, by the Greek part of the inscription on the cross, by the Roman officers in Acts 21:37-39 and 23:16-22, and by the decree on tomb robbery probably from the time of Claudius; perhaps also by the well-known temple inscription which forbids entrance to pagans, though, more probably, Greek is here the common language of the foreigners addressed. Still later the children of the house of Gamaliel were permitted to be taught Greek 'owing to their relation with the government'.[1] We should not, therefore, be astonished that legal documents of the second century c.e., even in the region round the Dead Sea, were in Greek, such as a re-marriage contract between Jews 124 c.e.[2], a marriage contract,[3] and the various documents of the Babatha archive. The Avroman parchments, which are contracts of loan between pure Iranians are an instructive parallel: in the Parthian kingdom they were drawn up in Greek, in 88 b.c.e. and 22/21 b.c.e.[4] In all likelihood, then, the census of Luke 2:1-3 was carried out in Greek, and Pilate's conversation with Jesus may have been in Greek too.

The relevant writings as mentioned above continue only the preceding Greek-Jewish literature, which is supposed to have been composed or translated in Palestine b.c.e., such as I Maccabees, Judith, Testaments of the XII Patriarchs, Tobith, Susanna, Testament of Job, parts of I Enoch. This indicates that in first century Palestine Greek literacy and translation work rested on a tradition which may have gone back to pre-Hasmonean times.[5] We are informed about this in so many words by the additions to the Greek Esther 10:3 (1), which say that one Lysimachus of Jerusalem translated the book for the Egyptian Jews and that a priest named Dositheus took it to them by way of festival letter. The letter of Aristeas, too, says that the LXX-translators were priests from Jerusalem (ch. 47-50), and on the whole it seems more natural to suppose that if translations were necessary among Diaspora Jews, the first-class mastery of Hebrew needed for making them was hardly to be found outside Palestine. Jerusalem, then, must still have been a centre of Greek learning in the first

and the inscription on the cross of Jesus, the Hebrew(?) of which may have been exceptional.
[1] T. Sotah 15:8. Cf. P. T. Shabbath vi, 7d and T. B. Sotah 49b.
[2] DJD ii, no. 115.
[3] Ibid., no. 116.
[4] JHS xxxv (1915), pp. 22ff.
[5] See Hengel, pp. 161ff. and 186ff.

century C.E., where men like Josephus (who visited the empress Poppaea when he was only 26 years of age), James the brother of Jesus, and Paul might have acquired the command of Greek needed either for their writings or their missions. And if we are to judge from the continuity in this kind of literature, we must also conclude that the destruction of the temple and Jerusalem was not on the whole disastrous to Greek learning. In all probability it was at Jabneh, which now became the centre of Jewish studies under Johanan b. Zakkai, that instruction in literary Greek was continued. According to the Tosefta, members of the Sanhedrin should have knowledge of 70 languages, and two should be able to speak them.[1] In the Court of Jabneh four members spoke them: R. Eliezer, R. Joshua (who visited the emperor Hadrian and stayed at Athens), R. Akiba, the teacher of Aquila[2] and R. Simeon of Teman. The former two are said to have examined Aquila's translation of Scripture.[3]

We must keep in mind, however, that the main purpose of instruction in Greek was the publication of Jewish religious works and the maintaining of contacts with the Diaspora. Knowledge of Greek wisdom was not on the whole the aim. This is borne out by Josephus' statement to the effect that the Jews did not hold polyglots in high esteem, since even slaves could learn foreign languages (in Palestine?), they esteemed people 'who have an accurate knowledge of legal matters and are able to interpret the meaning (δύναμιν) of the Holy Scriptures'.[4] A century later Origen says more or less the same thing: 'Jews are not very well (or: not at all) versed in Greek literature'.[5] The passages quoted above on the teaching of Greek to the house of Gamaliel probably reflect such an aversion from Greek philosophy and literature – after the destruction of the temple – which has its parallels in the prohibitions to teach Greek wisdom or Greek as such to children, which were issued during the wars of Hyrcanus II and Aristobulus II,[6] and during the war of Quietus (117 C.E.).[7] The very fact, however, that R. Joshua (circa 100 C.E.) is asked whether Greek wisdom may be studied,[8] may underline the fact that some people wished to do so.

---

[1] T. Sanhedrin 8:1; cf. P. T. Shekalim v, 48d and T. B. Sanhedrin 17a.
[2] According to Jerome on Isaia 8:14.
[3] P. T. Megillah 1, 71c.
[4] Ant. XX, 264.
[5] οὐ πάνυ μὲν Ἰουδαῖοι τὰ Ἑλλήνων φιλολογοῦσι (Contra Celsum II, 34).
[6] T. B. Sotah 49b and T. B. Baba Kamma 82b.
[7] M. Sotah 9:14.
[8] E.g. T. Abodah Zarah 1:20.

For the final question, as to what extent Greek was used as a second language by the Jews in Palestine, we depend almost wholly on the testimony of contemporaries, or of persons who at least had first-hand knowledge about linguistic conditions in Palestine.

First of all these authors do not mention the presence of any interpreters in situations where Jews have to talk to Romans or Greeks. The conversations between Jesus and the centurion[1], between Jesus and Pilate, between Peter and Cornelius,[2] between Paul's nephew and the officer,[3] between Titus and the inhabitants of Jerusalem,[4] all give the impression of having taken place without an intermediary. So do the conversations of Jesus and Philip with the 'Greeks',[5] of Jesus with the Gerasenes and Decapolitans,[6] of Jesus with the Syro-Phoenician woman,[7] who is expressly stated to have been a Ἑλληνίς 'a Greek (speaking?) woman' or 'a pagan woman', and not a Jewes. Titus, who is sometimes suspected to have had no command of Greek, can only have conversed in that language with Josephus and certainly with the Jewish princess Berenice, who was his mistress for some time. That during a riot in Jerusalem many rioters were supposed to understand Greek is perhaps implied by Acts 22:2, because they 'became still more quiet' when unexpectedly Paul spoke to them in their own tongue. This situation is more or less paralleled by the personal exhortation to surrender which Titus addressed to Jerusalem and his subsequent request to Josephus to do the same in his own language.[8] The Roman officer's amazement at Paul's knowing Greek must be understood in its context: he had first mistaken him for an Egyptian robber who of course could not be supposed to be so well educated. We are also told that people shouted remarks at the officer in reply to his questions, probably also in Greek (21:34). All this can only mean that Greek was understood by many Jews; it does not mean that they were also able to write it well. Peter probably spoke Greek,[9] but when he wanted to write, Mark may have been his secretary according to Papias[10] ἑρμηνευτής 'translator' or merely 'interpreter'?[11]

[1] Matt. 8:5.
[2] Acts 10.
[3] Acts 23.
[4] Josephus, *War* v, 360-361.
[5] John 12:20.
[6] Matt. 4:25; Mark 3:8; 5:1; 7:31.
[7] Mark 7:26.
[8] *War* v, 360-361.
[9] Acts 10.
[10] Fragment II, 15 (ed. Funk-Bihlmeyer).   [11] Cf. fragment II, 16.

In Acts 6 and 9:29 reference is made to the special group among Jews and Christians called the Ἑλληνισταί, who according to Sevenster and others were Greek-speaking Jews,[1] in all likelihood a mixture of Jews who had returned from the Diaspora and their descendants, and Jews who had assimilated in one of the Hellenistic towns in Palestine. It is, however, doubtful whether these people were wholly monoglot, that is, devoid of any knowledge of Hebrew or Aramaic; the cardinal point may have been that their knowledge of these languages was insufficient for them to understand the reading of the Hebrew Old Testament or an Aramaic Targum. As a consequence the Scriptures had to be translated for them; in other words, after the reading of the Hebrew text, the Septuagint or another Greek 'Targum' was read to these people. Compare the case of Philo, who in his learned commentaries on the Bible always bases himself on the Septuagint. This may explain why a Greek copy of the Bible was present in the Qumran community. We also think it likely that many if not most of the ossuaries with Greek inscriptions contained the bones of deceased 'Hellenists'.[2] We must agree with Sevenster that it cannot be proved that they belonged mainly to returned exiles, whose only desire perhaps it was to be buried in Israel.[3] The Mount Ophel inscription of the ruler of the Synagogue, Theodotus son of Vettenus (the name of a Roman gens) may be from such a Hellenist, perhaps even from a Libertine i.e. a freedman who had come back from Italy.[4] The inscription on Jason's tomb, which probably fell into disuse before 37 B.C.E., is a different case; the owner may have been one of those free-spending aristocrats, who considered it normal to have an inscription in Greek in their tomb; it runs: 'Be cheerful, you who live! for the rest: drink and eat as well!'. The same holds good of Antiochus son of Phallion, who could even afford a sarcophagus; he was probably a nephew of Herod the Great and the inscription is, of course, in Greek.[5]

As we have pointed out there was ample opportunity in Palestine for Jews to assimilate in the various Hellenistic towns, in which the majority of the inhabitants were not Jewish. Schürer has given a survey of these towns,[6] and if their territories were connected on the map by a line, the Jewish area is seen to be discontinuous. The

[1] Sevenster, p. 31.
[2] In CII 76 Greek ossuaries are listed against 102 Hebrew and Aramaic ones.
[3] Sevenster, pp. 147-148.
[4] Cf. Acts 6:9. See the discussion in Sevenster, pp. 131ff.
[5] SEG VIII, 46.
[6] Schürer II, pp. 94-222.

'Hellenistic' area would be as follows: the entire coastal strip from Raphiah to Ptolemais, plus the land of the Decapolis, including the towns of Gadara (the 'Assyrian Athens');[1] Pella, Scythopolis, Gerasa (the native place of the mathematician Nicomachus) and Philadelphia. Moreover, a number of Hellenistic towns were scattered over the remaining territory: Phasaelis, in Judaea; Sepphoris and Tiberias, in Galilee; Caesarea-Philippi and Betsaida-Julias, in Batanaea; Heshbon and a second Julias in Peraea. The fragmentation of Jewish territory was still further marked by Samaria, which was shunned by the Jews,[2] except on special occasions, which were explicitly noted.[3] Moreover, its capital Sebaste was also an important Hellenistic town deriving its name from Augustus. We should also remember that Idumaea and its Hellenistic centre Marissa, Galilee and Peraea had only been Judaized by John Hyrcanus, Aristobulus I and Alexander Jannaeus, that is, for hardly more than a century.

In a linguistic territory, if we may so call the remaining Jewish country, which is so strongly fragmentated and has so many enclaves, the knowledge of Greek must have been much more widespread than the mere presence of some Greek schools and synagogues in Jerusalem might suggest. The New Testament and other testimonies point in the same direction. Moreover, the language of the aristocracy and the Roman government was Greek. Even one of the very last survivors of the revolt, a Judas in Masada, received a letter in Greek about such an ordinary affair as the supply of vegetables.[4] On the other hand, we must take care not to exaggerate: Greek remained a second language to the people at large.

Even in the Hellenistic parts we should not overestimate the number of monoglot Greek-speakers. It is true that a number of these towns have produced excellent men of (Greek) letters, like Gadara the birth-place of the poets Menippus, Meleager, and Philodemus, all three of whom contributed to the *Anthologia Palatina*, and the rhetor Theodorus, a contemporary of Strabo. Ascalon produced the grammarians Ptolemy and Dorotheus, the latter an Atticist who composed a lexicon entitled. Ἀττικαὶ Λέξεις. It was also the native place of some philosophers and historians. Josephus, however, sometimes mentions

---

[1] *Anth. Pal.* VII, 417: Ἀτθὶς ἐν Ασσυρίοις ναιομένα Γάδαρα (from a poem by Meleager who was born there).
[2] Cf. perhaps Jesus' detour in Mark 10:1.
[3] Josephus, *Ant.* xx, 18 and possibly John 4:4.
[4] *IEJ* xv (1965), p. 110.

large minorities of Jews in these towns who were slaughtered at the outbreak of the revolt; so at Caesarea Maritima and Scythopolis. In Ashdod, Jabneh, Joppa and Tiberias Jews may have outnumbered non-Jews. No doubt some Jews lived in all these towns, but apart from the last mentioned, we hear only of small minorities in Ascalon, Dora, Gadara, Gerasa and Ptolemais. And we should not think that all non-Jews in these towns spoke Greek, much less were Greek. From later times we have some information, precisely about these Hellenistic towns, which shows that Aramaic, or 'Syriac' as it is often called, was still the native language there. In Scythopolis, around 286 C.E., the Syriac version of Eusebius' *De martyribus Palaestinae* says that Procopius had to perform three tasks in the local church: Scripture reading, translation into Aramaic, and the imposition of hands for the exorcizing of demons.[1] We hear of the same thing with regard to the church in Jerusalem 385-388 C.E., from the *Peregrinatio* of Aetheria (*ch.* 47): the bishop knew 'Syriac' but preached in Greek, his sermon and the Scripture reading were translated into Syriac because only some of the audience were monoglot speakers of Greek, while the others spoke only Syriac or at best a little Greek. It need not therefore surprise us that when farther to the south, some inhabitants of Elusa asked the hermit Hilarion to bless them, they said: '*barech*' id est: 'benedic'.[2] In Gaza, as late as 402 C.E., a Christian child is reported to have said in Syriac and later in Greek that the temple of Marnas was to burn down. His mother afterwards declared that neither she nor her child spoke Greek.[3] Apparently Greek was the official language of the Church:[4] tombstones of Christians are usually in Greek, like the 140 from still later times found in the neighbourhood of Bîr-es-Seba', not far from the Elusa mentioned above.[5] They all date from the fifth and sixth century C.E., but again, this is also the time when it was still necessary for the Melkites to have the Gospel translated into 'Christian Palestinian Aramaic'. Even among the Jewish intelligentsia the mastery of Greek was not such a matter of course as we might be inclined to believe on the basis of talmudic testimonies about rabbis who were so well versed in Greek,[6] or on the

---

[1] *PG* xx, p. 1459, note 5.
[2] Jerome, *Vita Hil.* 25.
[3] Marcus Diaconus, *Vita Porphyrii*, 66-68.
[4] Bardy, p. 17.
[5] A. Alt, *Die griechischen Inschriften der Palaestina Tertia westlich der Araba* (1921).
[6] *P. T. Megillah* I, 71b; *P. T. Ketuboth* VII, 31d; *P. T. Peah* I, 15c; *Genesis Rabba* 14 (p. 127).

basis of the inscriptions of Beth Shearim, those for instance in the catacomb of the sarcophagi.[1] In connection with a damaged passage in a Greek legal document we are told that Rabbi Huna, who had come from Babylonia, it is true, did not know Greek,[2] and had to ask others about possible emendations of the numeral... κοντα.

BIBLIOGRAPHY

The interest in Koine Greek dates from Antiquity: in the time of Augustus, Minutius Pacatus and Demetrius Ixion wrote on the dialect of Alexandria, but their works are lost. The Renaissance period was mainly concerned with New Testament Greek and the question whether it was purely Attic (Purists) or not (Hebraists, the first being Erasmus). A second point of debate was whether Koine Greek was a separate dialect (Hellenistic Greek). The nineteenth century witnessed the birth of the study of Koine and modern Greek and their relationship, while Atticism was also paid attention to; moreover the Egyptian papyri were discovered, and also their linguistic resemblance to the New Testament (Deissmann). In the twentieth century there is a renewed interest in the Semitic background of the New Testament. On the history of Koine study see: J. ROS, *De studie van het Bijbelgrieksch van Hugo Grotius tot A. Deissmann* (1940); S. G. KAPSOMENOS, 'Die griechische Sprache zwischen Koine und Neugriechisch,' in *Berichte zum XI.internationalen Byzantinisten-Kongress* II, 1 (1958); H. CREMER and J. KÖGEL, *Biblisch-theologisches Wörterbuch der Neutest. Gräzität* (10th ed. 1915), pp. 1220 ff. (bibliography).

General works: A. THUMB, *Die griechische Sprache im Zeitalter des Hellenismus* (1909); F. ALTHEIM, 'Die Weltgeltung der griechischen Sprache,' in *Neue Beiträge zur Geschichte der Alten Welt* I (1964), pp. 315 ff.; W. SCHMID, *Der Atticismus in seinen Hauptvertretern* (1887-97); J. FRÖSÉN, *Prolegomena to a Study of the Greek Language in the first Centuries A.D. The Problem of Koiné and Atticism* (1974); W. MICHAELIS 'Der Attizismus und das Neue Testament,' in *ZNW* XXII (1923), pp. 91 ff.; J. VERGOTE, 'Grec Biblique' in *Dictionnaire de la Bible Supplément* III (1938), cols 1320-69 with observations on separate authors; F. BLASS and A. DEBRUNNER, *Grammatik des neutest. Griechisch* (11th ed. 1961); L. RADERMACHER, *Neutest. Grammatik. Das Griechisch des Neuen*

---

[1] *ZDPV* LXXVIII (1962), pp. 7off.
[2] *P. T. Baba Bathra* X, 17c (4th cent. C.E.).

Testaments im Zusammenhang mit der Volkssprache (2nd ed. 1925);
J. H. MOULTON, W. T. HOWARD and N. TURNER, *A Grammar of New
Testament Greek*, 3 vls. (1908-65); L. RYDBECK, *Fachprosa, vermeintliche
Volkssprache und N.T.* (1967); A. DEBRUNNER, *Geschichte der griechischen
Sprache* II: *Grundfragen und Grundzüge des nachklassischen Griechisch*
(1954); L. RADERMACHER, 'Besonderheiten der Koine-Syntax,' in
Wiener Studien XXXI (1909), pp. 1 ff.; J. HUMBERT, *La disparition du
datif en grec (du Ier au Xe siècle)* (1930).

Inscriptions on stone and graffiti: B. LIFSHITZ, 'Beiträge zur palä-
stinischen Epigraphik,' in *ZDPV* LXXVIII (1962), pp. 64 ff.; id.
L'Hellénisation des Juifs de Palestine. A propos des inscriptions de
Besara (Beth-Shearim),' in *RB* LXXII (1965), pp. 520 ff. (on the language, pp. 523-26). H. J. LEON, *The Jews of Ancient Rome* (1960),
esp.ch. 4 (language); id. 'The Jews of Venusia,' in *JQR* XLIV (1953-54),
pp. 267 ff. (pp. 274-6 language); S. APPLEBAUM, 'The Jewish community
of Hellenistic and Roman Teucheira in Cyrenaica,' in *Scripta Hierosolymitana* VII (1961), pp. 27-51 (hardly any remarks on the language,
see p. 42); H. LIETZMANN, 'Jüdisch-griechische Inschriften aus Tell el
Yehudieh,' in *ZNW* XXII (1923), pp. 280 ff. (edition with linguistic
remarks).

Numismatic inscriptions: B. V. HEAD, *Historia Nummorum* (1911), pp.
783-812 (Coele-Syria, Palestine and Arabia Petraea); G. F. HILL,
Catalogue of the Greek coins of Palestine (1914); A. REIFENBERG, *Ancient
Jewish coins* (3rd ed. 1963).

Papyri, ostraca and parchments: J. N. SEVENSTER, *Do you know Greek?
How much Greek could the first Jewish Christians have known?* (1968).
A survey of papyri outside Egypt is given by R. TAUBENSCHLAG,
'Papyri and Parchments from the Eastern Provinces of the Roman
Empire outside Egypt,' in *JJP* III (1949), pp. 49 ff. See further:
E. MAYSER, *Grammatik der griechischen Papyri aus der Ptolemäerzeit*
(1906-34); S. G. KAPSOMENAKIS, *Voruntersuchungen zu einer Grammatik
der Papyri der nachchristlichen Zeit* (1938); L. R. PALMER, *A Grammar
of the Post-Ptolemaic Papyri I: Accidence and Word Formation* (1964);
CPJ I, pp. 30-32 (about the adoption of Greek by Egyptian Jews);
A. H. SALONIUS, *Die Sprache der griechischen Papyrusbriefe* (1927);
id. *Zur Sprache der griechischen Papyrusbriefe* (1943); cf. H. LJUNGVIK
in *Eranos* XXVII (1930), pp. 166 ff.; F. PREISIGKE and E. KIESZLING,

Wörterbuch der griechischen Papyrusurkunden mit Einschluss der griechischen Inschriften, Aufschriften, Ostraca, Mumienschilder usw aus Ägypten (1925-71); J. H. MOULTON and G. MILLIGAN, *The vocabulary of the Greek Testament, illustrated from the papyri and other non-literary sources* (2nd ed. 1952).

Septuagint: G. DELLING, *Bibliographie zur jüdisch-hellenistischen und intertestamentarischen Literatur 1900-1965* (1969); H. st JOHN THACKERAY, *A grammar of the Old Testament in Greek according to the Septuagint* I: 'Introduction, Orthography and Accidence' (1909); R. HELBING, *Grammatik der Septuaginta. Laut- und Wortlehre* (1907); F. M. ABEL, *Grammaire du grec biblique suivi d'un choix de papyrus* (1927); M. JOHANNESSOHN, *Der Gebrauch der Kasus und der Präpositionen in der Septuaginta* I: *Gebrauch der Kasus* (1910); R. HELBING, *Die Kasussyntax der Verba bei den Septuaginta. Ein Beitrag zur Hebraismenfrage und zur Syntax der Koine* (1928). On translation Greek see: J. M. RIFE, 'The Mechanics of Translation Greek,' in *JBL* LII (1933), pp. 3 ff.; H. S. GEHMAN, 'The Hebrew Character of Septuagint Greek,' in *Vetus Testamentum* I (1951), pp. 81 ff.; R. A. MARTIN, 'Some Syntactical Criteria of Translation Greek,' in *Vetus Testamentum* X (1960), pp. 295 ff.; id. 'Syntactical Evidence of Aramaic Sources in Acts I-XV,' in *NTS* XI (1964-5), pp. 38 ff.

Semitizing non-translated works: H. PERNOT, *Études sur la langue des Évangiles* (1927); J. C. DOUDNA, *The Greek of the Gospel of Mark* (1961); M. ZERWICK, *Untersuchungen zum Markus-Stil* (1937); S. ANTONIADIS, *L'Évangile de Luc. Esquisse de grammaire et de style* (1930); E. A. ABBOTT, *Johannine grammar* (1906); E. C. COLWELL, *The Greek of the Fourth Gospel* (1931), rejects Aramaisms, see p. 12; J. DE ZWAAN, 'The use of the Greek language in Acts' in *The beginnings of Christianity* II, ch.2 (1922); M. BLACK, *An Aramaic approach to the Gospels and Acts* (3rd ed. 1967); M. WILCOX, *The Semitisms of Acts* (1965); R. A. MARTIN, 'Syntactical Evidence of Aramaic Sources in Acts I-XV,' in *NTS* XI (1964-5), pp. 38 ff.; R. H. CHARLES, *The Revelation of St. John* I (1920), pp. CXVII ff.; F. G. MUSSIES, *The Morphology of Koine Greek as Used in the Apocalypse of St. John* (1971); K. BEYER, *Semitische Syntax im Neuen Testament* I: *Satzlehre* (1962); M. SILVA, *Semantic Change and Semitic Influence in the Greek Bible* (1972), cf. *NTS* XXII (1975), pp. 104-10.

Non-Semitizing and Non-Atticizing Literature: H. G. MEECHAM, *The Letter of Aristeas, a Linguistic Study with Special Reference to the Greek Bible* (1935), on pp. 325-8 a lexicilogical comparison between Aristeas and the fragments of Aristobulus and Eupolemus); T. NÄGELI, *Der Wortschatz des Apostels Paulus* (1905); R. BULTMANN, *Der Stil der paulinischen Predigt und die kynisch-stoische Diatribe* (1910); A. WIFTRAND, 'Stylistic problems in the Epistles of James and Peter,' in *Studia Theologica* I (1947-8), pp. 170-182. For Barnabas see : H. REINHOLD, *De graecitate patrum apostolicorum* (1898) .

Atticizing literature: L. TREITEL, *De Philonis Judaei sermone* (1872); J. JESSEN, *De elocutione Philonis Alexandrini* (1889); L. COHN, *Philonis Alexandrini libellus De opificio mundi* (1889), pp. XLI ff.: 'Observationes de sermone Philonis'; C. SIEGFRIED, *Philo von Alexandria als Ausleger des Alten Testaments. Nebst Untersuchungen über die Gräcität Philo's* (1875), pp. 32-136: lexicological; W. SCHMIDT, *De Flavii Iosephi elocutione observationes criticae* (1893); H. St JOHN THACKERAY, *Josephus the Man and the Historian* (2nd ed. 1967), pp. 100 ff.: 'Josephus and Hellenism: his Greek assistants,'; B. SNELL, 'Die Jamben in Ezechiels Moses-Drama,' in *Glotta* XLIV (1966), pp. 25 ff.; id. 'Ezechiels Moses-Drama,' in *Antike und Abendland* XIII (1967), pp. 150 ff. esp. p. 151; E. OLDENBURGER, *De oraculorum Sibyllinorum elocutione* (1903).

Greek loan words: S. KRAUSS, *Griechische und Lateinische Lehnwörter im Talmud, Midrasch und Targum* (1898), cf. G. ZUNTZ in *JSS* I (1956), pp. 129 ff. and H. ROSÉN in *JSS* III (1963), pp. 56 ff.; S. LIEBERMAN, *Greek in Jewish Palestine. Studies in the Life and Manners of Jewish Palestine in the II-IV Centuries C.E.* (1942); id. *Hellenism in Jewish Palestine* (1950); M. SMITH, *Tannaitic Parallels to the Gospels* (1951), ch.1.

Greek names: M. HENGEL, *Judentum und Hellenismus. Studien zu ihrer Begegnung unter besonderer Berücksichtigung Palästinas bis zur Mitte des 2.Jahrh.v.Chr.* (1969), pp. 114 ff.: 'Das Vordringen griechischer Namen'. Egypt: *CPJ* I, pp. 27-30; Rome: H. J. LEON, *The Jews of Ancient Rome* (1960), ch. 5; Venosa: H. J. LEON, 'The Jews of Venusia,' in *JQR* XLIV (1953-4), p. 280.

Greek in Palestine: The works by Sevenster and Lieberman mentioned above; besides: A. SCHÜRER II pp. 84-9; Th. ZAHN, *Einleitung in das Neue Testament* I (3rd ed. 1906), pp. 1-52; G. DALMAN, *Worte Jesu*

(2nd ed. 1930); H. BIRKELAND, *The language of Jesus* (1954), pp. 16 f.; H. OTT, 'Um die Muttersprache Jesu,' in *Novum Testamentum* IX (1967), pp. 1 ff., survey of research 1930-1965; G. BARDY, La question des langues dans l'Église ancienne (1948), pp. 1-18, first—fifth century Palestine.

Greek in the Diaspora: K. TREU, 'Die Bedeutung des Griechischen für die Juden im römischen Reich', in *Festschrift für Endre Ivánka* (1973-4), pp. 123-44.

Chapter Twenty Three

Paganism in Palestine

At no time in history was Judaism the only religion of Palestine. In the time of the First Temple, though paganism and pagans were strictly proscribed by the Bible, there were not only pagans in the country, but their influence was so strong that many Israelites did not escape it. The pagans were still there in the Second Temple era, there was an influx of Greek and Roman colonists in the Hellenistic and then in the Roman period, and Greek cities were founded. The local paganism and its gods were Hellenized, and new additions made to the pantheon. In the first century, therefore, there were three elements to be reckoned with: the paganism of the Hellenized Cannaanite population, that of the Macedonian and Greek settlers and an influence from Roman paganism.

There had been a two-way movement in ancient times. Greek paganism, as is well known, was influenced by the oriental religions, and the local gods were then identified with Greek gods, very often with the same gods as had influenced the Greek ones. To show how the process worked, we may instance the city of Beth Shean, which was then called Scythopolis in Greek. In the Hellenistic and the Roman periods, until the Jewish war broke out, relations between Jews and pagans in the city were very good. Judas Maccabeus marched against Scythopolis, 'but when the Jews who dwelt there bore witness to the good will which the people of Scythopolis had shown them and their kind treatment of them in times of misfortune, they thanked them and exhorted them to be well disposed to their race in the future also'.[1] Even during the pogroms which the Jewish war occasioned, relations were still so good, in contrast to what was going on elsewhere, that the Jewish citizens took the side of their pagan fellows, and sallied out along with them against the rebellious Jews who were attacking the city. In the end, however, they were surprised by the pagans and slaughtered.[2] Beth Shean could also be called *Skython*

[1] 2 Macc. 12:29-30.
[2] On this and the following, see Schürer II, pp. 170-3.

polis, the 'city of the Scythians', which suggests that Scythians had once occupied it. The Byzantine historian George Syncellus who had good sources at his disposal, says that the Scythians had invaded Palestine and conquered the city of Beth Shean, which was therefore called Scythopolis.[1] The 'Hegesippus', a 4th century Christian of Jewish origin[2] who produced a Latin recension of Josephus' Jewish War, says that the city was dedicated to the Scythian Artemis, because it was founded by the Scythians and named after them.[3] This seems to be more than mere etymology and suggests that the city had had a temple of Artemis. Even so, erudite speculation had something to do with the statement, because the notion of a Scythian Artemis comes from the *Iphigenia in Tauris* of Euripides. 'Hegesippus' picked up the learned surmise somewhere. It is also in the *Chronicle* (*Chronography*) of John Malalas, c. 491-578, an author who had good sources but used them carelessly.[4] His version is that when Thoas, king of Scythia, heard that Iphigenia had taken the golden statue of Artemis and fled with it, he sent out a large number of Scythians in pursuit, telling them not to come back if they could not produce the statue. They looked everywhere and so finally came to Palestine, to the town of Nysa, formerly called Tricomia. There they heard that Iphigenia and Orestes had reached the sea-coast and sailed off, so finding the place to their liking and being afraid to go back to the king, they settled down in the city, which they then called Scythopolis. Another thing they liked in it was its shrine to Artemis—which is the second reference to the worship of the goddess there.

Syncellus says the Scythians were invaders from Scythia, and Herodotus (I, 105) had spoken of such an invasion in the 7th century B.C.E. Possibly a group of such Scythians had settled in Beth Shean, but there are historians with grave doubts about the reliability of Herodotus here. The town could have got the name from Scythian colonists of a later date, maybe in the Persian or Hellenistic period. Scythians were renowned as archers and horsemen throughout the whole of antiquity. It is therefore possible that there was a core of veterans from Scythian units among the colonists settled in Beth Shean and the neighbourhood

---

[1] Syncellus I, 405.
[2] See *Hegesippi qui dicitur Historia libri quinque*, ed. V. Ussani, vol. II, praefationem Caroli Mras ... continens *CSEL*, (1960), p. XXXI-XXXVII.
[3] Op.cit. vol. III (1932), p. 19.
[4] Malalas, ed. W. Dindorf (1831), p. 140. See also Kedrenos, ed. A. Bekker vol. I, p. 237, and M. Avi-Yonah, 'Scythopolis,' in *IEJ* XII (1962), p. 126.

by Ptolemy II. Avi-Yonah has suggested a very probable date.[1] One of the *Zeno Papyri*, dated 21 September 254 B.C.E., says that Zeno was called upon to look after an embassy from Pairisades, King of Bosporus, on its way to Egypt. The Scythians in the Ptolemies' armies were probably subjects of this king. Possibly the embassy took the opportunity of settling some Scythians at Beth Shean, in the autumn of 254 B.C.E., and the town was given its new name.

One derivation supplied for the name has some interest here. It links Beth Shean with Greek mythology and the worship of Dionysos. According to Pliny the Elder, the town was once called Nysa, and the geographical lexicon of Stephanus of Byzantium (sixth century C.E.) says: 'Scythopolis, a city in Palestine, or the Nyssa of Coele-Syria'.[2] According to the coins from Beth Shean, the inhabitants were known as 'Nysaean Scythopolitans'.[3] This has a long history behind it, because we read in the *Iliad*[4] that Lycurgus 'drove away the nurses of the divine Dionysos to the sacred mount of Nysa (κατ' ἠγάθεον Νυσήιον). So Nysa, which has some connection with the name of the god, then became part of mythology, and the legendary place was sought in remote parts of the world.[5] Diodorus Siculus makes Arabia one of the possible sites (III, 4), where he also put the graves of Isis and Osiris (I, 27). This may be a pointer towards Beth Shean. Pliny explicitly links the Homeric myth with the latter place, saying that Scythopolis was once called Nysa because Dionysos buried his nurse there, having first brought Scythians to the place.[6] Solinus, who re-wrote much of Pliny, is more prolix: 'When Dionysos had buried his nurse, he founded the city, to make the burial-place more famous by giving it the more extensive walls of a city. There were no inhabitants, so he selected some of his followers, the Scythians, to settle it, and rewarded them by calling the city after them, to encourage them to hold out'.[7] This legend, therefore, makes Nysa Dionysos'

[1] See Avi-Yonah, loc.cit., pp. 123-34.
[2] Pliny, *Natural History* v, 18, 74. See below, note 5.
[3] Schürer II, p. 56. The whole quotation from Stephanus, Schürer II, p. 170.
[4] *Iliad* VI, 130-2. See also the Homeric Hymn to Dionysos XXVI, 5.
[5] Jane Harrison, *Prolegomena to the Study of Greek Religion* (3rd ed. 1922), pp. 367, 379-9; Guthrie, p. 160-1; Nilsson I, p. 628; II, p. 567, 581, 590; Apollodorus, *Bibliotheca*, ed. J. G. Fraser, vol. I, p. 321 and note 5 there (vol. III, 4, 3).
[6] Pliny, *Natural History* v, 18, 74: 'Scythopolim, antea, a Libero patre sepulta nutrice ibi Scythis deductis.'
[7] Solinus, ed. T. Mommsen, ch. 36: 'Liber pater cum humo nutricem tradidisset, condidit hoc oppidum, ut sepulturae titulum etiam urbis moenibus ampliaret. Incolae deerant: e comitibus suis Scythas delegit, quos ut animi firmaret ad promptam resistendi violentiam, praemium loci nomen dedit.'

nurse, who was buried by the god himself in Beth Shean and gave a new name to the city, which was finally called Scythopolis because of the Scythians put there to protect it.

What might be the kernel of fact behind this strange legend of the founding of a Palestinian city? The connection between the name Scythopolis and a group of Scythian colonists seems almost certain. And it is not surprising to find Scythians in Dionysos' train. Herodotus says that there were Scythians who celebrated a feast in honour of the god every three years, accompanying it with Bacchic dances: and that the Scythian king, Scytes, having become a devotee of the god, was driven out and killed by his people when they saw him in a frenzy along with his Bacchic rout.[1] The Scythian religion had markedly shamanistic traits. Hence it is quite possible that the Scythians brought one of their gods with them to Beth Shean, who was then identified with the Greek Dionysos.[2]

Since relations there were good for a time between Jews and pagans, it is conceivable that this was the place where the notion took hold that Dionysos was the real god of the Jews. Plutarch has his proofs for it, namely that the fast day (Day of Atonement) is celebrated at the time of the vintage, and is followed by the feast of Tabernacles. The huts are mostly constructed of vine and ivy branches, and there are many sorts of fruit on the tables and a procession to the Temple bearing the *thyrsos*—a Dionysiac emblem here identified with the *lulab*. The small trumpets are also linked with the worship of Dionysos and even the name of the Levites is given a fancy etymology for the same reason. So too with the word sabbath, apropos of which Plutarch says that the Jews invite each other to drink and make merry with wine, or if that is impossible they sip a little wine. The opening blessing of the sabbath thus becomes a sort of bacchanalia. The conclusive proof that the God of the Jews was really Dionysos is, according to Plutarch, or rather, his sources, to be found in the high priest's vestments. Another proof is that no honey was used in the temple liturgy. The resemblance between the *thyrsos* and the *lulab* is so great that even Jewish writers translate the latter by *thyrsos*.[3]

The worship of Dionysos was introduced into the desecrated Temple by Antiochus Epiphanes in 167 B.C.E. 'When the feast of Dionysos

---

[1] Nilsson I, p. 575; Herodotus IV, 79-80, 108.
[2] Plutarch, *Quaestiones convivales* IV 5, 2-6, 2; M. Stern, *Greek and Latin Authors on Jews and Judaism* I (1974), no. 258, pp. 546, 552-4, 556-62.
[3] See Stern, op.cit., p. 561.

came, the Jews were compelled to walk in the procession in honour of Dionysos, wearing wreaths of ivy'.[1] But this was only a brief aberration, and certainly could not have given pagans the idea that the Jews were really worshippers of Dionysos. And the comparison between the rites, along the lines drawn by Plutarch, was far too widely known to be explained in this way.[2] It was still familiar to the Byzantine writer John Lydos, from whose confused descriptions of antiquity some important pointers can be drawn: he mentions the bunch of golden grapes in the Temple and its purple and scarlet veil.[3] Tacitus too knows that the Jews were thought to worship Dionysos after his conquest of the East, since it was known that the Jewish priests chanted to the accompaniment of flutes and drums and wore wreaths of ivy and that a bunch of golden grapes had been found in the Temple.[4] But Tacitus disliked the Jews too much to accept this idea. There was no connection between the two religions, that of Dionysos containing solemn and joyous rites, while that of the Jews was silly and dirty.

According to one theory the comparison was due to the identification of the God of the Jews with the Thracian-Phrygian god Sabazios, who was himself often understood to be Dionysos.[5] Valerius Maximus says that the Jews were expelled from Italy (139 B.C.E) 'for having tried to infect Roman customs with the worship of Zeus Sabazios'.[6] Some scholars think that Sabazios had been—falsely—identified with *sabaoth*. But it is easier to suppose that the God of the Jews was first identified with Dionysos in Beth Shean, where Dionysos was an important figure and the Jews enjoyed exemplary relations with their pagan neighbours. More than a surmise, however, this cannot be.

The ancient name of the town, Beth Shean, occurs as early as the time of Pharaoh Thutmose III (1500-1450), meaning undoubtedly the sanctuary of the god Shean. Possibly he was really called Zan, like Zeus in Crete. The god may have been brought in by a non-Canaanite group. At any rate, the Philistines, part of the 'Peoples of the Sea' and probably, as is often held, from Crete, were certainly there later. More important for our present purpose is that a stele has been found

---

[1] 2 Macc. 6:7.
[2] See Stern, op.cit., p. 560.
[3] Lydus, *De Mensibus* IV, 53, p. 109. See Stern, op.cit., p. 560.
[4] *Histories* V, 5.
[5] See Stern, op.cit., pp. 560, 359.
[6] Ibid., no. 147b, p. 358, Valerius Maximus, *Facta et Dicta Memorabilia* I, 3, 3.

in Beth Shean, displaying the Egyptian architect Amen-em-Opet and his son as they adore 'Mekal, the god of Beth-Shean'. Both in appearance and clothing, Mekal is clearly Asiatic.[1] Originally, he need not have been a Canaanite god. At any rate, a bi-lingual inscription at Idalion in Cyprus identifies him with the Phoenician-Canaanite god Resheph,[2] who appears as a foreign, Asiatic god in Egyptian inscriptions also.[3] Amen-hotep II is said to have crossed the dangerous waters of the Orontes like Resheph. And elsewhere the Egyptians praise Resheph as 'the great God, the Lord of Heaven, the Ruler of the Ennead and the Lord of eternity'. The warriors in the chariots are said to be 'as mighty as Reshephs', who was evidently regarded as a fearsome and powerful god.

Some light is also thrown on his nature by biblical texts, where the word *resheph* occurs, but only in highly poetical contexts. This means that it came from Canaanite poetry. In the Bible it means plague, pestilence, and also flame and fire. And the great Canaanite god Resheph, known from the Ras-Shamra texts and an Aramaic inscription from Syria, is a baneful god who brings plague and pestilence, a devouring fire whose arrows are terrible.[4] He was worshipped by the Phoenicians and Carthaginians, and his fame reached Egypt. Apollo is an obvious parallel, with the dark side to his character which made him the god of pestilence, loosing deadly arrows, while at the same time so lightsome that he was linked with the sun as early as Aeschylus.[5] The identification of Resheph and Apollo, made on two inscriptions at Tamassus in Cyprus,[6] is not merely due to their similarity. Apollo is actually Resheph, at least to some extent. A bi-lingual inscription at Idalion, also in Cyprus, is dedicated in the Greek to 'Apollo Amyclus' and in the Semitic text to 'Resheph Mekal' (רשף מכל). Mekal we know from the Beth Shean inscription, and the identification with Resheph, which has survived only by accident in Cyprus and was later forgotten,

---

[1] Pritchard, *Ancient Near East in Pictures*, p. 249.
[2] Schürer II, p. 133, n. 159.
[3] Pritchard, pp. 244-5, 250.
[4] See now the article on *Resheph* by S. Loewenstamm, in *E.B.* It was still known, as late as *T. B. Berakoth* 5a, that *reshaphim* were either harmful demons or sufferings.
[5] Apollo, the god of illness and death, is also of course the safeguard against illnesses. Up to present, the best discussion of his ambivalent nature is to be found in Macrobius (c. 400 C.E.), where it is well documented (*Saturnalia* I, 17, 9-26). He bases himself, naturally, on the identification of Apollo with the sun, as was the common view in his times.
[6] Schürer II, p. 133, n. 159.

gave rise to the baneful elements of Apollo's character. The influence of Resheph was already at work in the Mycenaean period.

Resheph-Mekal is translated as Apollo Amyclos. Amyclai was a place where Apollo Hyacinthos had been revered since Mycenaean times, Hyacinthos being a pre-Grecian god later identified with Apollo. The later legend was that Apollo had accidentally killed a youth called Hyacinthos. This means that the Mycenaean god, Apollo Amyclos, was a killer. Further, the inscription does not say Apollo Amyclaios but Apollo Amyclos, which means that the name of the town was derived from Amyclos and not vice versa. So too Athens from Athene. It follows that the epithet Amyclos is not derived from the name of the city of Amyclai, but a Greek way of transliterating the Canaanite Mekal, the Graeco-Mycenaean form of the name. In other words, Resheph was identified with the Mekal whom we know from the stele of Beth Shean; or perhaps Mekal was originally another name for Resheph or an epithet which could be added. In Greek, Mekal supplied the epithet Amyclos for Apollo, which gave the town Amyclai its name, where the Apollo in question was also designated by the pre-Grecian name of Hyacinthos. It was in this way that the Canaanite god Resheph came to the Mycenaean Achaeans, and so Apollo became the bright but sinister god whose swift and deadly arrows brought plague and pestilence. How far this latter element remained characteristic of Apollo in later times cannot be gone into here.

This investigation was necessary because Resheph came back once more from Greece to his original country and was still known in our period. Pliny the Elder mentions the city of Apollonia in his description of Palestine.[1] Josephus tells us that in the time of Alexander Jannaeus it was in Jewish territory and was re-built by the Roman governor Gabinius.[2] According to the distances indicated by the Peutinger chart, Apollonia must have been on the site of present-day Arsuf, which is an Arabic name derived from that of the god Resheph. We cannot now tell what was the original Semitic name of the place,[3] but in any case the name Apollonia was connected with Resheph.

[1] *Natural History* v, 69. See Schürer II, pp. 132-4; Stern, op.cit., p. 474.
[2] *Ant.* XIII, 395; *War* I, 166.
[3] The place is now called Rishpon. This is based on H. Winkler's hypothesis, that the name Rishpun is to be read in Tiglat-Pileser's inscription. It is now known from parallel texts that this reading is incorrect (communication from H. Tadmor). But the identification of Arsuf and Apollonia still stands, as already proposed by Clermont-Ganneau.

Hence it was known in the locality that Apollo was Resheph. We do not know whether Apollonia was an ancient Canaanite city which had been Hellenized or a city founded in Hellenistic times. If it was a Hellenistic foundation, the name Apollonia must have later been translated back again, by the local Semitic population, into a name deriving from the god Resheph. Or the city was founded in the Seleucid period by the Phoenicians, who at the time were installed in the coastal regions as far south as Dor. In this case, the two names, the Semitic with the Resheph element, and the Greek Apollonia, would be one of the outcomes of the symbiosis of Phoenician and Hellenistic elements in Palestine.

Another very interesting example of the survival of Canaanite religions in Palestine is the worship of Baal Carmel, which is now particularly instructive as the result of recent discoveries.[1] The small collection in the possession of the monastery on Mount Carmel includes a marble fragment from the foot of a statue, which was from 3 to 3.5 metres high. The foot is on a partially-preserved base, which contains the following inscription: '[Dedicated to] the Heliopolitan Zeus Carmelos [by] G. Jul[ios] Eutychas, colonist from Caesarea'.[2] The inscription is from the end of the second century C.E. or perhaps from the beginning of the third. The name indicates that the devotee was a Greek or a Hellenized native, perhaps of Phoenician origin. The 'Gaius Julius' part of his name shows that his family had obtained Roman citizenship under the Julian dynasty, perhaps in the time of Augustus, when Caesarea was founded, or perhaps even earlier. More important than the man is the god to whom the statue was dedicated, and his epithets. The god Carmel is well known, especially for having predicted a brilliant future for Vespasian.[3] Since Tacitus affirms that there was neither statue nor temple, but only an altar on Mount Carmel (hill and god having the same name), Eutychas must have built the outsize statue after the historian's time. The god of Carmel had already been identified with Zeus by the geographer Scylax, and Zeus

[1] See M. Avi-Yonah, 'Mount Carmel and the God of Baalbak,' in *IEJ* II (1952), pp. 118-24. See also K. Galling, 'Der Gott Karmel und die Ächtung fremder Götter', in *Geschichte und Altes Testament; A. Alt zum 70. Geburtstag* (1953), p. 105-25.
[2] This important inscription reads:
ΔΙΙ ΗΛΙΟΠΟΛΕΙΤΗ ΚΑΡΜΗΛΩ, Γ. ΙΟΥΛ. ΕΥΤΥΧΑΣ. ΚΟΛ. ΚΑΙΣΑΡΕΥΣ.
[3] See Avi-Yonah, op.cit., p. 119-20; Schürer, Vermes, Millar I, p. 613-4. The texts are: Tacitus, *Hist.* II, 78f.; Suetonius, *Vespasianus* 5. Iamblichus, *Vita Pythagorae* III, 15, where the sacred hill of Carmel is linked with the life of Pythagoras, is also important.

is the Zeus of Heliopolis, Baalbek in Syria, in our inscription. Macrobius says, correctly, that the god of Heliopolis is none other than Hadad, which is another way of saying Baal.[1] We know from the Bible that he was worshipped on Carmel, so Elijah's feat merely interrupted the worship for a moment. The Phoenicians took it up again, so that one of the priests, with the Greek name Basilides (his Phoenician name being apparently a compound of *m-l-k*), could prophesy Vespasian's success. Since the Baal of Carmel, 'Carmelos', was identified with Zeus, while it had not been forgotten that he was really Hadad, he could later be identified with the Hadad of Baalbek, and be called in our inscription 'the Heliopolitan Zeus, Carmelos'. This is another proof of the hardiness of the local religions.

Macrobius knows that the goddess who is linked with Hadad is called Atargatis. The names appear together on a Greek inscription from the same region as the previous one.[2] It was found in Kafr Yassif, a village 9 kilometres north-west of Accho, the ancient Ptolemais, and is from Hellenistic times, probably about 150 B.C.E. It reads as follows: '[This altar was dedicated] to Adad and Atargatis, the gods who answer prayer, by Diodotos, son of Neoptolemos, on his own behalf and on behalf of his wife Philista and his children, in fulfilment of a vow'.[3] Diodotos and Philista are purely Greek names, so their bearers were Greeks or Macedonians, probably colonists from Ptolemais. There is a votive inscription from the same period from Samaria, dedicated to Sarapis and Isis by Hegesandros and Xenarchis and their children,[4] people with purely Greek names. But Isis and Sarapis were universally revered at the time, while Hadad and Atargatis were local Aramaic divinities. The inscription does not identify Hadad and Atargatis with Greek gods, which means that the ancient religions not merely survived in the Phoenician regions around Ptolemais but were adopted by the Greeks. Atargatis was also worshipped in Gaza, Joppa and especially in Ascalon.

---

[1] Macrobius, *Saturnalia* 1, 23, 10-19. In par. 17 he explains the name Adad as *unus unus*. Hence the popular etymology is Aramaic: חד חד.
[2] See M. Avi-Yonah, 'Syrian Gods at Ptolemais-Accho,' in *IEJ* IX (1959), p. 1-12. A later inscription, probably from the first century C.E., is to be published by A. Ovadya. It is on an altar dedicated to Atargatis, in the Golan.
[3] The inscription reads:
[Α]ΔΑΔΩΙ ΚΑΙ ΑΤΑΡΓΑΤΕΙ ΘΕΟΙΣ ΕΠΗΚΟΟΙΣ. ΔΙΟΔΟΤΟΣ ΝΕΟΠΤΟΛΕΜΟΥ. ΥΠΕΡ ΑΥΤΟΥ ΚΑΙ ΦΙΛΙΣΤΑΣ. ΤΗΣ ΓΥΝΑΙΚΟΣ ΚΑΙ ΤΩΝ. ΤΕΚΝΩΝ ΤΟΝ ΒΩΜΟΝ. ΚΑΤΕΥΧΗΝ.
[4] See J. W. Crowfoot, G. M. Crowfoot, M. Kenyon, 'The Objects from Samaria,' in *Samaria-Sebaste* III (1957), no. 13, pl. V, 1.

Another example of the survival of local divinities is the Idumaean god Kos.[1] The Idumaeans, as we know, were forced to adopt the Jewish religion by the Hasmonaean kings. When Herod came to the throne, he recognized Kostobaros as governor of Idumaea, gave him his sister Salome in marriage[2] and finally executed him, in 25 B.C.E. Kostobaros belonged to one of the noblest families of Idumaea, and his forefathers were priests of Koze (Κωζέ), 'adored as god by the Idumaeans', as Josephus says. So, at the time, many Idumaeans had retained their native religion. In earlier times, a king of Edom had the name Kos-geber,[3] which was probably the real name of Herod's brother-in-law, which is reached by a very slight change in the Greek majuscule script, from T to G.[4] Josephus says that 'Kosgobar's' forefathers were priests of Koze, who scholars think was a different god, found under the name of Quzah among the pagan Arabs.[5] If Josephus is right, and if there were really two such gods, the Idumaeans must have identified Kos with Koze.

According to Josephus, Kosgobar had plotted with Cleopatra, in the hope of gaining his independence with regard to Herod. In the same context (*Ant.* xv, 255), Josephus writes that Kosgobar thought that it was not well for Idumaeans to adopt Jewish customs. When this cautious expression is taken in combination with the fact that Kosgobar's forefathers were pagan priests, there is much to be said for the following surmise put forward by the medieval author who produced a Hebrew version, revised, of Josephus, under the title of *Josippon*.[6] Here we read that when endeavouring to free the Idumaeans from Jewish rule, Kosgobar 'installed the ancient idol of Edom'.[7] The medieval

[1] Th. C. Vriezen, 'The Edomitic Deity Qaus,' in *Oudtestamentische Studien* xiv (1940-65), pp. 330-53.

[2] Josephus, *Ant.* xv, 253-66.

[3] See Vriezen, loc.cit., pp. 330-1.

[4] See Josephus, *Works*, ed. R. Marcus and A. Wikgren, vol. viii (Loeb Classical Library, 1963), p. 119, where it is proposed, with other scholars, to change the name into Kosgabaros. Kosgobaros seems to us graphically easier and linguistically possible. But then Kostobaros, the name of a relative of king Agrippa, hence also an Idumaean (see Index to Josephus) must also be correspondingly changed. Vriezen also adduces instances of the name Qaus—gabri from Mesopotamia, op.cit., p. 131-2.

[5] Vriezen, op.cit., p. 334-5.

[6] For an account of this work, see D. Flusser, 'Der lateinische Josephus und der hebräische Josippon,' in *Josephus-Studien, Festschrift für Otto Michel* (1974), pp. 122-32.

[7] In my critical edition (now in the press), *Josippon*, ch. 49, lines 4-6; Josippon, ad fidem editionis ... Mantuae ante annum 1480 impressae, ed. Günzburg (1913), p. 297.

writer understood what Josephus had really meant, that Kosgobar was aiming at freedom and the re-establishment of the god of his priestly forefathers.

The worship of Kos was not confined to Edom. Up to the Persian period, there were personal names in ancient Mesopotamia containing Kos as an element. This is also true of the Nabataeans, from the fourth to the second century B.C.E., and the pre-Islamic Arabs were acquainted with the god. The name is also found in a tannaitic text from the Cairo Geniza.[1] Of the pagan divinities it says: ''You shall destroy their names' (Deut. 12:3). Change their names! When you hear the name Gadya, call it Gallya (dung); when you hear the name Pene-Baal (Face of Baal), call it Face of a Dog; when you hear the name Ein Kos (Well of Kos), call it Ein Koz (Well of Thorn).'[2]

We have already spoken of the Idumaean Kos. Gadya (or Gad) is an Aramaic name for the tutelary deity of men or places. It also occurs among the Nabataeans and is often mentioned in texts from Palmyra.[3] Gadya may also be a translation back into the original form, of a corresponding Greek Tyche or Roman Genius. The place called Gadyon, in Mishnah *Zabim* 1:5, is named after this god.[4] Undoubtedly, the most interesting name in the list is Pene-Baal (Face of Baal). 'The Face' (*panim*) is a hypostasis of God even in the Bible, where Gen. 32:24-40 shows how the face of the divinity can be given concrete form of a man. Hence the place where Jacob wrestled with the Man is called Peniel or Penuel, God's Face. Canaanite religion also had a person as hypostasis of Baal. Pene-Baal is the standard name of the Punic goddess Tanit, the wife of Baal Hammon.[5] In

---

[1] Published by S. Schechter in *JQR* XVII (1904), pp. 146-52, 695-7. The text was reprinted in *Midrasch Tannaim*, ed. by D. Z. Hoffmann. Our passage is on p. 60. There is a parallel to it in *T. B. Abodah Zarah* 43a, where we correct the meaningless בריה into גדיה, and read three times שמם instead of שמה.

[2]

ואבתם את שמם, שנה את שמם

שמעת ששמם גדייה, קרא שמם גלליא

שמעת שמם פני בעל, קרא שמם פני כלב

שמעת שמם עין כוס, קרא שמם עין קוץ

I owe the reference to Z. Safrai.

[3] See J. Starcky, in *Dictionnaire de la Bible, Supplement* VII, p. 1000.

[4] The correct reading seems to be 'from Gadion to Shilo', not 'to Shiloach,' i.e. Siloam in Jerusalem.

[5] See B. H. Warmington, *Carthage* (1964), pp. 156-8; Y. Yadin, 'Symbols of Deities at Zinjirly, Carthage and Hazor,' in *Essays in Honor of Nelson Glueck, Near Eastern Archaeology in the XXth Century* (1970), pp. 199-231, esp. pp. 216-24.

Carthage, the greatest of the Punic cities in North Africa, a Phoenician colony, Tanit is well attested from the fifth century B.C.E. on. How did she come to be termed Pene-Baal? Ought she be identified with the Canaanite Astarte (Ashtoret)? In the Ras Shamra texts, Astarte never appears as the wife of Baal, but the Tyrian religion links Astarte with Adodos (Hadad—Baal) and says that the couple were installed by Kronos (El) as rulers of the land[1]—and Tyre had given the first settlers to Carthage. Astarte is twice termed Shem-Baal (the Name of Baal), in a formula of malediction from Ras Shamra, and on the sarcophagus of a king of Sidon,[2] which means that Astarte is a sort of personification of Baal, just as Tanit is Baal's Face in Carthage. The goddess Pene-Baal was still worshipped as wife of Baal Hammon in Roman times, as appears from a votive inscription from Dacia, where someone from Palmyra addresses the divine couple as his native gods (*dii patrii*).[3] The same goddess, who was then called Tanit in Carthage, seems to have been already worshipped in the Canaanite town of Hazor. Some masks found there have parallels in Carthage, and so depict the goddess as the Face of Baal. And further, a shrine in Hazor (14th-13th century B.C.E.) contained a stele showing two raised arms supporting a circle with a lunar crescent. The latter is taken to be a symbol for Baal Hammon, while the two raised arms would be a stylization of the well-known symbol for the goddess Tanit, the outlines of a female figure with raised arms. The Canaanite origin of the goddess Tanit or Pene-Baal is also indicated by a discovery made to the south of Ashdod, which has produced a lead weight with the symbol for Tanit. But for our present purpose it should also be noted that the symbol is found on Roman coins from Ascalon, along with the image of a goddess and the Greek inscription φανηβαλος (Pene-Baal).[4] The coins are from the time of Augustus, Hadrian and Antoninus Pius. Thus the goddess was still revered in her Asiastic homeland in Roman times. This is proved by the coins from Ascalon, the votive inscription from Dacia and the rabbinical text where Pene-Baal appears as a divine name—designating an important goddess.

[1] See Eusebius, *Praeparatio Evangelica* I, 10, 31 (ed. K. Mras, vol. I, p. 49) and S. E. Loewenstamm, in *P. W. Suppl.* XIV, p. 594.
[2] I owe this reference to S. E. Loewenstamm.
[3] The inscription reads: 'Diis patriis Malagbet et Bebelamon et Benephal et Manawat.' See Y. Yadin, op.cit., p. 229, n. 92.
[4] See Y. Yadin, op.cit., and G. F. Hill, *Greek Coins of Palestine* (1914), pp. LIX ff., XIII, 18.

In Palestine and the neighbouring countries gods could often simply be called 'Lord' in antiquity, without mentioning their names. Hadad, for instance, is simply called Baal, and we do not in fact know the real (Syrian) name of the divinity called Adonis (from *adon*, Lord), by the Greeks. The God of Israel was also called Adonai, (my Lord). And the great god of the city of Gaza was called Marna(s), which really means 'our Lord',[1] who was worshipped there in the famous temple of the Marneion. The *Life of Saint Porphyrius of Gaza* by the Archdeacon Mark speaks of this form of worship and the destruction of the Marneion under Theodosius.[2] Until quite recently, the best proof of the worship of Marna came from a coin from the time of Hadrian.[3] An important pointer is given by the philosopher Damascius, who says that the Phoenician letter M was a symbol for Zeus among the people of Gaza.[4] This is the initial of the name Marna, and as described by Damascius, corresponds to the Aramaic letter *mem*, which appears in an archaizing form on coins from Gaza, in Seleucid and Roman times. Thus we have the passage from Damascius to confirm the supposition of scholars, that the *mem* on the coins stands for the great god of the town, Marna(s). Recently, coins struck in the years from about 410 to 300 B.C.E. have been found (not yet published), with the *mem* imprinted on them.[5] So the Semitic god Marna was already worshipped in Gaza at the time. A recently-discovered ostracon, apparently from near Raphia, and dating probably from about 300 B.C.E., contains the name עבדמראן (Abdmaran), 'the servant of Maran', which points to the worship of Maran/Marna. There is proof that at a later date, in the Christian era, the city of Hatra in northern Mesopotamia, revered the triad of gods מרתן, מרן and בר מרין (Maran, Marthan and Bar-Marin).[6] This is clearly the god Maran, his wife and their son: 'our Lord', 'our Lady' and 'our Lords' Son'.

Philo of Alexandria[7] tells of the use of the acclamation 'Marin' as a form of mockery by the crowds in Alexandria on the occasion of the

---

[1] See *P. W.* XIX, col. 1899-1906. On the following, see J. Naweh, 'פחלץ in a new Ostracon,' in *Leshonenu* XXXVII (1963), pp. 273-4 (in Hebrew).
[2] See Marc le Diacre, *Vie de Porphyre, évêque de Gaza*, ed. H. Grégoire and M. A. Kugener (1930). For the god Marna and other pagan religions in Gaza, see pp. XLVII-LVI.
[3] Ibid. pp. XLIX-L; the proofs for the worship of Marna outside Gaza are also there.
[4] Ibid., p. L.   [5] See Naweh, loc.cit.
[6] See H. Donner und W. Röllig, *Kanaanäische und aramäische Inschriften* (1964), nos. 246-8; see also J. Naweh, loc.cit., p. 273.
[7] *In Flaccum* 39.

visit of the Jewish king, Agrippa I. They brought an inoffensive lunatic called Carabas into the hall of the high school, tricked him out in imitation regal finery and paid homage to him, finally acclaiming him as 'Marin'. This was what 'the Lord' (κύριος) was called in Syria, and the Alexandrians knew that Agrippa was of Syrian descent and was king of a large part of Syria. The mockery of the acclamation is paralleled throughout by the way the Roman soldiers made fun of Jesus,[1] as was already remarked by Hugo Grotius.[2] What the Alexandrians said was in all probability מרי (Mari, my Lord).[3] Were the pagans jeering at the messianic hopes of Israel in the case of Jesus, and later on the occasion of Agrippa's visit to Alexandria, seeing in the king of the Jews only a subject for derision, or was this derision even more complex?[4] It is rightly accepted, with good reason, that Jesus was addressed as 'Lord' during his lifetime.[5] The Greek would be κύριος, but the corresponding Semitic title cannot be discerned with certainty. Had the designation of Jesus as Lord a messianic connotation? The designation gave rise to the well-known Aramaic cry used by the early Christian Church, maranatha.[6] The first two syllables mean 'our Lord' in Aramaic, and the cry is to be taken as an imperative, מרנא תא, 'our Lord (or more simply, the Lord) come', in the light of Revelation 22:20.[7] In our opinion, the cry does not stem from the primitive community. The fact that the word marana or maran was not used in the Palestinian Aramaic of the time already tells against it. And the character of the two texts in which maranatha appears makes such a Palestinian origin doubtful. Not only is the word given in a Greek transliteration, but both texts are addressed to Greek-speaking readers. The cry must have been already known and

---

[1] Mark 15:16-20; Matthew 27:27-31; John 19:2f.

[2] *Annotationes in Novum Testamentum* (ed. Groningen 1837) II, p. 356 (ad Mtt. 27:28-29). See also D. Flusser, *Jesus* (1968), pp. 128-33.

[3] Grotius writes, 'מרן enim Syrum est,' and the form *marin*, meaning 'our Lord', could be considered, if necessary. But Philo writes: ἐξήχει βοή τις ἄτοπος Μάριν ἀποκαλούντων. So the crowds called him *marin*, which may be a Greek accusative of *mari*. In any case, Philo says correctly that the word means 'the Lord.'

[4] Later, the same king Agrippa was to be acclaimed seriously as God, and having acquiesced, was punished by God, the sources say, with death (Acts 12:21-22; *Ant.* XIX, 343-6). Both accounts mention the magnificent robe which Agrippa was wearing at the time. This recalls the mock regalia of the beggar in Alexandria and of Jesus in Jerusalem.

[5] See F. Hahn, *Christologische Hoheitstitel* (2nd ed., 1964), pp. 67-125 and G. Vermes, *Jesus the Jew* (1973), p. 103-28.

[6] I Cor. 16:22; *Didache* 10:10; cf. Rev. 22:20.

[7] See Hahn, op.cit., pp. 100-2.

of some importance in Corinth before Paul wrote his epistle, and the text in the *Didache* is later than the grace before meals which precedes it. Some scholars have rightly designated *Didache* 10:6 as an appendix.[1] It is also hard to believe that the primitive community could have had the saying, 'May grace come and this world pass away', which is hard to imagine on the lips of Jesus' disciples. The 'Hosanna to the God of David' could only have come into use in circles which prayed in Greek since 'hosanna' has there become a liturgical cry and the original Hebrew meaning has been forgotten.[2] Hence the prayer *Didache* 10:6 is a liturgical appendix to the foregoing and was first used in a Christian community which prayed in Greek. The fact that the *maranatha* is found in the *Didache* and I Corinthians tells against its having been used in the primitive community.[3] We should propose to assume that the liturgical cry *maranatha* was possible because Jesus was already addressed as Lord, but the cry was first actually uttered apparently in Aramaic-speaking communities, which can also mean Syriac, and was then taken up by the communities in the neighbourhood who only spoke Greek. From there it spread to such distant communities as that of Corinth. (There were probably Christians in this sea-port town who understood Armamaic, but this does not affect our surmise).

If, however, we are mistaken and the cry really stems from the primitive community, the liturgical formula *maranatha* was undoubtedly also uttered by Gentile Christians who understood Aramaic. As has been proved above, the god Marna(s) was revered in Gaza and the god Maran in Hatra. It is therefore certain that when a Gentile Christian heard the formula *maranatha*, it did not strike him as something entirely new. He understood that it was the name of a god. It is also significant that the Syriac translation of the Hebrew Bible uses Marana for the divine name. If, as has been supposed, a certain syncretism was at work when the pagan Greek title of *kyrios* was used of Jesus 'the Lord', a similar tendency was at work to associate the pagan Aramaic *maran* with the Lord Jesus.

We have endeavoured to show that the ancient Canaanite religions still flourished in Palestine in the first century C.E., while in many

---

[1] See J. P. Audet, *La Didachè* (1958), pp. 410-24.
[2] The 'Hosanna to the God of David' of the *Didache* sounds better than the 'Hosanna to the son of David' in Matt. 21:9, but is as meaningless in Hebrew as it would be to say, 'Save us, please, to the God (or son) of David.' Audet, op.cit., pp. 420-3, has not noticed this.
[3] Audet, op.cit., p. 415, has another view.

cases the gods in question were not identified at all, or only in part, with the corresponding gods of Greece. Rabbinic sources show that the ancient Canaanite origin of much of the surrounding paganism was still recognized. In many texts superstitious practices are forbidden because they are 'Amorite ways'. In the Tosefta we read that the magical oath *dagan* is forbidden, because 'it is one of the ways of the Amorites'.[1] In biblical Hebrew *dagan* means cereal, but, 'Rabbi Judah says, Dagan is the name of the idol Dagon, as is written (Judges 16:23): To Dagon, their god, and to rejoice.' Rabbi Judah was right in saying that the word for cereal and the name of the idol were basically the same, so it is quite possible that pagans of the time swore by the Canaanites' god, Dagon.[2] The rabbinical formula 'Amorite ways' refers simply to the ancient Canaanites.[3]

The Greek story of the freeing of Andromeda by Perseus also takes us back to ancient Canaanite Palestine. This famous story was always situated in Jaffa, its homeland, so to speak.[4] It may be regarded as perhaps the most important contribution of Palestine to Greek mythology. The first author to give Jaffa as the setting is Pseudo-Scylax (fourth century B.C.E.).[5] The story itself is well known, and was made famous by a tragedy of Euripides (now lost). Andromeda was the daughter of the king of Ethiopia, Kepheus, whose wife Cassiopeia had angered the god of the sea by boasting of her beauty. The god sent floods over the land, and then a sea-monster, to which Andromeda was exposed. Perseus came on wings, killed the monster, freed Andromeda, used the Gorgon's head to turn Andromeda's bridegroom into stone, one Phineus, her father's brother, along with his retinue.[6]

The legend was originally attached to Jaffa and was linked at a later stage with the Greek hero Perseus,[7] but still in pre-classical times, since Sophocles wrote a tragedy about it as well as Euripides, and it is found on ancient Greek vases. In determining[8] when and how the

---

[1] *T. Berakoth* 7:2; the second word has reached us in a corrupt form; S. Liebermann explains it as 'cypress'.

[2] The shrine of the god Dagon in Ashdod (Azotus) is still mentioned in Maccabean times (1 Macc. 10:83-4). For the god Dagon, see *E.B.* II, pp. 623-5.

[3] *T. Berakoth* 7 (end); *T. B. Baba Metzia* 25b.

[4] See K. Kerenyi, *The Heroes of the Greeks* (1959).

[5] See Stern, op.cit. I, p. 474. Also in Strabo, *Geographica* XVI, 2, 28 (Stern, no. 114, p. 290) and I, 2, 35 (Stern, no. 109, pp. 285-6).

[6] See also Apollodorus, *Bibliotheca* II, 4, 3.

[7] Already noted in Roscher.

[8] Communication from M. Avi-Yonah.

story took on its present form, there is a clue to the date in the fact that Andromeda is daughter of an Ethiopian king, which indicates the 25th dynasty (Ethiopian) in Egypt, 715-656 B.C.E.[1] The Greeks in the neighbourhood, and those settled in Naucratis (as we know, since shortly before 700), then identified the princess' rescuer with their Perseus.

The story has seemingly left various traces on the ancient accounts of Jaffa. Pomponius Mela, in his Chronography of c. 40 C.E., can say that Jaffa was supposed to have been founded before the flood. Its ruler was Kepheus, as the people of the place demonstrated by the fact that his name and that of his brother could be seen on ancient altars there. And gigantic bones had been preserved, belonging to the sea-monster killed by Perseus when freeing Andromeda.[2] Pliny the Elder too can say that the 'Phoenician' city of Jaffa was older than the flood.[3] The reference is hardly to the Greek story of the flood under Deucalion and Pyrrha. It seems to be rather to a story known in Jaffa, going back to the ancient Canaanite inhabitants, since the ancient East, as is well known, had its own version. Pliny also says that the traces of Andromeda's fetters can be seen on a rock off Jaffa. According to Josephus likewise, the imprint of Andromeda's fetters were still being pointed out on the cliffs jutting out into the sea at Jaffa (*War* III, 420). St Jerome could still say that the holes through which the chains of Andromeda passed were still visible.[4] Pliny adds further that the fabulous Keto was still revered in Jaffa, a figure known from Greek mythology since Hesiod. Perhaps there was a certain version of the legend which identified the monster slain by Perseus with Keto. Or did Pliny mis-read his source? In Greek, the sea-monster is called *Ketos*, which is basically the same word as the fabulous Keto. Pliny says elsewhere[5] that Andromeda was supposed to have been thrown to the monster on an island in the Phoenician Sea, off Jaffa, where there was a town called Paria. The place is unknown, except for this reference in Pliny, but perhaps there was such a settlement on the rock off Jaffa. And this may be the

---

[1] See W. Wolf, *Das alte Ägypten*, (1971), pp. 165-9, 248. Other explanations of the connection between Kepheus and Jaffa are given by Lewy in *MGWJ* LXXXI (1937), pp. 65ff.
[2] Pomponius Mela, *Chronographia* I, 11, 64; Stern, op.cit., p. 371-372.
[3] Pliny, *Natural History* v, 69; Stern, op.cit., pp. 469, 473-4.
[4] Jerome, *Comm. in Jon.* I, 3.
[5] Pliny, *Natural History* v, 128; Stern, op.cit., p. 481-2.

locality to which Conon[1] refers (beginning of first century C.E.) in his rationalist version of the story, where Andromeda is carried off in a ship, from a small, uninhabited island off Jaffa. The name of the ship was Ketos, i.e. Sea-monster.[2] According to Pausanias,[3] there was still another remarkable sight to be seen in Jaffa: a spring yielding red water, exactly like blood. The spring was near the sea, and had retained the colour of the blood when Perseus had washed in it after killing the monster.

But it was the notorious Aemilius Scaurus who made the most of the credulity embalming the myth. As we have seen from Pomponius Mela, the gigantic bones of the sea-monster killed by Perseus were on display in Jaffa. The corrupt and avaricious Scaurus was with Pompey in Syria before 65 B.C.E., and became governor of Syria in 62.[4] Being also a collector of rare curios, he then took the bones of the marvellous creature slain by Perseus and carried them off from the Judaean city of Jaffa to Rome.[5] When he became aedile in 58, he organized a public exhibition of his curios, and the Romans could then see for the first time, among the rare beasts and objects, not only a hippopotamus and five crocodiles but also the skeleton of the fabulous monster from Jaffa. It was forty feet long, with ribs which rose higher than an Indian elephant, and its spine was a foot and a half thick.[6]

The story of Perseus and Andromeda gave occasion for curious tales. It was also used in a pseudo-historical theory of Jewish origins. Tacitus writes that some authors believed that the Jews were of Ethiopian descent, driven by fear and hatred to leave their homes in the reign of king Kepheus.[7] Did the authors used by Tacitus believe

---

[1] Conon, *Narrationes*, Photius, *Bibliotheca*, Cod. 186; Stern, op.cit., p. 353-354.

[2] See Stern, op.cit., p. 352.

[3] Pausanias, IV, 35, 9; The beginning of the story is printed in Th. Reinach, *Textes d'auteurs Grecs et Romains relatifs au Judaisme* (1895), p. 362.

[4] In an as yet unpublished calendar from Qumran Cave four, the murderous deeds of אמיליוס (Aemilius) are mentioned. See J. T. Milik, *Ten Years of Discovery in the Wilderness of Judaea*, (1960), p. 73; F. M. Cross, *The Ancient Library of Qumran* (1961), p. 123, n. 28; p. 126.

[5] See Pliny, *Natural History* IX, 11; Stern, op.cit., p. 484.

[6] Ammianus Marcellinus XXII, 15; 24 (see also Stern, op.cit., p. 484). The ancient historian is probably mistaken when he assumes that the exhibition was installed by Aemilius Scaurus' father, who was aedile in 123 B.C.E. Our view corresponds to that of Schürer, Vermes, Millar I, pp. 244-5 and of J. C. Rolfe in his edition of Ammianus Marcellinus II, p. 290, n. 1. The hippopotamus and the five crocodiles were exhibited alive, in a canal especially dug for this purpose; see Pliny, *Natural History* VIII, 96.

[7] See Tacitus, *Historiae* V, 2. See also H. Lewy, in *MGWJ* LXXXI (1937), pp. 65ff.

that the Ethiopians living in Jaffa began to fear and hate their king when he wanted to sacrifice his daughter, and then betook themselves into the interior, which would have explained for them the origin of the Jews? One thing is clear at any rate. We learn from Tacitus that there were writers who used the famous story of Perseus and Andromeda to draw conclusions about the origin of the Jews. In antiquity, mythology was often taken to be a reflection of pre-historic times, and often used to explain the origins of the various peoples. The rise of many nations was traced in this way, including the Jews, as may be easily seen from the sources. It should also be remarked that the story of the Ethiopian origin of the Jews speaks of the fear and hatred which the Jewish people engendered. So this was an explanation of Jewish xenophobia, for which other reasons are given in other forms of pseudo-scientific histories of Jewish origins.

We have seen the far-reaching conclusions to which the local legend of Jaffa could lead when the story became a noted element of Greek mythology. But it seems to have had important repercussions down to our own day. Lydda in Palestine possesses the grave of the famous Saint George, a martyr from the time of Diocletian, to whose story the legendary fight with the dragon was later added. The daughter of a king was exposed to a dragon, which the saint wounded with his lance, brought into the city and eventually killed, when all the citizens had been baptized. The pious legend could not, of course, terminate with the marriage of the princess to the saint.[1] It is highly probably that the pagan story from Jaffa came in due course to be attached to the Christian martyr from nearby Lydda.[2]

Up to the present, we have been dealing mainly with pre-Grecian gods and legends in Palestine. For the actual Greek religions, we begin by returning to Beth-Shean, Scythopolis, not because it became, like Jaffa, the setting for a Greek legend, but because an excellent article now exists about the Greek religions in this city.[3] When speaking of the legend linking Scythopolis with Dionysos, we expressed the opinion, shared by most scholars, that there was more to it than a legend, and that Dionysos was really worshipped there. It is generally

[1] According to Jacob of Voragine, *Legenda Aurea* (ed. Th. Graesse, 1890), pp. 259-64. In this version, the fight with the dragon took place in Libya, where it lived in a pool that formed a sort of sea.
[2] Politis, Λαογραφία (1913), pp. 220 f. H. J. Rose, *Oxford Classical Dictionary* (2nd ed., 1972), p. 64.
[3] A. Ovadya, 'Greek Religions in Beth-Shean/Scythopolis in the Graeco-Roman Period,' in *Eretz Israel* XII (1975), pp. 116-24 (in Hebrew).

supposed that the shrine from the third century B.C.E. which has been discovered was dedicated to Dionysos. But no proof of this has been found. The shrine lay on a high and conspicuous place, and one must rather suppose that the Olympian Zeus was revered there. He is mentioned on an inscription from Scythopolis, along with the 'saviour gods' (θεῶν Σωτήρων), who may be the Dioscuri. The king Demetrius who is named in the inscription is probably Demetrius II (145-138, 129-125 B.C.E.). Up to the present, only one inscription mentioning the god Dionysos has been found in Scythopolis. It is on an altar which originally stood in the theatre of the city. It is practically certain that the altar was built at the same time as the theatre, that is, at the end of the second or the beginning of the third century C.E. The Greek inscription runs: θεῷ Διονύσῳ Γερμανός, 'to the god Dionysos, [dedicated by] Germanus'. But how far does this inscription allow us to conclude to the worship of Dionysos in Scythopolis? If such an inscription had been found in a city where we knew nothing of any worship of Dionysos, such a mention of the god would hardly suffice to make us believe that he was offered any special worship there. In the nature of things, Dionysos and the theatre go together, and an altar dedicated to him there is only to be expected. So for proof of the worship of Dionysos in Scythopolis, one can only hope for further discoveries.

The Greek goddess Demeter appears on the coins from Scythopolis. And her name may be mentioned on an inscription from the first century C.E.[1] Possibly a district in the city was called after her. The most interesting Greek inscription, probably from Scythopolis, was engraved on an altar in the third century C.E.[2] The dedication is in two hexameters and runs: 'To Ares, the armour-bearer of the great king Zeus, I Seleucus, rejoicing in libations and incense have dedicated [this altar]'.[3] On the coins from Scythopolis under the emperor Gordian III, the Pious (238-244 C.E.), the war-god Mars/Ares is displayed, and he also appears on the imperial coins of the same emperor, several times with the epithet ὁπλόφορος (armour-bearer). The Seleucus who had the inscription engraved was probably a Roman soldier. He terms Zeus 'the great king', which is hardly a reminiscence of Pindar who applies the same term to Zeus.[4] Seleucus rather meant

---

[1] The inscription has only ΔΗΜΗΤΡ [...; this may also mean Demetrios.
[2] It was found in Zemach, and Ovadya remarks that it comes from Beth Shean. It was published in *RB* XXXII (1923), p. 118.
[3] ΑΡΕΙ ΟΠΛΟΦΟΡΩ ΔΙΟΣ ΜΕΓΑΛΟΥ ΒΑΣΣΙΛΗΟΣ ΣΠΟΝΔΑΙΣ ΚΑΙ ΛΙΒΑΝΟΙΣ ΧΑΙΡΩΝ ΑΝΕΘΗΚΑ ΣΕΛΕΥΚΟC.
[4] Pindar, *Olympian Odes* 7, 34.

that the really 'great king' was not the king of Persia, the hereditary enemy of the Romans, but Zeus, the father of the war-god Ares.

Palestine, like the neighbouring countries, was in the first century C.E. a place where non-Jews were pagan and still worshipped their ancient gods. Under the influence of the Greek religions, the local gods and goddesses were identified with the Greek divinities, even in the Latin west, as widely and thoroughly as the nature, particularities and importance of the local divinities permitted, and the phenomenon went hand in hand with the progress of Hellenization in a given town or region. At the same time, as we have already noted, the Greek settlers often adopted the local divinities, even in Palestine. The Egyptian goddess Isis and her son Harpocrates are a particular instance. The worship of Isis and other Egyptian divinities was widespread in the whole world of antiquity, as early as the Hellenistic age. Hence it was not just by reason of the proximity of Egypt that pagans in Palestine both knew of and adhered to the religion of Isis, with whom went the half-Egyptian, half-Hellenistic god of the Ptolemies, Sarapis. We have a good example of this worship which the rabbis knew from their ordinary experience.[1] Among the idols mentioned by the Tosefta, is 'an image of a woman suckling her child' (i.e. Harpocrates) and also Sarapis. In the Babylonian Talmud the woman giving suck is explained as Eve, who suckles the whole world, and an Aramaic etymology is invoked to identify Sarapis with Joseph in Egypt.[2] Since the same identification occurs in patristic literature, it may be supposed that speculation of a type common in Hellenistic Judaism was at work here. The theory was that the idolaters of Egypt had been led to develop their false religion by their misunderstanding of the true doctrine as held by the Jews. So the Egyptians turned the biblical Eve into the goddess Isis and Joseph, the benefactor of Egypt, into Sarapis. Here too the possibility of Judaeo-pagan syncretism would be excluded.

With regard to Greek divinities in Palestine, it is often impossible to decide whether we are dealing with a Greek interpretation of an eastern divinity, or with a Greek divinity which came in from abroad. We have mentioned the Greek war-god Ares. His is one of the names of Greek divinities which occur elsewhere in Palestine: Dionysos, Kronos, Heracles, Hermes, Ares, Pluto, Persephone, Ganymede,

---

[1] See Liebermann, pp. 136-8.
[2] *T. Abodah Zarah* 5:1 (a tannaitic source); *T. B. Abodah Zarah* 43a.

Athene, Tyche, Aphrodite, Nike, Eirene, the Nymphs and the Nereids.[1]
But it is often hard to tell whether these and other Greek divinities
were already installed in Palestine in the time of the Second Temple, or
whether they only came in after the catastrophe following Bar Cochba's
revolt, or still later, under the Severian dynasty. Thus, for instance,
a shrine in honour of Hadrian with a statue of the emperor and his
consort has been discovered recently near Scythopolis. Here we can be
certain that there was no such worship in the time of the Second
Temple. Herod, however, had erected temples of Augustus in the
newly-built cities of Sebaste and Caesarea.[2] The splendour of the
temple in Sebaste can still be admired at the present day. Herod built
many pagan temples,[3] but in pagan and not Jewish regions of Palestine,
since idolatry is forbidden among the Jews. To the latter, he excused
himself by saying that he did so unwillingly, being under orders. He
used a different language when addressing Augustus and the Romans.
He also built a temple of Augustus at Paneas (Banyas), at the source
of the Jordan, where there was a cave which was already consecrated
to Pan at the beginning of the Hellenistic age.[4] Though Herod's
conduct is explicable to some extent, it remains strange that a man so
energetic in promoting pagan religion should have been allowed by the
Jews to re-build the Temple in Jerusalem on such a magnificent
scale.—In Tiberias, however, which was founded by Herod Antipas,
there were no pagan temples before the fall of Jerusalem in 70 C.E.

We shall add here a few remarks to our survey of the pagan religions
practised in Palestine.[5] We do not try to be comprehensive, mainly
because excavations are constantly turning up new evidence and
because there was no fundamental difference between pagan Palestine
and the rest of the pagan world in the number of religions and divinities
held in honour. We have already spoken of the worship of Marna(s)
in Gaza. But a temple of Apollo is also mentioned there, in connection
with an earlier period, that of Alexander Jannaeus. The worship of
Astarte, the heavenly Aphrodite of the Greeks, lasted in Ascalon into
imperial times, having already been mentioned by Herodotus. The
Canaanite goddess Atargatis was also worshipped there, and there was
also a story that Herod's grandfather had been a hierodule there in
the temple of Apollo. In Ashdod in pre-Maccabean times there was

[1] Schürer II, pp. 45-6.
[2] Schürer, Vermes, Millar I, p. 306.
[3] *Ant.* XV, 329-30; *War* I, 407.
[4] Schürer II, pp. 204-8.
[5] Schürer II, pp. 27-56.

a temple of the Philistine god Dagon, who was also known in Gaza and Ascalon. The temple in Ashdod was destroyed by Jonathan Maccabaeus. From the time of Caligula and later the coins of Dor display the image of Zeus with the laurels, or the image of Atargatis. As early as before the Christian era, the coins of Ptolemais display the Greek Zeus. We shall speak later of the statue of Aphrodite in the baths there.[1]

This is only a small collection of the pagan gods to be found in Palestine. For Jaffa (Joppa) and Scythopolis, we have already shown that they appear in connection with Greek mythology, and in both cases it seems to be proved that the connection is not just the result of an erudite pastime. The remarkable etymologies given to the names of cities in Palestine, as preserved in the geographical lexicon of Stephen of Byzantium, are much less interesting, being erudite speculation on mythology. But the mythology could be of ancient date. In any case they go to show that the Greeks and the Hellenized pagans living in Palestine did not feel that they were strangers in the land, even from the religious point of view.

Roman gods were of course worshipped by the Romans living in Palestine, who included Roman soldiers and officials, but they too could of course revere their gods in their Hellenized form, which was common in Palestine, as the examples adduced above show. Roman religion did not influence the local religions, as far as I can see, with the exception of the idol Merkulis (מרקוליס) which is often mentioned in the Talmud.[2] This is of course the Roman god Mercury, the Hermes of the Greeks, and according to the etymology, Hermes means 'He of the cairns'.[3] Cairns are found all over the world, as is the custom that each passer-by should add a stone to the heap. They are still common in Sweden. There was an upright stone on top of the cairn, and this is the oldest form of the Hermes-column or the herm. According to Cornutus, 'stones are heaped up on the *hermae*, since each passer-by throws a stone on to the heap'.[4]

The references in talmudic literature fill out our knowledge of this type of herm, while the non-Jewish references which can be adduced help us to understand the talmudic texts properly. It is clear, for

---

[1] See below p. 1094.
[2] See the lexicons of Jastrow and of Levy.
[3] See Nilsson I, pp. 205-7; 503-5.
[4] Cornutus, 15 (ed. Lang, 1881), p. 24. Babrius, who was almost a contemporary of Cornutus, speaks (48) of a three-cornered Hermes on the side of the road, with a heap of stones underneath.

instance, what the Talmud means when it speaks of someone who 'throws a stone on Merkulis'.[1] Our sources make it clear that the herms in Palestine were not anthropomorph. There were no statues of Hermes on top of them. A small herm consisted of two stones beside each other with a large stone on top. A large herm had three stones with another on top, with a heap of stones below and around, to which the passers-by added their contribution. This corresponds to the form which is taken to be archaic. Possibly there were herms in Palestine in pre-Roman times, but since they were by the side of the roads—and the Romans were the great road-builders—the numerous cairns came to be called by Jews, and probably by non-Jews, by the Roman name of the god, Mercury, which then gave Merkulis as the form in which the name was taken over by the Jews. The herm only began to figure as an important idol in the eyes of the Jews after the Romans were installed, which is why the Talmud speaks of it so often. Jews did not enter pagan temples and so the herms, which were in the open air, were the more common object of idolatry, with which the Jews were confronted.

A few words must be said about the attitudes of the Jews of antiquity to idolatry and paganism. We begin with some rabbinical texts. Deuteronomy 12:2-3 reads: 'You shall surely destroy all the places where the nations whom you shall dispossess served their gods, upon the high mountains and upon the hills and under every green tree; you shall tear down their altars, and dash in pieces their pillars, and burn their Asherim with fire; you shall hew down the graven images of their gods, and destroy their name out of that place'. The sages deduced from this text that the obligation of uprooting idolatry was binding only in Palestine and not abroad: "You shall tear down their altars and dash in pieces their pillars ...' Are you perhaps commanded to attack them in foreign parts? But it is written, 'destroy their name *out of that place*'. You are commanded to attack them in the Land of Israel, but you are not commanded to attack them in foreign parts.'[2] This does not mean that it was regarded as a precept to destroy the shrines of idols even in Palestine. This was in fact quite impossible and would also have been very inadvisable, if the Jews wished to live in peace with the many pagans in the country. And the presence of paganism was a hard fact that had to be faced and was admitted. Under these circumstances, one can understand that the Mishnah can

[1] See *M. Sanhedrin* 7:6 and the note on this text by Albeck in his edition ad loc.
[2] *Midrash ha-Gadol on Deut.* 12:3 (p. 246); *Midrash Tannaim*, ad loc.

say: 'When someone sees a place from which idolatry has been eliminated, he utters [the following blessing], Blessed be God, who has eliminated idolatry from our land'.[1] According to another rabbinical text,[2] the sight of a place where idols are worshipped evokes the following blessing: 'Blessed be he who exercises patience.' And when a place is seen from which idolatry has been eliminated, the blessing is; 'Blessed be God, who has eliminated idolatry from our land. May thy will be done before thee, O Lord our God, so that thou eliminatest idolatry from every place of Israel and bringest back the heart of thy servants to do thee service'. Such language is inappropriate abroad, because most of the people there are not Jews. Rabbi Simeon (probably ben Eleazar) said that the blessing should also be uttered abroad, because foreigners will one day be proselytes. According to this view, it would seem that God should be praised wherever idolatry is seen, so that he may be patient with idolaters and not destroy them. The blessing in which God is asked to eliminate idolatry from all places of Israel is based on Deut. 12:2 which refers to pagan worship on all places, which were given to the people of Israel. Possibly the blessing, 'May thy will be done' etc, was often uttered abroad as well as in the homeland, in quarters or localities where a majority of Jews lived. Finally, however, the decision was taken not to utter the blessing abroad, since the majority there were not Jews. Rabbi Simeon, on the other hand, thought the blessing should be uttered everywhere, even abroad, because of the hoped-for conversion of pagans to Judaism. The blessing, 'Blessed be God who has eliminated idolatry from our land', could not of course be uttered abroad.

Hence there were three interlocking elements in the attitude of the Jews of antiquity to paganism: the notion of the holiness of the Land of Israel, the sense of living in a pagan world, and the religious opposition to paganism, which culminated in the hope that the peoples would embrace the faith in the one God of Israel at the end of time. As regards the relationship of Judaism to paganism, it should also be noted though the Bible is a great profession of faith in universal monotheism, scarcely a text can be found in it where the peoples are counselled to abandon their paganism at that time. In the ancient attacks on non-Jewish peoples and rulers, which can be read in the Bible, there is only sharp criticism of their immorality and social

[1] *M. Berakoth* 9:1 (p. 48), *Sifre Deut.* (p. 127).
[2] *T. Berakoth* 6:2 according to the first printed edition; the parallel texts in S. Liebermann, *Tosefta* 1 (1953), p. 33.

injustice, but the fact of their paganism is taken for granted without any criticism. This attitude was then adopted from the ancient Israel and was in vigour in Palestine. To rabbinical Judaism, all apologetics were so foreign that it took the existence of paganism in Palestine and in the world as a matter of fact. Though the Jewish sages were sharply critical of paganism when addressing Jews, they did not seek to enter into controversy with their pagan neighbours on the nature of religion. The Talmud does of course contain discussions about the nature of Judaism and paganism, carried on by rabbis with pagans, but it is the latter who take the initiative. In such cases, the Jews were obliged to find the right answer, which would be the best defence of their faith. Here too the words of Rabbi Eleazar ben Arach applied: 'Know well how you should answer an Epicurean (atheist)'.[1] A fine example of how pagan polemics was answered is furnished by Rabban Johanan ben Zakkai.[2] The questions put by the non-Jew were polemical in character, and Rabban Johanan's answer was a merely defensive one. He gave the full positive answer to his disciples when they put more questions. This was also Jesus' way, according to the Gospels, when he was interrogated by outsiders. The full answer was given only to the disciples.

One must have a grasp of the relationship between ancient Judaism and paganism, to understand the origin and spread of Christianity. Two points must be noted. Firstly, pagans all over the civilized world felt drawn to Judaism. In the Greek and Roman periods, then, the intrinsic, universal structure of Judaism and the essential opposition of Jewish monotheism to paganism had begun to influence the pagans themselves. It should be noted, secondly, that as early as in the Persian period, the Jewish people in Palestine and elsewhere had become completely immune to the attractions of the paganism against which the prophets had thundered. The cry could be heard at the Feast of Tabernacles, 'Our forefathers, in this place ... used to worship the sun towards the east (Ezek. 8:16)—but we bow down to the Lord and it is to the Lord that our eyes are turned'.[3] Sun worship was common at the end of the First Temple era. A later Rabbi, Rabba,

---

[1] M. Aboth 2:14.

[2] See W. Bacher, Die Agada der Tannaiten I, (1903), pp. 36-9. The questioner's name was apparently Ignatius, and he was a hegemon, which means that he was a Roman commander. S. Safrai suggested (in a personal communication) that hegemon perhaps meant bishop, and that therefore the non-Jewish biblical scholar could have been the famous Ignatius of Antioch.

[3] M. Sukkah 5:3.

(c. 300 C.E.), summed up very well the transformation that came about in the Persian period. He explained the text in the Book of Esther which ran, 'they fulfilled [it] and took it upon themselves' (cf. Esther 9:27), by saying that it was then that the Jews finally took it upon themselves to observe fully the Torah.[1] And there is an edifying legend to the effect that 'the Jews in the time of Nehemiah rid themselves of the inclination to idolatry'.[2] The later view of history was therefore correct in attributing the elimination of all leanings towards paganism to the Persian era. The most important, and indeed the most ancient testimony to this change of heart is the Book of Judith, which is itself probably from the Persian era. The action takes place after the return from the Babylonian exile, and Judith says: 'For never in our generation, nor in these present days, has there been any tribe or family or people or city of ours which worshipped gods made with hands, as was done in days gone by—and that was why our fathers were handed over to the sword, and to be plundered, and so they suffered a great catastrophe before our enemies. But we know no other god but him, and therefore we hope that he will not disdain us or any of our nation'.[3]

There were Hellenized Jews in the country before the rising led by the Maccabees, but as our sources show, they had not lapsed into paganism. And if there were Jews who sacrificed to idols under the coercive regime of Antiochus Epiphanes, they did so under compulsion and did not persevere. We know from rabbinical writings that there were some Jews who apostatized and lived as pagans, most of them probably under compulsion or for personal gain. But they must have been comparatively few, and most of them were probably assimilated Jews from the Diaspora. How rare such cases were can be seen from the fact that the sources yield only two names of apostate Jews.[4] The first of them lived in the third century B.C.E., and our information about him comes from 3 Maccabees 1:3. He was an Egyptian Jew, 'Dositheos, called the son of Drimylos, by birth a Jew, afterwards an apostate, who abandoned the law and disdained the rulings of his ancestors'. He became a high Egyptian official and even a priest of the divinized Alexander. The second was the famous Tiberius

---

[1] *T. B. Shabbath* 88a.
[2] *T. B. Sanhedrin* 64a.
[3] Judith 8:18-20; cf. Y. M. Grintz, *Sefer Yehudith*, (1957; in Hebrew).
[4] See M. Hengel, *Judaism and Hellenism* (1974) I, p. 71 and II, p. 25. He holds that the anti-Jewish rhetor Helicon was a Jew. There are no grounds for this in Philo, *Legatio ad Gaium* 170.

Alexander, Philo's nephew, who achieved considerable success in his career in the Roman civil service.

Thus the Jews in Palestine and elsewhere were not attracted by paganism and remained faithful to their God and their distinctive way of life. Judaism became a great spiritual force by which the pagans were fascinated. The great proselytizing movement and the phenomenon of the 'God-fearers' (who adopted the Jewish faith but not the whole law) lie outside our present scope. We shall only touch upon these matters insofar as they can throw light on the nature of paganism in the first century.

We have already pointed out that the Jews and pagans of the time continued to go their separate ways, even though living side by side. But then there is the problem of explaining the coercive measures of the later Hasmonaean rulers, in consequence of which the Idumaeans and Ituraeans became Jews by compulsion. It appears to be correct to say that the Hasmonaeans considered these subject peoples as royal slaves, and that when they were emancipated they became Jews as was the custom.[1] This would be, however, merely the Halakah on the matter. The real reason which decided these kings, it seems, was political expediency. They were, in fact, Sadducees. How successful this policy was may perhaps be seen from the fact that these Idumaean descendants of Esau had as one of their leaders a man with the name of Jacob, who belonged to the radical nationalist 'right' during the Jewish War. His Idumaeans allied themselves to the Zealots, whose attitude to paganism was uncompromisingly hostile.[2] We learn from Josephus that three Roman officers who were captured by the rebels managed to save their lives by promising to become Jews and be circumcised. One was in command of the citadel of Herod (Antonia) in Jerusalem, and the two others were officers under Agrippa II, who were saved by placing themselves under Josephus' protection.[3] This attitude of the Zealots accords very well with the highly-coloured picture of them which the ancient Christian writer Hippolytus, drawing on an unidentified source, has inserted into his description of the Essenes.[4] There it is said that the Zealots are so extreme in their observation of the precepts that they do not even

---

[1] Personal communication from S. Safrai.
[2] See M. Hengel, *Die Zeloten* (1961), pp. 190-211.
[3] See Hengel, op.cit., p. 203.
[4] Hippolytus, *Refutatio omnium haeresium* 9, 26, *GCS*, ed. P. Wendland (1916) III, p. 259; reprinted in *Antike Berichte über die Essener*, ed. A. Adam (1961), pp. 47-8. See also Hengel, op.cit., p. 73.

touch a coin, their reason being that it is forbidden to carry or look at or fashion an image.[1] And they never enter a city, for fear of passing through a gate surmounted by statues. They think it is wrong to pass under statues. When one of the Zealots hears an uncircumcised person speaking about God and his laws, he watches out for him to catch him alone and then threatens to kill him if he does not let himself be circumcised. If he refuses, he is shown no mercy but is put to death. This is why they adopted the name of Zealots. They are often called *sicarii* (dagger-men). The Talmud speaks of a rabbi who would not even look at the image on a *zuz* (silver coin) and had never in his whole life let his eyes fall upon a statue.[2] This was, for a Jew, a very extreme position, as we can see, for instance, from the passage in the Gospel about the paying of taxes.[3] When the observers sent by the high priests ask whether it is lawful to pay tribute to the emperor, they are shown a dinar, and Jesus asks whose image and inscription is on the coin. It follows that people in general were not upset by the fact that Roman coins bore the image of the emperor. But the Jews and the Roman governors avoided coins with images.

Thus Jewish life in Palestine, as has been said, normally went on without contact with paganism. The Jews were tolerant towards it in the pagan parts of the country, though they longed for its final disappearance and when they saw it gone from some place in Palestine, they uttered a blessing, since idolatry defiled the Holy Land. But for all their actual tolerance of paganism in the Land of Israel, the Jews were very careful to see that there was not even a trace of paganism in Jewish regions and settlements, and for the most part, the Roman governors respected such religious feelings on the part of the Jews. Anything of a pagan character in Jerusalem was of course regarded as a blow to Judaism as a whole. Needless to say, the Jews were in revolt against Caligula's plan of installing an idol in the Temple. Pilate, who seems to have been a convinced pagan, used the nighttime to bring into Jerusalem the standards of a military unit which were

[1] Luke 20:20-6 and parallels, shows that this extreme view was not commonly accepted.

[2] Hengel, op.cit., p. 200. The passage also says: 'When king Jannaeus' house was destroyed, non-Jews came and set up a Merkulis (Hermes) there.' Jannaeus is often used in rabbinical texts as a derisive name for king Agrippa. This suggests that the passage refers to the Roman period and provides no proof for the existence of the Merkulis in pre-Roman times.

[3] Luke 20:20-6 and parallels. See Hengel, op.cit., pp. 198-200. I cannot agree with his interpretation. On coins struck by Pilate with heathen symbols, see chapter six p. 350.

adorned with the image of the emperor.[1] Josephus says that the Jews 'were deeply disturbed at the sight, since it meant that their laws were being trampled on, as these laws prohibit the setting up of any graven image in the city'.[2] It was therefore the general opinion that the prohibition in question did not apply to non-Jewish regions. After a demonstration by the Jews lasting five days, Pilate finally removed the standards from Jerusalem. Later, apparently, Pilate brought gold-plated shields to Jerusalem. They were consecrated to the emperor Tiberius, but displayed no image. All they showed was an inscription with the donor's name and the name of the emperor honoured by the consecration.[3] But the mere fact that Pilate wished to bring a votive offering of a pagan character into the Palace of Herod[4] was enough to make the Jews insist, successfully, that the shields should be removed again from Jerusalem.

This co-existence of Judaism and paganism in Palestine does not of course mean that the Jews had not to be careful to keep their distance from idolatry and pagan customs, even though they were personally, as we have said, on the whole immune to paganism. Even at the present day, when a Jew—or a Christian or a Muslim—is living in a country were pagan religions are practised, or if he visits such a country, he sees how easy it is to commit an offence against his own monotheism. And it is for this very reason that the Merkulis (the Hermes-column) is mentioned so frequently in rabbinical writings, since there was usually a Herm by the side of the roads which the Jews had to use. Another occasion where Jews were confronted with a form of idolatry was when they entered the baths. When Rabban Gamaliel had visited the baths of Aphrodite in Accho, a pagan philosopher called Proclus asked him: 'Why are you using the baths of Aphrodite'? Rabban Gamaliel first asked him to leave the baths, since Jews are forbidden to speak of religious matters there. Outside, he answered: 'I did not come into her territory, she came into mine. And it is not said that the baths were erected in honour of Aphrodite, but that Aphrodite is there to decorate the baths'. He went on to explain that the statue in the baths was not an object of worship, since no one

---

[1] See chapter six, pp. 351-2.
[2] *War* II, 170.
[3] If we believe Philo, *Legatio ad Gaium* 299, there were therefore no divine names on the shields.
[4] An inscription from Caesarea shows that Pilate himself put up a building there (the Tiberieum) in honour of Tiberius. See chapter six, p. 316.

would at any price appear before a real idol if he was naked and covered with suds. And then, he said, when Scripture speaks of 'your gods', this means that the god who is treated as a god is forbidden, but that a god not so treated is permissible.[1]

The quasi-segregation of Jews and pagans also follows from the fact that Jesus only speaks once of paganism, and then incidentally, when he says, 'And in praying do not heap up empty phrases as the Gentiles do; for they think that they will be heard for their many words'.[2] By speaking so, it was not necessary that the speaker knew much of actual paganism. It would have almost been enough for him to have read his Bible, where the priests of Baal are said to have prayed in vain to Baal from early morning to midday. And when we read about the primitive Church in Palestine we get no information about its relationships with pagans and paganism.

Jesus finds fault with some abuses that had come in among the Pharisees, which were also criticized in rabbinical writings. One of his reproaches has no parallel there, 'Woe to you, scribes and Pharisees, hypocrites! for you traverse sea and land to make a single proselyte, and when he becomes a proselyte, you make him twice as much a child of hell as yourselves'.[3] This would be more apt in the case of Hellenistic Judaism, even though the reproach is exaggerated. But there may have been such Pharisees in Palestine. As a rule, proselytes and 'God-fearers' were welcome by the Jews and regarded very highly, but there was in Palestine no active propaganda to further the cause of proselytism. This was one of the points in which the ancient Judaism of the Land of Israel differed from that of the Hellenistic Diaspora and from Christianity. In the latter two cases, active efforts were made not only to refute paganism, but also to convert pagans by their propaganda. Relations between Jews and pagans in the first century seem to have been much the same as those revealed by the first Latin Christian poet, Commodian, in his polemical writings.[4] Commodian was a minor poet but a great hater of Jews. It is certain that he lived before the triumph of Christianity under Constantine and after the death of the emperor Decius, in the second half of the third century C.E. He called himself Gaseus, and since the situation of Judaism, as he described it, corre-

[1] M. Abodah Zarah 3:4.
[2] Matt. 6:7. Cf. 1 Kings 18:26-27.
[3] Matt. 23:15.
[4] See Carmina (ed. J. Martin, Corpus Christianorum cxxviii) . For Commodianus, see especially J. Martin, Studien zur Erklärung und Zeitbestimmung Commodians (1913); id., 'Commodianus,' in Traditio xiii (1957), pp. 1-17.

sponds to that of Palestine, the epithet must mean that he came from Gaza. He seems to have been a son of a Roman official. All his poems which deal with Jews are very instructive. For our present purpose, the important thing is that he saw how attractive Judaism was to pagans, He knew of Judaizing pagans: 'So? You wish to be half-Jew and half-pagan? ... You are a blind man yourself and you are fool enough to enter the company of the blind! ... You go to people from whom you can learn nothing, and they leave you to go to idols. Ask first what is commanded in the Law! They should tell you whether the gods may be adored. But they tell you nothing about God's commandments, but only recount marvels'.[1] The Christian poet therefore finds fault with the Jews because they do not explain to the interested pagan that he should abandon idolatry. They do not explain the Law of Moses to the pagan, but only relate legends. What Commodian fails to see is that these Jews were ready to welcome pagans, but unlike Christians, did not make positive efforts to convert pagans and win them away from paganism. In spite of this attitude of forbearance, heathens, as is well known, were attracted by Judaism and many of them became converts who kept the law wholly or in part.

There were many reasons for this religious tolerance of paganism on the part of the Jews. They found it natural to be living in pagan surroundings, but leading their own separate religious and social life. And then, they were a people with their own ancestral laws, who felt no imperative impulse to make religious propaganda. But in addition, even in Palestine they were quite certain that paganism, being an ungodly phenomenon, would disappear at the end of the world and that humanity would acknowledge the sole sovereignty of God. This conviction was expressed in their prayers, especially in the introductory hymns of the *malkiyoth* (kingship hymns) of the Jewish new year: 'Therefore shall we hope, o Lord our God, to see soon the glory of thy power, so that abominations disappear from the earth and the idols be abolished, to prepare for a world in the kingdom of the Almighty'. In one of the scrolls from the Dead Sea, part of which is preserved in a medieval copy,[2] King David sings, referring apparently to his second, messianic, coming:[3]

[1] *Instructiones* I, 37.
[2] The text from the Cairo Geniza was published in *Ha-Goren* (1910), pp. 82-5. I hope to prove elsewhere that it is a medieval transcription from one of the Dead Sea Scrolls.
[3] For belief in the eschatological coming of David, see P. Volz, *Die Eschatologie der jüdischen Gemeinde* (1934), pp. 206-7.

'Rulers will gather and all earthly kings,
princes of the world and lords of mankind,
to see the mighty deeds of thy hand,
and to understand the mystery of thy holy words.
All shall acknowledge thy power,
that thy hand, o Lord, has wrought all this.
The righteous shall rejoice to see this,
and rejoice before thee in songs and praises.
All the inhabitants of the earth shall learn from me,
they shall return to thy way and serve thee truly.
They shall greet thy face thankfully
with song and chant and praise,
they shall extol thy glory in their dwellings
and acknowledge that thou, o Lord, hast made them.
All worshippers of signs shall be ashamed
of their knowledge of statues,
They shall no longer adore the idols
nor bow down to the works of their hands.
The idols shall all disappear,
they shall lose all value for ever.'

Here it is important to note that in the era of the Second Temple Judaism both in Palestine and the Diaspora always linked the hope of the disappearance of paganism to the hope of the manifestation of the kingdom of God: idolatry will vanish and God will be the sole king of the world.

Hellenistic Judaism was not content with defending itself against the widespread anti-Jewish feelings of the surrounding world. It also developed an offensive against paganism. The principle that pagans were not to be insulted was accepted. Hence the words, 'You shall not curse God' (Exod. 22:27) were translated as 'You shall not revile the gods' in the Septuagint. But the directive was not followed in the writings of Hellenistic Jews. They were eager to show up the immorality and senselessness of idolatry and display the rationality and sublimity of Jewish monotheism. Hellenistic Judaism had an apologetic and proselytizing ideology. We cannot say how many pagans were fully converted by this propaganda, but there were many 'God-fearers', who accepted the one God of the Jews but not all the law. Hellenistic Judaism had almost succeeded in making Judaism a world religion in the literal sense of the words. Early Christianity then won the victory over paganism, using Jewish weapons. Christianity was in fact oriented towards a missionary goal, and one of its advantages as against Judaism was that it could wage an all-out war upon sacrificial worship, while Judaism merely jeered at the futile sacrifices offered to the gods, but spoke favourably of the sacrifices of the Temple, even after its destruction.

Christianity could win the struggle against paganism because in the first and second centuries paganism was colourless, lacking any meaningful ideology. Among the intellectually-minded above all the many gods of pagan beliefs, the immoral mythology and the adoration of idols had long given rise to misgivings, and the majority of Greek philosophers spoke of the one God or the one divinity. These views had been to some extent popularized, and the propaganda of Hellenistic Judaism, drawing to some extent on the philosophers, was a further help, and an efficacious one, because the God it preached was not a thinker's model but a personal God to whom prayer could be addressed. If one studies the Christian writings of the second century, it becomes clear that Christianity did not so much spread under the guise of a religion of redemption, by reason of its Christology, but rather as a radical rejection of paganism, offering instead an instructive belief in God and a morality worked out on the basis of Judaism. It was only later, from 200 C.E. on, that Christology, redemption by the divine Christ, began to be important for Christians who had been brought up in the faith. This was also the beginning of the first profound Hellenization of Christianity.

The start of this Hellenization also coincided with the renaissance of paganism. Monotheistic and syncretist trends set in, and the problem of the conflicting claims of the gods of paganism was solved, either by regarding the various gods as aspects of the one godhead, or by identifying the gods with one particular god or goddess. Mythology was explained as so many allegories pointing to higher truths, any sort of immoral interpretation of paganism was abandoned, and paganism made its peace with philosophy and entered into an alliance with it. The Neo-Platonists became the champions of paganism. Marinus, who succeeded Proclus as head of the Platonic Academy in Athens in the second half of the 5th century C.E., came from Neapolis (Nablus) in Palestine. Paganism finally became a religion adapted to the cultured, and indeed found its strongest supporters among thinkers. The various mental climates in the course of Greek paganism may be assessed from the character of three philosophers from the Palestinian region. Menippus of Gadara (first half of 3rd century B.C.E.) was a Cynic whose criticisms of society were couched in satirical terms. Antiochus of Ascalon was an eclectic, a contemporary of the early Hasmonaeans (born between 130 and 120 B.C.E., died c. 68 B.C.E.) who became head of the Academy in Athens and endeavoured to reconcile Platonism, Stoicism and Aristotelianism. The third was the Neo-Platonist Marinus mentioned above, and it may be assumed that he was the most religious-minded of the three pagan philosophers. Thus paganism came to maturity just as it was being crushed by Christianity.

What changes did this apogee of paganism bring with it in Palestine? Even in earlier times there was no world-famous pagan temple there. The new upsurge of paganism after 200 C.E. brought about many changes in Palestine, such as the further spread of the religions in vogue there and the admission of new gods to the pantheon, but we know little about all this, because our actual sources tell us little about the earlier period. But there are three interesting discoveries at any rate, dating from precisely the turning-point mentioned above. A statue of the Artemis of Ephesus has been found in Caesarea. There too, quite recently, a large *Mithraeum* of about 200 C.E. has been excavated. Even some parts of frescoes have been preserved. The *Mithraeum*, one may surmise, was used by Roman officers, a list of whom has been found nearby. Possibly foreign visitors also took part in the worship, disembarking in the port of Caesarea. The third find is an inscription from Sebaste, in honour of Kore/ Persephone, from the same period: 'One God, the Lord of all, the Great Kore, the Invincible'.[1] This inscription has an exact parallel in an inscription from Rome dedicated to the Sol Invictus (the invincible sun).

Perhaps the most remarkable feature of Palestinian paganism is that paganism and Judaism co-existed in the Land of Israel in the Hellenistic and Roman periods. The Jews seem to have known more about paganism than pagans did about Judaism, though they had Jews as neighbours and felt the attraction of Judaism. Pagans also displayed the same remarkable ignorance with regard to early Christianity in Palestine. Neither Judaism, nor Christianity in its initial stages, felt the impact of paganism as a living religion.

---

[1] D. Flusser, 'The Great Goddess of Samaria,' in *IEJ* (1975), pp. 13-20.

BIBLIOGRAPHY

On the survival of ancient eastern religions in Palestine see the collection of texts by J. B. PRITCHARD, ed. *Ancient Near Eastern Texts* (2nd rev. ed., 1955; supplementary volume 1969).

The basic work on Greek religion in the Hellenistic and Roman period is M. P. NILSSON, *Geschichte der griechischen Religion* II (2nd rev. ed., 1961). See also J. H. ROSE, *Handbook of Greek Mythology* (6th ed., 1958); W. H. ROSCHER, *Ausführliches Lexikon der griechischen und römischen Mythologie*, 10 vols. (1884-1937); A. B. COOK, *Zeus. A Study in Ancient Religion*, 3 vols. (1914-40); W. K. C. GUTHRIE, *The Greeks and their Gods* (2nd ed., 1954); G. MURRAY, *Five Stages of Greek Religion* (3rd ed., 1951); E. ROHDE, *Psyche* (English translation 1925).

On the Roman religion see J. BAYET, *Histoire politique et psychologique de la religion romaine* (1957); F. CUMONT, *The Oriental Religions in Roman Paganism* (translated from the 2nd French edition, 1911).

On Persian religions see G. WIDENGREN, *Die Religionen Irans* (1965); C. CLEMEN, *Fontes historiae religionis Persicae* (1920).

On the influence of paganism on Judaism and early Christianity see P. WENDLAND, *Die hellenistisch-römische Kultur in ihren Beziehungen zu Judentum und Christentum* (2nd ed., 1912); E. HATCH, *The Influence of Greek Ideas and Usages on the Christian Church* (1890); M. HENGEL, *Judaism and Hellenism* (translated from the 2nd German edition, 1974); S. LIEBERMANN, *Hellenism in Jewish Palestine* (1950); C. H. DODD, *The Interpretation of the Fourth Gospel* (1953).

On the Jewish attitude towards paganism see E. E. URBACH, *The Sages. Their Concepts and Beliefs*, 2 vols. (1975); A. BÜCHLER, *Studies in Sin and Atonement* (1928, repr. 1967).

Chapter Twenty Four
The Jews in Greek and Latin Literature

Introductory remarks

The ties between Palestine and the Greek world came into being in ancient times when the Phoenicians and the people of the Palestinian coast made commercial contact with the Aegean Sea and Greece. Greek products found markets in Palestine as contacts multiplied between the Greek and Eastern worlds even before the Achaemenids came to power in the Persian empire, and multiplied further during its heyday, when it ruled the lands of the East. Archaeological excavations and discoveries in Palestine from Tel Abu Hawam and Athlith near Carmel to Tell Jemmeh near Gaza in the south as well as at inland sites have brought to light imported Greek ceramics, especially Attic (black-figured and red-figured pottery from the sixth to fourth centuries B.C.E.),[1] which, in the course of time, were copied locally. In Palestine in the fifth century B.C.E. the Athenian coinage circulated widely, and in the fourth century the Athenian drachma was copied by the local Persian satraps. This process can also be seen in Judaea with its famous Yahud coins.[2]

Ancient Greek literature also mentions contact between Greece and Palestine in pre-Hellenistic times, due especially to traders and soldiers. The first mention of a place in Palestine in Greek literature seems to be in the lyric poet Alcaeus (end of the seventh century B.C.E.). The poet's brother Antimenidas was a soldier who served the king of Babylonia and took part in the siege of Ascalon.[3] In the fifth century B.C.E. Herodotus too visited the Palestinian coast and spent some time in Gaza. The Palestinian coast is also described in the *Periplous* of Pseudo-Scylax, who refers to the Palestinian coast in the myth of

---

[1] See the summaries by D. Auscher, in *Vetus Testamentum* (1967), pp. 8-30; Hengel, pp. 32-35. See also E. Stern, *The Material Culture of the Land of the Bible in the Persian Period* (1973; in Hebrew).

[2] See Y. Meshorer, *Jewish Coins of the Second Temple Period* (1967), pp. 35-40.

[3] See E. Lobel and D. Page, *Poetarum Lesbiorum Fragmenta* (1955), fragment 48, l.11, p. 134; J. D. Quinn, in *BASOR* CLXIV (1961), pp. 19-20.

Andromeda.[1] The Athenian orators Isaeus and Demosthenes mention Greek businessmen in Ptolemais.[2] None of these writers, however, with the possible exception of Herodotus, mentions the Jews.

The relations between Greece and Palestine in pre-Hellenistic times are reflected to some extent in the Bible itself. The island of Cyprus, close to Palestine, was an important link. The name Kittim, seemingly derived from Kition, the well-known Cyprian city, came to be regarded by the Jews as synonymous with the Greek world and the West in general.[3] Yavan is mentioned by Ezekiel among the nations with commercial ties with the Phoenician cities.[4] The prophet Joel even chastises Tyre and Sidon for selling Jews to the Greeks.[5] There is a reason to believe that Jews lived in Asia Minor before Alexander (e.g. in Sardis),[6] and that there were also Jews in Cyprus. Yavan is mentioned in the prophecy at the end of Deutero-Isaiah which speaks of the ingathering of Jewish exiles from all the countries of their dispersion.[7] The first Jew definitely known to have been in Greece was at Oropus, on the border between Attica and Boeotia.[8]

In Greek literature information about the Jews first appears at the beginning of the Hellenistic period. A characteristic of this literature is the high honour in which it holds the peoples of the East in general and some specific groups among these peoples.

The Greeks were conscious of their supremacy in philosophy. They were proud of their own way of life and government, which nurtured free men as opposed to the people of the East who were subject to the will of a despot. And they had a well-grounded belief in the effectiveness of the Greek warrior. Nonetheless, Greek writers and philosophers came to respect the ancient civilizations of the East, first and foremost that of Egypt, and to some extent, that of Persia.[9] It is difficult to assess to what extent the writers and thinkers of Greece were

---

[1] See Müller, *Geographi Graeci Minores* I, p. 79 = K. Galling, in *ZDPV* (1938), p. 90; see also id., *Studien zur Geschichte Israels im persischen Zeitalter* (1964), pp. 185-209.

[2] See Isaeus, *Oratio* 4, 7; Demosthenes LII, 20 (*In Callippum*).

[3] See chapter three p. 154.

[4] Ez. 27:13.

[5] Joel 4:6.

[6] See chapter three p. 143.

[7] Is. 66:19.

[8] *SEG* xv, no. 293; see also D. M. Lewis, in *Journal of Semitic Studies* (1957), pp. 264-6.

[9] Cf. e.g. passages like Herodotus, *Historiae* II, 143 or Plato, *Timaeus* 22 b. For the influence of the *magi* on Greek culture in the sixth century B.C.E. see M. L. West, *Early Greek Philosophy and the Orient* (1971), pp. 165-242.

directly influenced by the culture of the East.[1] In any case, at about 300 B.C.E., a deep respect for some of the achievements of Eastern civilization is evident among Greek writers. The first stage in the history of Greek attitudes towards Jews was undoubtedly influenced by this mood, and it was this which determined the image of Judaism in the Greek literature of early Hellenistic times. Signs of the enmity which sprang from the conflict between Jews and Greeks in Palestine and the Diaspora during the following ages had not yet appeared.

The Early Hellenistic Period

The first possible mention of the Jews is in the historian Herodotus, who was already understood in ancient times to be speaking of the Jewish people. Herodotus included the history of the Near East in his great work and described the civilizations of Egypt and Babylonia. He also visited the lands of the East. The second book of his history centred upon a description of Egypt, its customs, religion and history. His point of view as revealed in this book is essentially Egyptian. In the fifth decade of the fifth century B.C.E. he also visited the Palestinian coast and Phoenicia.[2] He specifically mentions his visit to Tyre and it is almost certain that he was in Gaza, which he calls Kadytis. He compares the size of the city to Sardis. Since he was in Egypt only for a short period,[3] there is no reason to believe that he spent much time on the Palestinian coast. There is nothing to suggest that Herodotus reached the inland regions of Palestine.

Herodotus does not specifically mention the Jews or Judaea. However, what he writes about the Syrians in Palestine, namely, that they are circumcised, and acknowledge that they learned about circumcision from the Egyptians, was interpreted even in ancient times as referring to the Jews. Josephus also accepts this interpretation.[4] This contention

---

[1] See Jaeger, pp. 128-30. Oriental influence on Greek philosophy is put at a minimum by Th. Hopfner, *Orient und griechische Philosophie* (1925); J. Kerschensteiner, *Platon und der Orient* (1945). For the problem of Greeks and barbarians in general see J. Jüthner, *Hellenen und Barbaren* (1923); H. C. Baldry, *The Unity of Mankind in Greek Thought* (1965); a special volume is devoted to this subject in the volumes of Fondation Hardt *Grecs et Barbares, Entretiens sur l'antiquité classique* VIII.

[2] See F. Jacoby, in *PW, Supplementband* II, p. 266; P. E. Legrand, *Hérodote. Introduction* (1932), p. 25.

[3] See T. S. Brown, in *American Journal of Philology* (1965), p. 60; J. A. Wilson, *Herodotus in Egypt* (1970), p. 1.

[4] See Herodotus, *Historiae* II, 104; Jos. *Ant.* VIII, 262; *Against Apion* I, 168-71.

seems plausible since Herodotus mentions the Phoenicians separately and knows the difference between Arabs and Syrians. Thus it is reasonable to assume that when Herodotus writes of the circumcised Syrians he is in fact referring to the Jews.[1] It is also possible that in the section in which Herodotus deals with the battle between Pharaoh Necho and the Syrians, describing the Egyptian victory and conquest of Kadytis, he is in fact referring to the events connected with Josiah and the battle near Meggido.[2]

Herodotus is really the only Greek writer before the Hellenistic period whose writings include some reference to the Jews. The 'Solymites' described by the epic poet Choirilus should not be identified with the people of Jerusalem. This identification stems from the apologies of Hellenistic Jews.[3] Nor does Aristotle, in any of his surviving works, mention the Jews, nor does he deal anywhere with the monotheistic character of their religion, although this should have interested him in view of his metaphysical system.[4]

On the other hand, in his *Meteorologica*, Aristotle specifically mentions Palestine (Παλαιστίνη) in connection with a lake in its territory:[5] a man or animal thrown into it would not sink, but float on the surface. This lake is bitter and salty and no fish can live in its waters. It is clear that Aristotle is referring to the Dead Sea. A description of this lake became a permanent feature of all accounts of Judaea in Graeco-Roman literature, a clear expression of an interest in curiosities.[6]

The first mention of Jews by name in Greek literature is found in the work of one of Aristotle's greatest pupils, Theophrastus (372-288/7 B.C.E.). A native of Eresos on the island of Lesbos, the father of botany

---

[1] It seems that A. Wiedemann, *Herodots zweites Buch mit sachlichen Erläuterungen* (1890), p. 412, goes too far in his censure of Josephus.

[2] *Historiae* II, 159. In fact Herodotus speaks here of a victory of Pharaoh Necho over the Syrians at a place called Magdolus, and its identification with Megiddo is only a conjecture of modern scholarship: Cf. e.g. Ed. Meyer, *Geschichte des Altertums* III (1937), p. 162; W. W. Cannon, in *ZAW* (1926), pp. 63-4. Ed. Schwartz, *Gesammelte Schriften* II (1956), p. 255, n.1 even thinks that the reading Magdolus is due to a mistake of the copyists. For another view which denies any allusion here to the battle of Megiddo see Th. Nöldeke, in *Hermes* (1871), p. 451; F. M. Th. Böhl, *Opera Minora* (1953), p. 114.

[3] See *Against Apion* I, 172-5; cf. I. Lévy, in *Latomus* (1946), pp. 334-9.

[4] See the argumentation of W. Jaeger, p. 130.

[5] See *Meteorologica* II, p. 359 a.

[6] Aristotle locates the lake in Palestine. Thus in his eyes Palestine included the interior and not only the coast. However, Aristotle seems to have only a vague idea of the lake and it is very likely that the *Meteorologica* was written before the conquest of the East by Alexander. See I. Düring, in *PW, Supplementband* XI, pp. 247-8.

and a versatile writer, Theophrastus describes the Jews in his *On Piety*, when surveying the history of sacrifices.[1] Theophrastus was a leading opponent of animal sacrifices. In his view this custom developed gradually. As proof of this he cites the Jews as saying that they sacrifice animals but do it differently from the Greeks, for their sacrifices are always holocausts.[2] These they sacrifice hurriedly at night so that the all-seeing sun will not know of it. Throughout the sacrifice they discuss the nature of God and gaze at the stars and pray. Theophrastus sees the Jews as the first to sacrifice animals, and even human beings,[3] but does not take them to task for it, because they did it reluctantly. This section of Theophrastus' work is the only part of the remnant of his writing dealing specifically with the Jews.[4] The general impression one gets from Theophrastus is that he treats them with respect. They are part of the Syrian people and are defined as philosophers. Even the act of observing the stars is an accepted element of philosophical religion.[5] There is no reason to believe that Theophrastus depended on Hecataeus, the other writer of the early Hellenistic period who gave much attention to Jews.[6]

Hecataeus was undoubtedly one of the outstanding writers and thinkers of his time. During the reign of Ptolemy I he visited Egypt, travelling even to the southern part of the country. Although a disciple of Pyrrhon the Sceptic, we cannot place him in any specific philosophical school, but we can see him as a representative of the ideas and trends which were popular in the transitional age in which he lived.[7] His best known work was the one on Egypt, an enthusiastic description of the culture, history and political and religious life of the country.

---

[1] See Porphyrius, *De abstinentia* = W. Pötscher, *Theophrastos, Peri Eusebeias* (1964), fragment 13; see also J. Bernays, *Theophrastos' Schrift über Frömmigkeit* (1866); A. Büchler, in ZAW (1902), pp. 202-28; W. Jaeger, *Diokles von Karystos* (1938), pp. 134-53; id., in *Journal of Religion* (1938), pp. 131-6; A. D. Nock, in *HTR* (1944), p. 174; Y. Gutman, *The Beginnings of Jewish-Hellenistic Literature* (1958; in Hebrew), pp. 74-88.

[2] On the difference between Greeks and Jews in the matter of sacrifices see Philo, *Legatio ad Gaium* 356; see also E. J. Bickerman, in *Classical Philology* (1965), pp. 64-5.

[3] W. Jaeger, *Diokles von Karystos*, p. 143, n.1 suggests that Theophrastus knows something of the biblical story of the attempted sacrifice of Isaac.

[4] See also Jos. *Against Apion* I, 166-7 and some passage of the *Historia Plantarum*. See Stern, nos. 5-9.

[5] See Jaeger, p. 133. See also *Aristotelis Fragmenta* ed. Rose (1886), nos. 10-11.

[6] See M. Stern, in *Zion* (1969), pp. 121-125 (in Hebrew); see also *Journal of Egyptian Archaeology* (1973), pp. 159-63.

[7] On Hecataeus see now P. M. Fraser, *Ptolemaic Alexandria* (1972) I, pp. 496-505.

It was the principal source for the description of Egypt in the first book of the *Bibliotheca Historica* of Diodorus Siculus. From Diodorus we learn that Hecataeus was interested in the Jews in connection with the migration of Egyptians to other lands.[1] But a much more detailed description of the Jews has reached us by way of the *Bibliotheca Historica* book XL, which has been preserved in the *Bibliotheca* of Photius.[2] From this description, which is quite comprehensive, we learn that Hecataeus' point of departure is Egypt. The Jews, according to Hecataeus, were expelled from Egypt and this expulsion left its mark on their laws and customs. Moreover, some of their customs and institutions closely resemble those of the Egyptian as described by Hecataeus himself. In his description of the Jews, Hecataeus was influenced by Egyptian tradition as well as what he learned from Jews themselves. This can be proved by Hecataeus' evaluation of the personality of Moses and by an almost direct quotation from the Bible.[3] However, in his summary of the history of colonization, Hecataeus follows the Greek scheme of colonization rather than the Jewish tradition. In accordance with the Greek scheme Hecataeus describes the arrival of Moses in Judaea, his founding of Jerusalem and his codifying of Jewish law.

Hecataeus emphasizes the monotheistic outlook of Judaism and its rejection of anthropomorphism. He is also familiar with the social structure of Judaea and with the hegemony of the priestly class. He is even aware of the division of the people into twelve tribes, although he totally ignores Jewish history from Moses to the period of Persian rule. This gap may be simply due to the fact that Diodorus omitted to use Hecataeus here, just as he omitted some Jewish customs and institutions. Hecataeus mentions that certain changes took place in traditional Jewish customs as a result of Persian and Macedonian rule, but he does not evaluate these changes. In general Hecataeus is completely free of anti-Jewish bias. He describes the beginning of the Jewish people against the background of a plague in Egypt. The

---

[1] See Diodorus, *Bibliotheca Historica* I, 28, 2.
[2] Diodorus, *Bibliotheca Historica* XL, 3. Cf. some of the studies on Hecataeus and the Jews: M. Engers, in *Mnemosyne* (1923), pp. 229-241; H. Lewy, in *ZNW* (1932), pp. 117-132; A. T. Olmstead, in *JAOS* (1936), pp. 243-4; W. Jaeger, *Diokles von Karystos* (1938), pp. 134-153; idem, in *Journal of Religion* (1938), pp. 127-43; J. Bidez et F. Cumont, *Les mages hellénisés* I (1938), pp. 240-2; B. Schaller, in *ZNW* (1963), pp. 15-31; N. Walter, *Der Thoraausleger Aristobulos* (1964), pp. 172-7; 187-194; J. G. Gager, in *ZNW* (1969), pp. 130-9; O. Murray, in *Journal of Egyptian Archaeology* (1970), pp. 144-5; 158.
[3] *Bibliotheca Historica* XL, 3, 6. Cf. Lev. 26:46; 27:34; Num. 36:13.

Egyptians attributed the plague to the anger of the gods at the strangers in the land, who introduced new religious customs and undermined the native religion. A decision was therefore taken to expel the strangers. The most famous of them, under Cadmos and Danaos, reached Greece. The majority, led by Moses who excelled in wisdom and courage, migrated to Judaea which at that time was completely desolate. After taking over the country, Moses established a number of cities, the most famous of which was Jerusalem. He also built the Temple and laid down the ritual and the laws. He divided the people into twelve tribes because this was considered the most perfect number. Moses was opposed to anthropomorphism and identified the deity with the heavens. His regulations on sacrifice differed from those of other nations as did the entire way of life of the Jews. Because of their expulsion from Egypt, they set up a regime which was conspicuous for its hatred of strangers. The people whom Moses thought most suitable to lead the nation he appointed as priests, and made them responsible for justice as well as for the safeguarding of laws and customs. The Jews therefore have no kings and the leadership of the people is in the hands of a priest who excels in wisdom and virtue. He is called the high priest and the people believe that he is a messenger who transmits to them the will of God. This is why all the Jews treat the high priest with great respect.[1] Moses devoted special attention to matters of war, and fostered courage and endurance among the youth. Moses himself also went to war against the neighbours of Judaea and conquered a great deal of land, dividing it into equal portions. He gave larger tracts of land only to the priests so that they would have a substantial income and be able to concentrate on the service of God. He also forbade the Jews to sell the parcels of land given them, which would ensure them against impoverishment.[2]

---

[1] See also F. R. Walton, in *HTR* (1955), pp. 255-7.

[2] Also according to the Torah, the sale of land was only of temporary validity, and it returned to its original owners in the year of jubilee (Lev. 25:13). However, there is no reference to the continued existence of the jubilee in the period of the Second Temple. Tcherikover, p. 122-3 assumes a promulgation of a law whose purpose was to preclude the concentration of land in the hands of rich landowners. Cf. Neh. 5 on the return of mortgaged lands to their former owners. On the other hand, it stands to reason that Hecataeus wrote here under the impression of the conditions prevailing in the Greek world, where unequal property of land was thought to constitute one of the main reasons of social crisis. See Aristotle, *Politica* II, 1266A, where we learn of Phaleas of Chalcedon's intention to keep equality among the estates of the citizens. See in general D. Asheri, *Distribuzioni di terre nell'antica Grecia* (1966).

Hecataeus also emphasizes that the Jews were forbidden to expose their children, which meant that the population increased.[1]

No one doubts the authenticity of the portions of Hecataeus included in Diodorus' work; the problem arises only with respect to the passages of Hecataeus cited by Josephus in his *Against Apion*.[2] Josephus declares that he has taken his quotations from a special work by Hecataeus devoted to the Jews. The existence of such a work is also mentioned by Origen.[3] Another work attributed to Hecataeus is supposed to deal with Abraham, or Abraham and the Egyptians. This last work is without a doubt a creation of Jewish apologetics since it includes monotheistic verses falsely attributed to Sophocles.

Opinions are less unanimous with regard to the chapters of Hecataeus in the *Against Apion*.[4] These are cited as memoirs of Hecataeus which refer to such Jewish personalities as the high priest Hezekiah and the Jewish military officer Meshulam whom Hecataeus met. There are also sections dealing with the great devotion of the Jews to their laws, even to the extent of sacrificing their lives, the large population of Judaea and a description of Jerusalem and the Temple. Various arguments have been brought against the authenticity of the passages attributed to Hecataeus in the *Against Apion*. Scholars who have pointed out that the Jewish apologists attributed at least one book to Hecataeus which was not written by him (the book on Abraham). It has been argued that the passages cited by Josephus include anachronistic details which reflect the situation in Judaea after the Hasmonaean revolt and that the general spirit differs from that which pervades the passages of Hecataeus on the Jews which were cited by Diodorus. While Hecataeus as cited by Diodorus has an objective and sober approach, in Josephus he is a panegyrist. Moreover, those who reject the authenticity of the sections in the *Against Apion* argue that as early as the second century C.E. their authenticity was questioned

---

[1] The Jewish habit based as it was on religious duty to rear all new-born children glaringly contrasts with the Greek habit of exposure of new-born children. See M. P. Nilsson, *Geschichte der griechischen Religion* II (2nd ed. 1961), p. 291; R. Tolles, *Untersuchungen zur Kindesaussetzung bei den Griechen* (1941). See also Tacitus, *Historiae* v, 5. For the Jewish view see also Philo, *De specialibus legibus* III, 110; *De virtutibus*, 131-2; Jos. *Against Apion* II, 202; I. Heinemann, *Philons griechische und jüdische Bildung* (1932), pp. 392-8; S. Belkin, in *JQR* (1936-7), pp. 7-9.

[2] *Against Apion* I, 183-204.

[3] *Contra Celsum* I, 15.

[4] Schaller, op.cit. denies the authenticity of the fragments of Hecataeus included in *Against Apion*, and Gager, op.cit. defends it.

by Herennius Philo.[1] Most of these contentions can be convincingly refuted. It is true that there was a pseudepigraphic work on Abraham attributed to Hecataeus, but that does not mean that Hecataeus did not write a work *On the Jews* or that the work *On the Jews* is identical with *On Abraham*. It is also difficult to prove beyond dispute the existence of anachronisms in the work of Hecataeus as cited by Josephus. It is true that the tone here is more panegyrical than in the chapters of Hecataeus cited by Diodorus. However, when Hecataeus is cited by Diodorus, he is full of respect for the Jewish code of law and for the personality of Moses. We must also take into account the fact that the description in Diodorus was taken from a general work of Hecataeus on Egypt, written from an Egyptian point of view, while Josephus depends here, according to what he himself wrote, on a special work, *On the Jews*. The doubts of Herennius Philo need not be taken seriously, since they express the personal feelings of a man who lived in the time of Hadrian, and who could not believe that a great Greek writer could possibly praise the Jews. Then too, Hecataeus was a contemporary of Theophrastus, Clearchus and Megasthenes, all three of whom respected the Jews and their religious tradition. The scholars who argue against the authenticity of sections of Hecataeus in the *Against Apion* admit that these sections are very sober compared to the usual pseudepigraphic works of the day.[2] On the other hand, among the writings attributed to Hecataeus there is at least one item which is difficult to attribute to the authentic Hecataeus: he approves of Jews destroying pagan temples and altars set up in Judaea. One can assume that Josephus had a copy which had been modified by Jewish editors. They made the work a panegyric which completely identifies itself with the Jewish people.

Besides Theophrastus and Hecataeus there were two other writers at the beginning of the Hellenistic period whose comments on the Jews have been preserved: Megasthenes and Clearchus. Megasthenes was a contemporary of Seleucus Nicator, the founder of the Seleucid kingdom, and visited India in the beginning of the third century B.C.E.[3] The result, *Indica*, became the authoritive work on the subject. From the third book of this work a passage has been preserved in

---

[1] See Origenes, l.c.

[2] That is admitted by *Schürer*, III p. 606.

[3] See O. Stein, in *PW* xv, p. 232; A. Dahlquist, *Megasthenes and Indian Religion* (1962), p. 9. Megasthenes' reference to the Jews is to be found in Clemens Alexandrinus, *Stromata* I, 15, 72, 5.

which Megasthenes places the Jews on the same level as the Indian Brahmans. The Jews, he writes, are the philosophers among the Syrians, as the Brahmans are among the Indians.

There is a similar evaluation of the Jews in the writing of Clearchus of Soli in Cyprus. Clearchus, like Theophrastus, was of the Peripatetic school. Among his works is a dialogue *On Sleep* in which Aristotle himself is one of the participants.[1] The discussion is about the immortality of the soul. In the course of the dialogue Aristotle tells of a Jew of Coele-Syria, and identifies the Jews as the descendants of the Indian philosophers. While the philosophers of India are called Calani, the philosophers of the Syrians are called Jews. The name of their country is Judaea, and their city is called by a strange name, Hierusaleme. Aristotle adds that this Jew came from the Asian hinterland to the coast of Asia Minor, but was already a Greek by language and mentality. His cultural level was so high that he had more to tell people he met than to learn from them. It is difficult to accept the authenticity of the meeting between Aristotle and the Jew in the dialogue *On Sleep*. We know that Aristotle did spend some time in Asia Minor, but the meeting is as legendary as similar meetings in ancient literature which tell of contact between the wise men of Greece and those of the East, such as the meeting between Socrates and a wise Indian, described by Aristotle's disciple, Aristoxenus.[2] The description of the meeting between Aristotle and the Jew merely reflects Clearchus' image of the Jewish people.[3] Clearchus could have known Jews in his homeland, Cyprus, since Jews surely reached there in early times. However, what he says about Jews does not necessarily mean that he had direct knowledge of contact with them. His attitude is typical of the ideas prevalent among the Greeks at that time about the wisdom of the East and about the great influence of the priestly class there. His notion of the Jews stemming from the philosophers of India is similar to his notion that the Indian gymnosophists stemmed from the *magi*.[4] It is not necessarily the case that Clearchus was directly influenced by Megasthenes in his writing on the Jews.[5] Their

[1] See Josephus, *Against Apion* I, 176-183 = F. Wehrli, *Die Schule des Aristoteles* III (2nd ed. 1969) fragm. 6.
[2] See Eusebius, *Praeparatio evangelica* XI, 3, 8 = Wehrli, op.cit. II (2nd ed. 1967) fragm. 53.
[3] On Clearchus and the Jews see also I. Silberschlag, in *JBL* (1933), pp. 66-77; W. Jaeger, *Diokles von Karystos* (1938), pp. 140-2; H. Lewy, in *HTR* (1938), pp. 205-35; A. J. Festugière, in *RHR* CXXX (1945), pp. 29-31.
[4] See Diogenes Laertius I, 9.
[5] This is the view of Jaeger.

accounts differ. As opposed to Clearchus, and as far as we can deduce from the scrap of evidence which has come down to us, Megasthenes did not know about the supposedly Indian origin of the Jews. Moreover, it is worthwhile considering Clearchus' presence in Bactria. A Greek inscription has been found testifying to that effect.[1] We can assume that Clearchus could form his own impressions by comparing what he himself knew or heard from different sources, without having to rely on Megasthenes.

In sum, we can say that the impression given by the fragments of the Greek writers from early Hellenistic times is that their attitude towards the Jews was one of respect. Most of them pictured the Jews as a philosophical-priestly sect and part of the population of Syria. One also has the impression that these writers did not have direct contact with the Jews in Judaea, and that even Hecataeus, who describes Jewish society in Judaea in detail, reflects only to a limited extent the real situation. Above all his writing is stamped with the prevailing contemporary philosophical and political theories.

Graeco-Egyptian literature

Egypt was perhaps the most important centre of the Jewish Diaspora and the focus of its literary activity. In Alexandria the Bible was translated into Greek and writings on the history of the Jewish people as well as on apologetics and philosophy were meant to inform both enlightened Jews and non-Jews. In Hellenistic Egypt the Jews reached important positions in the political, military and economic life of the country. On the other hand it was in Egypt that there was a lengthy struggle between the Jews and the Greeks over civil rights in Alexandria, and here too there were signs of anti-Jewish activity among the Egyptian population as early as the Persian period. Moreover, the story of the exodus as it appears in the Bible does not do credit to the Egyptians and it begs for an Egyptian reply. And so as early as the third century B.C.E. an anti-Jewish version of the origin of the Jews and their expulsion from Egypt was developed. This account took shape among the local priests and was written down in Greek by one of them, Manetho. It became the prevalent version in Graeco-Egyptian literature and we can trace its development during the entire great age of Judaism in Hellenistic and Roman Egypt. Its

---

[1] See L. Robert, in *Comptes rendus de l'Académie des Inscriptions et Belles Lettres* (1968), pp. 422, 441-54.

influence reached beyond the borders of Egypt and can be found in the work of Greek writers who were not from Egypt, as well as in Roman literature. The notion that the Jews were originally lepers and morally debased was formed in Egypt. Here, too, without a doubt, the belief was that Jews worshipped an ass, as well as other anti-Jewish concepts.

Manetho played an important rôle in this development. He was the first Egyptian to write the history of his country in Greek. A native of Sebennytos, and an Egyptian priest, he knew the Egyptian tradition well from within. Parts of his *Aegyptiaca* have been preserved in Josephus' *Against Apion*. Josephus gives the impression that he did not come by Manetho's text directly, but came to know it from excerpts made by Hellenistic Jews.[1] They sought assistance in their struggle against anti-Semitism in Alexandria in the work of Manetho, but tried to contradict some of his premises. The importance of Manetho's work from the standpoint of its influence on succeeding generations must be rated highly, since it is the first literary expression of the anti-Jewish trend in Hellenistic-Roman Egypt. He was a writer who played an all-important rôle in the spread of anti-Jewish themes which from then on continued to re-appear in ancient literature. But many scholars deny this, and differentiate between the Manethonian and pseudo-Manethonian elements in the passages adduced by Josephus.[2] In their opinion the authentic Manetho did not refer at all to the Jews, and only pseudo-Manetho had anti-Jewish leanings. The fragments of Manetho in the *Against Apion* can be divided into two main groups.[3] The first describes the history of Hyksos rule in Egypt. The Hyksos, in accordance with accepted Egyptian tradition, are described as a people of lowly origins who set fire to the cities of Egypt, destroyed the temples of the gods and treated the population mercilessly. After their expulsion from Egypt they came to Syria, and in order to meet the danger of an Assyrian attack they built a city in the country in the time of Manetho called Judaea, which they called Jerusalem. Although Manetho does not here specifically mention the Jews in connection with the Hyksos, the connection between them can be deduced from what he says. The fact that Manetho writes that the Hyksos migrated to Judaea, which in his

[1] See Ed. Meyer, *Aegyptische Chronologie* (1904), p. 71.
[2] See W. Bousset, in *Berliner Philologische Wochenschrift* (1907), p. 1166; Ed. Meyer, op. cit., p. 77; R. Weill, *La fin du Moyen Empire Egyptien* (1918), p. 101; Laqueur, in *PW* xiv, p. 1071.
[3] *Against Apion* I, 73-91; 228-52.

time was not identical with all of Palestine, and attributes to them the founding of Jerusalem, can only be based on the identification of the Hyksos with the ancestors of the Jewish people. There was nothing special about Jerusalem in the Pharaonic period for it to be described as the centre of the Hyksos after their expulsion from Egypt except that it later became the capital city of the Jews.[1] Manetho's second version cited in Josephus' work had greater influence. According to Josephus himself Manetho differentiated between the two versions. The second is based on fables and current reports (μυθευόμενα καὶ λεγόμενα). In this account Amenophis had a great desire to see the gods. In order to achieve this he decided to cleanse Egypt of lepers and all other unclean people. He gathered about 80,000 of them and set them to work in the stone quarries. Later he deigned to give them Avaris, the former capital of the Hyksos where, at one time a priest named Osarsiph became their leader. Osarsiph ordered them not to worship the gods, to eat the meat of animals holy to the Egyptians and to develop ties only with their countrymen. He also sent a delegation to the inhabitants of Jerusalem who had previously been expelled from Egypt. By the joint forces of the exiles and the unclean, Egypt was conquered and the conquerors treated the Egyptian population with even greater cruelty than did the Hyksos in their time. At the end comes an identification of Osarsiph with Moses. Some scholars deny that Manetho had anything to do with this second version, and others reject only the identity between Osarsiph and Moses.[2] In this way they try to refute the argument that Manetho was a man of strong anti-Jewish bias. But the rôle assigned by the story to the Solymites (i.e. Jerusalemites), even without this identification of Osarsiph with Moses, is enough to establish his anti-Jewish leanings. In any case, there is no reason which would convince us to deny Manetho all of his story or even this identification. In the story there are features known to us from the Egyptian *Tale of the Lamb* or the *Potter's Oracle*,[3] which could easily be given an anti-Jewish

---

[1] In fact the connections of Jerusalem with Egypt are reflected already in the Tel el-Amarna tables. See J. B. Pritchard, *Ancient Near Eastern Texts relating to the Old Testament* (2nd ed. 1955), p. 488. However, nothing referred to in this correspondence makes it conspicuous among other cities of the land.

[2] It has been surmised that the name Osarsiph is an Egyptian form of the name Joseph, where the name of the Jewish God was superseded by that of Osiris.

[3] For the *Oracle of the Potter* see U. Wilcken, in *Hermes* (1905), pp. 544-60; R. Reitzenstein and H. H. Schaeder, *Studien zum antiken Synkretismus* (1926), pp. 39-40; *P. Oxy.* XXII, no. 2332; L. Koenen, in *Zeitschrift für Papyrologie und Epigraphik* 11 (1968), pp. 178-209.

colour,[1] especially since the Jewish version of the exodus required an answer sooner or later even in the period before the translation of the Bible into Greek, since it could have been circulated in some form or other earlier. It seems that Manetho was not the first who combined the Egyptian traditions on the expulsion of the unclean and the strangers from Egypt with the tradition of Moses and the Jews. We have seen that the work of Hecataeus had already implied a connection between the expulsion of the strangers from Egypt and the origins of the Jewish people. It seems, therefore, that Manetho used popular Egyptian traditions in his work but he gave them his own stamp. His version, however, was not unique, and parallel traditions can be seen in the work of other writers in Ptolemaic and Roman Egypt.

The earliest of these writers whose work has reached us seems to be Lysimachus.[2] It is conceivable that Lysimachus belongs to the Hellenistic period and lived and worked in the second or first century B.C.E.[3] With the possible exception of Apion, Lysimachus is the most extreme representative of the anti-Jewish trend in Graeco-Egyptian literature. Like Manetho, Lysimachus did not write a special work on the Jews, but dealt with them in his work on the history of Egypt. According to him, the Jews were not only diseased beggars but degenerates who delighted in murder and desecration. Even the name of their city testifies to their character: 'This town was called Hierosyla because of their sacrilegious propensities'.[4] The name of Pharaoh Bocchoris which appears in Lysimachus' work and the absence of all mention of the Hyksos and of the Egyptian origin of Moses, prove that his version is different from that of Manetho or the version reflected later by Chaeremon. In the passages of Lysimachus' work cited in the *Against Apion* there is no mention of Jewish rule over Egypt or of crimes committed by the Jews there, but only of the crimes committed by them in Judaea after they had settled there. Lysimachus' work reflects, it seems, the tense atmosphere which accompanied the struggle between the Greeks and the Jews on the soil of Palestine in the period of the Hasmonean conquests.[5] Josephus correctly defines Lysimachus as a sworn enemy of the Jews (συντεθεικὼς κατὰ πολλὴν ἀπέχθειαν).[6]

---

[1] See *CPJ* no. 520.   [2] See Jos. *Against Apion* I, 304-11.

[3] See P. M. Fraser, *Ptolemaic Alexandria* II (1972), p. 1092, n. 475.

[4] Τὸ δὲ ἄστυ τοῦτο Ἱερόσυλα ἀπὸ τῆς ἐκείνων διαθέσεως ὠνομάσθαι.

[5] See H. Lewy, in *MGWJ* (1933), pp. 84-99; 172-80.

[6] Jos. *Against Apion* I, 304. Güdemann, in *PW*, XIV p. 35 takes rather a too lenient view of Lysimachus' attitude to the Jews.

We do not know to what extent Apion was dependent on Lysimachus but it would appear that his influence was substantial. Apion (first half of the first century c.e.) was a writer and scholar of Egyptian origin. Like Manetho and Chaeremon he played quite a prominent rôle in the cultural and political life of his time. He mainly won fame as an expert on Homer and as the author of a history of Egypt. During the reigns of Tiberius and Claudius he was active as a teacher in Rome. In the time of Gaius Caligula he travelled to Greece, a journey which had widespread repercussions.[1] He was not born in Alexandria but came there from the Egyptian hinterland.[2] He won Alexandrian citizenship, however, and stressed this fact. As a citizen of Alexandria he also represented the Greeks of the city when he appeared before Gaius Caligula, as counsel for the prosecution against the Jews who were represented by Philo. Like his younger contemporary Chaeremon, Apion was at the meeting-place of two worlds, the Greek and the Egyptian, his function being to teach educated Greeks and Romans about Egypt and its past. His views on the Jews and their religion come in the third and fourth books of his *Aegyptiaca*. He did not write a special work against the Jews, as some scholars conclude from Clement of Alexandria.[3] It seems more probable that he devoted a certain part of his history of Egypt to the exodus of the Jews from Egypt and its outcome.

Josephus vigorously denounced Apion in the apologetic work, known as *Against Apion*. He describes Apion's accusations as revolving around three points: a) the Jewish exodus from Egypt; b) arguments concerning the civil rights of Jews in Alexandria; c) contempt for the holiness of the Temple in Jerusalem and for the customs of the Jews. The description of the exodus in Apion's work reflects above all the views common in Greek circles in Alexandria, such as the story about the lepers and the Egyptian origins of Moses. It is also noteworthy that Apion found it necessary to include in his writing the biblical tradition of Moses' spending forty days on Mount Sinai.[4] Since Apion was a writer well known to the educated classes of his time, even

---

[1] See Seneca, *Epistulae morales* 88, 40.
[2] See I. Lévy, in *REJ* XLI (1900), pp. 188-95.
[3] See Clemens Alexandrinus, *Stromata* I, 21, 101, 3. From the literature on Apion see A. Sperling, *Apion der Grammatiker und sein Verhältnis zum Judentum* (1886); A. v. Gutschmid, *Kleine Schriften* IV (1893), pp. 356-371; B. Motzo, 'Il κατὰ 'Ιουδαίων di Apione', in *Atti dell' Accademia delle Scienze di Torino* (1912-3), pp. 459-68; Gager, pp. 122-4.
[4] *Against Apion* II, 25.

though not all of them respected him to the same degree,[1] and his work on the history of Egypt became one of the authoritive works on the subject, he was a real danger to the Jews. It is not surprising that Josephus chose Apion as the prime target of his polemics in his apologetic work on the Jewish people and religion. It seems that Pliny the Elder also used Apion as a source and that he also coloured the Egyptian traditions as given by Plutarch.[2] On the other hand, it is doubtful whether Tacitus was directly dependent on Apion.[3] A light and flowing style helped turn Apion into a popular writer.[4]

Chaeremon was somewhat younger than Apion and was even more representative than Apion of the Graeco-Egyptian tradition initiated by Manetho. Chaeremon was an intellectual, proud of Egyptian culture and one of its standard-bearers. He is sometimes mentioned as an Egyptian priest (ἱερογραμματεύς) and we have a description from him of Egyptian priestly customs.[5] On the other hand he is called Chaeremon the Stoic and was tutor of the emperor Claudius.[6] He seems also to have been a member of the Alexandrian delegation to Claudius in 41 c.e.[7] The section on the Jews which has been preserved from Chaeremon deals with the exodus.[8] This essentially follows the Graeco-Egyptian tradition as presented by Manetho, but differs somewhat in names and details. Moses and Joseph are mentioned as the leaders of the Jews, and according to Chaeremon were Egyptian priests whose Egyptian names were Tisithen and Peteseph.[9] An important part is played by the goddess Isis who appears to king Amenophis in a dream. Chaeremon, like Manetho, pictures the Jews as unclean and debased, and states that their departure from Egypt was a religious necessity.

---

[1] The Emperor Tiberius called Apion 'cymbalum mundi.' Cf. Pliny, *Natural History*, *Praefatio* 25.
[2] Apion undoubtedly exercised some influence on Greek and Latin literature, see M. Wellmann, in *Hermes* (1896), pp. 249-53; I. Lévy, in *Latomus* (1946), pp. 339-40; (1951), p. 161.
[3] This is the view of Gutschmid, op. cit., p. 367.
[4] See e.g. the story of Androclus and Lion as related from Apion by Aulus Gellius v, 14, 5.
[5] See Porphyrius, *De abstinentia* IV, 6-8.
[6] See Suda s.v. Ἀλέξανδρος Αἰγαῖος. See also H. R. Schwyzer, *Chairemon* (1932).
[7] See H. I. Bell, *Jews and Christians in Egypt* (1924), p. 23 = *CPJ* no. 153.
[8] See Jos. *Against Apion* I, 288-92.
[9] See Schwyzer, op. cit. p. 57; Th. Hopfner, *Plutarch über Isis und Osiris* II (1941), p. 145.

A negative attitude towards the Jews which echoes the Graeco-Egyptian tradition can be seen in the work on the Jews by Nicarchus son of Ammonius. The only sentence preserved from this work refers to Moses and describes him as a leper.[1] This was repeated by other later writers such as Ptolemy Chennos and Helladius.[2]

The historian Timagenes (first century B.C.E.)[3] was exceptional among Greek writers in Egypt in his attitude towards the Jews, as far as can be ascertained from the passages which have reached us by way of Josephus. He was born in Alexandria and brought to Rome by Gabinius. In Augustan Rome he taught rhetoric and entered the prominent social circles of the city. Timagenes won fame as a historian, one of his works being a universal history centred on the kings of the Macedonian dynasties.[4] In the course of his narrative he also touched on the Jews, and three passages have been preserved which show his interest in Jewish matters. The first has to do with the attack of Antiochus Epiphanes on Jerusalem, and the last with the war of Ptolemy Lathyrus against Alexander Jannaeus, while the second deals with Aristobulus I, the Hasmonean king. Timagenes evaluates sympathetically the work of Aristobulus, explains the political reasons for the conversion of the Ituraeans, and remarks that he was a kindly person who did good for his people. This contradicts the impression received from Josephus' principal narrative which is based on the universal history of Nicholas of Damascus, an anti-Hasmonean. It is possible that all these passages are drawn from that part of Timagenes' work which tells the history of the Seleucid kingdom. But one should not discount the possibility that Timagenes devoted special chapters to the Jewish kingdom, including a discussion of its history, religion and land. This would become a certainty if, as many scholars believe, the Latin historian Pompeius Trogus depended on Timagenes when writing about the Jews. But this is itself uncertain.

[1] See Photius, *Lexicon* s.v. ἄλφα in R. Reitzenstein, *Der Anfang des Lexikons des Photios* (1907), p. 83.
[2] See Photius, cod. 190, p. 151 b; cod. 279, p. 529 b.
[3] See Jos. *Against Apion* II, 83-4; *Ant.* XIII, 319; XIII, 344.
[4] On Timagenes see C. Wachsmuth, in *Rhein. Museum* (1891), pp. 465-79; J. Kaerst, in *Philologus* (1897), pp. 621-57; R. Laqueur in *PW*, Series II, vol. VI, p. 1063-71; G. W. Bowersock, *Augustus and the Greek World* (1965), pp. 125-6; H. R. Breitenbach, in *Museum Helveticum* (1969), pp. 156-7; P. M. Fraser, *Ptolemaic Alexandria* (1972) I, pp. 518-9.

Asia Minor, Syria and Greece

Graeco-Egyptian literature was remarkable for its antipathy for, and its intense struggle against, the Jews and Judaism. This was not, however, the case in other parts of the Greek world, either in Asia Minor or Syria, where Jewish centres were populous, or in Greece itself where there were fewer Jews. The interest in the Jews felt by writers in Greek from Asia Minor, which is reflected in the number of works dealing specifically with the Jews (we know of at least three) can be explained by the size and prominence of the Jewish communities, as well as by the central rôle which Asia Minor played in the cultural life of the Hellenistic period and of the Roman empire in general.

Greece is represented by two famous writers, the historian Polybius in the Hellenistic period, and Plutarch in the imperial period. Syria is represented by two, Posidonius and Nicholas of Damascus. Among Greek writers from the Hellenistic cities of Palestine, Meleager of Gadara was familiar at least with the customs of the Jewish sabbath. Among the writers of Asia Minor, only Apollonius Molon can be regarded as clearly anti-Jewish. He came from Caria and worked in Rhodes. Mnaseas of Patara in Lycia is representative of the Graeco-Egyptian tradition, since he says Jews worshipped an ass. The attitude of Posidonius, of Apamea in Syria, is unclear. On the other hand Strabo, of Amaseia in northern Asia Minor, expresses admiration for the personality of Moses and for early Judaism, but makes reserves about later developments of the Jewish religion. Polybius condemns Antiochus' attack on the Temple in Jerusalem, and Plutarch discusses the Jewish religion objectively. Dio Chrysostom praises the Essenes. More than all the others, the anonymous author of the famous work of literary criticism *On the Sublime* had words of praise for the Jewish lawmaker, and quoted from Genesis as an example of the sublime. We do not know however, where he lived. Among the writers from Asia Minor, the first in chronological order is Hermippus of Smyrna (ca. 200 B.C.E.).[1] Josephus and Origen, when affirming Pythagoras' debt to Judaism, base their arguments on Hermippus.[2] Josephus mentions the first book of Hermippus on Pythagoras, according to which Pythagoras was told by the ghost of one of his pupils not to pass a certain place where a donkey had fallen on its

[1] See Fraser, op. cit. II, p. 656, n. 52.
[2] Jos. *Against Apion* I, 162-5; Origenes, *Contra Celsum* I, 15, 334.

knees, and to abstain from thirst-causing water[1] and from slander. Afterwards Josephus quotes, seemingly directly, passages of Hermippus in which Jewish and Thracian influence on the Greek philosopher is stressed. In conclusion Josephus adds that Pythagoras is said to have included Jewish ideas in his philosophy. Origen is vague on the influence of Judaism on Pythagoras and it is not evident that Origen depended on Josephus, since he may have used another work by Hermippus.[2] In any case, there is no reason to suspect the authenticity of the passage cited by Josephus from Hermippus, since nothing in it leads to assume that a Jew composed it. The Jews are compared here to the Thracians in their influence on Pythagoras, but there is no exaggerated praise for the Jewish people. The influence on Pythagoras attributed here to the Jews fits in well with the various bits of information, whatever their value, on his connections with the East, and especially with Egypt.[3] Moreover, we have seen that at the beginning of the Hellenistic period the Jews were respected by Greek thinkers and writers, and Hermippus reflects this attitude.

A different picture is presented by Mnaseas of Patara in Lycia, a pupil of Eratosthenes.[4] Among his works we find a collection of myths arranged geographically.[5] When he writes of how Jews were viewed in ancient literature, Mnaseas is particularly interesting because he is the first writer known to us to affirm that they worshipped an ass, and he is quoted on the subject by Apion.[6] Mnaseas states explicitly that the Jews worshipped the ass's head. Since Eratosthenes, Mnaseas' teacher, died in the nineties of the second century B.C.E.,[7] Mnaseas may well have written his account of the Jewish-Idumaean war, where the story of ass-worship occurs, even before the time of Antiochus Epiphanes.[8] Mnaseas certainly spent some time in Egypt and it is likely that it was there, and not in Asia Minor, that he heard

---

[1] διψίων ὑδάτων is taken by S. Liebermann, *Ha-Jerushalmi Kiphshuto* I, I (1934), p. 49 to imply uncovered water.
[2] Origenes refers to a work *On the Legislators* known also from Athenaeus, *Deipnosophistae* IV, 41, p. 154 D; XIII, 2, p. 555 C; XIV, 10, p. 619 B; Porphyrius, *De abstinentia* IV, 22.
[3] See Th. Hopfner, *Orient und griechische Philosophie* (1925), pp. 3-6; I. Lévy, *La légende de Pythagore de Grèce en Palestine* (1927).
[4] See *P. Oxy.* XIII, No. 1611, fragm. 2, col. I, 11, 128-9.
[5] For Mnaseas see Laqueur in *PW* XV, p. 2250-2; Fraser, op. cit. II, p. 755, n. 41.
[6] See Jos. *Against Apion* II, 112-4.
[7] See Fraser, op. cit. II p. 489, n. 205 for the date of the death of Eratosthenes.
[8] On Mnaseas and Jewish ass-worship see A. Jacoby, in *Archiv für Religionswissenschaft* (1927), pp. 265-82; Tcherikover, pp. 365-6; see also L. Vischer, in *RHR* CXXXIX (1951), pp. 14-35.

of ass-worship. It seems that this idea took shape in certain anti-Jewish circles in Egypt. The ass was sacred to the god Typhon, the enemy of Osiris, and in those circles the story of the origins of the Jewish people was connected with Typhon. The story of the Jews' worship of the ass was linked in Hellenistic Egypt to the struggle between the Jews and Idumaeans, basically a Palestinian affair, though there were large Jewish and Idumaean communities in Ptolemaic Egypt.[1]

Agatharchides, who lived some decades later, was one of the great historians of the middle Hellenistic period (second century B.C.E.). A native of Cnidus in southwestern Asia Minor, he spent some time in Alexandria during the reign of Ptolemy VI Philometor and Ptolemy Physcon. The great historical works which made him famous were his voluminous histories of Asia and of Europe. During his stay in Egypt, if not earlier, he had the opportunity of getting to know the Jews of that country for whom the second century B.C.E. was a golden age. Like Theophrastus and Clearchus, Agatharchides was a member of the Peripatetic school. From one of his larger works a fragment has been preserved dealing with the conquest of Jerusalem by Ptolemy I.[2] It has reached us in two versions: a more complete one quoted in the *Against Apion*, and the other in Josephus' *Jewish Antiquities*.[3] We do not know whether Agatharchides expanded his writing on the Jews in other parts of his historical works which have not been preserved, nor whether he became an authority on Jewish matters in the eyes of later Greek writers,[4] a supposition which seems wholly unwarranted. In the fragment which has survived Agatharchides deals with the Jews in passing, in a non-Jewish context. In a description of the death of the princess Stratonice who sparked off a rebellion against king Seleucus II and lost her life, Agatharchides writes that she could have escaped by sea, but being detained by a dream, was arrested and executed. Agatharchides considers her behaviour as stemming from superstition. As another example of the harm done by superstition he mentions the Jewish people. Although they live in a very strong city, Jerusalem, they allowed it to fall without resistence into

[1] See U. Rapaport, in *Revue de Philologie* (1969), pp. 73-82.
[2] It may derive either from the *European History* of Agatharchides or from his *History of Asia*.
[3] *Against Apion* I, 205-11; *Ant.* XII, 5-6. On Agatharchides and his views see H. Leopoldi, *De Agatharchide Cnidio* (1892); E. A. Wagner, *Agatharchides und der mittlere Peripatos* (1901); O. Immisch, *Agatharchidea* (1919).
[4] See Wagner op. cit. p. 5-6.

the hands of Ptolemy, son of Lagos. All this because of their custom
to cease all work on the seventh day and to pray until evening in their
temples.[1] Thus a harsh ruler conquered their land. It seems that
Agatharchides had more precise knowledge of the customs of the
Jews than his predecessors in the early Hellenistic period. He is the
first among the Greek writers to mention the rest on the seventh day.
But he does not make the mistake of later Greek and Roman writers
who thought that the sabbath was a fast day. It is difficult to determine whether Agatharchides used the Septuagint in his work on the
Red Sea (*De Mari Erythraeo*) as some scholars maintain.[2] It seems to
me that there is no reason to see in Agatharchides one of the fore-
runners of ancient anti-Semitism. In principle, he denounces the
superstitions of the Jews no more than those of Stratonice.[3]

A contemporary of Agatharchides, the historian Polybius, touched on
the history of Palestine in his *Universal History*, which of necessity
included the struggle between the Ptolemaic and Seleucid kingdoms.
In his fifth book Polybius describes the fourth Syrian war, which
reached its climax at the battle near Raphia in Palestine. However,
although he describes the war in detail, including military activity in
Samaria, he completely omits contemporary events in Judaea. In
this omission he resembles Hieronymus of Cardia, the great historian
of the Diadochi period whom Josephus mentions as not referring to
the Jews.[4] The fact that Polybius does not mention the Jews in
connection with the fourth Syrian war can be explained by the minor
rôle played by the Jews in this war. However, we know from the
twelfth book of Josephus' *Antiquities* that Polybius dwelt specifically
on the relations between the Jews and Antiochus III during the fifth
Syrian war, and affirmed that the Jews living around the Temple,
called Jerusalem, sided with Antiochus.[5] On that occasion Polybius
declares that although he has much to write about the Temple and its
renown, he would do so in another context. It seems that this was to
be done in his history of Antiochus Epiphanes and his policy towards
the Jews. As can be adduced from the *Against Apion*, Polybius
specifically said somewhere that when Antiochus Epiphanes was in

---

[1] The doubts of E. L. Abel, in *REJ* cxxvii (1968), pp. 253-8 as to the historicity
of the event seem unwarranted.
[2] See Fraser, op. cit. i, p. 517; ii, p. 783, n. 204.
[3] For the interest taken by Agatharchides in irrational human behaviour see
A. Dihle in *Grecs et barbares-Entretiens sur l'antiquité classique* viii, p. 223.
[4] *Against Apion* i, 214.
[5] *Ant.* xii, 136.

financial trouble he broke his treaty with the Jews and looted the Temple which was filled with gold and silver.[1] Polybius was interested in everything that happened in the Hellenistic east from the time he was one of the young statesmen of the Achaean league. In 180 he was chosen to be one of the emissaries of the league to the court of king Ptolemy V Epiphanes, but the appointment was cancelled on the death of the king. He even tried to influence the Achaean league to intervene on behalf of Ptolemaic Egypt at the time of the invasion by Antiochus Epiphanes which endangered the very existence of the Ptolemaic kingdom. Later he did a great deal to help Demetrius I to conquer the Seleucid kingdom from Antiochus' son.[2] Some time after 145 he visited Alexandria, but it is still unclear whether he knew parts of the Syrian or Palestinian coast at first hand.[3] From what remains to us of Polybius' writings, it is impossible to evaluate his attitude towards Jews and Judaism. We can only deduce from his manner of expression that he had feelings of respect for the Temple in Jerusalem, which to him was the central institution of the Jewish people. It is also clear that he was not sympathetic to the policies of Antiochus Epiphanes in Judaea. This agrees with his general antipathy towards Antiochus and with the fact that Polybius belonged to the political circles opposed to Antiochus. Polybius saw Antiochus' actions in Jerusalem as an effort to recoup his finances, rather than an idealistic effort to Hellenize Judaea. The description of the Jews by Polybius clearly left its mark later historians. Polybius' influence on Livy cannot be denied. What is less obvious is the relationship between Polybius and Strabo in this respect.

In the Hellenistic period the cities of Phoenicia and Palestine produced a number of influential writers of Greek. However, only in the work of one of them, Meleager of Gadara (first century B.C.E.),[4] is there any hint of the writer's knowledge of Jews and Judaism.[5] Meleager himself writes that he was born in Gadara, grew up in Tyre and spent his old age on the island of Cos.[6] But there is no way of proving the

---

[1] See *Against Apion* II, 83-4.
[2] On the negative attitude of Polybius to Antiochus Epiphanes see F. Reuter, *Beiträge zur Beurteilung des Königs Antiochos Epiphanes* (1938).
[3] Polybius certainly visited Alexandria some time after 145 B.C.E.; see P. Pédech, *La méthode historique de Polybe* (1964), pp. 561-2.
[4] See for the date A. S. F. Gow and D. L. Page, *The Greek Anthology: Hellenistic Epigrams* I (1965), pp. XIV-XVII. An earlier date is argued by L. A. Stella, *Cinque poeti dell' antologia palatina* (1949), pp. 232-8.
[5] For Meleager and the Jews see also N. Bentwich, *JQR* (1932-3), pp. 183-4.
[6] See *Anthologia Palatina* VII, 418.

theory that Meleager left Gadara and went to Tyre because Gadara had been conquered by Alexander Jannaeus.[1] In one of his love poems he mentions the cold sabbath: 'If thy lover is some sabbath-keeper no great wonder! Not even love burns on cold sabbaths.'[2]

Posidonius of Apamea (135-51 B.C.E.), a philosopher, historian and scientist, was one of the great figures in the culture of the late Hellenistic period. He came from Syria and was later active in Rhodes. No complete works of Posidonius have been preserved, and there are only a few fragments of his works dealing with the Jews.[3] In fact, all that we know of Posidonius' attitude towards the Jews is contained in a declaration by Josephus that together with Apollonius Molon, Posidonius supplied the material for Apion's attacks on the Jews.[4] In Strabo's *Geography* there is a passage taken from Posidonius on the production of bitumen from the Dead Sea.[5] From what Josephus writes in the *Against Apion* we can deduce that Posidonius, like Apollonius Molon, blamed the Jews for not worshipping the gods accepted by others. He also spread slanders about the Temple in Jerusalem and, as has been said, together with Apollonius Molon supplied Apion with anti-Jewish material. Then, Josephus adduces examples of these slanderous statements from Apion's writing, referring to the worship of the ass's head and the story of the annual murder of a Greek in the Temple—a murder which was discovered when Antiochus Epiphanes entered the Temple. Josephus does not differentiate between Posidonius and Apollonius Molon in holding them responsible for supplying this material to Apion. The source of Josephus' knowledge of Posidonius' viewpoint is unclear. It is not certain from his wording that he compared the writings of Posidonius and Apollonius Molon with the work of Apion and so reached the conclusion that the Alexandrian writer quoted him. It seems more plausible that Apion himself wished to show his affinity with the great Posidonius. It is also interesting to note that Josephus does not reveal any sign of direct knowledge of Posidonius' writing in any other place

---

[1] That he left Gadara because of its capture by Alexander Jannaeus is maintained by C. Radinger, *Meleagros von Gadara* (1895), p. 5.

[2] See *Anthologia Palatina* v, 160; see also A. Pelletier, in *Vetus Testamentum* (1972), p. 441.

[3] On Posidonius see I. Heinemann, *Poseidonios' metaphysische Schriften* I-II (1921-8), K. Reinhardt, *Poseidonios über Ursprung und Entartung* (1928); idem in *PW* XXII, pp. 558-826; M. Laffranque, *Poseidonius d'Apamée* (1964); L. Edelstein and I. G. Kidd, *Posidonius* I, *The Fragments* (1972).

[4] *Against Apion* II, 79.

[5] *Geogr.* XVI, 2, 43, (p. 764).

in his works.[1] Posidonius was a profilic writer and it is therefore difficult to determine precisely in which of his works he deals with the Jewish Temple, although undoubtedly his *History* is the natural place. We know that it included events beginning in the forties of the second century B.C.E.[2] From this we can deduce that the slanders which Josephus attributes to Posidonius and which influenced Apion cannot have been part of the description of the relations between Antiochus Epiphanes and the Jews but were found in a context dealing with later times, perhaps in a digression centred on later developments. It seems to us that this contention is supported by a part of the thirty fourth book of the *History* of Diodorus Siculus, who describes the struggle between Antiochus VII and the Jews. According to this account, the enemies of the Jews in Antiochus' camp tried to bring him to uproot the Jewish religion, and pointed to the precedent of Antiochus Epiphanes. The historian does not sympathize with them. He praises the king for not paying attention to his advisors and contenting himself with imposing a tax and destroying the walls of Jerusalem. 'But the king, being a magnanimous and mild-mannered person, took hostages but dismissed the charges against the Jews, once he had exacted the tribute that was due and had dismantled the walls of Jerusalem.'[3] Most scholars hold that Diodorus, from book thirty-three of his work onwards, depended on Posidonius, but this theory raises difficulties in the matter under discussion. As mentioned above, Josephus, in *Against Apion*, attributes an anti-Jewish outlook to Posidonius, but the section in Diodorus praises Antiochus VII for his refusal to accept the suggestions of the sworn enemies of the Jews. It is possible that Apion purposely blurred the fact that what was said against the Jews in Posidonius' work was really the view of the king's advisors, and does not express Posidonius' own view. Josephus, who did not know Posidonius' work directly, was led astray by Apion and thought that Posidonius was a sworn enemy of the Jews. Moreover, we should not forget that the dependence of part of Diodorus' work on Posidonius is based on mere supposition. More problematic is the attribution to Posidonius of the description of the origins and development of the Jewish religion as presented in the sixteenth book

---

[1] See R. Scheppig. *De Posidonio Apamensi Rerum Gentium Terrarum Scriptore* (1869), pp. 33-4.
[2] For the history of Posidonius see Reinhardt, in *PW* XXII, pp. 630-41; M. Laffranque, op. cit. pp. 109-51.
[3] See Diodorus XXXIV-XXXV, 1, 5.

of Strabo's *Geography* (see below p. 1131). We also know something about the attitude of Posidonius' native city, Apamea, towards its Jewish inhabitants at the end of Second Temple times. According to our sources, the attitude was friendly, and the Jews of the city did not suffer at the hands of their neighbours at the time of the great revolt,[1] unlike the Jews in most Syrian cities. Numenius, the second century C.E. philosopher and the forerunner of Neoplatonism, who showed a particularly sympathetic attitude towards Judaism, also came from Apamea. In conclusion, it is hard to evaluate the attitude of Posidonius towards Judaism since no unequivocal material exists on this point.

The attitude of Apollonius Molon (first century B.C.E.) towards the Jews is clearer. He was born in Alabanda in Caria and was one of the greatest rhetors of his time. Later he moved to Rhodes which became the principal center of his activities. Among his desciples were some of the greatest men of Rome such as Cicero and Julius Caesar.[2] Apollonius Molon is the first Greek writer after Hecataeus who is said to have written a special book on the Jews. The main surviving fragment of this work is found in a contemporary of his, Alexander Polyhistor, who was also from Asia Minor. Polyhistor's writing was preserved by the ecclesiastical writer Eusebius in the ninth book of his *Praeparatio Evangelica*.[3] Following Josephus, one tends to view Apollonius Molon as a bitter opponent of the Jews, like Apion whom he influenced. Josephus[4] tries to degrade his intellectual and moral stature, while Plutarch praises him. From the fragments preserved in Josephus we learn that Apollonius Molon accused the Jews of shutting themselves off from the outside world and hating strangers; in his view Moses was a fraud and there was nothing good in the Jewish Bible. He attributed to the Jews both cowardice and the courage of despair. Moreover, according to Apollonius, the Jews, more than all barbarians, are devoid of talent; they are a people who have contributed nothing to human civilization.[5] Josephus, in fact, says that Apollonius did not compose a single lengthy denunciation

---

[1] See Jos. *War* II, 479.
[2] See Cicero, *Brutus* 316; Plutarch, *Cicero* 4, *Caesar* 3; on his influence on Cicero see F. Portalupi, *Sulla corrente rodiese* (1957), pp. 16-17; J. C. Davies, in *Classical Quarterly* (1968), pp. 303-14.
[3] *Praeparatio Evangelica* IX, 19, 1-3.
[4] See Jos. *Against Apion* II, 255.
[5] See Jos. *Against Apion* II, 16; 79-80; 89; 91-6; 145; 148; 236; 255; 258; 295.

of the Jews. The accusations are scattered throughout his work.[1] Moreover, the main surviving fragment in Eusebius does not contain any anti-Jewish comments. What it mainly says is this: The man who survived the flood (i.e. Noah, whose name is not mentioned) left Armenia with his sons after he was expelled by the local people. He finally reached the mountainous part of Syria which was then desolate. Three generations later Abraham was born; his name means 'friend of God.'[2] Abraham was wise and went to the desert.[3] He married two wives, one local, and one an Egyptian maidservant. The Egyptian wife bore Abraham twelve sons who divided Arabia amongst themselves. His lawful wife bore him one son whose name in Greek was Γέλως (laughter).[4] Gelos had twelve sons, the youngest of whom was Joseph, and Joseph's grandson was Moses.[5] Apollonius' narrative is based on some form of the biblical story which probably came to him indirectly, from Hellenistic Jewish circles. It is noteworthy that Apollonius Molon does not seem to have been influenced by the Graeco-Egyptian tradition of the origins of the Jewish people, but stresses only the connection between the beginning of the Jewish people and Syria. Apollonius Molon probably came into contact with Jews in his native town of Alabanda, and he could certainly have met Jews during his stay in Rhodes.[6] The importance of Apollonius is considerable because he was the teacher and mentor of some of the greatest men from the end of the Roman republic, although there is nothing in Caesar's political dealings with Jews or in Cicero's attitude which shows the influence of Apollonius Molon.

Among Greeks of Asia Minor who wrote about the Jews, Alexander, known as Polyhistor, deserves special mention. Born in Miletus, he was brought to Rome as a slave and later freed by Sulla.[7] He was interested in the Jews as part of his general history and also as coming into prominence with Pompey's capture of Jerusalem. His work on the Jews was only one of his many works on various nations

---

[1] *Against Apion* ii, 148.
[2] See L. Ginzberg, *The Legends of the Jews* v, p. 207, n. 4.
[3] On the motif of retirement into the desert see M. Hengel, *Die Zeloten* (1961), pp. 255-61.
[4] For the Greek proper name Γέλως see L. Robert, in *Hellenica* ii (1946), p. 6, line 28.
[5] A similar tradition is to be found in Iustinus xxxvi, 2, 11 (deriving from Pompeius Trogus; here Moses is stated to be the son of Joseph).
[6] See chapter three, p. 153.
[7] On Alexander Polyhistor see J. Freudenthal, *Alexander Polyhistor* (1875); Schwartz, in *PW* i, pp. 1449-52 = *Griechische Geschichtsschreiber* (1959) pp. 240-4.

and other subjects. His compilations included quotations from various authors linked by connecting passages which he wrote himself. The remnants of Alexander's work on the Jews have been preserved in the ninth book of Eusebius' *Praeparatio Evangelica*. From it we know that Alexander Polyhistor read about the Jews in a large number of Jewish and non-Jewish writeis. Among the Jewish writers were Demetrius, Eupolemus, the epic poet Philo and the dramatic poet Ezekiel. Among the non-Jewish Greek writers he used Timochares and Apollonius Molon. But it is interesting to note that Alexander Polyhistor also mentioned the Jews in works devoted to other nations. Sometimes, the information he brings obviously contradicts that of the Jewish source he himself cites in his work on the Jews, but such contradictions did not disturb him.[1] Josephus quotes Alexander Polyhistor only once, citing an extract quoted by Cleodemus, but it is possible that this passage was not from Alexander's work on the Jews, but from his work on Libya. However, it is likely that the debt owed by Josephus to Alexander Polyhistor is greater than may be supposed from this single quotation.[2]

In addition to Apollonius Molon and Alexander Polyhistor, a third writer from Asia Minor of the first century B.C.E. who wrote about Jews was Teucer of Cyzicus. We know hardly anything about Teucer. Our sole source is in Suda which states: 'He wrote about gold-producing land, about Byzantium, five books about the achievements of Mithridates, five about Tyre, five of Arabian history, a Jewish history in six books, three books on the training of ephebes at Cyzicus and other works.'[3]

Diodorus came from a different part of the Greek world. He was born in Agyrium in Sicily, and wrote a universal history. The value of this work lies mainly in the fact that it is a compilation of works by earlier historians which adhered slavishly to their original content and attitudes.[4] But we cannot always determine the sources which he used

---

[1] See Suda s.v. Ἀλέξανδρος ὁ Μιλήσιος. Cf. Heinemann, in *PW*, XVI, p. 360; Gager, p. 20.
[2] See G. Hölscher, *Die Quellen des Josephus* (1904), pp. 43-52; E. Norden, *Kleine Schriften* (1966), p. 269; B. Motzo, *Saggi di storia e letteratura Giudeo-Ellenistica* (1924), p. 193.
[3] See Suda s.v. Τεῦκρος ὁ Κυζικηνός. The number of the books of Teucer's *Jewish History* should not surprise us if we compare it with the five books of his *History of Tyre* and the five books of his *Arabian History*.
[4] Diodorus' original contribution consisted mainly in changes of style and to some occasional comments. See J. Palm, *Über Sprache und Stil des Diodoros von Sizilien* (1955).

in the passages on the Jews. His main discussion of the Jews, their history and their religion is included in a description of the conquest of Jerusalem by Pompey.[1] Here Diodorus mentions Hecataeus as his source. But the source of Diodorus' narrative of the end of the Hasmonaean kingdom and of the appearance of Jewish emissaries before Pompey in Damascus,[2] is a matter of conjecture. It is interesting that in giving a list of lawgivers, including Minos, Lycurgus, Zathraustes (Zarathustra) and Zalmoxis, Diodorus mentions Moses last. These claimed to have received the laws from the gods. The name of the Jewish divinity appearing here is Iao.[3] What was Diodorus' source for this is an open question.[4]

Among the descriptions in ancient Greek literature of Judaea and the Jewish religion, that of Strabo's *Geography* stands out as the fullest.[5] Strabo was born in Amaseia on the river Iris in Pontus about 64 B.C.E. He came from an honourable background, and according to his own testimony, travelled a great deal: 'I passed in a westerly direction from Armenia to places in Tyrrhenia opposite Sardinia, and southward from the Black Sea to the borders of Ethiopia.'[6] He knew at least some of Asia Minor, had visited Corinth, and had spent some time in Cyrene, Egypt and Rome. On the other hand there is no mention of his ever having visited Palestine.[7] Strabo could have met Jews in his homeland, Pontus, and might well have visited the main centres of the Jewish Diaspora (Alexandria, Cyrene, Rome and the cities of Asia Minor), and could have learned about the Jews at first hand. Strabo claims to be a Stoic, and the Stoics were in his eyes 'our people' (οἱ ἡμέτεροι). He was undoubtedly close to various Roman personalities and we hear especially of his connections with Aelius Gallus, prefect of

---

[1] Diodorus XL, 3.
[2] Diodorus XL, 2.
[3] Diodorus I, 94, 1-2.
[4] Some scholars derive this passage from Posidonius. See I. Heinemann, in *MGWJ* (1919), pp. 117-8; G. Pfligersdorffer, *Studien zu Poseidonios* (1959), p. 145. On the other hand J. Bidez et F. Cumont, *Les mages hellénisés* I (1938), pp. 20-1 hold the view that it derives from Hecataeus. However, already Schwartz in *PW* v, p. 670 expressed his opinion that is hardly possible to detect the ultimate source of the passage. See also W. Aly, *Strabon von Amaseia* (1957), pp. 200-1 who also disagrees with the view that the name Iao in Diodorus comes from Hecataeus.
[5] The relevant passages are scattered through the sixteenth and seventeenth books of the *Geography*, but mainly to be found in the sixteenth book. See Stern nos. 110-24.
[6] *Geogr.* II, 5, 11 (p. 117).
[7] See Aly, op. cit. p. 48.

Egypt, and it is perhaps possible to trace further connections between him and the great men of Rome.[1] He saw his literary creation as a guide for men of political action and as useful to society. He was important both as a historian and as a geographer, and his historical work preceded his *Geography*. As a historian he continued where Polyhistor left off (145/144 B.C.E.), and he seemingly completed his work with the conquest of Alexandria by Augustus (30 B.C.E.), although it is possible to date the end of the events described by him a few years later.[2] The major part of the work comprised forty-three books, to which a summary introduction dealing with the period preceding 145 and comprising four books (προκατασκευή) was added. Unfortunately, only a few fragments have been preserved of Strabo's comprehensive historical work. Since most of the fragments were preserved through being cited in Josephus' *Antiquities of the Jews*, they deal with Jewish matter. This should not, of course, lead us to exaggerate the attention he gave to the Jews, compared to his general coverage of events. One would naturally expect the historian from distant Pontus to have a different approach to the affairs of Judaea than that, for instance, of his contemporary Nicholas of Damascus. Nicholas was influenced by the contacts between the kingdom of Judaea and Hellenistic Syria, from which he stemmed, as well as by his personal status as one of Herod's close friends. On the other hand, Strabo was not involved in the events of Palestine in the times of the Hasmonaean and Herodian dynasties, either emotionally or actually. The fragments of his historical work therefore reveal a substantially different approach from that of Nicholas. Chronologically, the first event of the Jews mentioned in these fragments is the looting of the Temple by Antiochus Epiphanes in 169 B.C.E., while the last event is the execution of Antigonus, the last Hasmonaean king, at Antony's order (37 B.C.E.). In the first passage Strabo is mentioned together with Polybius, Nicholas and a number of other Greek writers as a historian who condemned the looting of the Temple by Antiochus, describing it as unprovoked aggresion. The next section belongs chronologically to the reign of John Hyrcan and deals with the period following the Jewish conquest of Samaria. Josephus, who connects the success of the Jews in Judaea with the condition of the Jews in Egypt at the time of Cleopatra III, cites the passage from Strabo which deals with the struggle between the queen and her son Ptolemy

[1] See G. W. Bowersock, *Augustus and the Greek World* (1965), pp. 128-9.
[2] See R. Syme, in *Harvard Studies in Classical Philology* (1959), p. 65.

Lathyrus. Strabo says that most of the soldiers sent by the queen to Cyprus deserted her and went over to her son. The only ones who remained loyal were the Jews in 'the land of Onias.'[1] Of particular interest is the section describing the reign of Aristobulus I. Here Strabo bases his remarks on Timagenes, who says that Aristobulus was of great benefit to the Jews.[2] This favourable appreciation contrasts with the image of the Hasmonaean ruler given in Josephus' main narrative, which is based on the work of Nicholas of Damascus. One can see how Hasmonaean rule is described in sources not dependent on Nicholas' *History*. One of the most important fragments of Strabo's historical work deals with the Jews of Cyrene and the organization of the Jews of Egypt. Strabo states that the Jews are one of the four elements in the population of Cyrene.[3] The other three are the citizens, the farmers and the *metoikoi*. Events in Cyrene caused Strabo to comment generally on the condition of the Jewish people who, he said, had penetrated all the cities, so that it was not easy to find a place in the inhabited world which did not include this people and was not ruled by it (μηδ' ἐπικρατεῖται ὑπ' αὐτοῦ).[4] Strabo saw the Jews as originally Egyptian. This idea is repeated in his geographic work. In his *History*, he also mentions the conquest of Jerusalem, and it was from Strabo that Josephus learned that the city was conquered on a fast day.[5] His account of the campaign which saved Julius Caesar in Alexandria (47 B.C.E.), sheds light on the condition of the Jews at the time of Hyrcan II. Josephus' principal narrative, which is dependent on Nicholas, mainly stresses the rôle played in these events by Antipater, Herod's father. Hyrcan's personality and his rôle in these events were blurred and Antipater was allowed to overshadow him. Here too, as in the case of Aristobulus I, Strabo's material enables us to interpret events in a way which differs from the pro-Herodian narrative of Nicholas.[6] As mentioned above, the last section which has been preserved from Strabo's *History* deals with the execution of Antigonus the Hasmonaean by Antony in Antioch.[7] Strabo

---

[1] *Ant.* XIII, 287. [2] *Ant.* XIII, 319.
[3] See *Ant.* XIV, 115.
[4] For interpretations of the passage see I. Heinemann, in *PW, Supplementband* V (1931), p. 16; A. G. Roos, *Mnemosyne* (1935), pp. 236-7. However, it seems that Strabo exaggerates in order to stress the pervasive Jewish influence.
[5] *Ant.* XIV, 66.
[6] See *Ant.* XIV, 138-9. Cf. B. R. Motzo, *Studi Cagliaritani di Storia e Filologia* I (1927), pp. 1-18.
[7] See *Ant.* XV, 8-10. Bowersock, op. cit. p. 125, n. 5 suggests that Strabo derives here from Timagenes.

states that this is the first time the Romans resorted to beheading, and that Antony did so only because he saw no other way of influencing the Jews to accept Herod as their king. This unusual death, beheading, was meant to render the king odious. On the other hand, Josephus' main narrative, which is based on Nicholas, attempts to belittle Antigonus by presenting him as a coward pleading for his life.[1] From Strabo's writings, however, the king emerges as a man who was respected by his people and preferred decisively to Herod.

As seen from his *History*, Strabo's attitude towards the Jews can be summarized as follows: 1. His attitude towards the Hasmonaean dynasty is more balanced than that of Josephus. 2. Strabo is very impressed by the numbers of Jews all over the world and by the strength of the Jewish people. 3. According to Strabo the Jews are Egyptians in origin. 4. Strabo is ignorant of Jewish customs, and like other classical writers thought that the sabbath was a fast day. However, Strabo's *Geography* provides the main information on his view of the Jews and Judaism, particularly the sixteenth book, the second-last of the work.

His *Geography* was written later than his *History* and is aimed at the same enlightened audience of men of action. He included a great many historical facts about the countries described. The work deals mainly with the reign of Augustus, its trends and events, although some information from the reign of Tiberius is included. We can assume that it took a long time to gather the material and write the *Geography*.[2] It is not clear where Strabo wrote and published his *Geography*, but it was probably in one of the cities in the eastern part of the Roman empire.[3] Naturally, space is devoted to a description of Palestine in the framework of the general survey of Syria. At the beginning of this discussion Strabo lists the parts of the country: Commagene, Seleucis, Phoenicia and inland Judaea. Here Strabo comments that some divide Syria among the Coelo-Syrians, the Syrians and the Phoenicians, and maintain that four other nations are mingled with these: the Idumaeans, the Gazaeans, the Azotians and the Jews. The Syrians and Coelo-Syrians cultivate the land, while the Phoenicians are merchants. This reflects the situation in the second century B.C.E., for the Idumaeans lost their special identity in the twenties of that

---

[1] *Ant.* XIV, 481.
[2] See E. Pais, *Ancient Italy* (1908), pp. 379-428.
[3] See J. G. C. Anderson, in *Anatolian studies presented to Sir William Mitchell Ramsay* (1923), p. 13.

century, the Azotians lost theirs in the time of John Hyrcan, while Gaza was conquered by Alexander Jannaeus about 96 B.C.E. On the other hand, the situation which arose with the expansion of the Hasmonaean kingdom is evident later,[1] when Strabo comes to define the boundaries of Coele-Syria in their broad and narrow sense. He says that the inland part of the country beyond Phoenicia up to Arabia, between Gaza and the Anti-Lebanon, is called Judaea. This description reflects the change which took place in Palestine as a result of the conquest of most of the country by the Jews. In describing the coast of Palestine, Strabo does not usually show any knowledge of the situation in his time. Of Joppa, he says that it was a harbour of pirates and a den of robbers,[2] which is an insulting comment on the Jews. His description of Judaea begins with the Idumaeans who, he says, hold the western part of the country. The Idumaeans, he maintains, are really Nabataeans who left their country because of internal trouble, joined the Jews, and agreed to share their customs.[3] There is no parallel in any other source to the information that the Idumaeans were originally Nabataeans. Nor is there any other source which gives the same impression as Strabo on the Judaization of the Idumaeans. From Josephus it is clear that conversion was forced upon the Idumaeans, while Strabo states that it was voluntary.[4] Strabo regards the people of Palestine as of mixed origins, including Egyptians, Arabs and Phoenicians. This is the make-up of the populations of Galilee, Jericho, Philadelphia and Samaria (Sebaste). His predominant view of the Jews is that their ancestors were Egyptians. This concept of the Egyptian origin of the Jews, which we have already encountered in Strabo's *History*, is the background for his description of the development of the Jewish religion and his famous chapter on Moses. According to Strabo, Moses was an Egyptian from lower Egypt who deplored the situation in his homeland and who attracted many followers who respected the deity. Moses opposed the picturing of the deity in the form of man or animal and was convinced that the deity was an entity which encompassed everything—land and sea—an entity which 'we call heaven, earth, nature, everything.' As the leader of intelligent people, Moses reached the site of Jerusalem and conquered it easily. Since the area was rocky, it was not the object

---

[1] Strabo, *Geogr.* XVI, 2, 21, p. 756.
[2] Strabo, *Geogr.* XVI, 2, 28, p. 759.
[3] Strabo, *Geogr.* XVI, 2, 34, p. 760.
[4] Jos. *Ant.* XIII, 257.

of jealousy nor did it motivate anyone to fight for it tenaciously. Temples and the deity served Moses instead of weapons, and he promised his followers a ritual which would not be a burden to anyone by expensive foolish customs. Moses became famous and the neighbouring population joined him of its own will (here again joining the Jews by choice and not by force). His heirs continued in his way for a time, they were righteous and true believers in God. But in the course of time people with superstitious beliefs arose and took over the priesthood.[1] Later people of tyrannical character took over. Superstition brought about the abstention from certain foods as is customary among Jews up to now, the custom of circumcision for males and females[2] and other such customs. From the tyrannical rule sprang robbery and all the other evils which harmed the Jews' own country as well as the neighbouring ones with such exploits as capturing the lands of foreigners and enslaving a large part of Syria and Phoenicia. In this way Strabo distinguishes the different stages in the history of Judaism: the first stage is the time of Moses and his direct heirs; the second marks the beginning of the decline resulting from the growth of superstition; while the third is that of robbery and tyranny. But even in this final stage, the Temple of Jerusalem continued to be surrounded by an aura of sanctity. With regard to the personality and accomplishment of Moses, Strabo discusses other famous lawmakers and describes their achievements. He describes Moses as the same type of man as Minos of Crete, Lycurgus of Sparta and others who claimed divine inspiration. His positive and unequivocal appreciation of Moses' personality is among the most sympathetic in all ancient literature. His portrayal of Moses is reminiscent of the writing of Hecataeus who in the beginning of the Hellenistic period described Moses as a man who excelled in wisdom and courage. But while according to Strabo the decay of the Jewish religion was the result of an internal process within Jewish society, Hecataeus argued that the internal changes occurred in Judaea as a result of changing political situations. Both writers contrast the Jewish deity with anthropomorphic gods, and both emphasize the unity of God. But while Hecataeus just notes that the Jews refrain from making any idols and reject anthropomorphism, Strabo seems to agree with the

[1] On the attitude of Strabo towards superstition see P. J. Koets, *Deisidaimonia. A contribution to the knowledge of the religious terminology in Greek* (1929), pp. 63-5.
[2] On circumcision of females among Jews see also Strabo, *Geogr.* XVI, 4, 9, p. 771; XVII, 2, 5, p. 824. Yet Strabo, in contrast to other Greek writers, does not state that the Jews derived circumcision from the Egyptians.

teachings of Moses on this matter. Opposition to the cult of images was a long-standing tradition in the Stoa.[1] Here Strabo the Stoic gives expression to a trend in Greek philosophical thought. Without any reservation Strabo states that Moses was a priest from lower Egypt, and that his followers were also Egyptians who left their homeland and migrated together with him to Judaea. Strabo differs here from Hecataeus who saw the Jews as strangers who were in Egypt temporarily. On the other hand, there is a parallel with the Graeco-Egyptian literary tradition, beginning in the third century B.C.E., for in both Manetho and Chaeremon Moses appears as an Egyptian priest. According to Celsus too (second century C.E.) the Jews are rebels against the religious tradition of Egypt.[2] Strabo differs from the others in that he regards the departure of Moses from his nation's former tradition as a positive step. It should be added that Strabo had already formulated the idea that the Jews were of Egyptian origin in his earlier historical work, and when he discusses this point in his geography it is no longer new to him.

The question of the source of Strabo's views on Moses and the development of the Jewish religion has been extensively discussed by many scholars. This discussion has been nurtured by the increasing interest in the personality of Posidonius (see p. 1123). In the 19th century, and to a greater extent at the beginning of the 20th, scholars began to link Strabo's writing with Posidonius.[3] In 1919 Heinemann presented his opinion with the arguments for it.[4] His views were not known to Norden who published an article in 1921, which made a greater impact than Heinemann's study. In Norden's view, Strabo's source was someone who was particularly interested in geography and ethnography. He was a Stoic philosopher, historian, geographer and ethnographer. The obvious candidate seemed to be Posidonius. However, Norden also suggested that Polybius was a source for part of Strabo's description. The compromise conclusion is that Polybius was in fact the original source for Strabo's work, but that his views reached Strabo through Posidonius.[5] Norden won many followers, although

[1] See H. v. Arnim, *Stoicorum Veterum Fragmenta* (1921) I, fragm. 264; B. de Borries, *Quid Veteres Philosophi de Idolatria Senserint* (1918).
[2] See Origenes, *Contra Celsum* III, 5.
[3] See Reinach, p. 89; R. Reitzenstein, *Zwei religionsgeschichtliche Fragen* (1907), p. 77, n. 2; J. Geffcken, *Zwei griechische Apologeten* (1907), p. XI, n. 5.
[4] See I. Heinemann, in MGWJ (1919), pp. 113-21.
[5] As Norden (p. 296) states: 'der primäre Autor des strabonischen Abschnitts war Polybios, aber er liegt vor in der Überarbeitung und Erweiterung des Poseidonios.'

most of them passed over Polybius as the primary source contenting themselves with Posidonius alone.[1] It would appear that there are sufficient grounds to accept Posidonius as Strabo's source for the passages under discussion. Strabo frequently used Posidonius as a source in his geographical work and even in the 16th book he writes that Posidonius was the greatest scholar among the philosophers of his time.[2] Once he mentions him specifically with regard to the production of bitumen from the Dead Sea.[3] However, we know little of Posidonius' attitude towards the Jews, and those scholars who believed that the chapters on the origins of the Jewish people in Strabo's work are based on Posidonius felt somewhat uncomfortable when they had to determine where they occurred in Posidonius' lost *History*.[4] It should also be pointed out that there are a number of other difficulties in making Strabo dependent on Posidonius here: 1. One of the main elements in Strabo's view of the Jews is their Egyptian origin. However, we have seen that Strabo accepted this as fact when he wrote his *History* which was earlier than his *Geography*. It is not clear that he used Posidonius' *History* in writing his earlier work.[5] 2. Among the list of prophets included in Strabo's section on Moses is Decaeneus the Seer of the king of the Getae who was active in the forties B.C.E., in the time of Julius Caesar. It seems that Posidonius was no longer alive then. But even if it were possible to argue away the difficulties which arise in attributing the chapters on Moses to Posidonius, the fact remains that there have been no conclusive arguments to prove him the author of these chapters. At most it can be assumed that the chapters on Moses owe something to Posidonius' general views of religion, but it is not certain that Posidonius himself stated these views when speaking of the Jewish religion. Some scholars feel that Strabo used a Jewish source here, and the idea has also been aired that Strabo's digression on Judaism depends on a work written by a Jew who knew Posidonius' views.[6] The Hellenism

[1] So e.g. J. Morr, in *Philologus* LXXXI, pp. 256-79; H. Strasburger, in *JRS* (1965), p. 44. Cf. also F. Wehrli, *Studies in Memory of Ph. Merlan* (1975), pp. 254-5.
[2] Strabo, *Geogr.* XVI, 2, 10, p. 753.
[3] Strabo, *Geogr.* XVI, 2, 43, p. 764.
[4] Reinhardt and Pohlenz, *Die Stoa* II (2nd ed. 1955), p. 105, even suppose that Strabo derives not from the *History* of Posidonius, but from a special monograph written by him on Pompey. Yet the very existence of such a monograph is extremely doubtful. See Aly, op. cit. pp. 94-7.
[5] On the Egyptian origins of the Jewish people see already the passage from Strabo's historical work quoted in *Ant.* XIV, 118.
[6] A. D. Nock in *JRS* (1959), p. 9.

of this Jew, as opposed to that of Philo, was not absolutely subjected to the Scriptures. A Jew of this sort was possibly unhappy with the legalism and militancy of the Hasmonaeans. But this view runs into difficulty because Strabo's *Geography* not only contradicts the Bible, but also would make us attribute to this Jew the idea that an Egyptian priest and Egyptian people laid the foundations of Judaism. We know of Jews like Artapanus who were so eager to emphasize the contribution of Judaism to human civilization that they were even ready to attribute to Moses the creation of Egyptian ritual, but we have not found an ancient Jewish writer who described the opposite process, that is the contribution of Gentiles to the foundation of Judaism. It therefore seems preferable to make Strabo dependent on non-Jewish sources. In fact there is no reason to deny Strabo all originality here. He may be not only derivative here. Thanks to his broad learning and widespread travel, including long stays in centres of Jewish population, and to his relatively great preoccupation with Jews in connection with his historical work, Strabo could have come to know some views on the origin of Judaism and the development of the Jewish state. He could easily have merged this information with general contemporary views of religion. The contrasts between the lofty and philosophical character of the original religion of Moses as pictured by Strabo, and then the specific laws which he treats as superstitions, and finally the aggressive spirit which in his eyes brought about the ruin of the Hellenistic cities of Palestine, can be explained with the help of philosophical theories on the process of decline in matters of religion and ritual. This type of explanation was not limited to Posidonius and can already be seen among such earlier thinkers as Theophrastus. It is of course possible that Posidonius had great influence on Strabo, just as it is possible that other thinkers in his time and earlier influenced him and directed his mind along these lines. Like most Greek and Roman writers from Hecataeus to Tacitus, Strabo skips the early Judaean kingdom, but unlike them he does not mention in his geography the foreign domination of Judaea either by the Persians or the Greeks. The Romans are the first conquerors who appear in his historical survey of the country. The first personality he mentions by name after Moses is Alexander Jannaeus, whom he sees as the man who exchanged the priestly government for a monarchy.[1] He dwells somewhat on the conquest of Judaea by Pompey and describes the

---

[1] *Geogr.* XVI, 2, 40, p. 762.

strength of Jerusalem.[1] Since he has already written about the Jordan and Sea of Galilee, in this context he discusses only the Valley of Jericho and its produce, balsam and dates, whose quality he also mentions elsewhere.

We have discussed Strabo at such length because his personality and his attitude towards the Jews are of great interest. He is important as the spokesman of one of the decisive periods of ancient history, the beginning of the Roman Principate. His interest in the Jews and Judaism is part of a wider phenomenon. They aroused great interest in Asia Minor in the Hellenistic period and in the first decades of the Roman empire.

There were many reactions to the Jewish impact on the Greek and Roman world. To concentrate only on some major Latin writers who lived in the time between Nero and Hadrian and to speak mainly of some Graeco-Egyptian writers who were active at the centre of the major conflicts of the Diaspora would not do justice to all the aspects of the Jewish-Gentile confrontation as reflected in Graeco-Roman literature.

Nicholas of Damascus was a contemporary of Strabo. Nicholas'[2] attitude towards the Jews was naturally much influenced by his milieu. He was a Syrian Greek, proud of Damascus and representing the aspirations of the Greek cities, and also a member of the royal court of Judaea and a confidant of king Herod. He could thus learn more about the Jews than any other Greek writer. His closeness to Herod inclined his sympathies towards the Jewish people, and gave him an interest in their past. He was their spokesman in 14 B.C.E., when he confronted the Roman statesman Agrippa. From the fragments of his universal history we can see that Nicholas was also interested in the biblical tradition: he sometimes mentions great figures of the Jewish past, such as Abraham, in an essentially non-Jewish context. He is the first of non-Jewish writers before the spread of Christianity to mention King David.[3] In one section he also mentions that he intends to deal with the descendants of Abraham elsewhere: 'But not

---

[1] He may have used here the work of Theophanes the freedman and friend of Pompey. See on him F. P. Rizzo, *Le fonti per la storia della conquista pompeiana della Siria* (1963), pp. 35-7; on the other hand M. Dubois, *Examen de la géographie de Strabon* (1891), p. 327 suggested a dependence of Strabo on Posidonius in the narrative of the activities of Pompey in Judaea, but without proving his case.

[2] See chapter one, pp. 29-30.

[3] See Jos. *Ant.* VII, 101.

long after, he left this country also with his people for the land then called Canaan but now Judaea, where he settled, he and his numerous descendants, whose history I shall recount in another book.'[1] But this item has not been preserved and we cannot know with certainty in what context Nicholas went more fully into the history of the Jews. All we know is that he wrote a circumstantial and laudatory history of the reign of Herod, and that Josephus based himself on this in his story of Herod. Nicholas also wrote about Judaea in Hasmonaean times in his universal history, and his treatment of the subject is also reflected in Josephus' work. Josephus took from Nicholas both the factual material and, to a great extent, his point of view. For the *Jewish War* Nicholas was practically Josephus' sole source, and in the thirteenth book of *Jewish Antiquities*, his major source, to whom he adds others such as Strabo, original documents and Jewish traditions. It is often easy to identify these different sources, while Josephus' main narrative is obviously influenced by Nicholas with regard to everything connected with this period. Josephus' dependence on Nicholas explains the odd fact that despite his national pride and his family connections with the Hasmonaean dynasty, he presents an unsympathetic picture of the main characters of the Hasmonaean dynasty, such as Aristobulus I, Alexander Jannaeus and his wife Salome-Alexandra. In the *Antiquities*, he is even sympathetic to Gaza, the Greek city conquered by the Jews. The prosopographical material is much richer on the Greeks than on the Jews.[2] Moreover, it seems that there was a deliberate attempt to gloss over the victories of Alexander Jannaeus.[3] These characteristics of Josephus' treatment of the Hasmonaean kings can be explained on the assumption that Josephus was greatly influenced by Nicholas. Nicholas of Damascus, as a Graeco-Syrian, had many reasons for disliking the Hasmonaeans who were the enemies and destroyers of the Hellenistic cities and belonged to a dynasty exterminated by Herod. An example of Nicholas' approach is his description of the reign of Aristobulus, the first Hasmonaean king, which runs counter to the spirit of the short

---

[1] See *Ant.* I, 160.

[2] Thus he knows the names of the Greek leaders at Gaza and their internal struggles. See *Ant.* XIII, 358-64.

[3] See e.g. *Ant.* XIII, 389-91 with Syncellus I (p. 559 ed. Dindorf) which is here presumably independent of Josephus where we read of a victory of Alexander Jannaeus over Antiochus Dionysus and not of a defeat as related by Josephus. On the value of Syncellus as an historical source see H. Gelzer, *Sextus Julius Africanus* I (1880), pp. 255-68.

section on the subject written by Strabo, in dependence on Timagenes (see p. 1130). In sum, as can be expected of a historian who was friend and adviser to a Jewish king and who defended the rights of the Jews in the cities of Asia Minor, Nicholas is more appreciative of the Jewish past and traditions than most Graeco-Roman writers. But his description of the Hasmonaean dynasty was influenced by his close connections with Herod and by his natural sympathy with the inhabitants of the Graeco-Syrian cities. It seems that Nicholas did not directly influence any later Greek or Latin writers on the Jews, other than Josephus.

The translation of the Bible into Greek had very little effect on Greek literature. But some echo of it can perhaps be found in the neo-Pythagorean work attributed to Ocellus Lucanus (c. second century B.C.E.). Here one idea propounded is that man's sexual drive was given him not for pleasure but to ensure the continued existence of the race. Man should therefore fulfil his obligations not like animals but to fill the earth with good people. Ocellus' wording here (πλείονα τῆς γῆς πληροῦσθαι) is reminiscent of Genesis 1:28 (Αὐξάνεσθε καὶ πληθύνεσθε καὶ πληρώσατε τὴν γῆν).[1] The Septuagint seems to have also influenced the anonymous author of the great book of literary criticism, *On the Sublime*, which has been wrongly attributed to Longinus.[2] Most scholars agree that the author lived in the time of Augustus or Tiberius, an assumption based on the impression gained from the spirit, style and general atmosphere of the work.[3] It was

---

[1] See Ocellus Lucanus, *De Universi Natura* 45-6 (ed. R. Harder 1926, p. 22 = *The Pythagorean Texts of the Hellenistic Period*, ed. H. Thesleff, 1965, pp. 135-6). For the date of Ocellus Lucanus see Thesleff, in *Eranos* (1962), pp. 10-11; H. Dörrie, in *PW* xxiv, p. 272. For the question whether Callimachus or Theocritus had any knowledge of the Greek Bible see P. M. Fraser, *Ptolemaic Alexandria* II (1972), p. 1000, n. 255.

[2] See *On the Sublime* IX, 9.

[3] See the discussion of the date by M. J. Boyd, in *Classical Quarterly* (1957), pp. 39-46; *Longinus, On the Sublime*, edited with introduction and commentary by D. A. Russell (1964), pp. XXII-XXX; G. P. Goold, in *Transactions of the American Philological Association* (1961), pp. 168-78. See also on the work H. Mutschmann, in *Hermes* (1917), pp. 161-200; Rhys Roberts, in *Philological Quarterly* (1928), pp. 209-19; J. P. Hoogland, *Longinus, Over het verhevene* (1936), pp. 91-4; W. B. Sedgwick, in *American Journal of Philology* (1948), pp. 197-200; E. Norden, 'Das Genesiszitat in der Schrift vom Erhabenen', in *Abhandlungen der Deutschen Akademie der Wissenschaften zu Berlin* (1954); W. Bühler, *Beiträge zur Erklärung der Schrift vom Erhabenen* (1964), pp. 34-7; G. J. de Vries, in *Mnemosyne* (1965), pp. 234-5; Gager, pp. 56-63; for a recent identification of the writer with the genuine third-century Longinus see G. Luck, *Arctos* (1967), pp. 97-113.

written in reply to another work of literary criticism by Caecilius of Caleacte, a Jew from Sicily who lived in the time of Augustus.[1] All attempts to identify the author of *On the Sublime* with one of the known living literary critics of the time have failed.[2] The writer quotes the first verses of Genesis as an example of the distinguished style which presents the nature of the deity in a manner suitable to this pure and great being. The verses are quoted immediately after Homer's description of Poseidon. The writer does not mention Moses by name but calls him 'the Lawgiver of the Jews' (ὁ τῶν Ἰουδαίων θεσμοθέτης). 'A similar effect was achieved by the Lawgiver of the Jews—no mean genius, for he both understood and gave expression to the power of the divinity as it deserved when he wrote at the very beginning of his laws. I quote his words: 'God said'—what? 'Let there be light. And there was. Let there be earth. And there was.''[3] The author writes about Moses, who besides Cicero is the only non-Greek writer quoted in the work,[4] with far more admiration than even Greek writers who treated Moses with respect, such as Hecataeus and Strabo. But there is not enough evidence to prove that the writer was either a born Jew or a proselyte. There are arguments to demonstrate that he was not a Jew and considered himself a Greek[5] and we must recognize the fact that here is a Greek writer who showed greater admiration for Moses and the Bible than any other pagan writer of his time. This admiration should not surprise us if we remember that the greatest expansion of the Jewish religion in ancient times was then taking place and that it penetrated different social strata. It is only natural for this phenomenon to be reflected in ancient literature, and not only unfavourably as in Seneca, Quintilian, Tacitus and Juvenal. Some scholars think that this favourable attitude of the author of the *On the Sublime* can perhaps be explained by the influence of the rhetor Theodorus of Gadara.[6] However, I find it hard to accept that Theodorus, a native of a Hellenistic city captured by Alexander Jannaeus, would be sympathetic towards the Jews. It is more probable that

[1] See on him Suda s.v. Καικίλιος (ed. Adler III, p. 83).
[2] See e.g. G. C. Richards, Classical Quarterly (1938), pp. 133-4 who identifies the author of 'De Sublimitate' with the literary critic Gnaeus Pompeius.
[3] The translation is according to Russell.
[4] See *On the Sublime* XII, 4.
[5] See ibid., (ἡμῖν ὡς Ἕλλησιν).
[6] So e.g. Rhys Roberts, op. cit. However, the presumable influence of Theodorus of Gadara seems rather questionable. See G. M. A. Grube, in *American Journal of Philology* (1959), pp. 356-65.

Pseudo-Longinus' information on the Jews came directly from a Jewish source.[1]

The only Greek writer of the early Roman empire who was a native of Greece itself and who wrote about the Jews was Plutarch. He was born in Chaeronea, the son of a respected Boeotian family who served as a priest at Delphi. Since Plutarch travelled and read widely, it is difficult to determine precisely his sources for the Jews. He could have learned about them from books, but he could also have met Jews in places with notable Jewish minorities, such as Alexandria, which he visited, or Rome, where he lived for a considerable time.[2] Plutarch's birthplace, Boeotia, had a large Jewish community dating from early times.[3] The main discussion of Jewish religion is in his *Quaestiones Convivales*,[4] a work apparently written c. 110 C.E.[5]—in any case during the reign of Trajan, at about the same time as Tacitus wrote his *Histories*. But the tone of the two writers is completely different.

The Jews are discussed in the above-mentioned work by Plutarch during a symposium at a place (Aidepsos) in the island of Euboea. In the course of the discussion Plutarch's brother, Lamprias, mentions that his grandfather was surprised by the fact that the Jews refrained from eating the most legitimate food, in other words pork. The problem then discussed is whether the Jews refrain from eating pork because of their respect for the animal or because of their revulsion for it.[6] One of the participants, Callistratus, argues that the attitude of the Jews towards the pig derives from their gratitude to the animal for its rôle in the development of agriculture, just as they were grateful to the donkey, which helped them find water during their wandering in the wilderness. Lamprias disagrees with Callistratus and says that they are afraid of leprosy which can be contracted from pork. Futhermore, Lamprias states that Adonis, whom he identifies with Dionysius, was killed by a wild boar. This comment leads to other remarks by the participants, and Moiragenes of Athens goes even further and tries to prove a similarity between the Jewish and the Dionysian ritual.

---

[1] Norden e.g. thought that the author was influenced by Philo.
[2] See C. P. Jones, *Plutarch and Rome* (1971), pp. 20-1.
[3] For Jews in Boeotia in the first century C.E. see Philo, *Legatio* 281.
[4] See *Quaestiones Convivales* IV, 4, 4-6, 2 (pp. 669 C-672 B).
[5] See also C. P. Jones, in *JRS* (1966), pp. 72-3 who dates the book after 99 and before 116 C.E.
[6] For Lamprias' view that the Jews abstain from pork out of fear of leprosy see also Aelianus, *De Natura Animalium* x, 16.

The part of Moiragenes' argument which has been preserved is mainly concerned with the Dionysian character of the Feast of Tabernacles. The description of the Feast of Tabernacles in Plutarch's work is at least partly derived from a source which dates from before the destruction of the temple. It has also been suggested that Plutarch was influenced by the customs of contemporary synagogues, and this possibility cannot be excluded.[1] Plutarch also touches upon the Jews in other works. In one of the essays written at the beginning of his literary career, *On Superstition*[2] he mentions the keeping of the sabbath as one of the many foreign customs which the Greeks adopted.[3] In the same work Plutarch tells that the Jews' avoidance of all activity on the sabbath brought destruction to Jerusalem.[4] But it should be emphasized that the Jews are not the only people criticized by Plutarch for superstition. He willingly joins the condemnation of the Egyptians by the philosopher Xenophanes and sharply criticizes the Gauls, the Scythians and the Carthaginians whose ritual includes human sacrifice.[5] In any case, the description of the Jews as tending towards superstition is a long-standing Graeco-Roman tradition dating back at least as far as Agatharchides, and is also known to us from Horace and Apuleius. But while Apuleius[6] considers the Jews the *superstitiosi* par excellence, both Plutarch and Agatharchides do not consider superstition to be specifically Jewish. In his work on Isis and Osiris, Plutarch was influenced by the Egyptian tradition which connects the beginnings of the Jewish people with the myth of Seth-Typhon.[7] However, Plutarch does not take things at face value but remarks: 'Those who relate that Typhon's flight from the battle was made on

---

[1] This view is expressed by E. R. Goodenough, *Jewish Symbols in the Greco-Roman Period* VI (1956), p. 134. For the interpretation of the whole passage see A. Büchler, in *REJ*, XXXVII (1898), pp. 181-94; B. Latzarus, *Les idées religieuses de Plutarque* (1920), pp. 161-9.

[2] On its relatively early date among the works of Plutarch see R. Volkmann, *Leben, Schriften und Philosophie des Plutarchs von Chaeronea* I (1869), p. 78; K. Ziegler, in *PW* XXI, p. 708.

[3] See *De Superstitione* 3 (p. 166 A). Plutarch uses the word σαββατισμοί. It is found also in Hebrews 4:9. See also A. Pelletier, in *Comptes rendus de l'académie des inscriptions et belles lettres* (1971), pp. 75-7.

[4] See *De superstitione* 8 (p. 169 C). On this essay see also G. Abernetty, *De Plutarchi qui Fertur de Superstitione Libello* (1911); H. A. Moellering, *Plutarch on superstition* (1963).

[5] See *De superstitione* 13.

[6] See Apuleius, *Florida* 6.

[7] See *De Iside et Osiride* 31 (p. 363 C-D); see also J. G. Griffiths, *Plutarch, De Iside et Osiride* (1970), pp. 418-9.

the back of an ass and lasted for seven days, and that after he had made his escape he became the father of sons, Hierosolymus and Iudaeus, are manifestly, as the very names show, attempting to drag Jewish customs into legend.'[1] The biographies of Plutarch which mention certain facts in the history of Judaea make no general remarks on the Jews or Judaism.

Epictetus and Dio Chrysostom, both from Asia Minor, were contemporaries of Plutarch. From the writings of Epictetus (50-130 C.E.)[2] one learns that relations between Greek intellectuals and Judaism at the end of the first century show none of the tension which often characterizes Latin literature of the period. As opposed to Seneca, the hostile Latin Stoic of the previous generation, Epictetus, the Stoic from Phrygia, is objective about the Jews. He lists the attitudes of the Jews, Syrians, Egyptians and Romans and mentions the difference between them.[3] He also considers these four nations equals. He presents them as agreeing in principle that one should strive for holiness, but divided on the details of how to go about this, thus e.g. as to whether the eating of pork affects the issue. Epictetus knew the custom of the baptism of proselytes, and we should not think that he confused Jews and Christians.[4] The overall impression from Epictetus' writing is of a correct and objective attitude towards the Jews who in principle are no different from other nations such as the Syrians, Egyptians or Romans.[5]

From the famous Sophist Dio Chrysostom from Bithynia no texts on the Jews have been preserved. But in a passage which has been preserved in the *Life of Dio* by Synesius, we read that Dio praised the Essenes, a people who live in a happy city near the 'Dead Water' (i.e. Dead Sea) in Palestine near Sodoma.[6] In this passage Dio does not relate the Essenes to the Jews, but we should not jump to any

---

[1] It is clear that this story arose among anti-Jewish circles who attributed ass-worship to the Jews. Plutarch himself dwells on the connection between the ass and Typhon.

[2] The setting of the discourses of Epictetus at Nicopolis is dated c. 108 C.E. See F. Millar, in *JRS* (1965), p. 142.

[3] See Arrianus, *Dissertationes* I, 11, 12-13; I, 22, 4.

[4] *Dissertationes* II, 9, 19-21.

[5] It seems that the Galilaeans of Arrianus, *Dissertationes* IV, 7, 6 are not to be identified with the Zealots. It seems preferable to think here of the Christians. See Ed. Meyer, *Ursprung und Anfänge des Christentums* III (1923), p. 530, n.1; A. von Harnack, *Mission und Ausbreitung des Christentums* (1924), p. 412, n. 1.

[6] See Synesius, *Vita Dionis* in Arnim's edition, vol. II, p. 317; see also J. R. Asmus, in *Byzantinische Zeitschrift* (1900), p. 86; K. Treu, *Synesios von Kyrene* (1958), p. 42.

conclusions from this, since we do not have Dio's own words but only a brief reference to the Essenes in Synesius.

Latin literature

The earliest information about Judaism in Latin literature, and the first reactions, are from the last period of the republic, in the writing of Cicero and Varro. Cicero's attitude towards Judaism is particularly interesting if we consider the major influence of his writings on the development of European culture. To begin with, it is remarkable that none of his philosophical writings mention the Jews and their religion. Had Cicero been at all interested in Judaism we would expect some mention of it in a work such as *De Natura Deorum*. In this Cicero differed from his contemporary Varro who expressed his appreciation for Judaism because it forbade all images or statues representing the deity. He also differed here from such later writers as Seneca and Tacitus who reacted with hostility to the impact of the Jews. Even in Cicero's extensive correspondence only the nickname Hierosolymarius for Pompey the conqueror of Jerusalem can be found,[1] with no concrete information on the Jews, or any reaction to Judaism. In fact, Cicero refers to the Jews in only two of his speeches, the *Pro Flacco* (59 B.C.E.) and the *On the Consular Provinces* (56 B.C.E.).[2] On both these occasions the Jews were in the opposing camp. The first speech was in the law-court where Cicero defended his friend Flaccus who had been brought to trial by the cities of the Province of Asia. The Jews took an active part in accusing Flaccus, who had confiscated money which they had collected to send to the Temple in Jerusalem. In his speech Cicero had to answer these charges. He did this in two ways, firstly by arguing that Flaccus' action had not violated the law, and secondly by stressing the shortcomings of the Jews and their religion. Cicero defines the Jewish religion as superstition.[3] He also explains to the judges that Pompey's restraint in not looting the Temple in Jerusalem did not stem from any feelings of respect for the Jews who were the enemies of the Romans, but from the nature of the man and from political considerations. Cicero ends his outburst against the Jews by speaking of the difference between

[1] See *Ad Atticum* II, 9, I.
[2] See *Pro Flacco* 28, 66-9; *De Provinciis Consularibus* 5, 10-12.
[3] On the concept of superstition see R. Freudenberger, *Das Verhalten der römischen Behörden gegen die Christen im 2. Jahrhundert* (1967), pp. 189-99.

the Jewish religion and the traditional institutions of Rome, and the recent war fought by the Jews against the Romans. In order to evaluate correctly the anti-Jewish part of the speech, we must consider the legal context and the advocate's practice of blackening his opponents as the situation demanded. One of the methods he considered acceptable was to ridicule the national characteristics of witnesses. In other speeches he did so with the Sardi and the Gauls and in the *Pro Flacco* with the witnesses from the cities of Asia Minor whom he called Phrygians, Mysians, Carians and Lydians. These are presented in no more favourable a light than the Jews. In fact, Cicero himself points out the difference between his private opinions and those he expresses as a lawyer.[1] Sometimes one can even find contradictions in Cicero's evaluation of the same personalities in different parts of his speeches.[2] Therefore much of Cicero's anti-Semitism should be discounted. Despite the fact that Cicero was a disciple of the rhetor Apollonius Molon, he was not influenced in his *Pro Flacco* by the specific points raised by Apollonius against the Jews. He does not accuse the Jews of hating mankind, nor of contributing nothing to human civilization, nor of lack of talent, as does Apollonius.[3] Cicero's oration *On the Consular Provinces* in which he refers to the Jews and the Syrians as having been born to slavery 'publicanos tradidit in servitutem Iudaeis et Syris, nationibus natis servituti,' is along similar lines. But even if we cannot call Cicero an outright anti-Semite, his attitude towards the Jews[4] was different from that of his contemporary, the great scholar of the Roman Republic, Varro (116-27 B.C.E.). The few surviving passages from Varro[5] place him among the writers who showed sympathy and understanding for Judaism rather than with much Latin writers as Seneca. From the surviving fragments, mostly in Augustine, we learn that Varro identified the Jewish deity with Jupiter, and that he argued that the Jews' aniconic worship could serve as an example of a pure and helpful ritual which is like the religion of ancient Rome. In Varro's opinion those who make images

---

[1] See *Pro Cluentio*, 139.
[2] Cf. the usual evaluation of Cicero's great enemy Catilina in Cicero's speeches with his remarks in *Pro Caelio*, 12.
[3] Cf. above p. 1125.
[4] On Cicero's attitude to Jews see in general J. Lewy, in *Zion* VII (1941-2), pp. 109-134.
[5] See Augustinus, *De civitate Dei* IV, 31; *De consensu evangelistarum* I, 22, 30; Lydus, *De Mensibus* IV, 53 (pp. 110-11, ed. Wünsch). See also Stern, nos. 72a-b; 75.

and statues of the gods only lessen the worshippers' respect for them.[1] Varro's censure of the cult of images follows an ancient philosophical tradition. One can only guess the source of Varro's information on the Jewish religion (perhaps Posidonius or Antiochus of Ascalon). It is very likely too that Varro knew some Jews directly, since in his day the Jews were settling in most Mediterranean countries. Varro could have known them in Rome, and in Asia Minor where he spent some time, although there is no reason to think that he visited Syria and Palestine.[2]

Some of the great Roman poets of the time of Augustus also knew about the Jews. Virgil, however, (70-19 B.C.E.) does not mention them at all, and only once mentions the date palms of Idumaea (Idumaea = Judaea). On the other hand there is no firm foundation for the view that Virgil was influenced in his Fourth Eclogue by Jewish messianic ideas.[3]

There are many more direct allusions to the Jews in Horace. Most are in his satires. Horace (65-8 B.C.E.) was familiar with the sabbath and the custom of circumcision,[4] he alludes to Jewish missionary fervour[5] and mocks the credulity of Jews.[6] There is no convincing evidence to lead us to believe that Horace was of Jewish or eastern origin.[7] Ovid too knew of the Jewish sabbath.[8]

The most thorough discussion of the Jews in Latin literature in the Augustan age is in the historian Pompeius Trogus.[9] His great work

[1] Varro's sympathetic attitude to Judaism stands in marked contrast to his displeasure at the diffusion of the Egyptian deities at Rome. See Servius, *In Aeneidem* VIII, 698.
[2] See C. Cichorius, *Römische Studien* (1922), pp. 195-6; 203-4.
[3] Much has been written on this subject. Jewish influence has been argued e.g. by H. W. Garrod, in *Classical Review* (1905), pp. 37-8; T. F. Royds, *Virgil and Isaiah* (1918). Against this view see E. Norden, *Die Geburt des Kindes* (1924), pp. 52-3; H. J. Rose, *The Eclogues of Vergil* (1942), p. 194; J. Carcopino, *Virgile et le mystère de la IV églogue* (1930), pp. 29-30.
[4] *Sermones* I, 9, 60-78.
[5] *Sermones* I, 4, 139-43.
[6] *Sermones* I, 5, 96-104.
[7] See F. Dornseiff, *Verschmähtes zu Vergil, Horaz und Properz* (1951), p. 65; O. Seeck, *Kaiser Augustus* (1902), p. 134; K. Mras, in *Wiener Studien* (1936), pp. 70-85; W. H. Alexander, in *Classical Philology* (1942), pp. 385-397. Scepticism is shown by R. Hanslik, *Das Altertum* I (1955), p. 231.
[8] See Ovidius, *Ars amatoria* I, 76, 416.
[9] See *Historiae Philippicae, Prologus*, libri XXXVI; Iustinus, *Epitome* XXXVI, I, 9-3, 9; *Historiae Philippicae, Prologus*, libri XXXIX; Iustinus, *Epitome* XL, 2, 4; see on Pompeius Trogus, O. Seel, *Die Praefatio des Pompeius Trogus* (1955); idem, *Eine römische Weltgeschichte: Studien zum Text der Epitome des Iustinus und der Historik des Pompejus Trogus* (1972); J. Morr, in *Philologus* LXXXI,

Historiae Philippicae has not been preserved, but its content is known to us from the prologues to the various books of the work and from Justinus' epitome which was written hundreds of years later. It can be seen with certainty that Pompeius Trogus dealt with the history of the Jews in connection with the Seleucid kingdom. As background he uses the history of king Antiochus Sidetes who fought against Judaea at the time of John Hyrcan (book 36). From the prologue to book 39, it seems that he also deals with the further history of the Hasmonaean kingdom. But the principal description of the Jews by Pompeius Trogus is in book 36. There are three main parts to his description: a survey of ancient Jewish history and the formation of the nation, a geographical description of Judaea and a history of the Jews from the Persian period onwards. The description of ancient Jewish history, to judge by what has been preserved in the epitome of Justinus, was very detailed. Three sources can be recognized: one is very close to the biblical tradition; another connects the origins of the Jewish people with the city of Damascus; and the third is identical with the Graeco-Egyptian tradition which is known to us since Manetho and is hostile to the Jews. All three elements left their mark on Pompeius Trogus' narrative. Since Pompeius Trogus, it seems, did not always succeed in unifying these different elements which came to him from different sources, he presents them side by side and an inconsistent picture sometimes emerges. In any case, his description of ancient Jewish history ends with a favourable comment on the efficiency of the Jewish government as it developed over the years: 'and by uniting justice with religion, it is almost incredible how powerful they became'.

Trogus begins his description of the Jews by noting their origin in Damascus. The name of the city, according to Trogus, was the name of its first king, who was succeeded by Azelus, Adores, Abraham and Israhel. This last was the most famous because of his ten sons among whom he divided his kingdom. He called all of the Jews after Judas, who died immediately after the division. The youngest of the sons was Joseph. His brothers, fearing his great talents, sold him to traders who took him to Egypt. Here, thanks to his talents he became a master magician and gained the good graces of the king. He was

pp. 278-9; I. Heinemann, *Poseidonios' metaphysische Schriften* II (1928), pp. 80-1, P. Treves, *Il mito di Alessandro o la Roma d'Augusto* (1953), pp. 43-4; E. Cavaignac, in *Mélanges bibliques rédigés en l'honneur de André Robert* (1957), p. 350; G. Forni, *Il valore storico e fonti di Pompeo Trogo* (1958), pp. 80-1; Gager, pp. 48-56.

the founder of the science of interpreting dreams.[1] Egypt would have perished in a famine had not the king, at the advice of Joseph, stored grain in the previous years. Joseph's son was Moses who, besides the knowledge he inherited from his father, was outstandingly handsome.[2] Up to this point Pompeius Trogus seems full of praise for the Jews, but from here on we can feel the influence of the Graeco-Egyptian tradition. According to this tradition the Egyptians, who had been smitten with leprosy, expelled Moses with all the people who were infected with the disease. Moses, who led all the exiles, took the liturgical accoutrements of Egypt with him, and the Egyptians who pursued them to retrieve these items, had to return home because of storms. When he reached Mount Sinai, after suffering for seven days, he sanctified the seventh day as a fast since on the seventh day after the exodus from Egypt their wanderings were over. Moses' son Aruas inherited his position and was also appointed king; this was the origin of the Jewish custom of having the same man serve both as king and priest. This reflects the situation under Hasmonaean rule. In the geographical description which follows, Pompeius Trogus speaks mostly of the Jericho valley and its balsam-trees, which grow by the Dead Sea, and its bitumen. It is possible that in the original description there was much more material and that it was greatly shortened in Justinus' summary.[3] The succeeding historical survey is very meagre. It recounts the stages of foreign domination of Judaea. The most interesting fact in political history mentioned here is the connection between Judaea and Rome in the time of king Demetrius I.[4] Pompeius Trogus independently confirms the more detailed story found in the First Book of Macabees.[5] Pompeius Trogus undoubtedly

---

[1] It is also stated (Iustinus XXXVI, 2, 10): 'tantaque experimenta eius fuerunt, ut non ab homine, sed a deo responsa dari viderentur'. This remark is to be related to a tradition deriving from a syncretistic environment which is reflected in various later works. See Tertullianus, *Ad nationes* II, 8; Firmicus Maternus, *De Errore Profanarum Religionum* 13; Suda s.v. Sarapis (ed. Adler IV, p. 325). It emerges from this tradition that Joseph was considered worthy of divine worship under the name of Sarapis. For parallel talmudic tradition see Y. Gutman, *The Jewish-Hellenistic literature* II (1963; in Hebrew), pp. 109-10.

[2] It may be that the reference to Moses' beauty is to be explained by Pompeius Trogus' statement that he was descended from Joseph (so. I. Heinemann, in *PW* XVI, p. 362). However, also Josephus refers to the beauty of Moses. See *Ant.* II, 231.

[3] On the method of Justin see L. Ferrero, *Struttura e metodo dell' Epitome di Giustino* (1957).

[4] See Iustinus XXXVI, 3, 9.

[5] See I Macc. 8; E. Täubler, *Imperium Romanum* (1913), pp. 239-54; T. Liebmann-

depended on Greek sources, and he probably knew the work of his contemporary Timagenes, although it is debatable how much he resorted to him (see above p. 1117).

The description of the Jews in Pompeius Trogus' work is an example of what a well-educated Roman of the time of Augustus might have known about the Jews and their history.[1] The arrangement of the material is somewhat reminiscent of the description in the more famous digression of Tacitus in his *Histories*. However, this does not mean that Tacitus depended on Pompeius Trogus or even that they used the same sources. The resemblance stems mainly from their common approach to ethnography. It should also be stressed that there is a basic difference between the approaches of the two writers, one essentially objective and the other hostile. They even used the hostile Graeco-Egyptian tradition differently, which corresponds to the change of atmosphere in Rome between Augustus and Trajan.

The most famous historian of the Augustan age was Titus Livy, who also touched upon the Jews. But this was in his lost books, and we learn that Livy dealt with the conquest of Jerusalem by Pompey in 63 B.C.E. and its conquest in the time of Antony, 37 B.C.E. only from abstracts (*periochae*) of some of his books.[2] In the first instance he discusses the Jewish religion and the Temple in Jerusalem, which he still speaks of in a Polybian style.[3] It is evident that Livy, like Varro, was impressed by the fact that the Jews do not make images of their divinity and do not give it human form: 'neque ullum ibi simulacrum est, neque enim esse dei figuram putant.'[4]

In the period between Augustus and the philosopher Seneca there is no significant mention of the Jews and Judaism in Latin literature. Valerius Maximus tells of their expulsion from Rome,[5] Celsus the physician mentions a Jewish physician in his work,[6] the agricultural writer Columella describes a Jewish giant who was brought to Rome and presented before the people, a giant who was taller than any German,[7] and Seneca Rhetor refers to the conquest of Jerusalem by

Frankfort, *L'Antiquité Classique* (1969), pp. 101-20; A. Giovannini and H. Müller, in *Museum Helveticum* (1971), pp. 167-9.
[1] See e.g. the letter of Augustus himself to Tiberius, as quoted by Suetonius, *Life of Augustus* 76.
[2] *Periochae* 102; Jos. *Ant.* xiv, 68; *Periochae* 128.
[3] Jerusalem is still considered a temple (*fanum eorum Hierosolyma*).
[4] See *Scholia ad Lucanum* ii, 593; Lydus, *De Mensibus* iv, 53 (p. 109, ed. Wünsch).
[5] Valerius Maximus i, 3, 3.
[6] Celsus, *De Medicina* v, 19, 11; v, 22, 4.
[7] Columella, *Res Rustica* iii, 8.

Sosius in 37 B.C.E.[1] But all these wrote about Jews only in passing, without expressing their views.

Seneca (died 65 C.E.) was different; he was the first Latin writer who had harsh words for the Jews and Judaism, without the humorous touch which we find in Horace. We cannot explain his approach by any special reason, legal or political, such as was behind Cicero's comments on the Jews. Seneca objected in general to the spread of eastern religions in the Roman world.[2] He wrote against the Jews mainly in his later works, towards the end of his life, in the sixties of the first century C.E., at the height of the proselytizing movement in the Roman empire.[3] That a defeated nation should emerge the victor angered Seneca: 'Meanwhile the customs of this accursed race have gained such influence that they are now received throughout all the world. The vanquished have given laws to their victors.'[4] He also remarked that while the Jews at least knew the reasons behind their customs, most of the people who followed them did things which none of them understand: 'Illi tamen causas ritus sui noverunt; maior pars populi facit, quod cur faciat ignorat.'[5] He includes Judaism among the superstitions in his *Epistulae Morales*, and the Jewish religion is the prime target of his censures: 'Let us forbid lamps to be lighted on the sabbath, since the gods do not need light, nor do men take pleasure in soot.'[6] He sees in the Jewish sabbath a waste of a seventh of man's life.[7] Seneca's criticism of Jewish customs and ceremonial religion has special significance. It is an answer to the challenge of abstract Jewish

[1] See *Suasoriae* II, 21; cf. E. A. Sydenham, *The coinage of the Roman Republic* (1952), p. 199, no. 1272.
[2] See e.g. his censure of the Galli connected with the cult of Cybele in the fragment of *De superstitione* in Augustinus, *De civitate Dei* VI, 10; R. Turcan, *Sénèque et les religions orientales* (1967); M. Lausberg, *Untersuchungen zu Senecas Fragmenten* (1970), pp. 211-25.
[3] The *De Superstitione* is dated by K. Münscher, *Senecas Werke* (1922), pp. 8off. to the last years of Seneca though Turcan, op. cit. pp. 12-14 argues for an earlier date (40-41 C.E.). For the date of *Naturales quaestiones* and *Epistulae morales* see K. Abel, *Bauformen in Senecas Dialogen* (1967), pp. 167-69.
[4] See *De superstitione* in Augustinus, *De civitate Dei* VI, 11. There is no reason to assume that Seneca preferred Christianity to Judaism, as Augustine l.c. suggests.
[5] The *illi* are the Jews while by *maior pars populi* the non-Jews who adopt Jewish customs are meant. For a different explanation see Turcan, op. cit. p. 23.
[6] See *Epistulae Morales* 95, 57.
[7] See also Tacitus, *Historiae* v, 4. Otherwise Seneca knows to appreciate the importance of relaxation. See *De Tranquillitate Animi* 17, 7.

monotheism, which was the pride of the Jews.[1] Here Seneca argues that Judaism is not a philosophy but a superstition shackled by ceremonial worship.[2]

Similar views were held by Persius (34-62 C.E.), a younger contemporary of Seneca and the great satirist of Rome at the time of Nero. Persius was influenced by Stoic philosophy and was a pupil of the philosopher Cornutus. He knew Seneca personally but was not deeply impressed by him.[3] As a pupil of Cornutus and an exponent of first century Stoicism, he had lofty notions of the principles of religious ritual. However, he completely ignored the moral side of the Jewish religion. In his opinion its customs were an example of the superstitions which came to Rome from the East, and in this he did not differ from most of the educated classes of Roman society in his day. Persius expressed this view in his fifth satire, in which the Jewish religious customs are the prime target of the poet's barbs, even more so than the superstitions of the Phrygians and Egyptians. The Jewish custom which Persius chose as the target of his satire was the sabbath, or as he called it the day of Herod (*dies Herodis*).[4] Persius gives a description of the sabbath which is probably closer to reality than other such comments in ancient Greek and Roman literature, where the sabbath was often a fast day. Persius connects the sabbath with the lighting of lamps and the eating of fish, which is in fact customary in Jewish tradition: 'But when the day of Herod comes round, when the lamps with violets wreathed and ranged round the greasy window-sills have spat forth their thick clouds of smoke, when the floppy tunnies' tails are curled round the dishes of red ware, and the white jars are swollen out with wine, you silently twitch your lips, turning pale at the sabbath of the circumcised.'[5] The custom of circumcision is the mark of the Jewish people in the *Satyricon* of Petronius,[6] who considers the pig the Jewish deity.[7]

---

[1] See e.g. Jos. *Against Apion* II, 190-2.
[2] Philo also calls sometimes Judaism a philosophy (*De Somniis* II, 127; *Vita Mosis* II, 216; *Legatio ad Gaium* 245).
[3] See the *Vita* of Persius in Clausen's Oxford edition of Persius and Iuvenalis, p. 32.
[4] *Dies Herodis* should be identified with the sabbath. See F. Villeneuve, *Essai sur Perse* (1918), p. 486; W. Fink, *Der Einfluss der jüdischen Religion auf die griechisch-römische* (1932), p. 16; T. F. Brunner, in *California Studies in Classical Antiquity* (1968), pp. 63-4.
[5] See *Saturae* V, 176-84.
[6] *Satyricon* 68, 4-8; 102, 13-14.
[7] See Petronius fragm. 37 Ernout.

Jews are viewed unfavourably in the literature of the Flavian age. Pliny the Elder (see also chapter one, p. 32) was somewhat interested in other aspects of Judaism, apart from his geographical description. Among the schools of magic he gives considerable attention to Moses and the Jews,[1] and he speaks of a river in Judaea whose waters run dry every sabbath.[2] But his negative attitude towards Judaism is expressed in only one place: when describing the date-palms in Judaea he says that the Jews use an insulting word for the dates which the Romans serve their gods. In this connection he says that the Jews are a notably blasphemous nation: 'nam quos ex his honori deorum damus, *chydaeos* appelavit Iudaea gens contumelia numinum insignis.'[3] A strange ignorance of Jewish customs and of course of the war against Rome marks the work of Frontinus, a Latin writer of the Flavian age. Although Frontinus was close to the Flavian dynasty and held administrative posts in Rome, he reveals complete ignorance of the character of the Jewish sabbath as observed in his day—the period of the Roman-Jewish war under Vespasian and Titus. In his work *Strategemata* Frontinus says that Vespasian attacked the Jews on the sabbath which is the day when they are forbidden to do anything serious and therefore defeated them.[4] We know that the Jews at the time of Vespasian did fight on the sabbath; the situation as described by Frontinus had prevailed before the Hasmonaean rebellion, before Mattathias had amended the regulations, as we learn among other things from Agatharchides of Cnidus (see p. 1120-1 above).[5] Quintilian is unequivocally hostile to the Jews. The fact that

---

[1] *Natural History* XXX, 11: 'est et alia magices factio a Mose et Ianne et Lotape ac Iudaeis pendens'.

[2] *Natural History* XXXI, 24; see also *T. B. Sanhedrin* 65b; *Genesis Rabba* 11 (p. 93).

[3] *Natural History* XIII, 46. For the expression *contumelia numinum* see also Pliny the Younger, *Panegyricus* 11, 2.

[4] *Strategemata* II, 1, 17.

[5] For the regulation of Mattathias see 1 Macc. 2: 41. This regulation allowed only defensive operations on sabbath. Still, even after this proclamation the enemies of the Jews found it advisable to attack the Jews on sabbath, because they expected the Jews to be less ready for fighting on that day. See M. D. Herr, in *Tarbiz* XXX, p. 248. During Pompey's siege of the Temple mount the men of Jerusalem defended themselves only when directly attacked and did not react to the building of mounds by the besiegers which proved disastrous to them. See Jos. *Ant.* XIV, 63; *War* I, 146. However, the view that military operations should not be confined to cases of direct aggression became prevalent at a later period. See M. Hengel, *Die Zeloten* (1961), pp. 293-6; an extremist view against fighting on sabbath is represented by the *Book of Jubilees* 50: 12-13. Cf. C. Albeck, *Das Buch der Jubiläen und die Halacha* (1930), p. 11.

he wrote in the reign of Domitian may have had some influence on him in this matter.[1] However he was obviously not influenced by the fact that his patron Flavius Clemens was sentenced to death for following Judaism.[2] Quintilian's attitude is expressed in a passage in the chapter *De Laude et Vituperatione*. Here he alludes unfavourably to Moses as the father of Jewish superstition, although he does not mention him by name: 'The vices of the children bring hatred on their parents: founders of cities are detested for concentrating a race which is a curse to others as, for example, the founder of Jewish superstition.'[3] On the other hand, his mention of queen Berenice[4] is neutral in character.

Martial, the Latin writer who was born in Spain, like Seneca and Quintilian, was not very sympathetic towards the Jews. In his *Epigrams* he does not make general statements about the Jews or Judaism. He does not even refer to the problem which most disturbed Roman society: the spread of Jewish religion among the different levels of this society, which troubled such men as Seneca, Juvenal and Tacitus. The Jews, however, often appear in Martial's *Epigrams*, second only in frequency to the castrated Galli of the Phrygian religion. His attack is aimed particularly at Jewish circumcision,[5] but he also mentions the Jewish sabbath which he thinks is a fast day.[6] A Jewish beggar is also one of the types who enliven the cast of characters in Martial.[7]

The most ardent Roman exponent of a hostile attitude towards the Jews is undoubtedly Tacitus (see also chapter one, pp. 33-34). His great digression in the fifth book of his *Histories*, together with the writing of Pompeius Trogus, constitutes the principal survey of the origin of the Jewish people, its religion, history and land which has come down to us from Latin literature. As is customary among ancient historians, Tacitus comes to deal with the Jews in connection with the decisive military confrontation between the Jews and Rome, the history of which he relates. Diodorus (see p. 1128) discussed the Jews against the background of the conquest of Judaea by Pompey;

---

[1] See J. A. Hild, in *REJ* XI (1885), pp. 166-9.
[2] See M. L. Clarke, *Greece and Rome* (1967), p. 35 thinks that Quintilian inserted the anti-Semitic passage after Clemens' fall.
[3] *Institutio Oratoria* III, 7, 21.
[4] *Institutio Oratoria* IV, 1, 19.
[5] *Epigrammata* VII, 30; VII, 35; VII, 82; XI, 94.
[6] *Epigrammata* IV, 4.
[7] *Epigrammata* XII, 57.

Pompeius Trogus gave the Jews a place in his history in connection with the victory of Antiochus Sidetes over the Jews. Tacitus does likewise when he comes to tell the history of the conquest of Jerusalem by the Flavians: 'However, as I am about to describe the last days of a famous city (*famosae urbis*), it seems proper to give some account of its origin.'[1] The description of the conquest of Jerusalem by Titus has not been preserved, only the chapters describing the first stages of the siege. Because of Tacitus' fame as one of the greatest Roman writers, and because of his great influence on later times in Europe from the Renaissance onwards, this digression has perhaps won far greater importance than its intrinsic merit commands.[2]

Tacitus presents a number of versions of the origin of the Jews; some are neutral, one is favourable and the last extremely hostile. The first version links the Jews and the island of Crete. The Jews were refugees from Crete who left the island with Saturn when he was expelled by Jupiter. The origin of the name Iudaei is 'Ida', a mountain in Crete.[3] The second version is reminiscent of Plutarch's story (see p. 1143) in which Hierosolymus and Iudaeus were the leaders of the overspill from Egypt which emigrated to neighbouring countries. In another version the Jews are of Ethiopian origin.[4] Others, according to Tacitus, relate that the Jews were landless refugees from Assyria who at first took over part of Egypt and only later founded their own cities. This is quite close to the biblical tradition. Then Tacitus recounts the version which he thinks favourable to Jews: 'Clara alii Iudaeorum initia: Solymos carminibus Homeri celebratam gentem conditae urbi Hierosolyma nomen e suo fecisse.' Finally Tacitus relates the version which, he declares, reflects the opinion of many (or most) writers, and it is in fact identical with the Graeco-Egyptian tradition about the Jews. They were hated by the gods, became diseased, were led by Moses, whom wild asses helped to find water. In this connection Tacitus affirms that Moses laid down religious

---

[1] *Historiae* v, 2. *Famosa* may have a neutral meaning as in *Historiae* I, 10 or Horatius, *Ars Poetica*, 469. The excursus of Tacitus is included in *Historiae* v, 2-13.

[2] See e.g. on Spinoza's debt to Tacitus Ch. Wirszubski, in *Scripta Hierosolymitana* II, pp. 176-86. For the polemics of the seventeenth century Marrano thinker, Isaac Cardoso against Tacitus see Y. H. Yerushalmi, *From Spanish Court to Italian Ghetto* (1971), pp. 417-9.

[3] 'Inclutum in Creta Idam montem, accolas Idaeos aucto in barbarum cognomento Iudaeos vocitari'.

[4] On the Aethiopian origins of the Jews see H. Lewy, in *MGWJ* (1937), pp. 65-71.

customs contrary to those of all other religions and that 'the Jews think profane all that we think holy.' They sanctified the image of the ass and refrained from eating pig-meat because they remember the disease from which they suffered. The seventh day and seventh year Moses dedicated to idleness. Here Tacitus breaks off this version of the origin of the Jews and their religion, in order to evaluate it: 'Hi ritus quoquo modo instituti antiquitate defenduntur: cetera instituta, sinistra, foeda pravitate valuere.' And he gives us the reasons for his anger at the Jews: 'Nam pessimus quisque spretis religionibus patriis tributa et stipes illuc congerebant ... transgressi in morem eorum idem usurpant nec quidquam prius imbuuntur quam contemnere deos, exuere patriam parentes liberos fratres vilia habere.' Tacitus refers to the movement of proselytization which led Romans to desert their religion and society and join the Jewish people. Misanthropy and separatism are characteristics of the Jews, and the proselytes follow them. The first thing they learn from the Jews is contempt for the gods, rejection of their homeland and scorn for their relatives. Tacitus knew Jewish monotheism and the Jews' refusal to worship the emperor, but he rejects the comparison between the customs of the Jews and the worship of Dionysos: 'quippe Liber festos laetosque ritus posuit, Iudaeorum mos absurdus sordidusque.' Tacitus formally refrains from stating his preference for any of the versions, in keeping with the ethnographic tradition of ancient times. When he leaves the versions to expound his idea of contemporary Jewish beliefs he expresses doubts about the ancient traditions: (hi ritus quoque modo inducti). However, the relative length of the last version as compared to the previous ones, the prominent episodes included in it, the fact that only this version includes aetiological explanations of existing phenomena in the Jewish religion and its resemblance to other parts of Tacitus, all lend extra weight to the last version, which seems to be the historian's preferred view. In any case, Tacitus does not conceal his total rejection of Jewish religion. As mentioned above, he does not ignore the monotheism, but refrains from evaluating it in relation to the Jews. The geographical description of Judaea by Tacitus is in no way remarkable. Like others, he concentrates particularly on the Dead Sea, the balsam and the bitumen. This summary of Jewish history completely ignores Jewish independence in the biblical period and describes the Jews as a people who were always enslaved by foreign powers. King Antiochus was prevented from eradicating Jewish superstition only by the war against the

Parthians.[1] Later a favourable political conjuncture allowed the Jews to establish a state of their own, of a priestly character which fostered superstition. The state took on the evil characteristics of an oriental monarchy. When concluding the story of Roman rule over Judaea, Tacitus does not condemn the Jews for their rebellious nature, nor does he hold them responsible for the great rebellion. Tacitus makes it clear that the Roman procurators were responsible. If the Jews took up arms in the time of Gaius Caligula, it was only after he ordered them to place a statue in their Temple. The procurator Felix was harsh, but the Jews bore all patiently till Gessius Florus took over: 'Duravit tamen patientia Iudaeis usque ad Gessium Florum procuratorem: sub eo bellum ortum.'

What were the sources of Tacitus' ancient history of the Jews? Some have pointed to Apion,[2] others to Pliny.[3] Mucianus has been proposed for the geography; he was legate in Syria.[4] In any case, Tacitus' sources for ancient history are not necessarily those he used for the siege itself. And there is no reason to assume that all his versions of the origin of the Jews had already been collected in a single source. It seems more probable that he used more than one source.[5] But there is likewise no reason to assume the contrary, that all the opinions he offers came from different sources which Tacitus used directly. He probably found most of his material in the work of earlier Latin writers, although it is likely that he also had recourse to written Greek sources. The *Annals* were written after the *Histories*,[6] and the later

[1] Tacitus seems to combine here in one sentence activities pertaining to two Antiochi. See Jacoby *Fragm. Hist.* II C, p. 208; W. Otto, *Zur Geschichte der Zeit des VI. Ptolemäers* (1934), p. 85, n. 3.
[2] So e.g. A. v. Gutschmid, *Kleine Schriften* IV (1893), p. 367.
[3] So e.g. H. Nissen, in *Rheinisches Museum* (1871), pp. 541-3; he was refuted by D. Detlefsen, in *Philologus* XXXIV (1876), pp. 43-5. Nissen's view is adopted also by Ph. Fabia, *Les sources de Tacite dans les Histoires et les Annales* (1893), pp. 247-259.
[4] So e.g. W. A. Spooner, *The Histories of Tacitus* (1891), p. 21.
[5] From the studies concerning the attitude of Tacitus to the Jews and the sources used by him see J. A. Hild, in *REJ* XI (1885), pp. 174-84; G. Thiaucourt, in *REJ* XIX (1889), pp. 57-74; XX (1890), pp. 312-4; G. Boissier, *Mélanges Cabrières* (1899), pp. 81-91; G. Theissen, *De Sallustii, Livii, Taciti Digressionibus* (1912), pp. 76-80; Ed. Norden, in *Neue Jahrbücher für das klassische Altertum* XXXI (1913), pp. 637-66 (= *Kleine Schriften*, pp. 241-75); K. Trüdinger, *Studien zur Geschichte der griechisch-römischen Ethnographie* (1918), pp. 156-9; J. Morr, in *Philologus* LXXXI, pp. 271-9; F. Dornseiff, in *ZNW* (1936), pp. 143-55; J. Lewy, in *Zion* VIII (1942-3), pp. 1-34; 61-84; Hospers-Jansen; E. Paratore, *Tacito* (2nd ed. 1962), pp. 653-68; A. Toaff, *La Rassegna mensile di Israel* (1963), pp. 394-408.
[6] See chapter one, pp. 33-4.

books at least were composed after the fierce Jewish revolts in the time of Trajan. But it is hard to see how this rebellion affected his treatment of the Jews. It is true that he considered the loss of Jewish life as *vile damnum*,[1] but in his description of the riots in Judaea in the time of Cumanus and Felix he holds the procurators and not the Jews responsible.[2] In the celebrated chapter on the growth of Christianity Judaea is called *origo eius mali*, but Tacitus does not add any comment here on Judaism. Tacitus' hostility towards Judaism is in keeping with Latin literature from the time of Seneca. Like Seneca, and Juvenal, a contemporary of Tacitus, Tacitus' antipathy is not confined to Judaism but applies to the other eastern religions which had penetrated Rome at that time. The Egyptian religion is, in his mind, no less a *superstitio* than Judaism. What to him was dangerous, as it was to Seneca and Juvenal, was the spread of Judaism which threatened the entire structure of Roman society. In Tacitus' view this was more of a threat to Roman society than the Jewish rebellions in the period from Nero to Trajan.[3]

Juvenal (60-130 C.E.) too was very bitter about the foreign elements which were taking over the city of Rome, and the foreign atmosphere forced upon Rome as the capital of the empire: a Greek atmosphere, and even more so, an Eastern one.

'Non possum ferre. Quirites
Graecam urbem; quamvis quota portio faecis Achaei?
iam pridem Syrus in Tibrim defluxit Orontes?'[4]

Juvenal detests the rôle played in Rome by Syrian and Egyptian parvenus. Above all others he hates the Egyptians, and their barbaric behaviour seems to him to be completely opposed to the cultural atmosphere which characterized the western part of the empire at that time.[5] It is only natural, therefore, that a poet with such views would include the Jews in his *Satires*. First of all his *Satires* suggest that Judaism was spreading throughout Rome, that entire families were being caught in its net. He stresses the customs peculiar to the Jews, the sabbath, circumcision and abstention from pork. The worst effect of Judaism was, in his view, the scorn to which Roman in-

[1] *Annales* II, 85.
[2] *Annales* XII, 54.
[3] I don't think that we have to accept the view of W. L. Knox, in *JRS* (1949), p. 30 that the antipathy displayed by Latin writers of the type of Tacitus towards the Jews had to do with the Jewish support of the principate.
[4] *Saturae* III, 60-3.
[5] *Saturae* XV, 110-6.

stitutions were being subjected; like Tacitus, he stresses the misanthropy which characterizes the Jews:

'Quidam sortiti metuentem sabbata patrem
nil praeter nubes et caeli numen adorant
nec distare putant humana carne suillam
qua pater abstinuit, mox et praeputia ponunt;
Romanas autem soliti contemnere leges
Iudaicum ediscunt et servant ac metuunt ius,
tradidit arcano quodcumque volumine Moyses:
non monstrare vias eadem nisi sacra colenti,
quaesitum ad fontem solos deducere verpos.
Sed pater in causa, cui septima quaeque fuit lux
ignava et partem vitae non attigit ullam.'[1]

---

[1] *Saturae* XIV, 96-106. See also *Saturae* III, 10-18; VI, 542-7; Cf. G. Highet, *Juvenal the Satirist* (1954), p. 283, n. 3; G. Hirst, in *Classical Review* (1924), p. 171; R. L. Dunbabin, in *Classical Review* (1925), p. 112; A. Cameron, in *Classical Review* (1926), pp. 62-3; B. L. Ullman, *Classical Tradition, Literary and Historical Studies in Honor of Harry Caplan* (1966), pp. 276-7; J. Lewy, *Studies in Jewish Hellenism* (1960), pp. 200-3 (in Hebrew). The expressions *metuentem sabbata patrem* and *Iudaicum metuunt ius* in *Saturae* XIV, lines 96 and 101, probably allude to the 'fearers of heaven' in the rabbinic literature and the σεβόμενοι or φοβούμενοι τὸν θεόν in the New Testament and Josephus ('Ιουδαίων καὶ σεβομένων τὸν θεόν) and the *metuentes* of the Latin inscriptions, and it seems that it is not by chance that out of the dozen cases where Juvenal uses the verb *metuere* two occur in our passage (c.f. L. Kelling and A. Suskin, *Index verborum Iuvenalis*, 1951, p. 74). The 'fearers of heaven' were Gentiles drawn to Jewish religion who kept some of the observances of Judaism, mainly the celebration of the sabbath and the abstention from prohibited food, but did not become full proselytes and did not undergo the rite of circumcision. The existence of a specific term for that kind of people is proven beyond doubt by the rabbinic literature; cf. e.g. *Mechilta de R. Ismael* 22:20 (p. 312), *Midrash Tehillim* 29, 22 (p. 195); *Midrash Genesis Rabba* 28 (p. 264); *Pesikta Rabbati* 180a; *P. T. Megillah* III, 74a; *Midrash Debarim Rabba* 2. Cf. also I. Lévi, in *REJ* L (1905), pp. 1-9, LI (1906), pp. 29-31; *Strack-Billerbeck* II, pp. 715-23; S. Lieberman, *Greek in Jewish Palestine* (1942), pp. 68-90; and there is no cogent reason to deny validity of a terminus technicus to Josephus, *Ant.* XIV, 110: 'Ιουδαίων καὶ σεβομένων τὸν θεόν; cf. R. Marcus, in *Jewish Social Studies* (1952), pp. 247-50; H. Bellen, in *Jahrbuch für Antike und Christentum* VIII-IX (1965-6) p. 173, n. 19. The same holds true for the many σεβόμενοι (with or without τὸν θεόν) and φοβούμενοι τὸν θεόν in Acts; cf. e.g. K. Romaniuk, in *Aegyptus* XLIV (1964), pp. 66-91. Even K. Lake in Foakes Jackson and Lake, *The Beginnings of Christianity*, part I, vol. 5 (1933), pp. 84-88, who argued that there is no sufficient evidence for the view that the words have a technical sense, also admits (p. 87) that the question affects the use of words rather than the facts of history and that after all the application of these words in Acts to denote the class of 'sympathizers', speaks in the favour of them being *termini technici*. The arguments of H. J. Leon, *The Jews of Ancient Rome* (1960), p. 253

BIBLIOGRAPHY

The relevant texts with introductions and commentaries are now to be found in M. STERN, *Greek and Latin Authors on Jews and Judaism I: From Herodotus to Plutarch* (1974). The second volume, soon to be published, will include writers from Tacitus to the sixth century C.E. Among the studies of the subject which are of general importance, one should mention: M. RADIN, *The Jews among the Greeks and Romans* (1915); the illuminating articles of I. HEINEMANN, 'Antisemitismus,' in *PW, Supplementband* V (1931), and 'Moses', in *PW* XVI (1935), and the excellent monograph of J. G. GAGER, *Moses in Greco-Roman Paganism* (1972). See now the recent work of N. SEVENSTER, *The Roots of Pagan Anti-Semitism in the Ancient World* (1975).

See also the relevant chapters in Schürer III, pp. 529-45; V. TCHERI-KOVER, *Hellenistic Civilization and the Jews* (1959), pp. 357-77; M. HENGEL, *Judaism and Hellenism* (translated from the 2nd German edition, 1974), pp. 464-86; W. JAEGER, 'Greeks and Jews in the first Greek Records of Jewish Religion and Civilization', in *Journal of Religion* (1938), pp. 127-43; E. NORDEN, 'Jahve und Moses in hellenistischer Theologie,' in *Festgabe für A. von Harnack* (1921), pp. 292-301. See also A. M. A. HOSPERS-JANSEN, *Tacitus over de Joden* (1949); J. H. LEWY, *Studies in Jewish Hellenism* (1960; in Hebrew); A. MOMIGLIANO, *Alien Wisdom; the Limits of Hellenization* (1975), pp. 74-122; M. HENGEL, *Juden, Griechen und Barbaren* (1976).

against the connection between the 'fearers of heaven' and the *metuentes* is hardly convincing. The inscriptions bearing on the *metuentes* (*CII*, nos. 5, 285, 529) omit to mention the objects of worship. Cf. *CII*, I, p. LXIV; M. Simon, *Verus Israel* (2nd ed. 1964), p. 331; K. G. Kuhn and H. Stegemann, in *PW, Supplementband* IX, p. 1266. For an allusion to *metuentes* in Commodianus, see K. Thraede, *Jahrbuch für Antike und Christentum* II (1959), pp. 96-100.

Index of Sources

Division: 1. Hebrew Bible. 2. Apocrypha. 3. Pseudepigrapha. 4. Dead Sea Scrolls. 5. New Testament. 6. Philo. 7. Josephus. 8. Papyri and Inscriptions. 9. Targum and Midrash. 10. Mishnah. 11. Tosefta. 12. Palestinian Talmud. 13. Babylonian Talmud. 14. Early Christian Authors. 15. Greek and Roman Authors.

1. HEBREW BIBLE

Ezra		10:5	597
		10:9	379
1:5	597	10:23-24	597
2:29	79		
2:35	79		
2:36-39	588, 595	*Nehemiah*	
2:36	588		
2:40-42	596	1:1	837
2:61-63	590	2:1	837
2:64-65	624	2:7	78
2:64	109, 595	2:8	471
2:70	597	2:10	79
3:1	837	2:19	79, 80
3:6	837	3	79
3:8	597, 837	3:2	79
4:10	78	3:3	79
4:11	78	3:4	590
4:16	78	3:5	79
4:17	78	3:9	79
4:20	78	3:12	79
6:7	78	3:13	79
6:15	837	3:14	79
6:16-18	872	3:15-19	79
6:18	597	3:15	79
7:7	597	3:16	79
7:13	597	3:17-18	79
7:24	597	3:34	79
8:15-18	597	4:1	79, 80
8:15	596	5	1107
8:22	590	5:1-12	625, 634
8:29-30	597	6:1	80
8:36	78	6:15	837
9:1	597	7:2	471

3. PSEUDEPIGRAPHA

4. DEAD SEA SCROLLS

5. NEW TESTAMENT

6. PHILO

7. JOSEPHUS

8. PAPYRI AND INSCRIPTIONS

9. TARGUM AND MIDRASH

10. MISHNAH

II. TOSEFTA

(Ed. M. S. Zuckermandel, 1970; for *Zeraim, Moed* and *Nashim* also S. Liebermann, 1955-74).

12. PALESTINIAN TALMUD

13. BABYLONIAN TALMUD

14. EARLY CHRISTIAN AUTHORS

15. GREEK AND ROMAN AUTHORS

Geographical Index

Index of Proper Names

Subject Index

Hebrew and Aramaic Words

Greek Words

Latin Words

Survey of Contents
of Volumes One and Two

Editors and Contributors of
Volumes One and Two

SHIMON APPLEBAUM, born 1911 in England, professor of Jewish History and
Archaeology at the University of Tel Aviv. Publications: *Greeks and Jews
in Ancient Cyrene* (1969, in Hebrew); *Roman Britain* (1972)

MICHAEL AVI-YONAH, born Lemberg 1904, died Jerusalem 1974, professor of
Archaeology and History of Art at the Hebrew University 1963-74.
Publications: *Archaeology of the Holy Land* (1955, in Hebrew); *The Map
of Madeba* (1961, in Hebrew); *The Holy Land from the Persian to the Arab
Conquests* (1966); *Geschichte der Juden im Zeitalter des Talmud* (1946, in
Hebrew; German translation, 1962).

ZEEV WILHEM FALK, born Breslau 1923, associate professor of Law at the
Hebrew University, Publications: *Hebrew Law in Biblical Times* (1964);
Jewish Matrimonial Law in the Middle Ages (1966); *Introduction to Jewish
Law of the Second Commonwaealth* I (1972).

DAVID FLUSSER, born Vienna 1917, professor of History of Religion at the
Hebrew University. Publications: 'The Dead Sea Sect and Pre-pauline
Christianity,' *Scripta Hierosólymitana* 5 (1958); *Jesus* (German edition
1968, English edition 1970).

GIDON FOERSTER, born 1935 in Israel, senior lecturer of Archaeology at the
Hebrew University. Publications: articles on ancient synagogues and
other archaeological subjects in *Revue Biblique. Qadmonioth* and *Israel
Exploration Journal.*

MOSHE DAVID HERR, born Tel Aviv 1935, senior lecturer in Jewish History in
the Period of the Second Temple, the Mishnah and the Talmud, at the
Hebrew University. Publications: articles on the history of Halakah and
Jewish thought, in *Tarbiz* and *Scripta Hierosolymitana.*

MARINUS DE JONGE, born Vlissingen 1925, professor of New Testament and
Early Christian Literature at the University of Leiden. Publications: *The
Testaments of the Twelve Patriarchs* (1952, repr. 1975); *Testamenta XII
Patriarcharum* (1964, 2nd ed. 1970); *Studies on the Twelve Patriarchs* (1975).

GERARD MUSSIES, born The Hague 1934, lecturer in New Testament Greek at the
University of Utrecht. Publications: *The Morphology of Koine Greek in the
Apocalypse of St. John. A Study in Bilingualism* (1971); *Dio Chrysostom
and the New Testament* (1972).

CHAIM RABIN, born 1915 in Germany, professor of Hebrew at the Hebrew
University. Publications: *The Zadokite Documents* (1956, 2nd ed. 1958);
Qumran Studies (1957).

SHMUEL SAFRAI, born Warsaw 1919, professor of Jewish History in the Period
of the Second Temple, the Mishnah and the Talmud, at the Hebrew
University. Publications: *Pilgrimage in the Period of the Second Temple*
(1965, in Hebrew); *Rabbi Akiba ben Yosef. His Life and Teachings* (1970,
in Hebrew); *History of, the Jewish People in the Second Temple Period* (1970,
in Hebrew).

MENAHEM STERN, born Bialystok 1925, professor of Jewish History in the Period of the Second Temple at the Hebrew University. Publications: *Corpus Papyrorum Iudaicarum*, vol. 3 (1964); *Greek and Latin Authors on Jews and Judaism*, vol. 1 (1974).

WILLEM CORNELIS VAN UNNIK, born Haarlem 1910, professor of New Testament at the University of Utrecht. Publications: *Nestorian Questions on the Administration of the Eucharist in the Eastern Church* (1937); *Tarsus or Jerusalem* (1956); *Sparsa Collecta*, vol. 1 (1973).

HANS JULIUS WOLFF, born Berlin 1902, professor emeritus of Roman and Civil Law at the University of Freiburg im Breisgau. Publications: *Written and Unwritten Marriages in Hellenistic and Postclassical Roman Law* (1939); *Das Justizwesen der Ptolemäer* (1962, 2nd ed. 1970); *Beiträge zur Rechtsgeschichte Altgriechenlands und des hellenistisch-römischen Ägypten* (1961); *Die attischen Paragraphe* (1966); *Opuscula Dispersa* (1974).

Errata Volume One

and Volume Two

p. 32, note 2	read: *IGLS* VII
p. 35, line 16	read: problem
p. 42, line 7 from bottom	read: The Acts
p. 81, line 9	read: Mount Tabor
p. 85, line 3 from bottom	read: demographic
p. 87, line 12 from bottom	read: King Aretas
p. 99, note 5	read: Jos. *War* IV, 487, 503
p. 124, line 5 from bottom	read: Alexandria
p. 126, line 7	read: Avillius
p. 133, line 6 from bottom	read: Cleodemus-Malchus
p. 134, line 17	read: once again
p. 123, line 20	read: nor in the ancient world
p. 158, line 28	read: daughter of Nicias
p. 169, note 2	add: A. Ferrua, *Epigraphica* (1941), p. 43, doubts the Jewishness of the inscriptions from Pompei.
p. 148, note 1	read: On Anemurium
p. 148, line 6	read: Calycadnus
p. 159, line 14	read: a synagogue
p. 177, line 11 from bottom	read: brother
p. 209, note 7	read: Epiphanius
p. 211, note 4	read: Tiberias
p. 223, line 8 from bottom	read: in safe-keeping
p. 270, note 1	read: *Ant.* XVII, 134-45
p. 288, line 10	read: shields (instead of standards)
p. 295, line 3	read: as feasible
p. 303, line 29	read: to Rome (instead of home)
p. 327, note 1	read: E. Birley
p. 352, note 1	read: *War* II, 175-7
p. 360, line 17	read: and the high priests themselves
p. 365, note 2	read: B. W. Henderson
p. 373, line 14 from bottom	read: did not do so
p. 419, line 12	read: Jabneh and its Sages
p. 491, note 6	read: *P. T. Megillah* III, 71d,
p. 424, line 9	read: the middle of the third century
p. 436, line 5	read: and
p. 449, line 19	read: of the Jewish community
p. 482, note 4	read: Jos. *War* VII, 445
p. 518, line 7 from bottom	read: next-of-kin
p. 522, note 2	read: *P. T. Kiddushin* I, 59d?
p. 524, line 6 from bottom	read: created by
p. 525, bottom line	read: a lessee
p. 526, line 13	read: at a later stage
p. 544, line 9 from bottom	read: in force
Volume Two: p. 981 and 982	read: Kadmoniot V